The Which? Wine Guide 2002

WHICH? BOOKS

Which? Books is the book publishing arm of Consumers' Association, which was set up in 1957 to improve the standards of goods and services available to the public. Everything Which? publishes aims to help consumers, by giving them the independent information they need to make informed decisions. These publications, known throughout Britain for their quality, integrity and impartiality, have been held in high regard for four decades.

Independence does not come cheap; the guides carry no advertising; no wine merchant or producer can buy an entry in our wine guide; we also pay for the wine used in our tastings. This policy, and our practice of rigorously re-researching our guides for each edition, helps us to provide our readers with information of a standard and quality that cannot be surpassed.

ABOUT THE AUTHORS

Simon Woods (SW) swapped a career in electronics for one in wine in 1989. He co-ordinated *Wine* magazine's International Wine Challenge from 1990 to 1993 and now works as a freelance writer. He contributes regularly to *Wine, Square Meal*, the *Financial Times* 'The Business' magazine and several local newspapers, has appeared on TV and radio at home and abroad, and has judged at wine competitions in England, France, South Africa and Australia.

Susan Keevil (SK) has recently embarked on a freelance wine writing career after spending years on the other side of the fence, in the editorial seat. Her travels, post geography degree, firmly established in her mind that wine was the thing she knew most about and that no other career would do. She began with wine books and then joined the staff of *Decanter* magazine and became the editor. She has been freelance since summer 2000 following which, one of her most fascinating experiences has been working the 2001 vintage in Australia, where she learned the importance of wearing a dark T-shirt while making Shiraz.

The Which? Wine Guide 2002

SIMON WOODS and SUSAN KEEVIL

CONSUMERS' ASSOCIATION

The Which? Wine Guide voucher scheme

The Which? Wine Guide 2002 includes three £5 vouchers that readers will be able to redeem against a £50 wine purchase. (Look for the **£5** symbol after the Tastings and talks information in the Highly Recommended section, and at the end of the entry in the Also Recommended section to locate the participating merchants.) Only one voucher may be used against a wine purchase of £50 or more. Remember that your intention to use a voucher MUST be mentioned at the time of buying. The vouchers may not be used in conjunction with any other discount, offer or promotional scheme. Actual vouchers (not photocopies) must be presented. The vouchers will be valid from 1 October 2001 to 30 September 2002.

The Which? Wine Guide online

Internet users can find *The Which? Wine Guide* online at the Which? Online web site http://www.which.net. To access the *Wine Guide* you need to be a member of Which? Online, but you can visit the web site for details of how to take out a 30-day free trial to the service.

Which? Books are commissioned and researched by Consumers' Association and published by Which? Ltd, 2 Marylebone Road, London NW1 4DF Email address: books@which.net

Distributed by The Penguin Group: Penguin Books Ltd, 80 Strand, London WC2R 0RL

Copyright © 2001 Which? Ltd
This edition October 2001
First edition of *The Which? Wine Guide* published in 1981

Designer: Paul Saunders
Cover photograph: Price Watkins Design
Illustrations: Mandy Greatorex

British Library Cataloguing in Publication Data
A catalogue record for this book is available from the British Library

ISBN 0 85202 874 1

For a full list of Which? books, please write to:
Which? Books, Castlemead, Gascoyne Way, Hertford X, SG14 1LH
or access our web site at: www.which.net

Editorial: Lynn Bresler, Alethea Doran, Vicky Fisher, Rhys Jones, Barbara Toft
Production: Joanna Bregosz
Typeset by Saxon Graphics Ltd, Derby
Printed and bound in Great Britain by Biddles Ltd,
Guildford and King's Lynn

CONTENTS

Part III **What is wine?**

Part IV **Where to buy wine**

Part V **Find out more about wine**

FOREWORD

Can it really be 21 years since I sat in a garret writing the first edition of *The Which? Wine Guide*?

I have to admit that while it was quite daunting to put together such a comprehensive book from scratch, I had some first-class help in the form of a friend, now much more widely read than I: the romantic novelist Rosie Thomas, who was the first edition's Assistant Editor.

Edmund Penning-Rowsell gave the first edition gravitas by writing the Introduction, and the contributors, who wrote very detailed descriptions of the various regions with notes on vintages, producers and what exactly to buy, included Clive Coates MW, Tony Laithwaite (the man who has, I suspect, by setting up most of the mail-order wine clubs in Britain, made the most money from wine in the UK), Simon Loftus, David Peppercorn MW and Serena Sutcliffe MW.

Looking at the *Which? Wine Guide 1981*, I am struck by how similar its form is to this edition's, but also how extraordinarily limited our choices seemed then. Of the 100 pages allotted to 'What to buy', more than half were devoted to France, a mere seven to the 'New World'. Australia, described in the *Guide* as 'for long the "forgotten continent" as far as British wine lovers were concerned' was represented by the Australian Wine Centre in Soho, a distinctly moribund government-run shop that sold labels such as Ben Ean and Kanga Rouge.

And yet, and yet. The range of *different* tastes and styles of wine available was, I would argue, actually much wider then than it is today now that we can find Chardonnays and Cabernets from the likes of India, Uruguay, Ontario and Tunisia on our shelves. In the early 1980s, producers were still allowed to make the style of wine they wanted to from the grapes they were used to. Today, the tendency, in the UK anyway, is for a handful of important supermarket buyers to impose their ideas of what sells particularly well on all their suppliers – no matter where on the globe they may be. And this all too often means the same old handful of wine styles and 'international' grape varieties. International wine is as dreary as international cuisine. We are in danger of confusing geographical novelty with genuine originality.

Trust the continued noble tradition of the *Which? Wine Guide* to steer you towards real quality in a bottle.

Jancis Robinson

(See *www.jancisrobinson.com*)

INTRODUCTION

'Why, it may reasonably be asked, a *Which? Wine Guide?*' wondered
Edmund Penning-Rowsell (known as EPR or Eddie) in the introduction
to the first edition of this *Guide*. Much has happened in the 21 years
since that was written, but it's still a sensible question. And to be
absolutely truthful, most people who drink wine in the UK get by very
nicely thank you without any book on wine, never mind one with over
500 information-crammed pages that are thoroughly revised each year.

Even so, we still think that even seasoned drinkers need a little
guidance, although not for the same reasons they did when the first
Guide appeared. At that time, EPR said, 'Very few indeed of the
heavily promoted brands of table wines are consistent in style and
quality year after year.' Today, the opposite is true. Modern quality-
control in the winery is far more rigorous, and finding something
consistent and drinkable is no longer a problem.

However, the difficulty today is not avoiding the faulty wines,
but finding something with genuine character, as opposed to the
identikit Cabernets and Chardonnays that have displaced
Liebfraumilch from our shopping baskets. There's nothing wrong
with these wines, and for the vast majority of people, our advice is
to head to your local supermarket for a bottle of your favourite
tipple, or whatever is on special offer this week. But if you want to
derive the greatest enjoyment and stimulation from wine, then you
need to abandon the mainstream and expand your tasting horizons.

Wine is not a simple topic, although the message from some quarters
would seem to say otherwise. Most of the speakers at a seminar at the
2001 London International Wines and Spirits Fair agreed that
embracing brands – in other words going for the mainstream rather
than the esoteric – was the way forward for the wine industry. Mario
Micheli, president of Southcorp Europe, said, 'We should look
forward to a time when wines will be household names and will
thereby provide additional value to shareholders.' As critics and wine
lovers, we say forget the shareholders, what about the consumers?

SQUEEZING OUT THE GOOD?

Consolidation within the wine industry is increasing. Hardly a week
goes by without news of a Californian company investing in Italy, a

Burgundian producer entering into a joint venture in Canada, or another such partnership. Since the last edition appeared, two of Australia's largest wine companies, Southcorp and Rosemount, have merged, while another Australian giant, Mildara Blass, has joined forces with Beringer of California to become Beringer Blass, the world's third-largest wine company. In business terms, we assume such deals make sense, but again, our fear is that they are not good news for wine drinkers. Not only do these large concerns put the squeeze on much smaller and often more interesting producers, and indeed on wholesalers who just can't compete in price wars, they also encourage a one-stop-shop mentality among trade buyers.

Supermarkets are the most visible culprits of lazy buying practices, but they're not the only ones at whom we can point a finger. After 21 years of taking a close look at hundreds of UK merchants, we have become skilled at dissecting wine lists and seeing who has put together a range drawn from a handful of familiar sources, and who has boldly gone where no wine merchant has gone before. A quick look at a company's Bordeaux selection will tell you whether you're dealing with someone who hunts apart from the pack or a me-too. Anyone can put together a list of expensive wines from well-known châteaux and sell them on the back of the scores of influential commentators – the American Robert Parker in particular. Sourcing high-quality, reasonably priced (as in sub-£10) clarets that have escaped Parker's notice is much more of a challenge.

WHAT PRICE BORDEAUX?

We can't mention Bordeaux and not say something about the *en primeur* prices for the 2000 clarets. We're not talking here about the vast majority of wines from this generally excellent vintage. Prices for these are stable, and there are literally hundreds of very fine and affordable wines. However, for many of the top properties, and for wines which have been awarded high Parker points, the prices frankly have gone potty. If you fancy a case from one of the Médoc first growths, you'll have to pay in excess of £2,000 – perhaps rather appropriate, given the vintage. And to add insult to injury that doesn't include duty and VAT.

The justification from the château owners is that given the demand for the vintage, every case will sell easily, and that regardless of what they originally charged, the market would have eventually elevated the prices to these levels. And sadly, they are right. Léoville-Barton, a property that would be fully justified in raising the prices of its wines, sold its excellent 2000 at a fair price, and those who got in early paid less than £300 per case. The going rate today is around £800, and we've seen it on some lists at over £1,000. Impoverished claret lovers shouldn't despair however, providing (once again) they avoid the herd mentality. 2000 might be all the rage, but earlier vintages have been forgotten about, and prices remain reasonable. One case of 2000, or two cases of 1995 – you decide.

But where will the price hikes end? The irresponsibility and greed of the Bordelais haven't passed unnoticed in other parts of the world, and we won't be surprised to see increases for the 2000 vintage in other regions. Indeed, it's already happening. Lea & Sandeman, a London merchant, has recently delisted the wines of Querciabella in Tuscany, saying, 'Unfortunately, we could not agree with [the owner's] ambition to "reposition" Querciabella through implementing some quite dramatic price increases, without a corresponding increase in the quality of the wines.' Fortunately, many un-repositioned wines are still available, even in Bordeaux and Tuscany.

We mentioned last year how Old World wines often had more personality than those from the New World. Since then, we've been pleased to find more complexity and delicacy in many New World wines, especially those from South Africa and New Zealand. In Australia and America we can detect a backlash from both critics and producers against, as Hugh Johnson memorably put it, 'wines that have been designed for cigar smokers'. There will need to be a major upheaval before Barossa Shiraz can be described as subtle, but already there are growing numbers of wines that have graduated beyond fruity, oaky, alcoholic bodybuilder status and developed genuine *terroir*-based personality.

At one point, early in 2001, it seemed as though sales of Australian wines in the UK were set to overtake those of France. At the time of writing, this still hasn't happened, but we wouldn't be surprised to see the Australians gaining the upper hand in the near future. After years of complacency, the French are clearly worried by the threat from the New World, so much so that the government has employed a crisis manager, Jacques Berthomeau, to nurse the wine industry back to health. 'We have to be more professional,' he says. 'Marketing is a tool. We sold mineral water through branding. Why not wine?' We find this attitude disturbing, and hope that Monsieur Berthomeau finds a way to market not just cheap *vin de pays* but also Bordeaux Clairet, Côtes du Marmandais, Savennières, Côtes de Jura and all of France's other quirky and exciting wines.

THAT OLD CORK DEBATE AGAIN

Forgive us for yet another mention of the cork debate. Once again we have heard claims from cork companies that they have at last discovered how to prevent 'corked' wines, and once again, we've seen producers who have no faith in such claims turning to plastic corks and screw-caps. A group of eminent New Zealand producers, including the highly regarded Kumeu River, will be using screw-caps for several wines in the future. With each case of wine comes a note from the New Zealand wine writer Bob Campbell MW: 'I have one question for all the other winemakers who, for the time being, continue to use corks. If you know that screw-caps will produce better and more consistent wine than corks, how can you continue to short-change your customers?' How indeed.

Corked wine is one thing, but one of our favourite stories from 2001 was of the discovery of a bottle of what was thought to be Jacobean wine in the foundations of a seventeenth-century Surrey house. A tasting was organised in conjunction with a local vineyard, and expectations were high – but when the cork was pulled, the contents were found to be an eyelash, a handful of bent pins, pubic hairs and almost half a pint of urine. It seems to have been a folk charm to ward off a witch's curse.

So enough of digging up the past – it's time to look to the future. We hope to be able to produce many more editions of the *Which? Wine Guide* and to continue to do what we enjoy most – tasting, exploring and demystifying wine. In the meantime, let us head off into the sunset to celebrate 21 years of the *Guide*, where we'll be drinking something from a younger, cleaner and decidedly fruitier vintage than that Jacobean libation. *Santé*.

THE WHICH? WINE GUIDE AWARDS FOR 2002

We've been pleased to find an aura of intrepidity pervading the merchants' lists this year. Hot competition among them has led to a general 'branching out', heading away from the well-trodden Bordeaux–Burgundy–Australia path and venturing into new territory (for example, South America). These merchants are prepared to include different grape varieties (Verdelho, Malbec, Tannat and Pinot Gris, to name a few) and are brave enough to take on smaller, more interesting growers, even though we may never have heard of them before. We applaud all this wholeheartedly and hope it continues. Sameness in wine should never be encouraged, but adventurousness should be. The merchants listed below are those who have taken these things to heart and made the most creative strides within their field – we don't think they can be bettered!

Best Supermarket Award
Booths Supermarkets
For its good all-round range, and probably the best-trained staff you'll find in a supermarket, Booths got our vote this year.
Runner-up: Waitrose

Best High-Street Chain Award
Oddbins
Everyone's favourite chain continues to offer by far the most inspiring selection of wines on the high street, plus terrific annual wine festivals.
Runner-up: Sorry to say that at present, there's no competition

Best Mail-Order Merchant Award
Lay & Wheeler
The smart literature packed with high-class wines and backed up by sterling service make this East Anglian institution hard to beat.
Runners-up: Adnams, Tanners, The Wine Society

Specialist Awards

Bordeaux Specialist Award
Farr Vintners
A worthy winner not just for the vast selection of stellar classed growths that adorn the list, but also for the many affordable wines from up-and-coming properties.
Runners-up: John Armit, Justerini & Brooks, Nickolls & Perks

Burgundy Specialist Award
Morris & Verdin
An impeccable range of growers whose wares are promoted in a refreshingly forthright, unstuffy manner. M&V also provide the bulk of the burgundy range for several other merchants around the country.
Runners-up: Domaine Direct, Haynes Hanson & Clark, Justerini & Brooks, Howard Ripley

Rhône Specialist Award
Justerini & Brooks
The company has featured on several of our shortlists, but it is the depth of fine wines from top growers in the Rhône which caught our attention this year.
Runners-up: Croque-en-Bouche, Farr Vintners, Gauntley's, Yapp Brothers

German Specialist Award
Tanners Wines
We detect faint signs of a revival in the fortunes of Germany's wines. If you are wondering what all the fuss is about, the commendable selection at Tanners is the best place to start.
Runners-up: D Byrne, Howard Ripley, Justerini & Brooks, O W Loeb

Italian Specialist Award
Falcon Vintners
We're pleased to see more and more merchants taking Italy seriously. Few lists, however, are as serious as this star-studded range.
Runners-up: Ballantynes, Liberty Wines, Valvona & Crolla, Vino Vino

Spanish Specialist Award
Laymont & Shaw
John Hawes' selection puts excellence before any other considerations and is backed up with first-class service.
Runners-up: Direct Wine Shipments, Moreno Wines

New World Specialist Award
Philglas & Swiggot
Australia is still the main event at this friendly Battersea merchant, but there are also strong showings from several other countries.
Runners-up: Berry Bros & Rudd, D Byrne, Oddbins, Vin du Van, Noel Young

Fine Wine Specialist Award
Sommelier Wine Company
A company whose range keeps getting better, and whose selection of fine wine includes impressive showings from both Old and New Worlds.
Runners-up: D Byrne, Justerini & Brooks, Lay & Wheeler, La Réserve, La Vigneronne

Organic Wine Specialist Award
Vinceremos Wines and Spirits
This is our new award for 2002. Whether organic, biodynamic or holistically managed, we think kinder vineyard practices bring out brighter, fresher, cleaner grape flavours, and better wine. Vinceremos' globally sourced wine list gives us no reason to doubt our theory. An increasing number of merchants are hot on the heels of Vinceremos, but none yet offers quite such a wide range. However, at the current rate we expect more contenders for this award in the 2003 edition.
Runner-up: Lay & Wheeler

Regional Awards

LONDON
La Vigneronne
Competition here is fierce, but with its eclectic range of wines and excellent programme of tastings, La Vigneronne came out on top this year.
Runners-up: Lea & Sandeman, Philglas & Swiggot, La Réserve, Uncorked, Wimbledon Wine Cellar, The Winery

CENTRAL ENGLAND
Gauntleys of Nottingham
Not the largest set of wines you'll find, but few companies maintain such high standards of quality and interest throughout their ranges.
Runners-up: Bennett's, Connolly's, Tanners

NORTH OF ENGLAND
D Byrne & Co
Arguably the best range of wines in England, and certainly some of the keenest prices. The competition is closing in, but the Byrne family stands head and shoulders above the rest.
Runners-up: deFINE, Martinez Fine Wine, Portland Wine Company, Wright Wine Company

EAST OF ENGLAND
Noel Young Wines
A confident, stylish range backed up by strong opinions and good service, a model for small independent wine merchants everywhere.
Runners-up: Adnams, Lay & Wheeler, T & W Wines

SOUTH-WEST OF ENGLAND
Great Western Wine Company
A company that has come on in leaps and bounds in recent years, especially with its French and Italian ranges. Also great-value tastings.
Runners-up: Avery's, Nobody Inn, Christopher Piper, Reid Wines

NORTHERN IRELAND
Direct Wine Shipments
Few companies show the same eagerness to make wine more enjoyable, and there's a first-rate set of wines to support this.
Runner-up: James Nicholson

SCOTLAND
Valvona & Crolla
The vast selection from Italy is still the strength of this legendary Edinburgh emporium, but the range is now expanding successfully into other countries.
Runners-up: Raeburn, Villeneuve

WALES
Ballantynes of Cowbridge
Many modern merchants have a refreshingly unstuffy approach to wine, but few back it up with such a stunning range (especially from Burgundy and Italy) as this family company.
Runner-up: Terry Platt

Part I

Features

HIGHWAY '81 REVISITED

Do you remember 1981? Pope John Paul II and newly elected US president Ronald Reagan survived assassination attempts, IBM introduced its first personal computer and AIDS was first identified. Jenkins, Owen, Williams and Rodgers broke from the Labour Party to form the SDP, Brixton, Toxteth and Moss Side experienced riots, while Ian Botham and Bob Willis inspired a memorable Test Match victory at Headingley. We watched *Raiders of the Lost Ark*, *Chariots of Fire* and *Gregory's Girl*, read *Midnight's Children* by Salman Rushdie and were forced to listen to *Shaddap You Face* and *The Birdie Song*. Oh, and two people called Charles and Diana were married somewhere in London.

And what did we turn to for advice on what to drink? Why, to the *1981 Which? Wine Guide*, which began with editor Jancis Robinson saying, 'This handbook is meant for anyone who cares at all about the taste of the wine he drinks and about how much he pays for it.' These words are just as applicable now as then – but little else has remained constant on the wine scene. Have the changes been for the better or the worse? Read on.

In terms of what we drank in 1981, Europe reigned supreme. France took up half of the *Guide*'s 100-page section covering wine-producing countries, and the New World was huddled towards the end. California and Australia were beginning to make their presence felt and received reasonable coverage, but South America was summed up in half a page, and there were just six lines on a country that was '… only just emerging on the wine scene', namely New Zealand.

THOSE WERE THE DAYS

Several of the merchants featured in that first guide have long since disappeared, but many are still in existence. The comments on some of these are as relevant now as then. For example, Tanners – 'a most instructive and entertaining wine list'; Oddbins – 'one of the few companies that is really in touch with the curious wine buyer in the street'; Adnams – 'modesty is not one of Adnams' strong points'. Others have since improved out of all recognition, witness Farr Vintners, which at the time had 'a fairly restricted selection of Bordeaux'! Among the supermarkets, Waitrose attracted the most favourable comments, while Sainsbury's was 'one of the few stockists of Muscatel, useful for cooks' (they were lucky – Tesco didn't even appear in the book).

Also featured was Berry Bros & Rudd. Jancis described the Berry's list as a 'dear little price list which is much more reminiscent of a Psalter than a selling document'. Among the listings in the May 1981 edition of that 'dear little list' were 1970 La Mission Haut-Brion at £24.15 and 1966 Margaux at £28.75. Today, the prices at Berry's are £170 and £195, respectively. France received the lion's share of the coverage (although many of the company's French wines, burgundies especially, were actually being bottled in England) and there was good representation from Germany. Otherwise, there were five Italian wines, six from Spain, one from the Languedoc-Roussillon, and nothing from the New World apart from South African brandy and sherry.

THE NEW KIDS ON THE BLOCK

1981 was also when three well-known merchants, Majestic Wine Warehouses, La Vigneronne and Morris & Verdin, started trading. Majestic's Tony Mason looks back on the early days with nostalgia. 'Trading was easier then, and I certainly don't ever remember bothering to see if our prices were better or worse than anyone else's. Not only hadn't the supermarkets got their act together, they were buying particularly badly – they just weren't competitors until the mid-1980s. When we started out, Bulgarian Cabernet Sauvignon was *the* trendy wine, and we sold more of that than anything else. We did have a few Australian wines, such as Chateau Tahbilk. They used to be expensive, but we thought they were rather good.

'Most of the changes since then have been positive. Thanks to competition, both between retailers and wine-producing countries, the average quality level is much higher. I'd never have predicted the decline in the lower French *appellation contrôlée* wines, such as Muscadet, Côtes du Rhône, basic Bordeaux and burgundy. Other parts of the world can provide much better value for money at those price points. We've also seen German wines all but disappear. They used to be 25 per cent of our business; now they're less than 2 per cent.'

Mike and Liz Berry bought the South Kensington shop that was to become La Vigneronne in 1981, in what, according to Mike, was still very much bedsit land. 'In those days, 105 Old Brompton Road was a true off-licence, and we were rewarded for our good sales of beer by being lent the Löwenbrau Porsche for a week! It took us several years to evolve it into a wine shop, but we wanted to deal in fine wines from around the world, and were among the first to sell Grange, Sassicaia and Vega Sicilia. In those days, the allocation of Grange was 30 cases – now it is six bottles! In the last five or six years, we have moved to importing virtually all our wines direct, which as well as being the only way to survive is also much more interesting. For us, France still has the best wines, and there are still many new discoveries to be made.'

Jasper Morris set up Morris & Verdin with Tony Verdin in 1981 at the tender age of 23 when, he confesses, he was not particularly mature. 'We started off by visiting several French regions to see what we could find. This was something of a novelty, since at the time, most English merchants had typically one supplier for each region, bought through intermediaries, and hardly ever travelled abroad. The second trip to Burgundy was probably when my affair with the region and its wines really started. At that time the place was deeply unfashionable, especially for reds, and it was possible to get healthy allocations from virtually all the top domaines. In the beginning it used to be a real struggle to find decent stuff, red in particular, so to have quite so many people making good wine today is very exciting.

'It was in Burgundy that I first got turned on to New World wines. Someone gave me a glass of wine that I'd have sworn was a *premier cru* Volnay from Lafarge. It was 1985 Au Bon Climat Pinot Noir. I now import and drink a lot of Californian wine, which I'd never expected in the beginning. I also think that the rise of New Zealand Sauvignon Blanc has been brilliant but totally unforeseen. From virtually nothing, Marlborough has emerged to become the natural home for Sauvignon.

'I'm less happy with the trend towards high oak, high alcohol, high octane, high everything wines. I thought we'd seen the back of such wines after the Californian efforts of the 1970s. And I'm not keen on some of the price rises we're seeing now. If you're excited about wine, but don't have a huge budget, you just can't afford top claret any more. On the other hand, you used to have to drink classed growth claret in order to get something decent. Thankfully, that's no longer the case.'

THAT WAS THEN, THIS IS NOW

After the 1982 edition, Jancis Robinson handed the reins of the *Guide* over to Jane MacQuitty, now wine writer for *The Times*, for a two-year stint. 'It's definitely a much better time to be a wine drinker now than in the 1980s. We want bigger flavours to suit the more varied foods that we're now eating, and the producers have adapted their styles to suit modern palates. I was always convinced that interest in New World wines would take off, and I'm not surprised at the huge interest they now receive. I've heard people say that Australia is on the wane, but I don't see any reason why sales should slow down.

'I'm not so happy when greedy producers take short cuts. There are several instances where thanks usually to the intervention of Mr Accountant, production has soared and what was a glorious concentrated wine in the 1980s is now characterless and spineless. And I'd never have predicted that the top Bordeaux producers would have been as foolish, insular, arrogant and greedy as they have been. The whole of the 2000 *en primeur* campaign has been a circus, and I find it incomprehensible that they think it makes sound long-term business sense.

'But overall, the picture is much healthier than it used to be. I'm encouraged that women are now buying more wine than men, and also that we're drinking more red than white. That for me is a sign of a nation of grown-up wine drinkers. And I'm definitely pleased to see so many good-quality wines appearing from all over the world. More choice can only be a good thing.'

The job of editor for the 1991 *Guide* fell to Andrew Jefford, now columnist for the *Evening Standard*, *Decanter*, *Waitrose Food Illustrated* and *just-drinks.com*, and presenter of *Liquid Companion* on BBC Radio Four. How does he feel progress has been since his tenure? 'I'm pleased to see that small growers everywhere are increasingly literate (in winemaking terms), and that the prospecting of new *terroirs* is carrying on apace right around the world. There are still not many really great vineyards in the world, and the exploratory process is held in check to some extent by the mania for "technically correct", interventionist winemaking which erodes and obscures the natural differences between wines produced in different parts of the world.

'I find many Australian wines violent and unsubtle in flavour, hence difficult to drink. Chilean wines have also become duller as many of their large producers have chosen to pursue greater and greater profits, but both Argentina and South Africa are beginning to offer excellent, complex wines. I continue to admire the best Californian wines, since they represent passionate attempts to express vineyard origin. However, cheaper American wines are depressingly low in quality. France (in spite of global warming) still has the greatest vineyard sites in the world, and the best French winemakers understand better than any other nation the importance of maximum viticultural effort and minimum winemaking intervention. Italy offers wonderful alternatives to France's finest wines; Spain is beginning to do this too. My own personal passion is for red wines, and at the "bargain" level Spain and Portugal offer the best red-wine value in the world at present.

'Less encouraging is the huge rise in popularity of consistent but dull branded wines, sold on the back of lavish marketing and offering poor price-quality ratio. So inimical are brands to all that is best about wine, I never expected them to become important at all. But overall, now is a better time to be a wine drinker than 1991, especially if you can afford to buy bottles at £5 and over. The pool of fine wine – drinkable, digestible, intricate, complex and ageworthy wine which genuinely reflects its origin and vineyard site – is greater than it has ever been before.'

Jefford's successors for the 1992 and 1993 *Guides* were Rosemary George MW and Christine Austin. Rosemary, now chair of the Circle of Wine Writers, also feels that wine drinkers have never had it so good, but once again finds a few disturbing trends. 'Winemaking techniques and overall wine quality is much higher than it was, and it's been particularly encouraging to see the enormous improvement in New Zealand reds (especially Pinot Noir), the opening up of South Africa and the emergence of English fizz as a serious wine. But there is a risk of standardisation of winemaking practices, wine names – something called Cuckoo Hill could come from anywhere – and grape varieties. We've seen Chardonnay, Merlot and other well-known grapes being planted in favour of indigenous varieties in some regions. Also, if we don't have to pay duty when we cross the Channel with wine, why do we have to pay so much here?'

And since Rosemary's stint, I've been Contributing Editor and then Editor. Seven years may not seem a long time ago, but a quick look at the space devoted to Austria, Argentina, the Languedoc and Portugal in the 1995 *Guide* reveals quite how much the world of wine has changed. Sales of Australian wine in the UK had recently overtaken those of Spain, but Germany and France seemed a long way ahead. Today, Germany is (sadly, where the top wines are concerned) an also-ran, and the Australians are threatening to dethrone the French.

BIG, BIGGER, BIGGEST

Not everyone shares Andrew Jefford's distaste for Australia, but many who love wine find it disturbing that there is a generation of drinkers weaned on wines from Down Under for which big is beautiful, and subtlety irrelevant. This isn't the Australians' fault. They have brought simplicity, reliability and efficiency to wine, and their success comes as no surprise. What is disturbing, as Rosemary George mentioned, is that other parts of the world have sought to ape wines from Australia and other New World countries, both in their style and packaging. All those I've spoken to agree that there is more high-quality wine being made now than ever before, but our concern for the future is that, in Jancis Robinson's words from the first *Which? Wine Guide*, 'anyone who cares at all about the taste of the wine' might find the number of wines greater but the spectrum of flavours more limited.

SW

NIPS, TUCKS AND MOG

Wouldn't it be nice to think that wine was made from grapes, and grapes only? That what emerged from the winery was as natural and uncontrived a product as in biblical times – fermentation just left to go its own merry way, with minimal intervention and serendipitous, highly drinkable results? Sadly, however, wine today is subject to much more tinkering than many of us realise. Dip into this *Guide* and you'll see such comments as 'wines over-extracted in recent vintages', 'clean, simple fruity flavours to the fore', 'over-oaked of late' and, especially of more recent wines, 'a touch too sweet on the initial palate'. These are all signs of the men (or women) in the winery making their mark, and ensuring the grapes express themselves in the way they want them to – trying to make the wine more 'beautiful', but not always to good effect. How many times have you thought, after taking a sip of wine: 'Not bad, but what's that burning sensation?', or 'Hmm, nice and fruity, but there's something very plasticy about this'? – or maybe you've simply surprised yourself with an enormous sneeze? We believe that the more you can recognise these winemaking nips and tucks, the better equipped you will be to vote with your feet: that is, not buy the wine if you don't like the effects of the processing.

MATTER OTHER THAN GRAPES (MOG)

MOG, to use Australian parlance, normally refers to leaves, stems and the odd lizard (quickly fished out) finding their way into the collection vats. In fact, there's more than this. 'Matter other than grapes' also includes such outsiders as acid, tannin, bentonite and sulphur, added to refresh flavours perceived as missing from freshly picked fruit.

Acid is usually added in powder form to re-balance warm climate wines in which fruit often ripens to the point of over-fruity flabbiness (see 'The look, smell and taste of wine', pages

290–91). In Australia, for example, this additive goes in almost systematically, whether the wine is red or white; sweet, dry or sparkling. Added acid is invariably tartaric, citric or ascorbic acid, each of which is naturally present in the grape anyway, and readily melds with the juice. Similarly, added **tannin** (see 'The look, smell and taste of wine', page 292), which is used in a great many New World reds, is often extracted from pressed-out grape skins. When these things go in before fermentation begins, as a modest supplement, their effect on the taste of the wine is minimal and their integration practically seamless. Throw in a bit more (and a bit more) halfway through fermentation, however, and the problems start. Acid shows up separately on the palate, giving a burning effect. Added tannins become hard, chewy and 'awkward'. Flavours start becoming pinched and strained … Sound familiar?

Bentonite has a more medicinal function, and, thankfully, you won't taste it – you'll just miss what it removes. It's a clay (from Wyoming) that expands in water and has special absorptive powers. Its weight helps it to fall out of the grape juice, taking with it unwanted matter such as clumps of mould or rotten grape skins, which might come in with rained-on fruit. It is also used later in the winemaking process for clarification before bottling. Purists (well, non-purists) argue that the bits and pieces of grape skin give fuller flavours and that bentonite strips out texture and makes a wine taste neutral. But the good thing about it is, once it's fallen out of suspension there's no trace left.

Sulphur is the MOG factor that makes us sneeze or wheeze – particularly if there's too much of it (those who are allergic suffer particularly badly, but in strong doses sulphur can affect anyone). Added at the grape-crushing stage as metabisulphate, it acts as a cleansing agent, killing off bacteria and unwanted wild yeasts. (Winemakers who prefer their wine to be fermented by wild yeasts instead of cultured ones – see below – use smaller doses.) It also prevents oxidation, and thus is an all-round assistant to a rapid, clean fermentation, allowing the yeasts and grape juices to do their job undisturbed. You could say sulphur is the winemaker's ultimate control tool. Unfortunately, there are control-freak winemakers out there who use too much. Sulphur is a natural by-product of winemaking, so, as with acid and tannin, adding small amounts is fine. But adding sulphur right through fermentation leads not only to neutral (so-called 'reductive') flavours – too clean, too simple; boring and bland – but also to the occasional unpleasant whiff.

LIVE STUFF

We're not going to lean too hard on winemakers who add 'cultured' yeasts rather than using natural 'wild' ones, though we definitely prefer the more funky, spicy aromas and flavours imparted by the natural yeasts (see 'The look, smell and taste of wine', page 292). We also prefer the complex textures these yeasts generate on the palate – as in good-quality white burgundy or spicy Châteauneuf-du-Pape ... New World Chardonnay and simple Chilean Merlot just don't quite measure up in the flavour stakes. However, until a winery has built up its own reliable population of local yeasts (which live on the surrounding vines, grapes and in the soil, so the vineyards need to be well established for there to be enough), it is far more likely that 'packet' versions will complete the fermentation successfully, without spoilage. (Sometimes a wild yeast population won't tolerate wine-level alcohol, so stops working before the juice is fully fermented, leaving it susceptible to bacterial attack and re-fermentation.) Plus, some wines need to be kept fresh, simple and fruity. Take Riesling, for example: it doesn't need added spicy complexity or texture.

Our worry with the practice of adding 'live stuff' is that laboratory synthesising will be taken too far. Current state-of-the-industry wineries use selected freeze-dried natural yeast strains that have been found to work well in extreme conditions – they will, for example, happily ferment up to 17 per cent alcohol in Zinfandel, or chomp their way through sugary viscous Sauternes. But what happens when this process is taken a step further and these special assets are genetically modified? Yeasts developed for getting redder-than-ever Pinot Noir, or for creating the perfect long-lasting champagne bubble? As we don't yet know the full effects of such genetic modification, we'd prefer to know more about these additives, and be reassured that they have been rigorously assessed and approved, before they are used.

SIZE ISN'T EVERYTHING

Winemakers do adore big, strapping red wines that win prizes. And why not? We love some of those ripe, full-on flavours too. Unfortunately, however, in the race to wring the most flavour out of their grapes in order to achieve a gutsy great brew, we think some winemakers are going too far and forgetting that you are supposed to be able to drink the stuff. Some of these wines are so thick and mouth-coating, with overly high alcohol and big tannins, that they're impressive at the first sip but after that become quite overwhelming. Worse still, some red wine flavours have become stretched out and artificial-tasting as winemakers – New Worlders, Bordelais and Italians alike – try to make fruit into a bigger wine than it should be. This is also the stage at which the wine becomes too processed – when it is no longer a reflection of its region and its vineyard, but a reflection of the whims of the winemaker.

There are four basic methods for squeezing the best colour and flavour out of red grapes; all to do with managing the floating cap of grape skins that develops as the juice ferments:

1) Pushing down the skins with a pole (the old-fashioned way), regularly. This extracts their colour and flavours gently, resulting in the most delicately constructed red wine.
2) Pumping the wine from the bottom of the vat, out and back in over the top of the floating skins. This is a more aggressive, extractive method: it bashes the skins about in a fiercer way than the first method, releasing more colour and more tannins. (It can, however, be made slightly gentler by using a shower-head-like attachment to soften the impact of the wine returning into the top of the vat.)
3) Maceration – leaving the fermented juice with its skins for a week or two, so the alcohol brings out the flavours. This is very thorough. Cold maceration prior to fermentation is gentler and gives more fruit emphasis.
4) Allowing high temperatures during fermentation. This is the most aggressive way of extracting flavour.

Use all the last three methods above, and (if your grapes are ripe enough in the first place) you'll end up with a thick, black-coloured 'blockbuster' wine. However, if your grapes are not ripe enough in the first place – or if they're from vines that are simply too young to give any 'oomph' to the grapes, or if the yields are too high and the fruit too dilute – you can try to 'extract' all you want, but you won't end up with a balanced wine. In fact, it will taste downright odd. Ever tried a red with a bitter streak at the finish? Or one with thick black colour but not as much flavour as you would have expected? These are wines where the winemaker would have been better advised to coax out the flavours more gently.

The worst crime of all, in our eyes, is the lack of complexity these 'over-extracted' wines have. At best, they're a thick wall of fruit, but one-dimensional – there are no layers. Compare one of the pricier Chilean Cabernets with a decent Médoc Bordeaux and you'll see what we mean.

FINING AGENTS

All wines should be clear: cloudiness not only looks bad, but smacks of contamination and strange bacterial goings-on. Winemakers producing fine wines can afford the luxury of waiting – any bits of grape skin, dead yeasts, protein particles, etc. eventually fall out of vinous suspension in the vat or barrel. This is by far the best method, because all these bits and pieces tend to impart delicate flavours while they're hanging around. However, not all winemakers can afford to wait. To hurry things along a bit, 'glugging' wines will be filtered or centrifuged to clean them up. These are aggressive processes that strip out flavour, but at least the wine will be clean and stable. The alternative to filtering or centrifuging is to use fining agents such as isinglass, gelatin, casein (from milk) and egg white, which are used to absorb and precipitate any unwanted oddments in suspension.

These additives fall perilously into that grey area of 'processing aids' (as do yeast and malolactic bacteria) where, again, genetic modification could be used to make them more efficient, and may go unmentioned on the wine label. Added to which, none of them are substances we want to be tasting in our wine glass – wittingly or not. It's a tough call this: in these days of high turnover, a delicate egg-white addition – at as little as two parts per million – will have a far less flavour-stripping effect than pushing a fine wine through a centrifuge or narrow gauge filter, so this is an addition we don't object to. But we think the Burgundians have it right when they don't fine or filter at all; just let the wine settle out naturally, perhaps chilled down a little to speed things along.

Some merchants (see Vinceremos and Vintage Roots in 'Where to buy wine') go to a great deal of trouble to find out whether these fining additives have been used, so consumers – whether vegetarians, vegans, or anybody concerned – can decide for themselves whether or not they want to drink the wine. Many winemakers argue that these precipitates fall out of suspension naturally and are removed, but traces may remain. If their use were mentioned on the label (or wine list), it would give us the freedom to decide.

A SPOONFUL OF SUGAR

The piece of jiggery-pokery that is causing most upset at the moment is the practice of leaving a couple of extra grams of unfermented sugar in the wine (red or white) to give a sensation of ripe sweetness on the palate. The Americans and Australians are the worst culprits here, with the Bordelais not far behind. This extra sugar may be acceptable when it covers the multitude of flavours in cheap commercial wines, but in the rest, it blurs the true flavours of the grape and blocks out the wine's reflection of *terroir* – as in fact do all the other 'techniques' mentioned above. It is most shocking of all to see this being performed on expensive Bordeaux to make the wines drinkable when younger. Surely manipulating the classics is going too far?

BACK TO THE VINES

So, when you leaf through the 'Where to buy wine' section at the back of this *Guide* and see comments such as 'we're on the lookout for "agricultural", not industrial products', or 'we list wines made with the hands and the heart – not designed in a laboratory, made in a factory', then you'll know what they (and we) mean. Wine gets off to a far better start when it comes from healthy grapes and healthy vineyards; then there's less nip, tuck and tweak needed in the winery!

SK

Part II

A–Z of wine-producing countries

ALGERIA

Several areas in Algeria have an extremely friendly climate for making wine. Indeed, if the country was run by Australians, doubtless our shelves would be full of rich robust reds, some of which – thanks to the presence of venerable vines of Cabernet, Mourvèdre and Grenache – would be attracting the attention of influential critics. But it isn't, and the result is that of the thousands of wines we've tasted since the previous edition, not one has hailed from Algeria. An occasional bottle of the rustic Sidi Brahim has passed our way in recent years, but apart from that, there's little to occupy your time here.

ARGENTINA

Argentinian wine is selling more than well in the UK at the moment but we're worried this supply of decent wine is going to dry up. As the fifth-largest wine producer in the world, this might seem unlikely. Historic connections to Spain and Italy have ensured a magnificent array of grape varieties to draw from, over 2,000 producers, and a culture of day-to-day wine consumption that guarantees a ready market – so winemaking has been big business in Argentina for centuries. But this country is at a real vinous crossroads today and you can taste it in the wines.

It could, as it has done for years, satisfy itself with supplying its own very thirsty but undiscriminating consumers – who see little wine from other countries for comparison. It could follow Chile's success and make similar ripe, oaky Merlots and Cabernets – but we hope it won't. Or it could carve its own path and make wines with their own, essentially Argentinian character – speciality Malbec has been a good start here.

Argentina needs to have the confidence to avoid the first two paths or it might find the excitement its wines currently generate (in the USA as well as in Britain) suddenly dwindling. At grass-roots level, this means getting the growers to understand that the domestic and export markets have hugely differing standards. We hear stories of vines being irrigated right the way through to harvest. Water is a precious commodity in these desert conditions, but while the ability to continuously channel Andean snow-melt to irrigate apple orchards might be a good thing, after a certain point in the grape ripening cycle, it only dilutes flavours. Similarly, vines should be pruned to improve flavour concentration rather than ease the passage of pickers. Air conditioning and temperature control is required in the wineries. And so on. Instead of disparate pockets of innovation and foreign investment, there is a need for a few leading-light ambassadors of change (locals preferably) who will guide the way.

Massive external debt and over three years of recession, plus one or two multi-nationals who've gone in to churn out minimum-risk wines for cheap export, aren't helping things – but it isn't all bad news. We think Argentina's wines have a multi-layered kind of Burgundian rusticity – or spiciness – that's all their own, and with the right guidance they could get better and better. If you look out for Malbec, Cabernet with an individual twist, Bonarda or even Tempranillo, you'll be pleasantly surprised. Cool-climate whites such as peachy Torrontés from 'the highest vineyards in the world' in Salta or Cafayate, Viognier and Chardonnay from Tupungato and exciting new vineyards in northern Patagonia: they all offer new flavours and a new experience.

White wines – grape varieties

Torrontés
This peachy, aromatic grape is a little like a spicy Viognier. It's capable of producing some of Argentina's most distinctive wines, but sadly, many producers overcrop it and make something which is perky but seldom compelling. Head up to high-altitude Salta for the crisp, refreshing best.

Chardonnay
Several good examples exist, but great wines are thin on the ground. Even the finest speak of winemaking processes (usually oak and lees related) rather than of anything uniquely Argentinian. Chardonnay (sometimes with Pinot Noir) appears in some sparklers, but with the exception of Bodegas Chandon's soft creamy wines, few of these are exported.

Others
Experimentation continues apace, throughout the country, so you'll find Viognier, Semillon, Sauvignon Blanc, Chenin Blanc, Riesling and several other varieties. The greatest potential for any of these is in cooler regions such as Salta, Tupungato or San Rafael – there are even murmurings of Marsanne and Roussanne, too. Watch this space.

Red wines – grape varieties

Malbec

This variety, which struggles to excite in south-west France, is the one the Argentinians, rightly, rate the highest. Malbec comes in all guises from simple and juicy to full-bodied, complex and ageworthy – the price usually tells you which to expect. A slightly perfumed blackberry flavour pervades the wines, with the best, often with French oak in attendance, adding characters of damson, black cherry, liquorice and chocolate. Mature Malbec is the ideal foil to a plate-swamping Argentinian steak.

Cabernet Sauvignon

There's no such thing as a typical Argentinian Cabernet; they come in all shapes and sizes, depending on the aspirations of the producer. So while the best examples are on a par with the top Malbecs, they don't proclaim their nationality quite as loudly. Blends with Malbec and/or Merlot can be very good, although again, it's the producer who calls the shots.

Others

Thanks to the legacy of settlers from Europe, Argentina has a broad range of red grape varieties. Among these are Cabernet, Malbec, Merlot and Syrah from France; Tempranillo and Garnacha from Spain; and Nebbiolo, Refosco, Sangiovese, Bonarda and Barbera from Italy. Mature vineyards of all these grapes now exist, but Cabernet, Malbec and Merlot apart, growers have yet to exploit such resources fully, and many sites are poorly tended. Some good new wines, however, come from Syrah (often called Shiraz), Tempranillo (the 'grape of the moment'; let's see how it fares) and Bonarda which produces archetypal pizza wine – thin or slightly sour, spicy Beaujolais.

Just to confuse the issue even further, the above are also being put together in some interesting, if unconventional, blends. Look out for Sangiovese/Tempranillo or Merlot/Bonarda and prepare to be amazed.

The regions

More than 70 per cent of Argentina's wine comes from Mendoza – Mendoza province that is, not Mendoza City, which is its capital. Within the province, there is a wide variety of climates. Basically, as you travel towards the ever-present Andes, the higher and cooler it becomes, although all districts are basically desert, and depend on irrigation water in the form of snow-melt from the Andes for their survival. Tupungato is the highest, coolest area, and is gaining a reputation for Chardonnay, Viognier and well-balanced reds. Most of the highly rated districts for Cabernet and Malbec lie to the west of Mendoza City, among them Luján de Cuyo, Maipú and Guaymallén. If the lower-altitude vineyards to the east are sometimes considered inferior, this is perhaps more a reflection of the poor standard of the vineyards there than of the region itself. Three hours' drive to the south of Mendoza City, but still within the same province, is San Rafael, which, despite being rather hail-prone, is turning out to be a good home for whites – with Chardonnay, Sauvignon, Viognier and Rhône varietals Roussanne and Marsanne coming on stream.

The regions of Salta and La Rioja lie to the north of Mendoza. North generally means warmer in South America, but the higher altitude, especially in Salta, means that respectable reds and whites can be produced. In fact, Salta is generating so much excitement that suitable flat areas of the Andean foothills are being dynamited to make way for new vineyards – that's the power of a potentially good Cabernet site for you! Cafayate is a Salta sub-region at a lofty 1,700m with a growing reputation for fine Torrontés.

To the south of Mendoza is the cool Rio Negro region of Patagonia, which is causing the biggest stir of all. Cool is cool at the moment and fashionable growers are setting up new vineyards in this apple orchard-territory. Its chalky soils (as in Champagne) are an added attraction for fizz producers too.

Pick of the producers

La Agricola Large, export-minded and constantly experimenting winery owned by the Zuccardi family, turning out good-value, tasty wines under the Santa Julia and Pacajuan Peak labels. The Familia Zuccardi Q range, including excellent Malbec and Tempranillo, is a step up.

Bodegas Balbi Allied Domecq-owned operation based in San Rafael, but sourcing fruit from throughout Mendoza. Syrah rosé is delightful, whites are improving, but reds, topped by fine blend Barbaro and fruity Malbec, are the pick.

Bianchi The basic Elsa range is acceptable, but the high-end reds, especially the Familia Bianchi Cabernet/Merlot/Malbec blend, are first class.

Luigi Bosca From the 1998 vintage, the slightly tired wines of the past have given way to a much more impressive range of both reds and whites. Look out too for the stunning Viña Alicia reds (especially good Petit Verdot and Nebbiolo), made by a member of the same family.

Humberto Canale Rio Negro pioneer leading the pack in trendy northern Patagonia. Best known for traditional-style Malbec, but also succeeds with Semillon and Sauvignon.

Catena Dynamic producer making some of Argentina's finest Cabernet, Chardonnay and Malbec. Has recently launched a joint-venture with the Bordeaux Rothschilds. The range runs in ascending order of quality from good-value Alamos Ridge through Catena to top-notch (and top-price) Catena Alta. The sole criticism is that these are perhaps international rather than Argentinian wines. Also owns a variety of other labels, among them Libertad, La Rural and Argento, plus new vineyards in northern Patagonia.

Bodegas Colomé The spicy Cabernet/Malbec blend is the best Salta red we know – more like a Châteauneuf than a Bordeaux wine.

Etchart Owned by Pernod-Ricard, with vineyards in both Mendoza and Salta. Cafayate Torrontés is perhaps the most superior example around, while Arnaldo B Etchart Malbec/Cabernet blend is also outstanding.

Fabre Montmayou/Domaine Vistalba French-owned winery using the expertise of the famed Bordeaux consultant Michel Rolland to make high-quality, good-value reds and whites. Also produces the Infinitus wines from Patagonia.

Finca la Amalia Chardonnay, Cabernet and thoughtfully made Malbec from 1,000m-high Mendoza vineyards in the Andean foothills.

Finca la Anita Move over Australia. This Mendoza *bodega* makes superb Syrah, both straight and in a blend with Malbec. Fine, if expensive, Merlot too.

Finca El Retiro Mendoza estate benefiting from the winemaking expertise of Alberto Antonini, the former technical director of Antinori in Italy. Lovely rich reds, especially the Tempranillo.

Finca Flichman Elegant Chardonnay, spicy Syrah and ripe Cabernet Reserve are the most admirable of a large set of wines.

Bodegas Lurton Best of the flying winemaker projects in Argentina, with a spanking new winery making smashing reds, especially the Gran Lurton Cabernet. Also responsible for the Corazon label.

Medrano Exciting co-operative providing great value, especially for Malbec.

Navarro Correas Much improved with more sensitive use of oak; good reds with the stars being spicy Correas Malbec and Colección Privada Cabernet/Merlot.

Nieto y Senetiner Mostly known for its Valle de Vistalba range, but chunky, chocolaty, hedonistic top reds, called Cadus, are the pick.

Norton Reasonable whites, but reds, especially Reserve Malbec and Privada (Cabernet/Merlot/Malbec), can be first rate.

Terrazas New non-sparkling wine arm of Bodegas Chandon. Cabernet and Malbec from 1999, the first full vintage, promise much for the future. Basic range is Alto, then Reserva, then Gran Terrazas.

Trapiche Top winery of the giant Peñaflor, which also owns Santa Ana and Michel Torino (fine Don David Cabernet). Recently introduced top-of-the-range Merlot/Malbec Iscay is classy and now available in the UK; Medalla Cabernet and Merlot are also very good. Watch for new entry-level wine Astica, starting at £3.99.

Viña Patagonia Sister company of Chile's Viña Cono Sur based in Mendoza. Has La Chamiza vineyards in Maipú and Los Ponchos for white and lighter reds in Tupungato. Fruit-forward, spicy Malbecs especially good from the former.

Weinert The wines can occasionally be spoiled by extensive oak ageing, but otherwise, they are among the most satisfying in Argentina, densely fruity and more Old World than New in structure and flavour. Pick of an excellent range is the wonderfully perfumed Malbec.

Argentinian vintage guide

Another New World area where you might think vintage variation insignificant – but take care, it does exist. The terrible flooding caused by El Niño in 1998 proved the point. Though it doesn't have the same excuse, the 2001 vintage isn't looking much better, with rain and hail setting in towards the end of the ripening season. Fortunately for us, the rather undiscriminating local markets soak up much of the rained-out wines. Fortunately also, there's enough regional variation in Argentina for disastrous conditions in, say, Mendoza not to affect Cafayate or Salta. For the record, 2000 was an acceptable year, and 1999 was outstanding.

Most white wines should be drunk on release. Top Chardonnays can be kept for up to five years from vintage, but even these are probably at their best when younger. Cheaper reds too are mostly made for early consumption. However, some of the more expensive Syrah, Malbec and Cabernet-based wines often need a couple of years in bottle to settle down, and the best (especially from years such as 1999) will often last for a decade or more.

AUSTRALIA

Imagine that one big, giant company dominated an entire country's wine production, imposing its own ideas, values and range of flavours on every bottle that was made. Impossible? Well, until recently, there were five large companies in Australia. The merger, in early 2001, of two of those five – Rosemount and Southcorp – could well, however, change the status quo. The combined forces of these two estates will create the most powerful voice in the Australian wine industry by far – and the eighth largest in the world. We could console ourselves that one of the brains behind the merger is an ex-employee of that truly Australian organisation, Fosters. But then again, that is exactly our worry. Mildara-Blass' link with California's mighty Beringer estate looms equally threatening.

Is Australian wine going to go the same way as beer? Blended to the same recipe, with the same yeasts, by the same beer-maker,

with the same cheerful packaging? Will events such as the above merger help things along that route? When you have Chardonnay grapes coming in from all over the country, quantities ever-increasing as your vineyards expand, more again as your company amalgamates with another, what do you do with them all? There's an easy answer. Just blend them all up and put them in one big pot. Deal with them as one big batch. (Rumour has it that the first million-litre tank is under construction somewhere in the Barossa.)

We've talked to wine lovers, high-street merchants, restaurant wine waiters, Australian winemakers and marketing gurus both Down Under and here in rainy Britain – and we know that this doesn't make sense. Wine drinkers are ready to trade up. The 'anything but Chardonnay' voice is already filtering back to Australian vineyards. Grapes such as Riesling, Semillon and Verdelho are in demand for whites; Grenache, Mourvèdre, Pinot, and even more obscure varietals for reds. There's a huge call for more regional wines. Labels with Clare Valley, Barossa, Wrattonbully and Orange writ large are satisfying an increasing thirst for wine knowledge, from drinkers who want to get to grips with different flavours and aromas – why they happen and how.

We're worried, though, that a lot of the bigger wineries don't seem to realise this and are continuing to churn out the likes of cross-regional generic wooded Shiraz ad infinitum. There's even a term for it now: 'Chardonnisation'. Poor though we might be here in the dependable UK market, sooner or later we are going to be bored with this, really bored. Then Argentina and Chile will step in and offer something different at the same price. So, we ask, wouldn't it be better if the big Australian decision-makers got out of their private jets and listened?

As ever, it's the smaller wineries that have the broader, more interesting ranges (go to your wine merchant, not the supermarket, to find Cullen, Henschke, Grosset or Pipers Brook). On a smaller scale, the Australian have-a-go attitude invariably ends up with less formulaic winemaking more pertinent to the (dare we say it) *terroir* in question. Attention to detail in the vineyards has certainly stepped up, with leaf-plucking, green harvesting and improved canopy shapes all contributing to grape flavours outshining wood, concentration not dilution, ageability and complexity. Warm sunshine and plenty of rain usually preclude organic grape production in most Australian wine regions, but there has been a move towards it. Birds, though, are a perennial problem. Introducing 'spiders to catch flies' has always hit snags in Australia – but guinea fowl and chickens in the vineyards to attract birds of prey, which scare off the grape eaters, have been successful. Although, as ever seems the case Down Under, prey turns pest when the chickens learn to jump up and eat the grapes. But it's not so disastrous when (to use a Barossa example) they then lay Cabernet Sauvignon-flavoured purple eggs...

Australians are learning to be careful with their country. It's an ancient continent, its soils fragile and easily eroded. This is a thoughtfulness that's awakening in the wine industry too. Rejected products such as skins and stems are sent for recycling (to make marc, or extract alcohol and useful tartaric acid), pips are used for grape seed oil or for chippings on children's playgrounds. A shame then that this pattern of minimal disruption so often gets left at the cellar door when it comes to winemaking. Additions such as tannin and acid are still very much the everday norm, to the extent now that flavours are manipulated rather than adjusted. Again, we'd like to put out a call for winemakers to be less heavy-handed, and use more natural methods to balance their wines. We can, after all, taste what they're up to!

Red wines – grape varieties

Shiraz

Shiraz is Australia's most widely planted red grape, and is also responsible for many of the country's greatest wines. An amazing diversity of styles is produced in the different regions, from the Rhône-like wines of the Yarra and Lower Great Southern, through to the fragrant peppery reds of Central Victoria and on to the heady berry and chocolate concoctions of McLaren Vale and the opulent, ripe blueberry-spice wines of the Barossa Valley. In warmer regions, the ripe fruit and alcohol levels of some wines can overwhelm, but the best examples retain balance, and age extremely well. Some producers nowadays are blending Rhône-style and adding a tiny percentage of white Viognier, or even Chardonnay, to add complexity. There are also more new styles emerging from Western Australia – keep an eye out for Shiraz from Pemberton and Margaret River.

Cabernet Sauvignon

Cabernet Sauvignon can be almost as impressive. Again, the wines differ markedly from district to district. For elegance, go to Coonawarra, Yarra Valley and Margaret River, while for honest power, look at Clare and McLaren Vale. Cabernet/Shiraz blends are slipping out of vogue, but can be delicious. Malbec, Merlot and Cabernet Franc are also used as blending partners with Cabernet, and Petit Verdot and Malbec are creeping into more and more blends from the Bordeaux-centric Margaret River. Merlot plantings are increasing, but good varietal versions are still rare. Stand-alone Cabernet Francs can be pleasantly chunky yet perfumed.

Others

A growing number of producers are making use of the knobbly old vines of Grenache and Mourvèdre (known here as Mataro) which exist especially in the Barossa and McLaren Vale. These two varieties have traditionally been confined to the role of bulk provider, but they are now being treated with greater respect. The best wines tend to be blends, usually with a dollop of Shiraz, but there are some successful 100 per cent Grenaches from producers who manage to provide the depth of flavour to balance the often high alcohol levels.

The Australians continue to make steady progress with Pinot Noir. The Yarra Valley, Mornington Peninsula, Geelong, Adelaide Hills and Tasmania are the regions with the highest concentration of good Pinot, although as in Burgundy, the best are expensive and in short supply. Cheaper ones are better avoided. Plantings of Italian varieties such as Sangiovese and Nebbiolo are increasing, but few wines have been released so far.

White wines – grape varieties

Chardonnay

Australia's most poised, elegant Chardonnays undoubtedly come from cooler climate regions – including Clare Valley, Adelaide Hills, Margaret River – where they can gain in concentration without losing structure and becoming buttery, flabby monsters. We have high hopes that the latter will soon become a thing of the past as wines become more subtle with each vintage, especially as producers begin to take more care in their vineyards and cut their yields. Oak can still be excessive on occasions, but we're also in two minds about the vogue for unoaked Chardonnay. Many cheaper wines need the woody vanilla flavour otherwise they can be very bland. However, the best unoaked wines (Chapel Hill, Nepenthe, Pipers Brook's Ninth Island) have the substance to survive, nay, flourish in a wood-free form.

Semillon

Semillon is one of the best grapes for showing Australia's regional differences, but it's not as immediately luscious as Chardonnay and as a result hasn't been as commercially successful. The best-known Semillon region is the Hunter Valley, where they pick it very early to make a minerally low-alcohol wine – 10 per cent is not unheard of – with no use of oak, which needs five years at least to show at its toasty best. In South Australia, it is harvested riper and often treated like Chardonnay, with barrel fermentation and ageing. The result is more forward but again ages very well. Margaret River versions tend to this latter style, but often have a grassy edge. Fans of sweet

42

wines should try the opulent *botrytis*-affected Semillons of Griffith in New South Wales.

Semillon also plays a part in some regions in blends with Sauvignon Blanc. Much of Australia is too warm to make Sauvignon, but parts of central Victoria, Coonawarra, the Adelaide Hills and Margaret River have all shown that the variety can thrive in the right conditions. The best are like chubbier New Zealand versions.

Riesling
A grape that has shown its mettle in several parts of Australia is Riesling. The Clare and Eden valleys are the traditional strongholds, but many other regions make successful versions. The best start off tight and limey, but develop honeyed petrol and lanolin notes with time. Sweet *botrytised* versions are rare but be superb.

Others

Verdelho, one of the grapes used in the making of madeira, used to be confined mainly to Western Australia, but it is starting to appear elsewhere, making wines with aromatic peachy fruit and a nutty/savoury character. Marsanne, mainly found in the Goulburn Valley, provides more peaches, this time with hints of honeysuckle. Apart from at Houghton in Western Australia, Chenin Blanc seldom achieves anything of note. Many Australian producers are currently excited about the potential of Pinot Gris, and we've been favourably impressed with the wines from Pipers Brook, Henschke, T'Gallant and Mount Langi Ghiran. Viognier is proving just as much of a challenge in Australia as anywhere else, but after 20 years of experimentation, Yalumba has cracked it, with a rich, peachy wine.

Sparkling wines

Australia can make surprisingly classy fizz. In the past, producers have often made the mistake of getting too much flavour into their base wines before the bubbles go in – the result of using fruit which is more appropriate for table wines. But great strides are being made. The key is to source fruit from cool regions, and (amazingly) just about every state can lay claim to some of those. In Victoria, the Yarra Valley leads the way with Domaine Chandon's Green Point and Yarra Bank, and the Strathbogie Hills are showing promising signs. Tasmania is up there too, with Pirie from Pipers Brook and (relatively new on the scene) *brut* non-vintage from Stefano Lubiana. Brian Croser's Petaluma fizz from the Adelaide Hills is impressive, as is the multi-regional Yalumba D. Western Australia has cool spots; Orange (and a handful of other new areas) in New South Wales have potential, and even Queensland's Granite Belt isn't out of the question.

However, sparkling wine doesn't have to be made by the classic champagne method or with the classic grapes. Everyday, cheap and cheerful, summer-drinking wines, such as Yalumba's Angas Brut and Seppelt's Great Western, are fruity and lively but simple, with upfront flavour and lots of froth. Then there are the sparkling reds – real 'love 'em or hate 'em' wines. Shiraz is the favoured grape, although Cabernet and Grenache are also pressed into service. They're big, often quite sweet, rich, ripe and tannic, and they age magnificently. Quirky, but great fun, and a favoured partner for the Christmas turkey. Charles Melton's and Seppelt's are particularly good.

Australian 'sticky' wines

Stickies (sweet Australian dessert wines) fall into three groups – late-harvest wines; fortified, fruity 'port' styles; and Rutherglen Muscats. The good thing about all of them is that they're ripe, sweet, rich and fruity but they tend to have enough vibrant acidity to finish cleanly without getting sickly or cloying. Late-harvest and *botrytised* Semillons are the most visible on the market and tend to come from warmer regions – Noble One from De Bortoli is the classic example (and the most expensive); hot on its heels are Penfolds, Yalumba, Elderton and Fern Hill. Muscat and even Sauvignon grapes (from Windowrie) also make intense late-harvest styles, but the prize has to go to the Rieslings – who can resist that mouth-tingling lemony acidity? Mount Horrocks' Cordon Cut, Primo Estate La Magia and d'Arenberg's The Noble are the ones to watch. Oh, and all of them age well – so try to resist guzzling them straight away.

Fortified styles, called 'ports' and 'tawnies', don't tend to make it to UK shores in great abundance and have a much bolder fruitier style than the genuine articles – Penfolds Magill and d'Arenberg's Shiraz versions are good. The real classics though are the Rutherglen Muscats. These come from intensely ripe grapes fermented to a mere five per cent alcohol, fortified, then aged in barrels in a sherry-type *solera* (at one time this was in old tin sheds, so there was a lot of heating involved too). There are four grades – Rutherglen Muscat, Classic RM, Grand RM and (most hedonistic of the lot) Rare RM – that depend on the vineyards in question and the ripeness of the year. If you want a match for chocolate, it's these sumptuous monsters you should look to – particularly from Campbells, Chambers and Stanton & Killeen.

The regions

New South Wales

Proximity to Sydney rather than viticultural attributes led to the development of the Hunter Valley, New South Wales's most famous wine region. Australia's first commercial Chardonnay came from the Hunter in the early 1970s, and the Upper Hunter in particular, home of Rosemount, can still produce some great examples. However, it is another white grape, Semillon, which is behind many of the best wines. Hunter Semillon can seem rather 'so-what?' in its youth, with the same sort of steely austerity as a young Chablis, but ten years in bottle sees a rich, custard-on-toast character emerge to join the pithy limey fruit. Cleaned-up winemaking now means that the 'sweaty saddle' Hunter reds are a thing of the past, and the top wines such as Brokenwood Shiraz are magnificent.

Elsewhere in the state, Mudgee has been up and coming for several years, but quality remains erratic. Even so, wines such as Rosemount's Mountain Blue Shiraz/Cabernet show what the region is capable of. To the south, fine Chardonnay and Verdelho are coming out of Cowra, while Orange – the illustrious Rosemount estate once again acting as ambassador – is developing elegant Chardonnays, and rich but graceful Cabernet and Shiraz. The bulk region of the state is Riverina, also known variously as the Murrumbidgee Irrigation Area (M.I.A.) or Griffith. Amid simple varietals, here are some of the world's most unctuous dessert wines in the shape of *botrytis*-affected Semillon. Two more new areas to watch are cool-climate Hilltops and Tumbarumba – even cool enough, they say, for sparkling and Sangiovese.

Queensland

It should be too hot to grow grapes here, but the high altitude in the Granite Belt to the west of Brisbane means that temperatures are low enough for even fizz not to be out of the question. Ballandean Estate is the best-known winery, making decent rather than exciting Shiraz and Sauvignon/Semillon, plus surprisingly good late-harvest Sylvaner.

South Australia

Victoria has more wineries, but South Australia makes a larger volume of wine, as well as being home to virtually all of the country's major producers. While most of the output comes from the irrigated Riverland region, there are also a number of smaller, higher-quality districts. Clare Valley to the north of Adelaide is the source of rumbustious Shiraz and Cabernet as well as some of Australia's greatest, and finest, Rieslings. Wines from the Barossa

Valley vary from rather bland whites from hot valley-floor vineyards to outstanding old-vine Shiraz, often from hillside vineyards. The Eden Valley is a cooler sub-region of the Barossa, and vies with Clare to produce the state's most elegant Riesling. Again, Shiraz excels, especially in Henschke's Hill of Grace. The Adelaide Hills is also a cooler-climate region, already making crisp flavoursome Chardonnays and Sauvignons, and showing promise with Pinot Noir. Wines from the Lenswood sub-region are worth seeking out.

South of Adelaide are McLaren Vale and Langhorne Creek, sources of the type of open-faced honest reds which we most readily associate with Australia, the best of which are among the country's finest. Further south still brings you to a stretch of regions known collectively as the Limestone Coast. Most famous of these is Coonawarra – with its *terra rossa* soil – home of elegant Cabernet, great Shiraz and a couple of refined Sauvignons. The heated dispute about the precise definition of Coonawarra, with some vineyards, most notably one belonging to Petaluma, falling outside newly drawn-up official boundaries, has at long last been resolved – with Petaluma ending up in, not out. Padthaway to the north is just as cool but with slightly heavier soils in which Chardonnay thrives. Other Limestone Coast regions you may see on labels in the near future include Wrattonbully, which is making a name for red wines, and cooler, coastal Robe and Mount Benson.

Tasmania

Tasmania contributes less than one per cent to Australia's total grape crush, and the number of wineries on the island is small, with only Dr Andrew Pirie's Pipers Brook achieving anything like international recognition. However, the cool climate is ideal for grapes for sparkling wines, and several mainland companies now source Pinot Noir and Chardonnay from here to pep up their blends. Pirie's success with a variety of still wines shows that if the rest of the islanders can shrug off their cottage mentality, Tasmania could teach those across the Bass Strait a thing or two about elegance and complexity – but we're still waiting.

Victoria

Whatever style of wine you're looking for, chances are you'll find it somewhere in Victoria. The cheap and cheerful comes from vineyards along the Murray River in the north-west of the state. Travel eastwards along the border with New South Wales and you hit Rutherglen, home of luscious Liqueur Muscat and Tokay, and decent port lookalikes, as well as burly reds made from Cabernet, Shiraz and Durif. Across the centre of Victoria are several small regions, namely (from west to east) Great Western/The Grampians, the Pyrenees, Bendigo, Heathcote and Goulburn Valley. Each is home to only a handful of wineries, but a number of notable ones excel in reds, especially Shiraz. Goulburn Valley also has extensive plantings of Marsanne. The other main regions, Geelong, Macedon, the Yarra Valley and the Mornington Peninsula, are clustered around Port Philip Bay. Shiraz can be found here, but Pinot Noir and Chardonnay are the specialities, with both being used for still and sparkling wines (as is Shiraz for that matter). Further east, East Gippsland boasts few wineries, but is the source of the outstanding Pinot Noir from Bass Phillip.

Western Australia
Western Australia produces only two per cent of all Australian wine, but it's a remarkably good two per cent. While many of the large companies have vineyards in WA, none is based here, and most of the producers are medium-sized or smaller. The Swan Valley was the first region to be developed, in the mid-1800s, and still produces reasonable commercial styles, but the last 30 years have seen the establishment of wineries further to the south. Margaret River, at the south-western tip of the country, ranks as perhaps the most consistent fine wine region in Australia, with elegant Cabernets, refined Chardonnays, pithy Semillons and earthy Shirazes. The sprawling Lower Great Southern region along the south coast, encompassing areas we're hearing more and more about – Frankland and Mount Barker – is home to top-class Riesling and can also impress with Cabernet and Shiraz. Between here and Margaret River lies Pemberton, which is beginning to make a name for Pinot Noir and Chardonnay. Other new regions to look out for are Mandurah, Geographe, and the Blackwood Valley.

Pick of the producers

Tim Adams Clare Valley producer of great and powerful reds, especially the Fergus (Grenache) and Aberfeldy Shiraz. The creamy fat Semillon and limey Riesling are also delicious – and long-lived.

Amberley Small, quality winery in Margaret River for superb ageworthy Semillons; unusual Chenin Blanc is the mainstream wine, and reds are getting better and better.

d'Arenberg Most dynamic winery in McLaren Vale, offering a wide range of ever-improving reds at down-to-earth prices.

Bannockburn Geelong winery turning out Burgundian Pinot Noir and Chardonnay, plus an underrated peppery Shiraz.

Jim Barry Small Clare Valley winery with fine red range topped by the intense Armagh Shiraz.

Basedow Good-value varietals, especially Chardonnay and Semillon, from this Barossa concern, now widening its regional interest to the Adelaide Hills.

Beringer Blass see under Mildara Blass.

Bests Family-run winery in the Grampians, Victoria, making understated Shiraz, Riesling, Cabernet, and a Dolcetto – plus interesting Pinot Meunier from vines original to the homestead.

De Bortoli Opulent dessert wines including the intriguing Black Noble from Griffith; also elegant reds and whites from the Yarra Valley.

BRL Hardy Huge conglomerate whose brands include Houghton, Moondah Brook, Chateau Reynella, Yarra Burn, Stanley, Leasingham and Berri Estates, as well as Hardy's. The wines run the gamut from everyday ranges such as Banrock Station, Nottage Hill and Stamp Series to the very classy. Possibles for top wines include a trio of fine Shirazes, namely Eileen Hardy, Leasingham Classic Clare and Chateau Reynella Basket-Pressed.

Brokenwood Candidate for the finest winery in the Hunter Valley, with superb Graveyard Shiraz, substantial ageworthy Semillon and very acceptable second label Cricket Pitch. Also excellent Rayner Shiraz from McLaren Vale.

Brown Brothers Instrumental in bringing Australian wines to many Brits, and still very reliable. New Nebbiolo and Barbera are good, as are Riesling of all sweetnesses, Liqueur Muscat and sparkling Pinot/Chardonnay.

Grant Burge Fast becoming a Barossa institution, Burge makes good commercial wines at the lower end of the price spectrum but excels with satisfying reds, especially the new Holy Trinity (Grenache/Shiraz/Mourvèdre).

Campbells Rutherglen stalwart making great Liqueur Muscat and chunky reds – Bobby Burns Shiraz and The Barkly Durif.

Cape Mentelle Inspired reds (including a Zinfandel) and whites from Cloudy Bay's sister winery in Margaret River. Second label Ironstone uses fruit from other Western Australian regions.

Chambers Liqueur Muscats from Rutherglen with extraordinary depth and complexity.

Domaine Chandon Yarra Valley-based offshoot of Moët, making refined fizz and also impressing with still Pinot Noir and Chardonnay.

Chapel Hill Class across the board from Pam Dunsford, mainly from McLaren Vale fruit, with The Vicar, a Cabernet/Shiraz blend, being the pick.

Clarendon Hills Much-revered huge, idiosyncratic wines which often top 15 per cent alcohol. Astralis Shiraz competes with Penfolds' Grange, both in quality and price.

Coldstream Hills Chardonnay and Pinot Noir specialist in the Yarra Valley, founded by wine writer James Halliday, who still runs winemaking operations, but now owned by Southcorp (see *Penfolds* and *Rosemount*, below).

Cullens Award-winning mother and daughter team Di and Vanya Cullen make majestic Cabernet blends, rich powerful Chardonnay and pungent Sauvignon at their esteemed Margaret River winery.

Dalwhinnie Pyrenees winery making fine, elegant Shiraz, Cabernet and Chardonnay which all need time in bottle to show their class.

Devil's Lair Concentrated, stylish Chardonnay and Cabernet/Merlot from the Margaret River outpost of Southcorp. Second label Fifth Leg is trendy and tasty.

Fox Creek The Reserve Shiraz and Cabernet make this McLaren Vale red specialist one of Australia's most admirable small wineries.

Frankland Estate Finest producer in the Lower Great Southern, with tight limey Riesling, fragrant Shiraz and classy Bordeaux blend Olmo's Reward.

Grosset Clare Valley-based but also sourcing fruit from the Adelaide Hills, trump cards are tight, minerally Riesling and powerful, pungent Chardonnay. (See also *Mount Horrocks*, below.)

Henschke Stephen Henschke's winemaking skill combined with his wife Prue's viticultural talents have made this arguably Australia's best small winery. Hill of Grace Shiraz is the star, but if you can't find/afford it, any of the other wines, red or white, from Eden Valley or the Adelaide Hills, makes a lovely alternative.

Houghton Swan Valley-based winery, now owned by BRL Hardy. Best known in Australia for Houghton's White Burgundy (sold in the UK as HWB), also has good-value Wildflower Ridge range, classic WA Verdelho and top red Jack Mann.

Howard Park Based in the Lower Great Southern region of Western Australia, but now with a new winery in Margaret River. Riesling and Cabernet rank among the most satisfying in the state.

Jasper Hill Bendigo Shiraz specialist, currently engaged in joint venture with Chapoutier of the Rhône. Also lovely limey Riesling.

Katnook Estate Coonawarra winery with an impressive range topped by the Bordeaux blend Odyssey, Prodigy Shiraz and including one of Australia's most acceptable Sauvignons. Parent company Wingara also produces two other Coonawarra ranges, Riddoch and Woolshed, plus Deakin Estate from the Riverland.

Leeuwin Estate Margaret River showcase winery, the Art Series Riesling, Chardonnay and Cabernet are all very classy wines, while the second label Prelude range puts many others to shame.

Peter Lehmann No-nonsense wines from the Baron of the Barossa. Look out for good-value Vine Vale range, sappy Semillon with a touch of oak and sumptuous Stonewell Shiraz.

Lenswood The Adelaide Hills venture of Tim Knappstein, already first rate with Semillon, Sauvignon and Chardonnay and making strides with Pinot Noir. Also keep an eye out for Palatine red blend and rare Gewurztraminer.

Lindemans (see *Southcorp*, below).

McWilliams Large company making a broad selection of wines from various regions. Stick with the very traditional Hunter Valley Semillons and Shirazes.

Charles Melton Barossa maverick renowned for an original range – Nine Popes (Grenache/Shiraz), Rose of Virginia Grenache rosé and excellent Shiraz, sparkling as well as still.

Mildara Blass Has merged with mighty Beringer US estate. Parent company of several wineries including Wolf Blass (ripe, oaky commercial wines, impressive Black Label Cabernet/Shiraz and lovely Rieslings), Maglieri (classy McLaren Vale Shiraz), Quelltaler Estate (superb Rieslings) and Rothbury Estate (good Hunter Valley Semillon, Chardonnay, Verdelho and Shiraz).

Mitchelton Fat, peachy and remarkably ageworthy Marsanne is the best-known wine from this Goulburn Valley winery, but all the wines, including those under the Preece label, are good.

Morris The reds are big and rustic, but the class act is the Liqueur Muscat, bolstered by reserve wines dating back over 100 years.

Mountadam Now owned by Cape Mentelle. Adam Wynn's enterprising winery in the Eden Valley, making rich but subtle Chardonnay, fine-tuned Pinot Noir and complex fizz. Second labels are David Wynn and the organic Eden Ridge.

Mount Horrocks Fabulous Riesling (dry, and sumptuous Cordon Cut sweet) plus Chardonnay and Shiraz made by Stephanie Toole. Shares a winery (a converted dairy) in the Clare Valley with husband, Jeffrey Grosset (see above).

Mount Langi Ghiran Trevor Mast makes one of the most distinctive Shirazes in central Victoria, and his Riesling and Pinot Gris also merit attention. He makes the Four Sisters wines too, but using McLaren Vale fruit. Mast is now involved in a joint venture with Chapoutier of the Rhône.

Nepenthe Enjoyable Riesling, Chardonnay and Semillon from new Adelaide Hills producer. Surprisingly good Zinfandel too.

Noon With very little fuss, Master of Wine Drew Noon has transformed his family winery into one of the stars of McLaren Vale, with stunning Shiraz, Cabernet and Grenache (called Eclipse).

Orlando Mammoth, slightly lumbering Barossa operation owned by Pernod-Ricard, best known for Jacob's Creek, but also producing finer wines such as Steingarten Riesling, Lawson's Shiraz, Jacaranda Ridge Cabernet and the Saints range.

Penfolds Main brand of Southcorp (see below). Traditionally red wine specialists, with Grange Shiraz heading an impressive range, closely followed by 707 Cabernet and RWT Shiraz. Top white is Yattarna Chardonnay, but new Eden Valley Riesling is just as good – and a third of the price.

Petaluma Innovative winery headed by the forthright Brian Croser with very good wines from specially chosen sites throughout South Australia. Second label is Bridgewater Mill. Also owns the Knappstein Winery in Clare (great Cabernet Franc) and now have a stake in Stonier's in Mornington Peninsula.

Pipers Brook Largest, most important and best winery on Tasmania, thanks to the efforts of the studious Dr Andrew Pirie. Highlights of an excellent range (and an impressive second label Ninth Island) are the Pirie sparkling and the lush, complex Chardonnays, but don't ignore the aromatic varieties.

Rockford Robert 'Rocky' O'Callaghan of the Barossa uses ancient equipment and equally ancient vines to make huge, glowering Basket Press Shiraz, ripe Grenache, rich, petrolly Riesling and Semillon and glorious sparkling Shiraz.

Rosemount Long-popular family estate making history in 2001 for its leading role in the merger with Southcorp (see below), to make it the largest wine producer in Australia. Gained its stripes in the UK for the good-value 'Diamond Label' range, but also capable of immensely classy wines such as Balmoral Shiraz (McLaren Vale), Mountain Blue Shiraz/Cabernet (Mudgee), Orange Chardonnay (Orange) and Roxburgh Chardonnay (Upper Hunter). Marks & Spencer's Honeytree range comes from Rosemount. Watch this space.

St Hallett Shiraz is the speciality, with Old Block and Blackwell standing out, but everything from the good-value Poacher's Blend and Gamekeeper's Reserve upwards is a good, honest, flavour-packed Barossa wine.

Shaw and Smith Adelaide Hills white wine specialists making delicious crisp Sauvignons and fine Chardonnays – both oaked and unoaked.

Southcorp One of Australia's 'big four' wine companies – owner of prestige Penfolds estate, plus Coldstream Hills, Devil's Lair, Lindemans, Rouge Homme, Seaview, Seppelt, Wynns and others – as a result of the dramatic merger with Rosemount (see above) making it the largest producer in Australia – size-wise, eighth in the world! The merger is sending shockwaves through the industry. As the *Guide* goes to press, its full implications are as yet unknown.

Chateau Tahbilk Powerful, tannic and long-lived, if occasionally rustic, Shiraz and Cabernet; lovely honeysuckle-scented Marsanne.

Taltarni Good sparklers, including Clover Hill from Tasmania, and decent Sauvignon Blanc, but the stars are the reds from the Victorian Pyrenees, especially the Cabernet Sauvignon.

Tarrawarra Sexy, beautifully textured Yarra Valley Chardonnay and Pinot Noir; second label Tunnel Hill also commendable.

Tatachilla Now a sister winery of St Hallett, producing an admirable range topped by rich, chocolaty Foundation Shiraz.

Torbreck Dave Powell's Barossa reds are hard to find and not cheap, but their combination of power and balance makes them among the best in the region.

Tyrrells Hunter Valley stalwarts – bypass the rather ordinary Old Winery range and head for the Vat 47 Chardonnay, Vat 1 Semillon, Vat 9 Shiraz and Vat 8 Shiraz/Cabernet. Quality can be erratic.

Veritas Small Barossa winery making its own and contracted Shiraz (plus Grenache, and Mataro) from old bush vines. Hefty wines all, Hanisch, JJ Hahn, Heysen and Draycott, are all made by the irrepressible Hungarian, Rolf Binder.

Wirra Wirra Southern Vales winery with good whites and very good reds, Church Block, RSW Shiraz and the Angelus Cabernet being the pick.

Yalumba Barossa-based company best known for Angas Brut and Oxford Landing – the quality of both of which remains good – but with several more aces up its sleeve. Top reds are The Menzies Coonawarra Cabernet, Signature Cabernet/Shiraz and Octavius Shiraz, top whites are Rieslings from the Pewsey Vale and Heggies vineyards, and Virgilius Viognier. Yalumba D fizz is also recommended.

Yarra Yering Quirky Yarra winery owned and run by the bright-eyed Bailey Carrodus. Quality and interest level are both very high across the range, and all the wines benefit from extra bottle age.

Australian vintage guide

Yes, there is a variation in Australian vintages, although the technical expertise of the winemakers tends to diminish the effects of the lean years. Most wines taste good from the word go, but it's a mistake to think that, because of this, they don't age well. With whites, top examples of Riesling and Semillon are still in fine fettle after ten years – as are any of the sweeties – if you can resist them. Few Chardonnays are worth keeping for more than a couple of years, although a rest of 12 months after release for the oak to calm down is of benefit to many wines.

With reds, some Pinot Noirs can last for a decade, but don't necessarily improve. It's a different story with Shiraz and Cabernet. Many taste delicious on release, but only those who take the trouble of holding back the odd bottle or two, even of relatively humble wines, will be aware of just how well they age. Sparkling Shiraz is surprisingly good after cellaring too.

2001 A long, hot, growing season – mostly scorching in Barossa and Clare, totally rainless in Western Australia – made for easy vintage conditions and balanced, evenly ripened fruit. New South Wales had a trickier time, with rain arriving at harvest, but grapes brought in beforehand had the same long-ripened quality.

2000 A reduced crop, especially in South Australia, thanks to a poor spring and rain around harvest time. Even so, producers seem bullish about quality, and those in New South Wales and Tasmania are especially pleased with results.

1999 Frost in spring and autumn, drought, thunderstorms. To hear the Australians talk of 1999, it's a surprise there's any wine at all. 'Patchy' is the word they're using, although we haven't been disappointed with what we've tasted so far.

1998 Superb vintage, with producers throughout the country saying it's the best red harvest they've ever seen. Stock up on top Shiraz and enjoy it for the next 20 years. While whites are good, they are not in the same class, although some Semillons are delicious.

1997 Rain at harvest time in Margaret River and Hunter Valley caused a few problems with rot, while frost in the Riverland reduced crop levels there, but otherwise this was a good year, especially in South Australia.

1996 A large harvest, with the 'bulk' regions producing huge quantities of grapes. Temperatures were on the low side in the Yarra Valley and other cooler districts of Victoria, but conditions were more favourable in other parts of the country.

Respectable earlier vintages – Better Shiraz and Cabernet from 1990, 1991, 1992 and 1994 should all still be in good condition.

AUSTRIA

'A Taste of Artistry'. While the Austrian wine tasting at the Ambassador's residence in London's Belgravia in February 2001 may have had rather a pompous title, there was nothing remotely stuffy about what was on show. With no fewer than 63 different producers represented – roughly the same number as at the New Zealand tasting held in Chelsea the previous day – Austria could almost claim to have become a mainstream wine country. Indeed, some day very soon, the rather lovely venue will be too small to contain the event.

Translating this obvious interest into sales is a different matter. A letter to *Decanter* magazine in March 2001 bemoaned how hard it was to track down Austrian wines, despite the column inches written about them. It ended, 'So come on Oddbins, come on Sainsbury's, there are people out here who want to try Austrian wines and are prepared to spend our hard-earned cash doing so. Where are they?'

Their absence is partly explained by the dearth of lower-priced wines. Austria simply doesn't have the volumes of good sub-£5 wines that would make a UK supermarket sit up and think, 'We must have that.' It also isn't the easiest of countries to get to grips with. It's a lot simpler to ask for a bottle of Montana Chardonnay than it is to ask for one of Grüner Veltliner Weissenkirchner Achleiten Smaragd from Freie Weingärtner Wachau. Even if a supermarket were to be so brave as to stock even half-a-dozen Austrian wines, we don't feel that their customers are ready for them yet.

But serious wine lovers certainly are, even if they don't know it. Several merchants listed tell us that their customers are more and more keen to try something different. Austrian wines manage to be different without being *too* different. The flavours may echo those found in other countries, but they are unique, a blessing in a world of identikit wines. And while Austria doesn't dabble in the cheap and cheerful, there's plenty available for under £10, even if you'll have to do a little searching to find the wines in the first place. But when you have tracked them down (Bacchus Fine Wines, Ben Ellis, Morris & Verdin, Raeburn Fine Wines, T & W and Noel Young are good places to start; see *Where to buy wine*), you're in for a treat, especially with the high quality of the 1999 and 2000 vintages.

Red wines

If you imagined that Austrian reds would be rather thin and weedy, their high quality comes as a pleasant surprise. Yes, there are a few pale and not very interesting wines around, but there are also some remarkably full-bodied and well-structured wines made from both imported and native grapes which can age for a decade or more. While Cabernet Sauvignon is the most popular of the foreign grapes, several producers are beginning to experiment with Merlot, since it ripens more successfully. Pinot Noir, which has existed here for centuries, has yet to make a strong impression on us, although the occasional wine manages to pack a pleasant cherry-ish punch.

Austria has three main domestic red grape varieties. Blaufränkisch is sturdy and juicy, with a structure reminiscent of Cabernet Sauvignon, while St Laurent is a member of the Pinot family, and some versions have the sweet cherry and berry fruit of Pinot Noir. Zweigelt, a cross between these two, has juicy, earthy berry fruit and can bear an uncanny resemblance to Piedmont's Dolcetto. All three are often aged in new oak and can be impressive, either in pure form or in blends, but the pure, fruity and usually unoaked 'classic' styles (as the Austrians term them) deserve just as much attention.

Dry white wines

For a world bored with oaky Chardonnay, Austrian whites are like a breath of fresh air, even if the Austrians drink them too young and too cold for our liking. Chardonnay, sometimes known as Morillon, is grown, and there are some oaked wines which can proudly stand alongside foreign competitors. However, it also comes in a steely, dry and unoaked form which is like a slightly fruitier Chablis, and Pinot Blanc (Weissburgunder) and Pinot Gris (Grauburgunder) are often made in similar styles.

The most widely planted variety is Grüner Veltliner, a native grape that has flavours of grapefruit, white pepper and lentil (honestly). Lighter versions are perfect summer aperitifs, while richer wines are more serious and, with two or three years in the bottle, can begin to display the minerally characters found in white Burgundy. Grüner Veltliner's rival for making top-quality white wine is Riesling. The best versions lie between the Rheingau and Alsace in style, with the slaty, minerally intensity of the former and the weight of the latter. Welschriesling, a speciality of Styria, doesn't rise to the same heights, but can offer pleasant, crisp floral wines. Styria's other trump card is Sauvignon Blanc. The wines have evolved from the rather startling but ultimately underripe efforts of the early 1990s into extremely attractive wines that sit halfway between the flinty, earthy style of the Loire and the overt fruitiness of New Zealand. Shame they're so expensive.

Sweet white wines

Austria deserves its reputation as a source of high-class, sweet wines. Most are made from *botrytis*-affected grapes, often grown in the vicinity of the shallow Neusiedlersee lake in Burgenland, but you can also find a few examples of unctuous *Schilfwein*, made from grapes which have been dried on reed mats prior to crushing.

The wines are graded as in Germany by the sweetness of the must, so you'll find *Beerenauslese* (BA) and *Trockenbeerenauslese* (TBA) on the label. Austria has an additional category in the scale called *Ausbruch*, which sits between BA and TBA on the sweetness scale. *Ausbruch* is the speciality of the town of Rust on the Neusiedlersee, and has traditionally been made by adding fresh grapes to fermented must to reactivate the fermentation. However, much modern *Ausbruch* is simply TBA under a different label, although usually with a higher level of alcohol (and therefore lower residual sugar level) than a typical TBA. Eiswein also exists, although many producers look on it as a step down from *Ausbruch* and TBA.

Riesling and Grüner Veltliner are pressed into service for sweet wines, but you're just as likely to find wines made from supposedly inferior varieties such as Neuburger, Bouvier, Welschriesling, or from grapes not normally associated with sweet wines such as Pinot Blanc and Chardonnay. There are even some sweet red wines. All display pure, clean fruit flavours, backed up by fresh acidity. They're delicious on release, but have the structure to age well.

Sparkling wines

Austrian Sekt, often based on Welschriesling, is seldom great, but for uncomplicated drinking in a Viennese café, it's hard to beat.

The regions

Austria has four main wine-producing areas. The capital Vienna, where vines reach almost up to the city wall, is the smallest, and most of the wine is consumed in the local inns or *Heurigen*. Styria in the south makes tight, dry whites from Sauvignon Blanc and Welschriesling, with the occasional plumper Chardonnay. The highlight of Burgenland is the plethora of sweet wines produced in villages such as Rust and Illmitz around the Neusiedlersee. However, move not too far away from the lake, and the humidity drops, giving rise to good conditions for other styles, especially full-bodied reds. The fourth district, Lower Austria, is the largest. Its most famous sub-region is the Wachau, where Riesling and Grüner Veltliner thrive on the steep, terraced slopes hugging the northern bank of the Danube. Growers here also have their own classification system for dry wines. *Steinfeder* is for wines with less than 10.7 per cent alcohol, *Federspiel* for those under 12 per cent, and *Smaragd* for those with 12 per cent and above. The best wines of neighbouring Kremstal and Kamptal approach Wachau in quality.

Pick of the producers

Paul Achs Silky, full-bodied Burgenland reds made from blends of Cabernet and local varieties. Well-crafted Chardonnay too.

Braunstein Powerful Chardonnay and ripe, plummy Blaufränkisch are the best of an impressive range from Neusiedlersee.

Bründlmayer Working with fruit from prime vineyard sites in Langenlois, Willi Bründlmayer is one of Austria's most thoughtful and intellectual winemakers, crafting intense Riesling, long-lived Grüner Veltliner and rich Chardonnay.

Feiler-Artinger Burgenland producer with a well-deserved reputation for seriously high-quality, concentrated *Ausbruch*.

Freie Weingärtner Wachau A huge co-operative of nearly 800 Wachau grape growers which, despite its size, manages to produce some top-quality whites, especially from Grüner Veltliner.

Gernot Heinrich Full-bodied, tannic reds from Neusiedlersee. The Pannobile blend is Cabernet, Blaufränkisch and Pinot Noir; the Gabarinza is Zweigelt, Blaufränkisch and Syrah. Both are excellent. Not to be confused with up-and-coming Johann Heinrich from Mittel-Burgenland, another source of fine reds.

Schloss Gobelsburg Fairy-tale castle in Kremstal belonging to adjacent monastery, run since 1996 by Michael Moosbrugger and Willi Bründlmayer (see also *Bründlmayer*, above). The Ried Lamm Grüner Veltliner and Riesling Alte Reben (Old Vines) are the pinnacles of a splendid range.

Hirsch Organic estate in Kamptal excelling with rich, pure Riesling and Grüner Veltliner.

Fritz Hirztberger Benchmark Wachau whites, especially the well-focused Riesling and Grüner Veltliner.

Igler Smooth, creamy blends of Blaufränkisch and Cabernet Sauvignon made by Waltraud Reisner-Igler in Mittel-Burgenland.

Juris Axel Stiegelmar makes modern, New World-style *cuvées*, the powerful red St Georg and sweet wine in Gols, Burgenland.

Alois Kracher Some of the top Austrian *botrytis*-affected dessert wines made from several different varieties grown in Neusiedlersee. Kracher now numbers his *cuvées* 1–9.

Krutzler Ripe, upfront Burgenland Blaufränkisch.

Helmut Lang Another dessert wine wizard producing sweet wines from Chardonnay and Pinot Noir (yes, really) as well as from more traditional grapes.

Lenz Moser Despite management changes (Lenz Moser himself now works in the USA at Robert Mondavi), this remains a decent set of good-value wines and a fair introduction to Austrian grape varieties. Sappy, peppery Grüner Veltliner is our favourite; soft, lively reds are also worth a try.

Malat Wide range of well-made wines from Krems. Perfumed, acidic Riesling, Grüner Veltliner and forceful Chardonnay are highlights.

Gerhard Nekowitsch Up-and-coming maker of Neusiedlersee dessert wines; range includes first-rate *Schilfwein*.

Willi Opitz Eccentric winemaker (and great marketeer) turning out a range of unusual and innovative sweet wines from the Neusiedlersee. Red TBA, Eiswein and *Schilfwein* are among the bottlings.

FX Pichler One of the master-craftsmen of the Wachau excelling with low-yielding Grüner Veltliner, Riesling and Sauvignon Blanc.

Pöckl Excellent range of Neusiedlersee reds, especially Zweigelt varietals and the Zweigelt/Cabernet/Merlot blend Admiral.

Polz Large Styrian estate with fresh, sprightly whites including Chablis-like Pinot Blanc and crisp Sauvignon.

Salomon/Undhof Estate Fine steely Riesling and Traminer from one of Austria's top vineyards, Steiner Hund in the Kremstal region.

Schlumberger Austria's best-known Sekt producer, fetching up a froth in Vienna for 150 years.

Heidi Schrock Rust winery making superb *Ausbruch* from Furmint and Yellow Muscat; the dry reds and whites are also worth trying.

Sonnhof Jurtschitsch Langenlois wines of distinction, especially the Alte Reben (Old Vines) Rieslings.

Tement Styrian superstar excelling with Pinot Blanc, Pinot Gris and Chardonnay. Also involved (with FX Pichler and Tibor Szemes from Burgenland) in making tight, earthy red-blend Arachon.

59

Tinhof Modern, bright Burgenland range, including succulent blend of local reds.

Ernst Triebaumer ET, as he is unfortunately known, makes good, dry whites, but it is for his dense, fleshy reds and heady sweet wines that he is deservedly famous.

Umathum Organic, Burgenland red specialist, with impressive range topped by Ried Hallebuhl, Zweigelt with small amounts of Blaufränkish and Cabernet.

Weingut Dr Unger Fine Riesling, Grüner Veltliner and Pinot Gris from vineyards in the Wachau and Kremstal.

Fritz Wieninger Rich, complex wines from Vienna, especially the multi-layered, *barrique*-aged (and very pricy) Grand Select Chardonnay.

Austrian vintage guide

2000 Hot, dry vintage producing a smaller than usual crop. The whites are full-bodied but – despite the heat – not lacking in acidity, and the quality of both dry and sweet wines should be very good. Reds are also very promising, with some growers saying they picked the best fruit they had ever seen.

1999 The best vintage for many years has produced an embarrassment of riches, with intense, full-bodied reds, ripe, well-balanced dry whites and enough *botrytis* to keep sweet wine fans happy.

1998 Average for dry wines, since it rained hard at the beginning of September. Volumes are up, but the quality is only fair. There was more *botrytis* rot, however, so some decent dessert wines emerged.

1997 Billed by the Austrians as one of the greatest vintages for decades. A warm and dry ripening period lasted right through to the harvest and resulted in fine quality dry whites and reds. There was little *botrytis*, however, so don't expect great sweet wines.

1996 A troublesome year with cool, damp weather during the summer. Best for those producers who waited until later in the autumn to pick.

BOLIVIA

The only Bolivian wines you're likely to encounter in the UK are the rather respectable ones from La Concepción, which are imported by

Moreno Wine Importers (see *Where to buy wines*). La Concepción is one of the oldest wineries in the country, yet only sold its first wines in 1991 – testimony to quite how much of a novelty wine is in Bolivia. The Cabernet is the pick of the bunch. Even so, at the high altitudes (1700m and above) where most vineyards are found, the climate is not unfavourable to viticulture. So, who knows, this time next year we may be reporting on two Bolivian producers of note.

BRAZIL

Brazilian wines are noticeable by their absence on UK shelves at present, but that's not to say there's nothing to speak of wine-wise in South America's largest country. Production is on the up, increasing from 198 million litres in 1996 to 329 million litres in 2000, with forecasts of a further 50 per cent rise in the next five years. The main challenge for the wineries is to cope with the heavy rainfall, which causes many producers to pick their grapes before they have attained full ripeness, and while the acidity is still high. However, this is something of a blessing in disguise, as such attributes are exactly what is required for making sparkling wine. Testimony to this is that Moët & Chandon has a winery in Brazil. As for other styles, there's not much to report on at present, apart from an occasional flying winemaker project in conjunction with the Aurora co-operative in Rio Grande do Sul.

BULGARIA

The Bulgarian wine industry needs to have a rapid rethink if sales in the UK, already on the wane from the heady days of the early 1990s, aren't to slide even further. Coming to terms with the twenty-first century is going to be extremely difficult for wineries that are still in turmoil following the demise of the Communist regime and the return of the vineyards to private hands. Vineyards are being planted at a frantic rate in several New World countries, while the renaissance of southern European wines continues, and both factions provide far more reliable wines under £5, even under £4, than Bulgaria can.

The approach we see from Bulgaria, and from the importers of its wines to the UK market, seems wrong. The Bulgarian response hasn't been to make the most of points of difference, like the interesting indigenous varieties such as Melník, Mavrud and Gamza, or to return to the mellow, oaky-blackcurrant Cabernets and Merlots that won so many fans in the 1980s. Instead, it seems as if the Bulgarians want to downplay any Bulgarian-ness, so the names of regions and wineries are often notably absent from front labels in favour of the likes of Craftsman's Creek or Sapphire Cove. If, as wines such as Blueridge Bin 617 Merlot suggest, the idea is to assault Australia and other New World countries head on, then there's one major flaw in the game plan. The wines just aren't good enough. They're more consistent than they were, especially the whites, but very few rise above the level of competent to become genuinely interesting.

Domaine Boyar, owners of Blueridge, recently spent £500,000 on promoting the winery in the UK. For us, the money would have been far better spent in developing a wine that attracts the eye and garners serious critical acclaim. As it is, Bulgaria is firmly stuck in the cheap wine rut and, until the quality of the wines rather than the quality of the marketing improves, risks losing even more shelf space to wines from other countries. We hope that standards will improve as the wineries gain more and more control over their grape sources and develop their own vineyards, but at present we find it hard to think of any wineries that can be recommended wholeheartedly. If we have any advice, it is to try older reds, especially Haskovo Merlot and Cabernets from Suhindol and Sliven. They are seldom more expensive than younger *cuvées*, and can still hint at that lush warm fruitiness which first brought Bulgarian wines to our attention 20 years ago.

CANADA

Why do we see so little Canadian wine in the UK? Simple. The Canadians have used up all their marketing money fighting the EU courts to get the Icewine ban lifted. For the last few years, there's been no cash left for promotions, annual tastings or product launches because it's all gone to Brussels instead. It went something like this: EU: 'You can't bring Icewine into Europe because it's got more than 15 degrees potential alcohol.' Canada: 'But Austria and Germany can sell their sweet wines so why can't we?' EU: 'You don't make it the same way and besides, you're labelling your other wines with our names, Chablis and Champagne, so we're thinking about banning you altogether.' Canada: 'Hang on a minute! Look how much of your wine you sell in our country. And have you any idea how cold it gets out here? Would you cheat and make wine in a deep-freeze when it was –15°C outside?' etc, etc.

Well we have good news. In March 2001 the battle was won, and as of April 1st (no joke), Icewine became available in the UK.

Mission Hill's delicious 1997 Grand Reserve Riesling from the Okanagan Valley was first past the post and is now available at Berkmann Wine Cellars (see *Where to buy wine*) by the half bottle – and there are others to follow. Hallelujah! An agreement to lift the ban was finally reached on the basis (broadly) that Canadian Icewines are harvested from fruit frozen solid on the vine and pressed at –8°C. Not so difficult, as this was how it was made anyway.

As most producers have an Icewine, EU rejection was enough of a kick in the teeth to persuade them to sell the rest of their wines elsewhere. For the last few years Japan and the Far East have been a steadier market than the UK could offer, but we hope this will now change. As we've said before, Canadian wines are every bit as capable of wowing the international wine scene as are New Zealand's. They have the same varieties, the same acreage, the same price range and equally good quality. Two new viticulture and oenology research bases have been set up, at Ontario's Brook University and the University of Guelph, and new winemakers are now being locally trained. Plus there's a constant exchange of ideas with other New World countries and a steady stream of investment. We think Canadian wines will go down a treat in the UK, so let's hope in the next 12 months that we see more of them.

White wines

Serious wine production in Canada is still in its infancy, so it's no surprise to see that the main influence on the flavour of most wines is the winemaker. For example, Chardonnays often display plenty of oak, plus the influence of malolactic fermentation, which gives buttery characteristics. The tight, oatmealy wines of Ontario's Thirty Bench show what can be done when good fruit is sensitively handled.

Pinot Blanc, Pinot Gris and Sauvignon Blanc are thinner on the ground, and can impress, but Canada's undervalued trump card is Riesling, especially that from the Beamsville Bench overlooking Lake Ontario. In the right hands, the wines are rich, minerally, complex and ageworthy. Sadly, lack of popularity means that they are in short supply.

Riesling is one of the favoured grapes for Canada's Icewine. This can be interesting, but we've still to come across any examples with the refinement which Germany achieves. Now that Icewine is available in the UK, perhaps we'll get a better impression; until recently we've found the best (usually Riesling) balance copious sweetness and heady citrus and apricot fruit with cleansing acidity, but some are simply too much of a good thing. With the floodgates open, we'll reserve full judgement until next year.

Red wines

Merlot is Canada's most successful variety so far, largely because it is more difficult to get wrong than Cabernet Sauvignon and Pinot Noir. From what we've seen, any deficiencies in these latter two varieties are down to winemaking and viticulture, and as the producers become more experienced, and more adept at matching varieties to particular sites, we can expect better and more complex wines to appear. Also look out for the odd Syrah, Cabernet Franc and even Petite Sirah, as those who plant such grapes are usually serious about red wines, and the results can be amazingly satisfying. Hybrid vines such as Baco Noir and Marechal Foch can make full-bodied, rustic wines, but only go for those producers who have success with more mainstream varieties.

The regions

Ontario's vineyards, source of 75 per cent of Canada's wine, are on the same latitude as southern France. However, they certainly don't enjoy the same climate, and it is only the presence of Lakes Ontario and Erie which moderate the conditions and make grape growing possible. While this has traditionally been thought of as white wine country, a few producers such as Marynissen are showing that it is possible to make decent reds here. A few thousands miles to the west, most of the wineries in British Columbia can be found in the arid Okanagan Valley. Whites grow well in the northern stretches, with red grapes coming into their own in the southern parts close to the US border.

Canadian wines are in their youth, and there are plenty of teething problems. There are still those who prefer the easy route of making wine from inferior grapes, either hybrids such as Vidal and Baco Noir, or crosses such as Ehrenfelser and Kerner. Fortunately, the last year has seen a lot of regrafting over to quality *vinifera* varieties. There's also been progress in the winery – with two new research labs set up, a 'getting to grips' with over-oaking, and general positive communication with other New World winemakers experienced in pioneering new vinous territory. The overall feeling is that Canadians should carve their own way and focus on their own unique wine qualities. We can't argue with that.

Pick of the producers

Château des Charmes Ontario outfit whose best releases appear under the Paul Bosc and St David's Bench labels. Chardonnay, Cabernet Sauvignon, Cabernet Franc and Riesling (especially Late Harvest) stand out of a very good selection.

Henry of Pelham Ontario red specialist making chewy, perfumed Cabernet Franc, and a full-bodied Cabernet/Merlot blend. However, Late Harvest Riesling is arguably the best wine.

Inniskillin Despite highlights such as a fine Chenin Blanc Icewine, the British Columbia operation has yet to impress in the way that the Ontario winery does. There, veteran winemaker Karl Kaiser presides over an excellent range of wines, and success with Chardonnay and Pinot Noir has resulted in a collaboration with the Burgundy house Boisset. Watch this space.

Marynissen Niagara winery with competent whites, but much more impressive reds made from Cabernet Sauvignon and Franc, Pinot Noir and Petite Sirah.

Mission Hill Leaders of the 2001 Icewine influx producing a good commercial range of wines from the New Zealand winemaker John Simes, including the 49 North red and white; Merlot and Syrah are the most promising reds for the future.

Quail's Gate First-rate British Columbia winery with class across the range, and excelling with Pinot Noir and Chardonnay. Also makes one of the few good wines with the hybrid Marechal Foch grape.

Southbrook Triomphe Chardonnay is the pick of the table wines, but the stars are the fruit wines, especially the Cassis and the Framboise.

CHILE

Chile's evolution as a wine-producing country echoes that in several other New World countries. The 1990s was the era of the winery, in which the country's winemakers learned how to make good, clean, commercial wines. This was all very well for the cheaper end of the market, but it meant that the more ambitious offerings were often just oakier, riper, louder versions of the everyday wines. Today, we're in the era when far greater importance is being attached to what goes on in the vineyard. Wines are now appearing with flavours that cannot be attributed just to winemaking practices, varietal character or skilful blending (more of that later). Chilean *terroir* is now talking louder than it ever has before.

Part of the reason for not talking louder before is the sheer scale of most wine estates. It's not uncommon for a grower to have hundreds of acres of vines, and only recently has there been a move towards mapping out which parts of which sites are best suited to particular varieties. This also means that much more consideration has to be given to picking dates since, even where the same grape variety is concerned, different sections of a large vineyard can achieve optimum ripeness at quite different times.

Thanks to enthusiastic planting in recent years, the established producers now have several people wanting to sell them grapes, and are able to be more choosy as to what they select each vintage. We haven't quite got to a stage where the Chilean vineyards can be mapped Burgundy-style into *grands* and *premiers crus*, but already there's a considerable differential between the price of grapes from good sites and not-so-good ones.

Back in the winery, the winemaker's job has become more intensive but also far more interesting. Grapes now arrive in several small batches over a long period – and rather than being chucked together in one fermenting tank, are vinified separately, which gives the *terroir* a chance to express itself. Parcels intended for premium wines are treated differently from the start, and when the time comes to put together the final blends, the winemakers can pick which *cuvées* to include and – just as importantly – which to downgrade for lesser wines.

As a result, the prestige *cuvées* are better than they have ever been. However, there has also been a noticeable rise in quality of wines in the £6–£10 bracket, in no small way thanks to an increased appreciation of the art of blending. With a greater number of varieties at their disposal, the winemakers have more options to try out. If a wine based on the Bordeaux varieties (including

Carmenère – see below) benefits from a little Syrah, Petite Sirah or Zinfandel, then there's now no hesitation in adding a hefty dollop.

Our enthusiasm for Chilean wines is reflected in UK sales, which increased by more than 30 per cent in the year to June 2001. But before the Chileans pat themselves too hard on the back, there are a couple of points that aren't quite so commendable. Firstly, the 'Wines of Chile' office in the UK was closed in December 2000, because the Chileans felt that they had learned enough about our market to be able to handle the marketing and promotional campaigns themselves. As a source of information for both trade and press, Wines of Chile performed an excellent job, and many people feel that the decision to shut it down is a false economy. Secondly, in our tastings over the past year, it seems as if one or two wineries have let the quality of their entry-level ranges slip. Maybe it is the increased focus on the premium end of the market, maybe it is that rapid expansion is stretching the resources. But whatever it is, we hope it doesn't continue. It is those everyday wines that first won our hearts for their sheer drinkability, and which are genuinely cheap and cheerful. To neglect them now is a big mistake.

Red wines – grape varieties

Cabernet Sauvignon

Those who have never detected blackcurrant in Cabernet Sauvignon should try Chilean versions. Sometimes there's a hint of mint, sometimes tobacco, sometimes a dusty note, but the core of many wines is that lush cassis/blackcurrant pastille flavour. Blending and more sensitive winemaking is now resulting in more complexity in the wines, especially at higher price levels – but let's hope that Chile never gives up the joyous cheap versions at which it currently excels.

Merlot/Carmenère

It was only in the early 1990s that it became clear that much of what the Chileans understood to be Merlot was actually the obscure variety Carmenère, which hails from Bordeaux but is virtually extinct there. It's hard to understand how the two were ever confused. While there are visual similarities, Merlot gives softer wines, while Carmenère has more structure and fragrance, with an occasional overtone of soy sauce. It also ripens up to three weeks later than Merlot, and can sometimes struggle to attain full maturity. Today, a number of wineries make varietal versions of both grapes, and the two are also used in blends with Cabernet Sauvignon and/or Cabernet Franc. However, many wines labelled

Merlot still contain a very large dollop of Carmenère. As the typical Chilean 'Merlot' is rather good, we're not going to get too worried about this just yet.

Pinot Noir
Cono Sur and Valdivieso wooed us initially with Pinot, but now there are a number of producers who are capable of making attractive juicy wines brimming with silky berry fruit. As the Casablanca area develops, we can expect even better Pinots, although the stage where Burgundy, Carneros and Oregon need to begin worrying is still a long way off.

Others
We've encountered good Petite Sirah, Syrah, Sangiovese and Zinfandel in recent times, so it's no surprise to see more producers experimenting with these varieties. Carignan too can turn in surprisingly good wine. Many producers now grow Malbec, either for a single varietal wine or for blending. Cabernet Franc is also being used to good effect for blending, although Valdivieso has shown how successful it can be on its own.

White wines – grape varieties

Chardonnay
As with Cabernet, Chile's Chardonnays at the lower end of the scale delight, with simple fresh tropical and citrus fruit flavours very much to the fore. However, as one spends more and more, complexity seldom appears, although a growing number of wineries – notably Viña Casablanca, Concha y Toro, Errázuriz – do deliver the goods.

Sauvignon Blanc
While there is now a differentiation between Merlot and Carmenère in Chile, there's no move to distinguish between true Sauvignon and the inferior Sauvignonasse, which tires quickly in bottle. When real Sauvignon, from a cooler area such as Casablanca, has been grown without too much recourse to irrigation and has been picked at optimum ripeness, the wines are zippy, fresh and very attractive.

Others
Gewurztraminer, either from Casablanca or Bío-Bío in the south of the country, can be excellent. However, we'd urge you to buy some soon, otherwise the vineyard owners will replant with a more commercial variety. Semillon and Riesling can also be very good, both for dry and sweet wines, although again they are being

displaced from the vineyards in favour of other grapes. Viognier has a small but growing following, with Cono Sur's rich heady version showing what is possible.

Regions

Chile has three main wines regions, Aconcagua, Central Valley and Southern. Aconcagua is divided into Aconcagua Valley, home of just one winery (although a few others have vineyards there) and the Casablanca Valley, which lies between Santiago and the coast. The Central Valley spreads southwards from Santiago and is split into Maipo, Rapel (zones Cachapoal and Colchagua), Curicó (Teno and Lontué) and Maule (Claro, Loncomilla and Tutuven). Further south still, the Southern Region has Itata and the cool, wet Bío-Bío district as its sub-regions.

Within many of these delineated districts, there is a wide variety of growing conditions, ranging from well-drained limestone slopes at high altitudes to much lower, flatter alluvial plains. Because of this, factors such as the age of the vines, the extent of the irrigation and the skill of the producer, are currently far more important than the zone of production. This is true even in Casablanca, source of several of Chile's finest white wines, but also source of several mediocre ones. Rapel is another highly favoured region, particularly for Merlot, but despite what we say in the introduction, it's debatable whether we are actually tasting Rapel *terroir*, or just the influence of older, unirrigated vineyards.

Pick of the producers

Almaviva This firm, rich, oaky wine, the result of a joint venture between Concha y Toro and Mouton Rothschild, manages to pack the fruit of Chile into the structure of Bordeaux. From the same stable comes the more affordable but still impressive red blend, Escudo Rojo, and the Mapa varietal range.

Antiyal First solo venture for ex-Viña Carmen winemaker, Alvaro Espinoza, is a delightful blend of Cabernet Sauvignon, Merlot and Syrah, as complex as anything Chile has achieved so far.

Aquitania/Paul Bruno Maipo brainchild of Paul Pontallier (Château Margaux) and Bruno Prats (Château Cos d'Estournel) making Cabernet Sauvignon that, while showing some improvement, should be even better, given its pedigree.

Caliterra Improving wines from a winery owned jointly by Errázuriz and Robert Mondavi of California. New Arboleda range at

£12.99 outclasses most Chileans at the same price. (See also *Seña*, below.)

Canepa Continuing to offer good-value wines, despite upheavals in the mid-1990s that resulted in the loss of all its vineyards. Oak-Aged Semillon just one highlight of a very competent range.

Viña Carmen Very consistent Maipo producer making decent whites and even better reds, with inky rich Merlot, Winemaker's Reserve (Cabernet Sauvignon/Carmenère/Petite Sirah/Merlot) and Gold Reserve Cabernet the stars. Look out too for the Nativa range, made from organically grown grapes.

Casa Lapostolle Michel Rolland-inspired winery with good whites and superb reds. Cuvée Alexandre Merlot used to be the summit, now eclipsed by quite splendid Clos Apalta, a complex blend of Merlot, Carmenère and Cabernet.

Viña Casablanca Casablanca-based offshoot of Santa Carolina with some of Chile's finest whites and increasingly impressive reds from the Santa Isabel Estate. Also good reds from the Maipo and Rapel regions, including Fundo Special Cuvée.

Concha y Toro Huge company producing wines of exemplary standard, both under its own label and under the Trio (of which there are now six!), Terunyo and Explorer names. Amelia Chardonnay ranks as one of Chile's best, as does Don Melchor Cabernet. (See also *Almaviva*, above.)

Cono Sur Modern Concha y Toro-owned winery offering interest across the board, including quirky varietals such as Zinfandel, Viognier and Gewurztraminer. 20 Barrels range is especially good, with the Pinot being Chile's best. Wines under the Isla Negra label are also first class.

Cousiño Macul Famous for many years for its full-bodied if rather old-fashioned Antiguas Reservas Cabernet. The new flagship Finis Terrae is made in a more modern style from pre-phylloxera vines, but still lacks the complexity to be ranked among Chile's finest.

Dallas Conte Joint venture between Viña Santa Carolina (see below) and international wine group Beringer Blass. Supple juicy Cabernet is the pick so far.

Echeverria Curicó winery run by the scholarly Roberto Echeverria making good-quality Cabernet, Chardonnay and Sauvignon.

Luis Felipé Edwards 200-hectare Colchagua estate, source of some of Chile's best Chardonnay and Cabernet Sauvignon, and now with an ex-Penfolds winemaker in charge of the cellar. Top red Doña Bernada Privada has flavour and finesse.

Errázuriz Sole winery in the Aconcagua Valley, with high quality across the board from Californian winemaker Ed Flaherty. Best wines are the Wild Ferment Chardonnay (from Casablanca), Don Maximiano Cabernet and a fine Syrah. Sangiovese a new arrival in the range. (See also *Seña*, below.)

Gillmore Maule winery making classy reds, the best of which are Merlot and Cabernet Franc, but don't ignore the honest, juicy Carignan.

Gracia Increasingly classy red specialist with vineyards throughout Chile. The range is slightly confusing, with no fewer than five Cabernets, four of which carry the word 'Reserva'.

Viña de Larose/Las Casas del Toqui French-owned, and making fine Bordeaux-style Semillon and well-structured, fruit-packed Cabernet.

Montes The Montes Alpha reds, topped by the densely fruity 'M', are top class, and the Malbec and Syrah are also delicious, but other releases are more erratic.

MontGras Colchagua winery impressing with reds, especially Merlot and the top-of-the-range Ninquen releases. Chardonnays less convincing, but the Sauvignon is among Chile's best.

Viña Porta A new owner (who also owns Gracia), a new winery and new vineyards mean that only the Viña Porta name remains from prior to 1999. Silky Cabernet Sauvignon is the star so far of the new regime.

Viña Quebreda de Macul Rising Maipo star making serious but succulent Domus Aurea Cabernet Sauvignon from a single hillside vineyard planted in 1970.

Viña La Rosa Good-quality reds and whites under the La Palmeria and Cornellana labels, mainly from Rapel fruit.

San Pedro Large producer benefiting from the consultancy expertise of Jacques Lurton. Gato and 35 South (formerly 35 Sur) are the volume brands, Castillo di Molina Reserva is a step up, while Cabo de Hornos Cabernet is impressive but pricy standard-bearer.

Viña Santa Carolina Historic *bodega* based in Maipo, but with vineyards in several regions. Admirable Barrica Selection range includes fleshy Syrah and a Chardonnay that is far more subtle – or rather, less oaky than it used to be. Reservado wines are also good, while new Trébol (Cabernet/Merlot/Syrah) is astonishingly complex for £6. (See also *Dallas Conte*, above.)

Santa Inés Maipo winery offering both Merlot and Carmenère for those who want to compare and contrast. Legado de Familia Cabernet and Chardonnay stand out of an already good range.

Viña Santa Rita Large organisation continuing its climb in quality. Entry-level 120 range includes a delightful Cabernet Rosé, then come Reserva and Medalla Real ranges. Best wines are Casa Real, one of Chile's greatest Cabernets, and Triple C, a blend of the Cabernets with Carmenère.

Seña Joint venture between Mondavi and the Chadwick family, owners of Errázuriz and Caliterra, made with grapes from Errázuriz's Don Maximiano estate in Aconcagua. Wonderfully fleshy and ripe, but not cheap.

Tarapacá Major investment from California's Beringer (now Beringer Blass; see *Dallas Conte*, above) and new blood in charge of winemaking is transforming this Maipo winery. Has the potential to be among Chile's finest, but not as yet living up to it.

TerraMater Using fruit from vineyards that used to belong to the Canepa winery, Englishman David Morrison makes delicious commercial (in the best sense of the word) wines. On present form, stick with these in preference to the more expensive Altum range.

Miguel Torres Leading light in the 1980s for its whites, overtaken by others in the 1990s, but now reasserting itself with red wines. Manso de Velasco Cabernet is chewy and curranty, while Cariñena-heavy blend Cordillera is a full-bodied winter warmer.

Undurraga Impressive Maipo estate with good whites, especially Chardonnay and Gewurztraminer, and less convincing reds.

Valdivieso Famous in Chile for sparkling wines, but making a name overseas for still wines. Best are the single vineyard reds, the new 'V' Malbec and the multi-varietal, multi-vintage blend Caballo Loco. Are we alone in wondering whether the quality of some of the cheaper wines has slipped slightly in recent vintages?

Los Vascos Co-owned by Château Lafite-Rothschild. The wines so far have been rather hard and charmless compared with their compatriots, but the new top-end *cuvée* Le Dix de Los Vascos is a welcome step up in quality.

Veramonte Winery founded by the Californian Franciscan Winery, and now owned by its former boss Agustin Huneeus, who hails from Chile. Based in Casablanca with vineyards there, but also sourcing fruit from elsewhere. Look for the Casablanca Chardonnay and red blend Primus.

Villard Casablanca operation of Frenchman Thierry Villard, formerly of Orlando in Australia. Local fruit used for fine Pinot Noir, Chardonnay and Sauvignon, with Rapel grapes used for impressive Merlot.

Chile vintage guide

Whites – with precious few exceptions, drink the youngest available, especially the Sauvignon.

Reds – again, very few of the wines gain from further ageing after release, although the sturdier Cabernets, Carmenères and Merlots will take bottle age. Chile's vintages do not vary as much as in other countries, and while El Niño did affect certain parts of the country in the 1998 vintage, the effect was nowhere near as severe as in neighbouring Argentina. While 1999 was a good but small vintage, the gentle 2000 growing season produced plenty of wine. Where growers worked to reduce yields, the reds should be among the most subtle and complex Chile has made. The start of the 2001 season was poor, bringing yields down by as much as 30 per cent, but warm weather up to harvest meant that the grapes were picked in very good condition, so wine quality should be high.

CHINA

While China has a well-established wine industry that produces almost as much wine as Australia, the home market guzzles up all but a tiny fraction of what is made. The potential however is huge and, recognising this, a number of outside companies are involved in projects there. Rémy Martin provided input for the Dynasty range of wines, Pernod-Ricard did the same for Dragon Seal, while Allied Domecq is involved with the Huadong Winery, which makes the Tsingtao Chardonnay, one of China's best wines, and also one of the few to be exported in any quantity. Miguel Torres is even in on the act, with the Great Wall Torres Winery Co. Ltd, which is still to release its first wines. When we see them – *if* we see them – we'll let you know how good they are.

CROATIA

Grk, Dingač and Opol. No, they're not baddies from a fantasy novel, just names that we'll have to come to terms with if Croatian wine ever comes into fashion. This part of the former Yugoslavia has some fine vineyard sites, especially along the Adriatic coast, and a palette of interesting indigenous grape varieties led by the robust spicy Plavac Mali, which some think may be related to Zinfandel/Primitivo. California-based Croat Mike Grgich of Grgich Hills in Napa Valley makes a Plavac Mali (and a white from the Pošip variety) on the island of Korčula in the Adriatic, and Andro Tomic also produces a highly rated version. We'd like to see more of these and other Croat wines on our shelves, but with the political situation being what it is, we fully understand why UK importers are reluctant to do business here.

CYPRUS

Though the collapse of its Eastern Bloc sweet wine market came as something of a blow, Cyprus has moved on – and embraced a new culture of enticing varietal red wines. In fact, with no phylloxera, mountain viticulture on original rootstocks, and a host of characterful native grape varieties to draw from, there's every reason to assume these wines will go from strength to strength. Cyprus's mainstream varieties are its indigenous ones: Mavro (a widely planted, rugged red grape, particularly successful at higher altitudes, 800m and more, where it takes on more cherry finesse), Xynisteri (aromatic white Commandaria grape), Opthalmo (light, acidic red), and rich, dark Cabernet-like Maratheftico. Cabernet Sauvignon exists in small quantities, as do Mourvèdre, Carignan and Grenache, but the island mentality has led to strict quarantining and a reluctance to bring in new, potentially diseased international vines. For authenticity's sake, this has been a good thing.

Wines to look out for come from Keo, SODAP (Mountain and Island Vines brands), Etko and Loel, the main, public wine companies. Smaller wineries to watch are Vouni, Fikardos, Chrysoroyiatissa Monastery, Laona, Olympus and Mallia.

Australian winemakers have lately been a very positive influence in Cyprus – particularly at the larger wineries. Beer and ouzo being everyday local staples, the wine industry relies heavily on export, so an upgrade to international standards over the 1990s has been essential. Australians (used to working in similar hot conditions) have, among other things, transformed cellar technology, introduced controlled pruning and updated vineyard practices – and have even seemed content to stay rather than fly in and out for each vintage. Good news indeed.

Cyprus' long-established sweet wine, Commandaria, the wine of the Crusaders, is still hugely important to the island, and its similarity to Australian Liqueur Muscat makes it another reason for the Antipodeans to feel at home.

CZECH REPUBLIC

A hop across the border from Austria's Weinviertel brings you into Moravia, where more than 95 per cent of Czech vineyards are to be found. It comes as no surprise that many of the same varieties are grown as in Austria. Among the whites are Müller-Thurgau, Riesling, Welsch/Laski Rizling, Irsay Oliver, Pinot Blanc, Pinot Gris, Traminer, Grüner Veltliner and Neuburger, while reds include Frankovka (Austria's Blaufränkisch), St-Laurent and Pinot Noir. As yet, the standards have some way to go to catch up with those of its neighbour, but even so, we're disappointed to see so few Czech wines available in the UK. Not so very long ago, a number of supermarkets were selling lovely spicy Irsay Oliver and fresh sappy Frankovka for around £4. Where are they now? The only Czech wines that enjoy reasonable distribution are the Bohemia Sekt sparklers from near Prague, which come in white, pink and red guises. If you see them, give them a go. They won't strike fear into the makers of champagne, but they're really rather pleasant, in a frivolous frothy way.

ENGLAND

In 2001, England's productive area under vine remains unchanged, but its actual output of wine has increased. If this were anywhere else in the world we'd start to worry about rising yields, dilution and general greed, but in the UK it's a sign that viticulture is being taken more seriously. Hobbyists, smaller growers and weekend enthusiasts are turning over their plots of hybrids to the bigger estates, who are able to replant with better vines and generally afford better winemaking practices, and work more efficiently. But it isn't simply a matter of dismantling our cottage wine industry and starting again.

Britain's climate is cool and unpredictable and it takes skill to surmount the problems it creates in the vineyard. Global warming (if that is what is happening) is not an immediate solution; nor is it necessarily resulting in hotter summers and a warmer growing season. Temperatures in the British Isles were around half to one degree higher in 2000 but this increase was mostly at night, and during the winter, neither of which times helps with ripening grapes. According to Stephen Skelton, chairman of the UK Vineyards Association, global warming needs to give us earlier harvests, higher sugars, and more days over 30°C, none of which has yet happened.

The reason English wines are improving – with riper flavours and softer acidity – comes down to a handful of better techniques: increased disease control in the vineyard, better canopy management (to get more sunlight to the grapes), yeasts that convert sugar more efficiently, greater control over fermentation temperature, gentler pressing, and lighter use of wood (and wood chip) to round out flavours. But even these aren't enough for UK wines to stand up to, say, those of Chile and New Zealand on the supermarket shelf. Taste for taste, they might be just as good, but buyers don't yet have confidence enough to pick them up. This is nothing a powerful marketing plan couldn't change, but there just aren't the resources to put such things in place. A couple of wineries have had their fingers burnt trying this year, but most, sensibly, rely on tourist and local trade.

If England is to be taken seriously as a wine-producing nation, three things need to happen. Firstly, we need to show more confidence in the wines we produce. Secondly, we need to continue the trend away from odd-sounding Germanic hybrid grapes. And thirdly, we need to continue the exciting progress we're making with sparkling wine. Alongside Tasmania and New Zealand, the UK is one of the three places outside France with the potential to give the Champenois a run for their money and this is an opportunity not to be wasted. Nyetimber, Ridgeview and Valley Vineyards lead the way with distinctly Champenoise fizz, and show a heartening belief in what this country can do. There are now over 40 other producers joining the fizz force and, with careful techniques and continued steady improvement, we might eventually be able to make our mark internationally.

White wines

The predominance in English winemaking of lesser-known grapes of Germanic origin, including Reichensteiner, Kerner and Bacchus,

is gradually being eroded by plantings of Chardonnay and Pinot Blanc and, more interestingly, the noble Riesling. England's cool climate means that its wines will always be high in acidity, so don't expect everyday-drinking Chardonnays. Most Chardonnay and Pinot Noir will be used for sparkling winemaking, although the use of barrels nowadays suggests interesting blending possibilities with oak adding character to the basically fragile flavours on offer. Lastly, high acidity is not a problem with sweet wines. The English climate often leads to favourable conditions for *botrytis*, which creates sweetness, and works well when countered by a crisp, acidic tang. We certainly suggest trying any of these which you discover.

Red wines

Achieving sufficient ripeness in black grapes to allow successful red wines has always been a problem in the UK, due to the lack of sufficient sunlight. That said, some thoroughly impressive Pinot Noir and Dornfelder have emerged in the last few years from two estates in particular, Valley Vineyards and Denbies. Oak barrels and oak chips are also proving useful to round out some of the flavours. Other red grapes to watch out for are Syrah-like Rondo and tannic Triomphe – both of which make some flavourful blends.

Sparkling wines

The best of these, made traditionally with Chardonnay and Pinot Noir grapes, can be mistaken for champagne and are delicious. Given that some of England's vineyards are only one degree latitude above Rheims, with similar soil types, this is hardly surprising. There are now over 40 English sparkling wines, but only two of these come from vineyards planted specifically for making fizz. The next quality leap will come when, to quote the aphorism, 'great wine is made in the vineyard'.

Pick of the producers

Breaky Bottom Interestingly quirky property near Lewes, in Sussex. Anyone who thinks Seyval Blanc is an inferior grape variety should try Peter Hall's rich and ageworthy version. Also good Müller-Thurgau.

Chapel Down Fine range of whites, sparklers and the surprisingly full-bodied Epoch red made from Dornfelder. The crisp, smoky Bacchus Reserve could pass for a New Zealand Sauvignon. Recently joined forces with Lamberhurst and Carr Taylor: Chapel Down is the name they'll use in future.

Denbies Almost unbelievably beautiful 105-hectare estate in the Mole Valley, near Dorking in Surrey, currently battling hard to strengthen its place in the UK market. Has the potential to rival Germany with its crisp Rieslings and softly elegant Dornfelder reds when winemaking direction is firm. If nothing else, the visitor centre is well worth a visit.

Hidden Spring Let's hope this Sussex outfit maintains the quality of its wines, vinified at Valley Vineyards, and its quirky labels under its new ownership.

Nyetimber England's first vineyard dedicated solely to sparkling wine made from the traditional champagne grape varieties is run by a Chicago couple. The award-winning maiden release, in 1992, was a 100 per cent Chardonnay Blanc de Blancs. Pinot Noir and Pinot Meunier have featured in subsequent wines. Current vintages, 1993 and 1994, are showing superbly and look set to age. Would that others followed this shining example.

Ridge View New, purpose-built winery near Ditchling Beacon, high on the Sussex Downs, already producing prize-winning complex sparkling wines using solely Chardonnay, Pinot Noir and Pinot Meunier. The wines also appear under the South Ridge label.

Sharpham Eccentric Devon producer with good range of whites but best known for the Beenleigh red (or rosé in lesser years) made from Cabernet Sauvignon and Merlot grown under polytunnels.

Three Choirs The Reserve Schönburger and Madeline Angevine, the Reserve Brut and the Late Harvest are the best wines in a solid range produced from vineyards surrounding the cathedral cities of Gloucester, Hereford and Worcester.

Valley Vineyards The wines remain as reliable as ever from this Reading estate, particularly the impressive sparklers (Ascot, Heritage) and Clocktower, a delicious *botrytis* wine. Watch out also for Ruscombe red, a juicy raspberryish red from Triomphe, Pinot Noir, Dornfelder and Gamay.

Vintage guide

What the wettest winter on record will mean for the 2001 harvest is anyone's guess at this stage, but 2000 proves that even in a rainier than average ripening season it's possible to get it right with efficient canopy management and pruning. Wineries with good equipment and sound practices have made creditable wines from decent fruit. 1999 did not have the ripeness of 1998, but there were no significantly adverse conditions either and the wines are showing delicacy and finesse.

FRANCE

If you believe what you read in the press, then French wines are on the ropes. Their market share in the UK has been declining for a number of years, and by the time you read this, the Australians could very well have taken over the number one spot in the sales league table. Then comes the news from Bordeaux that, against the advice of countless wine merchants around the world, greedy château owners have hiked the release prices of the clarets from the 2000 vintage by more than 50 per cent, prompting many customers to abandon the region in favour of wines from other countries. Over in Burgundy, unscrupulous producers have been found guilty of adulterating their wines, and observers wonder whether these cases are merely the tip of a far larger iceberg. And down in the south, angry protestors hijack and destroy containers full of imported wine which they say is threatening their livelihood.

So has France lost the plot? *Non*. But it's a qualified *non*. With the possible exception of Italy, no other country offers quite such a splendid diversity of wines, and for this we have to thank the infamous *appellation contrôlée* system (AC). AC, which regulates the means of production and the grape varieties for a particular wine, is both a blessing and a curse. Without it, many of France's more obscure varieties – Courbu, Len de l'El, Counoise and Savagnin, to name but a few – might not be with us today. Anyone tired of a constant diet of Cabernet and Chardonnay need only head for places such as Jura or South-western France for some light relief.

However, AC governs typicity, not quality. This can be counterproductive, especially at the cheaper end of the market where France is losing out to Australia and other New World countries. Numerous weedy Bordeaux reds would be all the better for a slug of Rhône Grenache, while several tooth-stripping Loire Chenin Blancs would benefit from some riper Chenin from much further south. Such additions would mean that the wine would lose its AC status and could only be labelled *vin de table*, but with cross-regional blends being common in many countries, you'd be forgiven for asking, so what? And here, we're with you all the way. Don't get us wrong, we don't want to see the bastardisation of the great wines of France. Here, the AC system for the most part works very well, although a little more leeway in matters such as irrigation (currently a no-no) in hot years would be welcome in some districts. But for lesser vineyards, we've no objection to a little judicious blending, providing this is pointed out clearly on the label. At this level, indeed with all French wine, the name of the producer is of greater importance than that of the particular AC.

We wouldn't be surprised if French sales continued their slow decline for a few more years. What we hope to see emerge is a leaner, fitter France, devoid of the sour whites and charmless reds which used to populate our shelves, and focused much more on higher quality. Spurred into action in part by the challenge of the New World, and in part by the pursuit of quality whatever the cost, today's winemakers are better trained and better equipped than ever before.

Yes, the top wines (and not just of Bordeaux) will continue to be expensive and will rise even further in price. Yes, fraud will continue in Burgundy and elsewhere – that's just human nature. And yes, until they follow the quality rather than the quantity path, *vignerons* in the south will continue to complain about others challenging their livelihood. But France offers many more affordable alternatives to the pricy superstars; the vast majority of producers remain honest and make better wines with each vintage, and the renaissance of the Languedoc and other regions continues apace. As a result, if you offered us £10 to spend on a bottle of wine today, it would be to France that we head first.

ALSACE

It needs reinforcing – Alsace produces some of the best white wines in the world, they're not too expensive nor too difficult to track down. There are wines that are perfect as aperitifs and others that are ideal partners for a wide variety of foods; some that are delicious when young, and others that age magnificently. There are easy-drinking wines (at sensible prices too), and wines that appeal to the intellect; and wines that will strike chords with palates accustomed to both the New World and the Old World. There are sweet wines, medium wines, dry wines. Admittedly, Alsace has neither a lot of oak nor a lot of Chardonnay (although both can be found if you look closely), but we're certainly not going to hold that against the region. But otherwise, there is almost everything here that a white wine lover could want. That sales continue to be sluggish really is a crime.

Thankfully, many wine merchants in the UK continue to wave the Alsace flag. Few flap it more enthusiastically than John Gauntley of Gauntleys of Nottingham (see *Where to buy wine*), whose Spring 2001 Alsace offer featured wines from eight different growers. So how successful was the campaign? 'It went well. We have a core number of customers who buy large amounts each year, and a slow but steady stream of newcomers. We like Alsace, so we push it, and each year, we sell more and more, but we'd still like to improve our performance. The offer does well, but sales throughout the rest of the year are very slow.'

Getting acquainted with Alsace wines isn't too difficult. Most supermarkets stock competent wines labelled by grape variety – Pinot Blanc, Riesling, Gewurztraminer and Pinot Gris are the most popular – and usually hail from one of the number of quality-conscious co-operatives to be found in the region. If you like what you see and are interested in further exploration, you can always plump for more expensive wines from the same producers. However, as you move up the quality ladder, Alsace gets a little more complicated, and putting yourself in the hands of an Alsace-mad merchant such as Gauntleys is a smart move.

The complications arise for a number of reasons. The grape varieties remain the same, but new words begin to appear on the labels, some of which are simply brand names (Jubilee, Cuvée Caroline, for example) while others are vineyards. Burgundy is usually cited as the region in which *terroir* expresses itself most forcefully, but Alsace wines are also heavily influenced by where they are grown. Indeed, a few growers, notably Deiss, produce their top wines using a blend of grapes, since they feel that in certain sites, it is the *terroir* rather than the grape variety that has the greatest impact on the flavour of the wines.

Then there's the style of the wines. We are not alone in finding Alsace whites that we expected to be dry, actually having high levels of sweetness. Olivier Humbrecht of the highly rated Domaine Zind-Humbrecht makes no apologies for the often high sugar levels in his wines. He simply leaves them to ferment at their own pace, and if this means that some sweetness is left at the end, then so be it. We've no argument with such a stance, but what we would like to see is some indication on the labels as to what to expect in the bottles.

Even so, don't let these minor quibbles, nor the Germanic names and bottles, put you off jumping into the Alsace waters. Indeed, why not jump on the Eurostar and pay a visit to this beautiful region? And our other piece of advice? The food is just as good as the splendid wines.

Appellations and quality levels

There are three appellations in Alsace. AC Alsace is the basic appellation for still wine in the region, while AC Alsace Grand Cru, introduced in 1983, is used for wines at a higher level. The *grand cru* theory sounds good. A *grand cru* wine can only come from the best sites and be made from the best varieties, namely Gewurztraminer, Riesling, Pinot Gris and Muscat. In practice, however, there are too many *grands crus*. Not all of the 50 sites merit the higher designation, while others deserve it for certain grapes (including some outside the four listed above) but not others. Some famous monopole (single-proprietor) vineyards, such as Trimbach's Clos Saint Hune and Zind-Humbrecht's Clos Windsbuhl, don't even qualify for *grand cru* status, despite producing some of Alsace's finest wines. Also, several growers with *grand cru* vineyards don't promote their wines as such, either as a statement of their disagreement with the system, or because their yields are too high. So as in Burgundy, while the best wines still come from the best sites, the name of the producer is often a better guarantee of quality than the name of the vineyard.

The third AC is Crémant d'Alsace for sparkling wines from the region.

Styles

Vendange tardive Wine made from late-harvested grapes, which is sometimes medium-sweet and luscious, at other times dry with high alcohol levels. Potentially confusing.

Sélection de grains nobles Wines made from grapes affected by noble rot. *Botrytis* does not occur with any regularity in Alsace, and these wines are therefore rare, expensive and can be absolutely delicious.

White wines – grape varieties

Gewurztraminer

Anyone who has not yet tried Alsace Gewurztraminer should get hold of a glass, swirl it around and take a good sniff. A strong reaction is guaranteed – one way or the other. Gewurztraminer is Alsace's most distinctive and controversial varietal wine, with an extraordinarily exotic perfume propelling rose petals, powdered ginger, lychee and Turkish Delight up from the glass. If there is enough fresh acidity and a fruity citric core of flavour, the wine will taste as good as it smells, and be a great match for Thai cuisine. Poor examples are clumsy and flabby, with a scent horribly reminiscent of floral air freshener.

Muscat
The rarest of Alsace's four noble grapes (the other three being Gewurztraminer, Pinot Gris and Riesling), and often underrated, Muscat produces fresh, dry wines with the mouth-watering character of crunchy, green grapes. Alsace Muscat makes an ideal aperitif and, in the region, is traditionally matched with asparagus.

Riesling
Considered by Alsace producers to be their greatest grape, probably because with Riesling they can best express the subtleties of *terroir*. Fruity and bracing when young, Alsace Riesling is less steely than its German equivalent, although it can still display the same minerally notes and take on a rich, honeyed and sometime petrolly quality with age.

Tokay-Pinot Gris
No relation to the Furmint or Hárslevelű grapes used to make Tokaji in Hungary, Alsace's Pinot Gris epitomises the region's opulent style of white wine – rich and fruity with spicy, smoky depths. Despite an apparent lack of acidity, it matches food well and ages brilliantly. Choose with care, however, as there are plenty of one-dimensional, flabby examples around.

Pinot Blanc
Pinot Blanc isn't deemed worthy of producing *grand cru* wines, but while it may lack the extrovert personality of other Alsace varieties, this doesn't mean the wines are second-rate. Good examples, of which there are many, have fresh, tangy apple and melon flavours, plus a friendly creamy texture. If you find yourself in a restaurant looking for a wine to accompany four very different dishes, Pinot Blanc is a good choice.

Other white grape varieties
Auxerrois can be musky and red berry-flavoured in the hands of the right producer. **Sylvaner** is usually uninspiring, but a few wines made in the lean and racy style appeal. **Chasselas**, an Alsace old-timer, is now rarely encountered outside the region.

Blends
Blends of white grapes are traditionally bottled under the generic names Edelzwicker or Vin d'Alsace. Over the years these labels have become associated with cheap, boring wine, and quality producers increasingly choose their own names for specific blended *cuvées*. Some blends remain dull, but others, as we mention in the introduction, are inspired – so choose your producer with care.

Red wines

The only black grape cultivated in Alsace is Pinot Noir, which here makes a soft, perfumed, strawberryish red. Enthusiasts are trying to beef it up into a richer wine, sometimes using oak, although we've yet to be convinced of this approach. Chilled lightly and paired with fresh salmon, it makes an easy-drinking summer red; but even so, its delights are too simple to justify a price tag of around £10 a bottle.

Sparkling wine

AC Crémant d'Alsace is not the world's most characterful sparkling wine. It is made by the champagne method, often from Pinot Blanc, sometimes from Riesling or Pinot Gris. The result is a zippy, fresh sparkling wine with high acidity and hints of lemon and yeast. Again, the price tag can seem a bit steep when compared with sparkling wines from Spain and the New World.

Pick of the producers (Alsace)

Beblenheim Good-value, fruity co-operative wines, responsible for some of the best own-label wine in the UK.

Beyer Ancient house, with a relatively dry winemaking style and high-quality range. Long-lived, food-friendly Riesling stands out.

Paul Blanck et fils Increasingly impressive producer with an extensive range including reliable *crémant* and topped by superb Rieslings from the Fürstentum and Schlossberg *grands crus*.

Bott-Geyl Excellent wines from young Jean-Christophe Bott, particularly the Tokay-Pinot Gris.

Deiss Complex, intricately worked whites, with outstanding wines from the *grands crus* of Altenberg de Bergheim, Mambourg and Schoenenbourg.

Dopff au Moulin *Négociant* maintaining high standards, and doing well with fresh *crémant*.

Hugel The region's most famous producer. Lower end wines could be better, but the more expensive *cuvées*, especially the superb late-harvest wines, have bags of character yet also great finesse.

Charles Koehly et fils Good-value range, especially a limey Pinot Blanc, fresh grapey Muscat and spicy Gewurztraminer.

Marc Kreydenweiss Talented biodynamic producer from the northern part of the region.

Kuentz-Bas One of Alsace's best *négociant* houses, with 12 hectares of prime vineyard site. Especially good for Gewurztraminer, Tokay-Pinot Gris and *vendange tardive*.

Gustave Lorent Best known for Gewurztraminer, although the Pinot Blanc is worth a whirl too.

Albert Mann Rich wines, including a highly rated Pinot Noir.

JosMeyer Very well-crafted range, but most interesting for Jean Meyer's successful interpretations of minor Alsace grape varieties Chasselas and Auxerrois. The Pinot Blanc Mise du Printemps is an excellent wine for converting people to the Alsace cause.

Muré Serious Pinot Noir, fine *grand cru* Riesling (Clos St-Landelin), delicious Crémant d'Alsace and sumptuous *sélection de grains nobles*.

Ostertag André Ostertag is an exciting, maverick winemaker creating offbeat wines using low-yielding vines and, sometimes, new oak barrels.

Ribeauvillé One of Alsace's better co-operatives. Look out for uncommonly fine blends, such as Clos de Zahnacker, made from Riesling, Pinot Gris and Gewurztraminer.

Rieflé Excellent late-harvest wines, elegant Tokay-Pinot Gris and intricately worked Gewurztraminer.

Rolly-Gassmann Dedicated and unpretentious husband-and-wife team making characterful, rich wines, including a spicy Auxerrois and uncommonly tasty Sylvaner.

Schlumberger Extensive vineyard holdings in highly rated *grand cru* sites. Famous for Gewurztraminer.

Schoffit Finely crafted range from a serious young producer who reads *terroir* well and believes in keeping yields right down. The Rieslings from the Rangen *grand cru* are superb.

Trimbach Arguably the most impressive house of all, producing wine in a distinctive style – elegant, fresh, yet deeply complex. Trimbach's range of Riesling is a benchmark for the region, especially the long-lived, intensely fruity Clos Sainte-Hune, with full-bodied Cuvée Frederic Emile a more affordable alternative.

Turckheim Dynamic co-operative providing assured entry-level wines at decent prices. Especially good Tokay-Pinot Gris and highly affordable, tasty Gewurztraminer.

Weinbach The most mind-bogglingly extended family of wines on the shelves but nonetheless a serious set of Rieslings, Tokays and Gewurztraminers in particular. Worth a foray.

Wolfberger Large co-operative responsible for a variable range. Its *crémant* and wines under the Willm label are respectable.

Zind-Humbrecht Master of Wine Olivier Humbrecht offers high quality across the range, from the far-from-basic Pinot Blanc up to the splendid array of *grand cru* Pinot Gris and Riesling. Our only criticism is that the wines give no indication on their labels of the often high residual sugar levels.

Alsace vintage guide

2000 The vintage followed the pattern in much of France, with a cold July being the only interruption to the generally warm, sunny weather. A few showers fell during the last stages of picking, but the quality is generally high. The outcome is plump, fruity wines with sufficient balancing acidity, plus a few succulent *sélection de grains nobles* wines.

1999 A good spring and warm, dry summer led to a large crop. Quality, however, is somewhat variable, thanks to sporadic rain throughout the harvest. Those who worked earlier in the year to reduce their yields have made some lovely wines; others were less successful.

1998 A hot summer augured well, but rain in September meant a problematic vintage. Nonetheless early-picked whites, especially Muscat, are crisp and aromatic, and there were some superb *sélection de grains nobles* wines made. Still, this wasn't a classic year.

1997 Record hours of sunshine during September meant natural sugars beyond those of the previous record year, 1989. An excellent vintage with hot, dry days and cool nights right through the ripening and harvesting period. Top-quality dry wines all round, and late-harvest styles were excellent too.

1996 A late harvest due to cold weather in May and August. But a dry and sunny October brought grapes to a very good level of ripeness, and those who delayed picking until the warm late autumn found it paid off. First-class Pinot Gris and Blanc in particular have been noted whereas Gewurztraminer suffered during the cold patches and will not be at its best from this year.

1995 A producers' vintage – only the most meticulous were rewarded. A very hot summer was followed by a rainy harvest, but those who waited until October to pick benefited from late autumn sunshine. Low in quantity but some high-quality wines.

Fine older vintages 1990, 1989, 1988, 1985, 1983, 1981, 1976.

BORDEAUX

Well, we moaned a lot about 'fruit' last year – about too much of it, à la New World, at the top end, and also about a complete dearth of it at the bottom. This year, at last, it appears things have evened out a bit. There's been enough of a crisis at all levels of the Bordeaux spectrum over the last few years to ensure something was done, and things have changed.

Starting at the top, with the marvellous (but expensive) 2000 vintage, the producers were doing it properly, there weren't so many heavily oaked wines, overtly fruity and exotic tasting with that thick texture you get from using concentration machines.' You could argue that in a good vintage such as this, concentration machines (which remove excess water/rain by osmosis) wouldn't have been necessary, but nonetheless, the overriding feel was one of better wines, with greater elegance and restraint, that seem to have the layers of flavour that indicate they'll age well and evolve over time.

Two châteaux returned to the fold were Cos d'Estournel and Château Angélus in St-Emilion. Angélus' story is serendipitous. Hail in 1999 necessitated bringing the grapes in earlier than usual to avoid rot. Though it was less ripe than they'd wanted, the cellar team found an extra dimension of flavour in the fruit that they hadn't bargained for – and quite liked. So they decided to repeat the process again the next year, and (we hope) so on. It's this extra dimension of flavour, or the lack of it, that the UK trade has been whingeing about for so long. If, step by step, it begins to make a return, then that's a very good thing.

If there are welcome tales from the top of the tree, then those from the lesser Bordeaux ranks are to be doubly celebrated, for here the quality has been dire – not just inappropriate, but utterly dire. Underachievement, underinvestment and unenthusiastic winemaking having been producing thin, green, astringent wines that are nothing but an embarrassment to the French, sitting as they do, next to ripe easy Chilean and Australian wines at the same price.

Bordeaux is now beginning to wake up to more approachable wine styles, with better grape selection, subtle use of American oak, cleaner stainless steel and temperature control in the winery – and prove that it's capable of producing well-made, fruit-driven wines. However, this hasn't been without some help from Australian winemakers making a base in the region, and coaxing out their own easy-drinking styles. But we don't think that's a bad thing at this stage.

At *petits châteaux* level there are some good names emerging. Supermarkets have helped by putting together their own good, well-made brands. And in the Côtes (de Castillon, Francs, Bourg and Blaye), properties have also begun turning out some good, mid-price, fruity, supple clarets. What we recommend is to seek out a few good château names or brands and stick with them.

All this is easy to say from the stand-point of a recently launched good vintage. Though things might have improved, there's still a lot of sub-£3.99 wine out there with which the appellation might want to disassociate itself. Bordeaux is like a big, unwieldy ship, and turning the whole lot round is going to take some time. It isn't enough to just make monthly spot-checks in the winery and on the shop shelves, as was the Institut National des Appellations d'Origine's announced intent last year. And it isn't really enough just to bring in a few Australian winemakers. The realisation of what makes quality wine has to filter down to the vineyards and smaller farmers, many of whom still operate on a mixed-farming basis, alternating their attentions between grapes, corn and fruit trees. Getting 12,900 growers to adopt a new mentality isn't going to happen overnight; incentives and bonuses for growers yielding good grapes, however, are a good start.

So if Bordeaux was at a crossroads last year, stylistically it looks like it might have chosen the right direction. We won't know for sure until things are a little further down the road, but right now, things are looking good but wobbly. The 2000 vintage is receiving plaudits everywhere but, alas, the château owners have raised their prices by more than 50 per cent. It's uncertain whether consumers will tolerate yet another successive annual increase; it could be that the châteaux have commited collective suicide by raising their cash demand yet again.

Bordeaux classification

Bordeaux works on a unique pyramid structure of wine quality classification, with five tiers of *crus classés* – classed growths. There are a number of classification lists, but the most enduring and important is still that of 1855, when the best wines of Bordeaux were ranked according to the price they could command. (In 1855, Bordeaux was just the Médoc: the 'right-bank' wines of St-Emilion and Pomerol weren't of much importance.)

'Claret' is the term coined by the British to mean any red wine from the whole region; classed growth claret refers to the 60 or so Médoc wines from the 1855 classification. It's a bit like understanding the cast of a play with major roles taken by the first growths and the supporting players among the second to fifth growth wines. Continuing the 'dramatic' analogy, with every vintage not only can the quality of performance vary, but individual properties can become rising stars for a while, exceeding their designated status and acquiring a cult following in the process. As in theatre-going, it pays to be an avid enthusiast. If you choose to dip in and dip out, then it is vital to rely on the advice and reviews of trusted wine merchants.

Other regions within Bordeaux that have their own classifications include: Sauternes-Barsac (also 1855), St-Emilion (1955, reclassified 1967, 1985 and 1996) and Graves (1959). Ironically, the wines of Pomerol, which are some of the most expensive and most sought-after in the world, have no classification.

The regions

The vineyards of Bordeaux stretch along the left and right bank of the Gironde estuary and its tributaries, the Garonne and the Dordogne. The large, white wine-producing appellation of Entre-Deux-Mers is so called because it sits between the latter two rivers.

The Médoc

The Médoc is closest to the Atlantic coast of all the Bordeaux vineyards and, protected by the forests of Les Landes, produces some of the world's greatest and longest-lasting red wines – and almost no white at all. Within this grouping of left-bank appellations, lie the four star-quality villages of the Haut-Médoc (Margaux, St-Julien, Pauillac and St-Estèphe), where the most famous châteaux can be found and where the Cabernet Sauvignon grape flourishes on the well-drained, gravelly soil in close proximity to the Gironde estuary.

Driving north from Bordeaux along the N215, the first village, or commune, is Margaux. Key properties include the eponymous Château Margaux, as well as Palmer and Rauzan-Ségla. Purportedly the most feminine of all the wines of the Médoc, Margaux wines can be distinctively delicate on the nose as well as exceedingly powerful.

St-Julien comes next and is famed for its consistent, high-quality wines, although there are no first growths from this commune. However, the performance of Léoville-Las-Cases, Léoville-Barton and Gruaud-Larose in recent years belies their second-growth status.

The awesome vineyards in the commune of Pauillac, where nearly 90 per cent of the wines are classed growths, produce the most highly prized bottles of all. The first growths Latour, Lafite, Mouton-Rothschild; the excellent second growths Pichon-Longueville and Comtesse de Lalande; and the reputable fifth growths Grand-Puy-Lacoste and Lynch-Bages – all are here.

Lastly, St-Estèphe, a commune with a reputation for producing more tightly knit, tannic wines capable of great ageing. This may have something to do with the increased clay content of the soil and poorer drainage – the vine needs to work hard to produce good grapes and intensely dislikes being swamped. No first growths here, but Cos d'Estournel, Montrose, and Calon-Ségur are worthy of their following.

Apart from the famous names, the Médoc also produces vast quantities of generic Bordeaux for everyday drinking. For probably the best-value wine experience from this region, we recommend experimenting with the Crus Bourgeois (a large designated group of wines just below classed growth status) from the Haut-Médoc. Among these are well-structured, concentrated wines capable of ageing. Look out for Cantemerle, Coufran, Lanessan and Sociando-Mallet, or find a château whose style you like and follow it through the vintages.

Libournais

The Libournais, which includes the right-bank areas of St-Emilion and Pomerol, is known chiefly as the home of softer, more accessible, Merlot-based wines compared with the heavily structured Cabernet Sauvignon examples on the opposite bank. Right-bank wines are also capable of ageing, but do not have the same tannin content as their left-bank peers, and come to maturity up to a decade earlier.

The great Pomerol properties of Pétrus and Le Pin command stratospheric prices for these rich and velvety Merlot wines. The limited amounts of wine available from these small estates has also enhanced their rarity value and contributed to their reputation as the jewels in the crown of Bordeaux. Other well-known names snapping at the heels of these two, albeit from a fair distance, include Vieux-Château-Certan, Bon Pasteur, Lafleur, La Conseillante and Clinet.

St-Emilion, meanwhile, is one of the most confusing appellations of Bordeaux, as well as the most picturesque. The often uninspiring outlook of the Médoc finds a pleasant counterpart in the undulating vineyards surrounding the historic village of St-Emilion itself. Given the variations in soil types and the grapes grown, there is no such thing as a typical St-Emilion wine. While Merlot predominates, Cabernet Sauvignon and Cabernet Franc can also feature in a wine (for example, Cheval Blanc). The traditional winemaking infrastructure of smallholdings rather than large estates has led, in recent years, to the rise to prominence of many new and dynamic producers. The St-Emilion classification, revised every ten years or so, is complicated, grouping wine not just as *grands crus* (specific enough, you may think, but in St-Emilion of little definitive meaning), but also as *grands crus classés* and *premiers grands crus classés* (A and B). All in all, as in the Médoc, we are talking about 60 or so *crus classés*. Names to watch out for in St-Emilion include the great châteaux Ausone and Cheval Blanc, Clos Fourtet, Figeac, La Gaffelière and Laniote.

Nowadays it is certainly worth discovering the wines from the villages surrounding St-Emilion, some of which, such as Puisseguin and Lussac, can add their name to the appellation on the label. Côtes de Francs and Côtes de Castillon wines also make for excellent everyday drinking. Other quality improvements, and wines to watch, come from the Fronsac and Canon-Fronsac appellations – what's more, at sensible prices too. The Pétrus-owning Mouiex family have long operated in this area; one of their best properties is La Croix Canon. Others to look out for include La Vieille Cure, Moulin Pey Labrie and Fontenil.

Bourg and Blaye
Both these regions, situated directly opposite the Médoc, have much in common with those lesser appellations already mentioned, in that they are the source of many decent and improving, good-value red wines. Exceptional properties include Roc de Cambes in the Côtes de Bourg and Ségonzac in the Premières Côtes de Blaye.

Graves
Uniquely for Bordeaux, there are several châteaux in the Graves making acceptable white wines as well as red, although the majority of production is red. At the very top, the first growth Pessac-Léognan wine, Haut-Brion, is an historic reminder that the Graves (closer to the town of Bordeaux than the Médoc) has made wine longer than its more illustrious rival areas. Pessac-Léognan itself has five communes and, since the 1959 classification, it is generally acknowledged that the best wines of the region, both red and white, come from these. Examples are Haut-Bailly (Léognan), Smith-Haut-Lafitte (Martillac), La Mission-Haut-Brion (Talence), Pape-Clément (Pessac) and Bouscaut (Cadaujac). Below these famous names are many lesser-known properties which have

improved in recent years, and provide less-refined but concentrated and flavoursome alternatives to the wines of the Médoc.

Other reds

Classed growth claret and individual appellations, at the top end of the market, belie the fact that the majority of the region's production consists of basic Bordeaux and Bordeaux Supérieur blends – most of them destined for the French supermarkets. In the UK, these are the wines you will usually find with the word 'Claret' or a *petit château* on the label, expressly to give them a more upmarket and traditional feel. The quality of generic Bordeaux is the battlefield on which the reputation of the region is currently being fought over. Things are improving, or beginning to improve slowly. We feel the best way to enjoy a decent bottle is to find a good name and stick to it. It doesn't, unfortunately, pay to be too adventurous; but look to the Côtes de Bourg and Blaye, or the Côtes de Francs, or anything labelled with the 2000 vintage, and you could be off to a better start.

Second wines

These are the unimaginatively dubbed wines made from either the rejected *cuvées* of the *grand vin* blends or the fruit of younger vines, as yet not producing enough concentration for inclusion in the top wine. However, these are often scaled-down versions of the 'real thing' that offer an affordable sneak preview at very little less quality. Exclusion from the top blend can be owed to as meagre a force as a touch too much oak, or the wrong sort of pressings, the result of just a tiny difference in judgement – or a need to cut back on quantity. When as little as 40 per cent of production makes it to the *grand vin*, what you'll get in the 'second' bottle needn't vary much at all. And in lesser vintages second wines will receive even more juice from hallowed *terroir*. The second wines of Latour and Margaux (Les Forts de Latour and Pavillon Rouge), for example, are almost considered classed growths anyway, at a fraction of the price. Seize the day, we say!

Look out for: Clos du Marquis (Léoville-Las Cases), Bahans-Haut-Brion (Haut-Brion), Les Fiefs de Lagrange (Lagrange) and Sarget de Gruaud Larose (Gruaud-Larose) among others. Also look out for 'third wines' too, for similar reasons…

Red wine vintage guide

For more expensive clarets, say over £20 a bottle, our advice is always to check the vintage and the style of the wine. Some vintages, and nowadays some wines, are ready to drink sooner than others. Drinking young Bordeaux today isn't always like 'chewing nails', as many, even the most expensive ones, have softer tannins and are made to be ripe and approachable when young. Hefty classed growths will still require (and benefit from) a minimum of ten years' cellaring, but lighter vintages and right-bank Libournais wines may require less time to come round. When purchasing claret, check with your merchant as to when you should start to drink it, and always hold some back to sample at regular intervals, so you can enjoy its development and maturity. Most everyday claret, on the other hand, particularly bottles costing less than £7, are intended to be drunk young and will not benefit from ageing – indeed, the opposite; the freshness and any attractive fruit aromas will quickly fade.

2000 By all accounts a stunning year – and with three zeros, one to please the marketing men. Day after day of hot sunshine made for a perfect, rainless ripening season on both banks, and perfect conditions didn't waver during harvest. Merlots were picked, full of opulence and firm structure in mid- to late September; Cabernet Francs in early October were good news in St-Emilion where this grape features highly; and strong, structured Cabernet Sauvignons were harvested just before the rain set in on 10 October. The best vintage since 1990; not showy but one to last.

1999 September rains and a spectacular hailstorm in St-Emilion resulted in a patchwork performance across the region, after a promisingly bumper crop had materialised during the sweltering month of August. As 1998, this is a year where Merlot benefited from being harvested before the rains and the later-ripening Cabernet Sauvignon crop, particularly in St-Estèphe, was generally unable to provide its best. Properties from the Médoc with a higher proportion of Merlot in the blend will have produced better wines.

1998 A Merlot year, when September rains arrived after most of the Merlot had been picked but before the harvest of the two Cabernet varieties. Prior to that, August had been hot and dry, producing small berries with intense colour and flavour and no shortage of tannin. Pomerol is the star, closely followed by St-Emilion and other Libournais wines. The Médoc fared worst, and many wines, though deep in colour, are rather attenuated, even at properties which could afford to downgrade inferior batches of wine.

1997 The growing season had been very erratic, with cool spells, hot spells, high humidity and more. By the last half of August, Merlot had high sugar levels and low acid levels, but with unripe flavours and tannins. On 25 August rain came and panicked many growers into picking. Those who waited were rewarded with fine conditions from the end of September which lasted through into October, and most Cabernet Sauvignon was picked fully ripe. The wines are not concentrated due to the effects of the rain but they are charming, very accessible and made for early drinking. Pity about the horrendous prices.

1996 A year for Cabernet Sauvignon. The first two-thirds of September were warm and dry, but the last third brought further rain just as the Merlot and Cabernet Franc were being picked. The result was dilution of flavours. The Cabernet Sauvignon harvest took place after the vines had had a chance to dry out, and the result is a raft of wines from the Médoc with plenty of flesh and plenty of tannin. Like the 1986s, they will need lots of patience. A few Libournais châteaux which waited for the Merlot to dry out after the rain and ripen further have, in many cases, produced some fine wines.

1995 The best and most consistent vintage since 1990, with St-Julien, Pauillac, St-Emilion and Pomerol standing out. The wines fall halfway between 1985 and 1986 in style, with ripe, friendly fruit backed up by good structure.

1994 This was all set to be a great vintage before the cool, rainy September. However, while the lack of autumn sun meant that some châteaux had problems ripening their grapes as much as they would have liked, many decent, if rather sturdy, wines were made which are reasonable value but a long way off drinking.

1993 Rain at harvest made for dilute wines, but because the grapes had enjoyed almost perfect ripening conditions up until the rain, the flavours are not underripe. Not a vintage to keep, though some Pomerols have the substance to survive for another few years yet.

1992 There wasn't much sun, and the summer was the wettest for 50 years, so the wines were almost universally condemned. This doesn't explain why we occasionally come across remarkably pleasant and sensibly priced wines. Hmmm.

1991 A small, patchy vintage which, apart from those at the very top properties, is best forgotten.

1990 A brilliant vintage, initially underrated in the wake of the headstrong 1989 but now recognised as at least its equal and very probably its superior. The wines have been delicious since they were released, but those who wish to keep them will not be disappointed. The acids may not be the highest, but the wine has sufficient body of alcohol and ripe tannins to ensure a healthy existence for several years to come. Whether you can afford them is a different matter.

1989 A precocious vintage which prompted some growers to pick their Merlot too early. Cabernet Sauvignon was magnificent, and the best wines of the Médoc and Graves will be going strong for the next 30 years. Prices remain lower than for the 1990s.

1988 When the folk of the wine world refer to 'classic claret', 1988 is the sort of vintage they have in mind. Restrained, elegant wines with a slightly herbaceous, stalky edge, which need plenty of time to show their best, are more the order of the day than the fleshy excesses of 1989 and 1990.

Good older vintages
1986 Powerful vintage producing big, black wines. At less lofty levels, the tannins are often too weighty for the fruit content, and some wines seem destined never to come into balance, but the top Médocs are superb.
1985 Beautifully balanced, utterly captivating vintage – even at *petit château* level – which has been delicious from the word go and is still going strong.
1983 Pick your property well – the Margaux appellation had an excellent vintage – and you could have some of the best mature claret bargains around. However, several wines never seem to have fulfilled their initial potential.
1982 Spectacular vintage with extraordinary ripeness and now extraordinary prices. The best wines are full of fabulous rich fruit and are destined to join the legendary 1961s in the claret hall of fame.

Pick of the producers (Red Bordeaux)

As well as the reliable, and frequently very expensive, classics listed below (the 'wish list' if you like), the upswing in winemaking standards over the 1990s has meant that a new crop of châteaux names emerge every year – more familiar names, too, are shrugging off mediocrity and making splendid clarets to be proud of, both in modern and traditional styles. The following are a list of 10 good-value properties performing particularly well in the 2000 vintage.

Belgrave Much improved fifth growth Médoc château.
Côte de Baleau New-wave St-Emilion, also worth cellaring – tremendous value.
Fontenil New cult Fronsac, from a new cult winemaker, Michel Rolland.
Grand Corbin Despagne Really well-sited St-Emilion near Cheval Blanc, ever improving.
Haut Carles Another sensationally good Fronsac.
Kirwan Third growth Margaux, now up to second growth standard.
Lezongars British-owned property in the Premières Côtes making stunning wine.
Prieuré Lichine A new darling with the UK wine trade, great Margaux, be quick.
La Tour Carnet Every-improving Haut-Médoc wine.
La Tour Figeac Biodynamic St-Emilion château: lush ripe wines.

Angélus, *1er grand cru classé*, St-Emilion. A string of fine wines throughout the 1980s and, in particular, in the difficult vintages of the 1990s has made this large château one of the best of St-Emilion. A recent style change back to classic elegance is very welcome.

Ausone, *1er grand cru classé 'A'*, St-Emilion. One of St-Emilion's top two properties, an underperformer through much of the 1980s, but now, with Alain Vauthier at the helm and Michel Rolland as a consultant, is back and doing better than ever: 50:50 CabernetFranc and Merlot with 100 per cent new oak. Wonderful wine.

Beychevelle, *4ème cru classé*, St-Julien. This property can produce wines that are approachable in their youth but which also age well. Recent vintages have been erratic. Second label Amiral de Beychevelle.

Cantemerle, *5ème cru classé*, Haut-Médoc. Stylish, elegant wine which matures relatively early and is usually of exceptionally good value. Second label Baron Villeneuve de Cantemerle.

Chasse-Spleen, Moulis. Would probably be a fourth growth if the 1855 classification were to be redone. Solid wines with great concentration of flavour which age well. Was using too much oak, but now improving. Second label l'Ermitage de Chasse-Spleen.

Cheval Blanc, *1er grand cru classé 'A'*, St-Emilion. Wonderful property which is unusual in its high proportion – up to two-thirds – of Cabernet Franc. Wines are remarkably approachable from a tender age but live as long as any claret. Second label Le Petit Cheval (very like the *grand vin* but at a quarter of the price!).

Domaine de Chevalier, Pessac-Léognan. Classic elegant claret, as well balanced as any in Bordeaux. You'll miss the point if you drink it much before its tenth birthday. Second label Bâtard-Chevalier.

Clinet, Pomerol. The opulent, late-picked wines made in the last ten years by the late Jean-Michel Arcaute (aided by Michel Rolland) put this property near the top of the Pomerol tree.

Cos d'Estournel, *2ème cru classé*, St-Estèphe. Top property in its commune and one of the most concentrated of all clarets, yet managing to retain more than a vestige of elegance. New rigorous winemaking regime headed by Jean-Guillaume Prats is improving the wines. Second label Les Pagodes de Cos (Château de Marbuzet now from separate vines).

Ducru Beaucaillou, *2ème cru classé*, St-Julien. Back at the head of the St-Julien firmament (stunning 1996 and 2000) after a shaky period in the late 1980s. At its best, expect wonderful sweet cedar and blackcurrant refinement. Second label La Croix.

l'Eglise-Clinet, Pomerol. Old low-yielding vines and careful winemaking by Denis Durantou result in sumptuous silky wines of the highest class, and traditional style. Second label, La Petite Eglise, is a bargain!

l'Evangile, Pomerol. Powerful, silky, consistently fine Pomerol (up there with Pétrus) from the Lafite-Rothschild stable, whose only negative point is its phenomenal price.

de Fieuzal, Pessac-Léognan. The white is the sexiest wine, but the delicious supple red is not very far behind. A good buy.

Figeac, *1er grand cru classé*, St-Emilion. Property located close to Cheval Blanc and the Pomerol border with a high proportion of the two Cabernets. Slightly erratic, but the best (1982, 1990, 1998, 1999) are both accessible young and capable of ageing gloriously. Second label Grangeneuve de Figeac.

Gazin, Pomerol. Large (for Pomerol) estate which maintains quality by rejecting inferior *cuvées* for the *grand vin*. Performed splendidly throughout the difficult 1990s. Making great strides. Good value.

Gruaud-Larose, *2ème cru classé*, St-Julien. It's large, flamboyant, it's not too expensive, and the wine is of superlative quality. Very hard to fault. Second label Sarget de Gruaud-Larose.

Haut-Brion, *1er cru classé*, Pessac-Léognan. The top estate of the Graves, which lacks the showiness of some Médoc wines yet ages superbly to a state of pencil and cedar refinement and poise which few can match. Second label Bahans-Haut-Brion is 40 per cent of production, and very good.

Lafite-Rothschild, *1er cru classé*, Pauillac. Easy to misunderstand in its youth but will always emerge to a graceful, perfumed maturity and will keep for decades in the best vintages. High (93 per cent) in Cabernet Sauvignon. Excellent second label is Carruades de Lafite-Rothschild.

Lafleur, Pomerol. One of the sturdiest of the Pomerols and one of the few real rivals to Pétrus. Slow to mature: give it lots of time in bottle.

Lafon Rochet, *4ème cru classé*, St-Estèphe. Top quality in vintages since 1994 – buy now before prices rise. 2000 is best ever.

Lagrange, *3ème cru classé*, St-Julien. Revitalised by the Japanese Suntory group in the 1980s and now producing up to its third growth status at still reasonable prices. Upping its proportions of Cabernet Sauvignon as new vines come on stream. Watch for further change. Second label Les Fiefs de Lagrange.

Latour, *1er cru classé*, Pauillac. Powerful wine – increasingly so under Frédéric Engerer and François Pinault's direction – which lives for decades. The 1990 is the wine of the vintage; the 1995 and 1996 are also superb; 2000, according to Andrew Jefford of the London *Evening Standard*, is a 'satin-coated cricket ball'. Second label Les Forts de Latour is hardly less grand, from old vines and only a quarter of the *grand vin* price.

Léoville-Barton, *2ème cru classé*, St-Julien. Classic, classy claret, firm in its youth but ageing to cedar and blackcurrant perfection. The wines of the 1990s have all been among the best of the vintage; 2000 is tremendous but thanks to media hype now trades at extortionate prices. Prices for earlier vintages, however, are still very reasonable. Second wine La Réserve de Léoville-Barton.

Léoville-Las-Cases, *2ème cru classé*, St-Julien. A first growth in all but name, producing powerful, complex and intense claret of superlative quality. Second label Clos du Marquis – big and concentrated, a sneak preview, maturing sooner at a quarter of the price.

Lynch Bages, *5ème cru classé*, Pauillac. Widely acclaimed, and one of the easiest clarets to understand, with an almost Australian wealth of minty, ripe fruit, heaps of oak and the ability to be enjoyed from its fifth birthday onwards. Second label Haut-Bages-Avérous.

Margaux, *1er cru classé*, Margaux. Ever since the Mentzelopoulos family bought Margaux in 1977, this has been one of the top ten clarets each vintage; 2000 is no different. Fragrantly perfumed, yet backed up by intense fruit and powerful structure. Second label Pavillon Rouge of at least fourth growth quality.

La Mission Haut-Brion, Pessac-Léognan. Massive oaky wine, just falling short of the standard of its stablemate Haut-Brion but still of superb quality. Second label La Chapelle Haut-Brion.

Montrose, *2ème cru classé*, St-Estèphe. Vintages since 1989 have shown a string of powerful, highly extracted and flavour-packed wines, which show a return to form for what was once St-Estèphe's top château. When it's good, it's very, very good. Second label La Dame de Montrose.

Mouton-Rothschild, *1er cru classé*, Pauillac. A pencil-shavings, oak and cassis brick of a wine with a high – over 80 per cent – proportion of Cabernet Sauvignon. Consistently excellent, although prices, particularly for the 1982, have gone haywire. Shows its best earlier than the other first growths. American collectors will have to buy two different 1993s, since Balthus's original label, depicting a naked young girl of tender age, has been outlawed by US officials. Second label Le Second Vin de Mouton-Rothschild.

Palmer, *3ème cru classé*, Margaux. A star in the 1960s and 1970s, producing wines of perfume and class. Recent vintages (1995, 1996, 1998, 2000) show that it is currently second only to Château Margaux in the appellation. Second wine formerly Réserve du Général, now Alter Ego de Palmer: Merlot-dominated and earlier-drinking.

Pape-Clément, Pessac-Léognan. Since 1986 one of the classiest wines of the Graves, offering a combination of earth and tar, power and finesse.

Pavie, *1er grand cru classé*, St-Emilion. Sweet, modern-style, charming wine from one of the largest of the St-Emilion châteaux which was on form in the late 1980s, slipped up slightly but, under new ownership, is now right at the top of the Bordeaux ladder.

Pavie Macquin, *1er grand cru classé*, St-Emilion. Owned by the Thienpont family of Le Pin and Vieux-Château-Certan and making similarly rich, concentrated wines which need plenty of time to shed their tannic overcoat. Perhaps overpriced in recent vintages.

Pétrus, Pomerol. Still king of Pomerol, despite the mob of pretenders led by Le Pin. Not as flashy when young as some of the wannabees, always awesomely powerful and full-flavoured and needing 15 years to show at its best.

Pichon Longueville, *2ème cru classé*, Pauillac, aka Pichon-Baron. Reclaimed its rightful place as one of the Pauillac greats from the 1988 vintage onwards under the guidance of Jean-Michel Cazes and Daniel Llose. Second wine Les Tourelles de Longueville.

Pichon-Longueville-Lalande, *2ème cru classé*, Pauillac. Hiccups at this excellent château in the late 1980s, were smoothed out by 1994 and it's now one of the sexiest clarets around. More and more Cabernet-based of late, with an unusually high proportion of Petite Verdot in 2000. Second wine Réserve de la Comtesse.

Le Pin, Pomerol. Pocket handkerchief estate belonging to the Thienpont family of Vieux-Château-Certan and currently the wine in most demand in the world. Sumptuous, oaky, sleek, Merlot-based, and early-drinking. If you have to ask how much it costs, you can't afford it. (2000 is £6,000/case *en primeur*…)

Poujeaux, Moulis. On current form, the best of the Moulis châteaux, making spicy, rich, fruit-packed consistent wines which need plenty of time to evolve.

Rauzan-Ségla, *2ème cru classé*, Margaux. Improving with each vintage, thanks to cash from Chanel and inspired winemaking. The 1995 is splendid; 2000 is a top-class blockbuster. Second wine Château Lamouroux.

Smith-Haut-Lafitte, Pessac-Léognan. Up-and-coming property thanks to the efforts of the Cathiard family, making intense yet elegant claret. 2000 is decadent, seductive, right on track.

La Tertre Rôteboeuf, *grand cru*. A *premier grand cru classé* in any sane classification of St-Emilion; luxurious, silky wine of immense youthful charm – and price.

Trotanoy, Pomerol. Classic Pomerol with enough structure to support the lush fruit. Offers relatively good value in the light of demand for Pétrus and Le Pin.

Valandraud, *grand cru*, St-Emilion. The Le Pin of St-Emilion (before the arrival of La Mondotte), tiny quantities of an unfined, unfiltered boutique super wine. Second wine, Virginie de Valandraud, is very similar; third wine Axelle de Valandraud (from December 2000) and l'Interdit de Valandraud (made outside AC regulations) are priceless.

Vieux-Château-Certan, Pomerol. One of the leaner Pomerols, with 20 per cent Cabernet Sauvignon and 25 per cent Franc in the blend. Needs age to show well.

Dry white wines

Bordeaux today is redder than ever – 85 per cent so in fact – and those whites that make it have to be truly excellent. The region is as capable as any nowadays of producing well-made white wines at all levels, and while the classics carry on being classic (see the range of minerally, ageworthy, Sémillon-based Pessac-Léognan whites below), recent effort in the 'everyday' echelons is banishing the tired, over-sulphured underperformers of the 1980s. Straight Sauvignon is very much the watchword. Intelligent winemaking and careful picking can produce wines that are every bit as crisp and fresh as New Zealand's, with Sémillon taking very much a back-seat role. Some of the best of these Sauvignons (perhaps unsurprisingly) come from the cooler, marginal northern areas of the region, and are thoroughly into modernity; there's even a touch of American oak being used here and there to round them out. Some whites are still commercial and uninteresting, but up a level from basic Bordeaux Blanc, Entre-Deux-Mers and Graves are making rich, rounded, oak-aged wines which can rival some of the great Burgundian whites for style and elegance. It's also worth remembering that the best can be excellent to serve with food, whether young and fresh in style, or full and lingering, Sémillon-based classics from Pessac-Léognan. Watch out also, for the rare, interest-value whites from the great Médoc châteaux such as Margaux, Lynch Bages and Mouton-Rothschild.

Dry white vintage guide

2000 As good a year for the whites as reds. At premium level, some herald this as the best vintage for a decade, while others have more admiration for the vibrance of the 1996s. 2000s are richer and fuller and may do much to abate the gloom cast by previous rainy vintages and past over-production.

1999 Not a spectacular year, with rain – particularly in the Entre-Deux-Mers. However, quality-conscious growers (and there are ever-increasing numbers of them) managed to produce Sauvignon and Sémillon with attractive fruit and concentrated flavours. These wines will be worth paying that little bit more for. For the classic Pessac-Léognan whites, which were harvested ahead of the rains, think power rather than finesse.

1998 Hot summer conditions ensured good ripening. The showers at the start of September were generally too light to cause any damage, and the grapes were picked in first-class condition: fully ripe, with near-perfect sugar and acid levels and no signs of rot. The wines are good, some very promising, although not as high-quality as they would have been with a slightly less torrid August.

1997 Picking began on 18 August, the earliest start to a vintage since 1893, but humidity and rain at the end of the month caused rot in many vineyards, and a large amount of fruit was picked before it was fully ripe. Grapes that survived through to the sunny September had the chance to finish ripening, resulting in some high-quality Sémillon and aromatic Sauvignon.

1996 Sauvignon was picked in early to mid-September in fine conditions and came in with decent acidity and sugar levels, but Sémillon caught the rains later in the month and came in with slight dilution. The result is aromatic wines with high acidity which are decent but lack the body which Sémillon brings in great vintages.

Good earlier vintages (now only for the very top properties) 1995, 1994, 1990, 1989, 1988, 1986.

Pick of the producers (Dry white Bordeaux)

All Pessac-Léognan unless otherwise stated.

Couhins-Lurton The classiest of André Lurton's Bordeaux whites is a spicy, barrel-fermented Sauvignon.

Domaine de Chevalier Very concentrated but tight in its youth and heavenly at ten years old. Not always as expensive as other top Bordeaux whites.

de Fieuzal Exciting spicy 50/50 Sémillon/Sauvignon blend whose price is climbing steeply, despite its not being a classed growth.

Haut-Brion Rich, waxy and heady, this is 55 per cent Sémillon and 45 per cent Sauvignon which has been fermented and aged in new oak. Rare and expensive too.

Laville-Haut-Brion The 60 per cent Sémillon/40 per cent Sauvignon white of La Mission Haut-Brion is good but should be better given the prices asked. It does age remarkably well though.

La Louvière Another André Lurton smoky, spicy success for rather less money than some of the big names.

Margaux The Médoc is not renowned for its whites but Pavillon Blanc de Château Margaux (by far the finest) can take on any of those above or below. 100 per cent Sauvignon Blanc, it reveals the true capabilities of this grape: keep it for five years, or, if you can, for 20.

Pape-Clément Not a classed growth (unlike the red) but making deliciously rich, oaky whites.

Smith-Haut-Lafitte One of the most exciting properties in the whole of Bordeaux at present, making this superlative 100 per cent Sauvignon as well as excellent reds.

Sweet white wines

For most people, the epitome of sweet white wine remains the enticingly honeyed and intense examples of Sauternes, where *botrytis*, or noble rot, has concentrated the Sauvignon and Sémillon grapes to a degree of seductive sweetness that is unsurpassable in any other climate or with any other grape varieties. Although nowadays there are many unfortified Muscat or Riesling-based sweet wines available, none can really compare with Sauternes for ageing and development potential. Several merchants offer mixed case, *en primeur* selections, which will provide an interesting experience for enthusiastic amateurs.

Five villages – Sauternes, Barsac, Bommes, Fargues and Preignac – may use the name Sauternes; Barsac is also entitled to its own appellation. These wines are traditionally served to accompany foie gras and blue cheeses in south-west France, but equally can be served chilled with simple fruit desserts.

Bordeaux also offers some cheaper alternatives to Sauternes and Barsac, namely neighbouring Cérons (Château de Cérons, in particular), or, on the opposite bank of the Garonne, the wines of Cadillac, Loupiac, Ste-Croix-du-Mont and Monbazillac, near Bergerac. The tiny appellation of Saussignac, also near Bergerac, is now making waves in the sweet wine sector and is featuring on the lists of UK wine merchants. Also worth trying, particularly if you are on a budget, are Clos St-Georges (Graves Supérieures) and Château de Berbec (Premières Côtes de Bordeaux).

Sweet white vintage guide

That perfectly poised, apricot sweetness, cut through with a tingling balance of delicate acidity is the result of a most extraordinary set of climatic circumstances that have been timed to perfection – so precisely so that a good vintage seems almost miraculous. And even when that happens, there's often only enough juice for a couple of glasses per vine. Yet still we reject these wines. At very least, we should be buying them to lay down and drink at their marvellous best – in 20 years' time, maybe then will they be fashionable?

2000 While everything else benefited from the heat and good weather, Sauternes had a tougher time. Dry conditions meant *botrytis* took longer to set in, then rain on 10 October dashed most châteaux' hopes altogether. Tiny quantities of sweet wine were made by those who managed to collect some grapes before the downpours. The rest will have nothing at all.

1999 A reasonably decent vintage brought about by the hot, dry summer and with seemingly no adverse effects of picking in the damp conditions of late September. Healthy levels of *botrytis* have led to wines with good sugar levels, balance and fine quality. On a par with 1996 and 1997.

1998 There was no shortage of noble rot, and those who managed to pick before and after the main batch of rains at the end of September/beginning of October have made beautifully textured fleshy wines.

1997 The first pickings in early September were more to eliminate grapes with grey rot than to pick the nobly rotten ones. The weather was dry for the rest of the vintage, and the harvest progressed well, with the final pickings taking place in some cases in mid-November. Lovely pure wines, medium-bodied with fine acidity.

1996 September rain followed by a generally dry October gave grapes with high *botrytis* levels and little or no grey rot. The best vintage since the great years of 1988–1990, although not in the same league.

1995 A vintage that suffered none of the problems of grey rot which had caused havoc in the previous four years. Rich wines with reasonable levels of *botrytis* but lacking the concentration for greatness.

1994, **1993**, **1992**, **1991** With no *botrytis* in 1994 and 1993, little in 1992 and a tiny crop in 1991, these years are generally best avoided, although a few exceptions include the sumptuous 1991 Climens.

1990, **1989**, **1988** A superb trio, with 1988 classic and elegant, 1989 opulent and heady, and 1990 powerful and sweet. If you know of any back-to-back tastings of wines from these three vintages, please send us an invitation.

Good earlier vintages 1986, 1983, 1976, 1975, 1971, 1967

Pick of the producers (sweet white Bordeaux)

All Sauternes unless otherwise indicated.

Bastor-Lamontagne Not the greatest Sauternes but well-made, heady and above all very fairly priced wine.

Climens, Barsac. Concentrated, consistent, opulent yet managing to retain elegance. Textbook Sauternes – sorry, Barsac – which many regard as the finest after Yquem.

Coutet, Barsac. A larger property than neighbouring Climens, to which it is often thought to pay second fiddle. Coutet was on top form throughout the 1990s, however.

Doisy-Daëne, Barsac. Go-ahead property whose long-lived sweet wines have been stunning of late, made by Dennis Dubourdieu.

Doisy-Védrines, Barsac. Decent-value wine in a rich vein from former *négociant* Pierre Casteja.

de Fargues Yquem winemaking, Yquem style and not far from Yquem prices, but the wine is very impressive.

Gilette Made only in top vintages and aged in concrete tanks for decades before bottling. The unwooded style can seem out of kilter with more modern Sauternes, but the wine opens up remarkably if given plenty of time to breathe.

Guiraud High-quality estate which has been making top-notch wines since the early 1980s, albeit at a high price.

Lafaurie-Peyraguey One of the best-balanced Sauternes, matching oak and heady *botrytis* with fruit and acidity.

Rieussec Exotic Sauternes under the same ownership as Lafite and l'Evangile which is one of the best of the region on a good day.

Suduiraut Now owned by AXA Millésimes – which also owns Lynch-Bages, Pichon-Longueville and others – so expect a return to the form which almost made it a rival to Yquem.

d'Yquem Expensive but peerless, the greatest sweet wine in the world due to minute yields – a glass of wine per vine – and great care in the cellar. Compare the price to those of the top clarets and Yquem is a relative bargain. Now owned by luxury goods giant LVMH.

Other wines

Bordeaux Rosé or Clairet (very light red wines) have enjoyed something of a surge in popularity in recent years, helped also by improved vinification techniques, such as the gentle presses and cool fermentation employed for white wines. Château de Sours and Château Thieuley are fine examples of fresh, light and elegant pinks, perfect for alfresco dining.

BURGUNDY

The buzz word in Burgundy's vineyards at the moment is 'biodynamics'. As if this region isn't complicated enough, we're now supposed to take seriously growers who live by the tenets of

Rudolf Steiner, bury cows' horns and horse tails among their vines, and plan everything in synchrony with the phases of the moon. Is all this madness? On the face of it, the answer's certainly yes, but we also think these strange practices are rooted in a very deep-seated desire to improve quality. To make good the wrongs done by poor vineyard management in the 1960s and 1970s. And that has to be worthwhile.

As fashionable as Burgundy is today, it might seem hard to believe that after the Second World War growers were struggling to stay in business. Prices, frequently astronomical now, were then at an all-time low. So when the Americans opened up the market in the 1960s, with a huge demand for white burgundy, it's hardly surprising the reaction was to supply them at all costs – the customer was king. Yields crept up, bottles were churned out, and quality declined – Algerian, Tunisian and Rhône wine was blended into the reds to bolster them and integrity appeared to go out the window. The very worst crime, as it happened, was to bump up performance in the vineyards by adding potassium-based fertilisers. This had the effect of lowering the acidity structure of the fruit to the point of insipidity. And the disaster was that it remained in the vineyards for up to 20 years. Wine quality dived down and down.

So the adoption of biodynamics, it transpires, stems less from a desire to indulge in a 'happy drug' than a realisation that treating the vineyards badly could ruin them forever. As the character of Burgundy is so very dependent on soil type and specific vineyard plots, these efforts are all the more understandable. Phases of the moon and the position of Saturn aside, 'teas' made with disinterred cows' horns have the effect of restoring organic life to exhausted, over-worked soils.

Now we're not suggesting for a minute that people should only purchase biodynamic burgundy – far from it, and for three reasons. One, we don't know many people that can afford it. Two, for most practitioners this isn't a marketing ploy and they don't label their wines as being biodynamic for fear people won't judge them on their inherent merits – the wines that is, their aromas, flavours and complexity. And three, Burgundy is mostly too damp and cool a region not to need some rot or mould prevention in some form. (That biodynamic processes can be just too risky was discovered recently by an experimental grower in St-Aubin who, on refusing to spray it to prevent mould, lost his entire crop.) Nobody is even suggesting that biodynamics makes the wines taste better – although to those who feel strongly about these things, it's likely they will anyway. But what we are saying is, we 'like their style'.

Any monoculture is a worrying thing, with the potential to take too much of one thing out of the environment. In this respect, a more holistic approach to farming 'only vines' has to be good, whether it be organic, biodynamic, or the approach known as '*lutte raisonée*', by which as little as possible is done to intervene in the vineyards but in a year of dreadful rot, for example, remedial steps can be taken (spraying, dusting with sulphur).

Look to the likes of Leflaive, Comtes Lafon, Domaine Leroy and Roumier for the full-scale '*soixante-huiters*' as the biodynamists self-mockingly call themselves (1968 being the summer of peace and love…). But otherwise we suggest looking to merchant lists rather than labels for the growers taking part in this new wave of soil guardianship (be they organic, biodynamic or otherwise).

Not everyone, however, is striving to preserve the integrity of the sacred Burgundian vineyard site. Yet again, we find the increasing demand for burgundy is putting producers under pressure. *Négociants* and growers alike have been caught bulking up their wines with fruit from lesser vineyards. So far, none of the top growers has been involved (so stick to the growers you know and trust) and we very much hope the producers found guilty recently will turn out to be misguided loners.

Organisation of the trade

Burgundy's complex wine industry owes much of its structure to the French inheritance laws. For example, Vineyard X originally had just one owner, but two generations later, it has been divided between the 12 grandchildren, some of whom have sold their share to their siblings, while others have married into families which also had vineyards. It's easy to see how, today, a typical Burgundy domaine will be split into maybe a dozen or more plots spread over several villages, and perhaps ranging from a sizeable chunk of Bourgogne Rouge to just a couple of rows in a *grand cru* vineyard.

In the past, it didn't make economic sense for the grower to vinify and sell each wine separately, and this led to the emergence of *négociants*, merchants who would buy some or all of a grower's different batches of grapes, must or wine and then blend them with other similar batches in order to both guarantee continuity of supply and maintain their particular house style. It's easy to see how the *négociant* system could be abused, and it certainly was. For every honest *négociant*, there was at least one other whose wines bore little resemblance to what was claimed on the label. Many a pre-1970 Nuits-St-Georges was bolstered by matter from the Rhône and even Algeria.

Gradually, the growers began to realise that not only were such tactics damaging Burgundy's reputation, but that they could also make a better living by selling wines under their own label. With the increase in domaine bottling from the 1950s onwards, the reputation of the *négociants* slumped, to such an extent that come the early 1980s, no serious Burgundy lover would choose their wines in preference to that of a small grower. Many went out of business or were bought up by rivals.

Today, the distinction between grower and *négociant* is rather more blurred. The major firms still buy-in large quantities of wine and grapes, but they are also looking to expand their own vineyard holdings in order to guarantee both supply and quality. Winemaking standards have improved too, and the best wines stand comparison with those of the top growers – the *négociant* house Jadot is a good example.

There has also been the emergence of smaller companies known as '*micro-négociants*', who are prepared to pay high prices for the best grapes, and who then make, mature and sell the wine themselves focusing only on quality and individual plots. Not only does this allow talented new winemakers, such as Nicolas Potel and Jean-Marie Guffens at Verget, to break into a wine-environment dominated by historic families without owning any vineyards, it also, in an ironic twist, is a direct copy of the New World model of winemaking. (Penfolds, for example, frequently buy their fruit from other top-quality growers.) The other recent phenomenon is the rise of the *éleveur*. These are the *micro-micro-négociants* who buy in wine ready-made but not yet barrel-aged. Their role is purely to mature the wine in their cellars and coax it into perfect condition for sale.

Does this all sound rather confusing? Well, sorry, it is. But we say as long as the growers and *négociants* label clearly whether their wine is estate-grown or from bought-in fruit, then we'll know where we stand. So while we used to list the *négociants* separately from the growers, we've now listed them together later in this section.

The Burgundian hierarchy

Burgundy has well over 100 appellations ranging from blanket generics which cover the whole of the region to tiny *grands crus* of less than one hectare. At the top of the quality tree – and base of the quantity tree – come the 39 *grands crus*. The 24 red ones are, with the exception of Corton, all in the Côte de Nuits. Seven of the 15 white ones are in Chablis, one, Musigny, in the Côte de Nuits and the rest are in the Côte de Beaune. With the exception of the ones in Chablis, these will just bear the vineyard name rather than the village in which they can be found.

Then come the plethora of *premiers crus* vineyards which can be hard to keep up with – Beaune alone has 34. These annex their names to the village name, resulting in wines such as Puligny-Montrachet Folatières. The wines which bear no vineyard name and just say Premier Cru will be blends from a number of *premier cru* vineyards. Montagny used to be able to use the words if it reached a certain alcohol level, but is now in the process of making the appellation more vineyard specific. After this are the village wines, Meursault, Chambolle-Musigny, Givry. Finally come Bourgogne Rouge and Blanc, Bourgogne Passetoutgrains (Pinot Noir and Gamay) and Bourgogne Grand Ordinaire (lowest of the low). Beaujolais has a slightly different hierarchy which is dealt with later, although it too can also call itself Bourgogne Rouge.

Red wines

You can find small amounts of strange varieties such as César and Tréssot in the Chablis district. Then there is the frothy Gamay of Beaujolais fame. However, the grape responsible for great burgundy, the most sensuous red wine in the world, is Pinot Noir. Producers describe the cultivation of Pinot using words such as 'fickle' and 'capricious', but it's not that difficult to grow. What is difficult, however, is to grow it well. The sentiment is that it is impossible to produce great red burgundy unless yields are low, less than 35 hl/ha. Organic and biodynamic viticulture are becoming more and more widespread as growers realise that the chemical treatments of the last 30 to 40 years have resulted in very unhealthy vineyards. A vine that receives all its nourishment from artificial fertilisers doesn't need to stretch its roots far into the soil to obtain sustenance, and so the influence of *terroir* is reduced.

Having grown sound fruit, the general message in the winemaking is 'hands-off'. Definitions of this vary from cellar to cellar. Some highly rated winemakers let their grapes macerate at low temperatures for a few days before fermentation begins, some control their fermentation temperatures, some chaptalise (add sugar) even in good vintages in order to extend fermentation, some use only new oak, some fine and filter their wines before bottling. Others don't. There's no formula for great burgundy – and in a world of identikit wines, praise be for that.

Côte d'Or red

Côte de Nuits

Heading south from Dijon along the N74, nearly all the vineyards – and certainly all the serious ones – lie on your right in a narrow band, rising from the road up an east-facing marl slope. Marsannay and Fixin are the first villages you come to, and although the wines can be attractive in a light, perfumed way, they only hint at the pleasures to come. The stretch of vineyards from Gevrey-Chambertin down to Nuits-St-Georges produces wines that can take your breath away with their exotic blend of fruit, spice, undergrowth and more. Too much Gevrey-Chambertin is instantly forgettable, but good versions, from village level up to the nine Chambertin *grands crus*, show that wine can be powerful yet perfumed. Chambolle-Musigny, Morey-St-Denis and Vosne-Romanée are less robust, but more perfumed, although the best *grands crus* such as Richebourg, Musigny and Clos de la Roche certainly lack nothing in intensity. Nuits-St-Georges has no *grands crus*, but several great *premiers crus*. The wines need more time than other Côte de Nuits reds to open out. Lesser but rather more affordable wines can be found in the appellations of Côte de Nuits Villages and Hautes-Côtes de Nuits.

Côte de Beaune

The reds of the Côte de Beaune are often said to be more feminine than their Nuits counterparts. There is something in their fruit texture which is silky and soft, although many balance this with startling intensity and no dearth of tannin. The hill-vineyard of Corton is the only *grand cru* in the Côte de Beaune, but there are a number of *premiers crus* sites, especially in Pommard and Volnay, which are currently producing better wines. Of the villages around Beaune, Savigny is light and perfumed, Aloxe-Corton potentially powerful and intense but rather unreliable, while Pernand-Vergelesses, Ladoix and Chorey-lès-Beaune all offer fairly simple but good-value wines. Beaune itself can vary from sublime to dreary, but the best have fruit in abundance allied with good structure.

The powerful Pommard is Gevrey-Chambertin to the more elegant Volnay's Chambolle-Musigny, and although neither is the most reliable appellation, the top wines of each rival the best in Burgundy. The underrated Monthelie and St-Aubin give rather cheaper glimpses of the Volnay style. Red Chassagne-Montrachet is rather rustic while the best Santenay is satisfyingly full and fruity. The Hautes-Côtes de Beaune needs a good vintage to ripen the fruit properly but the wines can be excellent value.

Pick of the producers (Red burgundy)

Marquis d'Angerville Elegant Volnay, especially from the monopole Clos des Ducs. Not widely available. (Marquis d'Angerville pioneered estate-bottling in Burgundy.)

Domaine de l'Arlot AXA-owned estate making delicious Nuits-St-Georges in a modern style (fruit-based, but never over-oaked). Look for the *premiers crus* Clos de l'Arlot and Clos des Forêts-St-Georges.

Comte Armand The sturdy, fruit-packed and ageworthy Pommard from the organically cultivated Clos des Epeneaux is one of the great reds of Burgundy. Undergoing changes. Let's hope the quality is maintained.

Robert Arnoux Robust Vosne-Romanée, Echézeaux and Nuits-St-Georges. Not cheap wines but long-ageing and getting better and better.

Simon Bize One of the best growers in Savigny-lès-Beaune: old vines, low yields and ripe, spicy, succulent wines.

Boisset Burgundy's largest company also owns Bouchard Aîné, Jaffelin, Edouard Delaunay, Ropiteau, F Chauvenet, Pierre Ponnelle and a number of other brands. Those from the company's own vineyards now appear as Domaine de la Vougeraie. Modern-style wines from excellent sites, improving with the recruitment of winemaker Pascal Marchand in 1999. Looking good for the future.

Chandon de Briailles Important, quality domaine for both Savigny-lès-Beaune and (white) Corton.

Bruno Clair Producer of serious Marsannay, but reaching higher quality with his wines from Gevrey, Morey-St-Denis and, further south, Savigny-lès-Beaune.

Joseph Drouhin Now Japanese-owned, but Drouhin still very much in control. This is a fine source of burgundy. Good, honest wines at all levels exemplified by robust, ageworthy Beaune Clos des Mouches.

Domaine Dujac The top estate of Morey-St-Denis, making elegant perfumed wines, best of which are the three Morey *grands crus* of Clos de la Roche, Clos St-Denis and Bonnes Mares. When it's good, it's very, very good.

René Engel Vosne-Romanée domaine making sturdy, flamboyant wines, built to last many years – showing vast improvements since the early 1980s when Philippe Engel took the helm. Good even in poor vintages.

Michel Esmonin et Fille Father and daughter team in Gevrey-Chambertin making silky, elegant wines with immense attention to detail. Classy since the early 1990s.

Faiveley Reliable source of good if slightly chunky reds, ranging from very fine Mercurey up to great Chambertin Clos de Bèze.

111

Geantet-Pansiot Hedonistic, very stylish Gevrey-Chambertin made with a modern approach, maturing early but with structure to last. Reliable wines.

Vincent Girardin Santenay-based Girardin sources fruit both from his own vineyards and from other growers throughout the Côte d'Or (50 in total) to make lovely silky reds. Variable in the mid-1990s but now back on form.

Jean Grivot Since 1993, Etienne Grivot has been making some of the best full-throttle, powerful wines in the Côte d'Or from vineyards in Vosne-Romanée and Nuits-St-Georges. The Richebourg is superb. Dedication shows in top wines from lesser vintages, for example 1998.

Anne Gros Vosne-Romanée domaine making revered reds of intensity and finesse. Top-class Richebourg, Vosne-Romanée, Chambolle-Musigny and Clos de Vougeot. Anne Gros' reputation grows every year.

Hospices de Beaune Major Côte de Beaune landowner that raises money by auctioning its wine each year on the third Sunday of November. Brand new winery, but the *élevage* – literally 'bringing up' – of the wines is then the responsibility of the *négociant* or domaine which bought it, so some wines can be great, while others are not.

Louis Jadot Well-respected *négociant*-turned-winemaker, with notably holistic approach and spanking-new winery. Jacques Lardière's reds need time to show their undoubted class. The range is topped by the Chambertin Clos de Bèze, but the wines from Beaune – particularly Grèves and Clos des Ursules – are also special.

Michel Lafarge Silky but powerful Volnay which exhibits considerable class when young yet ages well. Find them if you can; Lafarge courts no publicity but dominates by reputation.

Comtes Lafon Better known for whites, but Lafon's Volnays get better and better each year – California training shows in rich, distinctive wines.

Dominique Laurent Youngster, and former chef, Laurent produces boldly flavoured, powerful reds. The *grands crus*, often heavily oaked, are rare, pricy and built for the long run, but village wines from appellations such as Monthélie and Chambolle-Musigny are affordable and very tasty.

Domaine Leroy Biodynamic viticulture, miserably low yields and total devotion to quality make this one of the greatest Burgundy domaines at present. Critics say that Lalou Bize-Leroy's astonishingly concentrated wines are atypical for Burgundy. If you can find and afford them, and then have the patience to wait the 20 years which some of the wines need, judge for yourself. Taste them, we're told, and you'll forget the enormous price.

Méo-Camuzet Fine estate popular in the USA making ultra-modern, chunky wines with lots of fruit, no shortage of oak and great richness. The Vosne-Romanée Cros Parantoux is of *grand cru* quality, while the Clos Vougeot is one of the best around.

Alain Michelot Ageworthy, reliable Nuit-St-Georges from a small but expanding domaine.

de Montille Aristocratic Volnay producer who advocates minimal chaptalisation and whose wines lack the showiness which would make them attractive when young. However, they age superbly into classic red burgundies without too much alcohol (12 per cent maximum).

Bernard Morey Reliable grower of Chassagne-Montrachet and Santenay.

Denis Mortet Classy if occasionally over-oaked wines from Gevrey-Chambertin.

Jean-Marc Pavelot Top Savigny-lès-Beaune domaine with wines of fruit and complexity, elegance and depth.

Nicolas Potel Son of the late Gérard Potel who ran Domaine de la Pousse d'Or in Volnay, Nicolas has his own *négociant* business and is gathering a strong reputation for splendid wines from Volnay and other Côte d'Or villages.

Domaine de la Romanée-Conti Is it competition from former co-owner Mme Bize-Leroy at Domaine Leroy which is spurring this exceptional estate to greater heights? Quality from the six *grands crus* is as high as it has ever been, and almost justifies some of the phenomenal prices. La Tâche and Romanée-Conti itself remain for many people the pinnacle of red burgundy.

Domaine Georges Roumier et fils Georges' son, the technically brilliant Christophe, makes the wines today and marvellous, full

113

and rich they are too. Chambolle-Musigny makes up the most part but his Bonnes-Mares wines are concentrated and impressive. (Also succulent Corton whites.)

Armand Rousseau Consistency, prices which never seem excessive, and top-rack, long-ageing wines have made this Gevrey domaine with considerable holdings of *premier* and *grand cru* vineyards a favourite with many. Rousseau grandson now at the helm and maintaining classic Burgundian style.

Tollot-Beaut Reliable, fairly priced wines at all levels with plenty of fruit and no shortage of oak make this Chorey-lès-Beaune estate a dependable bet. Highly dedicated to organic health in the vineyards.

De Vogüé Renowned Chambolle-Musigny estate which owns over two-thirds of the Le Musigny *grand cru*, and whose best wine is the Vieilles Vignes *cuvée* therefrom. Consistency was not always the order of the day in the 1970s and 1980s, but winemaker François Millet has since then gained himself a reputation as a wine 'poet'. Next in line to Domaine de la Romanée-Conti. Pity there's so little about.

Côte Chalonnaise reds

The finest reds of the Côte Chalonnaise can surpass those of the Côte de Beaune, so we're surprised that more producers don't feel challenged to expend a little more effort and make some really impressive wine. Red Rully is rarely seen, but Givry and Mercurey in particular are capable of making solid Pinot which age transforms from a chunky adolescent into something richer and more satisfying. The best estate is that of Michel Juillot in Mercurey, a source of supple reds which can confidently be aged for up to ten years, and very drinkable whites too. This is a region in a state of flux. As a new generation of growers take time to settle in, it's difficult to say whether things are on track or not.

Beaujolais

Nouveau can be fun, but drinking it so young means that you miss most of the magic of this gem of a wine with the sprightly cherry and plum fruit at its best. Basic Beaujolais and the rather better Beaujolais-Villages should be drunk in the spring and summer following the vintage rather than on the third Thursday in November after harvest. A further step up is found in the ten *crus* villages in the north of the region. They are as follows: St-Amour – attractive when young, watch out for price rises around 14 February; Brouilly – perfumed, fruity and reasonable value; Chénas – rarely seen, underrated; Chiroubles – small quantities of often indifferent wine; Côte de Brouilly – firmer (and pricier) than

Brouilly; Fleurie – overpriced although can be full and charming;
Juliénas – solid yet supple and needing a year or two in bottle;
Morgon – quite firm but fruity, ideally needs two years in bottle;
Moulin-à-Vent – potentially very good, the sturdiest of the *crus*, and
not too expensive; Régnié – yet to convince us that it should have
been promoted to *cru* status.

As with mainstream burgundy, there is a new generation of
growers taking hold in Beaujolais, who are far more globally aware
than their fathers were. The latter may have turned a blind eye as New
World competitors – the cheerful, fruity and cheap wines of Chile for
example – took away their market share, but the new kids are taking
up the challenge. As they become far more scrupulous in their grape
selection and winemaking, better and better wines should result.

Since Beaujolais is not the trendiest of wines, you should be able to
find good stocks in the shops. *Cru* wines from the best growers are not
much cheaper than village burgundies, but the standard is high. The
big name is Georges Duboeuf, who makes a remarkably reliable range
topped by the very good Morgon Jean Descombes and Fleurie
Domaine des Quatre Vents. Other growers to look out for include
Domaine Berrod, Nicole Chanrion, Fernand Coudert, Marc Dudet,
Paul Janin, Jacky Janodet, André Large, Jean-Charles Pivot, Château
Thivin and Château des Tours. The best Beaujolais we've tried recently
is the range of full-bodied and ageworthy, single-vineyard wines from
Louis Jadot-owned Château des Jacques in Moulin-à-Vent.

Red vintage guide

The higher up the ladder of generic, village, *premier cru*, *grand cru*
you go, the longer the wines should last, although there's certainly
nothing to stop you enjoying them in their exuberant youth. Red
burgundy can be charmingly fruity at five years old and younger,
and leathery and feral at 15 years and over. In between, most retain
their appeal, although some seem to go into a rather moody phase
out of which, as long as they have the stuffing, they should
eventually emerge. Don't be afraid to open the odd bottle of even
the *grands crus* before their seventh birthday. If they are delicious,
whether you drink them now or keep them is purely up to you.
However, if they are rather disappointing and don't open out in the
glass over the course of an evening, compare your experience with
that of the merchant from whom you bought the wine. It may be
that more time in bottle is all that is called for.

2000 It started cool but early buds survived July cold and hail for
what turned out to be the hottest vintage for ten years. Storms on
12 September quickly cleared and most growers avoided spoilage.
A good, if not abundant, harvest was made in cooler weather. Reds
not looking as fine as the 1999s but good nonetheless.

1999 Spectacular, close to perfection on the Côte de Beaune. A welcome combination of quality and quantity. Spring weather was irregular, but a hot summer brought a large crop of healthy fruit to full ripeness. Rain towards the end of the harvest may have affected some Côte de Nuits growers, but most are billing this as their 'vintage of the millennium'.

1998 A vintage to sort the men from the boys. It rained for much of the first fortnight of September, and was then dry for a ten-day spell. Those who managed to pick during the dry period and took pains to exclude rotten fruit have produced some good to excellent wines with forward, fleshy flavours.

1997 As in Bordeaux, this is a nice, forward, friendly, low-acid vintage producing wines to be drunk while waiting for the 1996s and 1995s to mature. Cool spring weather resulted in a small crop, and the hot summer ripened the grapes well. Rain in late August and early September may have diluted the wines, but the grapes were brought in ripe and rot-free.

1996 Even flowering promised a good vintage, and although August was rainy, strong winds in September dried the grapes out, preventing rot and dilution. Grapes were harvested in excellent condition, and the wines promise to be full bodied and long lasting.

1995 The uneven flowering due to spring frosts was something of a mixed blessing. The crop size was reduced, but it also meant that the grapes developed thick skins which were able to withstand the rain which fell in September after a fine July and August. The wines have turned out to be ripe and fruity and close to 1993 in quality.

1994 Ever so nearly a good vintage spoiled by rain just before harvest. Wines are on the light side, but they are not unripe.

1993 Not quite up to 1990 quality, but for those who favour robust wines which take several years to approach maturity, this is a good vintage. In some lesser wines, where the fruit isn't quite up to that chunky structure, there's not a great deal of joy to be had.

1992 Decentish vintage, but with no real weight. Now tiring.

1991 Hail spoiled the party, but amid a sea of mediocrity there are some incredibly concentrated wines around from those scrupulous producers who were prepared to harvest only top-quality fruit.

1990 Wonderful year, with the abundant ripe fruit of 1989 matched with the structure of 1988. The only problem is when to drink them, since that ripe fruit makes even the top *grands crus* deliciously approachable now. However, bargains are hard to find.

Good earlier vintages 1989, 1988, 1985, 1978, 1976, 1971, 1969

White wines

Yes, there is some Pinot Blanc, and some Pinot Gris (Beurot as it is known here), as well as some of that Burgundian oddity Aligoté which needs a ripe year to shed its veil of acidity. And there's some remarkably good Sauvignon being made in St-Bris near Chablis. But white burgundy is all about Chardonnay. Despite the profusion of Chardonnay from virtually every country where wine is made, nowhere has come close to approaching Burgundy for the sheer number of great wines. There may not be large amounts of them, two barrels of one grower's Le Montrachet, three of another's Meursault-Genevrières, and you'll pay through the nose for them, but that's a different matter.

The style of Burgundian Chardonnay varies as you travel throughout the region from Chablis to the Mâconnais, but what underlies all the best wines is the feeling that you are tasting something seamless, rather than a concoction of fruit, oak and winemaking techniques. Where do the flavours of nuts and honey come from? How can it be so rich and buttery yet be totally dry? Why does it taste so delicious when young yet still manage to age gracefully for several years?

Of course, such comments only apply to the very top wines. There is still plenty of Burgundian Chardonnay which does no favours either to the grape or to the region. But because it's now possible to pick up decent Chardonnay from other parts of the globe, the UK's wine merchants don't feel compelled to stock boring, underflavoured Mâcon. Encouragingly, the Burgundians themselves are now looking at the competition and adapting their techniques accordingly, picking riper fruit and cleaning up their winemaking. Where yields are high, some of the wines could easily pass for New World versions, but where yields are low, the results are best described as excellent modern burgundy.

Chablis

While many agree that Chablis is the perfect accompaniment to shellfish, no one is precisely sure how it should taste. A number of practices, including reduction in the levels of sulphur dioxide, more widespread use of malolactic fermentation and the use of oak barrels for fermenting and ageing wines, are producing wines which have little in common with the classic image of a steely, flinty, green-gold wine which needs years to reach its peak. Fruit, a warm appley fruit sometimes with hints of rhubarb, has come to the fore, and the wines can be charming at a very tender age. Purists are outraged by these new wines, saying that they are indistinguishable from other white burgundies, while the modernists say that the characters of the wines of the past were more to do with poor winemaking.

There is also heated debate on the matter of soil. The seven *grands crus* – Blanchots, Bougros, Les Clos, Grenouilles, Preuses, Valmur, Vaudésir – live up to their name, as do the majority of the *premiers crus*. However, it is the incorporation of new areas of land into the basic appellation of Chablis, and the development of *premiers crus* where once there was woodland, which has provoked the biggest arguments. The traditionalists maintain that proper Chablis needs to be grown on Kimmeridgian soil. The opposition argue that the wines made on other soils are every bit as good, and since the yields in both cases are usually too high for the effect of *terroir* to be felt, they are probably right. This one could run and run …

Pick of the producers (white burgundy)
La Chablisienne Large but good co-operative producing a third of all Chablis. Quality, reliability and value are often higher than the majority of the growers.

René & Vincent Dauvissat/Dauvissat-Camus A combination of good sites and good winemaking makes this one of the top Chablis producers. The wines from the *grands crus* Les Clos and Les Preuses are as sublime as Chablis gets.

William Fèvre/Domaine de la Maladière/Ancien Domaine Auffray Fèvre's style was to use oak for fermenting and ageing his wines, and it will be interesting to see whether that changes under new proprietor Joseph Henriot, who also owns Bouchard Père & Fils. Great vineyard holdings, including 15 per cent of the *grands crus*, which still belong to Fèvre but are being leased to Henriot.

Jean-Hughes Goisot Not Chablis actually, but wines from the neighbouring Auxerrois. If you want to see the other grapes Burgundy has up its sleeve, this is an excellent place to come. Sauvignon de St-Bris, Aligoté and Bourgogne Pinot Noir from the top of the alternative tree in St-Bris-le-Vineux.

Louis Michel Classy, classic unoaked Chablis which, given the chance, ages for 20 years or more, yet still retains its minerally core.

Jean-Marie Raveneau Whether with or without oak, top-class wines which need a minimum of five years age to begin to show their true class. Given that these are among the best wines in the region, prices are very reasonable.

Also look out for: **Jean-Marc Brocard**, **Jean-Paul Droin**, **Jean Durup**, **Domaines des Malandes** and **Laurent Tribut**.

Côte d'Or white
A few whites are produced in the Côte de Nuits, such as de Vogüé's famous Musigny Blanc and the Nuits-St-Georges from Domaine de

l'Arlot. However, the vast majority of the great white burgundies are made in the Côte de Beaune between Aloxe-Corton and Santenay. The best value can often be found with basic Bourgogne Blanc from top producers, but the villages of Pernand-Vergelesses, Santenay, St-Aubin and Auxey-Duresses are somewhat underrated. St-Romain is less reliable, Beaune can be good though pricy, while the majority of Aloxe-Corton is sold as the *grand cru* Corton-Charlemagne, which ages to sumptuous, buttery perfection, providing the grower isn't too greedy with his yields.

However, the villages of Meursault, Puligny-Montrachet and Chassagne-Montrachet produce the majority of the truly glorious white burgundies. The *grands crus* of Le Montrachet and Bâtard-Montrachet, both shared between Puligny and Chassagne, can be awesome. But wines from other *grands crus* and the top *premiers crus* such as Meursault-Perrières, Puligny Les Referts and Chassagne Morgeot can also be exceptional. Some would say that Puligny is the refined one, Meursault the rich fat one while Chassagne sits halfway between. However, don't let such generalisations cloud your appreciation of these wines. We would say, though, that considering the prices, make sure you know your grower before splashing out on large quantities.

Pick of the producers

Guy Amiot-Bonfils Guy Amiot's father leased out a lot of his Chassagne-Montrachet vineyards but now these agreements are coming to an end, son Guy (and his son Thierry) have increasing control over their own destiny – and wines. Reliable quality.

Jean-Marc Boillot Excellent holdings in Puligny and Chassagne, including a small parcel of Bâtard-Montrachet, passed to M Boillot when he married into the Sauzet family, and these have now been joined by other red and white vineyards in the Côte de Beaune. Top quality across the board, but expensive.

Bonneau du Martray Major landowners in the Corton-Charlemagne vineyard and making first-class, long-lived wine. Watch for still-available older vintages. This estate is burgeoning under the watchful eye of Jean-Charles le Bault de la Morinière.

Louis Carillon Not the most fashionable Puligny producer but it's hard to explain why; it's one of the better ones. Subtle, often sublime wines from village level up to *grand cru*.

Jean-François Coche-Dury Bourgogne Blanc that tastes like good Meursault, village Meursault that rivals the top *premiers crus*, and Meursault-Perrières and Corton-Charlemagne which are sensational.

Given that demand is so high, the prices asked for what is close to perfect white burgundy are very reasonable – if you can find any.

Didier Darviot-Perrin Delicious, reliable Chassagne-Montrachet and Meursault from old vines.

Michel Colin-Deléger Not cheap, difficult to find, but very fine, elegant wines including Puligny-Montrachet *premier cru* Les Caillerets and Chassagne-Montrachet Les Vergers.

Joseph Drouhin Famous company with extensive estate throughout the Côte d'Or and Chablis with marginally better whites than reds. Lesser appellations such as Rully are very good, but the highlight is the glorious Montrachet from the Marquis de Laguiche estate.

Jean-Noël Gagnard Increasingly fashionable producer of Chassagne, and rightly so given the superb quality.

Louis Jadot Fine pure whites at all levels from Bourgogne Blanc up to *grand cru* level. It's a toss-up whether the Corton-Charlemagne or the Chevalier-Montrachet Les Demoiselles is the top wine. Both live for years.

François Jobard Meursault which can lack showiness and opulence in its youth, but which at ten years' old is magnificent, particularly the *premiers crus* of Genevrières, Charmes and Poruzot. The wines live forever.

Comtes Lafon Dominique Lafon is deservedly famous for his rich, oaky and quite splendid Meursaults. Tiny amounts of Le Montrachet are produced as well. California-comes-to-Burgundy, modern-style, big Chardonnay.

Hubert Lamy-Monnot St-Aubin domaine at which son Olivier Lamy – now responsible for winemaking – currently leads a quality upgrade. Mid-way between traditional and modern, top-quality Criots-Bâtard- and Chassagne-Montrachet.

Louis Latour Best known for his Corton-Charlemagne, quality is moderate elsewhere.

Domaine Leflaive Biodynamic viticulture and the winemaking talents of Pierre Morey have re-established the reputation of this famous Puligny estate. Although Olivier Leflaive is co-owner, the wines bearing his name are from a separate *négociant* business.

Paul Pernot Expanding Puligny domaine, with good wines despite young vines. Mostly sold through *négociants* but own-label Bâtard-Montrachet is excellent.

Ramonet Wonderful if occasionally erratic Chassagne grower, perhaps best known for the Montrachet, but also offering complex, long-lived Bâtard and Bienvenues-Bâtard as well as stunning *premiers crus*.

Domaine Roulot Underrated and very reliable producer of rich, tasty gorgeous Meursault. Hard to find.

Etienne Sauzet Well-known Puligny producer, now smaller in size than in previous years but making up quantities by buying-in grapes. Under the winemaker Gérard Boudot, quality is as good as ever.

Verget Mâcon-based Belgian Jean-Marie Guffens makes some of the best and purest wines in Burgundy. He excels with Chablis and the *grands crus* of the Côte d'Or, but even his Bourgogne Blanc and Mâcon-Villages are stars.

Côte Chalonnaise whites
There haven't been massive improvements in the Côte Chalonnaise recently. Progress, in fact, has almost been backwards. But we say give it time. A lot of the very good older growers have retired and it's too early yet to say if the new generation are 'chips off' or maybe have a more modern approach. The village of Bouzeron produces Burgundy's best Aligoté, some of which in a ripe year is even too good to be mixed with Cassis to make Kir. The version from de Villaine is the best. As well as the reliable but not very widely seen Bourgogne Côte Chalonnaise, a number of villages produce white wine under their own name. Givry and Mercurey are better known for reds but can produce buttery, spicy whites, Montagny – in the vast majority of cases with the words Premier Cru – can be good if rather lean, while the rounded fruity Rully offers the best value.

Mâconnais
The Mâconnais has rows upon rows of mature Chardonnay vines with which someone should be able to make decent, concentrated whites costing under £10 a bottle. A few producers are currently making such wines, but with co-operatives and merchants who see the region as just a source of cheap white burgundy, progress is still slower than we would wish. The new appellation of Viré-Clessé (from 1999), which covers wines formerly labelled Mâcon Viré and Mâcon Clessé (from the region's top two villages), has a maximum level of residual sugar of 4 grams per litre, and some of the top

domaines, most notably Thévenet and Guillemot-Michel, routinely make wines which exceed this. Thévenet's 1998s fall under this level, but quite what he'll call his wines in a riper vintage is still not clear.

Most Mâcon Blanc is made to a price, an inoffensive, underflavoured and unmemorable wine. Anyone looking for character and flavour should try a step up to Mâcon-Villages or one of the more specific village appellations such as Mâcon-Pierreclos. Pouilly-Loché and Pouilly-Vinzelles are one rung up from Mâcon, while Pouilly-Fuissé is better still, a rich, creamy wine which can be excellent and not as overpriced as was once the case. Perhaps the best-value wine is St-Véran – Pouilly quality at a Mâcon price.

The Burgundian rule of producer first, appellation second applies more if anything in the Mâconnais than anywhere else. The best wines are in fact coming from mainstream Burgundy growers, such as Lafon from Meursault, who are beginning to invest in the region and show how things can, and should, be done.

Pick of the producers (white burgundy)
Domaine Vincent/Château de Fuissé The St-Véran is good but the Pouilly-Fuissé, particularly the Vieilles Vignes *cuvée*, is the star, and probably the best-known wine of the Mâconnais.

Guffens-Heynen Belgian duo Jean-Marie Guffens and his wife Germaine Heynen produce Pouilly-Fuissé and Mâcon-Pierreclos of astonishing concentration and complexity.

Guillemot-Michel An excellent Mâcon-Clessé Quintaine is joined in suitable years by a *botrytised* wine, Sélection de Grains Cendrés.

Jean Thévenet/Domaine de la Bon Gran Old vines, low yields and ultra-ripe fruit make for concentrated and long-lived Viré-Clessé, and others. Noble rot often plays a part, and sometimes a separate Cuvée Botrytis is made.

Also recommended: *André Bonhomme*, *Cordier*, *Domaine Talmard*. New venture, *Les Héritiers de Comte Lafon* – a recent purchase by the top Meursault estate – is one to watch.

White vintage guide
Much better selection of grapes in recent years has led to a series of excellent vintages. No bad thing when you consider, rather perversely perhaps, that white burgundy can be a more suitable candidate for extended cellaring than red. There are some bottles of white burgundy which will set you back considerably more than £100, yet which at anything under five years of age just seem large

and oaky. Even at village level, most wines benefit from being drunk at least four years after vintage. And of all white wines, burgundy is the one which needs the longest time to breathe. We're not in the 'open-the-night-before' league, but do let it have some time to develop, so you can fully enjoy the whole bottle rather than just the last glass.

2000 Where 1999 looked to be the vintage of the millennium for reds, 2000 may well do the same for white burgundy. A cool start to the season followed by a hot summer, and a protracted, cool harvest, led to concentrated aromatics, good ripeness, gentle acidity and very fine wines indeed.

1999 Not as good for whites as reds, but there'll be plenty of ripe, low acid wine which should drink well at an early age. While the large harvest may mean that some wines are dilute, growers who thinned their crop in summer will have made some rich, concentrated wines.

1998 Rain fell in the first half of September, but the hot August weather meant that the grapes harvested were generally ripe with low acidity, if sometimes affected by rot. Hail earlier in the year meant that the yields in several top Côte de Beaune vineyards were dramatically reduced, and the extra concentration shows in many wines.

1997 As with the reds, the 1997 whites are ripe, fruity wines with low acidity, making them extremely attractive even at this early stage. In some cases, alcohol levels seem high compared with the depth of flavour, but generally this is as friendly as burgundy gets, and is an ideal vintage for novices to the region.

1996 A fine vintage, with a large and healthy crop of full ripe grapes. High acidity bodes well for longevity, while the wines should be more perfumed than the 1995s.

1995 A better vintage for whites than reds, although you'll have to wait for the wines to show their best. Quantities were small, so don't expect many bargains.

1994 A year when rain diluted the flavours of ripe fruit. There's a healthy supply of decent wines at the lower end of the scale, which should be drunk sooner rather than later, and even the higher-priced wines have been remarkably forward.

1993 A more restrained vintage after the opulence of 1992. Watch out for high acidity. The top wines will benefit from it and could in many cases eclipse the 1992s with bottle age. However, wines with insufficient fruit to stand up to the acidity are not uncommon.

1992 The only problem with this ripe and concentrated vintage is whether the wines have the acidity to hold them together. They've tasted wonderful from the start, but a few are now beginning to show their age. If you have large stocks and haven't tasted them recently, pull a few corks to check on their progress.

1991 Rain at vintage resulted in rot, and while, as ever, the best producers made some decent wine, there are few real stars.
1990 Not quite in the same league as the reds of the same vintage, nor of the whites of the previous one, but still a generally impressive performance. Lowish acidity means that they've been attractive from the word go, but the best still have lots of life ahead of them.
1989 Plenty of heat throughout the summer, and especially at vintage time, resulted in some wines which are excessively alcoholic, low in acidity and which are really showing their age. However, the best wines are classics, impressive and weighty and will provide excellent drinking for the next ten years.
1988 Wines of structure rather than opulence which are still going strong. The fruit flavours are generally good, although there are occasional hints of underripeness.

Good older vintages 1986, 1985, 1983, 1982, 1979, 1978, 1976

Crémant de Bourgogne

With such widespread plantings of Pinot Noir and Chardonnay, it is no surprise that Burgundy also produces sparkling wine – but it ought to be significantly better than it is. Although the Burgundians have recently proposed a new appellation designating vineyards specifically for sparkling wine production – and therefore, one would assume, establishment of the special clones, appropriate sites, plus the pruning and training techniques needed to produce fine fizz – it so far appears they've only done it to guarantee supply, and not quality. Let's hope we're wrong. The wines are made the traditional way, mainly based on Chardonnay, and prices are attractive. Very few of the growers' wines ever appear in Britain, but the co-operatives of Bailly, Viré and Lugny produce goodish versions.

CHAMPAGNE

Champagne is so wrapped up in marketing opportunities, it frequently can't see its own success. In early 2001 waves of gloom crossed the Channel as it finally hit home that the millennium party was over. That perfect licence to sell champagne was now at an end and it was long faces all round. Why? – with overall sales of 327 million bottles!

Among the reasons to be cheerless were two obvious ones. It had become apparent throughout 2000 that the 'real' millennium night, 31 December 2000, wasn't going to generate quite the sales the 1999 event inspired. Also, the 2000 harvest was bedevilled with rain, cold, and a lack of sunshine. That wonderful opportunity to put

'2000' on the label just wasn't going to materialise without compromising vintage quality.

As you can tell, we think the Champenois are being just a little greedy. So what if sales figures have sunk back to their 1996 point – surely this is an accurate reflection of the three years of hype that built up to the biggest-ever New Year's Eve party. Besides which, how many times did we hear their complaining that there wouldn't be enough to go round, that stocks wouldn't last?

The fact is, while all this was going on, Champagne was actually experiencing a series of rather good vintages – albeit they culminated in the not-so-wonderful 2000. 1995 has been billed as 'as good as the 1990' though it'll be different in style; 1996 likewise is praised for its excellent Chardonnay contribution; 1997 didn't run so smoothly but turned out not too badly in the end; 1998's warm summer and autumn made for fine wines; and 1999 was abundant and good enough to ensure post-millennium replenishment of reserve stocks. Champagne vintages can be divided into 'greats' (1982, 1990, 1996), 'usefuls' (1992, 1997) and 'good ones to age' (1989). In basic terms, every harvest released since those the millennium drew from (1995 onwards) has been at the very least 'useful', which would imply the world isn't yet about to come crashing to an end in Epernay.

So now the millennium party is well and truly over, we think it's probably time to restock the cellar with champagne, and a good time to remind ourselves what to open, and when. Vintage champagnes, for a start, change with time in bottle. They are the expression of one particular year, and therefore are bound to vary according to date. 1989, for example, was rudely dismissed at the time of release, but which, if you ever spotted a bottle now, we'd recommend pouncing right away. It was and still is great; others can go the same way. You never really know how a vintage wine will turn out, so you need to keep a careful eye on the wine press – or ask your wine merchant – to find out how it's doing. Make the mistake of drinking it too soon, and you've missed out on a biscuity, multi-layered treat (and it can't be stressed enough how delicious and complex vintage champagne can be!); but drink it too late… If you like aged champagne, start drinking the 1989s, but go easy on the 1990s and 1992s, they've got further to go in bottle.

Non-vintage champagnes are less the individualists. They're blended as expressions of the house in question, and tend to have a similar style from bottle to bottle. They draw on reserve wines held back from different years (vintage and non-vintage) as well as more recent harvests, and are skilfully blended to reflect what that particular winemaker deems to be sparkling perfection. We all have our favourites.

One step further down the path of fizz knowledge is getting to know single vineyard wines, the expression of one particular plot of land. Ironically, these don't necessarily come from smaller producers – some of the co-ops are waking up to the interesting possibilities of *mono-crus*. If you want to understand how the components of a great champagne blend together, these wines show just how that happens. Drappier's Grande Sendrée is one example – from an Aube vineyard with 70-year-old vines (it was once woodland, but burnt down in 1838; the ash, though, still gives a distinctive character to the wines). Salon is the most famous, and expensive, *mono-cru*, but we highly recommend looking out for others, as this is likely to be a growing trend.

Now for the facts.

Grape varieties

Most champagnes are a judicious blend of three varieties, Pinot Noir, Chardonnay and Pinot Meunier. Of these, the best Pinot Noir comes from the Montagne de Reims and is acknowledged to be the grape which provides body and structure to the wine. The most sought-after Chardonnay flourishes on the Côte des Blancs and gives a light, floral elegance, but has a firmness that softens and adds complexity with age. Pinot Meunier is often referred to as the workhorse grape, being normally left out of the better blends and vintage champagnes, while providing balance and fragrance in the standard wines.

How champagne is made

The traditional method of making champagne is by secondary bottle fermentation. The term '*méthode traditionnelle*' now legally denotes this practice and can be found on bottles of sparkling wine from all over the world. The word 'champagne', however, can only apply to sparkling wines from the region itself and this right is fiercely protected by the Champenois.

Ironically, if the still wines of Champagne had not been made into sparkling wine, this famous region would have remained a quiet backwater producing small quantities of mediocre red wine and some very thin and acidic whites. As it is, producers realised hundreds of years ago that very gentle pressing of black grapes gave a light juice, which could be fermented to dryness and then bottled with a little yeast and sugar to allow it to re-ferment. The sparkle is created by trapping the fermentation gas within the bottles; these are thick enough to withstand up to six atmospheres of pressure. All this takes months, if not years to achieve, and at any one time there are millions of bottles lying in serried ranks below the streets of Rheims and Epernay and throughout the region. A quiet evolution of epic proportions.

In time, the yeast sediment – via a painstaking series of gentle twists (traditionally done by hand, but now, more often than not, by machine) – drops to the neck of the bottle, and is then frozen and removed. A final addition of sweetened wine adjusts the style of the finished wine, and the bottle is re-sealed with the distinctive mushroom cork and wire cage, to settle down again. When ready for sale, the bottle is dressed with its unique foil and label.

Styles

Blanc de blancs Champagne made entirely from Chardonnay grapes. Typically fresh, elegant and creamy.

Blanc de noirs White champagne made from the red grapes Pinot Meunier and Pinot Noir. Usually a reliably firm and fruity wine.

Brut The term for dry champagne with less than 15 grams per litre of residual sugar. The vast majority of champagne sold in the UK is Brut.

Demi-sec Confusingly, this means sweet.

Extra-dry Again, potentially confusing – dry, but not as dry as Brut.

Non-vintage The producer's standard blend. Non-vintage can be as young as one year old, though quality-conscious houses aim for a minimum of three years. Cheap, basic-quality non-vintage does not improve with keeping; the best examples may.

Prestige cuvée/de luxe cuvée The champagne at the top of each house range – the most expensive, and supposedly the highest quality. Many have glitzy or unusual packaging, such as Roederer's Cristal in its clear glass bottle, or Perrier-Jouët's Belle Epoque with its enamelled flowers. Moët's Dom Pérignon is the most famous *prestige cuvée*. Generally speaking, these wines have a more

127

powerful and complex character than most champagnes, and benefit from some age. They are not always made in such tiny amounts as their producers would have us believe.

Rosé Pink champagne, usually made by adding small amounts of red Pinot Noir wine from the Bouzy or Aÿ areas to the blend.

Vintage A champagne from just one good-quality year. The best are more complex and have a fuller flavour than non-vintage.

Pick of the producers (Champagne)

Billecart-Salmon Small, family-owned house noted for the elegance of its champagne. Non-vintage has a floral note; vintage Cuvée Nicolas François Billecart is also floral-scented yet powerful; rosé is particularly refined.

Bollinger One of the best-known houses, 'Bolly' is typically rich and powerful, and ages well. Grande Année vintage wine, made with two-thirds Pinot Noir, is top-quality champagne in an upfront and ripe style. Back on track after disgorgement difficulties mid-2000.

Canard-Duchêne Very popular in France, less well known in the UK. We don't rate the non-vintage highly, but vintage wines and Blanc de Noirs impress more and offer good value for money.

de Cazenove Wines gaining in finesse for a number of years now. Brut Azur and Stradivarius are top labels based mostly on Chardonnay.

Deutz Roederer-owned house producing reliable, well-balanced wines. Massive improvements, year after year.

Drappier Small, independent house from the south of the Champagne region, with a good following for its attractive, fleshy wines and interesting *mono-cru*.

Duval-Leroy Family-owned company with some of the best vineyards in the region. Consistent, likeable wines (most of Sainsbury's decent own-label champagne is from this house). Its Fleur de Champagne vintage champagnes regularly win awards.

Gardet Not terribly well known, but for our money one of the top champagne houses. Meticulously made, high-quality wines, especially the lemony, creamy vintage.

Pierre Gimonnet A rare exclusively Chardonnay domaine run by a family of grower-turned *vignerons* fanatical about champagnes that express their origins.

Gosset Small, often overlooked house with first-class range, especially long-lived, rich Grand Millésime.

Henri Goutorbe Excellent, rich champagne from a single, small grower. Good older vintages.

Alfred Gratien Family-owned firm using barrels for long ageing. Quality impresses, especially in vintage wine.

Charles Heidsieck Hugely improved, rich and aromatic range expertly put together by one of Champagne's most talented winemakers, Daniel Thibault. Thibault's *mis-en-cave* wines (non-vintage, but with ageing potential) are terrific value for money, and the chocolaty and rich 1990 vintage was one of the best from that year.

Henriot Elegant range, including especially well-balanced, creamy non-vintage. Older wines are often readily available from this house.

Jacquart Reliable, good-value brand from a major co-operative in Rheims, now being seen more widely in the UK.

Jacquesson Very underrated house with a consistently fine, fresh-tasting range, including elegant, aromatic Brut Perfection non-vintage and ripe, refined *prestige cuvée* Signature (less delicate than Billecart-Salmon, more so than Mumm).

Krug The most exalted champagne house of them all – and with good reason. Impeccable care is taken over fermentation in wood, blending and ageing. The result is great complexity and broadness of flavour. Grande Cuvée is always impressive and powerful enough to stem our desire for the terrifyingly expensive single-vineyard Blanc de Blancs Clos de Mesnil. Even the elegant, narrow-stemmed bottles mark out this *marque* (now owned by LVMH).

Lanson The well-known Black Label is as reliable as ever – though critics still mention the 1991 change of ownership and a drop in quality. We haven't noticed one. We also like vintage wines that age well, and Lanson's certainly do.

Laurent-Perrier We like these fresh and satisfying wines, although the non-vintage may not be as consistently good as it once was. Ultra Brut is a tight-knit, extra-dry style, and rich Grande Siècle comes from a blend of three years' wine.

Moët & Chandon By far the largest house, underrated for the incredible amount it achieves. Vintage wines are excellent and there's an impressive amount of character injected into its huge-selling Brut Impériale. *Prestige cuvée* Dom Pérignon combines power and fragrance, and is magnificent after ten years-plus.

Mumm A well-known house still undeservedly maligned for a recent disappointing phase but has improved tremendously of late – Cordon Rouge NV tastes a little more complex at last, while vintage Cordon Rouge positively sings with character and flavour. Do try the more sophisticated wines further up the range, such as Cuvée René Lalou or Grand Cordon. Purchased in June 1999 from Seagram by a Texan consortium and again in 2001 by Allied Domecq.

Bruno Paillard Rising star, still rising, and creating consistently fine, typically dry but creamy wines in a high-tech winery. (Has agreeable wines from Provence too.)

Joseph Perrier One of the most traditional smaller houses maintaining exceptionally high standards, particularly with rich, honeyed non-vintage wine.

Perrier-Jouët Produces disappointing non-vintage wine but fine and fruity Belle Epoque *prestige cuvée* in flower-strewn enamelled bottles. Purchased from Seagram in June 1999 by a Texan consortium, and again in 2001 by Allied Domecq.

Piper-Heidsieck Large house, not looking so impressive of late.

Pol Roger Much-loved family-run house with a refined range, including classy, dry White Foil non-vintage, complex, citrusy Blanc de Blancs and long-lived *de luxe cuvée* Sir Winston Churchill. Vintage wines are never released too early.

Pommery Crisp, elegant non-vintage is good value; *prestige cuvée* Louise Brut 1987 is rich and deep.

Louis Roederer Consistently high performer with a fashionable image. Well-judged, classy non-vintage (recent tastings suggest it is better than ever); luxurious *prestige cuvée* Cristal in clear glass bottle.

Ruinart Ancient house (now owned by Moët) with well-crafted range that includes the deeply creamy Blanc de Blancs Dom Ruinart.

Salon Small company based in the Chardonnay-producing village of Mesnil-sur-Oger producing tight-knit, fine Blanc de Blancs.

Taittinger Fashionable, Chardonnay-rich wines. The non-vintage has shaped up well of late, but Taittinger is rightly lauded for its Blanc de Blancs Comtes de Champagne.

Veuve Clicquot One of the greatest houses producing classic wines of grace and breeding, their style recently much more youthful. Satisfying, relatively complex non-vintage, long-lived vintages and powerful *prestige cuvée* La Grande Dame.

Champagne vintage guide

If you're lucky enough to find vestiges of the excellent 1989 and 1990 around, we recommend you snap them up immediately! Otherwise, most of the main houses are selling the 1993. A fair smattering of 1995s and a few 1996s are on general release, while you might still find the occasional 1992 from lesser-known names, particularly those with a high proportion of Chardonnay in the blend.

2000 A large harvest, not helped by July rains, nor saved by brief sunshine in August. Not a good year and, despite the temptation to put '2000' on the label, there will (and should) be few declarations.

1999 With stocks under pressure after the demand for millennium champagne, the abundant 1999 crop was very timely. Overall quality is good, despite early localised hailstorms and the odd late summer downpour. Most houses will declare a vintage.

1998 A cold and humid start to the summer was followed by extreme heat in August and heavy rain at the beginning of September. Good weather during the harvest saved the day for many growers, resulting ultimately in a fine vintage. Expect universal declaration of vintage wines.

1997 Changeable and problematic weather conditions during the year, although a sunny September and perfect conditions during harvest saved this from becoming a terrible vintage. The wines are variable and can lack elegance, but many houses will produce vintage wines.

1996 Generally considered to be an excellent vintage, especially for Chardonnay. Many outstanding and powerful vintage wines will be (and are being) released, on a par with the 1990.

1995 A classic vintage, and good for Chardonnay, although Pinot Noir was somewhat affected by rain. Will be universally declared; many are on the market already.

1994 Again, after a warm, sunny summer, this potentially great harvest was spoilt by light rain and rot a few days before picking in September. Euphemistically, a 'difficult' vintage with very few vintage wines made – among them, Roederer Cristal and Lanson.

1993 The quality of the grapes was extremely promising on the eve of the harvest, but a short but intense rainfall at the beginning of the picking led to a tricky harvest. Pinot Noir did best. Most houses released vintages.

1992 Very large crop with, yet again, rain causing some rot. The quality was reasonably good, especially for Chardonnay, however, and many producers have released promising vintage champagnes.

1991 Large quantities despite spring frosts. Pinot Noir fared particularly well, and those houses for whom this grape dominates (for example Veuve Clicquot) declared a vintage.

1990 Like the previous year, a classic year for champagne, marked by very warm conditions not seen since 1950. A very high-quality, ripe harvest led to brilliant and powerful wines – some believe the best for decades.

1989 Exceptional quality producing excellent, notably rich vintage wines. Will be remembered as one of the greatest of recent vintages, eclipsed only by 1990.

1988 A year characterised by a changeable climate, but which nonetheless produced high-quality wines – the first of a trio of exceptionally fine vintages in the Champagne region.

Other good vintages The superb 1985 wines provide a relatively mature and rich style; 1982 and 1976 are also outstanding older vintages.

CORSICA

The news this year isn't so very different from last, or the year before that. Despite its 2,500 years of winemaking history, favourable climate and a renewed interest in Mediterranean viticulture, there is still very little Corsican wine making waves in the UK. But there are deep-seated changes taking place that could bode well for the future. As we reported in the last edition of the *Guide*, since the mid-1980s the islanders have recognised that their future lies in using their own distinctive local grape varieties rather than foreign interlopers, and significant replanting has taken place. Southern French bulk-producers such as Carignan, Cinsaut and Ugnic Blanc are being replaced by spicy Sciacarello and robust, tannic Nielluccio for the reds, smoky, minerally Vermentino for the whites. The international varieties (Cabernet and Chardonnay, say) are no longer welcomed, with the only possible exception of Syrah – though purists seriously believe this variety should be delisted too. Twenty-two other local grapes are currently undergoing rigorous testing as to potential quality. Most are still waiting in the wings, though one, Bianco Gentile, looks set to make its debut soon. Exciting times!

Quantities of the new oldsters are tiny. The bulk of Corsica's wine is, as yet, *vin de pays*, and yes, a lot of generic rosé is around. But skirting the coast of the island there are nine appellations in which decent winemaking equipment, lower yields, use of oak, concerted effort and new grapes are beginning to improve quality. Patrimonio, Ajaccio and Vin de Corse are the most commonly seen, plus a *vin doux naturel*, Muscat du Cap Corse, granted AC status in 1993. In the north, Patrimonio's top growers are Domaines Antoine Arena (for delicious complex Vermentino), Gentile and Orenga de Gaffory; good growers from the south are Fiumicicoli in Sartène and Domaine de Torraccia in Porto-Vecchio. Christian Imbert of the latter is president of Uva Corse, a group clubbing together to improve production processes and promote exports. We haven't seen the wines yet, but as 90 per cent of the island's sales are reportedly to passing tourists, and the Corsican hospitality industry is currently going through bleak times … call us callous, but why can't they send the difference to the UK instead? Surely it shouldn't all go to France?

JURA, SAVOIE AND BUGEY

Given the stunning scenery of this part of France, it'll be little hardship to learn that if you want to taste these wines, the best way is to visit the region itself. We've spotted a few of them on merchants' lists, but mostly they're not made in sufficient quantity, and the trade perceives them 'too unusual' for import to UK shores. A shame. Some people call them 'strange', but we think they are intriguing.

Jura

Lying at similar latitudes to Burgundy, it comes as little surprise to find Chardonnay and Pinot Noir in the 80-km stretch of Jura's vineyards. The area has four main appellations. Arbois makes light reds from Pinot plus the local varieties, delicate Poulsard and robust Trousseau. Côtes du Jura covers the entire region and can be red, pink or white. More interesting are the *vins jaunes* – yellow wines – of l'Etoile and Château-Chalon. This peculiar *flor*-affected wine made with the rasping Savagnin grape is produced in other parts of Jura, but it is in these two appellations that it reaches its remarkable peak. Long-lived, yes, memorable, yes, but certainly not a wine which will appeal to all tastes. More accessible, but still an oddball, is *vin de paille*, a sweet wine made from grapes which have been allowed to dry out (traditionally on straw (*paille*) in order to concentrate their sugars and flavours). Names to look out for throughout the region are Château d'Arlay, Jean Bourdy, Durand-Perron, Château de l'Etoile, Jean Macle, Pignier, Jacques Puffeney, Rolet Père et Fils, André et Mireille Tissot and Labet Père et Fils.

Savoie and Bugey

Pinot Noir and Chardonnay make further appearances in these
Alpine regions along the upper stretches of the Rhône to the south of
Jura. Bugey also has plantings of Gamay, but the main variety for the
red Vin de Savoie is the sturdy, smoky Mondeuse. White varieties
include the generally rather boring Chasselas, the tangy, rich Altesse
(aka Roussette) and Jacquère and small amounts of Roussanne, here
known as Bergeron. The most interesting wines are the Jacquère-
based whites from the villages of Abymes and Apremont, Chignin-
Bergeron which is 100 per cent Roussanne and the sparkling Seyssel.
Chardonnay and Pinot Noir under the Vin du Bugey VDQS (Vin
Délimité de Qualité Supérieure) can also be very attractive. Savoie
producers to look out for include Pierre Boniface (under the Domaine
de Rocailles label), Raymond Quénard, André and Michel Quénard,
Château de Ripaille, Philippe & François Tiollier and Varichon et
Clerc. From Bugey, Philippe Viallet and Eugène Monin.

LANGUEDOC-ROUSSILLON

We all know about lies, damned lies and statistics. Statistics tell us
that the Languedoc-Roussillon is having a torrid time, with demand
for the wines falling in all markets. In France, consumption fell by
120 million litres in 2000, and around 80 per cent of the decrease
was of wines from the south. As a result, prices for basic *vin de pays*
and *vin de table*, in other words for the vast majority of wine made
in the region, fell by 20–30 per cent in the year to Spring 2001.
Growers organised protests to try and persuade the European
Union to grant distillation rights for an astonishing 500 million litres
of wine. Even Vin de Pays d'Oc Chardonnay, supposedly one of the
saviours of the Languedoc, is tumbling in price, and the regional
syndicate has proposed a reduction in the yield requirements in
order to cut production and improve quality.

But there's also another face to the Languedoc-Roussillon that
is much rosier. We're finding it increasingly difficult but extremely
rewarding to keep up with the growing number of estates making
first-rate wines, usually but not exclusively red. Arguably the best
source of southern French wines in the UK is the London merchant
La Vigneronne (see *Where to buy wine*). Hardly a month goes by
without the company introducing two or three more producers
whose wines simply cannot be ignored; and there's no shortage of
customers willing to pay sometimes in excess of £20 a bottle. These
estates often have little or no track record, but the quality is there in
the bottle for all to appreciate, and the prices are still cheaper than
comparable wines from other parts of the world.

What has been especially pleasing is a new maturity in the style of the wines. Much is made of the excellent 1998 vintage, and rightly so. It was a year that showed many outsiders that the Languedoc was a fine wine region in its own right. However, faced with an abundance of healthy, flavour-packed, tannin-packed grapes, many *vignerons* were rather brutal in their winemaking, and tried to squeeze just too much out of the fruit, producing huge but hard-edged wines. 2000 was also a fine year, and having learned from their mistakes in 1998, the producers adopted a more gentle approach to winemaking, and the improvement shows.

We've reported in the past on how *vignerons* from other regions and countries are flocking to the Midi, and this continues. The American producer Robert Mondavi suffered a setback this year when plans to develop an estate in the Hérault were thwarted by a vociferous but (in our opinion) rather pig-headed protest from locals. However, the Sardinian company Sella & Mosca recently bought an estate here, while the eminent Burgundian Jean-Marc Boillot has just released his first wines from Pic St-Loup. One of the reasons Boillot cited for branching out into the region was that the vineyards were 100 times cheaper than comparable ones in Burgundy. If the Languedoc-Roussillon continues to develop in the way it has through the 1990s, we wouldn't be surprised to see land prices rise in the years to come. By how much, we're not prepared to say. After all, there are lies, damned lies and statistics.

AC wines

Of the two areas – Languedoc and Roussillon – the Languedoc is rapidly becoming the more complex and enterprising with a variety of appellations and sub-regions, particularly those on rugged slopes at the foothills of the Cévennes as opposed to the flat plains nearer the Mediterranean. The vast majority of production is red, although the amount of Vin de Pays d'Oc Chardonnay available on supermarket shelves in the UK might convince otherwise.

The best reds from the Languedoc-Roussillon usually comprise a blend of Mourvèdre, Grenache and Syrah with some of the more ubiquitous and lesser Carignan and Cinsault. Carignan, however, is the most widely planted variety in the region and, at its best, can provide some marvellously robust and herby reds, particularly from old vines. Corbières and Côtes du Roussillon are particularly noteworthy in this case.

While whites are not the strength of the region, Clairette and Grenache Blanc can sometimes be persuaded to yield plump waxy wines, with the addition of the Rhône grapes Viognier and Roussanne adding depth and fragrance. The only AC permitting Chardonnay in the blend is Limoux, which has to be barrel-fermented and must include at least 15 per cent Mauzac, although some producers have been known to bend this latter rule. While on the subject of Limoux, the intriguing and rarely found sparkling wines, Blanquette de Limoux and Crémant de Limoux, made by the traditional method, may also have a proportion of Chardonnay in them, along with a predominance of Mauzac (Blanquette) and Chenin Blanc.

Of the Languedoc appellations, Fitou was first conferred its status in the 1940s, with Corbières, Minervois and the sprawling Coteaux du Languedoc not achieving the same until 1985. Today's wine map of the region also includes Faugères, St-Chinian and Cabardès. A dozen villages are allowed to append their name to the sprawling Coteaux du Languedoc appellation, including Pic St-Loup, Montpeyroux and La Méjanelle. Both Corbières and Fitou have vineyards scattered through the mountainous and semi-remote terrain of the Montagne Noire. Along with Limoux and Cabardès, these are vineyard areas sandwiched between the Mediterranean and the Pyrenees, with myriad individual micro-climates and potential for variety. Minervois and St-Chinian, in the north of the region, produce wines varying from the rich and soft to the full and robust – according to how far into the high and arid hills the vineyards are located. Many of the best wines of Minervois hail from the La Livinière enclave, which was recognised as a sub-region from the 1998 vintage.

Costières de Nîmes, formerly Costières de Gard, is another rather bitty appellation, enclosed in this case by the towns of Montpellier, Arles and Nîmes. Whether it is in the Languedoc or the Rhône is debatable both geographically and stylistically, since the wines often have elements of the flavours of both. The best wines are of high quality and well priced, and could pass for something rather more expensive from the Rhône – and in some cases, the northern Rhône. As we've mentioned, in what could be the first French venture for an Italian producer, Sella & Mosca of Sardinia now owns a vineyard here.

In Roussillon, mercifully, life is a little simpler; the Côtes du Roussillon appellation predominates, although 25 villages are allowed to append their own names to it. Grenache is the main grape in many cases and the wines are, as a result, warmer and earthier than their herby counterparts further east around the Mediterranean basin, particularly in the tiny individual appellation of Collioure. Grenache is also the base for excellent fortified red *vin doux naturel* as produced in Banyuls, Maury and Rivesaltes. These are fascinating wines and worth discovering. Rivesaltes also produces white *vin doux naturel* from the Muscat variety, although we prefer the more delicate Muscat de St-Jean de Minervois, from the Languedoc.

Vins de pays

Vins de pays are not an exclusivity of the Languedoc-Roussillon, but most of the 150+ designated regions can be found here. Some of these are very localised, while others, such as Vin de Pays d'Oc, cover a number of *départements*. Trying to familiarise oneself with all of them is difficult, and ultimately a rather pointless exercise. The French authorities had originally (1973) intended this to be an intermediary level between *vin de table* and *appellation contrôlée* and as a stepping stone to improving quality and acquiring AC status. However, the concept of *vins de pays* was well and truly hijacked by growers and producers on two fronts. On the one hand, there were those feeding the demand for keenly priced varietal wines, while on the other, there were those aiming for top quality who realised that they could legally produce blended wines using virtually whichever variety they chose. Nowadays *vins de pays* can be simple Cinsault-heavy blends, impressive Cabernets, Syrahs, Chardonnays and Viogniers, and excellent wines made from local grapes pepped up by Cabernet and Co. As a consequence, the name of the actual *vin de pays* has become almost irrelevant, while those of both producer and varietal have risen in importance.

Pick of the producers (Languedoc-Roussillon)

Abbotts Australians Nerida Abbott and husband Nigel Sneyd, both previously at Domaine de la Baume, make a range of fine reds in the Roussillon.

Gilbert Alquier The top estate in Faugères, making Syrah-dominated wines of sterling quality, especially the new oak-aged Les Bastides.

Baron'arques Joint venture between Baron Philippe de Rothschild and Aimery Sieur d'Arques of Limoux, making firm, fleshy, oaky blend of traditional Bordeaux grapes with Syrah and Grenache. Good but pricy.

Mas Baruel Organically farmed estate which produces a fine Syrah and a very classy Syrah/Cabernet blend, the Languedoc's answer to Domaine de Trévallon.

Domaine de la Baume The southern French arm of the Australian BRL Hardy corporation. Surprisingly crisp whites, including one of the south's best Sauvignons, and spicy, fruity reds.

Gérard Bertrand Impressive selection of Vin de Pays d'Oc, topped by Cigalus Blanc (Chardonnay/Viognier/Sauvignon) and Rouge (Cabernet/Merlot).

Mas Bruguière Pic St-Loup (Coteaux du Languedoc) reds of real class, particularly the Fûts de Chêne *cuvée*.

Cazes Frères Perhaps best known for their Muscat de Rivesaltes, but the Grenache-heavy Vieux Rivesaltes is a better wine. The Côte du Roussillon reds aren't bad either.

Chemins de Bassac Inspired Vin de Pays d'Oc reds and a tasty rosé made from Syrah, Cabernet Sauvignon, Grenache and Mourvèdre from former school teachers Rémi and Isabelle Ducellier.

CIRA Wines bearing this acronym are from the stable of *négociant* Caroline de Beaulieu, a dynamic, trained oenologist who represents some excellent and great-value properties from around the Languedoc.

Clos Centeilles/Daniel Domergue Mourvèdre, Syrah and Grenache go into Daniel Domergue's excellent Minervois, but he also makes an immensely attractive wine called Carignanissime made from – guess what? – the humble Carignan.

Domaine de Clovallon Admirable and slightly quirky range including arguably the finest Pinot Noir of southern France, delicious Mas d'Alezon red blend and an astonishing, heady, barley-sugar-y Rancio.

Comte Cathare Englishman Bertie Eden oversees production of a fine range of wines under various appellations and *vin de pays* designations.

Domaine des Creisses Venture run by two ex-Bordeaux winemakers making extremely classy wine, with top *cuvée* Les Brunes combining power with elegance, something still rare in the Languedoc.

Mas de Daumas Gassac Pioneer of high-class *vin de pays* – de l'Hérault in this case – with a full-bodied if rather tannic Bordeaux-inspired red and an exotically fragrant white blend of mainly Chardonnay, Viognier and Petit Manseng.

Château Flaugergues Source of well-made, big, smoky Coteaux du Languedoc reds.

Font Caude Rising star making sumptuous reds, finest of which is the 100 per cent Syrah l'Esprit de Font Caude. Also great success with Chenin Blanc, both dry and sweet.

Fortant de France Robert Skalli's Sète-based operation was a *vin de pays* pioneer which lost its way slightly through much of the 1990s. New F de Skalli Chardonnay and Cabernet show a welcome return to form.

Domaine Gauby Probably the best estate in Côtes du Roussillon, thanks to old vines and low yields. Huge ripe reds and a very attractive white from Grenache Blanc, Maccabéo and Carignan Blanc.

Domaine de la Grange des Pères Like Mas de Daumas Gassac, a Vin de Pays de l'Hérault, and currently surpassing that famous estate in the quality of its red wine, a blend of Syrah, Mourvèdre and Cabernet Sauvignon.

James Herrick Now owned by Australian giant Southcorp, although the eponymous Australian-trained Brit is still involved in making the chunky reds and quite subtle Chardonnay.

Domaine de l'Hospitalet Showcase winery in the Coteaux du Languedoc, producing first-class reds and a delicious, lightly oaked white.

Domaine des Jougla Alain Jougla's supple, fruity St-Chinian is the best wine of the appellation. Good value too.

Mas Jullien The impassioned Olivier Jullien makes splendid reds, whites and rosés, often using varieties which others eschew. Pick of the range is the dense, structured Les Cailloutis red, a Grenache/Mourvèdre/Oeillades blend.

Château La Roque One of the leaders in Pic St-Loup producing elegant wines, particularly from the Mourvèdre grape variety.

Château de Lascaux Top-class Syrah/Grenache blends from the Coteaux du Languedoc.

Domaine de Peyre Rose Muscular Coteaux du Languedoc reds from former estate agent Marlene Soria. The Cuvée Syrah Leoné is classy but pricy.

Domaine de la Rectorie Producer of the best Banyuls and also three different Collioure wines which age brilliantly.

Val d'Orbieu You'll find the name (or the initials VVO) of this organisation of co-ops and growers on several wines from throughout southern France. Don't expect great shakes from the cheaper wines, but the range of single-estate Corbières and the gutsy Cuvée Mythique red can be very good.

Vaquer Son Bernard is now in charge of winemaking at this Côtes du Roussillon property, and the reds have improved vastly. The legacy of the elder Vaquer, Fernand, is some splendid 100 per cent Maccabéo whites which at ten years old still taste superb.

Maurel Vedeau Widely distributed, wines bearing this name are the work of dynamic, young winemaking duo Philippe Maurel and Stéphane Vedeau, who have so far specialised in well-made, single varietal *vins de pays*. Currently turning their attentions to appellation wines as well.

Wild Pig Englishman Guy Anderson and Frenchman Thierry Boudinaud of the major Rhône producer Gabriel Meffre make one of the best ranges of *vins de pays*, formerly know as Galet. Also the source of Fat Bastard Chardonnay and Utter Bastard Red (usually Syrah).

Vintages

As we mentioned in the introduction, 1998 and 2000 were both excellent vintages in the Languedoc-Roussillon, producing substantial red wines that at best will age well for several years. Sandwiched between these two is 1999, which was less of a blockbuster, but which still yielded some splendid if less ageworthy wines.

THE LOIRE

If we're correct in thinking that people are currently seeking a little more subtlety in their wines, then the Loire could be set for a rise in fortunes. The region enjoyed considerable popularity both at home and abroad in the 1970s, but has since struggled to gain new consumers. It's partly because there's no wine that really jumps up and says, 'Ignore me at your peril'. True, the sweet Chenin Blancs of Bonnezeaux, Coteaux du Layon and Vouvray are world-class wines and are better than they have ever been. However, for some reason, sweet whites are not everybody's cup of tea (shame – we love them), and it is dry wines that attract people.

So what can the Loire offer? Sauvignon Blanc performs admirably, but New Zealand currently defines the genre, while Chenin Blanc in its dry and medium dry forms can be difficult to come to terms with. In the red department, Cabernet Franc, the grape responsible for the wines of Chinon and Bourgueil, seldom

rises to the heights of Cabernet Sauvignon, while Burgundy need never feel under threat from Pinot Noir as produced in Sancerre.

The danger is that because other regions make more assertive, louder wines, we forget the Loire. That's why it was a pleasure to attend the Spring 2001 Majestic tasting in London, which kicked off with no fewer than six Sancerres – all good, all subtle, all different. The Majestic buyers confessed that the decision to stock so many was a result of not being able to find one or two available in sufficient quantities to see them through the course of the year; but never mind, the diversity was noted and appreciated.

If Loire Sauvignons deserve another look, then the same is certainly true for Chenin Blanc. Better viticulture means grapes are being picked later and riper, while more sympathetic winemaking means the wines have lost the over-sulphured heaviness of the past, and now display their attractive appley fruit to much better effect. There will always be a nutty, waxy edge to Loire Chenin – one writer describes the taste as 'lacy' – which won't be to everyone's taste, but it does bring an extra facet to the wines, and is certainly a welcome relief from the confected flavours of much modern Chardonnay.

And as for Loire reds, well this introduction is being written on a warm evening in western France, where there's a light breeze and the sun is still shining at 9.30pm. A heavy red would have been inappropriate for tonight's lamb, but the lightly chilled Saumur-Champigny went down a treat.

The Loire is the longest river in France, rising in the Massif Central and winding north before veering due west to the port of Nantes, and more than 100 different wines can be found along its 1,000-km length. The reds and rosés from the upper reaches of the river, such as Gamay-based wines from the Côtes Roannaises or Côtes du Forez, are unlikely to have crossed your path unless you've visited the region. Further downstream, the wines fall into three convenient segments:

Central Loire

Before New Zealand got in on the act, this was where everybody turned to for crisp, herbaceous Sauvignon Blanc in the form of Sancerre and Pouilly-Fumé. The wines tend to be less immediately ripe and fruity and more flinty and earthy than New Zealand versions, and take a little longer to reach their peak. While Sancerre and Pouilly-Fumé can be hard to tell apart, Sancerre is probably the more concentrated and consistent of the two. Cheaper alternatives can be found in Menetou-Salon, Reuilly and Quincy. Pinot Noir is the favoured grape for the reds of the region. Most are rather thin and weedy, although the occasional red Sancerre from a good vintage can have attractive, slightly earthy raspberry fruit.

Pick of the producers (Central Loire)
Cotat Frères Tiny amounts of fine Sancerre built for ageing.

Didier Dagueneau Rare source of innovation and excellence within the Pouilly-Fumé appellation, especially with the barrel-fermented Silex *cuvée*.

de Ladoucette/Château de Nozet Highly fêted producer of Pouilly-Fumé and Sancerre (under the Comte Lafond label). Good wines, sometimes very good – the prices are less easy to swallow.

Henry Pellé Menetou-Salon's top man, with delicious whites, especially Clos de Blanchais, and reasonable reds.

Vacheron Consistently among the best – if not the best – for Sancerre, both white and red.

Also worth hunting down: *Henri Bourgeois, Pascal Jolivet, Masson-Blondelet, Alphonse Mellot, Silice de Quincy, Château de Tracy* and *Vatan*.

Anjou-Saumur and Touraine

While these two areas enjoy separate official status, they share the same grape varieties for their best wines. In the white department, Chenin Blanc reigns, and appears in dry, medium, sweet and sparkling guises. In this relatively northerly climate, the late-ripening Chenin needs a good site and plenty of TLC to grow well, otherwise, as with much Saumur and Anjou Blanc, its often searing acidity dominates the wine. Savennières is the classic dry Chenin, bracing in its youth and needing considerable bottle age before the apple and honey fruit begins to rise above the sharpness. Vouvray and Montlouis appear in various stages of sweetness, including the unfashionable but really rather attractively nutty, honeyed *demi-sec*. Again, these medium dry wines benefit from age and can last for several years. However, the real distance runners are the *botrytis*-affected sweet wines from appellations such as Bonnezeaux and Coteaux du Layon. Thanks to their astonishing richness, they can be enjoyed in their youth, but as a result of that Chenin acidity and the high sugar levels, they can age gracefully for 50 years or more.

Cabernet Franc is the favoured grape for reds. Again, it takes a decent grower and a decent vineyard to ripen the grapes fully, otherwise the wines have an unappealing vegetal flavour. Even the best have a slightly earthy, leafy – as in blackcurrant leaf – note to them, combined with rich, almost tar-like flavours. Bourgueil and Chinon are homes to the best reds, although St-Nicolas de Bourgueil and Saumur-Champigny can also point to a few stars. Cabernet Franc is also used for rosé in Cabernet d'Anjou. Alas, the ubiquitous Rosé d'Anjou is made from the very ordinary Grolleau grape variety and is typically insipid, semi-sweet and forgettable.

Pick of the producers (Anjou-Saumur and Touraine)

Domaine des Baumard Top-notch Chenin both bone-dry and honeyed and sweet from Savennières (Clos du Papillon), Coteaux du Layon (Clos de Ste-Catherine) and Quarts de Chaume.

Bouvet-Ladubay Decent sparkling Saumur, particularly the oak-aged Trésor, from this subsidiary of champagne house Taittinger.

Pascal Cailleau/Domaine Sauveroy Up with Richou and Daviau at the top of the Anjou league, the dynamic Pascal Cailleau makes a great range of reds, whites and pinks, the best of which is a wonderful Coteaux du Layon.

Christophe Daviau Under the Domaine de Bablut and Château de Brissac labels, good ranges of red, white and pink Anjou, including Cabernet d'Anjou ageworthy. Also impressive Coteaux de l'Aubance.

Couly-Dutheil The *négociant* business throughout the Loire results in reasonable rather than thrilling wines, but the best are the estate Chinons, especially Clos de l'Echo and Baronnie Madeleine.

Pierre-Jacques Druet Leading grower of Bourgueil, making a number of different and serious *cuvées*, all of which are worth looking out for.

Château de Fesles The best of Bonnezeaux, especially since 1996, luscious when young yet will outlast most of us.

Domaine Filliatreau Vying with Domaine des Roches Neuves for top dog in Saumur-Champigny. Look out for the deep, concentrated Vieilles Vignes *cuvée*.

Huet Top dog in Vouvray, with dry, medium, sweet and sparkling wines of the highest order. Gaston Huet himself is in his nineties, and the main winemaking responsibility now lies with his son-in-law, the talented Noël Pinguet. The Cuvée Constance Moelleux produced in the best years is exceptional wine.

Charles Joguet Star of Chinon, with a series of single-vineyard bottlings which age almost as well as classed growth claret.

Nicolas Joly Eccentric and meticulous producer making rich, dry, long-lived and expensive Chenin Blanc in the Savennières sub-appellation of Coulée de Serrant. Joly practises biodynamic winemaking.

Langlois-Château Bollinger-owned house in Saumur making reliable reds and whites as well as snappy, refreshing sparklers.

Richou Dynamic domaine in Anjou producing sound whites and reds, and excellent sweet Coteaux de l'Aubance.

Domaine des Roches Neuves A startlingly good range of Saumur-Champigny from Thierry Germain, formerly of Bordeaux. Look out for the Terres Chaudes, oak-aged Marginale (both red) and the white L'Insolite made from 75-year-old vines.

Pays Nantais

Or Muscadet country. Muscadet is made from Melon de Bourgogne, a rather ordinary grape that needs careful handling in order to make the most of the little character it possesses. Most wines fall into the CFDN bracket – crisp, fresh, dry, neutral – but the better examples are worth looking out for. The important things to look out for on the label are one of the sub-regions – Côtes de Grand Lieu, Coteaux de la Loire or Sèvre et Maine – plus the words *sur lie*. This latter term indicates that the wines have been aged on the lees to bring about greater depth of flavour and a slightly spritzy finish. Some oak-aged Muscadet even exists nowadays. Muscadet is better now than it has ever been, especially in the hands of producers such as Guy Bossard, Chéreau Carré, Donatien Bahuaud, Luneau, Louis Métaireau and Sauvion. However, while we applaud the improvements, we still struggle to get excited about the wines. And we usually go out of our way to avoid those made in the same region from Gros Plant, a variety which combines the acidity of Chenin Blanc with the neutrality of Melon de Bourgogne.

Other wines

While Vin de Pays du Jardin de la France may not enjoy the popularity of its southern equivalents, a run of recent good vintages has meant that some fresh and crisp, easy-drinking varietals (Sauvignon, Chardonnay and Cabernet Rosé) are gradually appearing on the (mainly supermarket) shelves. The itinerant winemaker Jacques Lurton has produced some pleasing examples in conjunction with the vast *négociant* business, Ackerman. The Cave Co-opérative du Haut Poitou is another, mostly reliable source of varietal VDQS (Vin Délimité de Qualité Supérieure) wines, especially Sauvignon and Gamay.

Loire vintage guide

2000 Humidity and hail were just two of the problems growers had to contend with in the run up to vintage, but with the end of August, the weather improved dramatically, turning what could have been a disaster into a reasonable year for Sauvignon Blanc and Cabernet Franc. The fine conditions continued into October, enabling those who waited to harvest their Chenin Blanc to make some very good, full-bodied dry whites, and some sumptuous sweet wines as well.

1999 Heavy rain in mid-September dashed all hopes of a great vintage, but since the grapes were almost fully ripe at the time, this only had the effect of diluting the wines. Growers with well-tended vineyards made wines with good acidity in the whites and appealing softness in the reds. Others struggled.

1998 By no means a disastrous year, but tread carefully. Again, wines from the best *vignerons* stand out after a vintage marked by very hot sun in August (some grapes actually burnt on the vine) and rain in September/October. Canny winemakers have managed to come up with a decent set of wines, with the high acidity typical of the region; others came a cropper.

1997 Among the sunniest and hottest in the past 50 years and compared to 1990 in terms of fruit ripeness. Wines are, in general, soft and attractive, opulent and rich. Dry whites, however, lack the crisp acidity of classic Loire wines.

1996 A second great year in a row throughout the Loire, with top-class reds, great sweet and dry Chenin Blanc, and Sauvignons which, thanks to slightly higher acidity levels, are better balanced than the occasionally top-heavy 1995s.

1995 Excellent year for wines made from Cabernet Franc and Chenin Blanc, with some stunning *botrytis* wines from the latter. A classic year all round.

Other notable vintages 1990, 1989

PROVENCE

Yes, there's still a lot of rosé around, but things are moving on. Not only has pink Provence wine improved greatly over the last ten years, with better winemaking techniques bringing about a huge quality transformation, but growers are becoming also far more regionally aware, and are playing to the white and red strengths of their vineyards. For whites, look to the coastal Cassis appellation for Marsanne and Clairette wines cooled by sea winds; also the new, semi-Alpine Coteaux de Pierrevert region and Côtes du Lubéron (where the Rhône adjoins Provence) for the nutty Rolle grape. Elsewhere the emphasis is on red. Bandol still deserves its top-rank reputation for herby, blackberry Mourvèdre – the vines have to be eight years old, the wines need a minimum of 18 months barrel age, and long maturation. Les Baux de Provence follows, its warm, dry vineyards bringing out the best in Syrah, Cabernet and Grenache Noir. Coteaux d'Aix is slightly cooler, with an enormous variation in wine styles produced: sensibly there's a 30 per cent threshold on usurper varieties, Cabernet, Sémillon and Sauvignon Blanc. Côtes de Provence wines, however, gain a positive lift from Syrah and Cabernet that makes all the difference to them. Coteaux Varois is a large appellation in which blended rosés are still the most important wines; Palette and Bellet are each much smaller, the former for serious ageworthy Château Simone, the latter somewhat buried in the suburbs of Nice. Where the varieties don't conform to the local appellation rules, Provence's wines usually appear under the Vin de Pays du Var label (as from top-rank Domaine de Triennes, see below).

We can forgive the tourist rosé – as long as it's well-made and gluggable, not just swig-me-quick mouthwash – as we understand cash flow is an important starting point for quality improvement – so we're not going to be too damning.

Pick of the producers (Provence)

Domaine des Béates Coteaux d'Aix producer now partly owned by Chapoutier of the Rhône and already close to the top of the Provence league. Top wine is Cabernet/Syrah blend Terra d'Or; Les Matines is for everyday drinking; Les Béates is a meaty, steak-ready mouthful.

Domaines Bunan The elegant Mas de la Rouvière Bandol made by brothers Paul and Pierre Bunan is seriously good red wine made from a four-hectare plot of 50-year-old Mourvèdre. Also watch for Moulin des Costes and Vin de Pays du Mont Caume labels.

Clos Sainte Magdeleine François Sack's Cassis is a delicious crisp blend of Ugni Blanc, Marsanne, Clairette and Sauvignon with a flavour of honey, nuts and lemon and a salty influence from the sea.

Domaine de la Courtade Rapidly improving estate on the island of Porquerolles to the south-east of Toulon, making ripe, smoky Mourvèdre-based red and fleshy white from Rolle. Top wine La Courtade is seriously ageworthy and guaranteed to warm up your winter.

Château de Pibarnon Concentrated, strapping Bandol which is virtually pure Mourvèdre from Henri de Saint Victor. Needs bottle age.

Domaine Rabiega Swedish owned, and one of the most enlightened estates in the region, with a classy white (Chardonnay/Sauvignon) and a number of lovely reds, best of which is the 100 per cent Syrah Clos d'Ière Cuvée 1.

Château Routas Exciting Coteaux Varois estate producing interesting whites and bold herby reds, especially the Cuvée Luc Sorin. Watch out for Mistral Cabernet-Syrah and pure Syrah, Cyrano, plus 100 per cent pure Carignan from 45-year-old vines.

Château Simone Rich, basket-pressed whites, serious rosés and substantial but elegant reds to age, traditionally made from old vines (average, 60 to 100 years). Covers 17 hectares of the 23-hectare Palette AC.

Domaine Tempier This family-owned property is probably the most famous of the Bandol estates, and still one of the very best, with the broad-shouldered Cuvée Tourtine being the high point.

Domaine de Trévallon Eloi Dürrbach makes arguably the finest wines in Provence. Trévallon red (a Syrah/Cabernet *vin de pays*)

147

bucks AC regulations by missing out Grenache Noir, and is a splendid smoky, fruit-packed wine which merits its high price and ages superbly. There's a rare, but great, full, nutty white too.

Domaine de Triennes The sideline activity of two eminent Burgundians, Jacques Seysses of Domaine Dujac and Aubert de Villaine of Domaine de la Romanée-Conti. Impressive Viognier, Chardonnay, 50/50 Cabernet/Syrah Les Auréliens, and even better Cuvée Réserve Cabernet and Syrah from top years only. All these are made outside AC rules, so not Coteaux Varois but Vins du Pays du Var.

Château Vignelaure High, cool vineyards making elegant, structured reds with the assistance of illustrious Bordeaux winemaker Michel Rolland. Cabernet and Merlot are best.

THE RHÔNE

We mentioned in the general introduction to France that if we had £10 to spend, a French wine would head our shopping list. Let us now expand on that and say that we'd probably zero in on the Rhône valley, which vies with the Languedoc as the source of the best-value wines in France. The single-vineyard Côte-Rôties of Guigal, and the fabled wines of Hermitage and Châteauneuf-du-Pape, may be out of our reach with our crisp tenner, but there are dozens of other wines which we'd gladly drink instead.

What makes the Rhône such a happy hunting ground at the moment is that the region has just enjoyed a fine trio of vintages from 1998 to 2000. A decade earlier, the vintages 1988 to 1990 were also excellent, but since then, the Rhône has matured in remarkable fashion. At the end of the 1980s, many estates in the northern, Syrah-dominated section of the valley were still picking their grapes too early, and not bothering to remove the stalks prior to vinification. The result was wines with forbidding tannic structures where the fruit struggled to make its presence felt. Cut to the present, and the typical northern Rhône red is more supple, more fragrant and more fruity. There's still a considerable backbone of tannin there, but the tannins are ripe and silky rather than harsh and green, meaning the wine can be drunk when young but will also age well.

The evolution in the south is even more remarkable. Ten years ago, most Châteauneuf-du-Pape was made in primitive conditions, and emerged rustic, alcoholic and volatile. Hardly anyone was aware of villages such as Gigondas and Vacqueyras, and as for Côtes du Rhône, the operative word was 'avoid'. Today, the southern Rhône is a hot-bed of activity. Many cellars now gleam with modern stainless steel tanks and have a few new oak barrels hiding in a corner. Ancient vineyards that had been all but abandoned have been resurrected, and are yielding top-notch fruit, while growers who used to send their grapes to the local co-operative have begun making their own wines. And for consumers, the quality of the best wines is well in advance of the prices demanded.

Further good news is that while most vineyards in the northern Rhône are now being fully exploited, there are still major areas further south just waiting to be redeveloped or – in the case of the Luberon and Ventoux – developed for the first time. The Rhône is one of the few French regions currently enjoying an increase in sales in the UK, in no small part thanks to an aggressive promotional campaign. However, for us it's the high quality and their friendly prices that make this one of our favourite sources of red wine.

The Northern Rhône

In wine terms, the valley is split into the northern and southern Rhône. Such titles conveniently forget that the river runs through the region of Savoie along the Swiss border, but no matter. For the wine world, the northern Rhône starts at Vienne with the appellation of Côte-Rôtie and runs southwards to St-Péray, just across the river from the town of Valence. This is the home of the Syrah grape, capable of producing dense, smoky wines packed with aromas and flavours of black pepper and spice, ripe berries, orange peel and with a rich, creamy texture. Although vines are grown on alluvial land next to the river, and a number of recent plantings, particularly in St-Joseph, have been on plateau land overlooking the river, the best vineyards are those clinging to the slopes of the valley, often on hard-to-manage terraces.

Red wines

On the evidence of wines currently being produced, Côte-Rôtie is arguably the greatest appellation, a mighty wine packed with black fruit, yet with a perfumed elegance, some but not all of which is derived from the addition of small amounts of the white grape Viognier. Overlooking the town of Tain l'Hermitage is the famous hill of Hermitage, source of blockbuster Syrahs, uptight and glowering in their youth and requiring a decade or more to open out fully. Crozes-Hermitage has *terroirs* varying from flat alluvial plains to slopes adjoining Hermitage, and the wine, too varies from powerful, potent mini-Hermitage to fairly easy-drinking. The dark, rich wines of Cornas, one of the most reliable appellations in the Rhône, rival those of Hermitage for strength and longevity, although they lack the same elegance. St-Joseph covers a very large proportion of the western bank of the river which isn't taken up by other appellations. Such a spread results in a small number of high-quality, complex wines but also plenty of rather ordinary ones. Pick your grower with care.

White wines

The white grapes Marsanne and Roussanne can constitute up to 15 per cent of the blend for red Hermitage and Crozes, but few producers use this option. Instead, these varieties are used to make small quantities of white wine, some of which (in St-Péray) is sparkling. Avoid the fizz, but approach the still wines with a more open mind. True, many are dull and flabby, but there are also fresher, fruitier wines from good growers in Crozes, along with quite majestic, richly textured, nutty, peachy and very ageworthy wines from Hermitage and to a lesser extent St-Joseph. A few growers dry their grapes on straw mats to make stunning *vin de paille*, one of the great unsung sweet wines of the world.

Hermitage's rival for the title of most interesting white of the region is the fragrant, opulent, peachskin-and-apricot wine called Condrieu, made from the capricious Viognier. Burgundians complain about the difficulties encountered with Pinot Noir. Viognier can be just as frustrating, being relatively easy to grow, but difficult to both grow and vinify well. The essence of Viognier is a ripe, creamy, floral, apricot and honeysuckle aroma, but this heady perfume doesn't develop properly unless the grapes are fully ripe, by which time the sugar levels are high and the acid levels low. Viognier picked too early is just another simple dry white wine. Viognier picked too late can be over-the-top, blowsy and alcoholic. Some growers choose to make sweet wines from this grape – they can be appealing but the aromas are all too often swamped in sugar and alcohol. Apart from Condrieu, the other world-famous Viognier comes from Château Grillet. The wines for a number of years have hardly been the stuff of legend, although they carried a legendary price tag. There has been a return to form of late, but we recommend you stick to the more dependable Condrieu.

Pick of the producers (Northern Rhône)
Cave de Tain l'Hermitage A reliable co-operative with stunning red Hermitage Gambert de Loche and delicious, long-lived *vin de paille*.

Chapoutier A company with major vineyard holdings in Hermitage and Châteauneuf-du-Pape which has been revitalised since the late 1980s by the efforts of the dynamic Michel Chapoutier. Biodynamic viticulture is now the order of the day, and the top wines from all appellations are superlative. The St-Joseph Les Granits, both red and white, are the best wines of the appellation. The labels are printed with Braille characters.

Gérard Chave Arguably the best producer of both red and white Hermitage. Expensive, perhaps, especially the top Cuvée Cathelin, but worth it. The bargain is the St-Joseph, a fraction of the price of the Hermitage yet displaying a lot of the same character.

Auguste Clape Old-fashioned Cornas which is dense yet dumb in its youth but outstanding at the age of ten years and older.

Clusel-Roch Source of fine Côte-Rôtie, especially the Les Grandes Places *cuvée*, and tiny amounts of superb Condrieu.

Colombo He's too brash for many Rhône *vignerons*, but the influence of oenologist Jean-Luc Colombo has been felt in cellars throughout the Rhône Valley in a generally positive way. He has vineyards in Cornas, including a 90-year-old plot from which the excellent Les Ruchets *cuvée* is made. He also buys in grapes from other areas including the Côtes du Roussillon. Quality is high – look out for authentic Rhône flavours minus the faults and the excess tannins.

Yves Cuilleron New star making appetising, if rather oaky, Côte-Rôtie, but excelling with Condrieu, especially the intensely fruity Les Chaillets Vieilles Vignes *cuvée*.

Château de Curson Exciting, modern Crozes-Hermitage producer Etienne Pochon makes bright, spicy, fruity reds and dry, floral whites in a 400-year-old castle.

Delas Revitalised, Roederer-owned company which thanks to new management in the cellar in 1997 is now exploiting its extensive domaine of vineyards to the full. Hermitage Les Bessards is the star.

Pierre Dumazet Viognier specialist, making *vin de pays*, Côtes du Rhône and two Condrieus. Low yields and ripe fruit ensure plenty of heady perfume.

Jean-Michel Gerin Up-and-coming producer advised by Colombo and producing impressive Côte-Rôtie Les Grandes Places and delectable Condrieu.

Alain Graillot Proof that Crozes need not be Hermitage's poor cousin. Full-flavoured, aromatic wines which are attractive while young yet develop very well, and a top *cuvée* called La Guiraude which is complex, brilliant and fairly priced. Fine Hermitage too.

Guigal Master of Côte-Rôtie, with a trio of single-vineyard wines – La Mouline, La Turque and La Landonne – that are the most expensive and probably the best in the appellation. Other stars of an extensive range are the Hermitage, Côtes du Rhône (always great value) and Condrieu too. Not content with this, Marcel Guigal also owns Vidal-Fleury, has recently acquired the estates of de Vallouit and Grippat in the northern Rhône, and is said to have his eye on domaines in Châteauneuf-du-Pape.

Paul Jaboulet Aîné Famous for the excellent Hermitage La Chapelle, but also a reliable source of wines from throughout the Rhône. The bargain is the long-lived Domaine de Thalabert Crozes-Hermitage.

Jamet Extremely concentrated, rounded, cassis-laden wines from Côte-Rôtie.

Jasmin One of the best Côte-Rôtie producers, making bold yet elegant wines of considerable class.

André Perret The Condrieu Coteaux du Chery is one of the finest in the appellation, and the red and white St-Josephs are also of note.

Gilles Robin Rising star of Crozes-Hermitage, making fine, fragrant wine.

Vernay Famous Condrieu producer whose wines, particularly from the Coteau de Vernon, are wonderfully scented essences of Viognier.

Noël Verset Although theoretically retired, Verset still makes small amounts of dense, traditional Cornas which can be stalky when young but which ages wonderfully.

Les Vins de Vienne High-class, new *négociant* venture for a trio of eminent producers, Cuilleron, Gaillard and Villard, making impressive wines from both northern and southern Rhône.

The Southern Rhône

After the last part of St-Joseph, there is not much of vinous interest except for a few little pieces of Côtes du Rhône before the southern section of the Rhône Valley begins below Montélimar. The valley opens out into a plain, and the vineyards spread out, mainly to the east. This is a scorched, arid region, and the Mistral and Sirocco sweep through most days of the year. Yet the southern Rhône is capable of great red wine and the occasional tasty white and rosé too.

Red wines

No fewer than 13 different grape varieties are allowed in the blend for the best-known and greatest wine of the region, Châteauneuf-du-Pape. This rich, alcoholic cocktail of sun-baked fruit, spices and herbs derives its power from ultra-ripe Grenache grapes, typically 80 per cent of the blend, backed up in varying proportions by the other 12 varieties, with Syrah and Mourvèdre being the most popular partners (Syrah is seldom used in the south as a 100 per cent varietal since the warmer climate tends to give wines that are just too hefty). Châteauneufs are currently bigger, better and more powerful than they have ever been, and although some now command rather high prices, most still represent excellent value.

Other wines of the southern Rhône follow along similar lines. Quality-wise, Gigondas is closest to Châteauneuf but, depending on the *terroir* and winemaking, can vary from elegant to rather rustic. Then come Lirac, Vacqueyras and wines from the named Côtes du Rhône villages such as Cairanne, Séguret and Sablet (at which Domaines Gramenon and Richaud excel). Côtes du Rhône itself can vary from declassified Côte-Rôtie from a top winemaker to a rather soft and weedy red resembling basic Beaujolais. Similarly styled wines are made in the Côtes du Lubéron and Côtes du Ventoux between the Rhône and Provence. Recommendations include La Vieille Ferme, Château Val Joanis and Château des Tourettes, owned by Jean-Marie Guffens of Burgundy fame. However, the best Lubéron wine we've tasted in the last year has been a £4.99 *vin de pays* Cabernet Sauvignon from Domaine de la Citadelle, which is owned by Yves Rousset-Rouard, producer of the film *Emmanuelle*.

White wines

Whites, made here from Clairette, Bourboulenc, Roussanne and Grenache Blanc, are very much in the minority. White Châteauneuf is typically a crisp, fresh wine with a nutty edge which is at its best when young, although it can be kept for up to five years, with the top wines such as Beaucastel's Roussanne Vieilles Vignes lasting much longer. Those weaned on a diet of New World Chardonnay may find that the flavour takes some getting used to – it's not particularly fruity, although it is a great partner for rich fish and poultry.

The southern Rhône is also home to one of France's most renowned *vins doux naturels*, the soft, grapey Muscat de Beaumes de

Venise which should be drunk as young as possible. The versions from Jaboulet, Domaine de Coyeux and Domaine de Durban are among the best. There is also a notable red *vin doux naturel*, the rounded, fleshy, almost port-like Rasteau.

Rosé

Serious rosé (well, as serious as rosé ever gets) is made in Lirac and Tavel using the same varieties as for the reds. These wines can be more concentrated and fruity than other rosés, but we would recommend you drink them within two years of the vintage.

Pick of the producers (Southern Rhône)

Château de Beaucastel First-class estate which uses all 13 permitted varieties for its Châteauneuf. The Mourvèdre-based Cuvée Hommage à Jacques Perrin is a classic, but then so is the regular wine. The star white is the rich and nutty 100 per cent Roussanne Vieilles Vignes. Other wines to look out for are the red and white Côtes du Rhône Coudoulet de Beaucastel and the Côtes du Ventoux La Vieille Ferme.

Henri Bonneau Thick-set, chunky Châteauneuf-du-Pape, the best of which is the Réserve des Celestins.

Les Cailloux Ripe, concentrated Châteauneuf-du-Pape, some from ancient vines.

Domaine du Cayron Smooth but hefty, purple-hued Gigondas packed with cassis. Old vines play a large part here.

Domaine du Grand Tinel Excellent but little-known property owned by Elie Jeune in Châteauneuf, making long-lived fruity, spicy wines using plenty of old vine Grenache.

Domaine de la Janasse Up-and-coming estate in Châteauneuf with concentrated, classy reds and slightly spicy dry whites.

Domaine de la Mordorée Based in Lirac, and making the best red, white and rosé in that appellation. Also Côtes du Rhône and Châteauneuf of considerable class.

Domaine du Pégaü Big, old-fashioned blockbuster Châteauneuf with loads of extract. Plan Pégaü is good value but only a *vin de table*, due to the Merlot in the blend.

Château Rayas Jacques Reynaud died in 1997 but the world-famous Rayas style from Châteauneuf lives on in the hands of his nephew

Emmanuel Rayas. Rayas and second label Pignan are concentrated, sweetly ripe reds made from 100 per cent Grenache from extremely low-yielding vines. The Rayas Blanc and Fonsalette Côtes du Rhône wines are commendable too.

Domaine St-Cosme Rising Gigondas star, whose sumptuous top *cuvée* Valbelle, was described by Robert Parker as the Château Le Pin of Gigondas. The Côtes du Rhône Les Deux Albion is as good a wine as you'll find for under £10.

Domaine Santa Duc Powerful Gigondas which manages to retain a vestige of elegance. Best *cuvée* is the sweet, sexy Hautes Garrigues.

Tardieu Laurent The 'Laurent' in question is Burgundian Dominique Laurent, but it is Michel Tardieu who is largely responsible for the range of forcefully flavoured and typically excellent reds from throughout the Rhône valley.

Domaine du Vieux Télégraphe Fairly light Châteauneuf which is attractive young but ages well. Drink the delightful, peachy white as young as possible. Since the 1998 vintage, the estate has been a part owner of Domaine Les Pallières in Gigondas.

Other wines

Falling into neither the southern nor northern Rhône are the wines produced around the town of Die on the river Drôme, a tributary of the Rhône. This is a beautiful rural retreat, its hillsides planted with lavender and vines, but if you can find the rare red and white Châtillon-en-Dios, don't expect to be thrilled. Crémant de Die, made from the lacklustre Clairette, is slightly better, while Clairette de Die Tradition, or Clairette de Die Méthode Dioise Ancestrale as it is now called is far more interesting. It's made from at least 75 per cent Muscat Blanc à Petits Grains by the Méthode Dioise Ancestrale, which involves halting fermentation partway through and bottling a wine with residual sugar, so the fermentation continues in the bottle, producing the bubbles. If you like Asti (and we know you all do), then you'll love this peachy, grapey fizz.

Rhône vintage guide

The wines of the northern and southern Rhône differ in many ways, and it doesn't always follow that a good vintage for one is also good for the other. In general, the Syrah-based wines of the north, especially Hermitage and Cornas, need more age than the southern offerings, being rather forbidding and tight in their youth. Wines from the south are approachable earlier, but better vintages of Châteauneuf (and occasionally Gigondas) from a top producer can age gracefully for 20 years or more. The top whites of the north should (in our view) be drunk either in their perfumed, peachy youth or after many years. Ten-year-old white Hermitage can seem rather flabby and flat, an expensive disappointment.

2000 The third great year in a row. Spring and early summer were cool, but with the exception of showers in mid-August, the rest of the growing season brought good weather, meaning that the fruit ripened well and was brought in in a very healthy state. Quality may not be as consistent as in the two previous vintages, but the best reds are of a similar standard, while the whites, especially those of the north, could be the finest for several years.

1999 If the southern reds slightly overshadowed those from the north in 1998, the opposite was true in 1999. Rain in mid-September coincided with harvest time in parts of the south, so there will be wines which though ripe are slightly dilute. The rain also panicked some northern growers into picking too early, but those who waited were rewarded with good weather through to mid-October, giving a large crop of high-class wines.

1998 A great vintage in the south and at least a very good one in the north. Frost and hail hit some northern vineyards, but the hot dry summer brought the fruit to full maturity. By the time rains came at the end of September, virtually all the grapes had been picked in the south, and the wines are exceptional. Some northern vineyards were hit by the wet weather, so the wines will not be quite so concentrated.

1997 Not an easy vintage because of the very hot spring followed by a dull cloudy summer. Fortunately, the sun came out for an Indian summer, and the conditions during the harvest were hot and dry. The wines are good to very good, and the reds should age well.

1996 The cool summer in the north meant that the Syrah did not ripen as well as in 1995, although sunny weather from late August onwards ensured grapes were by no means unripe. Quality is high, but not of the standard of 1995. The south was slightly more patchy, as grapes struggled to mature fully in the cool weather. However, whites from both regions were excellent.

1995 A classic. The summer was the driest and sunniest since 1990. Rain fell for two weeks at the start of September, but those who waited for it to abate produced some great wines, well-structured but with plenty of ripe fruit. Superb white wines as well, especially Condrieu.

1994 A difficult vintage spoilt in both north and south by rain in the autumn. There were a number of noteworthy wines, but there were also plenty of indifferent ones.

1993 Not great. Cool summer weather in the north meant that when rain arrived at the end of September, the grapes had not been picked. Scrupulous growers who were prepared to use only clean fruit made some light, reasonably attractive wines. In the south the overall quality was higher, if not quite great.

1992 In the north, rain at flowering restricted the size of the vintage, while further rain in October affected the final part of the harvest. The wines are generally sound but not made for keeping. Abundant rain in the south resulted in dilute wines.

1991 A classic example of the north and south enjoying different vintage conditions. A July storm wreaked havoc in the south, and subsequent uneven ripening produced wines which ranged from decent to mediocre (and worse) in quality. Meanwhile, the north produced some excellent wines for the fourth year on the trot, with Côte-Rôtie excelling.

Good earlier vintages Northern Rhône 1990, 1989, 1988, 1985, 1983, 1982, 1979, 1978. Southern Rhône 1990, 1989, 1988, 1985, 1981, 1979, 1978

SOUTH-WESTERN FRANCE

Fading advertisements from the 1920s and 1930s proclaiming 'Vin de Cocumont – Côtes de Bordeaux' can still be found close to the vineyards around Marmandais. Bordeaux itself is 100km away, but time was when this part of France was considered a satellite of France's most exalted wine region. The Bordeaux legacy is still important for wines of Marmandais and indeed many other wines of this part of France. Many are based on the same grapes as Bordeaux, and make wines which, in the case of the best of Bergerac, Duras and Monbazillac for example, can compare very favourably with those of their famous neighbour. Others seem like early stages in the evolution of Bordeaux. The wines are similar in weight and structure, but the raw materials – grapes such as Malbec, Tannat, Colombard and the two Mansengs – lack the nobility of the Bordeaux varieties. That's not to say that the wines can't be very good, just that it needs a remarkable *vigneron*, such as Alain Brumont of Madiran or Henri Ramonteu of Jurançon, to coax the best out of them.

But don't let that put you off this fascinating region. While Abouriou, Courbu, Negrette, Len de l'El, Fer, Servadou and Arrufiac aren't in the top league of grape varieties, they make a pleasant change from a constant diet of the familiar and shouldn't be ignored, especially as they are usually very good value. The only difficulty with some of the more obscure appellations is that you'll find them difficult to track down in the UK. Les Caves de Pyrène (see *Where to buy wine*) offers an excellent selection but otherwise you'd do better to go to the region yourself. The wines aren't the only reason to pay a visit – the foie gras is among the best in France!

Red wines

The red wines from the areas nearer Bordeaux, such as Bergerac (undergoing something of a quality renaissance at present), the Côtes de Duras and the Côtes du Marmandais, naturally have claret-like characteristics and share the grape varieties. Pécharmant, a sub-appellation within Bergerac, produces slightly heftier wines, such as Château de Tiregand, which benefit from bottle age. The legendary 'black wine' of Cahors – deeply coloured, tannic and practically undrinkable – is thankfully more appealing nowadays, as producers have succeeded in gaining depth of flavour from the Malbec without hanging on to the huge tannins. Styles vary from easy-drinking to structured and spicy. Côtes du Frontonnais, made mainly from Negrette, is lighter and not far removed in flavour from the Dolcetto of northern Italy. The wines of Madiran, Béarn and Irouléguy, down in the south-west, are made mainly from the chunky Tannat grape blended with Cabernet of some description, and typically need time in bottle to soften. Alain Brumont has been demonstrating for several years that Tannat can be tamed with good winemaking and new oak barrels, but few as yet have followed his example.

White wines

As a rule, the modern, basic dry whites of the south-west are extremely reliable despite being made mainly from the highly uninteresting Ugni Blanc, also the grape of Cognac. A good proportion of the floral, aromatic Colombard is usually used to pep up the blend or sometimes some Gros Manseng for structure. Humble Vin de Pays des Côtes de Gascogne was one of the success stories of the 1980s and is still going strong – Domaine du Tariquet and the wines from the co-operative at Plaimont are always worth following. Similar wines may be found from the Côtes de St-Mont appellation. In Gaillac, white wines are made to varying degrees of sweetness from the Mauzac and Len de l'El grape variety, and are fast improving in quality, we are able to report – particularly those from producers such as Plageoles or the co-operative at Labastide de Lévis. Mauzac also make the little-known sparkling wines of Gaillac, which has its own *méthode gaillacoise*, as well as those of neighbouring Limoux.

Sweet whites from south-west France are something of a revelation. Monbazillac and Jurançon tend to be the most recognised, although they are completely different animals. The grape varieties for Monbazillac, and the now extremely upwardly mobile Saussignac appellation not far away, are the same as for Sauternes. While *botrytis* may not affect the Sémillon, Sauvignon Blanc and Muscadelle here with as much frequency as it does in Bordeaux, careful winemakers are able to produce wines of great distinction and honeyed richness – for a fraction of the price. Discrimination is the watchword here, though, as many Monbazillacs in particular, can be just sweet and clumsy.

Jurançon wines offer a much more refreshing experience for sweet wine lovers. Here Gros and Petit Manseng and Courbu are harvested ultra-ripe but do not succumb to *botrytis*, remaining lighter and more delicately scented in style. The dry Jurançon Sec is also worth trying, particularly those examples now fermented in oak from Domaine Cauhapé. The last mention must go to the gloriously named Pacherenc de Vic Bilh, a tangy white from Madiran made resolutely from local varieties such as Arrufiac, Courbu and Petit Manseng with a permitted smattering of Sémillon and Sauvignon. In some cases the grapes are left to dry (*passerillé*) on the vines at the end of a warm vintage to be turned into sweet wines of great longevity.

Pick of the producers (South-western France)

Alain Brumont Brumont's three properties – Domaine Bouscassé, Château Montus and Domaine Meinjarre – produce some of the best Madiran, using a high proportion of Tannat and a courageous dose of new oak. New in 2000, Montus Cuvée La Tyre is a pure Tannat from the highest vineyards in the appellation. The dry Pacherenc de Vic Bilh from Bouscassé is good, but the Moelleux is excellent. The range of *vin de pays* varietals is less convincing.

Domaine Cauhapé Henri Ramonteu is the mover and shaker in Jurançon, making dry and sweet whites of consistently high quality, particularly the luscious Quintessence.

Clos du Cadaret Rising Côtes de Duras property which makes reds comparable with top St-Emilion (especially the Cuvée Raoul Blondin) and astonishingly complex whites.

Château des Eyssards The up-and-coming property of Pascal Cuisset, impassioned producer of astounding sweet Saussignac wines, especially the Cuvée Flavie, from 100 per cent Sémillon.

Domaines Grassa Yves Grassa was the man who established the reputation of Côtes de Gascogne in the mid-1980s, and is still among the top producers. Of the various labels, Domaines du Rieux, du Tariquet and de Plantérieu are the best.

Primo Palatum *Négociant* business producing small quantities of astonishingly concentrated wines from throughout the South-west (including Bordeaux).

Producteurs Plaimont Large co-operative organisation that makes reds and whites of good quality in several south-west appellations, but probably best known for white Côtes de Gascogne.

Elian da Ros Fairly new (1997) Côtes du Marmandais estate already on form with powerful chunky reds and a rather fine rosé.

Château Tirecul La Gravière Stunning Monbazillac buoyed up by a large proportion – 50 per cent – of Muscadelle. Most Sauternes struggle to keep up with the regular bottling, while the Cuvée Madame is mind-blowing (unfortunately so is its price).

Château Tour des Gendres Now the finest estate in Bergerac. Talented winemaker Luc de Conti produces rich but refined reds which repay keeping, as well as a range of lovely whites capped by the brilliant Anthologia, which can hold its own against almost anything from Pessac-Léognan.

GERMANY

Germany and France. No one would deny that there's a big difference between the wines made in each country; however, there is a similarity between the current state of the two wine industries. There is greater demand for the top wines than ever before, and as a consequence, the prices are on the increase. There are growers with holdings in some of the finest vineyard sites who are not making the most of their potential, and there are overachievers farming less favoured plots. There are exciting new estates emerging in places previously considered unsuitable for fine wines. In France, it's the southern Rhône and the Languedoc, in Germany it's parts of Baden and the Pfalz. And then there is a sea of wine which used to have a market, but which now, thanks to falling consumption and the rise of the New World, is surplus to requirements.

The impassioned *vignerons* of southern France (source of most of the surplus) reacted to this situation by overturning tankers of

foreign wine and wrecking government offices. And the Germans?
They are taking a much more measured, a much more German
approach. First of all, they gave us the relaunch wines, dry varietal
wines in clear Bordeaux bottles selling for less than £5 which were
launched – or re-launched – with seminars and presentations and
other fanfare. This they told us was what we should be drinking in
the post-Liebfraumilch era. The trouble was, most of the wines
weren't very impressive and they failed to excite both press and
consumers.

The latest initiative – 'How Germany is simplifying its dry-style
wine labels for consumers around the globe', according to the
German Wine Information Service – is Classic and Selection.
'Classic' is the designation for simple everyday wines made from
single grape varieties which are considered typical of each region.
For example, nine grapes are permitted in the Nahe, while only two
are allowed in the Rheingau. 'Selection' permits the same grapes,
but applies further regulations on such things as yields and
alcoholic content (a minimum of 12.2 per cent). In addition, the
wines must meet with the approval of a tasting panel.

The first Classic wines appeared in Spring 2001, while Selection
wines were set to appear in September 2001. At the time of writing

161

(June), we see very little move from UK retailers to embrace these new categories, and we can understand their reluctance. For us, the Germans are missing the point. It's almost as if every time they see a problem in their industry, the response is to produce another set of rules. More regulation is precisely what the Germans don't need. Indeed, a little more anarchy, as was the case with the Italian *vino da tavola* movement of the 1970s and 1980s, would be most welcome. That, and a willingness to acknowledge that other parts of the world can make cheap, dry (or dry-ish) white wines more efficiently. If we'd like to see the Germans plug anything, it is the superb Rieslings from the classic regions with which no one else in the world can compete. After all, if you spend all your time trying to improve your areas of weakness, you just finish up becoming average.

The German wine classification system

Around 98 per cent of Germany's production qualifies for the title of 'quality wine'. The fraction that doesn't comprises *Deutscher Tafelwein* and *Deutscher Landwein*. These are generally wines to be avoided, apart from some modern experimental ones which are only permitted to be called *Tafelwein* – their high price normally gives them away. The lower level of quality wine is *Qualitätswein bestimmter Anbaugebiete* (QbA), meaning quality wine from specific regions. QbA wines vary from the bland such as Liebfraumilch and friends to quite classy estate wines which in many cases may have been voluntarily downgraded from a higher quality level.

Süssreserve – unfermented grape juice – may be used after fermentation to alter the sweetness of the wine. Chaptalisation is permitted to increase the alcohol content of QbA wines. Indeed, some producers whose wines would qualify for QmP level (see below) opt for QbA status as they feel that chaptalising gives them a better wine. This is especially true for wines made in the southern reaches of the country from the Pinot family.

The higher level is *Qualitätswein mit Prädikat*. The QmP system categorises the wine according to the amount of sugar in the grapes at harvest rather than by the sweetness of the final wine. This means that from the same batch of grapes, a producer could make both a bone-dry wine and a sweeter wine which was lower in alcohol, and both would be labelled as *Spätlese*. The label gives few clues as to which style to expect, although the words *Trocken* (dry) and *Halbtrocken* (semi-dry) may offer some assistance (see also our comments in the introduction relating to Classic and Selection wines). Chaptalisation is not allowed for QmP wines, *Süssreserve* is, although its use is declining as the demand for drier wines grows.

QmP wines fall into one of six categories. The lowest grade is *Kabinett* (typically dry), then come *Spätlese* (off dry), *Auslese* (medium), *Beerenauslese* (sweet) and *Trockenbeerenauslese* (very sweet). The sixth category is *Eiswein*, which is made from grapes which have frozen on the vines after winter frosts and have been crushed before the ice has a chance to melt, thus concentrating the flavours. *Eiswein* is higher in acidity than the *botrytis*-affected *Auslese*, *Beerenauslese* and *Trockenbeerenauslese* wines.

According to this system, all vineyards and all grapes are created equal, so the finest Rieslings from sites on the slopes overlooking the Mosel and Rhine are thus given the same ranking as mass-produced Müller-Thurgau. This is patently nonsense, so the producers have taken things into their own hands. Founded in 1972, the Verband Deutscher Prädikatsweingüter e.V. (VDP) is a group of estates whose members have agreed to a set of regulations concerning preferred varieties, methods of viticulture, lower yields and a commitment to the higher-quality vineyards. Not all wines bearing the VDP symbol, a black eagle, on their capsules are great, and not all great estates have applied for membership of the organisation. However, the VDP stamp of approval is a more reliable measure of quality than anything in the wine laws.

Since the mid-1990s, some regions have taken this a stage further and come up with their own classification of vineyards, the *Erstes Gewächs* (first growths). The Nahe and Rheingau schemes stipulate that only Riesling is permitted, while the Pfalz system also includes Weissburgunder and Spätburgunder (Pinot Blanc and Pinot Noir). In order for a wine to be designated a first growth, it has to conform to certain requirements including yields and must be approved by a tasting panel.

As yet, these schemes are unofficial, and are by no means universally supported. Opposition naturally comes from those whose vineyards aren't included in the classifications, as well as from those who feel the system is too inflexible. Their argument is that if a site or a producer is superior to others the market will honour it over time regardless of whether it is classified or not. Such debate can only be healthy for wine lovers as both sides will be intent on making the best wines they can in order to plead their cause.

White wines – grape varieties and wine styles

Riesling

Apart from being unfairly tarred with the Liebfraumilch brush, Germany's greatest grape has also suffered in recent times from confusion of identity. Should it be made as a light and slightly sweet wine (often described as 'fruity'), or a dry (*trocken*) one? Adherents of both styles used a variety of historical evidence to back up their arguments as to which was the traditional Riesling wine.

At the heart of the debate is Riesling's acidity, which requires something to balance it. For quality producers, the alternatives are residual sweetness for the fruity style, and body – in other words alcohol and extract – for the dry or *trocken* styles. In cooler regions such as the Mosel, where the potential alcohol levels of wines even from good growers may only be 11 per cent, it makes more sense to make wines in the fruity style with around 8–9 per cent and some residual sugar. In warmer areas, where good growers have no problem achieving 13 per cent potential alcohol, there is a choice as to which style to make, and increasingly, the choice is to make a *trocken* wine. Even so, the *trocken* category permits up to 9 g/l of residual sugar, and most producers make full use of this allowance. (Those making cheaper, dry Rieslings resort to other means such as malolactic fermentation and occasionally oak ageing to knock off the gawky edges, but they are seldom successful.)

Providing they're well made, we enjoy both the full-bodied dry and the lighter fruity styles. The dry wines are better with food, although they need time in the bottle – three to four years at least – to flesh out. The fruity styles drink well from the word go, are the perfect summer aperitif, and usually outlast the dry wines. If you've had bad experiences with *trocken* Riesling in the past but are willing to give it another go, a good rule of thumb is to look for wines with at least 12 per cent alcohol.

The above comments apply to grapes which have not been affected by *botrytis*. Nobly rotted Riesling retains the citrusy, sweet 'n' sour flavours and fresh acidity and can vary from fairly delicate *Auslesen* to rich *Beerenauslesen* and *Trockenbeerenauslesen* which are not too far removed from liquid marmalade.

Müller-Thurgau
Or Rivaner as many now like to call it. Any change of name will do little to disguise the fact that this is not one of the world's great grapes. Unfortunately, it is widely grown, popular for its early ripening rather than for the vaguely flowery character of wines such as Liebfraumilch.

Silvaner
Solid, stolid even but capable of producing full-bodied, slightly earthy wines which sit very nicely with traditional German cuisine. Franken and the Rheinhessen produce the best examples.

Rülander/Grauburgunder
The Pinot Gris of Alsace also performs similarly in Germany, producing powerful spicy dry whites and luscious dessert wines, especially in Baden. Sometimes labelled Pinot Grigio.

Weissburgunder
Aka Pinot Blanc, another variety which has leapt over the border
from Alsace and is producing some full-bodied wines in the Pfalz
and Baden.

Scheurebe
Like it or loathe it, you can't ignore it. Dry versions from the Pfalz
are akin to liquid grapefruit and are falling out of favour. Sweeter
versions are less controversial and can be excellent.

Gewürztraminer
Never reaching the heady heights of Alsace, but capable of quite
charming scented wines in Baden and the Pfalz.

Chardonnay
Yes, it's there, but with Riesling around, one wonders why.

Red wines

The red wine boom which is sweeping the world has not passed
Germany by, and red varieties are now more widely planted than
Riesling. In particular Spätburgunder – Pinot Noir – is being put to
good use. Efforts in the Mosel and Rheingau generally fail to excite,
but some of the versions from Baden and the Pfalz are very good,
with supple cherry fruit and the occasional touch of Burgundian
silk. Shame they're so expensive. Names to look out for are Huber,
Hans Lang, Künstler, Fritz Keller, Vollmer, Dr Heger and Johner.
There is some Cabernet Sauvignon – avoid it; but do try Dornfelder,
Germany's answer to Dolcetto, and the spicy Lemberger.

Sparking wines – Sekt

Some of Germany's Sekts can command the same money as *prestige
cuvée* champagne on the home market. Even so, we're still hard
pushed to find many we enjoy. Some of the wines based on
Riesling are pleasantly fruity, but the assertive character of the
grape sits rather awkwardly with the bubbles. Those made from
the Pinot family are more promising, but few wines receive the
attention in production which quality sparkling wine demands.

THE REGIONS
Baden-Württemberg

With co-operatives dominating production, Baden is best known for
making large quantities of attractive easy-drinking Weissburgunder.

There are also some high-class estates making impressive Grauburgunder and Spätburgunder, although sadly, little of this ever leaves the region. Co-ops also dominate production in Württemberg, but once again, some quality-minded producers do exist. Reds are considered a speciality of the region, although sometimes it's hard to see why.

Franken
Bavaria is not just beer gardens and BMWs. The wines from Franken, often in the traditional *Bocksbeutel*, also deserve a try. Müller-Thurgau is the most widely planted variety, although the region is more famous for its rather earthy Silvaner which can take some getting used to, but goes splendidly with the hearty local cuisine. However, the best wines are made from Riesling.

Pick of the producers
Juliusspital Large and famous estate belonging to a hospital with holdings in all five of what are considered to be Franken's best vineyards. Riesling, Rieslaner, Silvaner and Weissburgunder all deserve attention.

Wirsching, Hans Elegant wines from an estate in the Steigerwald region with fresh but powerful Silvaner and Riesling.

Mosel-Saar-Ruwer
If you've never drunk a chilled Mosel *Kabinett* on a fine summer's day, you've missed out on one of life's greatest pleasures. This north-westerly region is the source of the quintessential German Riesling with a touch of sweetness, seemingly light but packed with flavour. With estate wines from great vineyards such as Wehlener Sonnenuhr and Ürziger Würzgarten still available at very reasonable prices, there is no reason to drink the dreary Müller-Thurgau which is still produced in large quantities.

Pick of the producers
Deinhard Taken over by the giant Henkell & Söhnlein corporation in 1997, at which point the great vineyards which formed the Wegeler-Deinhard estate reverted to the Wegeler family. Subsequent efforts have focused on larger-volume, cheaper wines from regions further south. D No.1, a Riesling/Pinot Blanc blend, is fleshy, aromatic and remarkably successful.

Robert Eymael/Mönchhof Classic wines from Ürziger Würzgarten and Erdener Pralat. Some of the Mosel's more convincing *trocken* styles, but the sweeter wines surpass them.

Friedrich-Wilhelm-Gymnasium Reliable, good-value Rieslings from vineyards bequeathed by Karl Marx's old school.

Fritz Haag Text book minerally Mosel Rieslings from Brauneberger Juffer-Sonnenuhr.

Reinhold Haart Theo Haart makes proper Piesporter from the Goldtröpfchen vineyard, with fleshy fruit in abundance.

Heymann-Löwenstein It's hard to find a more vocal supporter of dry German Riesling than Reinhard Löwenstein anywhere in Germany. Schieferterrassen – slate terraces – is his (very good) basic *cuvée*, and he also makes some fine *botrytis* wines.

Carl Aug. Immich-Batterieberg Firm, steely wines which need time in bottle to open out from vineyards blasted out of the rock face.

Jordan & Jordan Peter Jordan's wines from Scharzhof, Wiltingen and Ockfen are a delicious combination of minerals, acidity and fruit, and are proof that the Mosel can provide power with grace.

Karthäuserhof Superb, tangy, steely Rieslings from Christof Tyrrel's estate in the Ruwer.

Reichsgraf von Kesselstatt Large, reliable estate with extensive vineyards in various parts of the region, including Graach and Scharzhofberg.

Dr Loosen Ernie Loosen is one of the finest ambassadors for quality German wines. Everything, from the tangy Riesling QbA up to the *Auslesen* from Erdener Prälat and Ürziger Würzgarten, is of exemplary quality, and the clear labelling also deserves praise.

Egon Müller-Scharzhof Classic wines from the Saar, delicate, pure and long-lived.

J J Prüm Excellent wines from Graacher Himmelreich and especially Wehlener Sonnenuhr which are firm and fleshy in their youth and age brilliantly.

Max Ferd. Richter Dirk Richter's vineyards include parcels of Wehlener Sonnenuhr and Brauneberger Juffer. Wines range from dry and spicy to exquisite *Eiswein*.

Schloss Saarstein With fruit to the fore, these wines are accessible when young but also age well.

von Schubert Understated, impeccably balanced and fragrant wines from the Maximin Grünhaus estate overlooking the Ruwer.

Dr H. Thanisch, Erben Thanisch The better of the two Dr Thanischs in Bernkastel producing impeccable pure Riesling in the Badstube and Doktor vineyards. The latter is labelled Berncasteler Doctor, a tradition stemming from the time when these wines were very popular in England.

Nahe

The forgotten region of Germany, lying between the Mosel-Saar-Ruwer and Rheingau districts, lacking its neighbours' popularity but often competing with both in producing pure racy Riesling.

Pick of the producers
Paul Anheuser Attractive, forward and fruity wines from Kreuznach and Niederhäus.

Schlossgut Diel In a range where oak is often no stranger, Armin Diel's best wines are his Rieslings from the Goldloch, Burgberg and Pittermännchen vineyards in Dorsheim. Diel is also co-author of the Gault-Millau *German Wine Guide*.

Dönnhoff Memorable slatey Rieslings with magnificent fruit flavours from the Niederhäuser Hermannshöhle and Oberhäuser Brücke vineyards.

Staatliche Weinbaudomäne, Niederhausen-Schlossböckelheim The Nahe State Domaine has some of the best vineyard sites in the region, but in recent times has only occasionally realised the full potential of the vineyards.

Rheingau

The sun-kissed northern slopes of the Rheingau are potentially the source of Germany's greatest dry Rieslings, full-bodied, with fairly high alcohol, minerally intensity and ripe fruit flavours. That the many well-sited estates are not fulfilling this potential was shown in the early 1980s when the Charta group began to plug its drier wines. Many were simply not full-flavoured enough to stand up to such a style. The introduction of *Erstes Gewächs* (described earlier) will, we hope, turn growers' attention back to producing better fruit and improving quality in those glorious vineyards.

Pick of the producers
J B Becker Fine, racy Riesling and surprisingly good Spätburgunder.

Breuer Excellent, full-bodied dry Rieslings from the Rauenthal Nonnenberg and Rüdesheim Berg Schlossberg, as well as exquisite sweet wines and a fine sparkler.

Künstler Up-and-coming estate making finely structured Riesling and one of the region's best Spätburgunders.

Balthasar Ress Hattenheim-based Stefan Ress makes well-balanced wines from a number of vineyards.

Schloss Johannisberger Historic estate now owned by Henkell & Söhnlein whose drier Rieslings are improving to match the quality of its extremely good sweet wines.

Schloss Schönborn Large but inconsistent estate, capable of magnificent, intense wines but often falling short of its potential.

Robert Weil Power and delicacy are the hallmarks of this range, which excels in all styles from dry to sweet. Kiedricher Wasseros and Gräfenberg are the finest vineyards.

Rheinhessen

On one bank of the Rhine are sprawling vineyards of Müller-Thurgau destined to become Liebfraumilch and other similar wines. On the other are better-situated slopes, the source of some excellent Riesling and Scheurebe. Silvaner can be good, providing it comes from those south-facing slopes.

Pick of the producers
Gunderloch Classic and simply labelled Rieslings from the Rothenberg (red hill) vineyard in Nackenheim.

Heyl zu Herrnsheim Organically farmed estate based in Nierstein producing delicious fragrant wines.

Pfalz

This is arguably Germany's most dynamic wine region, where newer independent producers such as Lingenfelder, Koehler-Ruprecht and Müller-Catoir, who don't confine their activities to Riesling, rub shoulders with rejuvenated traditional estates such as Bürklin Wolf, von Buhl and Bassermann-Jordan. The three 'B's, as they're known, are now fully exploiting their first-class sites and have also shown that they too are not averse to a spot of innovation. If/When Germany finally re-establishes itself in overseas markets, the Pfalz could very well lead the way.

Pick of the producers

Bassermann-Jordan Stylish, well-balanced classic Rieslings from vineyards in Deidesheim and Forst – and a surprisingly good Chardonnay.

Reichsrat von Buhl On form since 1995 after years in the doldrums. The Armand Riesling *Kabinett* manages to combine the best of the ancient and modern aspects of German wines, while the wines from vineyards in Deidesheim and Forst are back among the finest in the region.

Bürklin-Wolf There are a few quirky wines such as a Cabernet Sauvignon and a Riesling/Silvaner blend named each year after a different operatic character. But the most satisfying wines remain the classic Rieslings from Forst, Deidesheim and Wachenheim.

Lingenfelder Notable fruity Riesling, Scheurebe, Spätburgunder and Dornfelder from the innovative Rainer Lingenfelder.

Müller-Catoir Despite not having vineyards in what are considered the best Pfalz sites, Hans-Günter Schwarz's top-quality Riesling, Scheurebe, Weissburgunder and Rieslaner make him one of the stars of the region.

Other regions

Apart from Toni Jost's lovely Rieslings from the Mittelrhein, it is rare to see wines on sale in the UK from Germany's other regions, the Ahr, Hessische Bergstrasse, Saale-Unstrut and Sachsen (the latter two in the former East Germany).

German vintage guide

Although 1987 was no great shakes, you have to go back as far as 1984 to find a truly dreadful German vintage. However, tread with caution through German vintage charts. Riesling is a late-ripening grape, and several growers, worried by the weather conditions, often pick before their fruit has fully developed.

2000 Apart from a wet July and a rather hot August, the weather had been favourable throughout the season, and a large healthy harvest was in sight. Then in early September, it rained, and didn't stop until most varieties had been picked. Riesling had a chance to dry out after the rain, but even so, problems with rot were not uncommon. Those prepared to go through the vineyard several times and only pick healthy grapes will have made some very good wines.

1999 A very favourable growing season resulted in a large crop, and this was further increased by rainfall in late September, which caused some grapes to swell up. Those who picked at this point will have made ripe if slightly dilute wines. Those who waited were rewarded with a dry October, and late ripening varieties such as Riesling and Spätburgunder were gathered in excellent condition, with high sugar levels and ripe acidity.

1998 With temperatures as high as 41°C, Germany had a summer which if anything was *too* hot. Many vineyards suffered in the excessive heat, with some growers losing as much as a quarter of their crop. Rain came in October, but many grapes had already been picked. The wines are rich in extract and acidity and have a great future. *Beerenauslese* and *Trockenbeerenauslese* wines are rare, but a mid-November frost resulted in the production of some splendid tongue-tingling *Eiswein*.

1997 The frosts and a subsequent summer drought reduced the size of the total crop, but the later-ripening grapes such as Riesling, Silvaner and Scheurebe were harvested in excellent conditions, with some top estates picking through to the second half of November. There was little *botrytis*, but producers have high hopes for their *Eiswein*. The ripe fruit and low acidity make this a very user-friendly vintage.

1996 A cool season saved by good weather in October. Those who had the nerve to hang on harvested their grapes in perfect condition, rich in sugar with concentrated flavours. Few *botrytis* wines were made, but there are some splendid Eisweine.

1995 Again late harvesters were rewarded, with a clement October following the rather damp August and September. This encouraged the development of *botrytis* and there are some fine concentrated wines.

Good earlier vintages 1993, 1990, 1989, 1988, 1985, 1983

GREECE

Greece might have an army of its own grape varieties (250 and counting) but there's no doubt about it, it doesn't have the bottles to take on the world. While the wines are certainly interesting enough to outclass many a Chilean Cabernet or Australian

Chardonnay, the quantity just isn't there to challenge these New World regions. Plus, all the action is at boutique level, and unfortunately this means prices tend to top that crucial £5.99 a bottle mark, not something that will endear them to the great British public.

North of Athens there's a co-operative called Thebes. It's an exciting new development, apparently, that's busy night-harvesting its white grapes to keep them fresh, crisp and flavourful. The wines this co-op will produce, we're promised will be available for £3.99. And that's what we wanted, isn't it? Is it? Shouldn't we be ashamed of ourselves? On the one hand, we complain bitterly about boring Australian Chardonnay, then, with the other, we demand Greece joins that very same cheap and cheerful club.

Thankfully, not only has Greece recently shaken up its whole wine industry to produce some stunning, highly individual wines for the international market, it's also toned up the Retsina act too. Like it or loathe it, Retsina is certainly crisper, more aromatic, cleaner and more complex than it has been.

Starting with the white grapes, Greece is producing some stunning Chardonnay and Sauvignon from Patras on the Peloponnese (southern Greece). These are wines from cool, coastal vineyards, the coolest of which also have stunning Riesling. Look also to the inland hills and 'Mantinia' (ski-slopes aren't uncommon in this region), for wines from the local grape Moscophilero. This was thought to be related to Gewurztraminer and has a similar rosewater/Turkish delight perfume, but on the whole it's crisper, with balancing acidity and is a better partner for red snapper, salmon or seafood.

Rhoditis is the Retsina grape, but don't let that put you off. Without the resin, it has its own toasty herbaceous qualities that (with good concentration) make it stunning. Also on the Peloponnese (coastal again), there's Lagorthi: soft and buttery, delicately fruity and aromatic, like dry herbs. Lighter, more lemony whites come from the islands: on Santorini Aïdani Aspro, Assyrtiko and Athiri vines need to grow so close to the ground to keep out of the strong winds, that they curl around themselves in small baskets. Robola on Cephalonia makes more rounded, fleshy wines with a hint of limey fruit.

Starting at the top, Aghiorghitiko is Greece's best red grape. Also known as Saint-George, though, unfortunately, Greek wine producers are fairly determined we get to grips with their difficult grape names, so the latter isn't a name you'll see too often on the bottle. Aghiorghitiko is like a variation on Cabernet Franc, making anything from juicy, sappy rosés to full-on brambly black monster wines: delicious. 'Ag' comes primarily from the Peloponnese, and the surrounding vineyards are also well suited to strapping Cabernets and Syrahs. Mavrodaphne is also local, and though usually made to churn out Mavrodaphne de Patras ('poor man's port'), also makes robust, tannic dry wines.

Further north, in more Balkan territory (Macedonia), home of fruit orchards and one or two bears, Xynomavro is the prize red grape in the appellations of Naoussa and Goumenissa. Similiar in structure to Pinot Noir, it has strawberries to Pinot's raspberries – it's an equally cantankerous customer in the vineyard, so pick your grower with care. Merlot and Syrah are good grape neighbours.

For sweet wines, look to the delicious thyme-scented Vinsantos of Santorini (made from those three 'A' grapes again), and Muscats such as the oily, sun-dried Samos Nectar.

2000 was a great year in Greece, and what better vintage to start a new look at this country?

Pick of the producers

Arghyros Santorini producer with the oldest and finest reserves of Vinsanto, plus lemony, dry whites.

Gaia Progressive Peloponnese estate for superb Aghiorghitiko (rosé versions to rich, dark cherryish wine) and, dare we say it, the finest Retsina.

Gentilini Boutique Chardonnay, Sauvignon Blanc and Robola from Cephalonia, made by British horticulturalist, Gabrielle Beamish.

Gerovassilou Esteemed Macedonia producer of fabulous, new-wave Chardonnay and Viognier.

Kyr-Yianni Merlot, Syrah and Xynomavro: aromatic, flavourful reds from the northern Naoussa region.

Constantin Lazaridis Crisp Sauvignons, herbaceous Assyrtico and rich dark Merlot: gaining depth as the vineyards gain age.

Oenoforos Vibrant, steely Asprolithi whites from the coastal cliffs of Patras. Anghelos Rouvalis brings out the best in Greek grapes.

Papaioannou A mixture of Greek and international grapes. Top is peony-scented red Aghiorghitiko from Nemea, Peloponnese.

Sigalas Charismatic Santorini grower Paris Sigalas makes superb Oia Assyrtiko and tangy, honeyed Vinsanto.

Spyropoulos Energetic modern Mantinia producer; also with ripe, rich Cabernet/Merlot/Aghiorghitiko blend.

Strofilia Half and half, Greek and cosmopolitan varieties, from trend-setting winery near Athens.

Tselepos Delicate whites: Gewurztraminer and Mantinia – can you taste the difference?

Others *Ktima Katsaros*, *Skouros*, *Thebes* co-operative, *Ktima Voyatzis*, *Zitsa* co-operative.

HUNGARY

Last year we put out a cry for more quality wines from Hungary – in the £5 and over price bracket. This year we do the same. There's still not much at the top end, unless you count Tokaji/Tokay (and we do of course, so more of this later), but first what of the oft-promised premium, dry wines? All is well at the cheap and cheerful end of the spectrum, with occasional local surprises such as the almondy, white Zenit grape making a welcome appearance, or tonsil-tingling spice-and-limey Irsai Oliver. Sappy Zweigelt and gutsy Kékfrankos (Blaufränkisch) do the same for the reds. But it's the usual suspects (Chardonnay, Sauvignon, Pinot Gris, Gewurztraminer, Cabernet and Merlot again) that we are bored with. Though they can be enticingly fruity from Hungary, more often than not, they're over-produced, thin and dilute. A shame, as there's nothing wrong with the conditions they grow in – the vineyards, temperature and climate are perfect.

Such quality as there is can often be traced back to small, private estates, although few of these wines are as yet being exported to the UK. Improvements can often also be linked to a foreign influence, as with Tibor G'al, former winemaker at Tenuta dell'Ornellaia in Tuscany, who makes some of the best wines in Eger in the north of the country. (Thummerer is the other star wine producer of the region.) Another name to look out for is Franz Weninger, who has an estate in Austria's Mittelburgenland. Weninger began his Hungarian exploits in the Villány region close to Croatia with a joint venture with Attila Gere, one of the top names in this very promising area, and has since acquired an estate in the Sopron region close to the Austrian border. The reasons for his rapid success are simple – he knows how to make wine, and he realises the importance of a healthy, low-yielding vineyard. If others follow his methods, there's no reason why Hungary shouldn't be occupying several more pages in this *Guide* ten years hence.

The efforts of flying winemakers and inspired locals, most notably A'kos Kamocsay of the Hilltop Neszmély winery, are all commendable too, and we especially like the highly individual results they have achieved from making dry wines with the Tokaji grapes, crisp, resiny Furmint and aromatic, limey Hárslevelű. These have the richness of Alsace Riesling or Pinot Gris and a similar tangy acidity – excellent food wines. As with Sauternes, however, the dry wines are not the main event, and they also tend to be expensive. All in all, we still have the feeling that Hungary could do better in the middle ground.

Tokay
In the past decade, much of the international interest and investment has been focused on the fabled sweet wines of Tokaj in north-eastern Hungary. And rightly so, we say – how many other wines are reputed to have revived fading monarchs on their death beds? Currently, Tokaji ('Tokay' in its Anglicised form) is Hungary's most important contribution to the wine world. A blend of Furmint with maybe a third Hárslevelű and a small amount of Yellow Muscat, it is made by adding a paste of ultra-ripe, often nobly rotten, grapes (Aszú) to a vat of wine, which reinitiates fermentation. The finished wine is graded according to how much of the Aszú paste was added. Wines of 3 to 5 puttonyos – literally 'buckets' – are fairly common, 6 puttonyos is rarer, and Aszú Eszencia, an 8-puttonyos wine, is rarer still. Tokay Eszencia is made from the treacle-like liquid which oozes out of the Aszú grapes before they are crushed. It takes ages to ferment – we've heard of wines that only reach four per cent alcohol after three years. Compared with the Tokajis from the Communist era, modern wines, often made by foreign producers, have the same burnt apricot, marmalade and honey flavours, but are fresher and more concentrated, and fully deserve their place among the sweet wine elite. Purists argue that this modern, pure-fruit style is wrong and that minerally, oxidised notes are in keeping with tradition. As only a few tired wines exist from the happier times preceding the last political regime, it is impossible to say who is right.

Estates to look out for are Domaine Disznókö, Château Megyer, Oremus, Château Pajzos, The Royal Tokay Wine Company and István Szepsy. Vintages to watch for (noble rot only thrives in the better ones) are 1993, 1995, and yet to be released 1998, 1999 and 2000 – 1993 and 2000 being by far the best.

INDIA

'Chantilli, you'll agree is wine divine. It's not the rhyme that matters but the experience sublime… time after time…' Quite. As yet, we in the UK haven't been subjected to the pleasures of

Chantilli, a range of still wines from Château Indage, but it is possible to find the same company's rather attractive Omar Khayyam sparkling wine. Indeed, it's the only Indian wine that is widely distributed here. Other producers exist in India, among them Grover Vineyards which benefits from the input of French consultant Michel Rolland and Champagne house Veuve Clicquot. However, we at the *Guide* have never tried the wines – have any of you? Do write and tell us.

ISRAEL

Until recently we were unlikely to see more than one, maybe two, modern-style Israeli wines on UK shop shelves. The kosher products were (and are) widely available, but the flash-pasteurising necessary to fulfil religious requirements regularly makes them, well to our mind anyway, undrinkable. Today we're pleased to report the exciting news that not only is there a new winery in Israel but a new quality-wine region too – and we'll be seeing the fruit of each on our merchant lists very soon.

Despite the fact that most of Israel is desert, under irrigation, it is as adept at producing quality wine as is neighbouring Lebanon. Indeed, many of the best are made in similar, high-elevation conditions less than 40 miles from the Bekaa Valley. Israeli wines are more 'New World' in style, where Lebanon's are heavily French-influenced. Lebanon has its serious reds, but from Israel (the best wineries anyway) there are a plethora of crisp Chardonnay, Sauvignon, Syrah and Sangiovese-type varietals (from higher, cooler sites, there's even Riesling and Gewurztraminer too). The best wineries are Yarden, in the Golan Heights, Domaine du Castel near Jerusalem (improving Bordeaux-style wines), Tishbi, Dalton and Margalit.

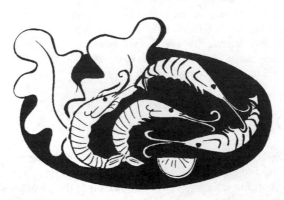

Back to that new winery. 'Galil Mountain' is a joint venture between Yarden and Kibbutz Yiron in the Upper Galilee. Being a peaks, streams and mountainside kind of area, the wines turn out very differently to those from the Golan plateau or the desert flats, and although it's early days yet (the first vintage was launched at Vinexpo 2001), signs are that the Merlot in particular is very good. (The added advantage of this site over the Golan Heights is that the vineyards are less likely to revert to Syrian control ...)

There are, too, new vineyards opening up all over Israel. Planting of quality rootstock has doubled over the last five years, firstly because more people are getting into wine, and secondly, because grapes are being seen as more successful than other fruit (dates or oranges, for example); the third factor clinches the deal: grapes need less water than other crops and water in the Israeli desert is expensive. Ever the optimists, we think these new plantings will go a long way towards improving the rather 'tired' kosher brands, and will also inspire other new wineries to follow Yarden, Domaine du Castel and Galil Mountain's footsteps. Let's hope so.

ITALY

Whatever your pocket or your palate, Italy has a wine for you. For those reared on the classic regions of France, there are structured, ageworthy reds from Tuscany and Piedmont, plus increasingly impressive whites from the north-east. For those more accustomed to the exuberant fruit of the New World, try the rich juicy offerings from the south of the country. There are classy sparklers, reds ranging from delicate to distinctly burly and whites of all sweetnesses. When it comes to the quality and sheer diversity of wines produced, only France can rival Italy.

If you don't hear more about Italian wines, the Italians themselves must take a fair amount of the blame. Other major wine-producing countries mount large campaigns to make sure that press, trade and consumers are kept up to date with the activities of their wine producers, but the generic promotion of Italian wines in the UK is almost non-existent. Indeed, in a UK wine trade calendar crammed to overflowing with tasting after tasting after tasting, the only event that presents the wines of Italy in a reasonable setting is organised independently by two Brits who have brought together the major importers of Italian wine under one roof. That tasting, however, is one of the most exciting of the year, not least because none of the wines sells for under £4.50 a bottle. Those who exhibit there are reporting that while sales of basic Chianti, Valpolicella and Soave are rather sluggish, interest in better-quality Italian wines is on the up, with restaurants leading the way. Better-off customers, who are interested in wine and looking for alternatives to either the classics or the New World, find Italy a happy-hunting ground. Indeed, thanks to their often high acidity and firm tannins, many Italian reds only begin to show their true colours when served with a meal.

Does this mean that you'll only find good Italian wines in a restaurant? Not at all. Over the past year, both Unwins and Oddbins (see *Where to buy wine*) have upgraded and enlarged their ranges, while many independent merchants are now confident enough to stock much more than a basic selection. Where once the shortlist for our Italian Merchant of the Year was a very short list, there are now several companies capable of making a coherent claim for the award.

We'd recommend you put yourself in the hands of one of these merchants since, despite the growth in popularity, Italy is still a challenge for the novice. There is nothing comparable to the 1855 Bordeaux classification or the Burgundian *grands crus* to tell you which are the best producers or vineyards. There are Chiantis that sell for £3.50 and others that cost £35. Great new wineries spring up every year; and there are over 2,000 different grape varieties, some of which deserve to be far better known and others of which deserve universal uprooting. But persevere with Italy, as it offers enough surprises, delights and top-class wines to satisfy even the most choosy of connoisseurs.

The Italian wine classification system

Italian wines are classified into four categories, the lowest of which is *vino da tavola* (VdT). Prior to 1996, many producers, especially those in Tuscany, chose to bypass the more rigid constraints of DOC and DOCG (see below) and release their top wines as *vini da tavola*. However, since 1996, a VdT can carry neither region of origin, nor grape variety, nor vintage (or at least that's the law – a few producers still choose to ignore it).

Today, most of the Super-Tuscans, as these wines from Tuscany became known, and the other top *vini da tavola*, belong to a new category called *indicazione geografica tipica* (IGT), although some now qualify for DOC or DOCG status. IGT is the equivalent of French *vin de pays* in that certain restrictions about grape varieties and production methods are required. As with *vin de pays*, quality varies from the basic to the sublime. For DOC (*denominazione di origine controllata*) wines, the regulations are more stringent, although this doesn't stop many dull wines receiving such a status. DOCG adds a '*garantita*', and quality is in general higher for these wines. However, with some – Vernaccia di San Gimignano, Albana di Romagna and Asti for example – the *garantita* is certainly not a guarantee of a high-class wine.

Vintages

Tuscany and Piedmont are the regions where it is most important to follow the vintages. Not that other areas are immune to the effects of the weather, it is just that the likelihood of their wines being kept for any length of time is rather less. Indeed, we would recommend that you drink up light Italian whites, and all but the best of the soft, fruity reds of the south, soon after purchase.

2000 was another fine vintage in Tuscany, with warm weather throughout the season making for an early harvest. Most grapes were picked before rain came in October, and quality is generally high. 1999 was potentially even better, although work in the vineyards was necessary to reduce yields. The best reds have the structure of 1998 and the plump fruit of 1997. 1998s are quite firm and lack the opulence of the vintages either side, but the best should age well and could surprise some critics. In 1997 it was very hot and sunny, and several splendidly ripe, fleshy wines with low acidity were produced. 1996 was more patchy, with some fair Chianti but other reds not quite up to scratch. The 1995 vintage was good, although low in quantity. As for older Tuscan vintages, look out for the great wines of 1988 and 1990, followed in rough order of merit by 1993, 1991, 1994, 1989 and 1992.

Fine conditions in spring and summer meant that Piedmont also had an early 2000 vintage. Rain fell in early October, but well-tended vineyards had already been picked by then. Early forecasts are for splendid reds. 1999 yields were as heavy as in Tuscany, and high August humidity in many vineyards may have caused some problems with rot. Even so, there is optimism about the quality. Rains towards the end of harvest caused problems in 1998, but while some reds are on the light side, the growers who had already picked most of their grapes before the worst of the weather have made excellent wines. 1997 brought very hot weather and very ripe grapes – wines made from fruit grown in cooler sites will keep best as the acidity will be higher. Still, this year was a fine one. 1996 was an excellent year for Barolo, in particular. The older vintages to look out for are 1988, 1989 and 1990. 1993 also produced reasonable wines although it suffered from autumn rain.

THE REGIONS
North-west – Piedmont, Lombardy

Piedmont is Italy's most mysterious and fascinating wine region. The softly sloping, fog-cloaked curves of the Langhe hills near Alba in Piedmont are home to Italy's most majestic and long-lived wines, Barolo and Barbaresco. Both of these graceful, perfumed giants are made from the Nebbiolo grape, and have high tannin and acidity levels which can jar on palates trained on soft New World wines. Persevere. These wines evolve from young treacly brooders to headily scented and surprisingly delicate, complex concoctions with a dazzling array of flavours – plums, raspberries, chocolate, tar, roses, game and more. Styles vary from modern, fruity-oaky wines to rather challenging and old-fashioned with more than a whiff of volatility. Choose your producer with care as style, quality and price vary enormously.

The Nebbiolo is used for an easier-drinking red from Roero in Alba, designed to be drunk in its youth, and also for the Nebbiolo Langhe DOC, which covers everything from light and friendly to really rather classy. The Nebbiolo-based reds Carema, Gattinara, Ghemme and Spanna are more easily approached than their sophisticated cousins in the Langhe, but quality is distinctly unreliable from these DOC and DOCGs.

When Nebbiolo is blended, its partner is usually the plump, plummy Barbera, and these wines can be immensely satisfying; Nebbiolo without the mountaineering. Barbera by itself has traditionally played second fiddle to Nebbiolo, being used for simple, fresh, everyday gluggers. However, a number of producers now award it more respect by planting it on the better sites, cutting the yields, vinifying it with care and dressing it in a new oak overcoat. The results can be stunning. Dolcetto, 'the little sweet one', is the third grape of Piedmont. It has traditionally behaved as the Gamay of Piedmont, producing fresh, bracing, cherryish reds for everyday drinking. But as with Barbera, a few producers are now giving Dolcetto a makeover, and producing chewy, chocolaty reds of some class.

White varieties play very much a secondary role in Piedmont, but a few are worth seeking out. Gavi DOCG is a rather neutral, acidic wine made from Cortese that commands a price rather higher than its quality often merits. The nutty, soft whites produced from Favorita grapes are better value, while the fuller, peachier wines made in Roero and Langhe from Arneis are better quality. Some modern, fruity Chardonnays are also made in the region. And then of course there is the fresh grapey Asti (the Spumante bit was dropped in 1994). It's one of the few sparkling wines we'd recommend with wedding cake, but most people are too snobby to serve it on such occasions. If Asti is just too naff for you, try the more refined, subtle, perfumed Moscato d'Asti.

Lombardy's best wines are also sparklers, namely those of Franciacorta, which are made by the *méthode champenoise* from the traditional champagne grapes (plus Pinot Bianco) and rank among Italy's finest. Still wines are less successful, although a few producers are making decent reds (from Cabernet Sauvignon and

Cabernet Franc) and whites (mainly from Chardonnay) under the Terre de Franciacorta DOC. Finally Lugana from along the shores of Lake Garda is one of the rare wines made from Trebbiano which has a little personality and elegance.

Pick of the producers (Piedmont, Lombardy)

Altare Master winemaker of Barolo, with full, rich Nebbiolo wines. Thanks (allegedly – a trial is under way) to a batch of faulty corks, don't expect to see several wines from 1997 and 1998.

Araldica/Alasia Large Piedmont co-operative which produces a modern, lively range, widely available in the UK at reasonable prices.

Braida/Giacomo Bologna Barbera specialist with a trio of very good, single-vineyard wines which are able to command Barolo-level prices. Also a partner in the Serra di Fiore winery, source of some of Piedmont's best whites.

Ca' dei Frati Delicious, lemony, nutty Lugana with Il Brolettino, an excellent, oak-aged *cuvée*.

Ca' del Bosco Lombardy estate making great Franciacorta fizz and fine, still wines including Bordeaux-style blend Maurizio Zanella and new Carmenero made from Carmenère.

Domenico Clerico Rising star making well-crafted Barolo, rich, ripe Dolcetto and sweet spicy Arte (Nebbiolo plus 15 per cent Barbera and Cabernet Sauvignon).

Aldo Conterno Master of Barolo, with top *cuvée* Gran Bussia being a real winner. The *barrique*-aged Il Favot, a Langhe Nebbiolo, is a fine and affordable introduction to the range.

Giacomo Conterno Powerful, traditional Barolo from Aldo's brother.

Fontanafredda Sleeping giant with excellent vineyard holdings, now back on track thanks to new management. Wines such as the Papagena Barbera d'Alba augur well for the future.

Gaja Influential producer who demonstrates that Nebbiolo can be internationally appealing without sacrificing its character. Highlights of an impeccable (but expensive) range are Sorí San Lorenzo, Sorí Tildin and Costa Russi, three single-vineyard wines that used to be sold as Barbarescos but have now been 'downgraded' to Langhe Rosso.

Bruno Giacosa Quality is high across the range of Barolo, Barbaresco, Dolcetto, Barbera and Arneis from traditional Piedmont producer.

Giuseppe Mascarello Admirable Piedmont reds – intense Barbaresco, Dolcetto and, of course, Barolo. The top Barolo, Monprivato, is deeply complex.

Oberto Highlights of an excellent range are the firm but fruity Barolo Vigneto Roche and the supple Nebbiolo/Barbera blend Fabio.

Prunotto Antinori-owned winery making grand Barolo Bussia and fine Barberas, especially Pian Romualdo. Occhetti Nebbiolo d'Alba is a good introduction to the range.

Bruno Rocca Barbaresco maestro, with two first-class but different _cuvées_, Rabaja and Coparossa. Chardonnay, Dolcetto and Barbera are also good.

Paolo Scavino The sumptuous, fragrant Bric del Fiasc and Canobric are among the finest modern Barolos, while the Barbera and Dolcetto also impress.

La Spinetta Superb throaty Barbaresco, equally fine Nebbiolo/Barbera/Cabernet blend Pin, plus delicious Barbera and Moscato.

Roberto Voerzio Modern Piedmont wines, brimming with fruit and new oak. Barbera, Dolcetto and Chardonnay all excel, but the Barolos, especially Brunate and Cerequio, are the stars.

North-east – Friuli-Venezia-Giulia, Trentino-Alto Adige, Veneto

Throughout most of Italy's wine regions, reds outshine whites. The north-east, however, bucks this trend, with its fresh, zesty whites being somewhat more serious than its light, quaffable reds. The best whites can be found in Friuli-Venezia-Giulia at the eastern edge of Italy on the Slovenian border, and in Trentino-Alto Adige, in the mountainous, German-speaking Südtirol. Friuli is the most highly respected region in Italy for single-varietal whites, and its fresh, pure Tocai Friulano, Pinot Grigio, Pinot Bianco and Sauvignon Blanc can be delicious, if sometimes pricy, particularly from the DOCs of Collio, Colli Orientali del Friuli (COF) and Friuli Isonzo. Reds are mainly soft, juicy Bordeaux blends, although there is a resurgence in popularity for the nutty, plummy Refosco grape.

Trentino-Alto Adige produces a wide range of whites, some from the German grape varieties Riesling, Gewürztraminer and Müller-Thurgau. Try Pinot Grigio and Chardonnay from the far north too – the German-influenced style is racy and crisp, lean and lemony. Here, as in Friuli, a small but significant band of producers are beginning to blend varieties to achieve extra complexity. Reds, again, are not terribly serious, but do try the local Teroldego Rotaliano, a deeply coloured, currant-packed and slightly bitter wine. Lagrein, another local grape, makes some excellent red wine and fair *rosato*, but you'll probably have to go there to find it.

Trebbiano vines growing on fertile plains provide the region near Verona with plenty of dull white wines, exemplified by the vast majority of Soave. The best wineries bypass the Trebbiano and instead squeeze much more character out of the native Garganega grape to produce a soft, lemon- and almond-oil-flavoured white. If you are looking for something cheap, the crisp, sherbety Bianco di Custoza is often a better bet. If you're looking for something sparkling, try the famous Venetian fizz Prosecco from the hills around Treviso, a light, again sherbety, wine which is made both sweet and dry. The best are known as Superiore di Cartizze.

The Veneto's most popular red is Valpolicella, which, like Soave, ranges from delicious to dire (the same is true of its close relative, the lighter Bardolino). Good examples are friendly reds with lively, cherry fruit, designed to be drunk in their youth, while better versions – where yields are lower, and the percentage of the region's best grape Corvina is higher – have more muscle and don't mind another three to four years in bottle.

More complex are the rich Amarone (dry and bitter) and Recioto (sweet) – late-harvest specialities made from grapes that have been dried before pressing to render them extra-concentrated. Recioto di Soave is the same idea applied to a white grape. All Recioto and Amarone wines are higher in alcohol than ordinary table wines – and they can be expensive too. It's worth trying them as they thoroughly deserve their Italian description *vini di meditazione* – buy a bottle and work out the translation for yourself. A halfway house between regular Valpolicella and Recioto/Amarone is the *ripasso* style, in which a young wine is passed over the detritus left after a Recioto/Amarone fermentation, and in the process acquires extra character and alcohol.

Pick of the producers (Friuli, Trentino-Alto Adige, Veneto)
Allegrini The top producer of single-vineyard Valpolicella, or IGT Veneto as it will now be labelled; also fine Amarone and Recioto, plus 100 per cent oak-aged Corvina La Poja.

Anselmi Fine range of IGT Veneto whites, which came under the Soave Classico classification until Roberto Anselmi withdrew them in protest about abuse of the DOC regulations. Some wines are barrel-fermented; also a toothsome, sweet Recioto called I Capitelli.

Bertani Large, reliable Valpolicella producer currently on great form.

Livio Felluga Whites that are slow to reveal their true colours, but which are as rich and concentrated as any in Friuli; also spicy, fruity Refosco.

Franz Haas Elegant, concentrated and fruity wines from Alto Adige.

Inama Superb, single-vineyard Soave and decent, modern Chardonnay.

Silvio Jermann Expensive, often brilliant, but sometimes rather pretentious range. Vintage Tunina is a juicy, white blend of five different grapes, while toasty, barrel-fermented Chardonnay is now labelled, 'Were Dreams, now it is just wine'.

Lageder Progressive Alto Adige winery turning out excellent but pricy Cabernet and Chardonnay. The more affordable Lagrein and Pinot Grigio are worth seeking out.

Maculan Superb range from Breganze in the Veneto. Maculan's luscious Acininobili and Torcolato are two of the country's great sweet wines, but the two Cabernets, labelled rather confusingly Fratta and Ferrata, are also great successes.

Masi First-rate Valpolicella Classico, Amarone and Recioto. Specialises in the *ripasso* style.

Pieropan Anyone bored with dull, dilute Soave should take a look at Pieropan's intensely ripe lemony examples, made with low-yielding vines.

Quintarelli Maverick producer using old-fashioned methods to craft intense and pricy Recioto, Amarone and Valpolicella. There's also a rare Amarone-style Cabernet.

Mario Schiopetto Pure, clean whites from Collio and COF, with Sauvignon and Pinot Bianco being especially successful.

Fratelli Tedeschi Superior range from the Veneto, including Amarone, Recioto and Soave.

Villa Russiz Superb range of powerful aromatic Collio whites, plus a rather good Merlot.

North-central – Emilia-Romagna

Emilia-Romagna is the broad swathe of land that stretches almost right across Italy just below the Po river. This is the land of Parma ham, Parmesan cheese, Bolognese sauce and balsamic vinegar, so it sounds as though the region should make a plentiful supply of easy-drinking wine to wash it all down. And it does, in the shape of Lambrusco – typically not the sweet, sickly stuff exported to the UK but a local, dry version, which is frothy and tart and a fitting match for the rich regional food. Co-operatives dominate its production – there are few boutique wineries here.

Otherwise, the rather ordinary white Albana di Romagna is an undeserving recipient of DOCG status, although the sweeter *passito* versions can be delicious. More noteworthy is Sangiovese di Romagna, the best versions of which can stand their ground alongside more expensive Chiantis.

Central Italy – Tuscany

For all Nebbiolo's intensity and complexity, Sangiovese remains the red grape that most outsiders associate with Italian wine. It may be more widely planted in Emilia-Romagna, but most people think of Tuscany as its spiritual home. Some of Italy's finest and most famous reds come from the hilly countryside to the south and east of Florence, and although only two wines have to be 100 per cent Sangiovese – Brunello di Montalcino and its less serious, younger brother Rosso di Montalcino – this grape lies at the heart of all the finest DOC and DOCG wines.

Chianti is the best-known wine but can be somewhat confusing to the novice. The wines, a blend of Sangiovese with Canaiolo and other grapes (both white and red), range from examples so dilute they could almost pass for rosé, to full-bodied wines similar in structure and ageing potential to claret. What most Chiantis have in common is a distinctive tea-leaf and herb note, plus the juicy cherry-meets-strawberry fruit of Sangiovese. The region has seven sub-zones, the best of which are Classico and Rufina. Since 1996, Sangiovese wines can be labelled Chianti Classico, something less law-abiding producers have been doing for several years.

Brunello di Montalcino is also well known outside Italy and commands a higher price than many Chiantis. It can range from one of Tuscany's most memorable experiences to one of the most disappointing, the latter usually a result of excessive oak ageing. Many producers choose to sell their wines as Rosso di Montalcino, which can be sold a year after vintage rather than after four years (five for *riserva*), two of them in barrel, which are the law for Brunello. Vino Nobile di Montepulciano, not connected with the Montepulciano grape of the Marches and Abruzzi, can be a decent halfway house between Chianti and Brunello, although it is not the most reliable of wines. Parrina is similar to a medium-bodied Chianti, with a herbal or minty hint, while the rarely seen Morellino di Scansano is beefier and more rustic.

Cabernet Sauvignon is becoming increasingly important in Tuscany. Sometimes it is blended with Sangiovese, as witnessed in the lesser-known appellations of Carmignano and Pomino and in numerous IGT wines, and sometimes it appears with Bordeaux bedfellows Merlot and Cabernet Franc, again often under an IGT. Some of the best Cabernet blends are made in Bolgheri, home of Sassicaia and Ornellaia. Merlot by itself is as erratic as it is anywhere in the world, but the best, such as Ornellaia's Masseto, give top Pomerol a run for its money. Syrah is not as popular but there are already some delicious examples.

As for whites, few exist that can compete with the reds of the region. Vernaccia di San Gimignano DOCG is a pleasant white with lean, limey flavours. Tenuta dell'Ornellaia makes a decent Sauvignon called Poggio alle Gazze, while several wineries listed below have risen to the challenge of creating successful Chardonnay. Tuscany's most intriguing white is still *vin santo*, the 'holy wine', a *passito* sweetie made from white grapes left to shrivel and dry before being squeezed of their concentrated syrup. The best are sweet (but not as sweet as many dessert wines) and strong, with flavours of nut oil and tart citrus peel.

Pick of the producers (Tuscany)

Altesino Smooth Brunello di Montalcino, pleasant Rosso and a relatively inexpensive Cabernet/Sangiovese blend, Alte d'Altesi.

Antinori Pioneering company, greatly influential in its use of Cabernet Sauvignon to create the Super-Tuscans Tignanello (Sangiovese/Cabernet Sauvignon) and Solaia (Cabernet Sauvignon), but also with fine Chiantis and, from the 1995 vintage, a Brunello from the Pian delle Vigne estate.

Avignonesi Upmarket Vino Nobile di Montepulciano and Super-Tuscan, Cabernet-dominated Grifi, plus admirable Merlot, Chardonnay and *vin santo*.

Badia a Coltibuono Rich, long-lived reds, especially 100 per cent Sangiovese Sangioveto, made at an historic abbey estate in Chianti Classico.

Banf Huge estate just outside Montalcino, built with money made from exporting Lambrusco to the USA. Wide range of decent wine, especially Brunello and Chardonnay.

Biondi-Santi Original producer of Brunello di Montalcino and responsible for its DOCG status. Traditionally rather old fashioned (and very pricy); more recent vintages, while sturdy, have shown much more fruit. Also good wines from sister estates Poggio Salvi (Brunello) and Castello di Montepo (Morellino).

Capezzana Historic Tuscan estate which almost single-handedly created DOCG Carmignano with its trail-blazing Cabernet and Sangiovese blends.

Castellare Chianti Classico estate best known for its excellent Super-Tuscan I Sodi di San Niccolò – Sangiovese with a touch of Malvasia Nera. Recently announced new joint venture on the Tuscan coast with owners of Château Lafite.

Castello di Brolio Chianti Classico of depth and majesty – the 1997 is a stunner – plus impressive if a little 'international' Sangiovese/Merlot blend Casalferro. The regular Brolio Chianti Classico is no slouch either.

Castello di Fonterutoli Another fine Chianti Classico estate, which also makes the juicy but powerful Sangiovese/Merlot blend Siepi.

Castello dei Rampolla Back on form after a shaky patch with Tuscan reds, both with the fulsome, easy-drinking Chianti Classico and the Sammarco *vino da tavola*, a Cabernet/Sangiovese blend.

Felsina Berardenga A name to seek out: lovely I Sistri Chardonnay, great, barrel-aged Sangiovese Super-Tuscan Fontalloro and rich Chianti Classico.

Fontodi Delicious 100 per cent Sangiovese Flaccianello della Pieve and fine Chianti Classico. Look out too for the Syrah.

Frescobaldi Aristocratic family of Chianti-producers with an ancient estate in Rufina. Classy wines, especially the Chianti Riservas and Cabernet-based Mormoreto; also a leading producer of red and white Pomino. (See also *Luce*, below.)

Isole e Olena Paolo De Marchi is resurrecting an old family estate in Piedmont, but Tuscany remains his passion for the moment. Great range including top-notch Chianti Classico, Cepparello (Sangiovese) and an excellent, rich Chardonnay.

Luce Joint venture in Montalcino between Frescobaldi and the Robert Mondavi Winery of California to make classy, if pricy, Sangiovese/Merlot blend. Second wine Lucente also good but still expensive.

Monte Vertine Best known for 100 per cent Sangiovese Il Pergole Torte, one of the most delectable Tuscan reds.

La Parrina Inexpensive and juicy reds based on Sangiovese and made on the coastal DOC of Parrina.

Poliziano Arguably the finest producer of Vino Nobile di Montepulciano, also excelling with Sangiovese/Cabernet Sauvignon blend Elegia and 100 per cent Cabernet Le Stanze.

Querciabella Chianti Classico and *vino da tavola* Camartina in the fruity, modern style.

Rocca della Macie Well-known and reliable Chianti Classico house.

Sassicaia This remarkable estate, near Bolgheri on the Tuscan coast, is home to probably the most famous of the Super-Tuscans. The blend of Cabernet Sauvignon and Cabernet Franc was first developed by the Marchese Incisa della Rochetta, and Antinori now markets the wine. Deeply sophisticated, world-beating red, which since 1994 has had its own DOC, Bolgheri de Sassicaia.

Selvapiana The leading Chianti Rufina estate, with a particularly impressive Riserva called Bucerchiale.

Tenuta dell'Ornellaia Top-class Bolgheri winery run by Lodovico Antinori, cousin of Sassicaia's proprietor, and part-owned by California's Mondavi. Ornellaia is a fulsome, classy Bordeaux blend, while Masseto is arguably Italy's best Merlot, with a price to match. New wine (from the 1997 vintage) Serre Nuove is a good, earthy, cheaper substitute, while Le Volte is even more approachable and immediately gluggable. Sauvignon Blanc (Poggio alle Gazze) is crisp and lean.

Tenuta del Terriccio Fine range of IGT Toscano includes rich peachy Rondinaia (Chardonnay/Sauvignon), densely structured Lupicaia (Cabernet Sauvignon/Merlot) and fragrant, juicy Tassinaia (Cabernet Sauvignon/Merlot/Sangiovese).

Fattoria Zerbina Top winery in Emilia-Romagna, making substantial Sangiovese di Romagna, dense, cherryish Marzieno (Sangiovese/Cabernet) and luscious Albana di Romagna Passito Scacco Matto.

Umbria, Abruzzo, Lazio

Each of these regions is responsible for an ocean of dull white wine. Orvieto comes from Umbria, where it dominates the local wine industry. More adventurous drinkers should instead look out for finer whites from Antinori's Castello della Salla project in the region. Other interesting Umbrian wines include the red Torgiano from Lungarotti, particularly the Rubesco Riserva made from Sangiovese and Cannaiolo, and the Amarone-like Sagrantino di Montefalco from Sagrantino.

The whites of Abruzzo are made predominantly from the uninspiring Trebbiano grape, so more yawns there. More exciting is the juicy red Montepulciano d'Abruzzo, pizza wine par excellence (no mean feat, that). The neighbouring province of Marches also uses Montepulciano in Rosso Conero, where it can be blended with Sangiovese. Bringing blessed relief after an excess of Trebbiano is Verdicchio, responsible for the zesty yet creamy wines of Verdicchio dei Castelli di Jesi.

Lazio's vinous claim to fame is Frascati, made mainly from Trebbiano and Malvasia and, as if you didn't know it already, all too often lacking in character (Castel de Paolis is an honourable exception). The other notable white – famous for its name rather than its quality, although wines have improved of late – is Est! Est!! Est!!! di Montefiascone. The admirable Falesco shows what can be achieved with a little effort in both the red and white departments.

Pick of the producers (Umbria, Abruzzo, Lazio)
Antinori Whites from Umbria under the Castello della Sala label are excellent, especially the fine Chardonnay, called Cervaro.

Bigi A rare Orvieto producer – one managing to inject some character into its wine.

Castel de Paolis Super estate which catapults Frascati into fine wine territory. Top *cuvée* is Vigna Adriana, made from Malvasia and Viognier. Also good reds based on Syrah, including firm but fruity Syrah/Merlot blend I Quattro Mori.

Falesco Lazio star owned by famous consultant winemaker Riccardo Cotarella, best known for sexy, spicy Montiano (100 per cent Merlot). Also the best Est! Est!! Est!!! in the form of the Poggio dei Gelso Vendemmia Tardiva, plus smooth peaches-and-cream Ferentano made from the local Roscetto grape.

Lungarotti Formerly the leading light of Umbria's Torgiano, which put the DOC on the map using Sangiovese and Cabernet for a wide range of high-quality varietals and blends. Now fading slightly.

Umani Ronchi Large, reliable range including rounded, nutty Casal di Serra Verdicchio, white, silky 100 per cent Montepulciano Cumaro and superb Montepulciano/Cabernet/Merlot blend Pelago.

Valentini Montepulciano and Trebbiano d'Abruzzo of real class, both of which age magnificently.

The South

As in much of southern Europe, the south of Italy is enjoying something of a mini wine boom, as wine drinkers all around the world get to know the fascinating local grape varieties. The best of these are Negroamaro, with its bitter chocolate and cherry flavours, and Primitivo, genetically the same (although a few disputes linger on) as California's Zinfandel. Puglia is perhaps the best source of good everyday reds, with modern, fruity wines often under the IGT Puglia, together with more leathery, raisiny offerings from the DOCs of Salice Salentino, Copertino and Squinzano.

Campania boasts two whites of interest, the dry, fruity Greco di Tufo and the concentrated, nutty Fiano d'Avellino, which ages well. For reds, Taurasi, made from Aglianico can be very good, but the grape reaches its apogee in Aglianico del Vulture, which, from a top producer such as d'Angelo, is one of Italy's best-kept secrets. Calabria's only wine of note is Cirò, which comes in red, pink and white and is made on the eastern Ionian coast of the region from the local Gaglioppo grape. Quality is not a strong point, although the reds from Librandi are very respectable.

Pick of the producers (the South)
A Mano Promessa Excellent, modern wines from Mark Shannon, with the Primitivo a dead ringer for a fine Zinfandel from his native California.

Candido Smooth, herbal-scented reds mainly made from Negroamaro in Salice Salentino. Relative bargains, but whites are less impressive than reds.

Cantina Sociale Copertino More great-value co-operative reds, mostly made from the Negroamaro grape to exacting standards.

Feudi di San Gregorio The current star of Campania, offering high-class modern Taurasi as well as some of southern Italy's best whites.

Librandi Top exponent of the light red Cirò Rosso, made from the Gaglioppo grape in Calabria.

Mastroberardino The best-known name of Campania can still be relied on for Greco di Tufo, Fiano d'Avellino and Taurasi. However, a recent family split has left one branch with the name and the winery, and the other, under the name Terredora, with the vineyards.

Taurino Delicious, smooth, fruity red from Salice Salentino.

Trulli Name used for wines made by the flying winemaker Kym Milne MW in conjunction with the local winemaker Agusto Càntele. All are commendable, with the refreshing, dry Muscat making a perfect aperitif.

The islands

While progress has not been as rapid as on mainland Italy, Sardinia and Sicily both have their movers and shakers who can turn their hands to local and foreign varieties with aplomb. Sardinia offers the tangy but usually rather bland Nuragus de Cagliari, as well as reds made from Cannonau (Grenache), Carignano (Carignan) and Monica, which is believed to be of Spanish origin. Where yields are low, both Carignano del Sulcis and Cannonau di Sardegna can be wonderfully rich, robust wines.

Sicily is more dynamic than it has ever been, with wineries such as Regaleali, Planeta, Settesoli and Terre di Ginestra now leading the way with fresh, modern wines. At Marsala, the local fortified wines are too often over-sweetened, but better versions from producers such as de Bartoli and Pellegrino still delight with their complexity and subtlety. Lastly, the island of Pantelleria, lying halfway between the mainland and Libya, offers a vinous speciality. Here Moscato grapes, known locally as Zibibbo, are used to make a honeyed, sweet *passito* wine.

Pick of the producers (the Islands)
Argiolas Fine range of Sardinian reds and whites, both dry and sweet, made from both famous and local grapes – ever heard of Bovaleddu? Top wine is sexy, oaky Turriga, a blend of Cannonau, Carignano, Sangiovese and Malvasia Nera.

Marco de Bartoli The best producer of Marsala, an ever-inventive, colourful local figure. Also makes the lovely Moscato Passito di Pantelleria, an unctuous dessert wine with hints of nut-oil and citrus peel.

Cantina Sociale Dolianova Sardinia's premier co-operative, making tasty Nuragus white.

Duca di Salaparuta Corvo Rosso isn't terribly exciting, but the Duca Enrico blend is smashing, one of the best in Sicily.

Salvatore Murana Murana's Moscato and Passito di Pantelleria are world-class dessert wines, with the Martingana Passito being astonishingly complex.

191

Pellegrino Fine Marsala producer, especially for dry styles.

Planeta Sicily's star winery, whose first vintage was 1994. High quality across the range, but the top wine is the red Santa Cecilia, a robust blend of local grape Nero d'Avola with Shiraz.

Regaleali Highly respected Sicilian estate using local grape varieties for richly flavoured reds, the most famous of which is the full-bodied Rosso del Conte, a blend of local varieties. Also fine, if expensive, Chardonnay.

Sella & Mosca Sardinian perfectionists, producing good DOC Vermentino and exciting Marchese di Villamarina red blend. Also make wine in France's Costières de Nîmes.

Cantina Sociale Santadi If you didn't think Carignan was capable of quality, try the Rocca Rubia *cuvée* from this first-class co-operative.

Cantina Sociale Settesoli Modern Sicilian wines. Look out, in particular, for the red Bonera and white Feudo dei Fiori, made from blends of local grapes. Mandrarossa is new premium range.

Terre di Ginestra Modern, fresh Sicilian table wines.

LEBANON

Far be it from us to seek out only the modern wines, but it appears that Chateau Musar's place at the top of the Lebanese tree is about to be toppled by its Bekaa Valley neighbours. Musar's classic Cabernet blend has long been synonymous with Lebanese winemaking, and has survived against horrific odds, trucking fruit across war-torn hills to its cellars north of Beirut. It is still, by far, the most widely available Lebanese wine in the UK, and still highly commendable, but, we feel that recent vintages have been a little too oxidised – that the wines are beginning to look old and tired a touch before their time. Better survivors of the baking Mediterranean temperatures are the new-wave producers we hinted at last year. Chateau Kefraya's wines run the gamut from thick-textured, nutty, surprisingly good white Cuvée d'Aïda (Sauvignon/Chardonnay/ Viognier), through delicate rosé, to powerful blueberry-blackcurrant reds that could give Barossa Shiraz or top Chilean Merlot a run for their money. Clos St Thomas, a newcomer in 1994, also has impressive, ripe, structured reds. Chateau Ksara, a little more classic in style, makes Cabernet blends that are a fabulous mix of spice, cedar and berries that need a fair bit of cellar time to soften. And finally there is Massaya, a partnership between a local businessman Sami Ghosn and three Frenchmen, Hubert du Boüard de Laforest (Château Angélus), Dominique Hébrard (ex-Cheval Blanc) and Daniel Brunier (Vieux Télégraphe). The wines (three reds, two whites, one rosé) are good rather than great, but we expect great things in the future.

LUXEMBOURG

Just as the Luxembourgers probably see precious little English wine, so you'll struggle to find anything from the vineyards along the banks of the Moselle, in the cantons of Remich and Grevenmacher, in UK shops. Yields of varieties such as Elbling and Müller-Thurgau are generally too high to produce anything of note, and although some better-quality varieties, notably Riesling, can be found, we've never tasted anything that excited us.

MACEDONIA

The birthplace of Alexander the Great offers growing conditions that are almost perfect for making high-quality wines, both red and white. However, wine production isn't high on the current Macedonian agenda, and the vineyards and wineries need considerable attention. In the right hands, grape varieties such as Vranac, Kratosija (both red) and the white Zilavka could no doubt be put to good use, and we've even tasted a decent Chardonnay. But as for finding them in UK shops, don't hold your breath.

MEXICO

Don't be surprised if you hear more about Mexican wine in the future. While much of the country is too hot for vines, there are regions where altitude and proximity to the sea provide good conditions for grape-growing. Most vineyards are on the Baja California peninsula, and top producers such as Château Camou, L A Cetto, Casa de Piedra, Monte Xanic and Santo Tomás make wines that improve with each vintage. Casa Madera from the Parras Valley in Monterrey is another name to look out for. Cabernet Sauvignon and Chardonnay are widespread, although other varieties such as Tempranillo (from Casa de Piedra, Nebbiolo and Petite Sirah (both L A Cetto) can be found.

The number of wineries is small, but growing, and in the future Mexican wines may well be more visible on UK shelves.

MOLDOVA

While several Eastern European countries have the potential to make high-class wines, none gives quite the same sense of so-near-yet-so-far as Moldova. Not only are there large plantings of popular grape varieties such as Cabernet Sauvignon, Merlot, Pinot Noir, Chardonnay, Pinot Gris, Riesling and Sauvignon Blanc, there are also a number of local varieties of note, among them Saperavi, Black Sereskia and Gamay Fréaux. The climate is favourable and the soils are good, but, sadly, it's the same story as elsewhere in this part of the world – the vineyards need attention, the wineries are poorly equipped, good wines are crippled by bad storage conditions before they see the inside of a bottle, the transport system is inefficient and the bureaucracy is a nightmare.

MONTENEGRO

We'd like to see some more of the chewy, spicy red Vranac that occasionally surfaces from this coastal region of the former Yugoslavia. A wine or two from the snappily titled co-operative Agrokombinat '13 Jul' sometimes pass our way, but otherwise we struggle to recall any other Montenegrin wines we've tasted.

MOROCCO

Strapping Moroccan wines were once widely used for padding out poorer French reds (most notably, burgundy), but independence from France and tighter appellation laws put a stop to all that in the 1950s and 1960s. After that, Morocco really only had tourists to cater for. Today, it looks as though the French are returning the favours once dealt them, with investors such as Castel working hard to restore the country's decaying vineyards. We'd even go so far as to say that you won't get a better accompaniment for your *tagine* than one of the new spicy, heart-warming Syrahs – though perhaps it's a little early to generalise. Good things are emerging from the Celliers de Meknès, which has long been among the more progressive growers (fruity, raspberryish Grenache/Cinsaut; black-fruited, smoky Syrah). Better still are the high-altitude (650m) wines from Atlas Vineyards, made with stainless-steel technology, low yields, French experience and more 'understood' varieties – Cabernet, Syrah and Merlot. Atlas Vineyards' Domaine Larroque and El Baraka premium labels are supple and delicious, and at around £5 a bottle, they're a steal.

Moroccan whites and rosés are improving, but it's the reds you should go for. The *appellation d'origine garantie* system, modelled on the AC classification in France, is a good pointer to quality, though poor labelling frequently means these are some of the hardest wines to sell.

NEW ZEALAND

In February 2001 the New Zealanders held their 20th annual trade tasting in the UK, with 65 producers and more than 400 wines on show. Developments in the Land of the Long White Cloud since the first such event in the early 1980s have been dramatic, and signs are that the Kiwis still have their foot firmly on the fast pedal. The area under vine has more than doubled since 1990, while the number of producers has soared in the same period from around 130 to almost three times that figure. Indeed, hardly a month goes by without a new winery being drawn to our attention.

What has encouraged us most in recent years is the way in which the wines themselves have matured. Time was when any new winery's portfolio would typically consist of a startling Sauvignon Blanc, two slightly sterile Chardonnays – one oaky, one not-so-oaky – and maybe a rather vegetal Cabernet-based red. Today, not only is the diversity much more marked, with varietals such as Syrah, Pinot Gris, Pinot Noir, Merlot and Riesling increasingly in favour, but there's also far more complexity to be found in the wines, even the Sauvignons.

Some of the improvement can be traced back to the cellar, where winemakers seem to be a little less clinical and formulaic in their techniques than was once the case. However, it's in the vineyards that the real developments are taking place. Much more thought is now going into which sites to exploit, which varieties will grow best there and how best to cultivate them. All varieties have benefited from the rise in standards of viticulture, but the improvement has been especially noticeable with red grapes. The wines now have much less of the underripe, green pepper character that used to make them so distinctive but not necessarily so enjoyable. It was with whites, Sauvignon Blanc and Chardonnay in particular, that New Zealand made its name, but don't be surprised if in the future the red wines capture more of the headlines.

As for which regions will prove most successful in the future, it's far too early to say. New Zealand is a long way away from grading its various *terroirs* in Burgundian fashion, but sub-regions are already beginning to make a name for themselves. Where once it was sufficient to know about Marlborough, Nelson and Hawke's

Bay, we now have to familiarise ourselves with districts within these, such as the Awatere Valley, Upper Moutere and the Gimblett Gravels. Gimblett Gravels, part of Hawke's Bay, is something of a first for New Zealand in that it is the only district whose boundaries are defined by soil type rather than by geographical features or roads. As yet, it is only an unofficial appellation, but the producers who form the Gimblett Gravels Association hope that that will change in the future. Certainly, several of Hawke's Bay's finest reds come from this 2,000-acre plot of deep stony soil.

Finally some corporate news. Some of New Zealand's largest wine companies have been changing hands in the past 12 months. The Austral-American wine conglomerate Beringer Blass now controls Auckland-based Matua Valley, while BRL Hardy has finally taken a controlling interest in Nobilo, also of Auckland. But it is Montana, New Zealand's largest wine producer, that has seen the greatest upheavals. Just as the 2001 edition of the *Guide* hit the bookshop shelves, the news broke that Montana had taken over its rival Corbans, the country's second largest wine business, to form a company that now makes more than half of the country's wine. Then in February 2001, Montana itself was subject to takeover bids both from the British drinks giant Allied Domecq and from the Australian brewers Lion Nathan.

Quite who will end up in charge of Montana had still not been settled as we went to press, but whoever it is, we hope that the new owners don't take any steps that could damage the quality of the wines. The standards Montana has maintained ever since that first annual trade tasting have been exemplary for such a large organisation, and go a long way to explaining New Zealand's extraordinary rise in fortune in the last two decades.

White wines – grape varieties

Sauvignon Blanc

Sauvignon and New Zealand are synonymous in many wine drinkers' minds. In particular, wines from the ancient stony riverbeds of Marlborough have grabbed the world's attention with their vivid flavours, variously described as gooseberries, asparagus, tomato leaf, freshly cut grass, mixed herbs, blackcurrant leaf, and even sweaty armpits. Today's wines are more restrained and complex than was once the case, and some producers blunt the gawky edges by using a touch of oak for fermentation and ageing, or by blending in some plumper Semillon. If you find Marlborough's flavours a little *too* overwhelming, try the wines of Hawke's Bay, which are rounder, riper and softer. If you'd prefer something in between, try Sauvignon from Wairarapa.

Chardonnay

For a while it looked as though New Zealand's Chardonnay was being overlooked by British drinkers in favour of its Sauvignon Blanc. But the excellence of Kiwi Chardonnay produced on both islands has now become apparent, and it is selling well in the UK. Chardonnay's malleability makes it hard to pin down regional styles. The further north you travel in New Zealand, the richer and riper the wines should become, but we've had wonderfully fleshy wines from Central Otago and equally rather weedy ones from much warmer spots on the North Island. Wines veer from the simple, fresh, tropical fruit salad in a glass to the quasi-Burgundian, in which the fruit flavours have been deliberately underplayed in favour of greater complexity. This is much more a function of winemaker than region.

Riesling

We're thrilled to see that Riesling plantings are on the increase (admittedly from a low base) – for us, the wines outclass Sauvignon almost every time. The style in the 1980s was to make wines with some residual sweetness, but many wines today are bone dry and can in some instances reach 14 per cent alcohol. Pithy lime and apple flavours run through many, and their dryness can make them quite reserved when young. At two years old, however, they blossom, and many are built to drink well for a decade or more. Good and great Riesling can be found in the Wairarapa and any of the South Island regions. *Botrytised* Riesling can also be delicious, but at present it can't be imported into the UK – ask your MEP why, because we don't understand it.

Others

As elsewhere, Pinot Gris is currently very trendy in New Zealand. Also as elsewhere, dull versions abound, but there are some fine, mineral-tinged wines from Central Otago, Marlborough and Wairarapa that hover between the crispness of Italian versions and the opulence and spice of Alsace. Gewurztraminer can also be wonderfully aromatic, but it's criminally unfashionable. A few producers make Chenin Blanc, either in a lemony, often oak-tinged, dry guise or as a sumptuous sweet wine. Müller-Thurgau, planted on bad advice in the 1960s, is thankfully disappearing from New Zealand's vineyards but still props up many a cheaper blend.

Red wines – grape varieties

Pinot Noir

Is New Zealand the only country where Pinot Noir is the most widely planted red grape? Much of it goes to sparkling wine production, but there are some wonderfully silky reds, often with slightly nutty, cherry flavours, being made throughout the South Island and in the Wairarapa. Better clones, better sites and better vineyard management mean that the wines continue to improve, and while the finest in the future will undoubtedly command Burgundy-level prices, we're pleased to see the efforts which big companies, and Montana in particular, are putting into making Pinot to sell at under £10.

Bordeaux varieties (Cabernet Franc/Cabernet Sauvignon/ Merlot/Malbec)

If New Zealand has historically had a poor reputation for its red wines, then Cabernet Sauvignon is largely to blame. Today, very few spots in the South Island are bothering with the variety, while further north, it takes exceptional sites such as the Gimblett Gravels region of Hawke's Bay and Waiheke Island to ripen it satisfactorily in most vintages. If Cabernet does appear in today's Bordeaux-inspired blends, it is often as the junior partner in wines where Merlot plays the dominant role, maybe with Cabernet Franc and Malbec in support. Merlot by itself can also work well, giving supple, plummy wines, and Malbec too can be thoroughly charming and chocolaty. In the past, producers of Bordeaux-style wines have been inclined to macerate their grapes for too long, extracting harsh, green tannins in the process, but this is now changing, and the wines of Hawke's Bay in particular have a promising future.

Others

A number of producers in Hawke's Bay make remarkably good Syrah, which at best has more than a little in common with the northern Rhône. We've sampled a couple of wines made from the Italian grape Montepulciano, but the message so far is don't hold your breath. However, if you see one of the rare Pinotages, try it, as some can be remarkably good – Babich are specialists, and make a juicy Pinotage/Cabernet blend that at £5.99 is very good value.

Sparkling wine

New Zealand now produces an admirable range of sparkling wine, mostly *brut* made by the *méthode traditionnelle*. Chardonnay and Pinot Noir from Marlborough are especially well suited to sparkling wine production, and the wines are excellent value for money. Some put the accent on fruit, while others go for a more complex, yeasty, champagne-like style. We recommend Hunter's Miru Miru and Deutz Marlborough Cuvée as the pick of the former style, while Cloudy Bay's Pelorus and Huia Brut head the ranks of the latter.

THE REGIONS

New Zealand's wine-producing regions stretch over a wider spread of latitudes than the vineyards of France, so it's reasonable to expect a wide variation in wine styles throughout the country. Some regions are a long way along the path to determining what varieties work best, and to discovering what flavours are the result of the *terroir* rather than the winemaking, but others have only just begun.

The North Island

The area around Auckland/Henderson remains the industrial centre of the country's wine industry, and many wineries have their bureaucratic headquarters and winery facilities there. Waiheke Island, half an hour by ferry from Auckland, is a hot spot in more than one sense. It basks in intense summer sun and has caused a flurry of interest in its rich Cabernet/Merlot blends from small boutique wineries. North of Auckland in Northland, a number of small estates (Okahu and Providence for instance) have also made classed growth Bordeaux lookalikes as well as high-class Chardonnay.

Gisborne is also a source of plenty of Chardonnay, much of it simple stuff, but with a few stunningly rich examples. Way down at the south-eastern tip is the Wairarapa, or Martinborough as it is often known. This is the home of some of New Zealand's finest Pinot Noir, as well as several classy white wines. But the most important quality area in the North Island lies between these two regions on the east coast. Hawke's Bay has a wide range of soils at various altitudes, so that the ideal spot can be found for virtually any grape variety from Chenin Blanc to Zinfandel. Bordeaux-style reds, with Merlot now dominating, can be brilliant, with many – but by no means all – of the top wines coming from the Gimblett Gravels (see introduction). But there are also several classy Chardonnays, and as the area is developed more fully, don't be surprised if Hawke's Bay gains a reputation for Syrah, Malbec and even Tempranillo.

The South Island

It's hard to believe that the first vines on this dramatically beautiful, glacier-strewn island were only planted in the mid-1970s. Since then, sunny, cool, stony-soiled Marlborough in the north-east has grown to become the largest wine region in New Zealand, with its Sauvignon Blancs attracting international acclaim. Chardonnay, Riesling, sparkling wines and, more recently, Pinot Noir are other strong suits, their pure fruit flavours a distinctive stamp on the wine.

Nelson lies just one hour's drive west and could best be described as a cooler version of Marlborough, enjoying success with similar varieties, especially Chardonnay. Canterbury, further south around Christchurch, is known for elegant Pinot Noir, Chardonnay and Riesling, with the Waipara sub-region being a particularly promising area. You would think that Central Otago, the country's most southerly wine region, was too cold for grapes to ripen, but a growing number of producers are making some of the most exciting, complex wines in the country. Pinot Noir, Pinot Gris, Chardonnay and Riesling are all being used to great effect, and the future looks bright for this most scenic of wine regions.

Pick of the producers

Alpha Domus Hawke's Bay winery with decent whites and very fine Bordeaux-style reds. Top releases are under the AD label.

Ata Rangi Small Martinborough winery producing one of New Zealand's most worthwhile Pinot Noirs to date. Watch out for Syrah in the future.

Babich High-quality and good-value wine from large Henderson outfit. Wide range, of which Irongate Chardonnay (from Hawke's Bay), rich Winemaker's Reserve reds (including a Syrah) and Patriarch Chardonnay and Cabernet impress the most, but Gewurztraminer and Pinotage are remarkably good.

Chancellor Impressive range of wines from the rapidly developing Waipara district near Christchurch.

Cloudy Bay Trail-blazing Marlborough winery, still one of the best. Sauvignon is the most famous wine, but the rest of the range is also very good, especially rich, mealy Chardonnay and Pelorus fizz. Recently introduced oaked Sauvignon called Te Koku divides opinion, but won't appear in the UK for a few years.

Collard Brothers Family-owned winery producing excellent Chardonnay, Riesling and Chenin Blanc in Henderson.

Corbans The full effects of the Montana takeover (see introduction) are still to be seen. Stars from the old portfolio were the Stoneleigh range from Marlborough (including absurdly good-value Riesling), complex Cottage Block Chardonnays from Gisborne and Marlborough, and the Cottage Block Bordeaux blend from Hawke's Bay.

Craggy Range Steve Smith's new enterprise is one to watch. Marlborough Riesling and Sauvignon are both rich and classy, while Seven Poplars Chardonnay from Hawke's Bay is already among the best in the region.

Kim Crawford Talented winemaker producing wines using grapes sourced from throughout New Zealand. Chardonnay, especially that from the Tietjen vineyard in Gisborne, is the pick of the range.

Delegat's Good-quality Hawke's Bay range from Henderson-based winery – look out for Reserve Chardonnay in particular. Marlborough wines appear as Oyster Bay.

Dry River Top-notch range of premium Pinot Noir, Pinot Gris and others made by Neil McCallum in Martinborough. Low cropping accounts for the concentrated style.

Esk Valley Decent whites, including dry and sweet Chenin Blanc and – from 2001 – Pinot Gris from this Hawke's Bay winery. However, it is for his outstanding reds that Gordon Russell is rightly known, with The Terraces, a powerful yet elegant Merlot/Malbec/Cabernet Franc blend, being among New Zealand's finest wines.

Felton Road Central Otago star putting out superb Pinot, Chardonnay and Riesling.

Fromm The Chardonnays and Rieslings are excellent, but the main focus is on reds at this Marlborough estate. Look out for intense Pinot Noir, plummy perfumed Malbec and rich, peppery Syrah.

Giesen Fine-tuned, elegant range from the three Giesen brothers in Canterbury in the south, where sophisticated Chardonnay and Riesling are produced. Recently built a new winery in Marlborough.

Goldwater Waiheke Island winery that made its name with intense, cassis-rich Cabernet/Merlot blend, but is now producing plummy Merlot (Esslin vineyard) and rich complex Chardonnay (Zell vineyard). Also a Chardonnay and a Sauvignon from Marlborough fruit.

Grove Mill David Pearce's Marlborough operation interests us most for its aromatic whites, notably Pinot Gris, Riesling and Gewurztraminer. Good-value second label Sanctuary.

Huia Claire and Mike Allen's Pinot Gris, Gewurztraminer and lively sparkler are among the best in Marlborough.

Hunter's Long-established Marlborough winery, producing complex, oaky Chardonnay and rich, creamy Sauvignon. Riesling similarly full-on; also great-value, fruity sparkler Miru Miru.

Isabel Estate Exciting estate excelling with some of the most subtly flavoured Riesling, Pinot Noir, Chardonnay and Sauvignon Blanc in Marlborough.

Jackson Estate Pungent Sauvignon, crisp Riesling, complex Chardonnay and top-quality *brut* from John Stichbury's Marlborough estate.

Kumeu River Master of Wine Michael Brajkovich produces Burgundian-style Chardonnays at his small, family-run winery north of Auckland.

Lawson's Dry Hills Aromatic wine producer of some distinction in Marlborough. Elegant Gewurztraminer and classic, flinty Sauvignon.

Martinborough Vineyard Martinborough pioneer, and still at the top of the tree with complex, silky Pinot Noir and rich, mealy Chardonnay.

Matua Valley Auckland-based winery, now owned by Beringer Blass, making good wines from throughout the North Island. Top releases are Ararimu Cabernet/Merlot and Chardonnay. Also a range from Marlborough under the Shingle Peak label, including appealing Pinot Gris.

Millton Vineyard A rare Gisborne boutique winery producing an interesting range of organic wines – award-winning, barrel-fermented Chenin Blanc is notable.

Montana The giant of the New Zealand wine industry has a remarkably reliable track record with whites and sparkling wine: Marlborough Sauvignon and Chardonnay, and best-selling fizz Lindauer are all reliable, well-priced wines. At higher levels, the reserve releases of all varieties (Pinot Noir included) are commendable, while at the top of the tree, the single-vineyard wines, especially 'B' (Marlborough Sauvignon) and 'O' (Gisborne Chardonnay) are superb, as are the Deutz Marlborough Cuvée sparklers.

Morton Estate Morton makes wines in Marlborough and Hawke's Bay and is much admired for its Black Label Chardonnay, in particular, although reds are fast catching up.

Nautilus Owned by Australian company Yalumba and producing fruity yet elegant Chardonnay, Sauvignon, Pinot Noir and fizz in Marlborough.

Neudorf The best winery in Nelson. Tim and Judy Finn craft wines of great depth and complexity, particularly from Chardonnay and Pinot Noir.

Ngatarawa Thoughtful Hawke's Bay producer with elegant citrusy Chardonnay and supple, complex Merlot/Cabernet blend. Top releases come under the Alwyn label.

Nobilo Commercially minded Auckland winery now owned by Australian giant BRL Hardy. Let's hope quality – which seems to have remained static for a few years – improves under the new owners.

Palliser Estate A mainstay of Martinborough, with premium, well-balanced Chardonnay, vibrant Sauvignon and blackberryish Pinot.

Pegasus Bay Splendid Waipara winery making classy, complex wines, best of which are the Pinot Noir, Chardonnay and Riesling.

Rippon Vineyard Best known for a highly acclaimed Burgundian-style Pinot Noir from Central Otago, but also excelling with Chardonnay and Riesling.

Sacred Hill Good wines across the board from Hawke's Bay winery. Top-tier 'Special Selection' wines are impressive, especially the Graves-style Sauvage Sauvignon and Riflemans Chardonnay.

St Clair Reliable, good-quality range from Neal Ibbotson that includes fine *botrytis* Riesling (if you can get hold of it . . .).

Selaks/Drylands Estate One of the quiet performers of Marlborough, making crisp, pithy Sauvignon and tangy Rieslings. Has belonged to Nobilo since 1998.

Seresin A new Marlborough star, already coming up with an accomplished range that includes weighty Pinot Gris and juicy Pinot Noir.

Sileni Ex-Villa Maria winemaker Grant Edmonds is chief winemaker at this new state-of-the-art Hawke's Bay operation. Semillon, Chardonnay and Merlot/Cabernets are all complex and satisfying.

Stonecroft Maverick Hawke's Bay producer specialising in Gewurztraminer and Syrah; also an astonishingly impressive Zinfandel.

Stonyridge Stephen White's cultish winery on Waiheke Island is best known for Larose – one of the country's best (and most expensive) reds. It's a Bordeaux blend of considerable concentration and complexity, but UK allocations are tiny.

Te Mata Wine industry spokesman John Buck makes benchmark Elston Chardonnay and consistently fine-tuned, complex Coleraine reds at this influential Hawke's Bay winery.

Tohu Maori-owned venture making ripe but fresh Marlborough Chardonnay and well-balanced Gisborne Chardonnay.

Trinity Hill John Hancock is looking forward to making Tempranillo and Roussanne as soon as the vines mature at his Hawke's Bay property. In the meantime, his broad, chunky Merlot and vibrant Chardonnays are excellent.

Unison Hawke's Bay red specialist making just two wines blended from Merlot, Cabernet Sauvignon and Syrah. They both have the finesse, complexity and flavour found in expensive Bordeaux wines.

Vavasour Based in Marlborough's deep south, the Awatere Valley, and producing an exciting range of intense whites and decent Pinot Noir. Second label Dashwood also impresses.

Villa Maria High-quality wines across the board, from the good-value Private Bin range up to the Reserve wines. The single-vineyard Sauvignons from Marlborough shows the diversity within the region, while the Marlborough Riesling, either dry or sweet, and Hawke's Bay reds deserve attention. Villa also owns Esk Valley (see above) and Vidal wineries in Hawke's Bay.

Waipara West Waipara operation of Paul Tutton of the Waterloo Wine Company (see *Where to buy wine*); lovely wines, especially Riesling and Pinot Noir.

Wairau River Phil and Chris Rose own some of Marlborough's oldest vineyards, producing a notably rich and pungent Sauvignon from them. Also lovely Chardonnay and decadent *botrytis* Riesling.

Wither Hills Ex-Delegat's winemaker Brent Marris makes some of New Zealand's finest Chardonnay, Sauvignon and Pinot Noir from vineyards established by his father John in 1975.

New Zealand vintage guide

New Zealand Sauvignons are at their best when youthful and crisp, although the best ones age into rich honey- and asparagus-edged maturity. Some Chardonnays gain complexity over two or three years, while the lushest of the reds will improve over five years and more.

New Zealand's wine-producing regions vary a great deal in terms of both climate and conditions and the grape varieties that are planted, so a poor vintage for, say, Marlborough whites, might be a great one for Hawke's Bay reds.

2001 A vintage of two halves. Those in Martinborough and on the South Island had an excellent year, with hardly any rainfall from early summer through to harvest. As in 1998, some Marlborough whites may be overripe, but producers are generally optimistic about quality. In Hawke's Bay, rain around the start of harvest caused rot in several white varieties, but growers seem optimistic about the quality of the reds.

2000 Irregular flowering in many regions meant that yields were down in several areas. Marlborough was badly affected, but the outcome was a small crop of intensely flavoured wines. Rain at vintage affected several North Island vineyards, so the Hawke's Bay reds and Gisborne Chardonnays are somewhat variable in quality.

1999 A good to very good year, producing first-rate intense whites but reds that lack the concentration of 1998. The summer was fine, but there was some cooler, wet weather towards the end of picking. Quantity is up.

1998 A hot, dry year led to ripe, full-bodied reds (some say the best New Zealand has produced to date), especially in Hawke's Bay. However, Marlborough whites needed picking early to avoid turning flabby and tropical rather than herbaceous and crisp, and very few wineries got it exactly right.

1997 Quality was more than satisfactory, but the quantities were down – about one-fifth less than average. An Indian summer in Marlborough meant especially fine Riesling, Chardonnay and Sauvignon Blanc.

1996 A good vintage, with a fair-sized crop produced after plenty of sunny weather. Reds from Hawke's Bay are excellent.

PORTUGAL

Wanted: adventurous wine merchant. The UK is blessed with several shops specialising in wines from Italy, Spain, Germany, various regions of France, and many of the New World countries – and if you're after Greek wines, Oddbins (see *Where to buy wines*) has an astonishingly good range. But we still aren't aware of any retail merchant who has jumped headfirst into the fascinating world of wines from Portugal. A few companies that act as UK agents for Portuguese producers may offer ranges that just about stretch into double figures, but, let's put it this way, we don't have an award for Portuguese Specialist of the Year because, at present, no one deserves to win it.

Why? Raymond Reynolds, ex-senior winemaker for Taylor's Port, has been importing Portuguese wines since 1990, and now offers a range of nearly 50 wines from 14 different producers. He puts it down to fear. 'Most merchants are still feeling their way with Portugal. The idea that they can find high-quality wine there is very new to them, but this is slowly changing. I recently took a group out to visit several estates, and the response was excellent. But even so, we're talking about companies who previously didn't stock any wines now putting maybe six or seven on the shelves. I can't think of anyone with a really extensive selection.' A quick look at Reynolds' web site, *www.winesfromportugal.com*, will reveal the extent of his selection. If you thought of Portugal as offering merely the cheap and the cheerful, be warned that there's little here costing under £6, and a number even top the £20 mark.

Commercially, we can understand the reluctance of merchants to become heavily involved with Portugal. Well-known grapes such as Chardonnay and Cabernet are thin on the ground, while unfamiliar words such as Alfrocheiro, Trincadeira (both grapes), *herdade* (estate) and *garrafeira* (reserve) abound. Pick up a bottle and there's little to tell you whether it should be £4 or £24.

But persist, as this is a country that hasn't bowed to international varieties and international tastes, and that is making some of the most interestingly different reds in the world. The vineyards are healthier, the wineries better equipped and the winemakers better trained than ever. Maybe begin with the simple, everyday wines of talented winemaking consultants Peter Bright, José Neiva and João Portugal Ramos, as they're good right across the board. Then look at the range of varietal wines made by the Australian David Baverstock at Herdade do Esporão, as these will help you get a handle on grapes such as Aragonês (Spain's Tempranillo), Bastardo, Trincadeira and Touriga Nacional. And do find time for the rich, violet-ish table reds produced in the Douro; the best have all the sumptuous flavour of port minus the alcohol, and are world-class wines.

And we close with a word of congratulations. And jubilations. You've heard of Cliff Richard, singer, but what of Cliff Richard, *vigneron*? The Peter Pan of Pop has had a vineyard in the Algarve for a number of years, and 2000 saw the first vintage being made with the aid of David Baverstock. Rather good it is too, by all accounts, although at the time of writing, it has yet to be bottled. Suggestions for names for Cliff's blend of Syrah, Aragonês and Trincadeira are apparently being welcomed – how about Livin' Dão?

Wine classification system

The wine classification system in Portugal is less than straightforward. There are, at the last count, around 15 regions designated *denominação de origem controlada* (DOC), followed by some 30 designated *indicação de proveniência regulamentada* (IPR). In practice, DOC and IPR are considered fairly close in Portugal, so short of a crash course in Portuguese geography, the easiest thing to remember is that these 50 or so regions are neither *vinho regional* (VR), equivalent to *vin de pays*, nor *vinho de mesa*, aka table wine. No, we take that back. The easiest thing to remember is a list of the best producers.

White wines

Making quality white wines in Portugal has always been something of a challenge, and we have rarely seen great examples despite the fact that whites represent 40 per cent of total production. To their credit, the Portuguese have resisted the lure of Chardonnay and its ilk and, where winery upgrades have allowed proper temperature-controlled vinification, we are now seeing some excellent and characterful wines made from indigenous grape varieties.

In the Douro, producers such as Niepoort (with Redoma) and Quinta de la Rosa make small quantities of very respectable white wine using grapes such as Gouveio (Madeira's Verdelho), Rabigato and Malvasia. The Arinto variety is responsible for the tight, pithy Bucelas from near Lisbon.

As far as single varieties are concerned, in Dão, the Encruzado variety is hitting heights given its fresh, rounded appley notes and ability to take oak ageing. Look for the wines from Quinta dos Roques and Quinta dos Carvalhais. Then there is Bical, planted extensively in Bairrada and Dão, and potentially Portugal's answer to Riesling with its propensity to develop from grassy youthfulness to petrolly maturity. The best examples are Casa de Saima, Luis Pato's Vinha Formal (both Bairrada) and Bela Fonte Bical from Beiras. José Neiva also makes exemplary limey and delicious wines in Estremadura from the workhorse Fernão Pires grape (also known confusingly as Maria Gomes). We recommend the Vale do Rosas label.

That best-known Portuguese white, Vinho Verde, appears sadly not to be keeping up with the times, despite the success of the Alvarinho grape (which together with Loureira makes the best Vinho Verde) just over the border in Spain's Galicia. A major revamp of this potentially fresh and floral wine would be very welcome on UK shores.

Red wines

For those who only remember the dreary, chewy fruit-free wines of the past, today's Portuguese reds come as a revelation. Established properties have improved their quality, while many growers who used to deliver their grapes to the local co-operative are now set up in their own brand-new wineries, thanks in no small part to generous EU grants.

Portugal's most consistent DOC is the Douro, where the same grapes used for port, especially Touriga Nacional and Tinto Roriz (also Tempranillo), are being put to good effect for intense red table wines with flavours of tobacco, leather, plums and berries all vying for attention. Those which blend in foreign grapes such as Cabernet Sauvignon forego the Douro name and are labelled Tras-os-Montes. Dão, a Touriga Nacional-heavy blend from a hilly, pine-forested region in the central/north zone, and Bairrada, made mostly from the tannic Baga and lying between Dão and the west coast, are slowly improving, thanks to the efforts of a number of the producers listed below; but we'd still approach a typical wine with caution. The venerated (in Portugal at least) red wine of the Buçaco Palace hotel is also largely Baga – shame you can only buy it in the restaurant there. Another variety to look out for here is the fruity, chocolaty Jaen – try the Bela Fonte and Quinta das Maias.

Further south are the central and eastern regions, where the revitalised co-operatives of Ribatejo, Estremadura, Palmela and Alentejo specialise in likeable, cherryish reds made from the local grape Periquita aka Castelão Frances. Finer reds are also appearing, either from revamped co-operatives, or single estates. French grape varieties, especially Cabernet Sauvignon, are often used for these, but the majority rely on local grapes. Even the humble Alicante Bouschet is being used to good effect. Look for José Neiva's Grand'Arte and the rare (and expensive) Mouchão.

Rosé

As the medium-sweet, spritzy and infamous Mateus declines towards insignificance, there is not much left in the Portuguese rosé department, although a few examples of Bairrada *rosado* can be found, notably from the Caves Aliança.

Pick of the producers

(As well as the producers listed below, Portugal has a number of co-operatives which turn out large quantities of excellent-value wine, the best of which is often scooped up by winemakers such as Peter Bright and José Neiva to offer under their own labels. Look out for *Atlantic Wines* (Bright Brothers) and *DFJ Vinhos* (José Neiva).

Quinta da Aveleda One of the best Vinho Verde producers. Casal Garcia is commercial but refreshing, while Aveleda is drier and lemony. Also very good varietal Alvarinho.

Quinta do Boavista Estremadura estate employing José Neiva as consultant. Quinta da Espiga is an appealing, cheaper quaffer, while higher-quality wines are produced under the Palha Canas, Bon Ventos and (for varietals) Santas Lima labels.

Bright Brothers Good-value wines from several regions made by the Australian Peter Bright. Chardonnay is strong, as are reds made from Portuguese grapes – spicy Palmela Reserva is deliciously heady.

Quinta de Cabriz Up-and-coming Dão estate, with fine range topped by Escolha Virgilio Loureiro *cuvée*.

Casa Cadaval Ribatejo producer with wide range including Pinot Noir and Cabernet 'foreigners' and good, single varietal Trincadeira.

Quinta do Carmo Single estate in Borba, now owned by Rothschild of Lafite. Produces mellow reds from the Alicante Bouschet grape.

Quinta do Carneiro Small and perfectly formed estate in the new DOC Alenquer making trusty, great-value wines with a nod to tradition.

Herdade de Cartuxa Large Alentejo estate making stunning Per Manca red, and almost as impressive Cartuxa Reserva. The creamy whites are good too.

Casa de Saima Model Bairrada property acquiring cult renown – hand harvesting, grape treading and unfiltered bottling gives you some idea. Watch for the delicious Garrafeiras.

Caves Aliança Bairrada-based producer of reliable, modern wines, including a fine, dry white; also makes soft reds in the Douro and Dão, plus supple Tinta Roriz in Estremadura.

Quinta da Cismeira Some of the best Douro red table wines – intensely flavoured and lushly fruity. Bordeaux's Michel Rolland is consultant here, so, unsurprisingly, there's excellent Cabernet too.

Cortes de Cima Unabashedly combining New World know-how with Portuguese grapes in the Alentejo, this property was completely revamped by the Danish Jørgenson family in the late 1980s, with the Australian viticultural guru, Richard Smart, consulting. The cheaper blend, Chaminé, likely to be more widely available.

Quinta do Côtto Another producer of richly fruity Douro reds, the best of which is Grande Escolha.

Quinta do Crasto The Australian David Baverstock of Esporão (see below) works at this Douro property to produce brilliantly rich, concentrated reds, especially the massive but fragrant Touriga Nacional. Small plots of old vines also make great Vinha Dapont, and watch too for the Maria Teresa label.

Herdade do Esporão David Baverstock makes one of Portugal's best, most consistent and most widely distributed ranges at this progressive Alentejo estate. Impressive, soft, peachy whites, but the reds, including varietal Trincadeira, Touriga Nacional and Aragonês, are even better. Second label Monte Velho.

Ferreira Port shipper, now owned by Sogrape. Soft, generous Barca Velha is one of Portugal's most prestigious (and expensive) wines, although it may be a little old-fashioned for some. In lesser years, a *reserva* is made. Fresher wines include Quinta da Leda and Callabriga, while Vinha Grande and Esteva provide an introduction to the range.

José Maria da Fonseca Sucessores Not to be confused with Fonseca Internacional, makers of the commercial wine Lancers, or with the well-known port house. This is one of Portugal's best table wine producers, based in the Setúbal peninsula near Lisbon. The range is wide-reaching and impressive – especially the rich red Tinto Velha (a successful blend of Cabernet Sauvignon and Periquita), full-bodied Quinta da Camarate, single varietal Periquita and cheap yet cheerful Terras Altas. Also notable is the fortified Muscat-based Setúbal, which is very good value.

Fiuza Ribatejo winery working in conjunction with Peter Bright on New World-ish, oaky Chardonnay, Cabernet and Merlot.

Quinta da Gaivosa Douro table wines with all the richness and concentration of port without the alcohol. Winemaker Domingos Alves de Sousa is also behind the first-class reds of Quinta Vale da Raposa.

J P Vinhos Palmela-based winery making impressive range, including oaky Tinta da Anfora, tight-knit traditional red Meia Pipa, fresh, fragrant João Pires Muscat and Cova da Ursa, one of Portugal's finest Chardonnays. Also makes rather tough Cabernet from the historic Quinta da Bacalhôa estate in the Setúbal peninsula.

Quinta do Lagoalva Good if slightly too oaky whites, but the reds from this Ribatejo estate are wonderful, especially the Syrah.

Quinta das Maias Exalted, traditional Dão estate.

Herdade de Mouchão Brilliant but hard-to-find red from Alentejo, made using a high proportion of the Alicante Bouschet grape. When it's good, it's very good.

Niepoort Port shipper whose Redoma table wines, a red based on the traditional Douro varieties and a barrel-fermented white made from Viozinho, Rabigato and Gouveio, plus a rosé, are among the finest in Portugal. Batuta is the label for top-of-the-range wines.

Quinta de Pancas The reds from this picturesque show estate in Estremadura get better and better under the direction of João Ramos. Special Reserva Cabernet and Touriga Nacional are splendid ageworthy wines.

Luis Pato Leading Bairrada producer, best known for long-lived reds and now making softer, easier styles of wine. The single-vineyard wines Vinha Barrosa and Vinha Pan are firm but very classy, as is the wine from Quinta do Ribeirinho. Pato is also experimenting with Cabernet and makes good fizz.

João Portugal Ramos Talented winemaker responsible for several Portuguese wines, but also with a splendid range under his own label.

Ramos-Pinto Another port house, now owned by Louis Roederer of Champagne, making damson and cherryish Duas Quintas (with a great *reserva*) Douro red, and also supple Quinta do Bons Ares, which includes some Cabernet and therefore has to settle for the Vinho Regional of Tras-os-Montes.

Quinta dos Roques Textbook modern winery in the Dão at the forefront of the region's renaissance: one to watch, making outstanding premium wines. Single varietal Encruzado and Alfrocheiro are extremely promising, if scarce.

Quinta de la Rosa Spectacularly sited Douro port *quinta* owned by the Swedish Bergqvist family whose forebears have been in the port trade since the early nineteenth century. Source of notable and popular red – *reserva* especially – and aiming to increase production.

Quinta de Saes Dão estate making gutsy and good Touriga Nacional and Tinta Roriz reds, and ripe, full-flavoured whites. Best wines are from Quinta da Pellada.

Caves São João Top-class, traditional Bairradas and Dão from this family winery.

211

Sogrape Huge, chameleon-like company with countrywide interests, responsible for Mateus rosé and Gazela Vinho Verde – both highly commercial, off-dry wines. Many exciting wines now emanate from the vast Quinta do Carvalhais winery in the Dão, alongside the Duque de Viseu label. Vinha do Monte from Alentejo also impressive.

Tapada do Chaves Alentejo estate challenging Mouchão for title of top red in the region. Also rich, full-flavoured white.

PORT

Anybody out there reading this after spring 2002 will be wiser than us on the port front. It's then we'll know for sure whether or not this famous Christmas tipple has really made it back into the fashion stakes. Americans couldn't get enough of the 1994 vintage, rich, ripe and fruity as it is, they bought it by the barrow-load to drink then and there, and the same with the excellent 1997. But after two dreary, rained-on years (1998 and 1999) the release of the marvellous 2000 vintage is due in early 2002. And will the Americans still be buying port then?

Port lovers are divided as to whether this American interest is a good thing. It's one thing to see this fabulous wine being appreciated for what it is, the growers supported and the market lively; it's another to see a wine, traditionally at its best 20 or so years after the vintage, being consumed on release. What a waste of all those fabulous mature flavours that could-have-been – and not all that convenient to have 'foreigners' pushing the prices up so high. We still think it's best to wait for vintage port and drink it in its fascinatingly complex 'old age'. Look out for 1983s and 1985s, which are just about drinking now – and catch any 1994 you can as these wines come back on to the market after the initial wave of investment.

Fortunately, port isn't all about the 'vintage' wines. The quality of the other styles is increasingly good too. (The Upper Douro, we're pleased to report, is now fully supplied with electricity – it wasn't for ages; but now it is, winemaking has improved dramatically.) We're as upbeat as ever about the quality and interest factor of the traditional LBVs (late-bottled vintage) and *single quinta* ports, which are readily to be found on wine merchants' shelves nowadays. And we have a lot of time for the aged Colheita wines too. Tawny port, long a favourite of wine lovers, is as deliciously raisin- and toffee-scented as ever and great to have to hand in the fridge during the summer months, not to mention Yuletide.

Styles

All red ports begin in the same manner: the grapes are crushed (they are rarely trampled by foot any longer, although the stone *lagares* that contained the grapes can still be seen here and there in the Douro Valley), and then brandy is added halfway through the fermentation process. The addition of the brandy halts the fermentation, and any remaining sugar is retained in the wine. After that, the many styles of wines split roughly into two categories. 'Ruby' ports are bottled early and do any maturing they have to in bottle, whereas 'Tawny' ports are aged for long periods in cask and are ready to drink as soon as they have been bottled.

Ruby
A wine labelled 'Ruby' is generally an inexpensive port bottled after two or three years spent maturing in big wooden vats. Drink it while it is young, and preferably fresh, for its fiery, fruity attack. Vintage character port is nothing more than a premium ruby.

Vintage port
The finest port from the best vineyards (only about two per cent of all that is made) is 'declared' and bottled after just two years in barrel without any treatment or filtration. Only two or three high-quality vintages each decade are deemed good enough by the shippers for a declaration. A question increasingly asked today is: when is vintage port ready to drink? Voracious Americans, as we've said, can't get enough of it soon enough and will drink vintage port straight after release, preferably with a well-cooked T-bone steak. Others like to drink it when it is still vigorously fruity and exuberant, but is just beginning to release its tannic grip – at about ten years of age. Others hang on for decades, although for many, 20 years is just the time to strike, when the extraordinary bundle of intense berry fruits, brooding tannins and dark hints of tar, herbs and chocolate is beginning to soften and mellow. Don't forget to decant vintage port as it throws a heavy sediment from a very young age.

Single quinta port
These are true vintage ports often from the estate – *quinta* – which provides the backbone of the company's regular vintage blend, or from a growing army of small, quality-conscious independent producers. Typically, those wines of the larger shippers are made in years not universally declared vintage and are ready to drink earlier than vintage ports. They are first-class value for money and enable you to drink top vintage port without paying top vintage prices.

Late-bottled vintage (LBV)

LBV is wine from a single vintage bottled after spending five or six years ageing in wood. Traditional LBV is bottled without filtration so that it throws a crust and needs decanting just like vintage port. These intense wines can represent good value. Regular, mass-market LBVs, on the other hand, have often been stripped of their character, with some no more interesting than vintage character port. Choose carefully.

Crusted/crusting port

Vintage-style port made from a blend of wines from more than one year. They are rare but can be excellent value.

Tawny

Proper tawny port, as opposed to the bland blend of white and red port which the French drink in place of vermouth, acquires its colour – and hence its name – from long-term cask maturation, acquiring on the way a mellow, nutty quality. Aged tawny comes in 10-, 20-, 30- and 40-year-old styles, and the older wines are well worth the high prices they command. Tawny port is delicious served lightly chilled as an aperitif in the summer.

Colheita

A tawny from a single vintage, the label of which will state both the year and the date of bottling. The port must be aged for a legal minimum of seven years before bottling. Colheitas are currently enjoying somewhat of a vogue – deservedly so, as they offer easy and pleasurable drinking.

White port

This is made from white grapes and is generally rather a dull drink. The port shippers drink white port as an aperitif, with tonic water and ice, and usually serve it with a bowl of salted almonds. This custom has tended to remain firmly in Portugal, however. In the UK, look out for Dows Extra Dry White or the outstanding Churchill's Dry White Aperitif, which is definitely too good to mix with anything.

The major port houses

Burmester Very good tawny and Colheita ports from house owned by Amorim cork producers.

Cálem Portuguese house making good Colheitas, an excellent *single quinta* wine – Quinta da Foz – and specialising in wonderful old tawnies. Quinta da Foz fruit provides the backbone for the vintage blend.

Churchill Rapidly expanding house founded in 1982. Enjoys a loyal following both in the UK and in America. Vintage wines from Quinta da Agua Alta are the best of a good-quality, full-bodied set, the excellent Dry White Aperitif sets itself apart from the crowd having been aged for an average of ten years.

Cockburn Owned by Allied-Domecq. Well known for the best-selling, undemanding Special Reserve (top seller in the UK), Cockburn makes more impressive vintage and tawny ports, though quality can be patchy.

Quinta do Crasto *Single quinta* best known for red Douro wines, also making good LBV and upwards.

Croft Light, commercial wines, although vintage ports are good and much-improved since the notable 1994 vintage. Currently being sold by UDV and attracting many illustrious bidders.

Delaforce Another house owned by UDV and currently up for sale. Best approached via its fine tawny His Eminence's Choice. (Again, very good since 1994.)

Dow A top house owned by the powerful British Symington family (see also entries for Warre, Smith Woodhouse, Quinta do Vesuvio and Graham ports and Madeira). The house style is intense and serious, and the *single quinta* wine from Quinta do Bomfim outclasses many true vintage ports. Also nutty, delicious ten-year-old tawny.

Ferreira Leading Portuguese house owned by Sogrape (see Portugal's table wines, above). Produces superior mid-weight vintage wines and rich 20-year-old tawny Duque de Bragança.

Fonseca From the Taylor's stable, Fonseca provides a splendid range, from fine vintage to affordable and full-bodied Bin 27 vintage character.

Graham Superb, sweetly fruity vintage wines among the best from the Symington group. Six Grapes is a ripe, fruity vintage character port, while the LBV is perhaps the best non-traditional version.

Kopke Oldest of all the port houses bottling small amounts of stunning Colheita ports. (Belongs to port shipper Barros Almeida.)

Niepoort Dirk Niepoort makes powerful, long-lived vintage wines and superb Colheitas at this small top-notch estate. Quinta do

215

Passadouro is a delicious *single quinta* port. Splendid Redoma table wines too.

Quinta do Noval Elegant, fragrant vintage wines and the justly famed, deeply concentrated Nacional (made from the fruit of ungrafted vines) from this French-owned shipper. Wines made from bought-in fruit are labelled Noval. Particularly good since AXA ownership began in 1993.

Offley-Forrester Now part of the large Portuguese Sogrape group, Offley produces powerful port with fruit from the ancient Quinta da Boa Vista.

Ramos-Pinto Renowned for its complex and classy aged tawnies and now owned by champagne house Louis Roederer. Also known for Duas Quintas red wine.

Quinta de la Rosa Family-owned and producing newly exciting, fine vintage ports as well as rich table reds.

Royal Oporto Wine Company Port house undergoing a revival. Tawny and vintage port much improved.

Sandeman Seagram-owned house which, at the time of writing, is up for sale – Sogrape and Amorim mooted as top bidders. Vau is new vintage port blend intended to be drunk earlier than the regular vintage wine (which is also accessible when young). Aged tawnies are even better.

Smith Woodhouse More Symington-owned port – this time an underrated house that supplies many UK chains with reliable own-label port. Particularly good at traditional LBV with vintage port very undervalued too.

Taylor, Fladgate & Yeatman Or Taylor's as most people know it. The grandest port house of them all, and its vintage wines are widely considered to be benchmarks. The *single quinta* wine, Quinta de Vargellas, is excellent.

Quinta do Vesuvio Historic *quinta*, now Symington-owned and already making its name for powerful, super-concentrated but complex vintage ports.

Warre Venerable brand, now owned by the Symington family, producing traditional, rounded vintage and lovely *single quinta* wine, Quinta da Cavadinha. 'Warre's Warrior' premium ruby also very good.

Port vintage guide

2000 An outstanding year: for the first time since 1997 there was no rain during vintage, yields were low and concentration very good. Most houses will declare in early 2002.

1999 Not an outstanding year – another one in which it poured with rain – and *single quinta* vintages only have been declared.

1998 A difficult, wet vintage after a warm summer caused volume and quality to drop. Not a declared vintage for the major shippers. The *single quinta* vintaged wines, such as Vargellas, Agua Alta and de la Rosa, show good promise.

1997 A short, high-quality crop, generally declared a fine vintage by all the main houses.

1994 An excellent year, the best vintage ports since 1985, with wines which are full-bodied, dark and rich, the products of a ripe vintage.

1992 Only declared by a handful of shippers, one of whom (coincidentally of course) also celebrated its 300th anniversary in the same year. The best wines are ample and fruity.

1991 A very dry year, declared by most shippers. Fine, perfumed wines to drink from 2010 onwards.

1985 Much hyped year declared by most shippers. Though priced too high on release, the best wines will be magnificent and approachable from now on.

1983 Powerful, concentrated wines which while opening up will still repay keeping. Undervalued.

1982 Not a universal declaration, with wines that are on the light side, but again, fairly priced and drinking well now.

1980 Not a highly praised vintage, but one that produced well-balanced, mature wines, ready for drinking now.

1977 A great vintage – drink lesser wines from now onwards, but the best still need time.

1975 Relatively light wines – drink up.

1970 Outstanding – drink from now onwards.

1966 Very good vintage but drink wines up now.

1963 Classic vintage producing massive wines. Drink from now onwards.

Earlier fine vintages 1960, 1955, 1948, 1945.

Madeira

The good news from the island of Madeira is that all bulk shipments of wine are being suspended as of the beginning of 2002. Not that we see much of the bulk-made stuff in the UK (the French drink most of it) but it means overall quality should improve and maybe, gradually, people's perception of the wine will change as a result. Maybe, or maybe not.

Madeira is designed to hang around; that's how it came into existence in the first place. Barrels of wine were stored in the holds of exploration ships as ballast – to be replaced later by treasures from newly discovered lands – and in transit through the tropics it became baked, burnt and caramelised. Eventually the sailors discovered that their 'ballast' tasted rather good – and so madeira came about. Today those sea journeys are replicated by heating the wine in tanks and lofts in a process known as *estufagem*. Because it is cooked, madeira wine is tremendously resilient; not only does it appear to last for ever in bottle, but the wine remains unspoilt for months after opening. And it isn't a heavy, sweet, sickly product, but one with bracing acidity and richness, in a range of styles from rasping dry to magnificently honeyed.

In a drive to attract new, younger drinkers, a fresh slant on madeira has recently hit UK shores. Blandy's 1994 Harvest (Colheita) Malmsey is a (relatively) young, single-vintage wine and a departure from tradition. It gives a taster of what top-quality madeira is all about, but without the high price – it has about five, rather than 20 to 100 years' barrel age, and costs around £12.

In case we haven't got the message across already, we'd like to say beware cheaper madeiras. Those labelled Sweet Rich or Pale Dry are made from the inferior Tinta Negra Mole grape and we advise you instead to confine your drinking to the premium madeira varietals – Sercial, Verdelho, Bual and Malmsey.

Styles and grape varieties

Cheaper madeira, usually made from Tinta Negra Mole, tends to be about three years old. These wines are put through a basic method of *estufagem* in a concrete tank and rapidly cooled. Quality varies – avoid coarse, sickly, inexpensive madeiras, some of them released as own-label supermarket wines.

Older and more expensive wines, however, usually carry the name of the grape used to make them and represent a huge leap in quality. Five-year-old madeira can be appealing, while the 10- and 15-year-old wines are usually complex and fine, more than justifying the price hike. These older madeiras are 'cooked' in the traditional manner – stored in wooden casks and left to develop slowly in specially heated rooms at the *bodega*. Traditionally, vintage or *solera* wines are not subjected to *estufagem* at all. These are the rarest and most precious madeiras and can take over 50 years to reach maturity. Visitors to the island can try to persuade the Madeira Wine Company to offer a few sips of ancient wine at the São Francisco Wine Lodge in Funchal.

Only a few madeira brands, but a fair range of own-label wines, are available in the UK. Blandy's, Cossart Gordon and Leacock's are all owned by the Symington family. Henriques & Henriques, H M Borges and Barbeito are independent marks.

Sercial and Verdelho
The driest and lightest of madeiras are made from the Sercial grape. Fine examples are nutty with a racy acidity. In Madeira, Sercial is often drunk lightly chilled as a refreshing aperitif. Verdelho wines are medium-dry and slightly less acidic with a nutty, tangy finish and are traditionally drunk with soups and consommés.

Bual and Malmsey
Bual achieves higher ripeness levels than either Sercial and Verdelho, producing a medium-sweet madeira with a hint of raisin. This is the madeira to match with cheese. Malmsey, the most famous style of all, is made from the Malvasia grape and is the sweetest, with rich raisin fruit, dates and figs in the flavour. It makes a superb partner for chocolate puddings.

ROMANIA

It looks as though the long-unrealised potential of Romania is slowly being recognised. There's a new generation of investors, a crop of modern designer labels, and a new wave of winemakers gaining in confidence with their Cabernets and Merlots, and going from strength to strength with their Pinot Noir. Improvements are slow, and wineries investing the money are still frustrated by the general rusticity of those around them. So we can't make any sweeping generalisations as to quality just yet, but there's definitely been a wealth of improvement, the fruits of which are making their way to UK supermarkets as we write – Safeway and Waitrose, in particular.

Estates to look out for are Prahova Valley, which produces lighter wines from the high-altitude Dealul Mare ('big hill') region: smoky smooth Pinot and minerally elegant Fetească Neagră. Vinartek, on the warmer Danube Terraces, makes chunky New World-style varietals: 100 per cent Cabernet Soara ('the sun') from 35-year-old vines is modern but with a Bordeaux-like twist. SERVE (Societé Euro Roumanie des Vins d'Exception) is another winery that show's what Romania can do when it really tries. We think, perhaps, that the latter is trying too hard with California-sounding names such as Bears Rock, Eagle Valley and Willow Ridge, but its 2000 Pinot Noir has everything Carneros has to offer at only £3.69, so we're not going to sound off too loudly.

And don't forget the local grapes. Spicy reds from Fetească Neagră and Burgund Mare ('big Burgundian', related to Pinot

Noir), and the white Tămaîioasă and Grasă – both capable of
making long-lived, sweet wines – are well worth trying. We need
to see more producers like the above before we make any
wholehearted recommendations, but this year the signs are
positive.

SLOVAKIA

When Czechoslovakia split up, Slovakia was the part which got the
best vineyards – it now produces over twice as much wine as the
Czech Republic. Our hope for the next few years is that the
influence of neighbours Hungary and Austria rubs off on the
Slovakian wine producers and spurs them on to greater heights.
In the west, there are plentiful plantings of Frankovka (aka
Blaufränkisch), St Laurent and Grüner Veltliner, all of which are
now being used to good effect in Austria. Cabernet Sauvignon and
Pinot Noir have also been planted. Most of production (65 per cent),
however, is of white wine. It seems that the more noble Irsay Oliver
and Pinot Gris varieties are encroaching on the large vineyard share
currently held by (insipid) Müller-Thurgau and Laski Rizling, but
we'll have to wait for the completion of privatisation and a great
deal of technical improvement before we can really vouch for any
quality. For 'signs of life', we're looking to the Bratislava-Raca,
Pezinoka and Nitra wineries and we'll keep you posted as to
progress. In the east, in Tokájská, sweet wines are made using the
same techniques and grape varieties as are employed over the
border in Hungary's great sweet wine region, Tokaj (historically, in
fact, Tokájská is part of the same region). We confess that we've
never tasted any Slovakian sweeties which are as good as Tokay,
but then there hasn't been the huge foreign investment which has
taken place on the Hungarian side of the border. We still wait in
hope for a renaissance of Slovakian wines as, until then, there'll be
little more than nothing reaching UK shores.

SLOVENIA

Rumour has it that some of the top Collio producers from across the
border in Italy's Friuli region (just north of Gorizia), have been
buying grapes from Slovenia for years. We're not sure. There are
certainly some similarly good crisp whites emerging from Slovenian
growers – such as Simcic, one of the few whose wines make it to the
UK. Sauvignon, Pinot Gris, Chardonnay, Tocai, and local varieties
such as Rebula, are all being made the modern way (fermented in

stainless steel, aged in *barriques*), though none of them is particularly cheap. The usual Merlot and Cabernet are around too.

Wines of the other regions, best of which is the Kontinentalna Hrvatska in the Sava and Drava valleys, are more tricky still to get hold of, and we can't comment further than to mention they exist. Should the necessary capital be injected, we have no doubt we will hear more from these regions in future, as the potential quality is apparently (and historically) very high.

SOUTH AFRICA

South Africa is working very hard at updating its image as a wine producer and all credit is due for its efforts – the wines we've seen of late have been superb. New clones available since the early 1990s, better vineyard management, and up-to-date winemaking practices, have all led to a dramatic turnaround in wine quality, with not a few distinctive grape varietals emerging as 'vinous ambassadors' to prove just what this country can produce. Shiraz and Sauvignon Blanc lead the fray at the moment.

On balance, South Africa has everything – climate, soil and, newly, the expertise – to create great wines, so we shouldn't be surprised that they are starting to make waves. Today, a vibrant, forward-looking industry is led by talented winemakers and businessmen, who have shrugged off the vestiges of over-controlled bureaucracy and welcomed a new era of enlightened and forward-thinking winemaking. Larger companies are being streamlined to focus more effectively on export markets, and initiatives such as the Wine Industry Trust and Vision 2020 fuel the desire for change and recognition.

At the heart of recent progress has been the impetus generated by a dynamic group of young winemakers who have gained from experience in other, progressive parts of the wine world, and have returned to carry out the developments. Bruwer Raats of Delaire learnt his skills in Bordeaux, California and Tuscany; Adi Badenhorst of Rustenberg trained in California and at Château Angélus in Bordeaux; Eben Sadie of Spice Route; Ian Naudé of Linton Park … these and more now have the practical knowledge to experiment, hone and fine-tune their wines; they are the driving force towards new and greater things.

In addition, the so-called black empowerment projects also continue to alter the face of South African wine. The likes of Freedom Road, Fair Valley, New Beginnings,Tukulu, Winds of Change (particularly good), Thandi (whose winemaker has just returned from Burgundy and Oregon) and Spice Route are increasingly available in major retail outlets in the UK. We are able to report that the wines from these joint ventures, set up to encourage the black workforce to have a more proactive role within the wine industry, are on the whole well made and worth trying, though quality-wise they may have had a shaky start.

A final tip: since South African wines tend to attract a loyal following once discovered, particularly amongst those who have actually visited the spectacular scenery of the Cape, the comprehensive, commercial web site *www.wine.co.za* now allows enthusiasts to remain bang up to date with matters vinous. Log on and see for yourselves.

Red wines

It may have been true in the past that red wines were not a natural strength for South Africa's winemakers, but the increase in quality we've seen over recent years implies they now have a sure grip. Very sure. Pinotage, the grape with which growers initially chose to lead their charge into the global wine market may not have been the ideal choice for showcase wines. Authentic and individual to South Africa yes, yet possibly less reliably appealing than Zinfandel in California or Shiraz in Australia. But we're now seeing signs of winemaking difficulties being overcome and very fine, quality wines emerging.

Pinotage is a tricky grape both in the vineyard and winery, allowing only a narrow margin of error before slipping into bubblegum-confected notes on the one hand, and outright bitterness on the other. Many estates have taken time to get it right, but the wines have improved dramatically over the last five years and the best examples are superb. Once a grower has mastery over the grape, the results are every bit the plum and spice standard-bearers South Africa wanted.

What we admire at the moment is that South Africa's growers appear to have finally recognised this grape's weaknesses. The drive in 2001 has instead been to develop a Cape Blend, a mixture of varieties focusing on Cabernet Sauvignon and Shiraz, along with Pinotage and Merlot, each in whatever proportion the grower wishes, to establish these as showcase wines, as proof of the country's ability to produce top quality. This is a good idea, in that the standard varieties appear to be easier to grow, but as we go to press no decision has been made as to what the official Cape Blend criteria will be. Not everybody feels the varietal proportions should be flexible. Some growers want no Pinotage at all; others feel it should make up the base of the blend. The debate runs on...

Whatever the outcome, we feel it shouldn't obscure the fact that Shiraz is making the biggest contribution to South Africa's red portfolio at the moment and that the Australians should watch their backs. Last year we spoke of the launch of the Cape's first super-premium wine, the Perold 1996 Shiraz made by KWV International, selling at £60 a bottle. Ostentatious as this sounds, it was (and is) good and is supported by a great many other quality examples – we've listed many of them in the producer details below. It might also be a relief to hear that most of them aren't nearly so expensive.

Of the other grapes, new virus-free clones of Cabernet Sauvignon are ensuring that the dusty, austere, gritty versions are a thing of the past; they are now full, almost minty wines, not unlike the Australian versions. Merlot, too, is popular with growers who are Francophiles – a couple of whom are aiming at Pomerol lookalikes. Pinot Noir achieves its best in the cool vineyards of Walker Bay (Hamilton Russell and Bouchard Finlayson are the names to look out for), and the lesser Cinsaut and Ruby Cabernet which are more often than not used in everyday generic reds or as part of a blend, also have a significant presence.

White wines

Traditionally, the vast majority of Cape wine was white – most of it, it has to be said, made from Chenin Blanc grapes, or 'Steen' as they were attractively known. Today Chenin is being grubbed up as if it were an embarrasing weed. While there's little doubt this grape has been responsible for some terrible wine, we think this reaction is a shame, and urge South Africa's winemakers to look (again) at the Australian example. In the 1980s the Australians were about to rip out all their Shiraz through similar embarrassment. It had been a bulk-producing workhorse, got them through tough times, but now they were ashamed of it. Similarly, just as decently farmed Shiraz can produce marvellous wine (and we're all agreed there), so can Chenin Blanc. Low-yielding, dry-farmed examples can be fantastically rich and honeyed as growers such as Ken Forrester in Stellenbosch and Villiera in Paarl are now proving. Not only this, there are also sumptuous sweet, sticky wines made – though few, unfortunately, reach the UK – and tangy, everyday-drinking examples which make refreshing aperitifs. Our message is two-fold: to the UK we say 'watch your grower'. To South Africa we say: 'Please don't pull it all out, it would be a huge pity!'

Our next lecture (sorry) is to extol the virtues of South African Sauvignon Blanc. We think this white grape is better here than almost anywhere at the moment, so good is that balance it achieves between New Zealand-style lemon-and-lime, racy acidity and tropical, warm-climate ripeness. It needs to grow in cooler regions – those not subject to South Africa's frequent bursts of heat, where it tends to lose its delicate aromatics. But a large number of growers are getting it right. Arch exponents are still Vergelegen and Springfield Estate in Robertson. Chardonnay has its pockets of greatness too – thriving in the cooler areas, just as Sauvignon does. We think the almost ethereally elegant wine from Thelema still leads the pack, although Danie de Wet in Robertson and Vergelegen also make impressive versions.

Méthode Cap Classique (MCC)

This is the South African term for sparkling wine made by the French *méthode traditionnelle*. While the method of production mirrors that of champagne, not all the wines are made from the classic champagne grape varieties (Chardonnay, Pinot Noir and Pinot Meunier). These sparklers are sadly not widely available in the UK, but Graham Beck Brut, Blanc de Blancs, made solely from Chardonnay in the hot, flat vineyards of Robertson, is well worth hunting down, and great value too. Boschendal and Clos Cabrière are two others to watch out for.

The regions

Generally speaking, the vineyards of the Cape are cooler than their proximity to the equator might suggest. This can be attributed to the climatically moderating influences of the Indian and Atlantic Oceans, and the Benguela current emanating from the Antarctic. Importantly, the varied topography of the Cape offers many different vine-growing conditions and the potential for *terroir* characteristics in the wines.

Constantia
This fashionable and affluent suburb of Cape Town is where governor Simon van der Stel established the first Cape vineyards in 1685 and set about making mainly sweet wines. The decision to plant vines here no doubt had much to do with the proximity to Cape Town. Some 315 years later Constantia's fortunes are being revived and it has become one of the best areas in South Africa for white wines – Sauvignon Blanc in particular. There is generally more to choose from as the number of growers and wines increases rapidly. It's also worth watching out for the reds; there's a lot of unrealised potential as some ripe, rounded Merlots have proved.

Franschhoek

Franschhoek, or 'French corner', was named after the French Huguenots who settled here in the seventeenth century. Strictly speaking, this is a sub-region of Paarl (see below), but its verdant valley location and a refreshing air of community collaboration mark it out as a separate entity. Since the valley runs east to west, producers can choose where to site vines – north-facing slopes for red grape varieties, south for white grape varieties, with those looking for cooler climates simply planting them up the slopes. There's much potential for elegance here, with alcohols invariably 1–1.5 per cent lower than in neighbouring Paarl and Stellenbosch, but as yet, it's not that often realised. Sauvignon and Semillon currently star as the best of the grapes.

Olifantsrivier/Orange River

These two wine regions would be far too hot for wine production if it wasn't for cooling breezes from the Atlantic Ocean in Olifantsrivier, while the Orange River, even further to the north and inland, exerts a tempering effect on nearby vineyards. Irrigation is widely practised, and yields can be very high. The giant Vredendal co-operative – the single, largest winery in South Africa – is to be found here, its overwhelming size not preventing a pioneering drive for quality.

Paarl

Paarl is often thought of as Stellenbosch's (see below) poorer cousin. While that is not strictly fair (some of the wineries are among the country's best), like a lot of generalisations it has a degree of truth about it. Paarl does not produce as many great wines as Stellenbosch but they tend to be riper and rounder, and it comes a close second. It's generally warmer than Stellenbosch, although the area contains a variety of vineyards from hot valley-floor ones to decidedly chilly mountainside plots. Its wide range of wines, and in particular Chardonnays and Cabernets, can be excellent. Although the KWV once dominated this region, smaller, good, innovative growers such as Fairview and Backsberg are emerging from its shadows.

Robertson

This is a hot, fertile, inland region, known touristically as the 'Valley of Vines and Roses'. Irrigation from the arterial Breede River is essential since the rainfall is only 200mm per year. Despite the high temperatures, Robertson has a name for white wine, with refined, impressive Chardonnay, Colombard and Sauvignon particularly successful on stony, lime-rich sites. Amazingly enough, there's even good sparkling wine and a passable Riesling from de Wetshof too. Reds are at long last beginning to emerge (Cabernet and Shiraz) – and we guess there'll be no stopping them!

Stellenbosch

While Stellenbosch is undeniably the source of South Africa's top red wines, white and sparkling stars are increasingly emerging too – thanks to the breezes from the ocean at False Bay which cool temperatures in the summer. Stellenbosch can offer excellent vineyard sites, particularly for those winemakers prepared to move off the plains and head for the hills, as it has over 50 different types of soil and terrain, ranging from steep, south-facing slopes to alluvial plains, not suited to quality wine production.

Some of the most successful new wineries in the Cape, such as Hazendal, are situated in the Bottelary Hills, north-west of Stellenbosch town. The towering Simonsberg Mountain, Jonkershoek Valley, Helderberg and Vlottenberg are also important new districts to watch for a new younger generation of growers who believe strongly in the individuality of the wines from these areas. In fact the air of complacency, which we have criticised Stellenbosch for in recent years, has largely given way to the wave of enthusiasm they have generated. We suspect it is the increasing competition, both within and outside South Africa, that has caused this. Whatever the reason, there are fewer mediocre wines emerging than ever before.

Swartland/Tulbagh/Malmesbury

Since the early 1990s, this hot and previously underrated wheat and tobacco region has been producing some top white wines as well as powerful reds. The cooler, coastal Malmesbury sub-region is now making fashionable waves, while inland, scenic Tulbagh is also expanding its range. As the vines are unirrigated, great concentration of flavour is possible. Some excellent value-for-money wines come from the local co-operatives and the few estates.

Walker Bay/Elgin

This cool, damp and humid area south-east of Cape Town encompasses the districts of Elgin and Bot River and has been subject to much hype since the 1980s, although there are only a few wineries of note. Stellenbosch-based Neil Ellis has produced splendid Sauvignon Blanc in Elgin, while Bouchard Finlayson and Hamilton Russell make particularly refined Pinot Noir and Chardonnay in Walker Bay. Hip and happening Wildekrans at Bot River, six miles further inland, is carving a reputation with its solid reds from a much warmer locality.

Worcester

Worcester is a warm, fertile area which contains nearly one-fifth of the country's vineyards but few producers of note, apart from some decent co-operatives. White wines are generally basic, but Pinotage can be respectable, and a few delicious Ruby Cabernets deserve a much wider audience. Problems with high cropping levels in the past indicate that it's worth watching carefully which producer you pick.

Pick of the producers

Backsberg Michael Back's range of reds and whites is one of the most reliable around. The Freedom Road Sauvignon Blanc (a result of the successful worker/management joint venture) continues to impress, and Simunye, a new joint venture with California, is also one to watch.

Graham Beck Convincing MCC sparklers from Robertson. We particularly like the creamy, soft Chardonnay Blanc de Blancs. Coastal Range vinified at Bellingham by Charles Hopkins is making waves with impressive Shiraz, Cabernet and Pinotage, plus new Merlot. Also look out for the easy-going, well-made and value-for-money Railroad Red and Waterside White.

Bellingham Charles Hopkins is fired up with enthusiasm for Cabernet Franc but also makes intensely flavoured Sauvignon and decent Chardonnay, Merlot and Cabernet Sauvignon. Stunning Pinotage Spitz in premium range.

Beyerskloof Boutique winery (only 12 acres) belonging to Pinotage king, Beyers Truter (see *Kanonkop*, below). The eponymous Bordeaux blend is deliciously complex, outstanding, with the Pinotage not far behind.

Boekenhoutskloof Exciting Franschhoek estate where the quiet but passionate Marc Kent makes superb limey Semillon and a Syrah that bears an uncanny resemblance to Côte-Rôtie. Also good-value second label Porcupine Ridge.

Boschendal The Cape's largest, now extensively revamped, estate; these might be old-timer wines, but their style is all modern. The rich Chardonnay and Merlot and crisp Sauvignon and MCC traditional sparklers all prove the point.

Bouchard Finlayson Good, crisp Chardonnay, almost like Chablis, very clean, steely Sauvignon and (consuming passion) the cherryish Galpin Peak Pinot Noir from Walker Bay.

Buitenverwachting Hermann Kirschbaum's excellent Sauvignon, Chardonnay, Riesling, and a very decent Bordeaux blend called Christine, are produced in Constantia.

Cabrière The enthusiastic and somewhat eccentric Achim von Arnim makes the elegant, fine-grained Pierre Jourdân MCC fizz and an impressive Pinot Noir in Franschoek.

Clos Malverne Exciting Stellenbosch winery dedicated to reds and doing well with Pinotage and Cabernet in particular.

De Wetshof Larger than life, Danie de Wet is the leading figure in Robertson and best known for his range of fruit-driven, upfront Chardonnays (labelled Bon Vallon, Lesca, Bateleur and d'Honneur); Sauvignon and Riesling are also classy. The fruits of the newly planted red grape vines (Pinot Noir and Cabernet Sauvignon) are still eagerly anticipated. We'll have more to report next year…

Delaire Youngster Bruwer Raats notched up vintages in California, Bordeaux and Tuscany before finally settling down at Delaire in the Simonsberg area of Stellenbosch – the Banhoek bench to be precise. Prices of his first wines matched those of the aforementioned classics but are snapped up anyway. Look out for delicious Chardonnay and Sauvignon too.

Delheim Stellenbosch winery for impressive Vera Cruz range: Pinotage, Merlot, Cabernet and, now, gamey Shiraz.

Dieu Donné Perhaps best known in the UK for the restrained mountainside Chardonnay, but the Sauvignon, Cabernet and Merlot are also quality wines. Shiraz and Pinotage to follow soon.

Neil Ellis Wines The first authentic, roving winemaker in the Cape, with a passion for producing the best wine from a particular locality (or nothing else), Neil Ellis now has a base in Stellenbosch (Jonkershoek Valley). Look out for his Reserve Reds (Cabernet Sauvignon, Shiraz and Pinotage), the whites from Elgin and the Stellenbosch range.

Fairview Across the board Charles Back is one of the Cape's best winemakers. We have been impressed by all of his range, which includes decent Shiraz and stunning Pinotage, as well as excellent Chardonnay and Viognier. Back is not only into all things Rhône – witness the irreverent Goats do Roam blend of Rhône varietals with a dash of Pinotage – but is also ready to take on the Californians with his new Zinfandel. His vision stretches beyond the Paarl estate where he's based, to impressively democratic dimensions with the Fair Valley empowerment venture and Spice Route (see below).

Grangehurst Winery Small but perfectly formed, Jeremy Walker's winery turns out some of the Cape's richest Pinotage and Cabernet/Merlot blends. Walker also has a hand in making the superb Hidden Valley Pinotage.

Groot Constantia Great Shiraz plus classic Chardonnay, Sauvignon, Riesling and Bordeaux-blend Gouverneur's Reserve from the original Constantia farm. New winemaking broom Bob de Villiers is pushing quality higher and higher.

Hamilton Russell Vineyards 'If they want cake, give them Pinot Noir!' says Anthony Hamilton Russell, one of South Africa's most opinionated winemakers. This Walker Bay estate now concentrates solely on Chardonnay and Pinot Noir, with immense attention to detail and some outstanding wines as a result. Second label, and vineyard, is Southern Right – named after the whales which annually return to Hermanus Bay.

Hartenberg Subtle rather than bold Shiraz (from older vines than many following this new star); classic-style Cabernet and new Zinfandel from progressive young winemakers in the Bottelary Hills (Stellenbosch).

Hazendal Acclaimed winemaker Ronell Wiid makes top whack Shiraz/Cabernet in the quality Bottelary Hills area of Stellenbosch. She's a newcomer but well worth watching.

Jordan The California training shows at this Stellenbosch winery. Kathy and Gary Jordan make extremely popular, classy reds and whites with immense attention to detail.

Kanonkop Beyers Truter's influential Stellenbosch Pinotage is the top example of this variety – spicy, brambly, powerful. Look out for the Paul Sauer Cabernet Sauvignon/Merlot/Cabernet Franc blend. There's no doubt Truter is one of the Cape's top producers of red wine.

Klein Constantia Judging by Ross Gower's Chardonnay and Sauvignon Blanc, his New Zealand training has stood him in very good stead. While textbook, ripe and forceful Cape Sauvignon is his hallmark, he makes satisfying Cabernet and Shiraz, but the most interesting wine is probably the sweet Vin de Constance, a non-*botrytis* dessert wine made from Muscat de Frontignan, an attempt to re-create the legendary Constantia wines of centuries past.

KWV International The recently privatised incarnation of the former, massive co-operative enterprise (with regulatory control to boot), declares its aim of 'becoming a major international player' with impunity. The basic KWV range are better than ever, particularly the Cabernet and Pinotage, while the flagship Cathedral Cellar range is also going great guns. New super-premium wine Perold intends to change the course of South African wine history.

Louisvale Best known for Burgundian-style Chardonnay but producing increasingly agreeable reds from Cabernet and Merlot in Stellenbosch.

Meerlust The Pinot Noir and Chardonnay from this Stellenbosch (Helderberg) estate may not be to all tastes, but the Merlot and the Rubicon Bordeaux blend are both stunning wines capable of long, graceful ageing.

Middlevlei Unpretentious, family-owned Stellenbosch winery producing excellent reds, particularly the front-running Shiraz, and a delicious Chardonnay. One to watch.

La Motte One of the best estates in Franschhoek and one of the most renowned in the whole of South Africa. Jacques Borman makes exemplary Shiraz, Cabernet, Chardonnay and a Bordeaux blend called Millennium, as well as convincing oaked Sauvignon Blanc (all with French role models).

Mooiplaas From 1996 producing one of the top ten Pinotages in South Africa. There's also delicious Sauvignon from these Bottelary Hills (Stellenbosch) vineyards.

Mulderbosch A top producer of Sauvignon Blanc, both oaked, and grassy and crisp. Match that with the splendid Chardonnay and the exuberant Faithful Hound Bordeaux blend and you have a Stellenbosch estate that's hard to beat. New Steen-op-Hout (Brick on Wood) Chenin, all concentrated flavours and light oak, is bang up to date and justifiably popular.

Nederburg Although the basic Nederburg range can be rather pedestrian, and the Private Bin and Auction Release wines are hard to keep up with, the sweet wines are exceptional, especially Edelkeur – Chenin Blanc – and the Weisser Riesling. Sourced from throughout the Cape.

Overgaauw Over-sized, bold Stellenbosch reds: Cabernet, Merlot, Shiraz and blended Tricorda. There's also new Cabernet/Touriga Nacional (port grape, here?). Big – but we like them anyway.

Plaisir de Merle Glamorous Paarl estate producing impressive, claret-like Cabernet and other red blends. The Bordeaux influence of Paul Pontallier of Château Margaux no doubt has something to do with the style of the impressive but firm Cabernet and the Graves-like Sauvignon Blanc. The Chardonnay is reasonable, too. Exciting new deep dark Petite Verdot is one to watch.

Rustenberg Utterly revamped and loftily ambitious, historic estate. Excellent flagship wines, Peter Barlow Cabernet Sauvignon and Five Soldiers Chardonnay, sit alongside Rustenberg and Brampton ranges.

Rust-en-Vrede High-flying Stellenbosch red wine specialist. Cabernet, Merlot, Shiraz and Estate Blend all noteworthy.

Simonsig Family-owned, sizeable estate producing consistently appealing dynamic reds (good Pinotage, Shiraz and Bordeaux-blend Tiara) and a notable Chardonnay.

Sonop This Paarl winery has made waves recently with its Winds of Change varietal blends – part of its workers' empowerment initiative – and also the ecologically sound African Legend range, of which the Shiraz and the Sauvignon are the best examples.

Spice Route Two ranges exist from this pioneering Malmesbury venture started by a group of South African wine gurus, but now solely owned by Charles Back of Fairview. Now in their third vintage, Spice Route 'flagship wines', made by young winemaker (and surfer) Eben Sadie, are world beating; neither are the 'standard' Chenin and Cabernet Sauvignon/Merlot to be passed over lightly. Look out, too, for the more broadly appealing Andrew's Hope Merlot-based blend and new Viognier.

Springfield Estate Relatively new Robertson winery run by the energetic and talented Abrie Bruwer. Chardonnay and Sauvignon in a minerally, elegant style; also fine Cabernet.

Steenberg The new kid on the old Constantia block, with a remarkable Sauvignon already, and more varieties in the pipeline for future vintages, including Nebbiolo and Shiraz. Merlot currently performing exceptionally.

Stellenzicht Finely crafted Stellenbosch wines across a wide range. Particularly of note are the intensely powerful, iconic Shiraz, ripe, oaky Pinotage and serious Founder's Private Release Cabernet; Sauvignon Blanc also a winner.

Thelema For many, the front-runner for the Cape's top estate. Whatever Gyles Webb turns his hand to is world class, whether it be full, fruity, minty Cabernet blends, piercingly flavoured Sauvignon or elegant Chardonnay – or new Pinotage. Good-value second label called Stormy Cape. There's a good supply of this in the UK yet Thelema's cellar-door sign invariably says 'sold out'. Enjoy this luck while it lasts. Grab it while you can.

Uiterwyk Historic Stellenbosch estate with excellent Top of the Hill Pinotage, Cabernet-based Cape blend and Shiraz.

Van Loveren Family-owned Robertson winery producing a range of good-value varietals, especially the unusually pinkish, sweet Red Muscadel and the more everyday River Red and Chardonnay Reserve.

Veenwouden Outstanding, new, boutique estate in Paarl, staking a firm claim to the title 'Super-Cape', with reds helped along by the influence of the renowned Michel Rolland from Bordeaux. Merlot predominates, gesturing towards the great right-bank wines of Pomerol. Tiny production, no expense spared and consequent sky-high prices. A cult classic.

Vergelegen The ebullient and deeply talented André van Rensberg now holds the reins at this state-of-the-art winery in Somerset West (Stellenbosch). Outstanding whites (delicious Semillon, serious Chardonnay and racy Sauvignon) are complemented by a bang up-to-date range of reds, particularly Cabernets. Gratifyingly well-distributed in the UK. A must-try, if you see them.

Villiera Solid range all round from Paarl, with particularly noteworthy Chenin Blanc, Sauvignon, Merlot, Gewurztraminer and sparklers. The Grier family has a progressive approach to both their vineyards and their workforce.

Vriesenhof The larger-than-life Jan Boland Coetzee makes hefty reds, although with more easy drinkability than they once had, with the Kallista Bordeaux blend being the best. All Stellenbosch grown.

Warwick Estate All change, as the younger generation takes the helm. Still making fine Cabernet Franc, Cabernet Sauvignon and Merlot from Stellenbosch, with the blend of all three called Trilogy even better. Look out also for the quite delicious Pinotage and Chardonnay.

Wildekrans Precocious Pinotage from this hot and happening estate in Walker Bay, now sits alongside some elegant Bordeaux-style wines – particularly the new blend Osiris. Definitely to be sought out.

Winecorp Not a name you'll see on bottles but this dynamic
company's brands include (in ascending price and quality order)
Capelands, Bay View, Longridge and Savanha. Look out too for the
stunning Cabernet (Naledi) and Merlot (Sejana) produced in
conjunction with Bordeaux *vigneron* Alain Moueix.

Yonder Hill Another new-wave Stellenbosch boutique winery,
making great Merlot influenced by the wines of Pomerol and
Australia – and aiming to repeat their powerful presence on the
world stage.

Zandvliet Robertson Shiraz specialists *par excellence*.

Vintages

Cape whites are traditionally not built to last, although the better-
structured Chardonnays might easily do so. As winemaking
improves and the fruit of virus-free vines begins to take on age, red
wines in particular will show more scope. Vintage to vintage,
weather doesn't vary vastly in South Africa but the following are
some guidelines as to what to expect.

2001 was less excessively hot than the previous two vintages:
there's real optimism about the wines, especially the whites, as we
go to press. The 2000 vintage will be remembered for the massive
wildfires which caused heavy damage to some of the Cape's best-
known wineries (with the inevitable resulting price hikes) and also
tremendous heat. 1999 was similarly hot and favoured early
ripening varietals brought in early; reds show concentration and
reasonable quality.

SPAIN

We'd love to have a crystal ball to see just where Spanish wine will
be in 50 years' time. Today, while Spain has more land under vine
than any other country in the world, it lags behind fellow European
giants, France and Italy, in terms of the complexity and diversity of
its wines. However, the last 20 years have seen rapid improvements
in both departments, and the next few decades promise to be just as
exciting.

In 1980, with very few exceptions, high-class Spanish wine –
table wine, since sherry is a different matter entirely – began and
ended with Rioja. Today, first-rate wines, both red and white, can
be found in a growing number of other regions around the country.

Ribera del Duero and Priorato lead the way, but Rias Baixas, Navarra and several parts of Catalonia can all point to outstanding wines. Where quality grape varieties are concerned, it once seemed that Spain offered little beyond Tempranillo. Now you'll find growers country-wide resurrecting grapes that have been almost extinct since phylloxera swept through Spain a century ago. No one has yet found a way of altering the weather in the huge, desert-like central plain. However, the development of irrigation systems (legal since 1996 and widely used prior to that) now means that growers can contemplate planting many more interesting varieties than the drought-resistant but ultimately dull Airén.

The evolution in winemaking styles has been no less impressive. The first stage involved moving from over-oaked, under-fruited reds, and dull, oxidised whites to the opposite, high-tech extreme of lively, oak-free wines that were clean but not exactly inspiring. The next stage involved finding a much happier medium, where wines weren't afraid to be oaky, providing they had the fruit to support the barrel-ageing, and this of course has led back to a greater interest in work in the vineyards. The tiers of Spain's appellation system as described below are still based on the way in which wines have been aged, but these are almost irrelevant for those looking for the finest modern Spanish wines. Today's top wines are identified by the name of the producer and increasingly by the name of particular vineyards.

   While progress in the past two decades has been swift, it hasn't been entirely problem-free. The desire to make up for lost time means that promising newcomers can occasionally be burdened with unrealistic expectations. Spain may boast some fine red wines, but in the search for high-quality whites, we're still not wholly convinced that grape varieties such as Verdejo, Albariño and Godello are quite as classy as some would have us think. We've also heard some people referring to the Somontano district close to the Pyrenees as 'the most exciting wine region in Spain'. It isn't, or at least it isn't yet. It seems to have the potential to produce great wines, but given that only a handful of producers are currently based there, it will take several years to fulfil that potential.

   Another issue has been fluctuations in wine prices. Rioja largely is to blame for this, since where Rioja leads, the rest of Spain follows. Problems began in the early 1990s, when sales started to increase rapidly. This led to a rise in grape prices throughout the decade culminating in the small 1999 harvest, when the going rate to the producers for a kilo of grapes was 440 pesetas as opposed to 70 pesetas only four years earlier. These increases were reflected in the prices of the wines, with some rising 20 per cent in a single year. In 2000, however, the world seemed to say, 'Enough is enough'. Bottles just stayed on the shelves, and sales plummeted. In such a situation, the large but fairly mediocre 2000 vintage was exactly what the producers didn't want. Price reductions have followed, and maybe lessons have been learned. Let's hope that both grape growers and wineries take more of a long-term approach to their prices in the future.

   One good thing that did come out of the price escalation was the emergence of different levels within the grape market – in other words, producers were willing to pay higher prices for higher-quality fruit. This may encourage growers in Rioja (and other regions) to produce smaller quantities of better grapes in the future. If this happens, and if progress continues apace in the vineyards and wineries, Spain could very well rise to the top of the European tree 50 years from now.

Wine classification

Spain's equivalent of French *appellation contrôlée* is *denominación de origen*, or DO for short. DO delimits the boundaries of wine-producing areas and controls matters such as grape varieties, pruning, maximum yields and minimum levels of alcohol. It doesn't however delimit wine quality. In 1991, a further category *denominación de origen calificada* (DOCa) was introduced. So far, only Rioja has qualified, even if some other DOs achieve a higher average standard. Within the DOs, the wines are further subdivided according to how long they have been aged prior to release. *Joven* or *sin crianza* wines can be sold as soon as the winemaker feels they are ready, while *crianzas* must spend at least six months in cask (a year in Rioja and Ribera del Duero) and can only be released after two full calendar years, i.e. a 1999 *crianza* cannot be sold before 1 January 2002. *Reservas* require three calendar years of ageing of which at least one must be in cask and another in bottle, while *gran reservas* undergo a minimum of five calendar years ageing, spending at least two of those years in cask and two in bottle. Below DOCa and DO come the categories of *vino de la tierra* (equivalent to French *vin de pays*, and potentially just as interesting) and *vino de mesa* or table wine.

NORTHERN SPAIN – RIOJA, NAVARRA, RIBERA DEL DUERO

Rioja

For many people, Rioja *is* Spanish wine. It originates from vineyards spread along the River Ebro, and is usually a blend of Tempranillo and Garnacha grapes supported by small amounts of Graciano (for finesse and tannin) and Mazuelo (aka Carignan, for colour and body). Cabernet Sauvignon does feature in certain wines, although it is only supposed to be grown for 'experimental' use.

The region is split into three zones, namely (in rising order of warmth) Rioja Alavesa, Rioja Alta and Rioja Baja, and many wines have traditionally blended fruit from all three to produce their wines. However, there is a slow growth in the popularity of single-vineyard wines, not least because it gives the producers far greater control over the quality of their grapes. There is also a move to bypass the traditional *crianza/reserva/gran reserva* system of classification. Many entry-level wines are now made in what the producers call the 'semi-*crianza*' style, to denote wines that have had a few months of oak influence, but not enough to be called *crianza*.

At the opposite end of the scale, several of the finest modern wines qualify for *reserva* rather than *gran reserva* status, by dint of spending less than 24 months in barrel, and it is the name of the vineyard or producer rather than the *reserva* status that receives the highest billing. Those barrels, traditionally made from American oak and used for several years, are now often new French oak, which imparts a large difference in flavour. Instead of a soft and oaky red with slightly jammy strawberry and vanilla flavours, high-class modern Rioja is firm and chewy, with fresh rather than cooked berry fruit, and requires several years in bottle before reaching its peak. While we enjoy wines in this modern style, we hope the Riojanas don't pursue them at the expense of the mellow, traditional style, which nowhere else does as effectively.

Not all Rioja is red. White Rioja is made predominantly from the rather neutral Viura grape plus Garnacha Blanco and Malvasia Riojana, and comes in a variety of styles. Ten years ago, the fashion was for clean-as-a-whistle wine that had no oak influence, and not much more flavour. At the other extreme, traditional white Rioja, deeply coloured and heavily oaked, and with a higher than normal proportion of Malvasia, provides a memorable, although not for some people pleasurable, experience. López de Heredia is one of the few *bodegas* persisting with such wines. The best whites of today lie between these two extremes, with oak- and barrel-fermentation being used with greater sensitivity to add substance and complexity.

Pick of the producers

AGE Huge operation, once best known for the insubstantial red Siglo Saco in its distinctive hessian cover. Its replacement, Siglo 1881, is a far better, fruitier wine. The *gran reserva* Marqués del Romeral is also very good.

Allende The prestige *cuvée* Aurus comes in not far short of £100 a bottle. Leave it for the label hunters and head for the excellent regular wine at a fraction of the price, which is one of the best of the new-wave Riojas.

Artadi Main brand of former co-operative Cosecheros Alaveses, making wines using mostly Rioja Alavesa fruit. All the range, from easy quaffer Orobio up to stunning Grandes Anadas Reserva, comes highly recommended.

Barón de Ley Single-estate wines displaying clever use of French oak and a little Cabernet Sauvignon in some blends.

Beronia Small, good-quality *bodega* owned by González Byass of Jerez, producing juicy but long-lasting *reservas*.

Marqués de Cáceres Successful commercial company making lively, modern wines plus top of the range wine Gaudium.

Campo Viejo Commendably high standards for such a large concern. C*rianzas* and *reservas* are worth looking out for. Albor is the lighter *sin crianza* style. Part of the Bodegas y Bebidas group.

Contino Excellent, plummy, single-vineyard wine from Rioja Alavesa made and marketed by CVNE (see below) as *reserva* and *gran reserva* only. The delicious Graciano shows the potential of this fine grape.

El Coto Small Rioja *bodega* making consistently appetising reds under the El Coto and Coto de Imaz labels.

CVNE (Compañía Vinícola del Norte de España) A fine name from Rioja Alta, producing classy, oak-aged white Monopole, first-rate, accessible Viña Real Reserva and outstanding Imperial Gran Reserva.

Faustino Martínez Large but reliable *bodega* in Rioja Alavesa, producing impressive whites, and sound, sweetly fruity reds, the best of which is Faustino I Gran Reserva. The frosted bottles and regal labels are garish, however.

Marqués de Griñón Ripe Cabernet Sauvignon is among the range produced at this go-ahead winery, based near Toledo. Professor Emile Peynaud of Bordeaux acts as consultant.

Viña Ijalba Impressive, concentrated red from a new-wave winery that has been organic since 1998. Try the peppery, single-varietal Graciano for a change.

López de Heredia Venerable *bodega* with a long history of making old-fashioned, long-aged reds and hugely oaky, waxy-yellow whites. If you like archly traditional Rioja, then try the Viña Bosconia and Viña Tondonia wines; those in search of youthful, fruity flavours should go elsewhere.

Martínez Bujanda Main label Conde de Valdemar is great for both whites and reds in a modern style with plenty of ripe fruit and soft oak to the fore. New single-vineyard wine Finca Valpiedra keeps standards high.

Miguel Merino Impressive recently established *bodega* with stylish, fruit-packed *reserva*.

Montecillo High quality across a wide range at this award-winning *bodega*, which uses French oak for complex, elegant reds. Owned by the Osborne sherry group.

Muga Historically known for its traditional, finely wrought reds that have a soft and old-fashioned appeal, especially Prado Enea Gran Reserva. Today reinventing itself with a delicious barrel-fermented white and new-wave Torre Muga Reserva.

Marqués de Murrieta Prestigious *bodega* making traditional, oaky reds and whites. Castillo de Ygay is long-lived and complex, the regular white label *cuvée* is back on form after a shaky period in the early 1990s. Recent introductions to the range are red Dalmau – big wine, big bottle, big price – and white Capellanía – ancient-meets-modern to good effect.

Bodegas Navajas Small producer of straightforward reds and oaky whites.

Palacio A modern operation making supple, concentrated, fruit-packed reds that don't necessarily fit into the rigid system of *crianza, reserva* and *gran reserva*.

Federico Paternina Large Haro-based *bodega*. We prefer the older, aged reds from its broad, good-value range.

Remelluri One of the best single-estate Rioja *bodegas*, with rich reds well suited to long ageing.

La Rioja Alta Large, admirable *bodega* successfully combining traditional values with modern know-how. Standards are high for *reserva*s and *gran reservas,* and citrus-flavoured Viña Ardanza white is attractive.

Bodegas Riojanas Traditional, family-owned winery making powerful, top-quality Monte Real *gran reservas.*

Marqués de Riscal Pioneer of modern Rioja, this house started breaking the rules over a hundred years ago. Long known (but not always liked) for its Cabernet component in the blend. Best wine is Barón de Chirel.

Bodegas Roda Recently built winery in Haro, causing a stir with richly concentrated, well-crafted *reservas*. Roda II Reserva 1995 is superb.

Rioja vintage guide
2000 The growing season had been very good, but as the harvest drew nearer, the weather turned colder and wetter, and the rain didn't stop until all the grapes had been picked. Don't expect anything memorable to result.
1999 'The worst frost for 60 years' eventually had less than its predicted effect, with only pockets of land being affected, and the vines caught up with themselves over the summer. Quality should be excellent.
1998 A large harvest spoiled by rain and low temperatures at the final stages of ripening. Given the conditions, the wines are quite satisfactory.

1997 A difficult vintage with a wet summer, saved only by warm, dry weather at harvest-time. Quality is erratic, and those who failed to put in the hours in the vineyards are easy to spot.

1996 Officially classified as 'very good', which means less exciting than 1995 and 1994. A sound year with decent quality and quantity.

1995 An excellent year. Despite heavy spring frosts, the subsequent warm weather meant the vines regenerated and produced high-quality grapes. Reds are rich and generous.

1994 Another great vintage, maybe even better than 1995, producing a smaller than average crop of wines with concentration, structure and plenty of fruit.

Good older vintages 1990, 1989, 1988.

Navarra

No longer known primarily for its cheap and cheerful *rosados*, the hauntingly beautiful region of Navarra has come up in the world. Its red wines, now the majority of production, continue to gain recognition and some of the best can even command higher prices than wines from neighbouring Rioja. An emphasis on modern winemaking leads to juicy, succulent, fruit-driven Tempranillo, often blended with Cabernet Sauvignon or Merlot. Some stunning Chardonnays are appearing which definitely outdo the local Viura-based wines. Just to reassure you that the world's varietal wines won't all taste the same, we can confirm that Navarra is still prone to lapses of consistency, so tread carefully. The *rosados*, full and flavoursome Garnacha wines, are still going strong and are often better than Mediterranean rosés from France. Sadly, they are a lot less easy to find.

Interestingly it is Navarra that is home to, and provides local government support for, Spain's most high-tech experimental winery – EVENA – source of inspiration for producers around the country. Overall, we tip Navarra for greater things.

Pick of the producers

Castillo de Monjardín Tangy, unoaked Chardonnay; the best of a lively modern range are the ripe, well-structured Merlot and Merlot Reserve.

Julian Chivite Leading Navarra producer, family-run for three centuries. The range of squeaky clean, elegant wines includes soft reds, crisp *rosado* and richly oaked Chardonnay.

Guelbenzu Serious reds in a fruity, modern style are produced from this stately, family-run boutique winery; try the juicy, everyday-quaffer Jardin before moving on to the more expensive bins.

Ochoa Modern company producing a quality range, including plummy Cabernet Sauvignon, and deeply perfumed Tempranillo, among others.

Palacio de la Vega Pernod-Ricard-owned *bodega* turning out consistently impressive reds plus fruit-driven Chardonnay.

Ribera del Duero

Home to the stars, Ribera del Duero only became a DO 20 years ago and is now one of Spain's most sought-after and emulated regions. Here the Tempranillo grape is known as Tinto Fino and is often blended with Bordeaux grapes. The loftiest names to buy are the venerable Vega Sicilia, and the comparative upstarts Pesquera and Pingus. In the last two decades, the region has boomed and a crowd of swanky new wineries has sprung up producing top-notch wine and sparking a fierce debate on the merits and demerits of pure Tempranillo versus Tempranillo/Cabernet blends. In fact, both can be excellent and these powerful, intense Ribera del Duero reds represent an often stunning alternative to the more strawberry and vanilla overtones of Rioja. The following producers are the most reliable. There is no DO for Ribera whites, although some wineries make zippy, young wines from the Albillo grape, which also finds its way into some of the reds.

Pick of the producers

Abadia Retuerta The vineyards fall just outside the official Ribera boundaries but so what? The wines are brilliant. If you can't afford the extraordinarily good El Palomar (Cabernet/Tempranillo) or El Campanario (Tempranillo), the basic Rivola *cuvée* at around £7 makes a far-from-disgraceful substitute.

Alion (see *Vega Sicilia*, below).

Hacienda Monasterio Young Dane Peter Sisseck makes superb reds, including the astonishingly concentrated (and priced) Dominio de Pingus.

Pago de Carraovejas Rising star making the most of excellent vineyard sites to produce intense, fruit-driven blends with up to 25 per cent Cabernet Sauvignon.

Pesquera Cult Ribera *bodega* owned by Alejandro Fernandez making concentrated, lengthily aged reds that command high prices, especially top *cuvée* Janus. Sister winery Condado de Haza is a state-of-the-art operation with 300 hectares of vines; wines made here are for earlier release. Standards are high across both ranges.

241

Bodegas Reyes Teòfilo Reyes has worked at top Ribera *bodegas* all his life and is now creating fine, richly concentrated reds from low-yielding vines at his own winery.

Vega Sicilia Legendary company making Spain's most venerable (and expensive) wine from a blend of Tempranillo, Cabernet, Merlot and Malbec. All wines undergo lengthy wood-ageing, and top-of-the-range Unico spends up to ten years in vat and barrel. Recently acquired and updated the Alion *bodega*, also in the region, and the results are impressive.

Other northern regions

Basque Country
Chacolí de Getaria and Chacolí de Bizcaia are the two DO sources of crisp and lean Basque white wines best suited to the local seafood cuisine, and only really ever found there.

Galicia
Galician whites have taken on 'it' status lately, particularly the Albariño wines of DO Rías Baixas, which at best are peachy and lime-scented, with a tantalisingly rich and crisp palate. This is probably Spain's best white wine, and as a result, demand is high, and prices can be expensive. Good as they can be – try Martin Códax, Lagar de Cervera or Santiago Ruíz – are we the only ones who think that they are slightly overrated?

DO Valdeorras is also worth watching for its light reds from the Mencia grape (akin to Cabernet Franc) and white from Godello, a high-quality, aromatic white grape.

Castilla y León
Although we have found Ribera del Duero, the most famous wine region of the vast province of Castilla y León, worthy of an independent entry of its own, there are others worth mentioning. One of them, DO Bierzo, is an up-and-coming region now making a name with Spanish enthusiasts for its reds and whites similar to those in neighbouring Valdeorras (see above). Closer to Ribera del Duero is DO Rueda, a source of crisp, fresh whites from Verdejo or Sauvignon. Lurton is the name to look for – either Hermanos Lurton for crisp, fresh wines, or Bellondrade y Lurton for richer, more ageworthy fare. Nearby DO Toro, not far from the Portuguese border, has made a favourable impression in the UK with some intense, gutsy reds made from Tempranillo, known locally as Tinto de Toro.

Pick of the producers
Con Class Great-value, zesty whites from Rueda, especially the crisp, grapefruity Sauvignon Blanc.

Bodegas Fariña The top producer in Toro. Gran Colegiata, a rich, sweetly ripe red made from Tinto de Toro (aka Tempranillo), is the best wine.

Bellondrade y Lurton Brigitte Lurton, co-owner of Château Climens in Barsac, makes rich, heady and ageworthy barrel-fermented Verdejo with her husband Didier Bellondrade which takes Rueda to a different dimension.

Hermanos Lurton The French Lurton brothers are making lively, good-quality whites in Rueda from Verdejo, Viura and Sauvignon Blanc varieties.

Lagar de Fornelos Rías Baixas *bodega* relaunched after huge investment by La Rioja Alta. Softly ripe Albariño called Lagar de Cervera has delightful lime and peach juiciness.

Pazo de Señorans Fine Albariño, a concentrated, rich mouthful of creamy peach flavour.

Marqués de Riscal Historic Rioja *bodega* but here the best bet is white Rueda, made from Sauvignon Blanc.

EASTERN SPAIN – CATALONIA, ARAGON, VALENCIA

Catalonia

The fiercely independent spirit of the Catalans has also pervaded the region's wine industry, which includes some of Spain's most dynamic and innovative producers. The Penedès DO, outside Barcelona, was little known until the energetic and forceful Miguel Torres introduced fashionable Cabernet Sauvignon and Chardonnay to his family *bodega* some 40 years ago. Since then, the area has not looked back. Watch out in the future for Torres wines made using Catalan white grapes such as Vermenti and Rosanna, and red grapes such as Garrut, Monastrell and Cariñena.

Penedès is also home to Cava, Spain's astonishingly successful and value-for-money, *méthode traditionnelle* sparkling wine made from the local white grapes Parellada, Macabeo (aka Viura) and Xarel-lo, in and around San Sadurní di Noya. As a party fizz, Cava is hard to beat, especially with a humble £5 supermarket price tag – its earthy base enlivened by appley characteristics and lean, fresh sparkle. The more expensive blends with Chardonnay in them, or vintage Cava, are not always worth the price difference, we find.

For our money, the jewel of Penedès is Priorato, or Priorat in Catalan. This stunning picture-postcard, historic DO, with mountainous terrain and stone villages, is home to a growing number of boutique wineries. Cold nights and long, hot summer days produce intensely concentrated, long-lived reds based on old-vine Garnacha. The traditional style in which oxidation and volatility were never far from the surface has given way to cleaner, more modern wines in which other varieties such as Cabernet and Syrah are sometimes used. These are some of Spain's finest red wines and command prices to match. Impecunious wine lovers should either seek out wines from the local co-op, Vinicola del Priorat (sometimes under the Onix label), or examine what's happening in neighbouring Tarragona, and in the sub-zone of Falset in particular. Here – for the moment – you'll find Priorat-style wines for a fraction of the price. Falset is set to get its own DO, which will probably be called Montsant.

Other Catalonian DOs of note are Costers del Segre, home of the huge progressive Raïmat winery; and Conca de Barberà, source of several simple fruity reds, but also home to two high-class, single-vineyard wines from Torres, Milmanda Chardonnay and the warm, spicy Grans Muralles red blend.

Pick of the producers

Albet i Noya Family-run estate in Penedès making delicious barrel-fermented Chardonnay, and top-notch, oak-aged varietal Cabernet and Tempranillo.

Cellers d'Anguera Tarragona Falset *bodega* making gutsy reds, best of which is the Syrah-heavy Finca l'Argata.

Cellers de Capçanes Tarragona Falset's star estate, making full-bodied reds from local grape varieties, Garnacha in particular, but using modern techniques. Cabrida and Mas Torto are the top *cuvée*s, while Mas Collet, which has a little Cabernet Sauvignon in the blend, is a great-value alternative.

Clos Mogador Long-lived Priorato reds from old Garnacha vines, hand-crafted and made in tiny quantities.

Codorníu Giant Cava house based in San Sadurní. Basic wines are unexciting; newer Chardonnay *cuvée*s much better.

Costers del Siurana Clos de l'Obac is one of the most concentrated of the new-wave Prioratos, while Dolç de l'Obac is an amazingly concentrated sweet version.

Freixenet Well-known Cava producer making fresh, historically rather characterless Cordon Negro, which has become tastier of late. Segura Viudas sparkling wines are some of the Freixenet group's best.

Juvé y Camps The best Cavas on the market come from this small, family-run operation. The complex Reserva de la Familia wine is well worth the high price tag.

Jean León This ex-Hollywood restaurateur pioneered Cabernet and Chardonnay varietals alongside Torres in Penedès. Pricy, New World-style wines.

Masia Barril Concentrated, thick, inky reds from Priorato. Some new-wave, *joven* wines are made here too, but we prefer the blockbusters.

Alvaro Palacios Massive reds from Priorato made with two particular strains of Garnacha. The top wines, L'Ermita and Finca Dofi, are long-lived, single-vineyard reds and command extremely high prices. Third wine Les Terrasses is made from Garnacha, Cariñena, and Cabernet Sauvignon.

Parxet Quality whites from the leading winery in the tiny DO of Alella on the outskirts of Barcelona. Still wines are creamy and floral and there's a crisp, snappy Cava.

Bodegas Pasanau Family-owned *bodega* making excellent, modern-style Priorato reds at almost everyday prices.

Raïmat Huge estate in Costers del Segre that is back on form with a wide range of modern, fruit-driven varietals after a poor patch in the late 1980s. Owned by Codorníu.

Scala Dei Boutique winery in Priorato, with cult status for its intense, alcoholic Cartoixa reds. Whites, both unoaked and barrel-fermented, are appealing too. There's a decent *rosado,* or try the Negre Scala Dei, a lighter red.

Torres Catalan family firm, led by the dynamic Miguel Torres, who has created one of Spain's most innovative companies; the single-vineyard range is, in places, world-beating (Mas la Plana Cabernet and Milmanda Chardonnay), while red Coronas, white Gran Viña Sol and Muscat/Gewurztraminer Viña Esmeralda are the best of the blends.

Aragón

Stretching from the Pyrenees in the north to the edges of Valencia and Castilla-La Mancha further south, Aragón embraces some of the current DOs to watch. Cariñena, Calatayud and Campo de

Borja have long made chunky, cheap reds, but we now perceive signs of distinct upward mobility. Campo de Borja, especially, is moving into better-quality production. Lovers of cheerful, everyday reds and value-for-money dry whites, make a mental note.

The most promising DO of all is Somontano, nestled in the cool foothills of the Pyrenees and turning out modern, elegant whites and reds from both local and international grape varieties. Happily, these are now making regular appearances on the shelves of UK merchants.

Pick of the producers

Enate An up-to-the-minute range of familiar varietals behind eclectic labels. All the range is good, with a dry but spicy Gewurztraminer being one of the best we've tried from outside Alsace.

Bodegas Pirineos Newly arrived in the UK, a large and appealing range of reds, whites and *rosados*, some under the Espiral label, from a revamped co-operative in Somontano.

Viñas del Vero Somontano producer making good varietals, particularly Chardonnay and Pinot Noir, plus more ambitious blends Clarion (white) and Gran Vos (red). Blecua (Cabernet Sauvignon/Merlot/Tempranillo/Garnacha) is recently introduced flagship red.

Valencia

This region, most famous for its sweet Muscat, also accounts for vast amounts of inexpensive sweet and dry white table wine that appears in the UK. Valencia's wines are, generally speaking, reasonable value and fairly reliable. The small inland DO of Utiel-Requena puts out strapping reds and lurid rosés made from the Bobal grape.

Pick of the producers

Vicente Gandia Valencia's slickest modern producer, making the inexpensive and workmanlike Castillo de Liria range. Also responsible for attractive, honeyed Moscatel hiding behind many supermarket own-labels in the UK.

The centre and the south

Never mind Don Quixote and the windmills, in wine terms, the limitless, baking hot central plain of Castilla-La Mancha has traditionally been the source of vast quantities of cheap plonk, much of it dull and oxidised whites from the indubitably downmarket Airén grape variety. Given the size of the region and improvements in winemaking practices, including cool picking and fermentation, there is much potential to exploit – and certain wineries are beginning to do so, witness the improving La Mancha reds and whites cramming UK supermarket shelves.

However, a handful of decent producers in the Valdepeñas DO, an enclave within La Mancha, make soft, appealing reds of distinct quality and at a reasonable price. These will also be found in your local supermarket or high-street off-licence alongside the many bargain, robust reds from Jumilla. While in Jumilla, port fans should look for the Dulce Monastrell from Bodegas Olivares – it's actually unfortified, but with its sweetness, ripeness and 16 per cent alcohol, you wouldn't know. Yecla, where the traditional Murcian full-bodied reds from Monastrell grapes are being toned down to suit the tastes of the export market, is also upping the quality of its wines. Our favourite Yecla wine is the exuberant sparkling red La Pamelita made by Pamela Geddes, an Australian-trained Scot.

Pick of the producers
Bodegas Agapito Rico Producer of well-made, not over-alcoholic Jumilla reds, working well with international grape varieties.

Bodegas Castano Yecla winery, new to the UK. Source of value-for-money Monastrell blends.

Los Llanos Great value from this reliable Valdepeñas producer – reds are better than whites.

Felix Solis Soft, ripe reds from the largest, and one of the best, producers in Valdepeñas, with Viña Albali Reserva the top of the range.

FORTIFIED WINES
Sherry

Younger consumers are beginning to discover the pleasures of sherry both as an aperitif and an accompaniment to food, although it's the drier, lighter styles of fino and manzanilla they are turning to, rather than the sweet concoctions of previous generations. As evidence, look no further than Gonzalez Byass's famous Tío Pepe, which recently received a multi-million pound makeover, and now comes in a smart, New World-esque bottle on which the word 'sherry' appears in very small letters. The advertising with the catchphrase, 'Always drink on the dry side of life,' and images such as a bottom-groping female, are firmly aimed at a younger market.

While such a move doesn't necessarily signal a sherry revival, it would seem as if the rot has been temporarily stopped. Many younger wine drinkers thankfully cannot remember the 'pleasures' of British sherry (neither 'British' nor 'sherry') and are discovering the real thing for the first time. Add in the avid wine enthusiasts, who have never needed much persuasion to drink fine sherry, and you have a drink whose day may not be too far away. And about time too, we say. Sherry is one of the world's great and classic wines – and certainly its most affordable.

Fino and manzanilla

These types of sherry, made from first pressings of Palomino grapes, are affected by the yeast-like fungus *flor* which exists naturally in the air of the sherry region, and which grows like a creamy blanket on the surface of the ageing wine. *Flor* is the magic ingredient in the sherry-making process – it protects the sherry from oxidation, while giving it a tangy ripeness. When chilled, a crisp, mouth-watering fino or manzanilla is one of the most delectable dry wines in the world.

The three sherry towns – Jerez, El Puerto de Santa María and Sanlúcar – all make fino-style sherry, but the character of their wines varies because the natural *flor* of each town is slightly different. Jerez's finos are the most lemony and taste stronger in alcohol. The finos of El Puerto de Santa María, nearer the sea, are more heavily influenced by *flor* and tend to taste saltier while their aroma is more pungent. Manzanilla is the name given to fino-style wines made in the coastal town of Sanlúcar, where the *flor* influence is the strongest of all. At its best, manzanilla is soft, slightly briny but with a well-defined yeasty, bready character. Both fino and manzanilla should be drunk fresh and chilled, and soon after the wine has been bottled. We recommend buying them by the half bottle, so that you crack open a fresh wine regularly.

Amontillado, palo cortado and dry oloroso

Amontillado is a fine, aged, dry sherry that starts out as a fino. It is fortified to about 17 or 18 per cent, thus killing off the *flor* and exposing the wine to the air. This should give the sherry an attractive amber colour and nutty, rich character. Sadly, many amontillados on the market taste like nothing of the sort, but sweetened young wine of low quality. *Caveat emptor*.

Palo cortado is a rare treat, the style of which falls between amontillado and dry oloroso. It is pale caramel in colour and tastes delicately nutty.

Dry oloroso is the most noble of dry sherries, a warming, aromatic, sipping wine with layers of fruitcake, spice and nuts. It makes an ideal accompaniment to strong, hard cheeses.

Sweeter styles

The sweeter sherries, medium, pale cream and cream, are sweet styles developed especially for the export market and (we are sorry to say) they still account for four out of every five bottles sold in the UK. The best contain good-quality, aged oloroso wine; the worst are masked by sugary sweetness. The Pedro Ximénez (PX) grape is used for its intense sweetness to make an unctuous wine with the character of black treacle and raisins, which is great with desserts and cakes with a hint of ginger. The Spanish soak raisins in it and pour the lot over vanilla ice-cream for a delicious treat.

Pick of the producers

Barbadillo The largest *bodega* in Sanlúcar, noted for its fine manzanilla, especially the yeasty, mature Solear bottling.

Domecq This distinguished Jerez *bodega* is rightly famous for one of the best finos, the elegant La Ina; also dry oloroso Rio Viejo.

Diez-Merito Producers of the excellent Don Zoilo fino, often seen in bars and on restaurant lists.

González Byass The most famous sherry producer of all maintains admirably high standards across a range that includes the yardstick fino Tío Pepe, rare and authentic Amontillado del Duque and opulent, raisined, sweet Matúsalem. The company has released a few precious, vintage-dated dry olorosos for sale.

Harvey's Commercial sherries, now repackaged in modern bottles. The less well-known 1796 range is much better.

Hidalgo Family-owned Sanlúcar *bodega*, best known for soft, fresh manzanilla La Gitana but look out for the amontillado Viejo Pastrana, a rare but wonderful single-vineyard sherry.

Lustau A wide range of *almacenista* sherries are bought from small family concerns and bottled by this Jerez *bodega*. Some are much better than others, but the top bottlings are divine.

Osborne Giant, family-owned company in El Puerto, with huge brandy interests, but offering fair-quality sherry. Fino Quinta is a full-flavoured, bone-dry sherry.

Valdespino Highly respected sherries from this traditional, family-owned Jerez *bodega*. The pungent Inocente fino, dry amontillado Tío Diego, fine palo cortado and dry oloroso all regularly top tastings.

Williams and Humbert Large concern with tangy Pando fino and Dos Cortados oloroso the best in the range.

Other fortified wines

Montilla-Moriles

The DO region in the hills south of Cordoba produces sherry-style wines in *solera* systems mostly from Pedro Ximénez (PX). PX attains higher sugar levels here than the Palomino of Jerez, and many of the wines remain unfortified. Most of the Montilla that reaches the UK is designed to compete with the cheapest sherry and as such is best avoided. Better-quality, aged Montilla in the amontillado and oloroso styles can be very good, but little reaches the UK.

Condado de Huelva

You may very occasionally see the wines of this lesser-known source of fortified wines in the sherry style in the UK. With less franchise in the UK than Montilla, and the attendant problems of the sherry market, it comes as no surprise that Condado de Huelva vines are now being replaced by other more profitable crops such as wheat or strawberries. Some fairly lowbrow, still white wine is also being attempted.

Málaga

Andalusian DO whose production of nutty, caramelly, madeira-like dessert wines has sadly declined to a dribble in the early twenty-first century. Málaga wine is a rare treat, even more so now that the Scholtz Hermanos *bodega* has ceased production.

SWITZERLAND

The Swiss are not known to be defeated by uphill struggles, and the difficult times we warned of last year are being met head on. Consumers today are more willing than ever to pay £6–£8 a bottle for wine, so it's now become worth that concerted effort needed to get Swiss wines into the UK. Growers are working hard to improve their rather chaotic labelling system, which isn't helped by the different languages used (French, German or Italian) depending on where in the country the wine is produced. We've also heard rumours that, despite the steep (spectacular) vineyards, expensive labour and a thirsty home market, which have in the past mitigated entirely against finding any bargain Swiss wines under the magic £5 threshold, today there are signs of cheap, cheerful and enticing wines beginning to emerge. (More on this next year we hope.) From the supermarket, merchant and restaurant lists we've studied while putting together this *Guide*, we can report that exporters are indeed making some headway – take a look in Harrods, at For the Love of Wine, or on the Virgin web site for starters (see *Where to buy wine* and *Online-only merchants*).

Interestingly, Switzerland makes over twice as much wine as New Zealand, but the most widely planted variety is the white grape Chasselas or Fendant which can be very bland unless vinified carefully. When good, it demonstrates the different nuances of the individual wine areas very clearly – it also has the kind of rich, waxy texture that goes brilliantly with fiery Thai flavours and spicy Asian food. Soft and easy-drinking reds are made from Pinot Noir or Gamay, blended together in the case of Dôle, a wine sometimes seen in the UK. Many local grape varieties are also grown, such as Aligoté around Lake Geneva; strong spicy Cournalin, Amigne, Petite Arvine and Humagne reds from the dry, mountainous Valais. Merlot and white Merlot grow in the Italianate Ticino region, and light, floral and sparkling wines are the specialities of Neuchâtel.

Wines to look out for in the UK are those from growers Favre, Mauler (four generations of winemakers in 170 years!), Provins and Jean & Pierre Testuz.

TUNISIA

We reported the good news about Domaine Nefris last year, and although we know there are a number of other decent producers in Tunisia (Château Thibar, Royal Tardi, Mornag), developments in their wines seem to be few and far between. Sicilian investor Calatrasi, however, is still doing admirable things with Nefris and obviously rank its wines alongside those of its other, trendy, Puglia and Sicily estates. The aim is to champion local grapes, old vines and higher vineyard sites, building on small-scale authenticity rather than bulk blends. Juicy, spicy Carignan/Mourvèdre and super-premium Selian (100 per cent Carignan) are the top wines of the estate, and look to be on course. (Though however appealing £6.99 might be as a price point, we think that 'super premium' might be overstating it.) Other grape varieties include the usual Cabernet Sauvignon and Syrah, plus Grenache, Cinsaut, Clairette and Beldi (who he?), mostly used in full-bodied reds and light rosés.

TURKEY

According to archaeologists, the wine grape *Vitis vinifera* has been grown in Turkey for over 6,000 years. Today Turkey is the world's fourth-largest grower of grapes, the vast majority (98 per cent) being table grapes and fruit for drying. Even so, Turkey makes as much wine as do Canada and New Zealand, mostly for tourist and home consumption, but we are seeing some in the UK, too: two producers are beginning to export, though largely to Turkish grocers and ethnic restaurants. Doluca, one of the most popular brands, is doing increasingly well with light, crisp wines made from the familiar varietals, plus interesting local grapes – limey, herbaceous Emir, floral, honeyed Narince in the whites, and robust plummy duo Oküzgözü and Bogazkere for the reds. Kavaklidere is the other exporter, but as yet only in tiny quantities. Turkey has a wealth of different micro-climates and indigenous grape varieties, and with winemaking taking a turn for the better, expect to see fresher, cleanly made, surprisingly light whites and robust tangy reds – both on holiday and (they're only moments away from clinching that big supermarket deal, we're told) at home.

UNITED STATES OF AMERICA

CALIFORNIA

Are all Californians overweight? It's a question we have to ask, as we taste those big-boned, bulky reds from the Napa Valley. It's a constant whinge this side of the Atlantic – and increasingly in America too – that we just can't drink more than a glass. Cabernets are too heavy on the palate to be able to appreciate more than a mouthful and the Zinfandels, at 15 per cent and more, are much too alcoholic. Not only this, the wines are also too fat. Winemakers are making sure there's a dollop of residual sugar in there to keep the palate sweet and give an appealing, rounded mouthful … which is all very nice for a generation brought up on burgers and lots of sugar, but we just don't think it's necessary. Where's the integrity of the fruit, the character from the vineyard? It's pretty much the same as smothering with too much oak: sugar, alcohol and sheer power are just different wine condiments that are being over-used. And it's not only the high-price 'Cult' wines we're accusing here, there are plenty of mid-priced 'monster' wines too.

Ah yes, those Cult wines. After revealing some of the astonishing prices they fetched last year, we're pleased to report the first signs that Cabernet fever is subsiding. News just in from US auctions is that there's been a distinct waning of enthusiasm. At the Zachy's Christie's 'California Only' auction in June 2001, Cult Cabernets struggled to meet their lowest estimates, and only 72 per cent of the lots sold. At other events the story's been the same: the annual Napa Valley Wine Auction we spoke of last year, this year took a drop in profits for the first time in ages. It could be that stock market jitters have persuaded bidders to be more cautious, or it could be that many of them have turned their attention to the much-lauded Bordeaux 2000s instead – but we have a suspicion that the tide is turning and people are asking for more than just top-whack, expensive Cabernet Sauvignon.

Indeed, California is in a state of flux. As Napa Valley's neighbour, Sonoma, continues to savvy-up, lose its country-cousin image and turn out just as many Cult-class blockbusters as Napa, people are looking to the Sierra Foothills instead for wines with a cosy, family-made feel. Sierra is the new Sonoma, in fact.

And in the Sierras, they've been quietly getting on with producing their own style of reds. Rhône and Italian varietals feature highly, and we recommend tracking down the Zinfandels, Syrahs and fruity, supple Barbera wines. Indeed, the enthusiasm for Syrah has been infectious and plantings are going in all over the state. Where Merlot was the grape of the 1980s and Cabernet turned gold in the 1990s, Syrah looks set to be the star of the 2000s.

If you listen to some commentators, all these chewy, chunky reds look set for doom and gloom as the plague Pierce's disease sweeps the state. We're told it's only a matter of time before its carriers, the glassy-winged sharpshooter flies, spread the bacteria to Napa and Sonoma. Pierce's has already caused widespread vine destruction in Temecula, east of Los Angeles, and the sharpshooters are making their way north. Once infected, the vine's vascular system is clogged up by Pierce's bacteria and the plant effectively starves to death. But people – the general public that is – have been called in to help in Operation Bugspot, thousands of sticky traps have been set up to catch the culprits, and every attempt is being made to prevent the encroachment. At the moment signs are positive and we're told the scale of disease has been vastly over-sensationalised. What we don't want to hear (and nor do the Californians) is that things have reached

'phylloxera proportions' and that full-scale wipeout is inevitable. Should the Florida labs continue their GM experiments to engineer the perfect resistant vine? Should scientists continue work on pesticides that are not 100 per cent effective and also present a danger to local population? We'd say this is a far knottier problem than conquering the auction scene.

White wines – grape varieties

Chardonnay

We are still concerned that after a period in the early 1990s when the ideal balance between oak, alcohol and sweet fruit appeared to have been struck, California Chardonnays seem to be getting bigger once again in all three departments – impressive to taste but a challenge to drink. Many of them are also very low in acidity, to the point of tasting like milkshake. A handful of progressive growers realise this, and are aiming to produce wines in a more balanced, minerally (they call it 'Burgundian') style. They are holding back malolactic fermentation which softens natural grape acids, and taking full advantage of newly planted, cooler vineyards. (Californians now seem to realise that their original Chardonnay vineyards were too warm, and so are seeking out cooler regions with their new plantings – there are good signs from Carneros, Russian River and the Sonoma Coast.) However, cool vineyards and better clones are not enough on their own. The winemaking has to be right too. And unfortunately, the progressive growers who are on the right tracks are very much in the minority. At the cheaper end of the market, we find the wines too sweet and under-flavoured, and more expensive ones are often oaky, clumsy and just plain overweight. Oh yes, and don't be fooled by the wines from the 1998 vintage: they might seem finer-tuned, but this is a sign of uneven ripeness that year, not necessarily of less oak.

Sauvignon Blanc

We're pleased to say that California Sauvignon has evolved in recent years, largely because many people who were never very enthusiastic about the variety have simply stopped making it. In addition, those who have continued have honed their winemaking to good effect. Wines used to split into two categories – flabby with oak and flabby without oak – but today, more of Sauvignon's crisp, grassy nature is evident in the wines. The fruit flavours are typically richer, riper and more tropical in nature than in Sauvignons from the Loire and New Zealand. The best oaked wines, the best, mind you, often labelled Fumé Blanc, can be very good, like fleshy, white Graves. The worst generally come from Napa and regions that are far too hot for this grape.

Viognier

The prime beneficiary (in the white wine department at least) of interest in Rhône grape varieties is Viognier. It will never be 'the new Chardonnay', but the Californians have quickly learned how to make wines which have plenty of Viognier's heady pearskin and apricot kernel aromas and flavours. As with the Chardonnays, some are just too weighty for their own good. However, some delicious wines are made, as many perhaps as in the northern Rhône. While most are expensive, Fetzer's version shows that good Viognier doesn't have to break the bank.

Others

The growing interest in and therefore pursuit of Rhône grape varieties has resulted in the gradual appearance of Marsanne and Roussanne which are making steady progress, with some producers (Alban especially) touching on greatness. Sadly, Riesling is increasingly rare, although a few producers still use it for opulent late-harvest wines. The abundance of Chardonnay means that Colombard and Chenin Blanc are appearing less and less, although Dry Creek Vineyards still makes a lovely Chenin. The rise in popularity of Italian red varieties has not been mirrored in whites, although we've tasted reasonable Malvasia and Tocai Friuliano; Pinot Grigio (Pinot Gris) doesn't do nearly as well as it does over the border in Oregon. Muscat in its various forms is being put to good use, most notably by Quady and Bonny Doon.

Red wines – grape varieties

Cabernet Sauvignon

Some of these wines are so massive that we wouldn't know what to do with them. The best, from Napa, Sonoma and a few spots south of San Francisco Bay, are deeply serious wines offering a level of complexity second only to Bordeaux. But many of the rest are gigantic, alcoholic 'blockbuster' wines that win prizes and fetch top auction prices, but even a whole glassful is difficult to drink – if you like them, we suggest you try the wines from Napa's hillside vineyards, which are some of the biggest mouthfuls! Producers have made great progress in making wines with more friendly tannins, and the result is Cabernets are now drinkable very young and can also (we're told) age well. But we're not so impressed by other tricks in the winery – leaving a slug of sugar in the wine to make it enticingly sweet tasting and playing with the acidity to the same effect. Many of the wines that result are too simple to merit their £10 (and higher) price tags. Signs are that people aren't prepared to pay as much for these monsters as they have in the past and, as with Chardonnay, there are a few growers attempting to make more elegant wines that go well with food. We like the best of these. There's something of the cassis note of claret, but the flavours are often more reminiscent of berries and plums, with notes of mint, olives, herbs and sometimes all three. It was Cabernet from the Napa Valley that first established California as a potentially great wine region, so let's hope Napa can put Cabernet back on track again.

Merlot
The great California Merlots are as good as almost anything from Pomerol, with a wealth of lush, plummy fruit and the structure to age for ten years or more. Unfortunately, Merlot is a victim of its own success, and the average standard is well below that of Cabernet Sauvignon. Cheaper versions are pulpy, soft and dilute, while more ambitious wines mistake enthusiastic extraction and lots of new oak for high quality.

Other Bordeaux reds
Many Bordeaux-inspired reds from California are now blends including Cabernet Sauvignon, Merlot, Cabernet Franc and even Petit Verdot and Malbec, some of which go by the ghastly name Meritage (rhymes with heritage). As with straight Cabernet, there's a gaping gulf between the good and the bad and the ugly. Single-varietal Cabernet Franc is rare but can be very tasty. Ironstone makes a cracker, while the more upmarket Bordeaux blends from Niebaum-Coppola, Sinskey, Schug and Lang & Reed have both intensity of flavour and the all-important perfume.

Pinot Noir
Many of the best California Pinot Noirs don't reach the UK, as they are made in quantities which would seem small even to a Burgundian. However, we see enough – from producers such as Saintsbury, Au Bon Climat or Calera – to know that places such as Carneros, new vineyards on the Sonoma Coast, Russian River Valley and Santa Barbara County are capable of making Pinot Noir with the sensual appeal of great burgundy, even if the fruit flavours are somewhat riper. Unfortunately, we also see too many inferior wines which are too jammy, dilute, or too oaky, and poor value at any price. Sterling's Redwood Trail and Ramsey Estate's delicious wine sell at around £10 a bottle, but sadly we can't think of many others over here to recommend.

Zinfandel
Although now confirmed as being identical to southern Italy's Primitivo, Zinfandel can fairly be called California's own grape. It comes in all versions from pink (or 'white' as the marketing types would have it) to fortified, but the best are robust, juicy reds with

plenty of gutsy berry-fruit. Just a minor complaint, however. We realise that Zinfandel was never meant to be elegant, but with more than a few wines now weighing in at 16 per cent alcohol or more, it seems that some producers are playing a rather childish game of 'mine's bigger than yours'. Strangely enough, the prices for these big wines are getting bigger and bigger too.

Syrah

Watch out Australia. Syrah in California has just gone crazy. It's arguably better suited to many existing wine regions than Cabernet, and we've been very impressed by most of what we've tasted so far. The worry now, unfortunately, is have growers been greedy and planted too much? Over the last few years over 8,000 new hectares have gone in, and if there aren't quite as many takers as they anticipated it could be a disaster for quality. But, let's not get too pessimistic. The general style is for full-bodied, fruity wines similar to those of Australia, but which veer a little more towards the elegance and perfume of the Rhône. As we say, we've been very impressed. Again, kudos to Fetzer for a delicious, sensibly priced version.

Others

Syrah isn't the only Rhône variety enjoying popularity. Thanks to the activities since the 1980s of a band of producers who call themselves the Rhône Rangers, Grenache and Mourvèdre, often sourced from ancient vineyards, have risen in popularity. There is also the Cal-Ital brigade, producers who have planted Italian grapes such as Sangiovese (Noceto is delicious) and Nebbiolo (look for Il Podere dell'Olivos), and are also beginning to take more of an interest in the many old Barbera vines dotted around the state.

Sparkling wines

The enthusiasm for California's sparklers remains muted, a shame as the best can be very good indeed. Each year we hear of several new wineries specialising in Bordeaux- or Burgundy-style wines, but there are few newcomers who choose to concentrate on fizz. Indeed, many of those who set up as specialist fizz producers are now including still wines in their portfolio, simply because they make more money by doing so. We wish this weren't the case as the best wines, usually based on Pinot Noir and Chardonnay from cool-climate regions such as Carneros or Anderson Valley, are only a whisker away in style from the French originals, and can be eminently confusing. Look especially, for those linked to France's top champagne houses – Cuvée Napa Mumm, Domaine Carneros from Taittinger and Roederer Estate have all the skill and wines with not a little pizzazz.

The regions

Wines labelled 'California' must have been produced from grapes entirely from the state. If 75 per cent of the grapes (85 per cent for wines entering the EU) come from one of the state's 58 counties (Sonoma for example), that county can be named on the label. Approved Viticultural Areas (AVAs) are distinguished by their geographical features alone, not by the quality of the wines.

Napa Valley

California's most famous wine region is only 20 miles long, but it contains a large number of AVAs: Stags Leap, Oakville and Rutherford among them. Napa is known primarily for Chardonnay and Cabernet, but beware over-hyped wines – not everything from Napa merits its high price tag. There are wide variations in climate depending on whether a vineyard is on a hillside or the valley floor, and also whether it lies at the cool, southern end or the warm, northern end. The hillside vineyards (the Howell Mountain, Mount Veeder, Atlas Peak and Diamond Mountain AVAs) are fast gaining a reputation for producing the brawniest Napa wines of the lot, but a few growers outside these areas are, thankfully, making wines with more elegance. Much hard graft is currently taking place out in the vineyard, where a large number of Napa wineries are moving over (or moving closer to) organic viticulture, and/or testing new clonal material. But in case you see any, we say avoid Napa Sauvignon Blanc!

Sonoma County

Just over a hill from Napa, but often seemingly a world apart, Sonoma has in the past been more laid-back than its over-hyped neighbour, but it's catching up fast. It's a much larger region, boasting everything from ancient Zinfandel vineyards in the Dry Creek Valley, to brand-new plantings of top-grade Pinot Noir and Chardonnay in the cool Russian River, Alexander Valley has something of everything as soil and climate vary so much, but the real region to watch is the new Sonoma Coast AVA – where all the most fashionable Pinot Noirs and Chardonnays are beginning to be made. Most grapes grow well in Sonoma, and the standards are high – Zinfandel, Chardonnay, Pinot and Shiraz are all better here than in Napa. As a region, it might have nearly as much shoulder-padding as Napa these days, but fortunately it still has more charm.

Carneros

The relatively cool Carneros Valley at the southern end of Napa and Sonoma is shared between them and offers good sparkling wine, complex Pinot Noir as well as elegant Chardonnay.

Mendocino and Lake Counties

These two northernmost California wine counties both provide good-value wines. Mendocino is a cool coastal region where Fetzer and a couple of top sparkling producers are at work; Lake County is making a splash, particularly with Sauvignon Blanc. As it becomes increasingly expensive to buy land in Napa and Sonoma, it's likely we'll see more and more from these areas.

Central Coast

A huge AVA which stretches from San Francisco to Los Angeles and incorporates:

Edna Valley A cool valley in San Luis Obispo, making some of the most exquisite Chardonnay around.

Monterey Coolish coastal spot south of San Francisco; generally underrated but becoming better known for Pinot Noir, Pinot Blanc and Chardonnay.

San Joaquin Valley Part of the baking hot Central Valley, where much of the bargain-basement California jug wine is made.

Santa Cruz Mountainous district south of San Francisco, home to a handful of off-beat wineries such as Ridge and Bonny Doon.

Santa Maria and Santa Ynez Valleys Part of the relatively cool-climate Santa Barbara County, these up-and-coming areas make fantastic Chardonnay and Pinot Noir, and increasingly impressive Syrah.

Sierra Foothills

Is Sierra the new Sonoma? Vineyards were in fact established in the Sierra Foothills (to slake the thirst of local gold miners) long before they were in Napa. All but the highest, coolest sites are warm and best suited to red varieties: Zinfandel, Syrah and other Rhône grapes work best. There are also good results from Italian varieties – we definitely like the results from juicy, low-tannin Barbera. As yet, this is still a very under-appreciated region, so the wines tend to be cheaper!

Pick of the producers

Au Bon Climat One of the best Santa Barbara wineries, producing Burgundian-style Pinot Noir and classy, ageworthy Chardonnay. Owner Jim Clendenen also makes fine Italian-style wines under the Il Podere dell'Olivos label.

Beaulieu Vineyard Historically important Napa estate which was overtaken by others in the 1980s but is now showing a classy return to form with Private Reserve Cabernet, classy red blend Tapestry and an all-Carneros Chardonnay.

Beringer Huge Napa operation producing admirably accomplished wines across a wide range. Reds from the Bancroft Ranch on Howell Mountain are deeply sophisticated, and the Chardonnays are consistently ripe and fruity, rather than over-rich. Recently joined forces with Mildara-Blass.

Boeger High-elevation Sierra Foothills vineyards producing elegant wines – from 25 varieties including Riesling. Warmer sites produce great reds: signature Zinfandel and Barbera are especially good.

Bonny Doon Splendid, if erratic, collection of eccentricities based on anything that isn't a mainstream variety. Rhône, southern French and Italian varieties feature, as does Riesling. Winemaker/ philosopher/ dude Randall Grahm's Rhône-style wines are probably his best.

Bonterra (see *Fetzer*, below).

Cain Chris Howell's complex and subtle Bordeaux blend Cain Five is one of California's most underrated wines. Also delicious Sauvignon Musqué from a perfumed clone of Sauvignon.

Calera Monterey producer of palatable and ageworthy Pinot Noir, especially the single-vineyard wines. Also fine Chardonnay and Viognier.

Caymus Special Selection has been at the top of the Napa Cabernet tree for many years. Sauvignon Blanc is also produced, as is a sweetish white blend.

Chalone Wine Group Parent company for a number of wineries. These include Chalone itself and Acacia, both sources of lovely Chardonnay and Pinot Noir; Jade Mountain which specialises in Rhône-style reds; Carmenet which specialises in Bordeaux-style reds and whites; and Edna Valley Vineyards, which excels with Chardonnay. Quality vastly improved since arrival of new winemaker in 1998. A new top-end Napa Cabernet is to be launched in the near future.

Domaine Chandon Moët-owned sparkling operation in Napa making admirable progress in recent years.

Cline Cellars Specialists in big, powerful reds based on Rhône varietals from ancient vineyards.

Clos du Val Pioneering Stags Leap operation run by a Frenchman, Bernard Portet, and now producing delicious reds with none of the harsh tannins of early vintages.

Cuvaison Swiss-owned winery turning out tasty Carneros Chardonnay and improved reds, including juicy Pinot Noir.

Diamond Creek A range of single-vineyard Napa Cabernets which are tight when young but age splendidly. Quality in 1995, 1996 and 1997 is superb.

Dominus Increasingly impressive Napa wines produced under the guidance of Christian Moueix of Château Pétrus.

Duckhorn Big, concentrated Howell Mountain Merlot is the jewel in the crown at this Napa winery. Paraduxx (geddit?) is the separate brand for chunky Zinfandel. Big investments are beginning to pay off.

Dry Creek Large, well-made range of Sonoma wines including dense-packed, old-vine Zinfandels, unusual Chenin Blanc and hefty Petite Sirah. Good, long agers.

Fetzer Large Mendocino winery with a vast portfolio, most of it commendable. Look out for the organic wines under the Bonterra label and the top-of-the-range Private Collection.

Frog's Leap Organic viticulture produces delicious juicy Zinfandel and Cabernet among others, at this jolly Napa operation. John Williams' aim is for his wines to be 'less Jennifer Lopez, more Coco Chanel' – they are, indeed, more classy than many.

E & J Gallo Mammoth organisation making more wine than the whole of Australia. Avoid the cheaper labels such as Turning Leaf, Indigo Hills and Garnet Point and head for the Gallo Sonoma wines, especially the complex Chardonnays.

Grgich Hills Beret-clad Mike Grgich arrived in the USA from Croatia in 1958 and has since made consistently fine, structured wines without any concession to modern 'sweetness'. They're unostentatious, but show the best of the Napa Valley.

Harlan Estate Napa estate producing small amounts of powerful, ageworthy Cabernet. Cult stuff.

Hanzell Progressive, neo-Burgundian winery established in the 1950s, and always ahead of its time. Exceptional and long-ageing Chardonnay and Pinot Noir. Snap them up if you see them.

Hess Collection Cabernet is the main attraction here, especially the Napa Valley Reserve; the Chardonnays also impress. Not flashy wines, but worth a look!

Jordan Sonoma winery; the 'J' sparkler ranks highly.

Kendall-Jackson The Vintners Reserve range is a best-seller in the USA, while the single-vineyard wines, especially the Camelot Chardonnay, are top-notch. Also owns other brands such as Cambria, La Crema, Matanzas Creek (a recent purchase) and Stonestreet.

Kistler Sonoma specialist in single-vineyard, very expensive Chardonnay, but also lovely Pinot Noir. Resting on laurels: they need to be challenged.

Landmark Sonoma grower of supremely good Chardonnay and Pinot Noir: 'all decisions are based on palate, not chemistry' says winemaker Eric Stern.

Marcassin Helen Turley, described by the wine critic Robert Parker as a winemaking 'goddess', is consultant winemaker for some of California's finest (and most expensive) wines. This is her own label, under which she releases small amounts of opulent Sonoma Coast Chardonnay and Pinot Noir.

Marimar Torres Miguel Torres' sister Marimar makes opulent and ever-improving Chardonnay and Pinot Noir in Sonoma.

Peter Michael Chardonnays and a Bordeaux blend of considerable class are the best wines from ex-pat Sir Peter Michael. Wines come from cooler vineyard sites in Knights Valley and Sonoma Coast. Helen Turley (see *Marcassin*, above) was original consultant for first (1987) vintage.

Robert Mondavi Founder of the modern Californian wine industry, still at the top, and experimenting continuously to find ways to improve. Bypass the so-so Woodbridge range (mostly from the Central Valley) in favour of the wines from Napa and other coastal districts. Cabernet, Chardonnay, Zinfandel and Pinot Noir all impress. Look out also for the Italian varietal range La Famiglia di Robert Mondavi. Has joint ventures in Chile (Seña, with Errázuriz),

Tuscany (Luce, with the Frescobaldis), with the Rothschilds in California (see *Opus One*, below) but ventures in the south of France have not yet been as successful.

Mumm Cuvée Napa Reliable, fruity sparklers from Mumm's West Coast operation, with top-of-the-range DVX made in conjunction with Champagne Devaux.

Newton Fruit from coolish mountain vineyards makes complex, well-balanced Cabernet, Merlot and Chardonnay.

Niebaum-Coppola Film magnate Francis Ford Coppola's wine holdings now encompass the Inglenook winery, producing serious reds with high kudos – and price tags. Rubicon is the top, prestige blend, while Coppola Family wines are good and good value.

Opus One Illustrious and expensive joint venture from the Mondavi and Rothschild empires. Style is Napa Valley crossed with Bordeaux. Delicious, ageworthy Cabernet-based blends.

Pedroncelli Fourth- and fifth-generation Sonoma growers: specialists with an intriguing range of Zinfandels.

Joseph Phelps Admirable pioneer of single-vineyard Cabernet, classy Bordeaux blend Insignia and Rhône varietals, including Syrah and Viognier. Unsurprisingly, this classy winery now has a new venture in the trendy Sonoma Coast.

Quady Eccentric Central Valley producer of quirky dessert wines and port-style fortifieds – and Vya Vermouth.

Qupé More Rhône varietals, including Marsanne and Syrah, from this Santa Barbara innovator.

Ravenswood Sonoma winery rightly famed for its rich, fruity Zinfandels.

Renaissance Classy Sierra Foothills estate for steely, crisp Sauvignon, Cabernet and even late-harvest Riesling.

Ridge Working high in the Santa Cruz mountains to make some of the state's most complex and concentrated Zinfandels and Cabernets, Paul Draper is one of California's most dedicated winemakers. Very reasonable prices (in Californian terms).

Roederer Estate Mendocino County offshoot of the champagne house Louis Roederer. Top wine Quartet is one of the West Coast's finest sparklers.

Saintsbury Dynamic duo Dick Ward and David Graves specialise in lovely Pinot Noir and Chardonnay from Carneros.

Sanford Top-notch Santa Barbara Pinot Noir, Chardonnay and Sauvignon characterised by intense, pure flavours – the Pinot Noir is almost more Rhône than Burgundy…

Schramsberg Glamorous Napa producer of super, sparkling wines.

Schug Carneros grower of Pinot Noir and Bordeaux blends. Walter Schug has moved on from an illustrious career making high-price Napa heavyweights, to producing wines under his own label, with far more elegance and finesse.

Screaming Eagle Sadly, only 6,000 bottles of Jean Phillips' seductively rich and extremely cultish Napa Cabernet are made in a typical vintage. Of the Cult wines, this is one of the best – it's not just about new oak!

Shafer Stags Leap winery specialising in supple, sweetly ripe reds, best of which is brilliant Hillside Select Cabernet. Also notable Sangiovese/Cabernet blend called Firebreak. Red Shoulder Chardonnay (token white) is a strapping wine.

Simi Sonoma producer of excellent Chardonnay and Sauvignon; Cabernet much improved recently.

Sonoma-Cutrer Chardonnay specialist – the intricate, single-vineyard Les Pierres Chardonnay is top of the pile.

Sinskey Robert Sinskey's wines are as organic, elegant and as 'Bordeaux' as he can make them. He's looking for food matchability, not the 'cherry dollops' other Napa growers achieve.

Sobon Estate Dense, concentrated Zinfandel and Sangiovese from old Sierra Foothills vines – also good Barbera and Syrah. Shenandoah is second label for still impressive reds.

Stag's Leap Wine Cellars Superb Cask 23 Cabernet, with the SLV and Fay *cuvées* not very far behind.

Sterling Vineyards Huge, Seagram-owned Napa winery capable of producing good-value wines – but tread carefully. Soft, easy-drinking Redwood Trail Pinot Noir is a good place to start.

California vintage guide

California wines are drunk young, but the most serious Cabernets require several years – as much as a decade in some cases – to reach ideal maturity. Beyond ten years the jury's still out on how long they'll last. Fine Chardonnays can also benefit from two years' bottle age for the oak influence to calm down, but after that extra age is not necessarily beneficial.

2000 A mild vintage with two heat peaks and a 5.2-rated earthquake, plus a dash of rain at harvest, could have been tricky but in fact yielded sound, strong reds of consistent quality and white and sparkling wines that benefited from the initial coolness. Yields were about average but tonnage up by 23 per cent due to increased plantings. Expect to see more California wine than ever!

1999 'Late, small and great', was the verdict from one producer. A long, cool growing season, with vintage as much as six weeks behind schedule in some areas, resulted in a reduced crop of small, intensely flavoured grapes. Expect rich, powerful reds and well-balanced whites.

1998 The effects of El Niño resulted in record rainfall together with record lows and highs of temperatures, and the harvest was also one of the latest on the books. Fine autumn weather saved the vintage from being a complete write-off, but several wines are not up to their usual standards – so tread with caution.

1997 After two small vintages, this was a record harvest for California. Initial worries that it would make dilute wines have proved groundless, and quality is very good across the board, with the Cabernet vying with 1994, 1991 and probably 1999 for the best of the decade.

1996 Just like the previous year, this was a short vintage – up to 30 per cent down on average crops. Quality, however, was high, especially for Chardonnay and Merlot.

1995 Heavy rain, cool temperatures and hail all contributed to a small vintage (down 20 per cent) but due to a warm, dry harvest, the quality was ideal. Excellent reds.

1994 The prolonged growing season made for intense dark reds, with Cabernet and Pinot Noir being especially fine.

1993 A late, difficult harvest with reduced quantities in many areas, but first-class Chardonnay, and structured Cabernets which appeal more to European palates than American.

1992 After several years of drought, 1992 saw copious winter rain. A hot summer followed and the harvest was gathered in superb conditions. A small crop of ripe, forward wines, which should now be drunk up quickly!

1991 Generally very good-quality reds, with tannins which will preserve the wines for several years to come.

1990 Wonderful year producing extremely rich Chardonnay and ageworthy Cabernet.

OREGON

It is inevitable that the Oregonians compete with the Californians – they're direct neighbours. But in the face of all that California glitz, don't rule out these plucky 'northerners', who can do certain things better; Pinot Noir, for example. It makes up 80 per cent of Oregon's vine plantings and in its heartland, the northern Willamette Valley, growers take it very seriously. A few California Pinots *are* better, but when Oregon gets it right the seamless, silky pleasures of the Côte d'Or flood the senses. Sadly, we think the Oregon growers are getting a little greedy and their hit-rate is slipping. When these wines are carefully made, on an 'artistic' scale, they are good, but when they're churned out by the 'factory-load' we're not so impressed by some of the quality or value for money. Just like Burgundy in fact.

Hiding in Pinot Noir's shadow is a grape the Californians really cannot do well – Pinot Gris. In Oregon this has been the standard white grape for around 25 years, well-made, by many, but totally under-appreciated. It was initially used as a cash crop, for cheap gluggable wine to fill in the gaps while the Pinot Noirs matured in cask. This state's cooler climate means that more natural acidity is retained in the grapes. Some Pinot Gris are fermented in stainless steel and bottled when young, giving a sprightly, spicy wine, while others are fermented and aged in oak barrel, which results in a fuller, richer version, like a gingery Chardonnay. Our hot tip is to look out for these wines before the Californians get hold of them all, and the Oregonians realise they're on to a good thing and bump the prices up.

The other news story in Oregon at the moment (and as it is everywhere!) is Syrah. Further south than the Willamette Valley are the Umpqua and Rogue Valleys, where the weather is warm enough to ripen varieties such as Cabernet Sauvignon and even Zinfandel: it's here Syrah is doing really well. Compared with California's, Oregon's Syrah is less 'fruit-ball', more Old World in texture, and less generally Shirazy. Its huge style advantage is that it shows well even from lesser growers. The last three vintages (the small 1998, big 1999 and 2000) have really put this grape on the map, and the Californians in their place.

Riesling, Viognier, Marsanne, Roussanne and Sangiovese (hot on the heels of Syrah), are also showing positive signs in Oregon. In other US states a varietal wine only needs 75 per cent of a grape in the blend to take its name, but from Oregon the minimum is 90 per cent. So you get more of what you think you are getting!

Pick of the producers

Adelsheim Growing winery (15 to now 164 acres) in third decade, with new Pinot Gris and Pinot Blanc to add to Pinot Noir, Chardonnay and Riesling. Smooth, balanced wines.

Amity The heavily bearded and hippyish Myron Redford is one of Oregon's greatest characters. His ripe, cherry-flavoured Winemaker Reserve Pinot Noir and spicy Dry Gewurztraminer are both delicious.

Beaux Frères Exciting producer of pure, rich Pinot Noir. The American wine writer Robert Parker is a shareholder.

Bethel Heights Well-made Pinot Noir from Willamette, since 1977. Chardonnay, Pinots Blanc and Gris all aim at Burgundy style.

Domaine Drouhin French know-how combined with Oregon fruit makes for very fine Pinot Noir, especially the Laurene *cuvée*. Recently introduced Chardonnay also excellent.

Elk Cove Decent Pinot Gris and relatively rich Pinot from this winery in the north-west corner of the Willamette Valley.

Erath Vineyards Leading producer of consistently well-balanced Oregon Pinot Noir, Pinot Gris and Chardonnay.

Eyrie Well known for ground-breaking Pinot Noir back in the 1970s, and today notable for particularly fine whites as well – try the Pinot Gris or Chardonnay if you spot them on a wine list.

Henry Estate Based down south in the Umpqua Valley, Henry Estate is notable for its ripe Pinot.

King Estate Oregon's largest producer, providing the consistency with Pinot Noir which others in the state often lack. Reserve bottlings very good, as are those of Pinot Gris.

Ponzi Founded by Dick and Nancy Ponzi in 1970, with second generation now champing at the bit. Pinot Noir and Riesling are top rank; plus Pinot Gris, Chardonnay and Italian varietals.

Sokol Blosser Innovative producer of top Pinot Noir, Chardonnay and Riesling. The 'Randall Grahm' of Oregon. (See *Bonny Doon*, California, above.)

Willamette Valley Vineyards Sound, rather than exciting, range of wines from one of the state's best-known operations. The OVB –

Our Very Best – wines are, er, the very best they do, with the Pinot Noir being the pick.

Ken Wright Wright's range of silky Pinot Noirs sets him among the most notable producers in the state. Pinot Gris also amazing.

WASHINGTON STATE

Syrah is everywhere this year, but few places are doing it better than Washington State, whose versions are outrightly characterful, full of bright, earthy fruit, with more background structure and less overripe jam than those down south in California. But how come this is the case – Oregon excels with that cool-climate grape Pinot Noir, and Washington is further north again, so it ought to be cooler. So how does a big, red grape like Syrah do so well?

In Washington, the vineyards of the Columbia River Valley lie on the dry, eastern side of the Cascade Ranges, in stark contrast to Oregon, where they're on the coastal west – which is more lush and damper. This is one of the most arid, empty, sun-bleached spots in North-West America, yet as you fly across it, heading east from Seattle, you suddenly spot enormous green circular vineyards among the pale, scrubby wasteland. On each circle sits a long metal arm, like the hand of a huge clock. This is the irrigation pipe that keeps the vines verdant in this otherwise desert landscape. This is where those marvellous Syrahs grow.

The vineyards started life in the early 1970s, planted near to the Yakima and Columbia rivers for that essential irrigation water. The first company to plant here was called Associated Vintners – now Columbia Winery – followed by Chateau Ste Michelle. Just like the Oregon pioneers, most wine industry folk who settled here were on the look-out for suitable alternative vineyard sites outside expensive California. The long periods of hot, sunny weather and cooler nights meant that the Yakima Valley fitted the bill. Besides, the land was cheap.

The best wines are all reds – Syrah, Merlot, Cabernet Sauvignon and Grenache – both in the Columbia River Valley and further east in Walla Walla (generally speaking the home of smaller, boutique wineries). As growers learn to control the irrigation and let the vines benefit from the reliably dry, end-of-vintage weather, some stunningly accessible wines are emerging. (We even hear they're beating the Bordeaux *crus classés* and California's Opus One in blind tastings.) Look out too for wines of the new AVA Red Mountain. This warmer pocket is making reds that are even bigger, more powerful than many. Riesling has always done well in terms of whites, but today we think Cabernet Sauvignon-based wines are doing better still.

As vineyards and winemaking evolve, Washington's wines are becoming more complex, all the while retaining the pure, sunny, fruit flavour which seem to be the state's hallmarks. Since 1997, there have been no poor vintages – so we say, go for it!

Pick of the producers

Chateau Ste Michelle One of the state's pioneers, producing premium wine in Washington for 30 years. Best known for Merlot and Cabernet, although we think highly of the fruit-packed Chardonnay too. New joint venture with Antinori (Italy) has produced impressive Col Solare, while another very successful collaboration is that with Ernst Loosen of the Mosel in Germany to produce the wonderful limey Eroica Riesling. Parent company Stimson Lane also owns Columbia Crest for entry-level wines.

Columbia Winery English Master of Wine David Lake is the founding father of Syrah in Washington State: when he first planted it in 1985, he was thought to be misguided. A very good range, including a lovely Syrah from the Red Willow vineyard.

Delille Bordeaux blends (red and white both excellent) from Woodinville Francophiles. Ageworthy Chaleur is the top label Cabernet/Merlot blend; delicious, approachable D2 (named after the main road through the Médoc) is number two. New Syrah coming on stream.

L'Ecole 41 Beautifully crafted, flavour-packed wines from small producer based in Walla Walla. Don't miss the creamy, ripe Semillon if you ever get the chance to sample it – there are three different styles, best of which is Bordeaux-blend Apogee. Good Chenin and Merlot also splendid in a rich, oaky way.

Hedges Fine, all-round selection topped by full-bodied but supple Three Vineyards Cabernet/Merlot and superb Merlot-dominated, structured Red Mountain Reserve. (Hedges led the drive to establish the new Red Mountain appellation.)

Hogue Cellars Successful large operation making a modern, 'fruit-forward' (their description) range, including a crisp, citrusy Fumé Blanc Sauvignon, juicy Chardonnay, rich Syrah and well-structured Merlot. The top-of-the-range Genesis varietals are outstanding. Entry-level Syrah and Viognier sell like hot cakes.

Leonetti Rare but fabulous Cabernet and Merlot, both of which benefit from ageing. Also successful with Sangiovese.

Quilceda Creek Well-made Cabernet Sauvignon with lots of finesse from a tiny Puget Sound winery, where Alex and Jeanette Golitzin, their son Paul and son-in-law Marv are at the helm.

McCrea Puget Sound winery for especially good Syrah, Viognier and Grenache and other Rhône varietals. Complex, elegant wines made within sight of Mt Rainier.

Andrew Will Rarely available in the UK, but if you come across the classy Cabernets and Merlots made by Chris Camarda, snap them up. They're all boutique-quality, from individual vineyard sites.

IDAHO

Idaho has been making wine since the 1860s, so is far from being a newcomer. The 14 wineries, that initially started up along the cool Snake River Valley, took a knocking during Prohibition, but, gathering some reflected glory from neighbouring Washington and Oregon, at long last things are beginning to pick up again. With just over 700 acres planted, there's a long way to go before we see many of these wines in the UK; but the aim is high – to make Nampa Idaho as popular as Napa California! Wineries to watch out for are Pend d'Oreille, Camas and Ste-Chapelle, but more are springing up almost as we write. We're told Idaho has better Rieslings than almost anywhere and reds that'll soon be on a par with those in Washington. Watch this space.

OTHER STATES

The most important and prolific after California, Washington State and Oregon is undoubtedly New York State. Coolish-climate vineyards alongside the Finger Lakes in upstate New York can produce palatable, oaked Chardonnay and quite appealing Riesling, often as a late-harvest wine. This coolness is also an asset for making great, traditional sparklers, especially at Lamoreaux Landing, and also at Glenora estate. For still wines, grower names to look out for are Fox Run and Wagner.

Closer to the Big Apple, on Long Island, a few boutique wineries are producing increasingly impressive Chardonnay and Merlot in a rich, fruit-driven style. With a huge wine-quaffing metropolis less than three hours' drive away, the Long Island winemakers are in no rush to export their wines; if you find yourself in New York, we recommend you sample them, especially those from Bridgehampton, Hargrave, Peconic Bay and Pindar.

Of the remaining 46 states, 36 of them (including Hawaii) produce wines. Our experience of these has ranged from an excellent Zinfandel from Callaghan Vineyards in Arizona, a couple of decent, sparkling wines from Michigan and a surprisingly good Texan Gewurztraminer, to a quite dreadful, murky red from Missouri. There are also small-players making good Riesling in Colorado and New Mexico, we're told. But as far as winemaking on a serious scale is concerned, we're still waiting for news from Virginia and Maryland where signs are promising. Once more wines from these states are available in the UK, we'll tell you more about them.

URUGUAY

The Uruguayans arc going to have to tone it down a bit – the tannins in their Tannats are just too huge. This thick-skinned, rot-resistant variety might do very well in Uruguay's relatively damp climate and, there's no doubt about it, they've chosen the right unique selling point, as this grape really blossoms away from its spiritual home (Madiran in South-western France, where it's sturdier still and more severe). But at the moment Uruguayan versions are steak-friendly and chewy; we prefer the Tannats made with French advice, which are softer, structured and thick with tarry berry and plum fruit – even softened up by adding Merlot or Cabernet Franc – but without the rough prominent tannins that the locals have got used to. Look out for Casa Luntro and Casilla Dorada, made by the Frenchman, Jacques Lurton, and Juanico's wines (made by the Australian, Peter Bright), plus Filgueira, Pisano, Irurtia, Castillo Viejo and Castel Pujol, and you'll see what we mean. On the other hand, seek out Vino de El Colorado's (admittedly delicious) Tannat, if you want to see the monster version – it's a meal in itself. We also prefer the younger vintages as, contrary to expectations, the tannins tend to fall apart very quickly with age. In short, there's more work to do, but let's hope the Uruguayans continue to strive for elegance.

As well as Tannat available in the UK, there are also some muscly Syrah and Cabernet, plus Merlot and Pinot – the latter can be a bit jammy and boring but the best have plenty of easy-going 'Chilean' appeal. Chardonnay and even Sauvignon have an increasing presence too.

It's too early to seek out definitive regional characteristics, but from the Rivera region in the north of Uruguay expect more powerful reds from hotter soils; from the south, around Montevideo, where vineyard temperatures are tempered by Atlantic breezes, you'll see fruitier, more supple, styles emerge.

271

ZIMBABWE

The troubled political situation in Zimbabwe is unchanged, and the great potential this country has for making wine is the least of local concerns. We hope that, in the not too distant future, the winemaking practices that showed so much improvement before the unrest will be put to good use again – but at the moment progress is looking unlikely. Zimbabwean wines won't be making it to the UK for the foreseeable future.

Part III

What is wine?

GRAPE VARIETIES

PREMIER LEAGUE

The following grapes have probably given more pleasure to wine drinkers over the centuries than any others. Whether currently in vogue or not, these are the classic grape varieties that most consistently provide the best wine.

Red

Cabernet Sauvignon

Could this be the most uniformly successful grape variety of all time – the class swot who excels at everything? Certainly, we cannot think of anyone who dislikes the deep colour and blackcurrant, mint and cedar character of fine Cabernet Sauvignon. Winemakers adore it, so much so that any estate in the Iberian peninsula, southern France or the New World that turns its attention to Cabernet seems suddenly to have arrived. And Old World Cabernet has been clasped to the bosom of British wine drinkers for many years, as it is a major component in one of the UK's favourite wines – claret.

In Bordeaux, while hardly ever giving an entirely solo performance (1994 Lafite was a recent exception, apparently), Cabernet plays the starring role in the great wines of the Médoc and Graves. The wines it creates here range from the rustic *petits châteaux* to elegant *crus classés*, the latter beautifully poised and dusty dry, with plenty of Cabernet's cassis character held rigid when young by a magnificent structure of tannins.

A reasonably hardy grape, Cabernet has travelled well, and now appears in many shapes and forms. Californian, South African and Australian Cabernets can be first rate in a hefty, rich style, with lush, ripe fruit to the fore. More recently, Argentina and Washington State have impressed us with the best of their Cabernets. And Chile seems to have an effortless ability to turn out affordable examples that sing with pure blackcurranty varietal character.

Back in Europe, the south of France has proved it can turn out juicy, ripe Cabernet at fair prices, while Italy creates some of the most sophisticated, multi-layered Cabernet blends. In Australia, Cabernet is successfully blended with Shiraz, in Tuscany with Sangiovese, and in Spain with Tempranillo. But Cabernet's most regular bedfellow is Merlot, favoured in Bordeaux because its lush, plummy character softens up Cabernet's toughness. Most of the world's best Cabernet is aged in French oak *barriques,* but American oak has produced some excellent examples in California and in Rioja.

Merlot

High-class grape or fashion victim? Merlot plays both roles convincingly. In its home of Bordeaux, it's traditionally been an understudy to the more serious Cabernet Sauvignon, fleshing out Cabernet's rather austere nature. However, the last 20 years have seen a surge in quality of the wonderfully plummy, Merlot-heavy wines of St-Emilion and Pomerol, and with it a huge upturn in demand. The result is that all parts of the world have jumped on the Merlot bandwagon, eager to produce Château Pétrus lookalikes. Some, especially in California, Washington State and Hawke's Bay, have enjoyed great success. Others have only made large quantities of rather anonymous, simple, jammy wines. The problem is that given the right conditions, Merlot goes wild in the vineyard, and produces plump but largely flavourless grapes. The result is that much cheap Merlot tastes just that – cheap. Exceptions exist, especially in southern France, parts of Eastern Europe and Chile. Be warned about Chilean Merlot though. As we explain earlier in the book, much of it is made from an unrelated variety called Carmenère. This can be terrific – but Merlot it ain't.

Pinot Noir

Pinot gets a bad press for being one of the most difficult varieties in the world. This is indeed a fickle and exasperating grape, especially in comparison with the accommodating Cabernet. It suffers partly from being thin-skinned and sensitive to poor conditions, but also because expectations of it are so high. On a good day, Pinot Noir can be truly beguiling. As a fine young red, it is gorgeous, raspberry-scented, silky and winsome. When it ages, it takes on a voluptuous, earthy character, turning more pungent and animal-scented all the time. And as a component in champagne and premium sparkling wine, it adds red-berry fruitiness and perfume.

Shame then that it so often refuses to be seduced. The winemakers of Oregon, once heralded as Pinot's home from home, are familiar with the quixotic nature of the grape, and its inability to withstand less-than-perfect weather conditions. The Australians have managed to make elegant Pinot Noir only in relatively cool spots, such as Victoria's Yarra Valley or Tasmania, while in South Africa and Chile just a few good examples exist to prove that it may have a future there.

New Zealand provides more exciting Pinots – indeed, it is the most widely planted red variety. Several plots on the South Island plus Martinborough at the foot of the North Island are already enjoying considerable success with the grape, and the best may be yet to come. Parts of California where the warm sun is tempered by cool Pacific breezes have also proved ideal for Pinot. Regions such as Carneros, Russian River and Santa Barbara County are able to coax it into consistently lush, concentrated wines.

However, it is in Burgundy, if the weather is right and the winemaking shrewd (pretty big 'ifs'), that Pinot Noir is at its best, with a smooth, lush, red-berry youth and a farmyard-rich maturity.

Sensitive in all things, Pinot yields need to be kept low, and oaking should be relatively light. And it is almost always expensive – at the lower end of the price spectrum look out for a few pleasant Romanian wines from the region of Dealul Mare and a few examples from Chile.

Syrah/Shiraz

Syrah scores a double whammy – it is both a star variety in a classic European region (the Rhône Valley), and in Australia, where it goes by the name of Shiraz. After years of kowtowing to Cabernet and Pinot, it is finally receiving the recognition it deserves, and more and more countries are planting Syrah in their vineyards. Good Syrah combines the structure of Cabernet with the wild perfume of Pinot. It ages to herby, spicy, leathery complexity, and is a brilliant partner for red meat, roast poultry and cheese.

In the northern Rhône, Syrah is worshipped, producing great wines such as Côte-Rôtie and Hermitage. Plantings in the south of France have increased significantly over the past 15 years or so. Some wines produced from these have been ripe and satisfying, and it is successfully blended with Cabernet, Merlot, Grenache and Mourvèdre. The Languedoc region of southern France has impressed in recent years with its concentrated, rich *vin de pays* Syrahs. In the southern Rhône, Syrah makes a small but invaluable contribution to most of the great wines of Châteauneuf-du-Pape and Gigondas.

The Australians, on the other hand, despite the success of Penfolds Grange (which typically is 90 per cent Shiraz), only recognised it as their greatest traditional red grape towards the end of the twentieth century. Shiraz from ancient, gnarled Australian vines is inky black, hugely concentrated and rich (too rich, in some instances), while the fun, red sparkling Shiraz is an Australian speciality worth trying.

Where once Australia and France had a virtual monopoly on quality Syrah, good versions can now be found in Chile, Argentina, Spain, Italy, Greece, New Zealand and even Morocco. And while the Australians may currently be the New World Syrah champions, the quality of wines being made now in California and Washington State pose a serious threat to their crown.

White

Chardonnay

Well, it's still overload time as far as Chardonnay is concerned. The grape is everywhere – from Corton to Conca de Barberá in the Old World – and, we reckon, just about every New World grower either has some, or is within a stone's throw of some, vines. But that's no reason to turn our backs on it – even if we could. We really don't think that, however much there is, Chardonnay will ever be as bad as Liebfraumilch. To begin with, it not only thrives in almost any environment, but at almost any yield (high or low), any winemaking style (still or sparkling), with or without oak, it makes a cheerful, palatable wine. And when it lifts its game beyond the cheap, bulk-made offerings, the results can be superb.

Wine buyers and growers alike are really waking up to the ABC (Anything But Chardonnay) movement. Sauvignon, Viognier, Sémillon and Pinot Gris are all being planted, even in Chardonnay strongholds such as Australia (where, for a while, we were worried the message wasn't going to sink in). And that's great. That gives us more variety, more options. But we still think that people who say they're bored with Chardonnay don't fully realise the range of flavours and styles this grape offers. We heartily recommend that detractors trade up or trade across.

Chardonnay is such a chameleon that it makes an excellent display piece for *terroir*. In other words, it reflects exactly the vineyards in which it was grown. So for understanding the different flavours that come from different parts of France, California or Australia, choose a Chardonnay from each and compare the effects of this or that valley, hillside or village.

The Côte d'Or, as Burgundy is known, is Chardonnay's real home territory. Within that region there are the steely, flinty wines of Chablis; the toasty hazelnut Chardonnays from Meursault; and, somewhere between these two styles, the minerally, buttery ones of Puligny-Montrachet – vastly different wines, but all from the same grape. The New World wines tend to be fuller on the palate and more powerful, but the same diversity shows through. In Australia, for example, Barossa Valley Chardonnays are rich, toasty and fat; from Clare they are leaner, creamier with crisper acidity; and from Margaret River they're minerally and elegant, different again.

We're impressed with cooler-climate Chardonnays from New Zealand, South Africa and the Pacific North-west (Washington State and Oregon). There are also ripe, modern styles emerging from South America and Spain; Italian and southern French examples tend to be lighter and more structured. In all cases, cheaper versions can be dull, but, particularly from the New World, deciding on a specified region will increase your chances tenfold of making a good choice.

We're also pleased to report, that the global trend for over-oaking is at last subsiding. Winemakers are still tinkering and experimenting, and as well as a few more delicate, unoaked Chardonnays coming on to the market, tricks such as lees-stirring and natural yeast fermentation are giving richer, nuttier, more textured, complex wines. We're hearing more and more complaints such as 'I like Chardonnay but I don't like oak!' – so these new techniques and new flavours are certainly to be applauded.

All in all, we'd like to see both winemakers and consumers taking Chardonnay less for granted. We'd like to see fewer 'churned out', bland wines (generic blends, sourced from anywhere and everywhere); fewer-still of the oaky options; and we'd like to see many more regional choices. But otherwise, we still think Chardonnay is a good thing.

Riesling

We have no hesitation in listing Riesling up among the grape royalty. It is a versatile vine, easy to grow, produces distinctively racy, honeyed wines – and, if it really has been grown on the banks of the Mosel since Roman times, it's been around long enough to deserve a little respect!

Liebfraumilch and Niersteiner have, without doubt, spoiled the Riesling show for a great many would-be consumers, but we now hope the stage is set for change. On the other side of the world, there is a new generation of Australians who have no reason to doubt Riesling. Many weren't even born in the 1970s (the peak of the German wine flood), so, as well as being a long way away, they're children of the Chardonnay boom, who may never have seen or tasted unlovely Liebfraumilch.

Today, Germany produces fantastic Rieslings, ranging from steely and very dry (the version currently very fashionable locally), to delicate, floral wines with a touch of residual sugar sweetness, to delicious, intricately sweet examples. All of them have a firm, nervy acidity that balances any sugar and frequently leads to great ageing potential. You'll have to look further than your high street to track the best of these down: the image of German wine has been so tarnished that most merchants tuck these wines away until they're asked for. But we're pleased to say that we're seeing more and more good ones on restaurant and even supermarket wine lists, proving that a return to Riesling is beginning – and that people are realising just how good it is with (especially spicy) food.

Austria and Alsace produce finely tuned Rieslings which can demonstrate fascinating differences in soils and micro-climates (for those interested in the esoteric). The best New World examples, such as those from Australia's Clare and Eden Valleys, are riper, rounded, with a little more alcohol than their German counterparts, but have the same racy acidity and delicate petrolly, floral notes. The best can be outstanding. Cheaper examples can offer attractively ripe, lemon/lime characteristics.

Some of the world's greatest sweet wines are *botrytis*-affected Rieslings, such as the *Beeren-* and *Trockenbeerenausleses* of Germany. The rare *Eisweins* from Germany and their Canadian equivalent (Icewines) can be sublime.

Sauvignon Blanc

One of the most distinctive (if not always distinguished) grapes in the white firmament; that steely thread of limey acidity crops up in almost every wine, whether from Sancerre or Central Otago. The same goes for the straightforward, simple, appley green fruit. You can spot a Sauvignon (we normally drop the Blanc) a mile off. This was the grape that the ABC brigade first turned to in their flight to escape Chardonnay. We admit that it's not as outrightly 'acceptable' as Chardonnay, not as versatile or varied. It can be 'grubby' if poorly made, harsh and green if unripe, and doesn't have the same easy relationship with sweet, toasty oak. The gooseberry and nettle fruit – cat's pee to its detractors – is also something you either like or you don't. So as second-in-line to Chardonnay it can be disappointing. But if you were totally disappointed you'd be wrong.

Classic Loire Sauvignon (the best examples) are elegant and stunning. Look out not only for Sancerre and Pouilly-Fumé, but Quincy, Reuilly and Menetou-Salon – the latter are Sauvignons from smaller, lesser-known appellations where growers try harder and the wines are frequently better made. New Zealand is the other Sauvignon stronghold. Flavours are more vibrant, grassy and powerful, but these are balanced and long, and are invariably great food wines. We also like the new wave of Sauvignons emerging from South Africa: they seem to fall halfway between the Loire and New Zealand in weight, but add in a creamy, honeyed dimension, where others can seem simple and linear (boring?). Where California and South America are concerned we have our doubts. This grape needs a cool climate to thrive – too much heat and it loses its poise and becomes hard and clumsy. Chile's Casablanca Valley is the one possible exception. The continuing vogue for oaked Sauvignon called Fumé Blanc in the States is not something with which we've been particularly impressed.

Without doubt, the wine that proves this grape's class is Pavillon Blanc de Château Margaux. A hundred per cent Sauvignon that can age 20 years and develop the most fabulous minerally, spicy complexity. And while this wine isn't easy to get hold of, it goes some way to proving what Bordeaux can do. Though Sauvignon is traditionally blended with Sémillon here, there are more and more pure Sauvignon Blancs emerging from this region – we'll be interested to see how they develop.

FIRST DIVISION

These grape varieties are capable of producing fine wine, either alone or in blends. They do not, however, achieve top quality consistently, or are virtually unique to certain regions.

Red

Cabernet Franc

While it is unfair to think of Merlot as Cabernet Sauvignon's poor cousin, it is a description which we are happy to apply to Cabernet Franc. Except, that is, in France's cool Loire Valley, where it can produce serious reds. This is not a particularly rich grape but its combination of fresh raspberry fragrance, crunchy, red-fruit flavour and hints of green bell pepper and leaf is most appealing. Northern Italian Cabernet Franc is also grassy and light. These perfumed wines benefit from a light chill. Otherwise, Cabernet Franc's main role is as the third most important red grape in Bordeaux (after Cabernet Sauvignon and Merlot).

New World producers have been slow to take up the challenge, and so far only a handful of decent wines has emerged from Australia, California and New Zealand. A grape whose day is yet to come? Perhaps, especially since the general trend is moving away from blockbuster wines.

Grenache/Garnacha

Time was when Grenache was merely the red workhorse of Spain and France. It is the world's second most widely planted grape variety (Airén being the first), and many of us will have quaffed a good deal of Grenache without knowing it, either as cheap and cheerful French carafe wine, as holiday *rosado* in Spain, even as basic Australian red. Now the grape is gaining more respect. In Australia, you'll find seriously rich if occasionally jammy varietals or gutsy GSM – Grenache/Shiraz/Mourvèdre – blends, while in California the Rhône Ranger crew also produces enjoyable Grenache.

And about time too – the grape which makes up much of the blend in southern Rhône reds (including Châteauneuf-du-Pape) was always going to be good news given a bit of tender loving care. When its yields are kept low, and it is handled skilfully in the winery, raspberry and cherry fruitiness and a twist of black pepper emerge in the wine. This is a versatile variety, and one need look no further than Spain to witness a wide range of styles, from the hefty, thick-set reds of Priorato and Tarragona in Catalonia and Collioure in southern France, to the fresh, crisp *rosados* of Navarra, to the *vins doux naturels* of Banyuls. Grenache also blends well with grapes with more natural backbone, most famously with Syrah and Mourvèdre in the Rhône.

Malbec

If it were down to the French, Malbec wouldn't merit a great deal of attention. One of the lesser grapes of Bordeaux, where it is known as Cot, Malbec only comes into its own in Cahors, where it forms a minimum of 70 per cent of the blend of the robust local wines. But it is Argentina which has raised the profile of this grape in recent times, and which is responsible for our elevating it to First Division status this year. Argentina has more plantings of Malbec than the rest of the world put together, and here it can produce anything from attractive, fruity wines easy to mistake for Merlot, to serious, full-bodied, oak-aged reds with delicious black-cherry flavour and a rich, velvety texture.

Malbec is widely planted in neighbouring Chile, although few wineries as yet take it very seriously. In Australia's Clare Valley, some producers have preferred it to Shiraz as a blending partner for Cabernet, while across the

Tasman Sea in New Zealand, several Hawke's Bay *vignerons* use it to add seasoning and structure to their red blends.

Nebbiolo
Italy's great red grape is rightly famous for producing the heavyweight and splendid Barolos and Barbarescos of Piedmont. It takes its name from the *nebbia*, the fog that engulfs the vineyards of Alba in north-west Italy. Nebbiolo is extremely tannic and tough when young, and its wines can be slow to mature. When (and, in some instances, if) they finally soften, they are fascinating, complex and perfumed, inspiring the classic tasting note of tar and roses. Some people even claim to detect truffles in the wine, but then in Piedmont they may just have truffles on the mind.

Nebbiolo is also grown in Lombardy and further south near Brescia. Little is planted outside Italy, perhaps because winemakers find it hard to get to grips with such a darkly brooding variety. Nonetheless, it's enjoying a small but significant surge in popularity around the world. We've seen plantings in New Zealand and South Africa, although few wines have appeared so far. California is further along the Nebbiolo track, and has a band of producers who call themselves the Cal-Ital brigade. Already several very tasty wines have appeared, most notably from Il Podere dell'Olivos. The Australians are in on the act too – we recommend the wines from Brown Brothers and Garry Crittenden. And finally Argentina, which has quite extensive plantings, is beginning to make better use of this fine resource.

Sangiovese
The classic red grape of Tuscany, Sangiovese combines strawberry and red-cherry fruit with tobacco and tea-leaf to create distinctively Italianate reds. That great Tuscan wine Brunello di Montalcino is made from one specific clone, while in Chianti and Vino Nobile di Montepulciano Sangiovese is the principal grape in a blend of several different varieties. The grape is increasingly used in Super-Tuscan *vini da tavola*, either on its own or in combination with Cabernet.

It exists under various synonyms all over Italy (including Morellino, Prugnolo, Calabrese), but is rarely encountered elsewhere. But as with Nebbiolo this is changing. California now boasts several fine versions, and can also point to its own Super-Tuscan-style blends with Cabernet. Argentinian Sangiovese tends to be a little simple, but over the Andes in Chile, the debut wine from Errázuriz was remarkably good.

Tempranillo
Spain's most famous black grape and the mainstay of Rioja, Tempranillo ages well in American (and sometimes French) oak to produce lightly coloured, strawberry-scented, vanilla-packed red wine. It is usually blended with Garnacha (and perhaps some Graciano and Mazuelo) for Rioja, and is widely used elsewhere in Spain under local names such as Tinto Fino in Ribera del Duero, Cencibel in La Mancha and Tinto de Toro in Toro.

Tempranillo is also grown extensively in two regions of Portugal, the central Alentejo, where it is known as Aragonez and used in red table-wine blends of variable quality, and the Douro, where it is known as Tinta Roriz and mainly used, again in blends, to make port. The only other place you are likely to come across it is in Argentina, but the quality here is patchy.

Touriga Nacional
One of the red grapes of Portugal's Douro Valley and widely agreed to be the best grape for making port, Touriga is naturally low yielding and produces small, tough-skinned berries. Its young wine is packed with tannin and intense red-fruit flavour – and it has been compared closely to Cabernet Sauvignon. It ages brilliantly as a table wine, and is an important component in red Dão from northern Portugal. In Australia it is sometimes used for fortified wines.

Zinfandel/Primitivo
Zinfandel, at its most concentrated and inky red, should be on prescription for anyone bored with the classic red varieties; its exuberant bramble and strawberry fruit and spicy, leathery depths will soon revive a flagging interest. Zin produces some of California's most idiosyncratic and fascinating wine, often from ancient vines in Sonoma County and the Sierra Foothills. Unfortunately, it is still used to make oodles of insipid, sweet 'blush' wine labelled White Zinfandel. While California is Zinfandel's current home, DNA testing has confirmed that it is actually the same variety as the Primitivo of Puglia. Some Puglian Primitivos, especially A Mano made by Californian Mark Shannon, provide eloquent confirmation of this. Zinfandel outside California and Italy is rare but not uncommon. Cape Mentelle and Nepenthe make fine versions in Australia, and we've also enjoyed the wine from Chile's Cono Sur.

White

Chenin Blanc
Within the Loire Valley, Chenin Blanc produces an astonishing breadth of wine styles, from humble Anjou Blanc to long-lived, dry Savennières, from sparkling Saumur to honeyed dessert wines such as Coteaux du Layon, Bonnezeaux and Quarts de Chaume. Would that we could say, equally admiringly, that all Chenin Blanc wines were great. Sadly, they're not. Indeed, mediocre Chenin is possibly the worst of our pet hates. The best *vignerons*, often benefiting from generations of experience, know exactly how to exploit the naturally high acidity of Chenin – so beware carelessly made, mass-produced examples. There are no real distinguishing features of dry Chenin wines, apart from wet wool and some light floral overtones; if they are over-sulphured and badly handled to boot, almost no wine is worse!

Our advice therefore is to pick and choose, particularly in off vintages. In good Loire years, Chenin can come into its own, creating unique honeyed wines with the ability to age for years.

Outside France, South Africa has the major plantings of Chenin and the bulk wines it has produced in the past from this grape have gone some way to forming its poor reputation. In warmer climates, Chenin's high-yielding and high-acid tendencies make it perfect for neutral base wines for sparkling (Argentina) and, very often, wine for distillation into spirits. Today, however, a handful of South African growers are offering it a new lease of life. Pockets of greatness occur where some of them are taking more care in the vineyards and cellars. From older, low-yielding vines, we are pleased to say that we have tasted honeyed, rich, crisp wines showing exactly the way this grape should be. Serious results are coming from other New World regions too – California and Western Australia, for starters.

Gewürztraminer

If it's exoticism you're after, this is the grape for you. The best Alsace Gewurztraminer will assail your senses with pure aromas of lychees, roses or even ginger – sheer bliss! Rarely do other wines match up to the hedonistic 'Gewürz'. If, however, a nice crisp Chablis is your thing – be prepared to loathe it. One thing is for certain, there is no sitting on the fence. Often Gewürz is the first grape that wine lovers learn to recognise blind – try it if you haven't done so already. Ardent fans swear by Gewürz as the accompaniment for the delicate Eastern flavours of Thai food; we also love it chilled on a summer's evening.

The natural home of Gewürztraminer is Alsace, where its pinkish skin and capacity to ripen easily produces deep-coloured, powerful dry whites with a distinctive oiliness and sometimes a slight sweetness. The late-harvest *vendange tardive* wines of Alsace are naturally sweet, and the exceptional *sélection de grains nobles* can be outstandingly delicious. Elsewhere in Europe, Gewürz is generally lighter in style and can be found in Germany, Italy's Alto Adige, Hungary and Spain, where Torres makes a popular Gewürz and Muscat blend called Viña Esmeralda. The aromatic qualities of Gewürz (German for 'spice', incidentally) can often turn cheap-and-easy white wines into something a little more special. In the New World, Gewürz does better in cooler sub-regions, such as the Casablanca Valley in Chile or New Zealand's Marlborough. Henschke make a good one in Australia's Eden Valley.

Marsanne

In the northern Rhône, Marsanne, blended with a little Roussanne, is responsible for the enigmatic white wines of the staunchly red appellations of St-Joseph, Hermitage, Crozes-Hermitage and St-Péray. These are weighty, rich wines with an intriguing peach or marzipan aroma. Marsanne is also a permitted varietal in the Languedoc and producers there are increasingly coming up with good-value, inexpensive examples. The most interesting Marsanne enclave, however, is the Goulburn Valley in Victoria, Australia, where wines from Chateau Tahbilk and Mitchelton are sturdy with full-flavoured fruit. The likelihood is that there will be yet more from Australia, as the current Rhône trend really takes hold. There are experimental plantings in the Barossa Valley and Western Australia – together, of course, with traditional blend partner Roussanne. You may also find the odd Marsanne hailing from California.

Muscat

Truly the grapiest of grapes, aromatic Muscat is responsible, amongst others, for the light and frothy Asti and Moscato d'Asti in northern Italy; dry, scented Alsace Muscats; richly sweet Muscat *vins doux naturels* in the south of France; and the dark and raisiny fortified Muscats in Australia. In fact Muscat is not just one grape but a whole family of them with Muscat à Petits Grains generally accepted as being the best of the lot and behind the wines just mentioned. The next-most-popular Muscat, Muscat of Alexandria, gives us the sweet wines of Spain and Portugal (Moscatel de Valencia, Malaga and Setúbal) and crops up as Hanepoot in South Africa and Zibibbo in Sicily. Useful stuff for a wine quiz!

Pinot Blanc

Definitely a grape without vices, Pinot Blanc is easy to grow and makes easy-drinking, undemanding wines that rarely achieve great heights. In Alsace, the wines have an unusual intensity of flavour and we would argue that this is where Pinot Blanc performs best. In Germany, Pinot Blanc is known as Weissburgunder and does particularly well in southern areas such as Baden, where its adaptability and suitability for oak treatment allows growers to experiment with styles of wine which are not possible in the north. It thrives in Austria and is all over the place in northern Italy, where its neutrality also makes it suitable as a base for sparkling wines. We have occasionally come across the odd, and perfectly acceptable, Californian oaked Pinot Blanc.

Pinot Gris

Following closely on the spice route heels of Gewürztraminer, Pinot Gris makes dusky, smoky, dry Alsace wines (known as Tokay-Pinot Gris), sought after mainly as food wines. With extra ripening, it can also produce delicious *vendange tardive* examples.

In Germany, Pinot Gris is known as Rülander and occurs as a rounded, medium-bodied white wine mainly in Baden and the Pfalz. Rülander is also the name of Pinot Gris in Austria, whereas in Italy we find the more appealing-sounding Pinot Grigio, still neutral, but with a crisp, citrus palate. Winemakers have recently begun turning their attentions to Pinot Gris in the New World, especially in areas cool enough for it to retain its delicate acidity. Some seriously good wines are emerging from Oregon, where, we're amused to report, this grape has stolen Chardonnay's show. And we've also tried out an excellent example from Australia's Clare Valley – deliciously complex and mellow and eight years old. Looks like a case of spicy awakening!

Sémillon

Sémillon's (the accent is only required in France) greatest haunt is Australia, where it can occur just as easily in everyday quaffing Semillon/Chardonnay as it can in outrageously, full-bodied and flavour-packed, oaked Barossa Valley wines. The classic examples, however, come from the Hunter Valley. When young, they're nothing to write home about: thin, neutral, low in alcohol and not unlike grassy Sauvignon Blanc. But with time they develop into minerally, powerful wines with a creamy texture and a hint of honeyed beeswax, capable of great age, and well worth waiting for. From Margaret River in Western Australia, the style falls somewhere between these two: honeyed and ripe but with an elegant spicy crispness.

Sémillon in its classic role, in France, is mostly found as the co-varietal, with Sauvignon Blanc, in the whites of Bordeaux – both humble and classic, dry and sweet. In the Graves, Sémillon provides a soft, rounded counterpart to the crisp and zingy Sauvignon adding depth and intensity, as well as making the wines more suited to oak. The grape's susceptibility to *botrytis* is key to its greatest success in Sauternes and as part of the illustrious and expensive Château d'Yquem. In Barsac and neighbouring Monbazillac, it makes an equally sweet contribution.

Viognier

For a while there, in the late 1990s, Viognier was mooted as the 'new' Chardonnay but these claims were drastically premature. Attractive, fleshy and reliably peachy flavours make it fashionable and very appealing to wine producers and consumers alike, but, truth be told, it's a capricious beast and not as easy to pin down in the winery (or vineyard) as winemakers would like.Viognier's claim to fame lies with the full-bodied, fragrant, and highly sought-after, wines of Château Grillet and Condrieu in the northern Rhône. Light, easy-drinking facsimiles from the Languedoc are peachy, but mostly rather dilute when compared to the real thing. The best we have tasted lately came from Argentina, in fact. California and Australia are the other main sources but here there is a tendency for things to get overblown – over-oaked, and just too much of a peach-parcel. We think winemakers just haven't worked Viognier out yet. But sufficient effort is being made, and the time will come when they do work it out – with lower yields, less oak and cooler-climate vineyards. We certainly advise giving any that you see a whirl – be prepared for zesty, honeyed, apricoty wines at the cheap end and intensely lush and muskily developed wines for a few pennies more.

SECOND DIVISION

The grape varieties listed below have the potential to make good-quality wines, but they seldom create great ones.

Red

Baga

A sturdy, thick-skinned variety which forms the backbone of Bairrada reds in northern Portugal. Most versions are rather hard and tannic, although modern methods of vinification can produce fruitier reds with delicious blackberry character and a hint of spice. Luis Pato is the acknowledged master of the variety.

Barbera

Italy's most widely planted red grape typically produces easy-drinking, fruity wines. In Piedmont, Barbera plays second fiddle to Nebbiolo and as such is not usually planted on the best sites. In the right hands, however, it can make more serious, longer-lived reds, either on its own or in blends with Nebbiolo. New World versions are competent rather than outstanding, although Argentina is getting to grips with this variety, and some California offerings have been good.

Carignan

One of the workhorses of southern France, producing largely forgettable wine. However, low-yielding old vines can produce rather good, spicy wine. It is Spanish in origin but its use in Spain, where it goes under the names of

Cariñena or Mazuelo, is limited. One of the best examples elsewhere is the Carignano del Sulcis of Sardinia. It is widely planted in North Africa but does not produce wines of great distinction there.

Dolcetto
The 'little sweet one' produces some of Italy's most gluggable wines, refreshing, fruity and smooth, with a slightly sour cherryish twist on the finish. It is seldom seen outside Piedmont, although Best's in Australia produces a full-flavoured version.

Gamay
The jester to King Pinot Noir in Burgundy, Gamay is the ruby-hued, fruity grape responsible for Beaujolais, typically producing vibrant, strawberry-fresh wines for early consumption, although richer versions from *cru* villages can age well. Most Bourgogne Ordinaire is made from Gamay, while Passetoutgrains is a more attractive blend of Gamay with at least one-third Pinot Noir. A light version appears in Touraine, and a few Californians make reasonably decent versions.

Mourvèdre
A red grape used in blends for its firm structure and spiciness, Mourvèdre originated in Spain where, as Monastrell, it is the second most planted red variety after Garnacha and is used in pink Cava. However, it is now more famous in southern France, where it is used in blends and occasionally alone as in the strapping and long-lived wines of Bandol. It appears in a few Californian bottlings and pops up in Australia where a little is grown as Mataro.

Pinot Meunier
The 'other' Pinot of Champagne, where it is the most widely planted variety, contributing fruitiness to the blend but lacking the finesse of Pinot Noir and Chardonnay. Sparkling wine producers in other parts of the world have plantings too.

Pinotage
The Cinsaut/Pinot Noir cross developed in South Africa in the 1920s has yet to set the rest of the world on fire, but Cape versions get better and better. Styles range from simple, fruity Beaujolais lookalikes to hefty blockbusters such as the benchmark wine from Kanonkop Estate. The rough, tomatoey flavours of the past are slowly being phased out, but don't be surprised to detect a whiff of banana in many wines. The rare New Zealand Pinotages, especially those from Babich, are worth trying.

White

Colombard
With its roots in the Cognac region, Colombard was historically used in the production of brandy, but is now more likely to crop up in the blend of a crisp, fresh *vin de pays* des Côtes de Gascogne. Here it makes a floral counterpart to the essentially neutral Ugni Blanc. It also features in simple,

inexpensive quaffing whites from South Africa and California, which should definitely be drunk young.

Furmint
You won't find this grape outside Hungary, where it is the mainstay of the great, sweet white wine Tokaji, thanks to its high acidity and propensity to succumb to noble rot. Dry Furmint wines do exist; they can be good but are rare, and are not cheap.

Grüner Veltliner
The wines of Austria's Wachau show Grüner Veltliner at its very best. With its hallmark crisp, spicy, peppery character, Grüner Veltliner makes a welcome change from overtly fruit-driven wines so common nowadays – and, happily, is becoming slightly less of a rarity. Watch out for some interesting sweet wines too.

Macabeo/Viura
Mainly grown in the arc stretching from the Languedoc to northern Spain, Macabeo is widely used in white wines. As Viura, it is the principal grape of white Rioja, making occasionally delicious, but unusual, peachy, minerally wines. Its lightly floral character from cooler climates is possibly the reason why it is an important grape in the standard Cava blend.

Malvasia
Malvasia's main characteristics: a deep colour, high alcohol and propensity to oxidation, don't tend to put it high on anybody's list. However, in Italy, Malvasia (in many different forms) is widely planted and commonly blended with dull and neutral Trebbiano; for example, it lends fatness and fragrance to some of the best Frascatis. Malvasia is also grown in Spain and Portugal and can also crop up in California. Perhaps its best incarnation is in the sweet wines of *vin santo* and in Malmsey the richest of madeiras.

Palomino
For its role in the production of sherry, Palomino is certainly worthy of attention. Grown in the white *albariza* soils of Jerez, Palomino grapes make a low-acid, slightly flabby wine which would be nothing to write home about if it weren't for its propensity, once fortified, to transform – with *flor* – into extraordinarily tangy and elegant manzanilla and fino sherries. With oxidation as well, darker, nuttier amontillado styles are produced.

Outside Spain, Palomino can be found in most New World areas, particularly South Africa, where it has very lowly, still wine status. Where it is fortified outside Spain, the absence of *flor* keeps the wines well below par.

Roussanne
Roussanne is generally found with Marsanne in the aromatic white wines of the northern Rhône. It is also one of the main grapes in the curiosity-value, more southerly, white Châteauneuf-du-Pape (the Vieilles Vignes wine of Château de Beaucastel is entirely Roussanne). Roussanne can also be used in the whites of the Languedoc. Following its red Rhône cousin Syrah (Shiraz),

this grape is also making experimental appearances in cooler regions of Australia.

Trebbiano/Ugni Blanc

Ugni Blanc of south-western France originates in Italy as Trebbiano, where it has a multitude of strains, and provides a significant chunk of DOC white wines. Trebbiano/Ugni Blanc's main feature is, perversely, its almost total lack of character. Expect vapid neutrality and very little else from the quaffing whites it produces.

ALSO RANS

The following grapes are either widely planted but of only average quality, or have potential but are encountered infrequently.

Red

Cinsault/Cinsaut

Another widespread but frequently dreary grape of southern France. It is still widely planted in the Cape, but has little influence.

Montepulciano, Negroamaro

Two Italian black grapes. Montepulciano – not to be confused with the Tuscan town of the same name where Vino Nobile is produced – makes large amounts of easy-drinking, spicy, berryish wine plus the occasional silky stunner in central and south-east Italy. For some reason, a little has been planted in Marlborough, New Zealand. Negroamaro produces similarly friendly, burly wines in the south of Italy, especially Puglia. With a little care, some extraordinarily good southern Rhône-like wine can be made.

Periquita

This grape variety is the mainstay of central and southern Portuguese reds, particularly in the regions of Alentejo, Estremadura and Ribatejo, and is underrated. Progressive winemakers are squeezing pleasant, cherryish flavour from it.

Petite Sirah/Durif

There is increasing doubt as to whether these two are actually the same variety, but the wines produced certainly have similarities, both being tannic and not particularly refined. The grape appears in California, Mexico, Australia and South America.

Petit Verdot

A spicy, tough grape which is occasionally found in small quantities in Bordeaux blends, and in California. Bordeaux winemakers use it 'like salt and pepper', as one described it to us, to add a little zest and character to a blend. In Spain Marqués de Griñon has a varietal version, while Viña Alicia's Verdot from Argentina is extremely impressive.

White

Aligoté and Melon de Bourgogne

Aligoté, the second grape of Burgundy, is best known for its tart, white wine – the traditional choice to which you should add a splash of Dijon crème de cassis to make kir. Melon de Bourgogne is the grape of Muscadet and grown in the Pays Nantais, where it copes with the cold and can develop well with lees ageing. Made carelessly it can be execrable.

Müller-Thurgau, Silvaner and Welschriesling

A trio of everyday, reliably yielding Germanic grapes, generally used to make cheap, everyday whites from Germany, Eastern Europe and also England. Müller-Thurgau is capable of greater things in skilful hands (often outside its German home) and turns up in some pleasing blends in New Zealand. Silvaner does best producing crisp, racy Franken whites. Welschriesling (no relation to the noble Riesling) is grown widely in central Europe and Italy and is usually associated with cheap whites such as Laski Rizling, although it is responsible for some stunning sweet wines in Austria's Burgenland.

THE LOOK, SMELL AND TASTE OF WINE

What's the big deal about the making of this precious fluid, given that if you leave grapes in a bin in reasonably warm conditions they will turn into wine of their own accord? There must be something that makes an Australian Chardonnay different from Château Latour – so what is it? Throughout the A–Z of wine-producing countries we have tried to explain the differences that country, region and site can bring to bear on individual wines, and we introduced you to some of the winemakers who help to shape them. However, there is more to wine than places and people, so here we look at some of the other factors that determine what ends up in your glass.

APPEARANCE

'Good legs' is a classic comment which is made time after time about wine. It refers to the streaks of liquid seen on the side of a glass after swirling the wine around, described in a rare poetic moment by the Germans as 'cathedral windows'. These merely indicate that the wine has a high alcohol level.

Good colour is harder to fathom. If wine is bright, clear and does not show signs of premature ageing (brick-orange reds; dull yellow for whites) then that augurs well for the taste of the stuff. Clarity, just as with diamonds, is essential. No wine should ever be hazy. But good colour doesn't necessarily mean deep colour. A darker yellow, red or black is not always an indication of quality. Certain grapes have darker skins than others, for example, Syrah and Cabernet Sauvignon are naturally a much deeper purple-red colour than Pinot Noir. It is possible to increase the amount of colour in a wine by keeping the grape skins in contact with the juice for longer periods and by agitating the skins and juice, but since such procedures also extract other compounds such as tannin, the winemaker has to calculate the extent to which each is used

If young red wines show signs of browning, the chances are they have been poorly stored. Small, white tartrate crystals in white wines are harmless and indicate that the wine has not been over-filtered.

AROMA

Whether you're into one big 'sniff' or lots of little ones, it doesn't matter; stick your nose right in and go for it – you will come to no harm (unless you're sniffing Zinfandel or port, in which case, the alcohol might knock you sideways). And 'nosing' a wine is rather like foreplay, a necessary prelude to the main performance. If you've ever tried to smell fine wine with a heavy cold, you'll know that missing out on the aroma means you also miss out on a lot of the sensory thrill. Most of the wine's character that you will pick up on the palate is there to a greater or lesser extent on its perfume. Certainly, oakiness, alcohol level and faults such as cork taint, or excessive use of sulphur, are all apparent, and some people even claim to be able to spot tannin and acidity in an aroma. As a wine opens out, either with time in the glass or with vigorous swirling of the liquid, the scent develops further. (The pros and cons of decanting, swirling and airing wine are discussed in *Serving wine*.) Give a fine wine's bouquet plenty of attention – it deserves it!

FLAVOUR

Swallow a wine straight away and you will miss out on a multitude of flavours, undertones and textures. The alcohol will take effect, but that is about it. Instead, take a healthy slurp and swill the wine around in your mouth. Breathing in some air through your mouth while tasting can heighten the flavour of wine, but take care as it is easy to choke. Try to consider the flavours you are aware of – the level of acidity, the sweetness/dryness, any specific characteristics such as butter, fruit or toast. After you swallow or spit out the wine, assess the finish: how long the flavour stays in your mouth and whether it is, say, tannic, acidic or viscous.

The four main elements that affect the flavour of a wine are: which grape varieties were used, where and how they were grown, and how the wine was made – in short, variety, *terroir*, viticulture and vinification. (See below for a further explanation of *terroir*.) A fifth element is age. In mature wines, structural components – fruit, tannin, acidity, alcohol and oak – meld together and produce a range of different spicy secondary characteristics. The wine is said to gain in complexity, losing its primary grape characteristics and taking on a whole load more.

Acidity

Acidity lifts the flavours of a wine and also acts as a preservative. The great sweet Rieslings and Chenin Blancs rely on the high acidity levels of these grape varieties for their longevity, and to balance their sweetness. Contrary to popular belief, acidity does not necessarily soften with age. Taste certain red wines which are past their peak and one of the first things you will notice is the acidity.

Four factors are important in this respect: the grape variety itself; the time the grape is picked; its degree of shade or exposure to the sun; and the temperature of the region. Winemakers in warm areas where the grapes suffer from a lack of acidity have two options: to pick earlier, which could mean that the grape flavours are not fully developed – or to add acid (either tartaric or ascorbic), a procedure which is illegal in many European countries but is permitted in the New World (for more on this see the feature on pages 25–30). Winemakers in cool areas, on the other hand, have the opposite problem, and sometimes need to de-acidify by the addition of calcium carbonate. A further means of adjusting acidity is the use of malolactic fermentation (see *Glossary*), a bacterial conversion of malic acid – think of Granny Smith apples – to the softer lactic acid. Nearly all red wines go through the malolactic process, and the popularity of the process for whites, particularly Chardonnay, is increasing. The skill is to add complexity without turning the wine into buttermilk.

Acidity in a wine also helps it partner food. Think of Italian red wines, they almost all have it in good quantity, and it makes them tangy and mouthwatering. The crispness lifts the wine flavours and helps distinguish them from those in the dish. In contrast, a plump, fat Chilean Merlot sits happily next to a meal but doesn't have quite the same tangy contrast.

Sugar/alcohol

Sweet wines are made in a number of ways. Yeasts will only ferment up to a certain alcohol level, so if a wine reaches this level and still has some unconverted sugar, it will be sweet. Another method is to stop the fermentation process before all the sugar has been converted, either through the addition of spirit (as in port) or by chilling the must (see *Glossary*) and precipitating the yeasts out, a practice used in Germany. Method three is to concentrate the sugar in the grapes either by drying them in the sun (leaving them longer on the vine in the autumn for example), or through attack by a benevolent mould, *Botrytis cinerea*, which has the same dehydrating effect – especially on thin-skinned Sémillon and Riesling.

In winemaking sugar covers a multitude of sins. Liebfraumilch and Lambrusco are classic examples of wines whose blandness is often disguised behind a veil of sweetness, and numerous wines, especially those from hotter countries, are labelled 'dry' but still have residual sugar, making them seem rounder and fuller in flavour (for more about this, see the feature on pages 25–30). Alcohol, deriving from the fermentation of sugar, also makes for weightier wines. The hotter the region, the riper and sweeter the grapes, the more alcoholic will be the wine – Zinfandel in California can reach as high as 16 or 17 per cent quite naturally, but in Germany, wines achieve perfect balance at alcohol levels which can be as low as 7 per cent – although they usually have some unfermented sugar to balance the firm acidity. Without the acidity to balance the sugar, as in Liebfraumilch and Lambrusco, they are flabby.)

291

Methods to increase sugar levels include: training the vine canopy so that the grapes are exposed to the sun; allowing the grapes to ripen longer; must concentration; and – the easy option – tipping sugar into the fermenter, a process called chaptalisation (see *Glossary*). This latter process is permitted in cooler regions, such as Germany, parts of France and other northern and eastern European wine regions,where there's sometimes not enough sun for the grapes to reach full ripeness, but not in most parts of the New World.

Yeasts

The job of converting sugar to alcohol is done by yeast. In traditional winemaking, wild yeasts native to the vineyard and winery are used to start the fermentation. Nowadays, the use of cultivated yeasts is widespread, since they are more reliable and efficient at fermentation and reduce the risk of spoilage. However, critics say that they introduce a uniformity of flavour and point the finger at flying winemakers who use the same yeast strains the world over. Many of the most progressive wineries of the New World are switching back to wild yeasts, and there's no doubt, they do add interest to a wine, a kind of 'Burgundian' complexity. However, the funky, spicy, wild flavours they bring are not appropriate for every style.

After fermentation has finished, the wine may be left on the yeast lees – the words *sur lie* on a French wine label indicate a lengthier-than-usual period of lees ageing – in order to pick up something of their flavour. There is also a process called *bâtonnage* whereby the lees is stirred in order to impart more of its biscuity flavour.

Tannin

Tannin is the mouth-puckering quality found in some young wine, a bit like the taste of sucking on a wooden pencil. Sounds nasty? It can be if it is over-done or green and unripe, but tannins are essential to the structure of certain wines, and they diminish and soften with bottle age. Tannins are a group of complex organic chemicals found in the bark of some trees, and in some fruits. In wine, tannins derive from grape seeds, stems and skins, and also leach out of new barrels in which the wine is stored. Those from the seeds are not desirable, so care must be taken when pressing the grapes to avoid breaking the seeds and releasing their bitter character. Stems are more controversial; some winemakers ban them totally from the fermentation vats, some allow a few, while others positively encourage their addition.

Grape skins are the source of the majority of benevolent tannins. Extraction of these goes hand-in-hand with the extraction of colour, since that, too, is concentrated on the skins. The smaller the berries and the harder they are pressed, the greater the tannins will be. If a pressing is too aggressive, tannins will also be aggressive and bitter. If the grapes have been exposed to plenty of sun, the tannins will be riper and not as harsh as those in wines from cooler climates, which is why many New World wines often seem less tannic than their Old World counterparts. Ripeness is important, but get the fruit too ripe (we're talking California and Australia again) and winemakers often find they have to add powdered or liquid tannin to redress the balance. (For more on this, see the feature on pages 25–30.)

Oak

Oak is the most apparent of the winemaker's additions to a wine. Just like salt in cooking, if the amount is right it will enhance the wine, but if it is overdone the wine will be spoilt. Wines can be fermented and aged in oak barrels, or simply aged after fermenting in stainless steel or concrete vats. The smaller the barrel, the greater the ratio of surface area to volume, and so the greater the oak influence. The fashionable format is the 225-litre *barrique*, but barrels can vary in size from less than 100 litres to tens of thousands of litres. One factor which is seldom considered is that winemakers who use a 10,000-litre tank make just one wine, while those who use several 225-litre *barriques* can make several wines, all of them different, which can then be blended in any number of ways for extra complexity.

The character that oak lends to a wine depends on where the wood came from, where and how the wood was dried, and who the cooper was. The char in the inside of the barrel is also significant, with heavily toasted barrels giving a much greater vanilla and spice character to the finished wine than lightly toasted ones. American oak, widely used in California, Australia and Rioja, has a warmer, fuller and stronger vanillin flavour than French oak. French oak tends to impart more subtle flavours – especially from the Allier, Vosges, Tronçais and Limousin forests.

There are cheaper methods to give wood influence to a wine. Barrel staves are sometimes suspended in fermentation or storage tanks to add an oaky character, while oak chips, which are cheaper still, are also used. Staves and chips can be made from French and American oak, with different levels of tasting, and cost far less than proper barrels. Chips, in particular, used to give a crude, sawdust flavour to many wines, but as the winemakers have become more skilful in using the chips or staves and the quality of the chips has improved, so the quality of the resulting wines has increased remarkably. However, neither chips nor staves can duplicate the process by which a wine in cask 'breathes' through the sides of the barrel, acquiring extra complexity as it does so.

Water

It is shocking but true that water is the major component in every bottle of wine – even one priced at £1,000. And the more water a vineyard receives, the more water, and therefore less flavour, there will be in the finished wine. Even the classic areas suffer from wet vintages when grapes suck in too much water and become relatively dilute. (The Bordelais have got clever these days and found themselves a 'reverse osmosis' machine that sucks the water back out again so their harvest isn't ruined. This might lead to a rather thick-textured wine but it certainly won't be watery.) At the opposite extreme, and despite the cliché that vines should struggle to produce fine wine, a badly drought-ridden vineyard has an adverse effect on the finished product, inhibiting ripeness and reducing the yield heavily. Some drought is acceptable, but in this case, a judicious amount of irrigation is a good thing.

Other 'ingredients'

As you can see from the feature on pages 25–30, wine is not just grapes and yeast alone.

Terroir vs variety

Terroir and grape variety represent two different sides in a well-worn argument about the origin of a wine's character. Terroir is an ancient, quasi-mystical concept that defines wine as an expression of the soil, climate and cultural environment where it was grown. 'I do not make Pinot Noir, I make Volnay,' would be a typical remark from a Burgundian grower who is referring to the terroir of his vines. Until recently the attitude of a variety-driven New World winemaker would be that soil is just dirt. He or she would suggest that a competent winemaker should be able to produce decent wine no matter what grapes are brought to the winery, and where they are from. The two sides are coming closer together, however, with New World wineries increasingly bottling regional and single-vineyard wines. You'll even see Australians and Californians squabbling over specific vine plots, just as if they were grands crus in Burgundy. The Old World, on the other hand, is putting the accent on grape varieties as never before – witness the increasing number of single-varietal wines coming from the south of France.

THE LABEL

Information on all of the above is increasingly available on the wine label – especially (it's a New World trend) the one on the back of the bottle. Whether the wine contains four per cent Cabernet Sauvignon (usually detectable through its distinctive blackcurrant whiff, even in quantities this small); if the wine was barrel-aged; how much alcohol it contains; and what the winemaker was wearing when he made it (well, not quite). This isn't there merely to titillate the wine buffs (though it does that too), but to provide a useful clue as to how the wine will smell and taste. So now, more than ever before, you can gauge what you're getting before you open the bottle. We suggest you use this information wisely. Take the vintage date: even New World wines can fall victim to vintage variation – 1998's El Niño phenomenon, for example, had a beneficial effect in New Zealand but a disastrous, rainy one in California and Argentina. Taking a note of alcohol levels can make the difference between a sober supper and a sore head the next morning. More to the point, all this detail is a great help in matching a wine to an occasion – and making sure the lemon chicken isn't obliterated by a chunky Australian Shiraz.

STORING WINE

Setting up your own wine cellar at home can be straightforward. The basement of a house is ideal, provided it is not centrally heated or prone to flooding. The natural conditions of your average basement – a steady, fairly cool temperature (7–10°C/45–50°F), dampish environment, reasonable circulation of air and darkness – should keep your wine in pristine condition. Otherwise, look for a place where those conditions can be simulated: an old wardrobe, a disused fireplace, a cupboard under the stairs.

Remember to store the bottles away from a radiator or boiler, which will heat up one corner of a room, and away from anything with a strong odour, such as paint or paraffin. And at all costs, avoid the attic – or cupboards under the eaves if you have a loft conversion. These heat up like nobody's business in the summer and are generally the wrong side of roof insulation to avoid cold in the winter. If you're really stuck for a cool space, a wine fridge is a good idea. Though not cheap, they maintain the ideal constant temperature, and store anything from 50 to 200 bottles.

Wine racks are useful but not essential. The boxes in which the wine was packed will do almost as well. The important thing is to store the bottles on their sides, so that the cork stays moist and makes an effective seal. If you are interested in keeping and collecting the labels on your bottles, spraying them with odourless hair lacquer should help preserve them. Be careful not to tear them when pulling bottles from metal wine racks.

Contrary to popular belief, age in wine is not necessarily a good thing, even in reds. One of our more depressing duties is to inform well-meaning readers that their treasured bottles of, say, 1977 Beaujolais Nouveau are not only worthless, but also cadaverously dreadful. The good thing about the wines made today is that many are deliciously fruity right from the word 'go', and that includes those from Bordeaux as much as those from Chile.

Even so, a constant diet of in-your-face fruit eventually palls, and having a small store of older wine offers more variety. With bottle age, a wine loses what is called its 'primary flavours' and develops 'secondary characteristics'. Translated into plain English, this means that the fresh fruit flavours give way to notes of dried fruit, with additional nuances which might be gamey, earthy, leathery, spicy or honeyed. The oak influence also becomes less pronounced, while tannins (in red wine) will bond together to form longer and heavier molecular chains which eventually precipitate out as sediment, leaving a softer, more mellow wine.

Tasting the difference between a young, mouth-puckering Bordeaux or burgundy, and a fascinatingly complex one 20 years older, proves it's worth the wait. Alternatively, here are a few suggestions for affordable candidates that'll benefit from ageing:

- Riesling from anywhere
- Australian Semillon and Shiraz
- southern French reds such as Coteaux de Languedoc and Costières de Nîmes
- Côtes du Rhône-Villages
- Douro reds
- Spanish Rioja
- sweet Loire Chenin Blanc.

Don't forget that vintage champagne has the quality to improve deliciously over 10 to 15 years, and the same applies to white Bordeaux from the top châteaux, which is horrendously unfashionable and relatively cheap. This is not an exhaustive list, nor is every example of the wines listed built for the long haul. However, a year or two extra in bottle should let you see what age can do to them, and then it is up to you to decide at what age you prefer each.

Good wine merchants are always willing to give advice on which wines will benefit from further ageing – the best offer storage space in which they'll keep them in perfect condition for you. If you take up any of the tempting *en primeur* offers, by which young wine is sold while still in barrel at the château or estate, then it's definitely best to leave cellaring to the merchants. Any appreciation in price will quickly be lost if your treasures have been poorly stored (they check up these days!), so if you're unsure about your cupboard under the stairs and might want to re-sell your wine, leave it to the professionals.

Once your wine's ready to drink, don't guzzle it all at once. Try one bottle out of the case every year so you can gauge exactly how you like your tannins – soft or al dente!

Learn from every mistake and don't get too precious about your wine. It is there to be drunk, not worshipped.

SERVING WINE

To decant or not to decant?

There are two reasons for decanting red wines, one of which – believe it or not – applies to white wines too. There's no need for alarm here. If your decanter (assuming you have one) is a forgotten relic lurking unused at the back of a cupboard, serving more as a nostalgic reminder of wedding days than as a useful tool for entertaining, then that's fine. If you don't have one, that's fine too. Most red wines are now soft and fruity enough to be drunk straight from the bottle, and even Bordeaux isn't quite as crusty as it once was. It is a good idea to decant mature red wine or port, however, if it has a notable sediment. As well as making a thoroughly unpleasant, woody mouthful, this can be tannic and often bitter-tasting and is better removed. The best way is to stand the bottle of wine you wish to drink upright for at least a couple of days before decanting in order that the deposit settles to the bottom of the bottle. Then uncork the wine, ensuring that the rim is clean, by wiping with a damp cloth, and pour slowly and steadily into the decanter. If you wish to emulate a seasoned sommelier, then hold the bottle close to a source of light or to a candle and watch for the sediment as you pour. When the first signs of it appear, stop decanting and throw away the dregs. *Voilà*! Remember though, that wine will not keep indefinitely in a decanter; most open bottles will become undrinkable within a day or so.

The second reason for decanting is to aerate the wine and release the aromas and flavours that have been locked into the bottle. As airy-fairy as this might sound, for young, tight French reds, Bordeaux and young burgundies, and tightly knit California Cabernets, it really does work. For whites, too, where there's a lot of packed-in complexity (as with those oak-aged or concentrated by *botrytis*), decanting allows the wine to breathe and its full characteristics to develop.

Remember four things. One: if you don't have a decanter, pour the wine into a jug and then back into the same bottle – that way you can still show the label off too. Two: allow the wine to recover; pouring can give it a shock, so let it settle for an hour or two after decanting. Three: this trick can also work for wines opened before they're quite ready to drink, by allowing the fruit to open out and cover tannins which are still young and bony. Four: for the vast majority of everyday-drinking wines, none of this is relevant.

Does wine need to breathe?

The more austere, top-quality reds and whites do need to breathe, and decanting (see above) is a good idea. As a beneficial half-measure (for wines just a little bit closed) just opening a bottle a couple of hours before serving can help. Despite the fact so little of its surface is in contact with the air, this does give a definite reaction. Swirling the wine in an appropriate glass once it is poured will also have the same positive effect. Don't forget, if the wine is too cold or too warm all this effort will be wasted – chilling will close up the aromas, and heating makes wines soupy and over-blown. Fortunately there's a wide temperature range in the middle that works just fine; no precision is necessary.

The glasses

Especially when a lot of thought (and budget) has gone into the choice of wine, it is a shame to skimp on the glassware, knowingly or not. This does not mean that glasses have to be expensive – although they certainly can be – but rather that you stick to the best shapes for drinking certain types of wine.

The most appropriate wine glasses are always made of clear glass (avoid the recycled green or blue ones) and should have a long stem and a large bowl which tapers towards the rim rather like a tulip head. In fact, the larger the better, as swirling the wine in the glass is part of the pleasure of discovering a wine's merits. Contrary to classic British traditions, flutes are really the only style of glass for champagne or sparkling wines, as the lack of surface area for the wine allows the bubbles to last longer. Traditional 'copita' shapes are best for sherry. Paris goblets are robust enough for your wilder parties – or outdoor use – but their thick glass does good wine no favours.

If you are a total wine fanatic, then you probably have already heard of Riedel glasses, the *sine qua non* of drinking vessels. At the top of the range, the fabulously expensive, hand-blown examples are the ultimate in sophistication. Happily for most of us, a more reasonably priced machine-made range, called Vinum, is also available. In both, the glasses have been developed in many sizes and shapes to suit particular types of wine and to direct the wine to exactly the right place on your palate (for example, the flared rim of a Riesling glass directs the wine to the sides of your tongue, where your tastebuds will best appreciate this grape's greatest asset – racy acidity). Mature clarets, delicate Loire Sauvignons, esoteric Tuscans and others, are all represented. There's even a new range (Vinum Extreme) for New World wines, developed with a kink round the middle for extra swirling capacity, so that every dense-packed layer is unpacked and released.

Remember, always clean your glasses properly. This is vital. Vigilance pays. If they won't go in the dishwasher, glasses should always be washed separately in piping hot water with a tiny drop of detergent, rinsed in cold water and cleaned with a linen tea towel or glasses cloth specifically reserved for the purpose. Dirty glasses are a cardinal sin in wine terms and can ruin the aromas of a wine and therefore the pleasures of enjoying it.

Gizmos and gadgets

Much like any hobby, wine has its essential accoutrements for those in the know. There are avid collectors of corkscrews and wine paraphernalia the world over; the thousands of pages on the Internet devoted to this subject, let alone wine itself, must have opened up whole new avenues for enthusiasts.

The unbeatable must-haves for wine are a foil cutter and a reliable 'waiter's friend' lever corkscrew. Stoppers are fun to look at, but work best in a purely utilitarian role with sparkling wine; otherwise just replace the original cork. Anti-drip stoppers and collars are probably best left alone – better to perfect the natty little quarter twist of the bottle after pouring, which wine waiters do so well.

For picnics and alfresco summer dining, it is also a good idea to have a couple of padded cooling sleeves in the freezer. These are much quicker and less messy than an ice bucket and useful for all types of wines, including light reds.

If you want to drink only one glass of wine and save the rest of the bottle, the simplest way is to reinsert the cork and put the bottle in the fridge. This works for reds as well as whites, although you need to remember to take the reds out early enough so they can warm up. The wines may not be as fresh the day after, but they should still be drinkable (indeed, some young reds may even be better the next day). An alternative is the Vacuvin system, which pumps air out of the bottle through a special rubber stopper, creating a vacuum to preserve freshness. Critics feel it can also pump out flavour. A more reliable method is Wine Saver, a canister containing nitrogen which is squirted into a bottle, displacing the air.

FOOD AND WINE MATCHING

Most wines are reasonably satisfying with most food. But there are superlatives too, and so much decent wine is available nowadays that it is a crime not to experiment to your heart's content – either when entertaining at home or in a restaurant. One thing is certain though, decisions need to be made with confidence, and information about a wine is vital if you are not familiar with it. Good wine merchants and restaurant lists should provide details of the basic structure and taste you can expect and, increasingly, so should the labels themselves.

Broadly speaking – with simply too much vinous and culinary diversity in the world today to allow any – there are no rules. However, you do need to pay attention to the depth of flavours of a dish when considering a wine to go with it. This is the basic origin of the red wine with meat and white wine with fish and poultry routine, but such simplicity goes out of the window when you analyse cooking methods and sauces. Cooking? Think how different lamb tastes, for example, when roast as Sunday lunch, when barbecued as chops, in a casserole, or served cold. Each version needs a totally different approach. Add sauces and the palette is broader still.

Acidity, tannin and sweetness are the three main areas to keep in mind – the rest will inevitably be a journey of discovery. Consider matching the acidity of a dish with a complementary wine (for example, citrus or fruit flavours with crisp white wines or light reds). Or ensure that tannin, that mouth-furring component of robust and full-flavoured red wines, is paired off only with rich and robust foods, usually red meats. Remember that sweet wines are for sweet food in the main – could it be easier? (Actually just to ruin the plot, sweet wines are also renowned partners for salty flavours, Sauternes and Roquefort cheese or ripe Alsace Gewurztraminer with smoked salmon, for example.)

Another good rule of thumb is to choose a wine with a cultural link with the dish you are preparing or choosing. Mediterranean cooking goes well with southern French, Italian and Spanish reds, for pasta and pizza stay in Italy, French regional food has traditional links with many wines, manzanilla sherry and tapas suit each other, and so on. Modern fusion or spicy food are somewhat tricksier, but often this is where you can safely start with New World wines.

There are food and wine matching bugbears, however, and here are some of them to watch out for:

Eggs A not too oaky Chardonnay is your best bet here, as eggs are mouth-coating and need something to cut through them without clashing. Reds are definitely out unless the dish itself involves red wine or a particularly strong cheese element.

Chocolate Again, because of its mouth-coating qualities, generally never to be mixed with light wine. Dessert Muscat wines, in all their guises, can accompany sweet chocolate dishes perfectly though, and with dark chocolate, so can some Cabernets (New World ripe, sweet ones).

Tomatoes Try matching the acidity of the tomato with Sauvignon Blanc or, if you must have a red, then a crisp, young north-east Italian red, such as Valpolicella.

Fish Smoked salmon isn't difficult if you stick to a classic aperitif such as Chablis, Chardonnay or champagne, but with oilier versions (mackerel, kippers) go for something lighter still, and more acidic, such as Sauvignon or Muscadet – at all costs, avoid reds.

Spinach and artichokes These make wine taste metallic (in a similar way to red wine and fish). See 'Tricks of the trade' below, for how to avoid this.

Chinese and Thai food Match the delicacy and vibrancy in the dish with the same in the wine. Crisp, aromatic whites are the best accompaniment – Riesling, Alsace Gewürztraminer or (especially when there's lemon grass in the dish) New Zealand Sauvignon Blanc. Light reds such as Pinot Noir are also a possibility.

Indian food Richly flavoured New World whites, such as Chardonnay, Semillon or Verdelho, are excellent, or mellow reds which have plenty of fruit and not overpowering tannins, such as Zinfandel, Shiraz or Merlot – again from the New World.

Puddings and cakes Match the weight of sweetness in the wine to that in the food, and use the acidity of a sweet Riesling or the tang of a *botrytis* wine to match a dessert (for example, a lemony one) with equal bite. Strawberries go with red wine, but little else does.

Tricks of the trade

Professional tactics used to combat clashes include adding a condiment of some kind. By doing this, you expand your wine choices. Salt makes tannic wines seem even more so, but grind or shake some black pepper on to your steak, for example, and the wine will seem smoother and fruitier right away. Add salt to a dish to balance a particularly crisp wine – such as a young Sauvignon. And add lemon juice to temper the metallic-ness of spinach (that, or soften it by stirring in cream). Coriander in a dish can lift the fruitiness of many a dull Soave, and rosemary or mint can ease the relationships between many a Cabernet and its platter (Pinot Noir too, for that matter).

To see things as good as they get, we suggest trying Sauvignon, especially Sancerre, with goat's cheese; lamb and rosemary with top Bordeaux; Sauternes and Rocquefort cheese; port with Stilton. Plus, if ever you get the chance, champagne and oysters. But remember, if a different combination works for you, it works. Our palates are highly individual, and work in mysterious ways.

Part IV
Where to buy wine

EXPLANATION OF SYMBOLS

 Indicates the merchant operates case sales only.

 Mail order only.

 Where this symbol appears after information on tastings and talks, the merchant has elected to participate in *The Which? Wine Guide's* £5 voucher scheme. In the Also Recommended section the symbol appears at the end of the entry. For more information on this voucher scheme see the page opposite the Contents list. The terms and conditions of the voucher scheme are outlined on the back of the vouchers.

 The Which Web Trader Scheme is designed to make sure consumers get a fair deal when shopping online and to provide them with protection if things go wrong. For full details of the scheme and a list of traders currently registered see *www.which.net/webtrader*

 Denotes generally low prices and/or a large range of modestly priced wines.

 A merchant given this symbol offers exceptionally good service. We rely on readers' reports in allocating service symbols; this means that there may be merchants offering first-class service who appear here with no symbol because such distinction has gone unreported. Readers, please report!

 Indicates high-quality wines across the range.

 This award is given for a wide range of wines from around the world.

We have separated merchants into Highly Recommended (starting on page 304) and Also Recommended (starting on page 436).

Adnams Wine Merchants

Head office
Sole Bay Brewery, East Green, Southwold,   *Tel* (01502) 727222
Suffolk IP18 6JW   *Fax* (01502) 727223

The Cellar & Kitchen Store   *Tel* (01502) 727220
Victoria Street, Southwold, Suffolk IP18 6JW   *Fax* (01502) 727223

The Grapevine   *Tel* (01603) 613998
109 Unthank Road, Norwich, Norfolk NR2 2PE   *Fax* (01603) 622175

The Wine Shop   *Tel* (01502) 722138
Pinkney's Lane, Southwold, Suffolk IP18 6EW   *Email* wines@adnams.co.uk
                                                 Web site www.adnams.co.uk

Open Mon–Fri 8.45–6.30, Sat 9–12; shop times vary **Closed** Sun, public holidays
Cards Delta, MasterCard, Switch, Visa; personal and business accounts **Discount** 5%
on 5+ cases **Delivery** Free within 5-mile radius (min. 1 case); Nationwide service
available, charge £5, free for 1+ cases **Glass hire** Free with order, must return clean
Tastings and talks Regular tastings and events, phone for details **£5**

As we've said before, Simon Loftus has one of the shortest attention spans in
the industry, so when he outlines what he expects of a good wine (read on …),
that's what tends to end up on the list. We believe wholeheartedly in
Adnams' approach to wine, and Simon's own words best sum up what a
merchant's enthusiasms should be: 'One of the greatest pleasures of wine is a
sense of place. I want to be able to smell the aromatic *garrigue* of southern
France, taste the minerally slopes of the Mosel, remember the red earth of the
Barossa. Those vivid, distinctive differences are in danger of being lost.
Modern technology has made it easier to make wine without faults but has
resulted, far too often, in wine without character… safe options made and
sold by companies which prefer the middle road. I like the high ground and
the odd corners, local grapes and local flavours. I love vineyards untouched
by agrochemicals, wines which have not had the life filtered out of them. I
choose to work with individual winemakers, making individual wines.' His
enthusiastic team and his customers agree.

The wine list is divided into Adnams Classics and The Adnams Selection.
Even the classics must have that spark of individuality to make it on to the
core list. Nothing boring is admitted. This means you won't always see the
names you expect in the Bordeaux and Burgundy sections, for example.
They'll frequently be smaller domaines and châteaux, such as Château Le
Chec in the Graves, or Henri Germain in Burgundy for his elegantly
understated Meursaults. The larger likes of Langoa-Barton, Domaine de
Chevalier and Domaine Leflaive do make it, but you can be sure they'll have
been positively vetted, for style integrity, for value and for ethics.

It's not such an eccentric stance these days to promote an ecologically
sound list, but through both its ranges, Adnams does just this. A distinctive
green leaf marker picks out the likes of Aubert de Villaine, Tollot Beaut and
Thévenet from Burgundy; domaines Barret, de Villeneuve and André Perret
from the Rhône; and lesser-known names such as Viña Godeval from
Galicia and Viñas de Davalos from Argentina – who all strive for organic or
biodynamic status. Again, as we said last year, Adnams' motto might as well

be 'no passion; not interested', and that passionate care in the vineyards results in fine wines is amply reflected here.

If you aren't lucky enough to be in the wilds of Suffolk enjoying Adnams' wines in one of its Southwold hostelries – or beers within sight of the parent brewery – you'll do worse than take advantage of its Fine and Rare service (tempting regular mixed-case offerings) or Seasonal Cellar subscription (four deliveries a year chosen to complement each season). Adnams guarantee that if you don't like a wine, for whatever reason, return it within a month of purchase and it will be refunded without question or delay. They say this is one reason customers keep returning. Maybe so. The others would have to do with the wines themselves!

Look out for

- Australian favourites: Cullen, Charles Melton, Canoe Tree, Tim Gramp
- Spanish whites from Galicia and Rioja's Bagordi estate
- Bordeaux from 'owner-occupiers' (that is, châteaux not owned by insurance companies)
- Price per quality, a superb range of reliable Burgundy, including Leflaive, Sauzet, Thévenet
- Eco-friendly Alsace from classic domaines: Schoffit and Blanck
- Warming, tried-and-tested French country wines
- Rare California classics from Ridge, Saintsbury and Shafer
- Smart new web site for ordering your wines.

John Armit Wines

5 Royalty Studios, 105 Lancaster Road,   *Tel* 020-7908 0600
London W11 1QF   *Fax* 020-7908 0601
          Email info@armit.co.uk
          Web site www.armit.co.uk

Open Mon–Fri 9–6 **Closed** Sat, Sun, public holidays **Cards** Amex, Delta, MasterCard, Switch, Visa; personal and business accounts **Discount** Available, phone for details **Delivery** Free nationwide service available (min. 1 case) **Glass hire** Not available **Tastings and talks** Regular tastings and events, phone for details

There's none of the dusty packing-crate about this trendy wine merchant. Its Notting Hill venue simply seals its image as shiny, slick and way-to-go. (That's if its Studio Twenty designer list and packaging hadn't convinced you first.) And it's not cheap either – not if you're looking for bargain burgundy anyway. Armit people know who to talk to, where to go, what to drink and where to find it. In short, this is the 'It' wine merchant.

But look what wines there are! Hess Collection and Dominus Cabernets from California; Seresin from New Zealand; Rostaing and Chapoutier from the Rhône. You'll rarely find such a concentration of the world's finest. What followers really come to John Armit Wines for though (apart from the high standard of service) are Bordeaux, Burgundy and Italy. Supplying restaurant lists makes up an important part of the Armit business, and these three areas provide some of the best food accompaniments of all. Ornellaia, Sassicaia, Gaja, Romano Dalforno … you get the picture. Serving the on-trade means a high turnover, so the stash of back vintages isn't quite as deep as some; but the trend these days is for younger drinking and, as we said, 'trendy' is what Armit does best.

With 2001 came the launch of John Armit's own range of especially blended wines. There's even a John Armit Champagne, which is modestly listed in the catalogue among the top-10 'designer label' wines. But that's the sort of confidence that's gained this firm stratospheric success and the momentum to keep expanding, so we can't knock it. The year has also seen the introduction of a mixed case range, starting with a Party Wine case at £96, working up to 'Introduction to' cases for Spain, Italy, etc. and more expensive (£271 the priciest) Classic cases, all of which are impeccably chosen. There's also a 'Capsule Cellar' service for those just setting up, and a popular series of tastings for women.

We like it John. But all this – and still no web site?!

Look out for

- Burgundy from Faiveley, Roumier and Leflaive, plus 1970s and 1980s treasures from Maison Leroy
- Breathtaking Italian selection: Chiantis, Super-Tuscans, Amarone, Barolos …
- Right-bank Bordeaux: Vray Croix de Gay Pomerol and Belair Grand Cru St-Emilion
- Left-bank: Les Pagodes de Cos, Cantemerle and La Croix de Beaucaillou from 1995
- Glittering array of champagnes (e.g. Krug!)
- Delicious selection of top-name Sauternes including 1990 Filhot.

Asda Stores

Head office

ASDA House, Southbank, Great Wilson Street,	*Tel* 0113-241 9172
Leeds LS11 5AD	*Fax* 0113-241 7766
(230 branches nationwide)	*Web site* www.asda.co.uk

Open Mon–Sat varies between stores, Sun, public holidays 11–5 **Closed** Varies between stores **Cards** MasterCard, Switch, Visa **Discount** £1 on 5 bottles over £2.50 **Delivery** Via Asda Internet service only **Glass hire** Free **Tastings and talks** In-store customer tastings in addition to larger events

The time was when Asda was content with the cheap and cheerful, but wine marketing manager Gareth Roberts reports that customers are trading up, and are more open to experimentation. In transferring these sentiments to the shelves, the array of wines has been expanded by more than 50 per cent since the start of 2000 to around 500 lines. To help customers navigate through the enlarged range, they can consult the 'Discover a World of Wine' brochure, in which several of the wines are listed according to style ('dry zingy whites', 'juicy, fruity reds' and so on), complete with tasting notes and food-matching suggestions.

Being a supermarket today seems to mean that stocking well-known brands is a prerequisite. This is especially evident in the choice of New World wines, where the Californian range in particular is dominated by Gallo in its various guises. A few, more esoteric wines appear among the

Australians and South Africans, but the accent remains on the familiar. From Europe, too, most of the offerings are either brands or own-label wines. For a more entertaining selection, you need to look at the Spanish collection, or better still head for France, where the past year has seen the arrival of several offerings from the classic regions. Bordeaux now offers good wines at all levels from £5 (Peybonhomme Les Tours) up to £24.99 for 1997 Sociando Mallet. Of course, £25 claret is not what a supermarket is all about (and indeed only nine branches stock the Sociando Mallet), but the effort which Asda has expended in France in the past year deserves praise. We'd like to see this duplicated in other parts of the wine range, which for our palates is just too safe – especially with those adventurous customers.

If you do want pricy wines, head for one of the Asda/Wal-Mart Supercentres, where you'll find wines such as Rosemount Balmoral, Ridge Zinfandel, Beaucastel, Château Haut-Bailly and Dominique Laurent's Nuits-St-Georges. As with all of Asda's wines, prices for these are usually keen, and we even know of one London merchant who travelled to the Bristol store to clean out the annual supply of Grange.

Look out for
- Landskroon, Beyerskloof and Graham Beck from South Africa
- Australian Andrew Peace, Rymill and Peter Lehmann
- Baron de Ley, Fuentespina and Torres – all from Spain
- Much improved Bordeaux range
- Burgundies from Guy Mothe, Perruchot and Bernard Vallet
- Chileans Valdivieso, Casas del Bosque and TerraMater.

The Australian Wine Club

Freepost WC5500, Hounslow, Middlesex TW5 0BR   *Tel* (0800) 856 2004
Fax (0800) 856 2143
Email ukorders@austwine.co.uk
Web site www.austwine.co.uk

Open Mon–Fri 8–7, Sat, Sun 9–4 **Closed** Public holidays **Cards** Amex, MasterCard, Visa **Discount** Not available **Delivery** Nationwide service available, charge £4.99 per order (min. 1 case) **Glass hire** Not available **Tastings and talks** Annual wine tasting in May

We like your sense of humour, Craig. You came to the UK in 1974 for six months, found the weather so good you stayed! Fine. And your position at Australian Wine Club? 'Sitting down.' Well, thanks. There's no doubting that the AWC is an idiosyncratic setup – it couldn't be other with Craig Smith at the helm – but for a while there we were worried. Fortunately we can still report that the association with one of Australia's largest mail-order companies, Cellarmasters, hasn't dampened spirits one little bit.

The AWC began life by specialising in imports of high-quality, small Australian estates. In 2001, when we're seeing the big guys in Australia get bigger and bigger, the services of a merchant focusing on the other, niche end of the spectrum have become very precious indeed. We think individuality, quirky blends and interesting grapes should be encouraged and so have no hesitation in recommending the AWC as a safe haven from supermarket-style amorphous blends. South Australia was always the speciality here, and it still is. Big Barossa wines from Steve Hoff, St-Hallet and Torbreck, crisp Ashton Hills Riesling, Chapel Hill 'unwooded' Chardonnay, and Primo Joseph sparkling red are ample proof. New South Wales and Victoria are beginning to make an appearance with tasty Allandale Verdelho, Yarra Ridge Pinot Noir, and others, famous and undiscovered alike. And let's hope Western Australia and Tasmania aren't too far behind. We recommend seeing for yourself at the AWC's annual tasting in London, with over 300 wines on show – or taking advantage of one of the regular mixed case and featured wine offers.

Loyal followers might like to know that the indefatigable Frank Luff has now been promoted to wine buyer (F Luff, the cat, geddit?), his only qualification being that of dedicated wine drinker. Well, on the basis of this list, he looks to be more than qualified.

Look out for

- Fabulous Shiraz – Allandale, Tim Adams, Traeger and more
- Australian Rhône blends Theologicum, The Steading and The Fergus
- Off-beat whites: Verdelho, Riesling, Kapunda Road's 'sorbet fresh' Colombard
- 'Drama ... Intrigue ... superb quality dozens at rock bottom prices' (in other words, bargain mixed cases!)
- Top-notch Semillon from the Clare, Barossa and Hunter Valleys
- Sparkling reds and whites and 'sticky' *botrytis* wines.

Averys of Bristol

Head office
Orchard House, Southfield Road,
Nailsea, Bristol BS48 1JN

Tel (01275) 811100
Fax (01275) 811101

Cellars
9 Culver Street, Bristol BS1 5LD

Tel 0117-921 4146
Fax 0117-922 6318

Shop
8 Park Street, Bristol BS1 5HX

Tel 0117-921 4145
Email averywines@aol.com

Open Shop Mon–Sat 10–6.30, cellars Mon–Sat 10–7, office Mon–Fri 9–5.15 **Closed** Sun, public holidays **Cards** Amex, Delta, MasterCard, Switch, Visa **Delivery** Nationwide service available, charge £5.50, free for 2+ cases **Glass hire** Free with order **Tastings and talks** Tastings and masterclasses available, phone for details **£5**

This long-established merchant may be well into its third century, but it's certainly not living on past glories. The May 2001 list featured no fewer than 140 different wines from all over the world, and these have reinforced what was already a commendable selection. It's not a perfect range. Master of Wine John Avery (one of three MWs on the buying team) stuck his toe into New World waters long before many other merchants. Today, however, while you'll find representation from nearly all the relevant countries (Canada has recently slipped off the list), the choice is mostly confined to the wines imported by parent company Hallgarten. For the South African range, this is no bad thing, as a number of classy estates are featured. With the Australian wines, most of which come from Miranda, a little more diversity would be welcome.

Most of the new arrivals seem to have been in the Old World range. Here the Italian and Bordeaux selection remains as strong as ever, but the Rhône, Burgundy and Languedoc have all benefited from fresh blood. Traditional Averys' customers will be pleased to hear that there are no plans to shelve the old-fashioned wines from Remoissenet. Those of a more modern bent will appreciate the appearance of some new estates, especially Domaine de la Vougeraie. We would welcome a little more depth in the Spanish range, but we're not going to complain about the quality of the wines available.

If the regular list doesn't meet your requirements, ask for the fine and rare vintages supplement, where the Bordeaux range is especially strong. And if you're confused about the hundreds of wines on the list, you can settle for AfA – Automatically from Averys. Pay either £75 or £125 every three months and a mixed case of six different wines will arrive complete with tasting notes and background information. And finally – keep an eye out for the New Year Sale, when some of the treasures of the Averys' vaults are bundled together in attractively priced mixed dozens.

Look out for

- Burgundies from Domaine de la Vougeraie, Remoissenet and Morot
- Excellent selection from classy producers throughout Italy
- Hamilton Russell, Stellenzicht and Nitida from South Africa
- Swanson, Sonoma Cutrer and Clos du Val from California
- Rising Languedoc stars Château Veyran and Domaine Montlobre
- Rhône reds from Clos du Mont Olivet, Vernay and Courbis.

Bacchus Fine Wines

Warrington House Farm Barn, Warrington, Olney,	*Tel* (01234) 711140
Buckinghamshire MK46 4HN	*Fax* (01234) 711199
	Email wine@bacchus.co.uk
	Web site www.bacchus.co.uk

Open Mon–Fri 11–7, Sat 10–1.30, public holidays 11–4 **Closed** Sun, 25–28 Dec **Cards** Amex, Delta, Diners, MasterCard, Switch, Visa; personal and business accounts **Discount** Available, phone for details **Delivery** Free within 10-mile radius (min. 1 case); nationwide service available, charge £6 + VAT (min. 1 case) **Glass hire** Free with order **Tastings and talks** in-store and tutored tastings available **£5**

'We are not reticent to be "firm" with our advice.' Advice is of paramount importance in Russell Heap's shop, since there are many wines here that you simply won't find in too many other places. Even we haven't tasted them all. However, judging by those we have come across, we'd be happy to leave ourselves in Russell's hands. The Bacchus selection has expanded markedly in recent years, and now runs to more than 800 wines. Most of the major wine-producing countries are represented, and you'll find especially good selections from Burgundy, southern France, South Africa and Italy. However, Russell's current passion is for Austria, and his selection of around 50 whites and reds is one of the largest you'll find. Here, as elsewhere in the range, excursions above the £10 mark are the exception rather than the rule, although anyone wanting to splash out on a really special bottle certainly won't find themselves short of options. The first edition of the *Bacchus Gazette* in March 2001 heralded the return of the tutored tastings, which will now take place every two months. It also included a Discovery of the Month (Diamond Ridge Australian Chardonnay at £3.95) plus advice – firm, of course – on which wines to serve with a selection of recipes from Jamie Oliver's *The Return of the Naked Chef*.

Look out for

- Austrian wines from Heinrich, Achs and Preisinger
- Languedoc-Roussillon stars Alquier, Estanilles and St-Andrieu
- Californians Franus, Fife and Qupé
- Classy South African reds from Veenwouden, Claridge and Warwick
- Bremerton, Black George and Lost Lake from Australia
- Italians Nardi, Marcarini and Allegrini.

Ballantynes of Cowbridge

Regional Award Winner – Wales

---

3 Westgate, Cowbridge,
Vale of Glamorgan CF71 7AQ

Tel (01446) 774840
Fax (01446) 775253
Email richard@ballantynes.co.uk
Web site www.ballantynes.co.uk

Open Mon–Sat 9–5.30 **Closed** Sun, public holidays **Cards** Delta, MasterCard, Switch, Visa; personal and business accounts **Discount** 8% on 1 case **Delivery** Free within 5-mile radius (min. 1 case); nationwide service available, charge £4.95 per case/item **Glass hire** Free with order **Tastings and talks** Regular tastings and talks, phone for details **(£5)**

Richard Ballantyne is proud that even in his newly extended store, no 'token wines' adorn the shelves. Ever since the company was established in 1978, there has been a ruthless adherence to high quality, and the result is a range which ranks as one of the finest in Britain, with most of the wines being sourced directly from the producers. Most of those producers are based in France, where the Burgundy selection is especially impressive and the choices from the Rhône, southern France and Bordeaux are not too far behind.

Italian enthusiasts will also find their needs catered for with aplomb in a choice featuring high-class producers from throughout the country. Here, as in other sections of the list, there is a healthy mix of the affordable and luxurious, so if you can't stretch to 1996 Sassicaia at £75, several sub-£10 reds from Puglia and other regions may tempt you. The New World fare continues the theme of high-quality producers; some familiar, some less well known. Those from Australia form the largest range, but there's also much of note from California and South Africa. Indeed, this is one of those rare merchants where you could walk in and pick a dozen bottles from anywhere on the shelves, and be confident of finding something not just drinkable but very good indeed.

Look out for

- Inspiring Spanish reds from Reyes, Capçanes and Abadia Retuerta
- Extensive and high-class selection from Italy
- Bott-Geyl, Deiss and Burn in Alsace

- Burgundy from Perrot-Minot, J J Confuron, Tessier, Fichet and many more
- Rarely seen Australian stars such as Nicholson River, Bass Phillip, Mount Mary and Jasper Hill
- Southern French wines from Châteaux Pibarnon, de Cazeneuve and du Cèdre.

Balls Brothers

313 Cambridge Heath Road, Bethnal Green,
London E2 9LQ
(16 wine bars and restaurants)

Tel 020-7739 1642
Fax (0870) 243 9775
Email wine@ballsbrothers.co.uk
Web site www.ballsbrothers.co.uk

Open Mon–Fri 9–5.30 **Closed** Sat, Sun, public holidays **Cards** Amex, Delta, Diners, MasterCard, Switch, Visa; personal and business accounts **Discount** Available, phone for details **Delivery** Nationwide service available, free within Central London for 1+ case and throughout UK for 2+ cases (exc. Highlands and Islands); £6 for less **Glass hire** Free with order, charge for breakages **Tastings and talks** Regular tastings and events, see web site for details **£5**

'Our key strength is that we specialise in high-quality small producers. We are an independent, family-owned company and we ship, age and store our wines ourselves.' Perhaps this rather traditional introduction belies the fact that this upmarket wine merchant is one of the most modern and well equipped in the country. Its spanking new web site and fashionable London wine bar/restaurants put Balls Bros' best foot forward into the post-2000 wine world, appealing to a range of new, and young, wine consumers, making wine as accessible as it should be. Catering for 'those in a hurry' or 'stuck for ideas', *www.ballsbrothers.co.uk* offers pre-selected cases of good-value, benchmark burgundy, etc., from as little as £55 a case. It also offers a useful wine search option with 12 selection criteria (including likely food matches), as well as the more conventional list of mature Bordeaux and burgundy. The printed list encroaches on 'magazine-scale' usefulness, with panel notes ('The Knowledge') explaining various aspects of wine lore, wine gossip etc. 'The Chef' offers recipe options appropriate to the wines listed – snail and onion tart, for example, accompanies the superb range of Alsace wines on offer from Domaine Blanck. And down to the main business, the range of wines is excellent, particularly strong from the Old World, and far from disappointing from the New, bending constantly to customer demand. Surely the appeal to customers to come forward and ask for German wines shouldn't be resisted from a merchant as savvy as this?

Look out for

- Champagnes – first-rate selection from big and small names, vintage and non-vintage
- Burgundy back to 1984 (Voillot, Potel and Michel Lafarge)
- Bordeaux: plenty to choose from, from the excellent 1995 and 1996 vintages
- Loire favourites Riffault and Château de Tracy
- Delicious white and red Riojas from Marqués de Cáceres and Murrieta
- Pelorus sparkling and C J Pask wines from New Zealand
- Ornella Molon Traverso and Capaccia, plus more top names from Italy.

Barrels & Bottles

3 Oak Street, Heeley Bridge, Sheffield S8 9UB
Tel 0114-255 6611
Fax 0114-255 1010
Email sales@barrelsandbottles.co.uk
Web site www.barrelsandbottles.co.uk

Open Mon–Fri 9.30–5.30, Sat 9–5 **Closed** Sun, public holidays **Cards** Amex, Delta, MasterCard, Switch, Visa; personal and business accounts **Discount** 5% on 6 bottles, 10% on 1 mixed case, 15% on 1 unmixed case **Delivery** Free within 20-mile radius (min. 2 cases); nationwide service available, charge £7.50 for 1 case, £10 for 3 cases, free for 3+ cases **Glass hire** Free with order **Tastings and talks** In-store tastings, monthly vintner visits, dinners and tastings, phone for details **£5**

As we put the finishing touches to the *Guide* this year, Barrels & Bottles customers should be cruising along the canal in Sheffield enjoying a wine tasting prior to dinner at the WaterWays restaurant. There are several wines in the range that we wouldn't mind sipping (or even slugging back) on such an occasion, and we'd certainly opt for something from the extensive German range as an aperitif. Germany is the only country that could be called a speciality here, but competent choices are on offer from most major regions. Selections we'd steer you towards include the Loire, Australia and a lively Portuguese range, and there's also no shortage of claret. Elsewhere, good wines dot the list, but without quite the same depth of quality. Still, you shouldn't have a problem finding most of your requirements here. And if you're thinking of giving wine as a gift, take a look at the Alexander von Essen selection, denoted by the initials AVE on the list and web site. This is a range of wines (and grappas, eaux de vie, vinegars and olive oils) from some of the world's best-known producers in beautifully presented bottles.

Look out for
- German wines from Kühling-Gillot, Gebhardt and Schweinhardt
- De Fesles, Roches Neuves and Balland Chapuis from the Loire
- Rioja from Baron de Ley, Viña Salceda and Palacios Remondo
- Wirra Wirra, Cape Mentelle and Tarrawarra from Australia
- Quinta dos Roques, Niepoort, Cartuxa and Quinta de Abrigada from Portugal
- The Alexander von Essen selection.

Bat & Bottle

Knightley Grange Office, Grange Road, Knightley, Woodseaves, Staffordshire ST20 0JU
Tel (01785) 284495
Fax (01785) 284877
Email ben@batwine.com
Web site www.batwine.com

Open Mon–Thur phone for details, Fri 2–7, Sat 11–4 **Closed** Sun, public holidays **Cards** MasterCard, Switch, Visa **Discount** 5% on 1 case **Delivery** Nationwide service available, charge £4.99 per case/item, free for orders of £150+ **Glass hire** Free with order **Tastings and talks** Regular tastings, phone for details **£5**

'Our list is very brave,' says Ben Robson. 'No Bordeaux, a Californian list without Cabernet and an Australian one without Shiraz. We have, perhaps, lost the plot.' We disagree. This is one of Britain's most refreshing wine merchants, and deserves applause for steering into uncharted waters, particularly those of Italy. If you thought north-east Italy offered little beyond Valpolicella and Soave, Ben will introduce you to grape varieties such as Cividìn, Costa dei Fachi, Sciaglìn, Wildbacher and Torchato di Fregona. And they're not just there for novelty value either – they taste good too. Other parts of the country are also covered with aplomb, with most wines imported directly from the producer, keeping prices at reasonable levels. Outside Italy, Spanish fans will find some gems available, many of them courtesy of Laymont & Shaw (q.v.), and there are also several tasty, spicy reds from the Rhône, southern France and Portugal. Other countries do feature in the list, but Ben isn't one to include wines just for the sake of it. Indeed, at the time of going to press, he is considering delisting champagne in favour of alternative sparklers from Italy's Franciacorta and from England. Ben may have wandered from a mainstream plot, but the yarn he's spinning now is much more entertaining.

Look out for

- Inspiring collection of rarely seen, high-class Italian producers
- Riojas old and new from La Rioja Alta, López de Heredia and Martínez Bujanda
- New World stars Isabel, Il Podere dell'Olivos and Louisvale
- Alsace wines from Krick, Koehly and Ostertag
- The gutsy French reds of Puech-Haut, Montvac and Courbis
- Local apple juice from Ashgroves Farm – great with vodka, apparently!

Bennetts Fine Wines

High Street, Chipping Campden,
Gloucestershire GL55 6AG

Tel (01386) 840392
Fax (01386) 840974
Email enquiries@bennettsfinewines.com
Web site www.bennettsfinewines.com

Open Mon–Fri 10–1, 2–6, Sat 9–6 **Closed** Sun, public holidays, 25–28 Dec **Cards** Delta, MasterCard, Switch, Visa; business accounts **Discount** Available, phone for details **Delivery** Free within 10-mile radius (min. 1 case); nationwide service available, charge £6 per case/item (min. order £12) **Glass hire** Free with order **Tastings and talks** Tastings and regular wine dinners, phone for details

Charlie Bennett cites his qualifications for running one of Britain's finest independent merchants as '25 years of tasting great wines'. If this sounds immodest, it's not meant to be. Charlie and his wife Vicky have put together a range that quite simply is devoid of hangers-on. 'Every bottle has to be one we would personally drink' is the motto. This leads to entries in their list such as, 'We know people will criticise us for not having a comprehensive range from South Africa, but try as we might, we just can't find a bottle we would choose to drink with supper.' Given the quality of the selections from other countries, we'll forgive the Bennetts this time.

The quality-first approach doesn't leave much scope for those with only a fiver in their pockets, although a few wines just about creep into this price bracket. Once above this level, however, the goodies kick in. Wines from

South Africa may be thin on the ground, and if you're looking for an extensive selection of Eastern European or South American wines, you'll also be disappointed. Otherwise, there's almost everything here that a fine wine lover could ask for. Italy is the Bennetts' current area of passion, and now makes up a quarter of the range, but you'll find all the great wine regions of the world represented by high-class producers on the pages of the list. Even Germany is well covered, although we sense that trade is not the briskest. 'We felt the only logical response to slow sales of German wines was to add to the list a half bottle of Trockenbeerenauslese at £182.50.

That list runs to more than 50 pages, but it doesn't tell the full story. For this, you need to be in receipt of both the fine and rare supplement and the newsletters that give details of the many ex-cellars offers. If you struggle to keep up with the range, there are large summer and winter tastings in the Chipping Campden School Hall where dozens of top-class wines are available for sampling. Prices, as we have said in the past, can be on the high side, but since quality and service are on the *very* high side, don't let that put you off.

Look out for

- Italian wines from Allegrini, Fontodi, Aldo Conterno and many more
- Fabas, Clovallon and de Viella from southern France
- Fourrier, Raphet and Javillier burgundies
- Rhône reds from Domaine de la Mordorée, Belle and Remiller
- Kumeu River, Yarra Yering and Bannockburn from Down Under
- California stars Ridge, Cuvaison and Matanzas Creek.

Bentalls

Wood Street, Kingston-upon-Thames,
Surrey KT1 1TS

Tel 020-8546 1001
Fax 020-8549 6163
Email bentalls.online@bentalls.co.uk
Web site www.bentalls.co.uk

Open Mon–Wed, Fri 9.30–6, Thurs 9.30–9, Sat 9–6, Sun 11–5 **Closed** 25 Dec
Cards Delta, MasterCard, Switch, Visa; personal and business accounts, Bentalls card
Discount 5% for wine club members **Delivery** Nationwide service available, charges vary according to distance **Glass hire** Free to wine club members **Tastings and talks** Biannual wine fair for wine club members

---

Just as this edition of the *Guide* appears, Bentalls' wine buyer Jonathan Wenborn (formerly of First Quench) will be celebrating the end of his first twelve months in the job. He has inherited a fine range from his predecessor James Taylor (now at Fortnum's), and is looking to develop it further in the future. The wine club has been relaunched, giving members the option to buy standard, premium or deluxe wines of the month at a discount, and also get first stab at rarities such as Cloudy Bay Sauvignon.

Visitors to the Bentalls store will find a smartly laid-out wine department full of intriguing wines. The selection isn't huge, but scanning through the shelves reveals very few gaps in the range. Quality is high throughout, and the producers are a fine mix of the well known and the not-so-famous. If we had to point you in any particular direction to begin with, it would probably be the champagnes, where some top-notch small growers rub shoulders with the likes of Bollinger, Moët and Krug. There's not a bad wine in stock, and we'd happily follow the recommendations of Jon or any other member of the helpful staff. And when you've bought your wine, why not pop round the corner for a peek at the mouth-watering deli counter?

Look out for
- Champagnes from Selosse, Hostomme and Vilmart
- Tuscan reds from Avignonesi, Panaretta and Poliziano
- Girardin, Pascal and Lignier burgundies
- Australian selection featuring T'Gallant, Petaluma and Primo Estate
- Hamilton Russell, Meerlust and Thelema from South Africa
- Trévallon, Bunan and La Rouvière from Provence.

Berkmann Wine Cellars/Le Nez Rouge

12 Brewery Road, London N7 9NH

Tel 020-7609 4711
Fax 020-7607 0018
Email info@berkmann.co.uk
Web site www.berkmann.co.uk

Open Mon–Fri 9–5.30 **Closed** Sat, Sun, public holidays **Cards** Amex, Delta, Diners, MasterCard, Switch, Visa **Discount** Not available **Delivery** Free nationwide service (min. 1 case) **Glass hire** Not available **Tastings and talks** Not available

This is one of Britain's most successful wine importers, acting as agent for (at the last count) 36 prominent producers around the world. Dealing with the public is only a fraction of the business, but we're pleased to say that this hasn't stopped Berkmann from putting out a list with VAT-inclusive prices. There's no minimum purchase either, although orders of less than a dozen bottles are subject to a delivery charge. Given the wines on offer, assembling that full case should prove little problem. Those 36 wineries provide the bulk of the wines, and include such well-known names as Duboeuf, Beringer, Antinori (at the heart of a strong Italian showing) and Santa Rita. The selection also features wines from other producers, with the Burgundy section in particular benefiting from the inclusion of several serious growers. There may be merchants offering broader ranges of wines, and more extensive customer services, but we can't fault the quality on offer at Brewery Road.

Look out for
- Delas and Beaurenard in the Rhône
- Burgundies from Bernard Morey, Colin-Deléger and Girardin
- Masi, Maculan, Marco Felluga and Mastroberardino in Italy
- Buitenverwachting, Lievland and Groene Cloof from South Africa
- Antipodean wines from Morton Estate, Lenswood and Vasse Felix
- American wines from Norton, Santa Rita, Beringer and Hedges.

Berry Bros & Rudd

Head office
3 St James's Street, London SW1A 1EG

Tel 020-7396 9600
Fax 020-7396 9611

Order office

Tel (0870) 900 4300
Fax (0870) 900 4301

Berrys' Wine and Fine Food Shop
Hamilton Close, Houndmills, Basingstoke RG21 6YB

Tel (01256) 323566
Fax (01256) 340144

Duty-free shops
Terminal 3, Heathrow Airport TW6 1JH

Tel 020-8564 8361/3
Fax 020-8564 8379

Terminal 4, Heathrow Airport TW6 3XA

Tel 020-8754 1961
Fax 020-8754 1984
Email orders@bbr.com
Web site www.bbr.com

Open Mon–Fri 9–6, Sat 9–1 (times vary between stores, phone for details) **Closed** Sun, public holidays (exc. Heathrow) **Cards** Amex, Delta, Diners, MasterCard, Switch, Visa; business accounts **Discount** 5% on 1 unmixed case **Delivery** Nationwide service available, charge £7.50, free for orders of £100+ **Glass hire** £4.50 for 30 glasses **Tastings and talks** Regular events, tutored tastings and producer dinners, phone for details **£5**

A measure of the vast range of this long-established merchant is that the May 2001 list only featured wines appropriate for drinking during the Spring and Summer months, yet still ran to 600 wines. If you're interested in the complete collection, all 2,000+ wines can be found on the Internet, where Berry Bros has also been established for considerably longer than most other merchants. The current site is a model of simplicity, offering as much or as little information as you want, along with offers, tastings, news, and even a pronunciation guide.

As for the wines, they continue to impress. This may be the company which in 1923 provided 38 wines in miniature bottles for the cellar of Queen Mary's doll's house (at Windsor Castle), but not so very long ago, tradition hung heavy round its neck. Unless it was port, claret, hock, Moselle and old-fashioned burgundies you were after, Berry's had little to offer. However, since the new broom of Master of Wine Alun Griffiths appeared in the early 1990s, the cobwebs have all been swept away. The classics are still here in abundance, but some of the tired old wines, burgundies in particular, have been cast aside in favour of better wines from top-class producers.

As testimony to quite how far Berry's has come, one of the many merchant of the year awards for which the company is now in the running is that for the New World. Thanks to the peregrinations of the buying team, you'll find several classy wines here from all over the world that are simply not available elsewhere. If you're bored with the same old names from New Zealand, Australia and South Africa in particular, you'll find lots of new blood here. And while there's very little for under £5, there's plenty for under a tenner.

The new list also announces that, in the near future, visitors to the historic St James's Street premises will soon find three rooms with displays of champagnes, wines and spirits. 'The aim', according to Alun Griffiths, 'is to make shopping at BB&R an easier, more enjoyable experience.' This time next year, we're sure that we'll be reporting on even more evidence of the spring in the step of this sprightly oldster.

Look out for

- Vast array of clarets
- Burgundies from dozens of fine growers and domaines
- Von Buhl, Dönnhoff and Dr Loosen in Germany
- Rhône reds from Romero, Ogier, Jaboulet and Chapoutier
- Up-and-coming South African producers Waterford, Beaumont and Cordoba
- Mount Difficulty, Felton Road and Alana Estate from New Zealand.

Bibendum Wine

113 Regents Park Road, London NW1 8UR

Tel 020-7916 7706
Fax 020-7916 7705
Email sales@bibendum-wine.co.uk
Web site www.bibendum-wine.co.uk

Open Mon–Fri 8.30–6.30 **Closed** Sat, Sun, public holidays **Cards** Amex, Delta, Diners, MasterCard, Switch, Visa; personal and business accounts **Discount** Not available **Delivery** Nationwide service available, charge £10, free for orders of £100+ **Glass hire** £2.35 for 24 **Tastings and talks** Regular tastings, phone for details

Bibendum celebrates its twentieth anniversary in 2002, with what could be its best range of wines ever. Even if you're not a customer of this jovial north London institution, chances are that you've enjoyed a few of the wines it imports, either in a restaurant or at your local wine merchant. Bibendum started off in life specialising in wines from Italy and France, and these countries still offer the most enticing selections in the current range, with the choices from the Rhône, Burgundy, southern France and the Loire being especially good. In recent years, though, the company has branched out successfully into the New World. As in Europe, the average standard is high, and enthusiasts for wines from California, South Africa and Australia in particular will find much of interest.

Several of the wines are the result of projects that the roving Simon Farr has initiated with producers all around the world with the aim of tailoring wines specifically for the UK market. Such activities are usually focused on lower-priced wines from Australia, the Americas and southern Europe, but there are occasional forays to other places, such as Tunisia. However, for us, the best wines available are those where Bibendum is simply a middleman between high-class producers and interested customers.

There are a few drawbacks. For example, you may be able to mix a couple of wines in your case of 12 (the minimum purchase), but sales are normally by the full case only. There is now no comprehensive wine list for retail customers, so you'll have to browse through the web site, which isn't yet as detailed or efficient as the company would have us believe, and which quotes prices without VAT. But there are also advantages to being a Bibendum customer. The staff are friendly, clued-up and genuinely helpful. There's the fine wine desk for those interested in buying or selling blue-chip wines. Then there are the many tastings and dinners over the course of the year, often timed to coincide with the annual opening offers for wines from the Rhône/Languedoc, Burgundy and the New World. And finally there are the twice-yearly bin-end sales, where the full-case-only policy is relaxed. If you're a new customer, this is a good way to begin an exploration of the fine range that Bibendum offers.

Look out for

- A host of fine Burgundy growers
- Rhône producers such as Colombier, Goudray and Dumazet
- Rising Italian stars Alario, Bindella and Vecchie Terre di Montefili
- Paul Hobbs, Talley, Calera and many other top Californian estates
- Springfield, Grangehurst and Bouchard Finlayson from South Africa
- Champagnes from Billiot, Beerens and Paillard.

Booths Supermarkets

Head office
4–6 Fishergate, Preston, Lancashire PR1 3LJ

Tel (01772) 251701
Fax (01772) 255642

(Outlets throughout Lancashire, Cheshire, Cumbria, Yorkshire)

Email admin@booths-supermarkets.co.uk
Web site www.booths-supermarkets.co.uk

Open Mon–Fri 8.30–8, Sat 9–8, Sun 10–4 (times vary between stores) **Closed** 25 & 26 Dec, Easter Sun **Cards** Delta, MasterCard, Switch, Visa **Discount** 5% on 6+ bottles **Delivery** Not available **Glass hire** Free with orders of £25+, £10 deposit **Tastings and talks** Available, phone for details **(£5)**

Northerners may not have a Waitrose on their doorstep, but they do have access to Booths, one of Britain's more enterprising supermarkets. The stores can stock Mothers Pride with the best of them, but you'll always find something here that lifts the quality above everyday level and closer to the high-class grocer category. The wine department, presided over by Sally Holloway, but with close personal interest from a number of the directors, is no exception.

The size of the company – 25 stores at the last count – means that Sally is able to stock wines whose limited availability rules them out of other competitors' ranges. At the cheaper end of the market, as in most supermarkets, are the own-label *vin de table* and other rather anodyne bottles – but also wines from a number of individual domaines, which pack in a little more character. At much higher prices, you'll find some really rather serious wines, especially from Bordeaux and Burgundy (although in some cases, we're not sure how quickly these sell – 1986 Beauséjour-Bécot seems to have been on the list for rather a long time now). Between these two extremes, in the £5–£10 bracket, is where Booths excels – with the choices from Spain, southern France and Portugal deserving particular praise.

While only a quarter of the shops stock the entire range, in each you should find staff who have a fair degree of wine knowledge and in most cases have passed their WSET Higher Certificate. Also available is a fine range of beers that changes with encouraging regularity. If you can't find a decent tipple in a Booth's store, there's something wrong with you.

Look out for

- Artadi, Allende and Amezola de la Mora from Spain
- Vajra, Vallone and Viviani from Italy
- Enterprising selection of southern French reds
- Portuguese reds such as Cartuxa and Quinta de la Rosa
- Classy Australian fare from Capel Vale, Petaluma and Shaw & Smith
- Jordan, Spice Route and Bouchard Finlayson from South Africa.

Bottoms Up

see Thresher Wine Shops

The Butlers Wine Cellar

247 Queens Park Road, Brighton, East Sussex BN2 2XJ

Tel (01273) 698724
Fax (01273) 622761
Email henry@butlers-winecellar.co.uk
Web site www.butlers-winecellar.co.uk

Open Tue–Wed 10–6, Thur–Sat 10–7 **Closed** Sun, Mon, public holidays **Cards** Amex, Delta, MasterCard, Switch, Visa **Discount** Not available **Delivery** Free within 15-mile radius (min. 1 case); nationwide service available, charge £10, free for 3+ cases **Glass hire** Free with order (min. 1 case) **Tastings and talks** Regular talks and tastings, phone for details **(£5)**

It's business as usual at The Butlers Wine Cellar, according to Geoffrey Butler, who, with son Henry, runs this south-coast emporium. If you're not familiar with the company, this is a treasure trove of ancient and modern, where 1991 Australian Chardonnays and 1981 Hermitages are the rule rather than the exception. Not that there's nothing from current vintages. You'll find goodly selections from most wine regions, with the choices from southern France, Italy, Portugal and Burgundy (for whites more than reds) being perhaps the best. For us, however, the real reason to visit the shop (or the web site) is for the range of bin ends. As we said last year, this is the only place we know where the bin-end list is longer than the regular one. While some of it is given over to the last few bottles from recent listings, the bulk of the wines are much older. And while other merchants may be able to point to stocks of mature Bordeaux, who else has South African reds, California whites, Chiantis, German *Beerenauslese* and champagne from the 1970s? Moreover, the wines are priced at a level to make you think, 'Why not?' Those seven halves of 1990 *grand cru* Chablis at £9.75 could be rather good; ditto for those two bottles of 1981 Hermitage La Chapelle (£32.50) and that 1971 Fontanafredda Barolo (£25).

The Butlers' tasting programme is just as entertainingly offbeat. One month, it will be new wines from Spain, the next, a vertical of Beaucastel, and the next it will be Russian sparkling reds. There are also evenings when Geoffrey and Henry delve into their stock of venerable bottles, and for Brightonian wines lovers (and indeed those further afield) these should not be missed.

Look out for
- Southern French delights from Pietri-Geraud, La Forge and Château Routas
- Fontodi, Felsina and Vallone from Italy
- White burgundies from Chavy, Bouzereau and Bessin
- Australian reds from Grant Burge, Best's and Plantagenet
- Rodney Strong, Mill Creek and Bonny Doon from California
- The longest bin-end list in the world?

Anthony Byrne Fine Wines

Ramsey Business Park, Stocking Fen Road,
Ramsey, Cambridgeshire PE26 2UR

Tel (01487) 814555
Fax (01487) 814962
Email claude@abfw.co.uk
Web site www.abfw.co.uk

Open Mon–Fri 9–5.30 **Closed** Sat, Sun, public holidays **Cards** None accepted; business accounts **Discount** Available, phone for details **Delivery** Nationwide service available (min. 1 case), charge £6, free for 5+ cases **Glass hire** Not available **Tastings and talks** Available, phone for details

With 95 per cent of the business being wholesale, we'll forgive Anthony Byrne for his frill-free, picture-free, VAT-exclusive price list. Those private customers who do choose to deal with the company will find an eclectic selection of wines ranging from litre bottles of *vin de table* up to a vast array of clarets, including 12 vintages of Château Haut-Brion. It's not a fault-free range. For example, there are a few vintages of certain wines that should have been pensioned off by now, along with some rather basic wines at the sub-£5 level which seem to be aimed squarely at the restaurant market. However, those who possess the patience and knowledge to separate the wheat from the chaff will find plenty to keep them happy.

The company is a shipper or distributor for more than 50 producers, and wines from these form the backbone of the list. Most of those on offer are in France, with Burgundy and the Loire being especially well represented, but there are excursions to places further afield, such as Spain (Bodegas Lan), Germany (von Kesselstatt) and New Zealand (Palliser). Fans of Bordeaux and Italy can also indulge themselves at all price levels. Frequent tastings for both trade and private customers are held in London, Cambridge and Oxford, often with growers in attendance. And look out for the bin-end lists which appear throughout the year, and bring already reasonable prices down to even more attractive levels.

Look out for
- Madiran from Alain Brumont – the finest in south-west France
- Burgundies from Château de Maligny, Gagnard-Delagrange, Arnoux and dozens more

- Loire wines from Pinard, Druet and Crochet
- Rhône reds from Graillot, Nalys and Clos St-Jean
- South African selection including Lanzerac, Jordan and Hoopenburg
- Champagnes from Drappier and several major houses.

D Byrne & Co

Regional Award Winner – North of England

Victoria Buildings, 12 King Street,
Clitheroe, Lancashire BB7 2EP

Tel (01200) 423152
Fax (01200) 429386

Open Mon–Wed 8.30–6, Thurs, Fri 8.30–8, Sat 8–6, public holidays 10–4 **Closed** Sun,
25 & 26 Dec, Good Fri, Easter Sun & Mon **Cards** Delta, MasterCard, Switch, Visa
Discount £2 on 1 case **Delivery** Free within 50-mile radius (min. 1 case); nationwide
service available, phone for details of charges **Glass hire** Free with order **Tastings
and talks** Annual week-long in-store tasting; small in-store group tastings

No web site? No wine list? 'Our only concession to the modern day is the
acquisition of a telephone!' say the brothers Byrne. They still ring up sales
on the original brass hand-wound till, and fully admit that the best way to
get to grips with their wines is for customers to come and see for themselves.
And no, things have not changed since the last edition of the *Guide* (or for
110 years for that matter); they will still be in for a double shock.

Shock number one comes from the sheer scale and unpretentious
muddle of the whole thing – wine boxes stacked floor to ceiling, bottles on
display in every nook and cranny. It gives the sumptuous impression that
you're about to set off on a treasure-hunt, to find something lost and long-
forgotten by the Byrnes. When you get to the till – shock number two: these
prices are real. Again one must be careful not to get carried away.

How do you distil (in Tim Byrne's own words) 'an organised chaos of
thousands of the world's greatest wines' into a printed list? Answer: you
can't. For yet another year, the Byrnes can be forgiven this, and for flouting
every modern retail convention. We have their hefty, hand-labelled 'guide'
in front of us as we write and, such is its mammoth size, the term 'list' does
it an injustice.

Beginning at the beginning, claret vintages start with 1978 and continue
with not a few *crus classés* along the way (we even spotted some at less than
£25 a bottle!), finishing with magnums and double-magnums of Mouton-
Rothschild. 1990 Yquem comes in at £169.99 – a snip for such a wine.
Burgundies cover, by grower, Jadot, Faiveley, Comte de Vogüé, Trapet,
Leflaive and more. There's a whole page (40 or so wines) of delicious
Beaujolais; Rhône wines from Chave, Chapoutier and Guigal. Oddities, such
as Château Chalon Vin Jaune from the Jura, Alsace Pinot Noir from Bruno
Sorg and Zind-Humbrecht, sit alongside cases of Rhine and Mosel wines as
if to prove they never went out of fashion. There's a California selection to
leave you gasping: Frog's Leap, Hess Collection, Bonny Doon, Ridge, Stag's
Leap, Saintsbury … (not as stuck in the past as first appearances would have
us believe then!). Trendy southern Italy, Tokaji and, indeed, just about any
wine-producing country you care to mention, all get ample coverage. You
could even pick up a bottle of Australian wine from Queensland if you were
brave enough! For all else, we too recommend you visit.

Look out for

- Exceptional-value burgundy – watch out for the annual *en primeur* offers
- Prized allocations from the illustrious Napa Valley estates
- Australian classics: Grange, Magill and Yattarna, J J Hahn from Barossa, Henschke from Eden Valley
- Malbec from Argentina; Merlot and Carmenère from Chile
- Peru, Brazil, Mexico and Uruguay all listed
- Cutting-edge South African wines: Backsberg, Clos Malverne, Thelema
- Champagne, plus sparkling wine from Italy to India
- Impressive range of half bottle choices, including sweet wine.

Cairns & Hickey

854 & 856 Leeds Road, Bramhope,	*Tel* 0113-267 3746
Leeds LS16 9ED	*Fax* 0113-261 3826

Open Mon–Fri 9–9, Sat 10–9, public holidays 11–5 **Closed** Sun **Cards** Delta, MasterCard, Switch, Visa; personal and business accounts **Discount** Available, phone for details **Delivery** Free within 30-mile radius; nationwide service available, charged at cost **Glass hire** Free with order **Tastings and talks** Available, phone for details **(£5)**

Ernest and Peter Cairns are determined to outshine their competitors with better service, better prices and better wines. The fact that Cairns & Hickey's Burgundy and Bordeaux listings each have a healthy selection under £20 a bottle is testament to their doing a good job. (The likes of Léoville-Las-Cases, Mouton-Rothschild and Latour's Corton-Charlemagne forgivably sneak in a bit higher.) Ernest has 'enjoyed and survived' doing business for 34 years now and not a little of his success is attributable to the friendly and personal service he offers, as do his staff and his son (who now runs the buying side). The team see it as their duty to assist shop customers 'whose indecision is final' and such is Ernest's forthright turn of phrase, our guess is that buyers will know exactly what's what and what they're getting. Our advise to C&H is to get that newsletter up and running as soon as you can: the 'spade called a spade' approach is a prized thing in the wine world!

Cairns & Hickey have a superb New World range, from Australia, New Zealand and Chile, right through to bottles to try from Mexico. Of particular note in this edition of the *Guide* is the improved selection from Europe – French regional wines, the Rhône, Loire, Alsace and Italy. Perhaps that's a good thing if customers are tending away from 'upfront Aussie' choices? We'd still like to see more producer variation from California and Burgundy in particular – but keep up the old vintages, they're a nice touch!

Look out for

- Superb Bordeaux selection including 1982 and 1990 *cru classé* Pauillac
- Very reasonably priced Australian wines – and lots of them!
- Great sparkling selection, from Krug to Cloudy Bay Pelorus
- Rotllán I Torra, Guelbenzu and Murrieta from Spain
- Leventhorpe English wines from right there in Leeds
- A fine post-prandial choice of vintage ports and Highland malts.

Andrew Chapman Fine Wines

14 Haywards Road, Drayton, Abingdon,
Oxfordshire OX14 4LB

Tel (0845) 4580707/550707
Fax (0870) 1366335
Email info@surf4wine.co.uk
Web site www.surf4wine.co.uk

Open Mon–Fri (office only) 9–5.30, Sat 10.30–1 (open for collections and purchases from warehouse) **Closed** Sun (exc. by arrangement) **Cards** Delta, MasterCard, Switch, Visa; business accounts **Discount** Available, phone for details **Delivery** Free within Oxfordshire (min. 1 case); nationwide service available, charges per case: £4.99 for 1, £3.50 for 2–4, free for 5+ cases **Glass hire** Free with order **Tastings and talks** Range of tastings available, phone for details **£5**

Full marks to the enthusiastic Andrew Chapman for the up-to-date-ness of his wine list. It's constantly updated on the web site, and anyone without access to the Internet will be posted a hard copy whenever they require it. 'It's undoubtedly increased communication, efficiency and accuracy since we launched the concept three months ago,' says Andrew, and it's also had a positive effect on his sales figures. As for the wines on that list (whether printed or in cyber-space), they too show enterprise. Those from Australia form perhaps the largest chunk of the range, but there are also good selections from most other major countries and regions. We sense that Andrew is growing in confidence with regard to the wines he sells, and this has encouraged him to upgrade the choices from the Rhône, southern France and Austria in recent months.

If you don't have access to the brisk, friendly web site, you can keep in touch with the special offers, as well as the programme of tastings and events involving visiting winemakers, through the equally chatty newsletters. And if you're within the vicinity of Oxford, you're welcome to pop in on a Saturday morning for a browse, a quick taste and the chance to buy just a few bottles rather than the usual mixed case minimum. This is a merchant that seems genuinely interested in making the whole subject of wine as accessible as possible, and who backs up such a policy with a good (and improving) selection.

Look out for

- Rhône reds from Graillot, St-Cosme and de Ferrand
- Mas de Daumas Gassac, Mas Cremat and Clos Bagatelle from Southern France
- From Germany, J L Wolf, Dr Loosen and Heymann-Lowenstein
- Coriole, Tim Gramp and Plantagenet from Australia
- Antiyal, Villard and Finca El Retiro from South America
- North American powerhouses Ridge, Saintsbury and Au Bon Climat.

For an explanation of the symbols used at the top of some of the merchant entries, see page 303.

Charterhouse Wine Emporium

82 Goding Street, London SE11 5AW

Tel 020-7587 1302
Fax 020-7587 0982
Email charterhousewineemporium@ukgateway.net

Open Mon–Fri 10–7, Sat 10–5 **Closed** Sun, public holidays **Cards** Amex, Delta,
Diners, MasterCard, Switch, Visa; personal and business accounts **Discount** Available,
phone for details **Delivery** Free within 10-mile radius (min. 1 case); nationwide
service available (min. 1 case), charge £7 + VAT **Glass hire** Free **Tastings and talks**
Available on request, phone for details **(£5)**

With over 50 years of experience in the wine trade between them, John
Walker and Norman Price are well qualified to run this South Bank venture.
Their long service record might lead you to believe that they'd specialise in
the classic wine regions. Indeed, it's true that they offer a good range of
clarets that holds something for all palates and all pockets, some decent
burgundies (whites better than reds) and the ever-reliable German Rieslings
of Dr Loosen. However, it would be the New World selection that we'd steer
you towards first, especially the wines from Australia. 'We offer an extensive
range of wines not often seen in the multiples,' says Norman, and he's
absolutely right. If you thought Australian wine was dominated by Penfolds,
Hardy's *et al*, then a quick browse through these shelves will change your
mind. While no other country receives quite such enthusiastic coverage,
there's still plenty of note to be found.

Look out for

- Rhône reds from St-Cosme, Rostaing and Beaucastel
- Dozens of Australian wines from fine estates
- St Jerome, Ngatarawa and Fairhall Downs from New Zealand
- South African wines from Jordan, Vriesenhof and Neil Ellis
- White burgundies courtesy of Chavy, Verget and Valette.

Cockburns of Leith

7 Devon Place, Edinburgh EH12 6AL

Tel 0131-346 1113
Fax 0131-313 2607
Email sales@winelist.co.uk
Web site www.winelist.co.uk

Open Mon–Fri 9–6, Sat 9–5, Sun 12.30–5 **Closed** 25 & 26 Dec, 1 & 2 Jan **Cards** Delta,
MasterCard, Switch, Visa; personal and business accounts **Discount** Available, phone
for details **Delivery** Free within 30-mile radius (min. 1 case); nationwide service
available, charge £7, free for 3+ cases **Glass hire** Free, charge for breakages **Tastings
and talks** Available, phone for details **(£5)**

Self-confessedly 'long in the tooth' it may be, with 200 years' trading behind
it, but Scotland's oldest wine merchant should exude more confidence than
it does for its refreshingly honest approach and wealth of experience.
Though its web site (smartly designed) is not yet the comprehensive
reflection of the main list that Cockburns (and we) would like, and Italy still
proves a stumbling block following the death of a much-revered supplier,
improved opening hours, a new shop layout, plus a newsletter and

customer club (offering ten per cent discount) in the pipeline show there is forward momentum. Proof that modern wine trends do not escape this merchant comes also in the form of an expanded Rhône list, keeping in mind 'wines that can be drunk young despite their ability to develop with further ageing'. The claret list also questions tradition and disputes the merit of wines in the £15-to-£40 bracket, keeping its range resolutely below this in order to represent good value. (Arrangements can be made to get hold of *crus classés* if you're interested, of course.) A comprehensive range of Burgundy from Bouchard Père et fils is commendable, and reserves of the 1996 lying in Beaune present a good opportunity if you get in quick. But could there be other producer sources? Cockburns are pleased with Fouassier, their new supplier of Loire wines, and are rightly proud of their French regional selection. We also liked the conscientious food-matching notes with each wine. Overall the aim appears to be the pursuit of new classics rather than reliance on the 'old' – although 'other wines stocked' sections include these too. Best of all, there's no hard sell.

Look out for
- Bargain clarets
- 1996 Burgundy – a stash of this top vintage is cellared in Beaune
- Delicious Alsace selection: Kuentz Bas, Trimbach, Leon Beyer, Dopff au Moulin
- Chile's different regions well represented
- Excellent sparkling range
- Saint Clair Riesling and Chardonnay from New Zealand (not just Sauvignon Blanc!)
- California: steering away from sheer weight and opting for elegance, especially from Wente
- Top-notch malt whisky range too.

Connolly's Wine Merchants

Arch 13, 220 Livery Street, Birmingham B3 1EU

Tel 0121-236 9269
Fax 0121-233 2339
Email connowine@aol.com
Web site www.connollyswine.co.uk

Open Mon–Fri 9–5.30, Sat 10–4 **Closed** Sun, public holidays **Cards** Amex, Delta, MasterCard, Switch; personal and business accounts **Discount** 5%–10% on cash and carry (min. 1 case) **Delivery** Free within Birmingham area (min. 1 case); nationwide service available, charge £7.50 + VAT for 1–3 bottles, £10 + VAT for 4–12 bottles **Glass hire** Free with order, charge for washing if necessary **Tastings and talks** Tutored tastings throughout the year; tastings for corporate clients

As is the way of web sites, the Connolly's site – 'operational from 31/3/01' according to the company – was still not up and running at the time of writing in mid-May. This forced us once again to turn to the first page of the annual list, which as usual begins with one of Chris Connolly's 'poems' (we use the word loosely). Scooby Doo and Shaggy featured in this one. 'Fear not,' said Scooby. 'There's no need to panic, for wines with good structure but nothing too tannic ...' Enough said. As for the range of wines, this looks better than ever. Classicists will appreciate the selections from Bordeaux and Burgundy, and Chris persists with a small set of fine German wines, despite advice to the contrary from the company accountant. Spain and Italy are well covered too. In the New World, there are sprightly choices from all the relevant countries, with a good mix of the familiar and the more esoteric. Throughout the range there are wines to suit all pockets, and prices for some of the classier wines (burgundies especially) compare favourably with those at other merchants. For details of the programme of tutored tastings and dinners held either on the premises or in a local restaurant, give Chris a call. Or log on to the new web site.

Look out for

- Engel, Perrot-Minot, Large and Matrot from Burgundy
- South Africans Verdun, Jordan and Clos Malverne
- Southern French range from Château de Serame, Comte Cathare and Cazes Frères
- Artadi, Martínez Bujanda and Murrieta Riojas
- Australian wines from Mount Langi Ghiran, Lengs & Cooter and Cape Mentelle
- Healthy selection of clarets up to first-growth level.

The Co-op

Head office
PO Box 53, New Century House,   *Tel* 0161-834 1212
Manchester M60 4ES   *Fax* 0161-832 0817
(1,100 branches nationwide)
        *Web site*s www.co-op.co.uk (main site)www.grapeandgrain.co.uk
                    (wine and whisky site)

Open Mon–Sun 7–11 (times vary between stores) **Closed** Public holidays
Cards Delta, Switch, Visa **Discount** Not available **Delivery** 'Co-op 2U' service within 5-mile radius, charge £3 or free for orders over £25; nationwide service available via grape and grain web site **Glass hire** Not available **Tastings and talks** Regular in-store tastings and talks

The Co-op isn't just one company; more a collection of several smaller groups of companies (or societies) that all fall under the Co-op umbrella. These buy the majority of their wines through the Manchester-based Co-operative Group (formerly the CWS), which itself has over a thousand stores around the country, most of them licensed. The structure of the enterprise, plus the great variation in the size of the stores, makes talking about the Co-op wine range slightly problematic. Large stores in some parts of the country (notably the north-east) have wide ranges that extend beyond the CWS list and may include the likes of Cloudy Bay and Grange. Others have a far more limited selection, offering little beyond a few own-brand lines.

    Whatever the size of the store, the focus is on well-known names and value for money. This doesn't give the buying team too much scope for being adventurous, but you will find a few less familiar, more interesting wines and a growing number of organic offerings dotting the shelves of the larger branches. There is the Fairtrade Carmenère from Chile, which forms part of a range of products chosen not only for their quality but also for the ethics behind their production. We've tasted some decent wines in the Loire and Rhône ranges recently, and there is usually at least one classy estate-bottled German Riesling from a decent producer. But the main reason to pop into the Co-op is keen prices on well-known names, especially during promotions.

Look out for
- Weinert, Bianchi and Argento from Argentina
- Chilean wines from Casa Lapostolle, Valdivieso and Gracia
- Fairview, Longridge and Neetlingshof from South Africa
- Spanish reds from Torres and Berberana
- Familiar Australian fare from Rosemount, Hardy's and Lindemans
- Keen prices on champagne.

Corkscrew Wines

Arch No 5, Viaduct Estate, Carlisle, Cumbria CA2 5BN

Tel (01228) 543033
Fax (01228) 543033
Email corkscrewwines@aol.com

Open Mon–Sat 10–5.30 **Closed** Sun, public holidays, 2 weeks in Feb **Cards** Amex, Delta, MasterCard, Switch, Visa **Discount** Available, phone for details **Delivery** Free within 25-mile radius (min. 2 cases); nationwide service available, charged at cost **Glass hire** Free **Tastings and talks** 2 major tastings per year **(£5)**

We reported in the 2001 edition of the *Guide* that anti-French sentiment was causing Laurie Scott's customers to turn to his Chilean whites and Australian reds. This year, Laurie tells us that they have now overcome these prejudices. 'They are adventurous and quality-conscious, but they would like less alcohol in their wines!' We hope this means they don't bypass his selection of fortifieds, where the sherries in particular are very appetising. The Corkscrew range isn't the largest around, but unless your tastes are for the very expensive and esoteric, it's almost impossible to find any gaps in it. There's a good balance between the Old and New Worlds, and while there are plenty of well-known names, Laurie has also sought a clutch of less-familiar producers, particularly from southern France, Spain and Italy. Prices are reasonable, and while you have to pay £15 to join the Customer Club, the fee is worth it for the 20 per cent case discount in the January sale alone.

Look out for
- Chaume Arnaud, Guigal and Roger Combe in the Rhône
- Pineraie, Pennautier and Ramonfort from southern France
- Italian reds from Allegrini, Vallone and Brezza
- Cape Mentelle, Plantagenet and Pipers Brook from Australia
- New Zealand wines from Craggy Range, Isabel and Te Mata
- Clos Malverne, le Riche and Neil Ellis in South Africa.

Corney & Barrow

Head office

12 Helmet Row, London EC1V 3TD

Tel 020-7539 3200
Fax 020-7608 1373
Email wine@corbar.co.uk
Web site www.corneyandbarrow.com

Branches

8 Academy Street, Ayr KA7 1HT

Tel (01292) 267000
Fax (01292) 265903

Oxenfood Castle By Pathhead,
Midlothian EH37 5UB

Tel (01875) 321921
Fax (01875) 321922

Belvoir House, High Street, Newmarket,
Suffolk CB8 8DH

Tel (01638) 600000
Fax (01638) 600860

194 Kensington Park Road, London W11 2ES

Tel 020-7221 5122
Fax 020-7221 9371

Open Head office, Edinburgh Mon–Fri 9–6; Ayr Mon–Fri 9–6, Sat 9.30–5.30;
Newmarket, Kensington Mon–Sat 10.30–9 **Closed** Sun, public holidays **Cards** Amex,
MasterCard, Switch, Visa; personal and business accounts **Discount** Available, phone
for details **Delivery** Nationwide service available, free for 3+ cases or within M25 for
2+ cases; £9 + VAT for less **Glass hire** Available, phone Kensington store for details
Tastings and talks Available, phone head office for details

We repeat last year's friendly words of warning. Well might the wines of
Corney & Barrow start at £4 a bottle, but regular customers do not come
here for the enticing prices. They come to be nurtured in their hobby: to
seek out the finest châteaux via the super-efficient broking division; to take
advantage of wines, fine burgundy or otherwise, sold exclusively by this
merchant and nowhere else; and to be advised and assisted by the same
member of staff every time they call. Now that's service! Royal service?
Well C&B hold three royal warrants, so yes, we think that just about sums
it up.

But as the above, and the accessible, smart and welcoming wine bars
imply, there's stuff in here for us mere mortals too. You have to wade
around a bit in the beautiful but fiddly lists (though not when you're in the
trendy bars, obviously) but it's all there. Crus Beaujolais at under £100 a
case; snazzy South American wines; Giesen Estate and Cairnbrae from New
Zealand coming in with a similar price tag.

Price, though, really isn't the point. It's quality. You'll also still find that
the New World isn't really the point either. Corney & Barrow's ability is to
offer dependable *petits châteaux* from Bordeaux. Where else, too, will you get
wines to compare from the different communes of Meursault; vertical
(consecutive) vintage selections from top estates such as Marchesi Alfieri or
Tenuta dell'Ornellaia in Italy? More importantly, perhaps, C&B offer a
chance to realise your vinous dreams – or perhaps just the material to dream
them with …

Look out for

- Le Montrachet, Bâtard-Montrachet and Chevalier Montrachet

- L'Evangile, Trotanoy and La Conseillante 1998 Pomerol
- First- and second-growth Médoc – châteaux Latour, Léoville-Las-Cases and Pichon-Longueville
- Majestic, traditional German wines from Schloss Schönborn and Von Kesselstatt
- Sumptuous Spanish reds from Priorato's Alvaro Palacios
- Champagne: Delamotte, Guy de Chassey and the unmatchable Salon.

Croque-en-Bouche

221 Wells Road, Malvern Wells
Worcester WR14 4HF

Tel (01684) 565612
Fax (0870) 7066282
Email mail@croque-en-bouche.co.uk
Web site www.croque-en-bouche.co.uk

Open Any time by arrangement **Closed** 24–28 Dec, 1 Jan **Cards** Delta, MasterCard, Switch, Visa **Discount** Available, phone for details **Delivery** Nationwide service available (min. 1 mixed case), free within 10-mile radius for 2+ cases, otherwise £9.50 (exc. Scotland), free for orders over £400 **Glass hire** Not available **Tastings and talks** Not available

Be warned: Robin Jones' 'miniature' wine list has a vast selection of nearly 1,000 mature wines, and choosing between them isn't easy. If you're tempted to get to grips with the full-on restaurant version, book an early table for dinner at this restaurant-cum-wine merchant and give yourself plenty of time for perusal – you'll need it. On the other hand, it's more than likely that Robin will be around to assist your decisions. How better to plan your future wine-buying forays than in the environs of a Michelin-starred eatery?

For those of us too far away from Worcestershire to allow driving, reading and dining in one evening, Croque-en-Bouche's list is readily available via its speedy web site, on which 40 per cent of the company's business is now conducted. This really is the next best thing to being there, as there's plenty of pithy advice, background detail and tasting notes to delve into. The current hot tip at the time of this review was for Pinot Noir, and well it might be, with the Henschke, Cullens and Saintsbury versions leaping off the page at first glimpse (the list starts in the New World). Delve further back and you can pick up a *premier cru* burgundy (or 13), for less than £50, *grand cru* Clos Vougeot for not much more. It isn't the *premier* and *grand cru* names that are remarkable here though, it's the mature vintages, the astonishing prices, and the sheer amount of choice – off-beat and up-beat – that make the difference. Where else would you find 1976 Trimbach Riesling from Alsace, Guigal's La Mouline Côte-Rôtie from 1981, and Heitz Napa Cabernet from 1975 on the same list? Who else would offer classed growth mature claret for under £50 a bottle (still)? We reiterate our concern that recommending this merchant will encourage depletion of its marvellous stocks, but as Robin Jones himself suggests in his introduction to the list: 'Now it seems nearly everything can be drunk soon after release. It's only the exceptions that need time.' That means this list will no doubt get better and better. This reviewer is contemplating a move to Worcester …

Look out for

- 1980s Super-Tuscans Solaia, Sassicaia and Cepparello
- Classic Riojas and Ribera del Duero 1951 to 1999
- Fabulous, historic Australian wines from Wynns, Henschke and Penfolds
- Comprehensive Rhône library – Auguste Clape to Vidal-Fleury
- Château Lafite-Rothschild from 1948 (and more …)
- Champagne and other sparkling wines (including Seppelt's fizzy Shiraz and a Russian sparkler from Georgia)
- Late-harvest sweet wines from New Zealand, California, the Loire, Alsace and Burgundy
- 1963 port.

deFINE Food & Wine Ltd

Chester Road, Sandiway,	*Tel* (01606) 882101
Cheshire CW8 2NH	*Fax* (01606) 888407
	Email office@definefoodandwine.com

Open Mon–Fri 10–8, Sat 9–8, Sun, public holidays 10–6 **Closed** 25 & 26 Dec, 1 Jan
Cards Amex, Delta, MasterCard, Switch, Visa; personal and business accounts
Discount 5% on 1 case **Delivery** Free within 10-mile radius (min. 2 cases); nationwide service available (min. 1 case), charge £10 per case **Glass hire** Free with order
Tastings and talks Regular talks, tastings and visiting speakers; phone for details **£5**

'We have serious selections from areas we are turned on by,' says the somewhat unconventional Graham Wharmby. As a result, his claret selection in Spring 2001 wasn't even enough to make up a mixed case ('It's twice as many as we used to have!'), while he stocked more than a dozen Soaves, with more on order – 'You can't have too many Soaves, you know.' On our last visit to Sandiway, Graham's 'scruffy little corner shop' was undergoing a transformation. Out had gone the convenience foods to be replaced by, well, dust, paint fumes and polythene sheeting. But the building work has now been finished, and the Sandiway Wine Company had become the upmarket wine shop-cum-deli that is deFINE. Another development is the arrival of Jon Campbell, who in his previous job used to sell wine to Graham, but is now a partner in the business.

As for the wines, they remain as good as ever. Current passions are Italy (not just Soave), Spain and South Africa, while the choices from southern France, Australia and Burgundy are also excellent. Indeed, there's nothing on offer which isn't a good example of its style. If Graham and Jon can't find something they like from a particular region or country (Germany, for instance), they just bypass it. The result is an excellent range, sold with enthusiasm and a real sense of fun. With in-store tastings of both food and wine taking place most weekends, plus a vibrant programme of evening events of varying degrees of formality, deFINE customers are never bored.

Look out for

- Tuscan reds from Le Pupille, Argiano and Fontodi
- Spice Route, Thelema, Jordan and several other fine South African producers
- Australian wines from T'Gallant, Haselgrove and Charlie Melton

- Castel del Remei, La Rioja Alta and Joan d'Anguera in Spain
- A fine trio of Pic St-Loup – Mas Bruguière, l'Hortus and l'Euzière
- Champagne courtesy of Billecart Salmon, Jacques Selosse and Vilmart.

Direct Wine Shipments
Regional Award Winner – Northern Ireland

5–7 Corporation Square, Belfast,
Northern Ireland BT1 3AJ

Tel 028-9050 8000
Fax 028-9050 8004
Email enquiry@directwine.co.uk
Web site www.directwine.co.uk

Open Mon–Wed, Fri 9.30–6.30, Thur 9.30–8, Sat 9.30–5.30 **Closed** Sun (exc. Christmas period), public holidays **Cards** MasterCard, Switch, Visa; business accounts **Discount** Available, phone for details **Delivery** Free within Northern Ireland (min. 1 case); nationwide service available, phone for details of charges **Glass hire** Free with bulk order **Tastings and talks** Range available, including courses, tastings, wine dinners and themed events

The time is long past when a mere milk float could transport Direct Wine Shipments' wines to safety in a nearby garage. With nearly 1,000 to choose from, and anything up to 250 cases of each of those in stock, the move from central Belfast premises to a trendy dockside warehouse was necessary for 'size' as well as for security reasons. Paramilitary hold-ups, petrol bombs and devastating fires are now (we hope) a thing of the past, and the 'mental block' that got the McAlindons through the troubled 1960s and 1970s serves now as a firm resolve to make and maintain one of the best merchant's businesses in the country. The McAlindons are wine communicators extraordinaire. As well as imaginative courses for beginners, the wine trade or food matchers, there are enticing promotions ('Thirsty for Thirty?', 'Wine Dreaming in Oz'), and tasting competitions hosted by well-trained, wine-oriented staff. Every brochure is stylishly presented, entertaining, and with enough tasting notes and extensive detail to keep you happily browsing for hours – it might even dissuade you from your monthly wine-mag purchase. Though DWS finds it hard to meet its target of releasing an annual wine list – it's added to so frequently – a print-out is provided on request for those wishing to compile their own wish list. Otherwise, let the McAlindons do the choosing for you.

Travelling (well what would you do if your wine shop had been burnt down?), tasting and years of research have built up a strong list, covering the full wine range from Lafite-Rothschild, Langoa-Barton and Yquem in Bordeaux (over 100 wines), to Faiveley, Laroche and Amiot burgundy. The 150-strong Spanish section is a point of pride, but – if one has to pick fault – skimps on the trendy north-east. The classics of Italy are covered – with the next venture surely to be the deep south? Chile is superbly represented and no doubt Argentina will soon be too in response to growing customer interest in South America. DWS have also done extremely well to wheedle so many good wines out of the Californians – who mostly consume all the interesting ones themselves. An eye for the eclectic (and for good value) shows itself in less mainstream grapes, such as Riesling from New Zealand, Petite Sirah and Sangiovese from California, and Cabernet Franc and Verdelho from Australia, and reflects the justified confidence of the buyers.

331

Look out for

- Great Australian names: Cullens, Jim Barry, Rothbury
- Tantalising selection of Mosel Rieslings
- Excellent stash of Californian Pinot Noir from Calera, La Crema and Jensen
- Sparkling wines, from Bollinger to Brown Brothers' Aussie Brut
- Delicious range of Lustau sherries and Fonseca ports
- Chapoutier from the Rhône
- Château de Fesles and Jolivet from the Loire Valley
- Hugel from Alsace
- An eye for 'anything but Chardonnay'.

Domaine Direct

6–9 Cynthia Street, London N1 9JF

Tel 020-7837 1142
Fax 020-7837 8605
Email info@domainedirect.co.uk
Web site www.domainedirect.co.uk

Open Mon–Fri 8.30–6 **Closed** Sat, Sun, public holidays **Cards** MasterCard, Switch, Visa; business accounts **Discount** Not available **Delivery** Nationwide service available (min. 1 mixed case); free within London, otherwise £9.99 for 1 case, £12.93 for 2 cases, free for 3+ cases **Glass hire** Not available **Tastings and talks** Biannual themed tastings, charged at cost; private tastings, free to customers

This company moved to new premises in 2001, but what will not change is its passion for Burgundy, which has been the focus since it was established in 1981. Many merchants issue opening offers for burgundy in the first few months of the year, but none is as detailed in its vintage report and grower profiles as the Domaine Direct one. The range of growers is also excellent, and for all Burgundy's reputation as an expensive wine region, there are even some decent bottles to be had for under a tenner. However, this isn't just a one-region company. The DD extra newsletters feature wines from other French regions, Australia, South Africa and New Zealand, plus a first-rate range of Californian wines from producers you'll struggle to find elsewhere. It'll be the burgundies that get you hooked, but don't be surprised if you find yourself adding the occasional bottle of quality West Coast red to your mixed case.

Look out for

- Vast selection of high-class Burgundy domaines
- Viader, Etude, Havens and other California rarities
- Australian wines from Lost Lake
- Paul Prieur and Domaine Roches Neuves from the Loire
- Small but tasty set of clarets.

We love to hear your views on wine merchants. You can email your comments to us at: whichwineguide@which.net

Ben Ellis Wines

Brockham Wine Cellars, Wheelers Lane,
Brockham, Surrey RH3 7HJ

Tel (01737) 842160
Fax (01737) 843210
Email sales@benelliswines.com
Web site www.benelliswines.com

Open Mon–Fri 9–6 **Closed** Sat (exc. tasting days), Sun, public holidays **Cards** Delta, MasterCard, Switch, Visa; personal and business accounts **Discount** Available, phone for details **Delivery** Free within Central London & Surrey (min. 1 case); nationwide service available (min. 1 case), charge £10 per order, free for orders of £500+ **Glass hire** Free with order of 2+ cases **Tastings and talks** 'Semi-tutored' tastings available, phone for details **£5**

This is how a wine list should be. No reading between the lines necessary. Everything of interest in its own right. No also-rans. All the wines are carefully chosen, top-quality examples of their style, all equally delicious, and every one of them from a well-known grower with the best and gentlest of winemaking tricks up his (or her) sleeve. And as we said last year, there's nothing here we wouldn't be happy to drink.

Ben Ellis wines are sourced by two eminent Masters of Wine, Mark Pardoe and Lance Foyster, and that probably explains the excellent standards maintained at this merchant. You too can benefit from all that knowledge if you venture down to Surrey and attend one of the team's semi-tutored tastings – you are given a small talk and a guide booklet before being let loose to taste the wines yourselves. You are equally likely to benefit from purchasing a mixed case, of course, and with the impeccable array of fine wine to select from, that's no great chore. There's an alternative (and enticing) 'by style' listing to ease matters and compelling annual *en primeur* offers too.

Ben Ellis still focuses most strongly on France. ('All wines are from France unless otherwise stated' says the footnote on each page of the wines by style list.) The Bordeaux and Burgundy sections are little short of superb, and the Rhône section is succinct yet brilliant. Though the Alsace and Loire ranges might leave lovers of these regions disappointed, we think the ripe New World flavours that follow might well appease – and there shouldn't be too many of the overoaked kind here. We also like the selection of *vins doux naturels*, sweeties and stickies at the back of the list – a sumptuous finishing touch!

Look out for

- Fabulous range of Austrian wines, from minerally dry Riesling to full-on *Trockenbeerenauslese* sweeties
- New-wave Iberian 'wines to watch' from José Neiva (Portugal) and Telmo Rodriguez (Spain)
- Burgundy from Louis Jadot, Bonneau de Martray, Chandon de Briailles and more
- New World darlings: Ridge from California, Henschke and Charlie Melton from Australia
- Top port vintages dating back to 1959
- Claret going back to 1970.

European Wine Growers Associates

Head office
Challan Hall, Silverdale, Lancashire LA5 0UH

Tel (01524) 701723
Fax (01524) 701189

Shop
Wine Time, 37 Beetham Road, Milnthorpe, Cumbria

Tel (015395) 62030
Email enquiries@ewga.net
Web site www.winetime.ewga

Open Mon–Sun 9–6, all year **Cards** Amex, Delta, MasterCard, Switch, Visa; personal and business accounts **Discount** Not available **Delivery** Free within 75-mile radius (min. 1 mixed case); nationwide service available (min. 1 mixed case), charge cost + £6.50 per case **Glass hire** Free **Tastings and talks** Regular tutored, public and trade tastings **£5**

Deryn Moeckell of EWGA took us to task concerning our comments last year on her company, which, she said, seemed to imply that it was a case of a 'all play and no work.' Apologies for that Deryn – it's just that we like anyone with an enthusiasm for wine, and you and your staff seem to approach the subject with a good sense of humour. But we also recognise your considerable range of wines and are not surprised to hear that as well as supplying many high-class restaurants in the north-west, there are a number of better-known merchants in the south of England keen to raid your cellars for the stocks of older bottles.

As for wines from more recent vintages, there's also plenty of interest here. Rather than specialising in one particular region, the range covers most of the world to a reasonable depth, with good-quality wines. While much of the thrust is towards the restaurant trade (for which EWGA runs a number of courses and seminars throughout the year), retail customers are welcomed at the Wine Time warehouse in Milnthorpe, providing they are prepared to buy a minimum of 12 bottles.

If you are interested in sampling wines from the range, there is a large tasting each November, as well as an annual wine weekend in Lytham St Anne's. The 2000 session focused on 'Spain, Italy and Dessert Wines of the Med', and, at £165 for half-board and six tutored tasting, rather good value. And if you'd like to browse through the entire range, the list should soon be available on CD-Rom, following trials in Spring 2001. A quick glance should reveal that this is a serious wine company, albeit one with a smile on its face.

Look out for

- Pierre Ponnelle, Drouhin and Pascal Bouchard burgundies
- Van Loveren, Allesverloren and Meerlust from South Africa
- South American range including Casa Lapostolle, Las Condes and Terrazas
- Italian reds from Carpineto, Villa Caffagio and Duca di Castelmonte
- Wirra Wirra, Yalumba and Vasse Felix from Australia
- From Spain, every vintage of Vega Sicilia back to 1962.

Everton's

Shop and Delicatessen
Main Road, Droitwich, Worcestershire WR9 0EW

Tel (01905) 620282
Fax (01905) 621073

Warehouse
Ten Acres, Berry Hill Ind. Estate, Droitwich,
Worcestershire WR9 9AQ

Tel (01905) 775536
Fax (01905) 794660
Email sales@evertons.co.uk
Web site www.evertons.co.uk

Open Mon–Fri 9–5.30, Sat, public holidays 9–6 **Closed** 25 Dec, 1 Jan **Cards** MasterCard, Switch, Visa; personal and business accounts **Discount** Available, phone for details **Delivery** Free within 25-mile radius; nationwide service available (min. 1 case), charge £12.33 per case **Glass hire** £1 refundable deposit required **Tastings and talks** Tailored tastings available; visiting speakers by arrangement

The motto of Richard Everton, wine buyer and MD of the company founded by his grandfather more than 80 years ago, is 'personal attention at all times'. The Evertons' list is the only one we're aware of that comes with recipes for Possum Stew, Witjuti Grub Cappuccino and Beef with Cactus & Chilli Salsa. For the range of wines to continue along such eclectic lines would be something of a miracle, but with Uruguayan Tannat, Mexican Petite Sirah, Canadian Pinot Noir and Algerian red, it comes close. However, the majority of the bottles hail from more familiar territory – and jolly good many of them are too. No one with a preference for any particular region would feel short-changed by either the quality or quantity on offer, and someone with a passion for wines from Bordeaux or Australia would be especially happy. There's a decent selection of half bottles available too, not to mention the many fine foods from the deli counter. Why not pay the shop a visit and experience that 'personal attention'?

Look out for
- Italian range including Ascheri, Caparzo and Le Salette
- St-Cosme, Jaboulet and Chapoutier from the Rhône
- Klein Constantia, Backsberg and Nitida from South Africa
- Cimicky, Rothbury and Cape Mentelle from Australia
- Good selection of claret dating back to the 1970s
- Burgundies from Faiveley, Drouhin and Laroche.

Falcon Vintners

74 Warren Street, London W1P 5PA

Tel 020-7388 7055
Fax 020-7388 9546
Email eric@falconvintners.co.uk

Open Mon–Fri 10–5.30 **Closed** Sat, Sun, public holidays **Cards** MasterCard, Switch, Visa; personal and business accounts **Discount** Not available **Delivery** Nationwide service available, phone for details of charges **Glass hire** Not available **Tastings and talks** Available, phone for details

When a list opens with 32 choices of Sassicaia, with vintages dating back to 1968, you realise the merchant's claim to offer 'the best of Italy' is no hollow one. The choices, from Pergole Torte to Primitivo, through every kind of Brunello, are positively mouth-watering. We don't know anywhere else you'll find over 100 Barolos to choose from, or top Amarones – Dal Forno, Allegrini, Bertani, Masi – all on one list. These aren't cheap wines, by any means, but they're classy, and some of them are very hard to come by.

Beyond Italy, Bordeaux and Burgundy receive the same type of treatment; here's one of the few places you'll find the biodynamic nectar of Domaine Leroy for example. A case of this burgundy might set you back £2,569, but at least it's there! (And if you think that's steep, 1982 Château Mouton-Rothschild is getting on for twice that price...)

Most of Falcon's business is wholesale, and you'll need to buy by the case (don't worry, there are well-selected £10-ish bottles as well as the illustrious ones we've just mentioned). But we're impressed that this merchant has thought to include with- and without-VAT prices in its listings, in an attempt to welcome private customers – we can't, unfortunately, say the same for every wholesaler.

Champagne, the Rhône, Australia and Spain appear to be in the initial throes of development, but we don't doubt greater things will emerge from these countries in the near future. This might be a young merchant, just getting going, but it's already a haven for the 'cult classics', and we thoroughly recommend – especially the Italian fanatics out there – that you take a look.

Look out for

- Super-Tuscans in every manifestation: Antinori's Ornellaia, Solaia and Tignanello, Flaccianello from Fontodi, Saffredi from Le Pupille, and more
- Barolo and Barbaresco from Angelo Gaja
- 1990 Bordeaux: Talbot, Palmer, Pichon-Lalande and more
- Sauternes from the classic vintages 1988, 1989 and 1990
- Top burgundy domaines: Grivot, Ponsot, Domaine de la Romanée-Conti, Leroy and Laurent
- Crisp, quality Italian Sauvignon, Soave and Chardonnay from Inama in the Veneto.

Farr Vintners ✉

19 Sussex Street, Pimlico, London SW1V 4RR

Tel 020-7821 2000
Fax 020-7821 2020
Email sales@farr-vintners.com
Web site www.farr-vintners.com

Open Mon–Fri 9.30–6 **Closed** Sat, Sun, public holidays **Cards** Cheques and bank transfer only **Discount** Not available **Delivery** Nationwide service available, charged at cost **Glass hire** Not available **Tastings and talks** Occasionally, phone for details

1961 Lafite, a Nebuchadnezzar of 1986 Pichon-Baron, 1959 Latour? Name your heart's desire from any year and it'll probably be on this list somewhere. 'We feel that we continue to offer the UK's largest stockholding of classic wines with all the great wines of France and an increasing list of new classics from other countries,' says Stephen Browett modestly. What Farr actually do is deal in the world's most fabulous wines – and a lot more of them than any other merchant or auction house, anywhere.

But don't be intimidated by the grandeur of what you see on the page (or screen). Farr Vintners is not only renowned for the supreme quality and keen price of its wines but also for the friendliness and approachability of its staff. Stephen Browett might have been the wine buyer here for 20 years but there's not an ounce of pomposity in him. What we said last year about 'friendly unbiased advice' is still true today. One snag is that there's a £500 minimum spend if you want to shop here, though you won't be short of inspiration and you can buy by the bottle too.

Bordeaux makes up 77 per cent of business, but at nine per cent, Burgundy fans won't be disappointed by stocks of the likes of Domaine de la Romanée-Conti La Tâche and Leroy Richebourg. Nor will Rhône followers bemoan the Guigal, Beaucastel and Chapoutier selections, or Italophiles the long lists of Ornellaia, Sassicaia and Solaia. For the rest of the world, well, sales this year are up by eight per cent, and in the meantime supplies of Henschke Hill of Grace, Grange and Opus One aren't too disappointing.

Look out for

- *En primeur* offers: allocations from the finest Bordeaux châteaux come this way, and are now available by email
- Private collection stock: when Farr buy up an important cellar, there are often one-off bargains to be had from an unusual vintage or source (some wines under £20 a bottle!)
- Full condition reports and provenance details on any wine offered
- Ports and madeiras going back to 1845
- Vintages from the great Spanish estates, Vega Sicilia and Pesquera
- Jeroboams and *impériales* of brilliant gold Château d'Yquem.

Fine and Rare Wines

Units 17 & 18 Pall Mall Deposit,   *Tel* 020-8960 1995
124–128 Barlby Road, London W10 6BL   *Fax* 020-8960 1911
                                    Email wine@frw.co.uk
                                 Web site www.frw.co.uk

Open Mon–Fri 9–6 **Closed** Sat, Sun, public holidays **Cards** Amex, Diners, MasterCard, Visa **Discount** Not available **Delivery** Nationwide service available, phone for details of charges **Glass hire** Not available **Tastings and talks** Not available

When a merchant lists the following in bold capital letters on the cover of its list – Pétrus, Le Pin, Mouton-Rothschild, Yquem, Le Montrachet, Domaine de la Romanée-Conti, Domaine Leroy and Guigal – you know where you stand. Somewhere near the top. 'I firmly believe we offer one of the most comprehensive lists of rare wine available in the world today,' pronounces director Mark Bedini. A bold statement, but it can't be far from the truth.

Reading this list, you have to forget the price column to a large extent. Though the numbers are certainly no higher, on average, than any other fine wine specialist, the general calibre of what's on offer means you have to school yourself to expect a few more zeros – any figures under £100 for example are likely to be for a bottle, not for a case. What's great about this selection, however, is its breadth. Not that it covers the entire vinous world

– it doesn't. But as well as the usual first-growth clarets, you get added extras; little-seen producers such as Henri Gouges, Fréderic Esmonin and René Engel from Burgundy, Aldo Conterno, Paolo Scavino and Bruno Giacosa from Piemonte. Plus good-quality older vintages that add an extra dimension of choice. We'd say this is a great place to come to pick up a 'label', a big-name wine, but one with a difference. There are of course, the usual (same old!) Pétrus type wines too …

Look out for

- 1996 red and white burgundies (snap 'em up while you can, it's a top vintage)
- Well-priced, comprehensive selection of *en primeur* Bordeaux – each year
- Guigal's La Mouline, La Landonne and La Turque from a range of Rhône vintages
- Spanish 'royalty': Vega Sicilia, Pesquera and Artadi
- 1990 vintage champagnes from Bollinger, Perrier-Jouët, Roederer – plus 1988 Salon
- Biondi-Santi, Montevertine, and a fabulous array of Super-Tuscan Italians.

Fortnum & Mason

181 Piccadilly, London W1A 1ER

Tel 020-7734 8040
Fax 020-7437 3278
Email info@fortnumandmason.co.uk
Web site www.fortnumandmason.co.uk

Open Mon–Sat 10–6.30 **Closed** Sun, public holidays **Cards** Amex, Delta, Diners, MasterCard, Switch, Visa; personal and business accounts **Discount** 1 bottle free per unmixed case **Delivery** Nationwide service available, charge £6 per order **Glass hire** Not available **Tastings and talks** Available, phone for details

We're not going to reveal what the typical customer spends on a bottle at this Piccadilly institution, just that it exceeds the national average by a considerable amount. However, anyone looking for high-class wines off the shelf in central London will be hard pressed to find somewhere able to offer such an extensive range, from both classic wine regions and further afield. And you don't have to be a millionaire to shop here. While there's not much under a fiver and prices still err on the high side, there's plenty on offer for less than £10. James Taylor, who has recently returned to Fortnum's after a three-year stint at Bentalls (q.v.), sets as much store by quality at all price levels as did his predecessor Annette Duce. Although he has inherited an excellent set of wines, James is looking for reinforcements from Portugal and South America, and is also seeking out new producers in traditional regions. If you find yourself spoiled for choice, head for the own-label selection, which remains arguably the finest around (Harrods might dispute the point). The latest producer to appear under the F&M guise is Stefano Inama (of Soave fame). He joins a list of eminent contributors which includes Louis Michel, La Rioja Alta, champagne Billecart-Salmon and Château Palmer. And if you still can't make up your mind, ask the polite but friendly staff, who come complete with morning suits and are among the best-trained you'll find.

Look out for

- Excellent own-label selection
- Rhône reds from Santa Duc, Beaucastel and Jaboulet
- Extensive selection of claret, including ten vintages of Latour
- Grosset, Henschke, Leeuwin Estate and other top Australian wines
- Burgundian stars such as Chopin Groffier, Rousseau and Ramonet
- Mulderbosch, Meerlust and Thelema from South Africa.

Four Walls Wine Company

1 High Street, Chilgrove, nr Chichester
West Sussex PO18 9HX

Tel (01243) 535360
Fax (01243) 535418
Email fourwallswine@compuserve.com

Open Mon–Fri 8–5, Sat 8–1, Sun 9–12 **Closed** Public holidays **Cards** Delta, MasterCard, Switch, Visa; personal and business accounts **Discount** Available, phone for details **Delivery** Free within 20-mile radius (min. order £100); nationwide service available, charge £15, free for orders over 20kg **Glass hire** Free **Tastings and talks** Annual tasting, other tastings and talks by arrangement **£5**

If you've only recently become interested in wine, and find yourself frustrated with the dearth of older vintages in your cellar (or under the stairs), then you need to call Barry Phillips. His selection of wines from older vintages may not be quite as extensive now as it was in the days when he ran the White Horse restaurant in Chilgrove, but there are still some marvellous old bottles to be found on his list, at prices that mark him out as a wine lover rather than a businessman. The selections of Bordeaux and sweet wines from anywhere in the world provide the richest pickings, but there are mature gems from several other regions as well. Many of the older burgundies have now disappeared but there are dozens – no, hundreds – of wines from 1995 and younger vintages: the 2001 list featured no fewer than 46 different Puligny-Montrachets! Barry wouldn't deny that he is a Francophile, but that doesn't prevent him stocking high-class wines from other countries. So if you're starting a cellar, replenishing one or just looking for classy wines for current drinking, give him a call.

Look out for

- Vast array of burgundy and Bordeaux
- Alsace wines from Albert Mann, Schlumberger and Zind-Humbrecht
- More than 50 sweet Loire whites
- German Rieslings from von Schubert, Egon Müller and Bert Simon
- Rostaing, Romero, Champet and other top Rhône domaines
- Some of Italy's finest reds from Fonterutoli, Elio Grasso and La Spinetta.

Specialist and Regional Award Winners are listed on pages 12–15.

Gauntleys of Nottingham

Regional Award Winner – Central England

4 High Street, Exchange Arcade,
Nottingham NG1 2ET

Tel 0115-911 0555
Fax 0115-911 0557
Email rhone@gauntleywine.com
Web site www.gauntleywine.com

Open Mon–Sat 8–5.30 **Closed** Sun, public holidays **Cards** Delta, MasterCard,
Switch, Visa **Discount** Not available **Delivery** Nationwide service available (min. 1
case), charge £13 for 1 case, £8.50 for 2 cases, free for 3+ cases **Glass hire** Not available
Tastings and talks Not available **(£5)**

Gauntleys may have been purveyors of fine wine and tobacco to the people
of Nottingham since 1880, but don't let that fool you into thinking that this
is a rather friendly but bumbling provincial merchant. John Gauntley is a
passionate man who has put together a passionate selection of wines that
zeros in on his favourite regions and virtually ignores everywhere else. The
places he likes best are everywhere in France except Bordeaux, with
particular emphasis on Alsace, the Rhône and southern France. His *modus
operandi* here is to drive around meeting several producers until he finds one
he likes. As a result, you'll find plenty which is practically unavailable
elsewhere, despite being of the highest quality. John has also assembled
very respectable ranges from Italy and Spain, again with the thrust towards
top-notch but little-known estates. As for other countries, apart from
smatterings from Austria, Germany, Hungary and the USA, there's nothing
on offer. And we have the feeling that if you were to ask John to
recommend a Chilean Chardonnay at around £5, you would politely be
shown the door. But ask him about the Languedoc, or the southern Rhône,
or what's new in Burgundy, and you may have a problem getting a word in
edgeways.

Look out for

- Alsace whites from Barmes-Buecher, Burn and Boxler
- Rhône reds from Pégaü, Colombier and Trapadise
- Potel, Fourrier and Matrot in Burgundy
- The famous Bandol trio of Tempier, Vannières and Pibarnon
- Up-and-coming Languedoc estates such as Puech-Haut, Des Aires Haut
  and St-Andrieu
- Rare Spanish reds from Leda, Urbies Madero and Fra Fulco.

For an explanation of the symbols used at the top of some of the
merchant entries, see page 303.

Great Gaddesden Wines 👜 ✉

80 Lower Luton Road, Harpenden,   *Tel* (01582) 760606
Hertfordshire AL5 5AH   *Fax* (01582) 760505
       Email info@flyingcorkscrew.com

Open Not applicable (mail order only)   **Cards** Delta, MasterCard, Visa; personal and business accounts   **Discount** Not available   **Delivery** Nationwide service available (min. 1 case), free within 30-mile radius, 1–10 cases £13.50, 11–25 cases £1.35 per case, free for 26+ cases   **Glass hire** Not available   **Tastings and talks** Available by arrangement, phone for details **(£5)**

'Bad wine is always too expensive,' begins the wine list (quoting the illustrious Burgundian winemaker Henri Jayer). Too right, but you won't find it here. Paul Johnson started Great Gaddesden six years ago and his huge enthusiasm hasn't dimmed in the slightest in that time. When asked what he offers his customers, his reply is: 'Service with a smile; quality you can trust; a sense of humour; attention to detail, and a jolly good drink!' We like the sound of all of that, even though (as he himself admits) the smiling service isn't always visible on the telephone.

In terms of the wines, there's a whole booklet full. It's clearly laid out and covers everywhere from Greece to Austria and Mexico to Madeira, but starts with a hefty tranche from not just Bordeaux and Burgundy but the whole of France. There are a number of good-value producers from the Languedoc and Provence that we wouldn't mind trying out when we next have the chance, plus a few less mainstream Burgundy names we'd also be keen on dipping into. In fact this is another part of the service Paul likes to provide: 'The main reason I am proud of my range is that in almost every section there are exceptional bottles at affordable prices, as well as the high-priced famous producers.' (Sure enough, turn the pages and there they are: Guigal, Miguel Torres, Alois Kracher, Allegrini …)

Prices are dependably competitive and there's the add-on benefit of five pages of house wines, all under £5 a bottle, to finish off the list – plus a healthy smattering of half bottles and magnums too.

We still think Great Gaddesden's major successes are in Italy, South Africa, Argentina and Australia, but we'd add this year that we like the Spanish and Chilean sections very much too. Keep this up and the ten-year anniversary will be chart-topping…

Look out for

- Calatrasi and Promessa wines from Italy's trendy Puglia region, plus Calatrasi's chunky new wines from Tunisia
- Top California Pinot Noirs – Kent Rasmussen, Firesteed and Marimar Torres
- Fine Argentinian selection: Finca El Retiro, Bodegas Infinitus and Anubis
- South African Sauvignon Blanc: a wide range of this next-great-trend
- Illustrious Domaine de Triennes – top pedigree Provence wines from Burgundian gurus Jacques Seysses and Aubert de Villaine (Syrah, Cabernet and Viognier).

Great Northern Wine Company

The Warehouse, Blossomgate, Ripon,
North Yorkshire HG4 2AJ

Tel (01765) 606767
Fax (01765) 609151
Email info@greatnorthernwine.com
Web site www.greatnorthernwine.com

Open Mon–Fri 9–6, Sat 9–5.30 **Closed** Sun, public holidays **Cards** Amex, Delta, MasterCard, Switch, Visa; personal and business accounts **Discount** 10% on 1 case **Delivery** Free within 50-mile radius (min. 1 case), nationwide service available (min. 1 case), charge £5 **Glass hire** Free with order **Tastings and talks** Range of tastings, phone for details **£5**

With the closure in 2000 of the Leeds outlet and the moving of all operations to Ripon, Great Northern Wines is now, according to wine buyer Mark Ryan, 'leaner, meaner and keener'. The wine range itself doesn't seem any leaner. Those from Australia remain the most numerous, and there are a few new producers among their ranks who we don't remember seeing there before. Still in the New World, there are also good (but smaller) selections from New Zealand and South Africa, although a little more zip would be welcome in the Americas. In Europe, it's the Iberian range that we find most interesting, both for regular and fortified wines. Germany is slightly lacklustre, but the Italian wines are better, and the French better still, with some tasty Loire whites and decent burgundies on offer. Overall, our verdict is that a little more of the enterprise that has gone into the Australian and Portuguese range could transform what is a good wine company into a great (northern) wine company.

Look out for
- Engel, Matrot and Vallet Frères in Burgundy
- Modern Spanish reds from Artadi, Alion and Ochoa
- South African range including De Toren, Clos Malverne and Neil Ellis
- Portuguese reds from Quinta dos Roques, Casa de Saima and Cartuxa
- Less familiar Australian producers such as Margan, Viking and Brian Barry
- New Zealand wines from Trinity Hill, de Gyffarde and Alpha Domus.

Great Western Wine Company
Regional Award Winner – South-West of England

The Wine Warehouse, Wells Road, Bath BA2 3AP

Tel (01225) 322800
Fax (01225) 442139
Email post@greatwesternwine.co.uk
Web site www.greatwesternwine.co.uk

Open Mon–Fri 10–7, Sat 10–6 **Closed** Sun, public holidays **Cards** Amex, Delta, MasterCard, Switch, Visa; personal and business accounts **Discount** Available, phone for details **Delivery** Free within 20-mile radius (min. 1 case); nationwide service available (min. 1 case), charge £6 per case, free for orders of £180+ **Glass hire** Free, must return clean **Tastings and talks** Range available, phone for details **£5**

Philip Addis started Great Western Wines back in 1983, 'with what was (in hindsight) a terrible list of wines!' Nearly 20 years later, his selection has evolved into one of the best in the West Country. Not surprising, since this is one of those companies that sources its own wines, rather than relies on the same old band of UK wholesalers. We must admit that there are producers on the list whom even we aren't familiar with, but our experience of Philip's wines has always been favourable, so we'd be happy to follow any recommendation from him and his 'young, enthusiastic and passionate' staff.

The desire to boldly go where other merchants haven't gone before means that some parts of the wine world are covered more thoroughly than others. Francophiles benefit most from the forays abroad, so you'll find excellent selections from throughout France, including a set of fine Cognacs and Armagnacs. The fine wine list is also (at present) the sole domaine of France. Italian wines are less numerous, but still include some great finds. In other countries, familiar names are more the order of the day, but you'll still discover a few exclusivities such as Glaetzer (Australia), Chancellor (New Zealand) and Viña Alamosa (Chile). There's also an English trio from the nearby Mumfords Vineyard.

If you'd like to become more familiar with the GWW wines, several of the producers visit Bath each year for tutored tastings, which at around £7 per head are excellent value. Keep up with details of these and the regular special offers via the chatty newsletter or the web site. All in all, a company which isn't terrible, just terribly good.

Look out for

- Rhône reds from Bonnefond, Montez and Robin
- More than a dozen fine Loire domaines
- Bru Baché, Tour des Gendres and Capmartin in south-west France
- Chevalier, Boussey, Brenot and Jobard-Morey in Burgundy
- Italians Loacker, Beltrame and Castello di Poppiano
- Australian reds from Oakridge, Cimicky and Glaetzer.

H & H Bancroft

Matrix House, Cambridge Business Park, *Tel* (0870) 444 1700
Cowley Road, Cambridge CB4 0WT *Fax* (0870) 444 1701
Email sales@handhbancroft.co.uk

Open Mon–Fri 8.30–5.30 **Closed** Sat, Sun, public holidays **Cards** Delta, Switch, Visa; personal and business accounts **Discount** Not available **Delivery** Nationwide service available (min. 1 case), free within M25 and for 3+ cases; £7.75 for 1 case, £10 for 2 cases **Glass hire** Not available **Tastings and talks** Available, phone for details

The smart H & H Bancroft list kicks off with mixed cases of the favourite wines of four of the senior personnel – prices for which range from £127 to £172. If spending such an amount on a dozen bottles is beyond your budget, stop reading now. You *will* find cheaper wines here, even a few under £5, but the real meat of the list is in the £10+ range. Very tasty meat it is too. The list doesn't aim to be comprehensive – so, for example, you won't find anything from Germany, Austria or Eastern Europe, and there's also very little from South Africa or Portugal. However, when the company chooses to 'do' a region, it does it very well indeed. France (Burgundy and the Rhône in particular) and Italy have received the bulk of the attention in the past, but the growing Australian selection is also excellent. In most regions, several of the producers are well known, but there are also many emerging stars who deserve attention. If you're stuck for what to choose from this admirable set of wines, why not plump for one of those suggested mixed cases? It may not be the cheapest wine purchase you make, but it should be one of the most rewarding.

Look out for

- Fine array of top-class Burgundy growers
- Santa Duc, Gaillard, Villard and other top Rhône domaines
- Didier Dagueneau, Joguet and Marionnet from the Loire
- Italian masters Schiopetto, Rocca and Il Macchione
- Subtle Australian reds from Frankland Estate, Noon and Geoff Weaver
- The best of Pic St-Loup from Mas Bruguière, Mas Morties and Hortus.

Alexander Hadleigh Wine Merchants

19 Centre Way, Locksheath,   *Tel* (01489) 885959
Southampton SO31 6DX   *Fax* (01489) 885960
                            Email sales@alexanderhadleigh.sagehost.co.uk

Open Mon–Thur 10–4, Fri 10–7 (longer hours in summer and at Christmas), Sat 9–6
Closed Sun, public holidays   **Cards** Delta, MasterCard, Switch, Visa   **Discount** 7.5%
on 1 case   **Delivery** Free within 50-mile radius (min. 1 case); nationwide service
available, charged at cost   **Glass hire** Free with order   **Tastings and talks** Weekly
tastings, wine club tastings; group tastings and talks available **£5**

We're pleased to report that Del Taylor's plans to expand from a wholesale-only business to incorporate retail too have come to full fruition. Congratulations! The wines are as good as ever and now available to all. Even at first glimpse we can see that this list oozes quality. The 'house and everyday' selection kicking off the range on the first page lists delicious Canoe Tree Shiraz and Domaine de Terre Noires rosé; turn the page and top Alsace wines are followed by Yquem, Ausone and Cheval Blanc Bordeaux. Del doesn't stint on the back vintages either, and we're really impressed to see there's plenty to choose from all the way back to the 1970s (plus a 1945 Lafite in there somewhere).

We'd go so far as to say that Bordeaux is Alexander Hadleigh's strongest suit but we're pretty impressed by the Burgundy choices too, and it's an absolute joy to see Germany's delicious Mosel Rieslings taken so seriously. Italy's page includes a hedonistic smattering of Super-Tuscans (with a good handful of these in the Large Format section too), and New Zealand, Spain and South Africa are also well-represented. Grower choices aren't as plentiful from Australia, California or Argentina, but you can't win them all – the malt whisky and sherry selections almost make up for it!

Look out for

- Large Format clarets: everything from Haut-Brion magnums to a Nebuchadnezzar of Cos d'Estournel!
- Delicious Le Pergole Torte from Montevertine and other classics from Italy
- The illustrious Domaine de la Romanée-Conti from Burgundy, plus more attainable Tollot-Beaut, René Engel and others

- Well-priced Rhône wines, from sub-£10 Crozes-Hermitage to £29 Chapoutier Condrieu
- Champagne: vintage stock dating back to 1943
- Jordan, Simonsig and Overgaauw wines from South Africa.

Handford-Holland Park

12 Portland Road, London W11 4LE

Tel 020-7221 9614
Fax 020-7221 9613
Email james@handford-wine.demon.co.uk
Web site www.handford-wine.demon.co.uk

Open Mon–Sat 10–8.30 **Closed** Sun, public holidays **Cards** Amex, Delta, MasterCard, Switch, Visa; personal and business accounts **Discount** 5% on 1 case **Delivery** Free within Central London (min. 1 case); nationwide service available, charge £7.50 for orders under £120, free for orders of £120+ **Glass hire** Free **Tastings and talks** Available, phone for details **(£5)**

Handford customers continue to trade upwards and the wines keep on getting better and better; this dynamic young company is doing good business in some incredibly attractive wines. 'We select carefully and source small volumes unavailable to the high street chains or dotcom companies. And we can give a good service based on sound product knowledge and actually knowing our customers personally,' says David Penny. Both he and managing director James Handford do more than most to keep their customers up to date. Regular Handford Wine School seminars are available, with speakers such as Jancis Robinson and Riesling expert Matthew Boucher. There's a regular newsletter, a slick web site, frequent seasonal special offers, and plenty of no-nonsense tasting notes that give good guidance as to when to drink – and where a wine sits in relation to the 'classic' style. All genuinely helpful stuff.

Duck in here for a sub-£5 bottle if you wish (there are a good handful to choose from), but spend a little more and find that this list truly covers a range of good wine experiences. From fantastic Burgundy – basic Montagny to the illustrious Montrachet whites, seven different Volnays, Chambolle-Musigny, Echézeaux and Clos Vougeot for the reds – to spectacular Pétrus, Latour and Cheval Blanc Bordeaux. The rest of France is also well covered, in a range of warming, everyday Rhônes and interesting French country labels. The best pickings of the New World, from Pelorus sparkling wine from New Zealand to (sigh of relief) unwooded Australian Chardonnay, are all there, but we wouldn't be surprised if this selection expanded over the next year or so, to mirror the depth of the European range and include more growers.

Look out for

- Spectacular range of Ridge reds from California
- Trendy Spanish white wines from Rías Baixas and Rueda
- Top Australian reds from Henschke, Jim Barry and Hollick
- Côte-Rôtie La Mouline and delicious Châteauneuf-du-Pape from the Rhône
- Chablis, Beaujolais and the Loire: top growers represented
- Bordeaux vintages from the stunning 1982 to *en primeur* 2000s.

Harrods

Brompton Road, Knightsbridge,	*Tel* 020-7730 1234
London SW1X	*Fax* 020-7225 5823
	Web site www.harrods.com

Open Mon–Sat 10–7 **Closed** Sun, some public holidays **Cards** Amex, Delta, Diners, MasterCard, Switch, Visa; personal and business accounts **Discount** 6.5% on 1 case **Delivery** Nationwide service available, charge £5 per case **Glass hire** Not available **Tastings and talks** Available, phone for details

Not that we're snobs, but we do love this wine list. It isn't nearly as intimidating as people might think. Despite the unrelentingly starry credentials, even the Fine and Rare selection has the occasional bottle under £10; and there are, of course, pocket-friendly Australian and South American options in the main range too. Needless to say, you do pay more for the friendly and super-efficient service you receive here, but this is Harrods – there are 1,200 wines at the store's immediate disposal, but over 3,000 to which the staff have access for individual customer requirements.

For keen prices, it's definitely worth heading for the own-label 'Signature' products. As we've said before, these are repeated a few pages later in the list under the growers' own name but at higher prices, so they represent a good opportunity. For the rest, prepare to be dazzled but not fazed by the likes of 1945 Latour at £2,643 a bottle (a bottle?!), 1947 Cheval Blanc at £4,695 (what?) and 1989 Romanée-Conti at £3,100.

Take comfort in the fact that any wine you'd like (or would like to dream about) can be found at Harrods. Items as obscure as Swiss Petite Arvine, Barbadillo 'Sherry Relics' (aged for over 100 years in the original Sanlùcar *bodega*), and Hermitage Blanc from the Rhône feed the imagination. But there are 'normal' wines too. We'd perhaps like to see Harrods set an example and have more delicious Rieslings from Germany on sale. For this reason too, it would be good to see grapes beyond the more usual from the New World countries – and not just Chardonnays from Australia, Sauvignon from New Zealand, Merlot and Zinfandel from California – as Harrods is well placed to stretch their customers' awareness even further. (Having said that, we do notice a distinct lack of Australian Shiraz.) If the list is updated as frequently now as it has been in the past, we feel sure these quibbles will be quickly remedied. We shall watch and wait to see what the new wine buyer, Alistair Viner, has up his sleeve, and for the moment leave aside the numerous puns we could make about his surname.

Look out for

- Superb California choices: Ridge Lytton Springs and Geyserville Zinfandel, Stags Leap Vineyard Cask 23, Opus One and Shafer Hillside Select
- Illustrious burgundy, from Richebourg to Rully, Echézeaux and more
- 1996 and 1998 Bordeaux, including magnums of Château Siran and Alter Ego by Château Palmer, and many more vintages for current drinking (1993 back to 1945)
- Delicious South African reds from Hamilton Russell, Kanonkop, Hartenberg and Thelema

- Tantalising Loire whites from Baron de L Pouilly-Fumé to Château de Fesles Bonnezeaux
- Mas de Daumas Gassac, Château Simone and Domaine de Trévallon regional French reds
- Austrian sweet *Trockenbeerenauslesen* from Willi Opitz
- 1985 La Rioja Alta, 1997 Tirant from Rotllán i Torra and 1998 Les Terrasses from Alvaro Palacios, Spain.

Harvey Nichols

109–125 Knightsbridge, London SW1X 7RJ	*Tel* 020-7201 8537
	Fax 020-7235 5020
107–111 Briggate, Leeds LS1 6AZ	*Tel* 0113-204 8888
	Fax 0113-204 8080
	Email wineshop@harveynichols.co.uk
	www.harveynichols.com

Open Mon–Fri 10–8, Sat 10–7, Sun, public holidays 12–6 **Closed** 25 Dec, Easter Sun
Cards Amex, Delta, Diners, MasterCard, Switch, Visa; personal and business accounts
Discount Available, phone for details **Delivery** Free within Central London (min. order £25); nationwide service available (min. order £25), charge £10 per case **Glass hire** Not available **Tastings and talks** Available, phone for details

Compared with the buzzing Yo! Sushi bar and mouth-watering food market, the wine department is an air-conditioned haven of tranquillity on the fifth floor of Harvey Nicks. And the friendly, knowledgeable staff and stunning range make this a good place to shop for wines. (The Leeds store offers a much smaller selection of wines, but if there's anything from the London range that a customer would like, it can be sent up.) This being Harvey Nichols, the focus is on excellence rather than cheap and cheerful, so if you only have a fiver to spend, head elsewhere. However, if your budget is slightly larger and you're looking for top-quality wines from all over the world, chances are that you'll find them here. The company receives allocations from some of the most in-demand producers, and fans of Californian wines in particular will be delighted to find rarities such as Kistler Chardonnays and Turley Zinfandels on the shelves from time to time. California, Bordeaux and Burgundy are the three regions covered to the greatest depth, but there are first-rate wines from all around the world. And while many command the price per bottle that some people would spend on a case of wine, they are merely priced at the going rate. All in all, a great set of wines – and our only problem with the company is the efforts we have to go to each year to prise a list out of them!

Look out for

- Burgundy growers such as Dauvissat, Roulot, Bertheau and Arnoux
- Extensive selection of claret to suit all – OK, most – pockets
- Rare Californian wines from Alban, Viader and Neyers
- Australian range including Torbreck, Grosset and Leeuwin Estate
- Splendid array of prestige *cuvée* champagne
- Rhône reds from Chave, Combier, Graillot and Beaucastel.

Haynes Hanson & Clark

Head office
Sheep Street, Stow-on-the-Wold,   *Tel* (01451) 870808
Gloucestershire, GL54 1AA   *Fax* (01451) 870508
                                        Email stow@hhandc.co.uk

25 Eccleston Street, London SW1W 9NP   *Tel* 020-7259 0102
                                               Fax 020-7259 0103
                                        Email london@hhandc.co.uk

Open Mon–Fri 9–7 **Closed** Sat, Sun, public holidays **Cards** Amex, Delta,
MasterCard, Switch, Visa; personal and business accounts **Discount** Not available
Delivery Free within Central London (min. 1 case); nationwide service available,
charges per case: £9 for 1, £5.50 for 2–3, £5 for 4+; free for over £500 **Glass hire** Free
Tastings and talks Regular tastings available, phone for details

---

Haynes Hanson & Clarke have six tastings a year at a variety of City, West
End and country locations. When you hear of one, our advice is to get there,
by whatever means possible – these wines are impeccable.

Burgundy is without doubt the speciality. At the time of writing, there
was a fair smattering of its fabulous 1999 vintage reds still on sale (snap
them up while you can), but 1998 offerings (firmer, more awkward when
young) are plentiful too, plus abundant supplies of the maturing 1997s and
stunning 1996s. And what producers! Champy, Faiveley, Chandon de
Briailles, Roumier, Bonneau du Martray and more. Alongside the great
Burgundian Meursaults and Montrachets there are Mercureys and
Monthelies too, and not to be forgotten sparkling Crémant de Bourgogne
from Cave de Lugny. HH&C are also proud of their range of Loire wines
(especially Hureau and Bernard Baudry), plus champagne, classic Bordeaux,
perfumed Alsace and feisty Italian choices.

Three elements crop up continually: elegance, complexity and ageability.
This means that the New World wines on offer aren't those prize-winning
opulent monsters, but creatures with layers, texture and many levels of
flavour. Try C J Pask's Hawke's Bay Chardonnay from New Zealand, for
example, or Mount Langi Ghiran Shiraz from Victoria, Australia, or
Saintsbury's Carneros Pinot Noir from California.

We love the way this list finishes, Oh so traditionally, with oddities such
as ginger wine, 'wood port', vermouth and cups – not to mention sloe gin,
Aalborg akvavit, Underberg bitters and copies of Anthony and Rosi
Hanson's superb books. Progress on the web site is steady, apparently. We'll
be keen to see it, when at last it emerges, but this is, after all, a rather genteel
merchant and it's important to get things right, or not at all. Well, it works
for the wines ... and for us!

Look out for

- Quincy, Reuilly and Savennières: superb whites from the Loire
- Fabulous Sauternes: 1990 Yquem, 1995 Coutet, 1999 Rieussec and
  Climens
- *Grand cru* Bâtard-Montrachet burgundy from Marc Morey, Blain-
  Gagnard and Gagnard-Delagrange
- Corton and Corton-Charlemagne from Champy, Olivier Leflaive and
  Chandon de Briailles

- Bottles and magnums of 1999 and 2000 new vintage burgundy
- Delicious range of *grand cru* Alsace.

Hedley Wright

11 The Twyford Centre, London Road,
Bishop's Stortford, Hertfordshire CM23 3YT

Tel (01279) 465818
Fax (01279) 465819
Email hedleywine@aol.com

Open Mon–Wed 9–6, Thur–Fri 9–7, Sat 10–6 **Closed** Sun, public holidays
Cards Amex, Delta, MasterCard, Switch, Visa; personal and business accounts
Discount Available, phone for details **Delivery** Free within 20-mile radius (min. 1
case); nationwide service available, (min. 1 case), charge £5 **Glass hire** Free
Tastings and talks Range of tastings; winemaker evenings and cellar suppers (**£5**)

Sales are by the case at this Hertfordshire merchant, but assembling a dozen
from the range should not be too much of a problem. The shop used to be
the retail arm of wine importer HWCG, but although they still share the
same premises the two parted company in 1999. HWCG wines such as
Jackson Estate (New Zealand), Churchill Graham (Portugal) and Montes
(Chile) still feature prominently in-store, but the three-strong buying team
has also found space for plenty of other interesting lines. No particular area
could be called a speciality, but the Spanish, Italian and South American
selections are very good, while thanks to input from Seckford Wines (q.v.),
the South African and Australian choices are also worth a look. If you'd
prefer someone else to guide you through the range, you can sign up for the
bimonthly Mixed Cases which cost no more than £73 each (including
delivery), the aim being to offer good wine 'at considerable price
reductions'. Also bimonthly are the cellar suppers. The price of around £25
includes a tutored tasting of six wines, followed by a meal with wines to
match.

Look out for
- High-class Spanish wines from Palacios Remondo and Pago de
  Carraovejas
- Italian reds courtesy of Le Pupille, Allegrini and Vallone
- Montes, Weinert and Pisano from South America
- Classy South African wines such as Veenwouden, L'Avenir and
  Altydgedacht
- Bremerton, Coriole and Hollick from Australia
- The delicious Coteaux du Languedoc wines of Puech-Haut.

For an explanation of the symbols used at the top of some of the
merchant entries, see page 303.

Hoults Wine Merchants

10 Viaduct Street, Huddersfield,	*Tel* (01484) 510700
West Yorkshire HD1 5DL	*Fax* (01484) 510712

5 Cherry Tree Walk, The Calls,	*Tel* 0113-245 3393
Leeds LS2 7EB	*Fax* 0113-246 7173

Email robert@houltswinemerchants.co.uk

Open Mon–Sat 9–6, Sun 11–3, Good Fri, May Day 9–6 **Closed** Public holidays **Cards** Amex, Delta, MasterCard, Switch; personal and business accounts **Discount** 10% on 1 mixed case **Delivery** Free within West Yorkshire (min. 1 case) **Glass hire** Free with order **Tastings and talks** Available, phone for details

Rob Hoult cites his qualifications as 'Six years in the wine trade. And an ability to drink.' The business that his father David established in the 1980s has now gone full circle. The initial passion of David (now enjoying semi-retirement in Normandy) was for Australian wines, but as his and his customers' tastes developed, more and more countries and regions began to feature in the range. However, Rob tells us that Australia is back in vogue, that customers are now willing to spend more on their bottles from Down Under, and that Chile has taken over the mantle of 'provider of bargain quality wine'. The two countries provide some of the largest ranges in store, but there are also good selections from most other parts of the world. Rob finds space for some rather classy clarets and burgundies, but the focus, as it has always been, is on providing 'an excellent range of products at supermarket prices'. Tucked into a railway arch, the Huddersfield store faces a large branch of Tesco, so Rob has ample scope for daily comparison.

Look out for
- Ceravolo, Nepenthe and Plantagenet among more familiar Australian fare
- Chilean producers such as Luis Felipe Edwards, Montes and Concha y Toro
- Burgundies from Bessin, Carillon and Jadot
- Tidy little Italian range including Pieropan, Isole e Olena and Allegrini
- Loire Sauvignons from Brock and de Tracy
- Esk Valley, Isabel and Trinity Hill from New Zealand.

Specialist and Regional Award Winners are listed on pages 12–15.

Victor Hugo Wines

Head office

Longueville Road, St Saviour, Jersey JE2 7SA	*Tel* (01534) 507977
	Fax (01534) 767770
Cash & Carry, Longueville Road, St Saviour, Jersey JE2 7SA	*Tel* (01534) 507977
	Fax (01534) 767770
15 Weighbridge Place, St Helier, Jersey JE2 3NF	*Tel* (01534) 507991
	Fax (01534) 507991
3 Stopford Road, St Helier, Jersey JE2 4LB	*Tel* (01534) 507992
	Fax (01534) 507992
8B Quennevais Precinct, St Brelade, Jersey JE3 8FX	*Tel* (01534) 744519
	Fax (01534) 744519

Email sales@victor-hugo-wines.com
Web site www.victor-hugo-wines.com

Open Mon–Sat 8.30–6.15, public holidays 8.30–1 **Closed** Sun, 25 & 26 Dec, Good Fri
Cards Amex, Delta, Diners, MasterCard, Switch, Visa; personal and business accounts
Discount 5% on 6+ bottles **Delivery** Free within Jersey (min. 1 case) **Glass hire** Free
with order, charge for breakages **Tastings and talks** Regular talks and events, phone
for details **£5**

As Victor Hugo Wines is the main outlet in the Channel Islands, buyer and
director Martin Flageul has no trouble in sourcing a huge array of sole-
agency wines – Louis Latour and Anton Rodet from Burgundy for example,
Cloudy Bay from New Zealand and Hamilton Russell from South Africa.
Islanders have no difficulty getting hold of fine claret either. And although
we once billed this merchant as a New World wine specialist – we're still
particularly impressed with the range of South African wines on offer – it's
hard to say today whether the Old World selection (apart from Germany)
isn't just as good.

On the whole, we like the balance of this list, it's as broad as it is
spectacularly wide. Our one quibble, however: it's not especially deep.
Perhaps Martin has it too easy? There's something from everywhere, but
we'd like to see him going that extra mile occasionally and coming up with
wines that are a little unusual, or a few more top-notch estates.

On the substantial plus side, however, the level of communication at
Victor Hugo Wines is superb. Not only is the wine list full of helpful and
amusing detail about the growers, grapes and regions, but the monthly
newsletter is as packed with wine trade gossip as any magazine, and there's
an added 'Pro-Am' recipe section at the back – with wine to match and a
different guest chef each month. The wine club, at £80 for the annual
membership, is as enticing as ever, with regular tutored tastings (at least
four annually), two dinners attended by knowledgeable guest speakers, and
10 per cent discount on the wines. The web site doesn't play a major role in
proceedings but then we get the feeling the team are more hands-on, face-
to-face people than that. And we're glad they're trumpeting their selection
of Jersey wines a bit louder now too!

Look out for

- Good-value range of top *cru* Beaujolais from the best villages
- Delicious Italian reds, including Tedeschi Amarone and essential 1970s kitsch – straw-covered flasks of Chianti
- Superb New Zealand list: Oyster Bay, Giesen Estate, Villa Maria and more
- Wild ferment Chardonnay from Errázuriz, plus Concha y Toro and Almaviva from Chile
- Something from everywhere in Australia, from good-value Shaw & Smith Sauvignon to the occasional bottle of Grange
- Châteaux Cantemerle, Palmer, Cos d'Estournel and Mouton-Rothschild claret.

Jeroboams

(Incorporating Laytons)
Head office   *Tel* 020-7629 7916
8–12 Brook Street, London W1S 1BH   (Sales) 020-7727 9792
(7 branches in London, 1 in Cirencester)   *Fax* 020-7495 3314
Email sales@jeroboams.co.uk
Web site www.jeroboams.co.uk

Open Mon–Sat (times vary between stores), Sun (some stores) **Closed** Sun (most stores), public holidays **Cards** Amex, Diners, MasterCard, Switch, Visa; personal and business accounts **Discount** Available, phone for details **Delivery** Free locally; nationwide service available (min. 1 case), charge £10, free for orders of £150+ **Glass hire** Not available **Tastings and talks** Available by arrangement, phone for details

We've always quite liked Jeroboams'– or more correctly, Laytons' – own-label champagne, blended especially for the company by well-known champagne winemaker Daniel Thibault; but we're also impressed by the other sparklers on offer by this company. Chandon Australia is getting better and better, as is Miru Miru Brut from New Zealand (it means 'bubbles' in Maori, apparently), and we're never averse to a magnum of Bollinger or Veuve Clicquot either. In fact Jeroboams/Laytons sparkles quite a lot on the whole.

Just to clear up that dual nomenclature: the branches (all eight of them) are known as Jeroboams, but if you opt for mail order, you'll be dealing with Laytons. It's the same company and the same wines; just a different name. The advantage of ordering via the mailing list is that the best wines are often snapped up before the wines hit the shop shelves. That's how good they are. Bordeaux starts at £5.65 a bottle for Layton's own 'Jolly Good Claret', which sounds cheery, but the list quickly tackles the steep gradient up to *cru classé* level, peppered as it is with the likes of Montrose, Ducru-Beaucaillou and Lafon-Rochet – all priced considerably higher. The same is true of Burgundy: there's a lot in the mid-ranks, then a hefty helping of the big names too.

What particularly impresses us about Jeroboams is its ability to list small-production oddities such as the fascinating French Jura wines and the smaller estates of Western Australia. But in a range where quality and classic style are so important, we're disappointed that the top German wines don't get a good showing; and nor do the top Californian producers for that matter. Thankfully, the fine flavours from New Zealand, and a section on pudding wines at the back of the list, go some way to making up for this.

This is a bit of a 'gentlemans' list, with a lot of classics to appeal to a traditional type of client – with a largish wallet – but nonetheless, it's carefully chosen and presented, and almost certainly trustworthy.

Look out for

- Classic French whites: Château de Tracy Pouilly-Fumé, Petit Metris Savennières, Delas Condrieu, and Alsace from Domaine Schlumberger
- Australian wines with a difference: Moss Wood and Ribbon Vale from Margaret River; Alkoomi and Old Kent River from Frankland River
- California comes to South Africa: vibrantly fruity wines from the Jordan estate in Stellenbosch
- Affordable *cru bourgeois* and second-label claret: Réserve du Général from Château Palmer is stunning
- Helpful advice on vintages, plus books and Riedel glasses also on sale.

S H Jones

Head office

27 High Street, Banbury, Oxfordshire OX16 5EW	*Tel* (01295) 251179
	Fax (01295) 272352
121 Regent Street, Leamington Spa,	*Tel* (01926) 315609
Warwickshire CV32 4NU	*Fax* (01926) 315609
9 Market Square, Bicester, Oxfordshire OX26 6AA	*Tel* (01869) 322448
	Fax (01869) 244588

Cellar/order office

1 Tramway Road, Banbury, Oxfordshire OX16 5TD	*Tel* (01295) 251177
	Fax (01295) 259560
	Email shjones@btconnect.com

Open Mon–Fri 8.30–6, Sat 9–6 **Closed** Sun, public holidays **Cards** Delta, MasterCard, Switch, Visa; personal and business accounts **Discount** Available, phone for details **Delivery** Free within 40-mile radius (min. 1 case), nationwide service available (min. 1 case), charge £8.50, free for orders of £250+ **Glass hire** Free with order **Tastings and talks** In-store tastings, regular tutored tastings, suppers and distillery visits **(£5)**

This enthusiastic and expanding merchant (new shop in Cheltenham as of 2001) has an amazingly comprehensive range of wines. Although S H Jones might not get its hands on the very top-notch names, it has a sure knack of bringing in the 'best of the rest', and the bargains. For a start, look at the selection of *petits châteaux* from Bordeaux, with such reliable names as Tour de By and Lyonnat. It gets better on the next page of the list, with the choice of 'second wine' clarets, including Réserve du Général from Château Palmer and Sarget du Gruaud-Larose. Great names do crop up too – in France, there's Guigal from the Rhône, Huet from the Loire, and Trimbach and Schlumberger from Alsace. But this merchant's forte is breadth and value-for-money, and customers obviously like it that way.

We're particularly impressed by the monthly tutored tastings and food and wine trials on offer here. Turn up with a £5 note and you'll be regaled by the likes of Robert Steel, specialist in Italian and Swiss wines; for £25 try matching Pacific Rim fare with local Australian wine – food and wine tastings are hosted at a local Leamington restaurant. There's also a malt whisky club for warming winter snifters and plenty of advice on all subjects from friendly, hospitable staff.

Again, we like the adventurousness of this wine list. Not many others stock Greek Mantinia, Swiss Aligoté and Canadian Baco Noir. But it would be good to see a few more classic producer names and appellations added, to give drinkers an idea what the top brass can achieve.

Look out for

- Widely sourced Australian wines, plus some delicious sweet dessert wines
- Intriguing Italian Mediterranean reds from Sardinia and Puglia
- From England, Three Choirs, and Nyetimber and Chapel Down sparkling
- Superb selection of vintage and *single quinta* port
- Burgundy: good range of recent vintages for laying down (Leflaive, Sauzet, Latour and Colin-Deléger)
- Wide range of French country wines to try, at thoroughly decent prices.

Justerini & Brooks

Head office

61 St James's Street, London SW1A 1LZ

Tel 020-7484 6400
Fax 020-7484 6499

45 George Street, Edinburgh EH2 2HT

Tel 0131-226 4202
Fax 0131-225 2351

Open Mon–Fri 9–5.30, Sat (Edinburgh only) 9.30–5.30 **Closed** Sun, public holidays **Cards** Amex, Delta, Diners, MasterCard, Switch, Visa; personal and business accounts **Discount** Available, phone for details **Delivery** Nationwide service available, charge £9, free for 2+ cases **Glass hire** Not available **Tastings and talks** Available, phone for details **(£5)**

Justerini & Brooks offers everything you would expect from such a traditional establishment: the smartest clarets, the finest burgundies, *en primeur* offers, fine wine broking and cellaring services. The focus is primarily on classic wine regions: 'We have over 250 years' experience offering a tradition of excellence and quality in fine wines to suit every occasion and pocket (not just the deepest!),' say the marketing people. Indeed, the 2000 vintage clarets offered were not the most expensive we've seen while reviewing merchants this year, though they were certainly some of the most broad-ranging. Impressive too is the depth of the range, with Bordeaux vintages going back to 1895; all the favourites amongst them. (1895 Haut-Brion is on sale for £2,990 per magnum, in case you're interested.)

Furthermore, we don't think there are many better stockists of fine burgundy in the country. Who else could list over 30 growers and 18 vintages? More to the point, who else would have Domaine de la Romanée-Conti, Leroy, Méo-Camuzet, Jayer, Gros and Bonneau-du-Martray all on one list? As we've said before, there really is no dead wood here. J&B are equally strong on Alsace, German and Italian wines, not to mention Spain and the New World. Hew Blair and his buying team aren't content to stay with the predictable, or with the well known. For example, there are regular forays into South America to find new growers, and there's a real determination to represent the new-comer regions of the wine world with the highest-quality wines possible. Having said that, J&B will keep the selection short rather than compromise their high standards.

In the past we have accused this merchant of being expensive, but on close inspection there are plenty of thoroughly decent wines to be found under the £10 mark – and under the £5 mark for that matter. The format isn't quite the same as your everyday merchant, however, and if you'd like to buy some J&B wine, you're better off browsing through the superbly presented and expensive-feeling price lists and ordering your wine by mail order; that or call first before visiting the London or Edinburgh shop. Most of the wines are stored carefully at the company's vaults in Wiltshire so you won't necessarily be able to buy them and take them home straight away – although you'll more than likely get a taste of something decent that's been opened front-of-house.

Look out for

- Alternative New World growers such as Château Potelle and Chalk Hill from California; Dry River, Hunters and Ata Rangi from New Zealand
- Pétrus, Cheval-Blanc, Haut-Brion and Le Pin – Bordeaux' finest
- … plus, the illustrious second wines: Pavillon Rouge du Château Margaux, Les Carruades de Lafite, L'Hospitalet de Gazin, etc. – available at more affordable prices but comparable quality
- Very fine German estates, such as Fritz Haag, JJ Prüm, Egon Müller and Rheinhold Haart
- Top-notch Australian wines from Dalwhinnie, Clarendon Hills, Voyager and Picardy
- Old ports and whiskies, and madeira dating back to 1895
- Superb range of classic-style Italian wines: Chianti, Barolo, Brunello and more
- Regular offers of Rhône, top German wines, new vintage clarets and burgundies, etc.

Kwiksave

see Somerfield

Laithwaites

Head office (orders)
New Aquitaine House, Exeter Way, Theale,   *Tel* (0870) 444 8383
Reading, Berkshire RG7 4PL   *Fax* (0870) 444 8182

3 Holtspur Parade, Holtspur, Beaconsfield HP9 1DA   *Tel* (01494) 677564
Exeter Way, Theale, Reading RG7 4PL   *Tel* 0118 903 0600

121 Arthur Road, Windsor SL4 1RU   *Tel* (01753) 866192
     Email orders@laithwaites.co.uk
     Web site www.laithwaites.co.uk

Open Mon–Fri (order line) 8.30am–9pm (shops) 9–5.30, Sat (both) 9–6 Sun (order line)
9–6 **Closed** Sun (shops), public holidays **Cards** Amex, Delta, Diners, MasterCard,
Switch, Visa **Discount** Available, phone for details **Delivery** Nationwide service
available, charge £4.99 **Glass hire** Free **Tastings and talks** 40 tastings per year
throughout UK

Otherwise known as the *Sunday Times Wine Club*. The difference between
the two incarnations is negligible, apart from the face of Hugh Johnson on
the STWC mailings and that of Tony Laithwaite on the Laithwaites ones.
Whichever you choose to deal with, you will be doing business with a
phenomenally successful company – certainly the UK's most successful
mail-order merchant, and at the £10+ level, the leading retailer of wines to
private customers. One of the bedrocks of their performance is the high
standard of service. Considering the vast numbers of customers, we hear
remarkably few stories of deliveries going astray, incorrect orders or stroppy
voices at the end of the phone line.

As for the wines, the size of the range hovers around the 1,000 mark,
although you'd never guess this from the mailshots. These are designed to
get you to buy that month's special '12 for 10' deals or 'Superb mixed value
dozens from JUST £49.99'. There seem to be so many savings on offer that
it's only when you sit back and compare the prices with those at other
merchants that you realise that you're not getting a bargain after all. In early
2001, the least expensive wine (without discount) was £4.69. A typical
supermarket offers dozens, sometimes hundreds, of wines at cheaper prices.
If the quality merited the extra pound or two, we wouldn't be complaining,
but it often doesn't. We would tread with caution at the sub-£6 level.

At higher prices, quality is, as would be expected, much more consistent
– with Bordeaux, Burgundy, Germany and Australia being particularly
happy hunting grounds, especially if you head for the expanding fine wine
section. At this level, prices seem more in line with those at other merchants,
but stocks change rapidly, so you need either to ring up or access the web
site to find out precisely what's available at any time.

To summarise, then: full marks for service, and good marks for the higher-
priced wines. But as we've mentioned several times in previous editions, we'd
like to see Tony, Hugh and Co. putting a little more effort into the cheaper
end of the range, so that those glossy offers really merit the word 'special'.

Look out for
- More than 40 customers' tastings around the country throughout the year
- Annual Vintage Festivals in London, Nottingham and Harrogate

- Exemplary standards of service
- Constantly changing fine wines range
- Good choice of sensibly priced clarets, including La Clarière-Laithwaite.

Lay & Wheeler

Head office
Gosbecks Park, Gosbecks Road,
Colchester, Essex CO2 9JT

Tel (01206) 764446
Fax (01206) 560002

London sales office
47 Ludgate Hill, London EC4M 7JU

Tel 020-7329 0308

Lay & Wheeler Scotland
MacKeanston House, Doune, Perthshire FK16 6AX

Tel (01786) 850414
Fax (01786) 850414

The Bin Club
The Old Brewery, Station Road,
Wickwar, Gloucestershire GL12 8NB
(2 wine bars in London)

Tel (01454) 294085
Fax (01454) 294090
@Email:*Email* sales@laywheeler.com
Web site www.laywheeler.com

Open Mon–Sat 9–6 **Closed** Sun, public holidays **Cards** Amex, Delta, MasterCard, Switch, Visa; personal and business accounts **Discount** 10% on 5 cases **Delivery** Nationwide service available, charge £7.95, free for orders of £150+ **Glass hire** Free with order **Tastings and talks** Available, phone for details **£5**

Another of those excellent East Anglian merchants. A class act, oozing tradition (top burgundy and Bordeaux *en primeur*, plenty of cellaring advice), yet more than *au fait* with modern wines. What we like about Lay & Wheeler, apart from the jolly good wines it stocks, are the six plans it has for getting the best out of the bottle. First, there are the wine courses: L&W is an approved centre for the Wine & Spirit Education Trust teaching programmes (these are the ones most of the wine trade take – including Lay & Wheeler van drivers!). Second, the unsnobbish workshops: these are dinners or tastings hosted just about every week, with enticing themes such as '100 per cent Kiwi Fruit' (a focus on New Zealand wines), 'Naturally Napa' (everything from Cabernet classics to Leapfrogmilch from Frog's Leap vineyards), 'Clare, Victoria & Margaret too' (Australian wine regions) and 1997 Bordeaux. Third, stay at home and learn with Wine by Design: every two months a case of different bottles is sent to your door, complete with guidelines and tasting notes. Fourth, the Cellar Plan: a popular service whereby this merchant selects your wine to lay down and you spread your payments through monthly instalments. Fifth, Newsletters and offers: glossy mini-magazines full of estate profiles and up-to-date tasting notes are sent out every eight weeks. And six, investment advice: the 'blue chip' estates are all here and there's an efficient *en primeur* programme up and running. If investment is your thing (if you have cash to splash), the right people are here to guide you.

Back to those jolly good wines. We asked director Hugo Rose MW if he'd seen any recent trends emerging in his customers' buying habits. His reply? 'Pinot, Pinot, Pinot!' Well with all that lovely 1999 burgundy on offer at the time of this review, we're hardly surprised, but it goes further than France. Monticello and Pedroncelli from California; Fromm, Quartz Reef and La Strada from New Zealand; Groote Post Pinot Noir from South Africa's coastal Darling region (but none from Australia) – which all prove that the buying team know exactly where to look for the best of this grape. Other off-beat choices include a range of fabulous top estate Mosel and Rheingau Riesling, delicious 1999s and 1998s from Alsace, Tokaji from Hungary, a dozen different sherries, and unforgettable Barossa and Eden Valley Semillons from Australia.

Going mainstream, the illustrious clarets are all present and correct, listed by vintage. Plus, Lay & Wheeler now have their own bonded warehouse in Burton to ensure that private buyers' wines can all be stored in optimum condition. All in all, that winning combination of familiar and unfamiliar is still very much in place, although we'd still like to see the unfamiliar extend further when it comes to Chile, Argentina and California regions beyond Napa.

Look out for

- Burgundy from Olivier Leflaive and Jean-Marie Guffens, to name but two
- Delicious new-wave Bordeaux: châteaux Kirwan, Gruaud-Larose, Vieux-Château-Certan
- Magnums of Aloxe-Corton from Tollot-Beaut, plus châteaux Cheval Blanc, Haut-Brion, Bollinger Special Cuvée champagne, and more
- A long list of half bottles
- Olive oil
- New Zealand wines from L&W's own vineyards
- The Lay & Wheeler wine bar in London's Cornhill.

Laymont & Shaw

The Old Chapel, Millpool, Truro,
Cornwall TR1 1EX

Tel (01872) 270545
Fax (01872) 223005
Email info@laymont-shaw.co.uk
Web site www.laymont-shaw.co.uk

Open Mon–Fri 8.30–5 **Closed** Sat, Sun, public holidays **Cards** MasterCard, Switch, Visa; personal and business accounts **Discount** Available, phone for details **Delivery** Free nationwide (min. 1 case) **Glass hire** Free **Tastings and talks** Available, phone for details **£5**

'We have finished our brief flirtation with Languedoc,' says John Hawes, MD, and the 'Shaw' part (cue crossword fiends deciphering the 'Laymont' bit) of this Cornish company. Genial and gentlemanly on the surface, John has a streak of steel running through his being, and he's not one to suffer fools gladly, nor wines that just sit around and don't sell: so the southern French reds have disappeared from the range. In their place is a selection from South America, and more specifically Uruguay (we recommend the Castel Pujol reds). One flirtation that did prove successful was that with Portugal, and you'll find an array of classy wines from some of the country's top estates.

However, the L&S focus has always been and remains very firmly on Spain, and here the range takes in some of the best wines you'll find. There are old-fashioned Riojas, new-wave Prioratos, familiar names such as Torres and Marqués de Murrieta, and rising stars such as Joan d'Anguera (Tarragona) and Bodegas Borruel (Somontano). If you need guiding through the range, John or any other of the Spain-mad staff will be happy to put together a mixed case for you – or you could plump for one of the suggested dozens at the front of the list, or in the *Iberian Independent*, one of the best newsletters around.

Look out for
- Excellent selection of Spanish wines to suit all tastes and pockets
- Portuguese reds from Luis Pato, Quinta do Cotto and Quinta de Saes
- Uruguayan offerings from Castel Pujol and Pizzorno.

Laytons

see Jeroboams

Lea & Sandeman

Head office

170 Fulham Road, London SW10 9PR	*Tel* 020-7244 0522
	Fax 020-7244 0533
211 Kensington Church Street, London W8 7LX	*Tel* 020-7221 1982
	Fax 020-7221 1985
51 High Street, Barnes, London SW13 9LN	*Tel* 020-8878 8643
	Fax 020-8878 6522
206 Haverstock Hill, London NW3 2AG	*Tel* 020-7431 4412
	Fax 020-7431 1326

Email charles.lea@leaandsandeman.co.uk

Open Mon–Sat 10–8 **Closed** Sun, public holidays **Cards** Amex, Delta, MasterCard, Switch, Visa; personal and business accounts **Discount** Available, phone for details **Delivery** Free within Central London (min. 1 case), nationwide service available (min. 1 case), charged at cost, free for orders of £250+ **Glass hire** Free with order **Tastings and talks** Regular in-store tastings, tailored tastings by arrangement **£5**

Difficult as we found it to pull our nose out of the 1999 burgundy offer – the first of Lea & Sandeman's brochures to fall on our desk – we finally did, and were equally happy (as always) with the rest of what this merchant has to offer.

Charles Lea and Patrick Sandeman go out of their way to source wines of similar calibre to those of other merchants but at less cost. They do this by buying virtually all of their wines direct. 'We are able to offer the absolutely best quality domaines at prices competitive with bog-standard producers from other retailers who source via middlemen,' says Charles Lea. Special offers of Laurent-Perrier champagne at £16.95 a bottle (as opposed to the normal £21.95) illustrate the kind of thing we mean. Because of this approach, you may not recognise all the grower names. Well, so what? Dare to be different and you'll get a better price. And you can trust the judgement of this team to ensure there is no compromise on quality.

Charles and Patrick like the sound of their own drum best of all, as we've said before, and they are very successful at marching to it. Southern France, the Loire, the Rhône and Tuscany are all treated with the same alternative view, as is Champagne. (Ever heard of Benedick Brut or Legras Blanc de Blancs? No, nor had we.) New World countries get less of a showing here, but we feel that were they to make a bigger hit on this list, this team would manage to source some of the most interesting boutique wines and individual styles of the lot.

Join the Lea & Sandeman mailing list and we expect you'll enjoy the regular trickle of quality wine offers they send out – all enticingly presented and with frank, extensive and very readable tasting notes. Alternatively, pop into one of the four shops (a new branch has recently opened) and discuss your choices with one of the friendly and enthusiastic staff.

Look out for

- Burgundy from Laurent Pillot, Bonneau du Martray, Hubert & Olivier Lamy and Maroslavac-Leger, and more besides
- Outstanding range of Côte d'Or reds from the superb 1999 vintage (snap 'em up!)
- Delicious Italian reds, sourced from (top) Barolo to (unusual) Sicily
- Sumptuous dessert wines, including 5-puttonyo Tokaji from the Royal Tokay Wine Company and Pédro Ximenez Solera Superiore sherry from Valdespino
- Off-beat Bordeaux: Châteaux Pibran, du Maine, de Clairefont and many more
- Tiny but top-quality California selection: including Staglin, Sausal, Qupé and Limerick Lane.

Liberty Wines

Unit A53, New Covent Garden Food Market, London SW8 5EE	*Tel* 020-7720 5350
	Fax 020-7720 6158
	Email info@libertywine.co.uk

Open Mon–Fri 6.30–5.30 **Closed** Sat, Sun, 24–26 Dec, 1 Jan, Good Fri, Easter Mon **Cards** Delta, MasterCard, Switch, Visa **Discount** Not available **Delivery** Free nationwide service (min. 1 case) **Glass hire** Not available **Tastings and talks** Not available

---

It's four years now since Liberty Wines struck out primarily as a specialist wholesaler of Italian wines – as a descendant of the now-defunct Winecellars, it certainly had a good start in this direction. Its continued success is all credit to the immensely likeable David Gleave MW, who is also immensely knowledgeable about buying wine. David and his cheerful, capable team also sell direct to the public – by the case only, but this is an approach we thoroughly recommend taking.

Today Liberty's Italian list is virtually unmatched, and the rest of the range is growing almost daily. An eye to improving the North American selection has resulted in newcomers: the fabulous Zinfandels of Seghesio (not to mention its Barbera and Sangiovese) and the cool-climate wines of Testarossa. A look to France, and along came the beautifully poised

Vouvrays of Prince Poniatowski. Other arrivals have been Balnaves from Coonawarra and Meerea Park from the Hunter Valley, to add to the already impeccable Australian selection; plus breathtaking Rieslings from top German estate Schloss Vollrads. The big guys are flooding in.

The Italian choice, at the heart of everything, does nothing if not inspire confidence. Names such as Aldo Conterno and Allegrini from the north reek of quality. Isole e Olena, Conti Costanti, Calbello and La Torre Brunellos from Montalcino, and exciting new wines from the heel and toe area of Italy, do even more. (There's even a sideline in olive oil.)

Liberty wines are now well into their stride, and if they ever started running, with wines like these, they'd take over the world.

Look out for

- Top Chianti from Selvapiana, Castello di Farnetella and Petrolo
- Candia dei Colli Apuani from the Tyrrhenian coast; perfumed Alto Adige whites from Franz Haas
- Fabulous Mount Horrocks Riesling from Australia's Clare Valley
- Charles Melton's Barossa Shiraz (rosé, classic red and sparkling); plus Mount Langi Ghiran, Haselgrove and Shaw & Smith from Australia
- Luxury Col Solare Cabernet-Merlot from Washington State
- Off-beat, upbeat France: Domain Richaud Rhône, Château l'Euzière Languedoc and Liberty-blended Persimmon Vin de Pays d'Oc.

O W Loeb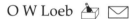

82 Southwark Bridge Road, London SE1 0AS

Tel 020-7928 7750
Fax 020-7928 1855
Email sales@owloeb.com
Web site www.owloeb.com

Open Mon–Fri 9–5.30 **Closed** Sat, Sun, public holidays **Cards** MasterCard, Switch, Visa; personal and business accounts **Discount** Available on 5+ cases, phone for details **Delivery** Nationwide service available (min. 1 case), charge £5 for one case, free for 2+ cases **Glass hire** Not available **Tastings and talks** Tastings available, talks for existing customers only

'We have increased our range of Rhône wines considerably this year, as well as increasing our standing in Burgundy,' says buyer and director Brough Gurney-Randall. Loeb is building on its already considerable strengths then. A look at the list, which is rich with detail, domaine profiles and characterful pictures of the growers, tells you the same. There are the usual trustworthy names plus smaller domaines, the latter of which sit alongside enough interesting information to give you the confidence to try them out: Pierre Damoy in Gevrey-Chambertin, Marius Delarche in Pernand-Vergelesses and Domaine Gilbert Picq in Chablis, for starters.

As well as the Rhône and Burgundy, German wines are a speciality here. The list is truly top class: Brauneberger Juffer Rieslings from Willi Haag, Wehlener Sonnenuhr from J J Prüm, Bernkasteler Doctor from Dr H Thanisch, and so on. It's not surprising, then, that the team at Loeb have seen a return to these wines in the last year. Anybody trying them would be sure to come back for more.

Such is the level of specialisation, however, that quantities of anything else pale into relative insignificance. Two Champagne houses are represented, two Australian estates, one Chilean, one from New Zealand and only two from Spain. Despite this, you can be sure that the quality will match those of Loeb's main-list names, and nothing less.

The arrival of the web site hasn't really changed things. Traditional one-to-one service is still very much the emphasis. And everyone at Loeb is so immersed in their subject that you know you're in good hands. Even the receptionist used to work at Domaine Henri Gouges in Nuit-St-Georges, and the latest arrival at the firm used to run his own estate in the Ventoux. The team know their stuff.

Look out for

- Monthly special offers – get hold of the newsletter and snap up the wines as soon as you see them, it's your only chance!
- Domaine Gallet and Domaine Jean-Michel Stephan Côte-Rôtie
- Château Rayas, Domaine de la Vieille Julienne and Domaine de Marcoux Châteauneuf-du-Pape
- Superb Rhône range from Paul Jaboulet-Aîné
- Vosne-Romanée burgundies from Anne Gros, Bruno Clavelier and Confuron-Cotetidot
- Tall Poppy Australian Chardonnay and Viognier: unlikely wines, from an unlikely source, in unlikely (unstylish) bottles.

Majestic Wine Warehouses

Head office

Majestic House, Otterspool Way	*Tel* (01923) 298200
Watford, Hertfordshire WD25 8WW	*Fax* (01923) 819105
(95 branches nationwide)	*Email* info@majestic.co.uk
	Web site www.majestic.co.uk

Open (Most stores) Mon–Fri 10–8, Sat 9–7, Sun, public holidays 10–5 **Closed** 25 & 26 Dec, 1 Jan **Cards** Amex, Delta, Diners, MasterCard, Switch, Visa; personal and business accounts **Discount** Available, phone for details **Delivery** Free nationwide (min. 1 mixed case), £5 charge for non-mainland **Glass hire** £1 refundable deposit per glass **Tastings and talks** Available, phone for details **(£5)**

Majestic's staff have noted a move in customer preference towards smaller growers who put an individual stamp on their wines, and this merchant is capable of supplying just those products. It is not impeded by having to stock the same range in every one of its 95 UK outlets, thus only buying its wines in bulk. In fact, Majestic studiously avoids widely available, entry-level brands – say, multi-state New World Chardonnay – and keeps resolutely to a more interesting, up-beat selection.

It's great to see such unusual grapes as Petit Verdot and Verdelho from Australia, for example. And top-quality but small-sized estates such as Bethany from the Barossa and Amberley from Margaret River in Western Australia. There are good names from South Africa, New Zealand and Chile too, so we were not wrong last year to withdraw our criticism of this merchants' New World range.

All the same, while the New World style rather suits Majestic's cheery, positive modern image, that's not what this company is about. A very serious list of 2000 vintage Bordeaux, with the likes of Châteaux Figeac, Angélus, Rauzan-Ségla, Palmer, Lafite and Latour, sits on our desk as we write, and Majestic also have the clout to put together an impeccable list of burgundy too – from everyday Chablis (starting at £5.49) up to the illustrious Bonneau du Martray Corton-Charlemagne (£46.99 a bottle if you get in quick). Loire lovers, Rioja drinkers and Nebbiolo tipplers will not be disappointed either. Plus, there's some very competitively priced champagne to be had.

All this is available on-line too. Majestic's web site has been souped up and redesigned, and is now faster than ever. Orders are delivered from your local store, with local staff answering queries (no dispassionate central switchboard here) and arranging convenient times for (free) delivery. Earth-bound browsers are welcomed too, with young, enthusiastic, well-trained staff on hand in each shop to inform, and to open bottles on request (if stock allows). The idea is to make buying wine as easy, as varied and as fun as possible. And here's to that!

Look out for

- Mixed-case offers on champagne: save 20 per cent when you buy six bottles or more
- Special-value wines for under £3 a bottle
- Fabulous range of Rioja Reservas from the 1994, 1995 and 1996 vintages
- Drostdy-Hof, Kanonkop and Fairview Estate Cabernets from South Africa
- Brunello di Montalcino, Barolo and Vino Nobile di Montepulciano – classic wines and top names from Italy
- Spicy, classic Urziger Würzgarten and Graacher Himmelreich Riesling from the Mosel.

Marks & Spencer

Head office
Michael House, 47–67 Baker Street, *Tel* 020-7935 4422
London W1A 8EP *Fax* 020-7268 2674
(350 branches nationwide) *Web site* www.marksandspencer.com

Open Varies between stores **Cards** Amex, Delta, MasterCard, Switch, Visa; personal and business accounts **Discount** 12 bottles for price of 11 **Delivery** Local service available, varies between stores, phone for details **Glass hire** Not available **Tastings and talks** Regular in-store tastings

---

Given that two of the Marks & Spencer team are qualified winemakers (one of them is a Master of Wine too), and that the range is one of the smallest of all the supermarkets', we could be more excited about the Marks & Spencer's list. At the top end, there are very few special-occasion bottles; at the bottom end, too many wines that are cheap but not necessarily cheerful – especially among the Italian and Spanish wines, the whites from southern France, and Australian wines under £5. In addition, we're not always convinced that the efforts of the buying team to produce its own *cuvées* are worth it, since the producers from which they source them – Southcorp and Rosemount (now bedfellows) in Australia, esteemed co-operative La Chablisienne and Montana in New Zealand, for example – usually make reasonable wines anyway.

However, that said, the range at M&S is not without its merits and we've seen encouraging developments in recent months. Time was when particular producers, such as Montana, Domaines Virginie in southern France and Girelli in Italy, used to dominate their respective section to the virtual exclusion of all others, but M&S seems now to be sourcing wine from more companies. Southern France, Burgundy, South Africa and Australia have benefited most from this policy, but there are now more diverse choices from most countries.

Another encouraging trend is a move away from companies making wine on an industrial scale to smaller concerns. The southern French selection which once offered little beyond basic *vins de pays* now contains a number of good single domaine wines that you'll struggle to find elsewhere. Up-and-coming Chilean producer Haras del Pirque provides a trio of excellent wines which we haven't seen at any other merchants, and while we commented on the dearth of special-occasion bottles, we'd happily settle down with the first-rate burgundies from Nicolas Potel. The focus on smaller estates often means that the wines aren't in stock for very long, and can be found only in the larger stores, but it does make the wine department a more dynamic place to shop.

We hope that the progress we've noted in the past year continues, and that the buyers can now find time to focus on the ranges from Spain, Germany and Italy, which are still rather pedestrian.

Look out for
- Burgundies from Potel, Monnier and La Chablisienne
- Own-label Australians from Evans & Tate, Geoff Merrill and St Hallett
- Plenty of characterful wines from the upcoming French Mediterranean regions
- Tasty South African wines such as Life from Stone Sauvignon and Monate Shiraz
- Pirque Estate Cabernet, Sauvignon and Chardonnay from Chile.

Martinez Fine Wine

Head office

35 The Grove, Ilkley, West Yorkshire LS29 9NJ	*Tel* (01943) 816515
	Fax (01943) 816489
20–22 Powell Street, Halifax HX1 1LN	*Tel* (01422) 320022
87 Town Street, Horsforth, West Yorkshire LS18 5BP	*Tel* 0113-281 8989
Corn Exchange Cellars, Harrogate,	*Tel* (01423) 501783
North Yorkshire HG1 2RB	*Email* editor@ilkley.co.uk
	Web site www.martinez.co.uk

Open Mon–Sat 10–6 Sun 11–4 (Dec only) (times vary between stores) **Closed** Sun (exc. Dec), public holidays **Cards** Amex, Delta, MasterCard, Switch, Visa; personal and business accounts **Discount** 5% on 6 bottles, 10% on £100+ cases **Delivery** Free within 10-mile radius (min. 1 case), nationwide service available (min. 1 case), charge £9.95 1 case, £6.95 per extra case **Glass hire** Free with order **Tastings and talks** Range of tasting events, including tutored tastings and guest speakers (**£5**)

The Martinez list starts with a 'no you're not dreaming' section of amazing bargains. Beginning at a mere £2.99 there are over 35 wines at under £5, plus three-for-£10 offers, or £40 a case – but in no way does this reflect a compromise. 'Our policy is quality before turnover' says marketing manager Mark Lascelles, and by page four of the wine list, you'll see what he means. Bordeaux might start at a cheerful £5.25 for a bottle of white Château Haut-Rian, but it builds up to the big guys before long (Gruaud-Larose, Mouton-Rothschild, etc.) and some pretty choice vintages.

They're not stuck on classics though, here at Martinez. Look past the (enticing) *en primeur* offers of burgundy, port and Bordeaux and you'll find cracking wines from California, New Zealand, Australia, regional France and even the Lebanon. Each of the four shops has its own area of expertise and knowledgeable, friendly staff to assist you in deciding between your Dão and your Douro red – in fact, even the van driver knows his stuff. And soon to be on-hand, for those guided by list only, will be a fully fledged web site. One comment, however: we'd like to see more from Germany.

Let's hope the newsletter, *Noble Rot*, makes it to the web site too, as this chirpy, bimonthly briefing makes good reading for any wine lover. Not only are there offers of recently stocked wines, and cellar profiles of something new you might like to try, there are ever-present Yorkshire witticisms – as dry as the wine list isn't – 'Glasses can make driving a lot safer, provided they're worn and not emptied,' for example.

Printed wine lists are available on request. It's the best way these days, when additions are so frequent. And locals should keep their eyes peeled for news of Martinez tastings and events. The words of illustrious speakers such as Georg Riedel, Dirk Niepoort and Paul Draper are not to be missed.

Look out for

- Vintage ports and madeiras – post-prandial heaven
- Ridge California wines: Lytton Springs, Montebello, Merlot and Petite Syrah
- Top Australian choices from Margaret River and Clare Valley
- Spectacular Italian selection from trendy Puglian Primitivos to Isole e Olena
- Great varietals from South Africa, including Simonsig Pinotage and L'Avenir Chenin Blanc
- Reliable, sub-£20 burgundy – red and white.

Mitchell & Son

21 Kildare Street, Dublin 2, Ireland   *Tel* +353 (0)1 676 0766
                                           Fax +353 (0)1 661 1509

54 Glasthule Road, Sandycove, Co. Dublin   *Tel* +353 (0)1 230 2301
                                           Fax +353 (0)1 230 2305
                                 Email wines@mitchellandson.com
                                 Web site www.mitchellandson.com

Open Mon–Sat 9–5.30 **Closed** Sun, public holidays **Cards** Amex, Diners,
MasterCard, Visa; personal and business accounts, wine club accounts **Discount** 5%
on 1 case **Delivery** Local service available within 10-mile radius, charge £4;
nationwide service available, charge £10 for 1 case, £5 per extra case **Glass hire** 13p
per glass (min. 48 glasses) **Tastings and talks** Weekly in-store tastings, regular themed
tastings for wine guild members, customer tastings with dinner **£5**

Following our comments last year about a slightly half-hearted Burgundy
selection, the folk at Mitchell & Son were anxious to show us how they had
revamped their range. Sure enough, the new list showed a distinct
improvement, and featured several rather classy wines, including a 1991
Romanée-Conti at a cool IR£1,500. Indeed, the entire range improves each
time we look at it. The well-known names that used to dominate the list
remain, but they share shelf space with less familiar but still good-quality
wines, especially from Spain, Australia and California. These sections, plus
the excellent array of Rhône reds and the growing band from the
Languedoc, are the ones we would steer you towards first of all, but really
there's very little in the range that we wouldn't happily drink.

Those wishing to learn more about wine might consider signing up for
the Wine Appreciation Courses that run over a six-week period. If these
whet your appetite, then the next stop is to join the Wine Guild. Members
pay a monthly sum by standing order (minimum IR£50), and the
accumulated funds are then used for wine purchases at discounted prices.
There are special tastings throughout the year, and members also receive
advance notification of wine trips. The September 2001 excursion to
Bordeaux and Cognac seemed very reasonably priced at IR£769 – or roughly
half the price of that bottle of Romanée-Conti!

Look out for
- Burgundies from Maroslavac-Leger, Gouges and Verget
- Rhône stars Graillot, Reynaud and Brusset
- South American producers such as Weinert, Alta Vista and Santa
  Carolina
- Spanish reds from Alvaro Palacios, Torres and La Rioja Alta
- Chateau Xanadu, Chatsfield and Katnook from Australia
- California wines from Sequoia Grove, Sean Thackrey and Caymus.

Mitchell's Wine Merchants

354 Meadowhead, Sheffield S8 7UJ

Tel 0114-274 5587
Fax 0114-274 8481

148 Derbyshire Lane, Sheffield S8 8SE

Tel 0114-258 3989
Email wine@mitchellswine.freeserve.co.uk

Open Mon–Sat 9am–10pm, Sun, public holidays 10–10 **Closed** 25 & 26 Dec **Cards** MasterCard, Switch, Visa; personal and business accounts **Discount** Available, phone for details **Delivery** Free within 25-mile radius (min. 2 cases); nationwide service available (min. 1 case), charge £10 **Glass hire** Available, phone for details **Tastings and talks** Available, phone for details **£5**

Thirty-two years in the family firm, and still going strong, John Mitchell continues to provide a good selection of wines and a very friendly welcome to the folk of Sheffield. In the past decade John has garnered several awards and honourable mentions in the Off-Licence of the Year competition, and is a three-times winner in the North of England section of the promotional body Wines from Spain's 'Best Spanish Wine List' competition. The accent in the wine range is on good-value wines at under £10, so as well as copious offerings from Spain, there is a healthy representation from most New World countries, and growing numbers of bottles from southern Europe. But while the thrust of the range is towards the value-end of the market, there are also some finer and rarer delights to be had in the Connoisseurs' Collection. A recent list included a host of clarets from the 1955, 1956 and 1957 vintages, several of the more-expensive Australian wines, plus other delights from around the world. And if you find that browsing through the shelves in Meadowhead makes you a little peckish, why not see what's on offer at the Green Peppercorn restaurant next door, where mine host is one J Mitchell.

Look out for
- Riojas from Muga, Riscal, Faustino, Murrieta and many more
- Cape Mentelle, Madfish and Katnook from Australia
- New Zealand producers such as Omaka Springs, Whitehaven and Framingham
- Dry Creek, Gallo of Sonoma and Toad Hollow from California
- Loire whites from Pabiot, de Tracy and Paul Thomas
- Wide range of sparklers, including Nyetimber from England.

For an explanation of the symbols used at the top of some of the merchant entries, see page 303

Montrachet Fine Wines

59 Kennington Road, Waterloo, London SE1 7PZ

Tel 020-7928 8151
Fax 020-7928 3415
Email admin@montrachetwine.com
Web site www.montrachetwine.com

Open Mon–Fri 8.30–5.30 **Closed** Sat, Sun, public holidays **Cards** MasterCard, Visa **Discount** On special offers only **Delivery** Nationwide service available (min. 1 case), charge (England & Wales) £5 + VAT for 1 case, free for 2+ cases, (Scotland) phone for details **Glass hire** Not available **Tastings and talks** Available, phone for details

The Australian wines have slipped quietly off Charles Taylor's list, leaving him with a range that is exclusively European. Indeed, with the exception of the 'magnificent seven' German estates and a handful of vintage ports, the entire range comes from France. Charles's passion is Burgundy, and more than 30 producers from the familiar (Girardin, Carillon) to the up-and-coming (Amiot-Servelle, Fery-Meunier) feature in his portfolio. However, his selection from other areas also merits attention. There's little – OK, nothing – from southern France, but the choices from the Loire, the Rhône and Bordeaux are of a high standard, while the lone Alsace representative, Domaine Bott-Geyl, is one of the stars of the region. The only drawback is that sales are by the unmixed case only (apart from the Germans, which can be bought by the half-dozen). But thanks to smart buying and an absence of frill, prices are reasonable, and the 'young, dynamic and highly knowledgeable' staff will be more than willing to cater for your requirements – unless, that is, you want something Australian.

Look out for
- Vast and inspiring range of burgundy
- Loire whites from Chatelain and Prince Poniatowski
- Bosquet des Papes, Sorrel and La Bouissière in the Rhône
- Bordeaux ranging from *petits châteaux* up to the top *crus classés*
- German wines from Lingenfelder, Ress and Richter
- Occasional in-house bin-end tastings and sales.

Moreno Wine Merchants

11 Marylands Road, Maida Vale, London W9 2DU

Tel 020-7286 0678
Fax 020-7286 0513
Email morenowi@dialstart.net

Open Mon–Thur 12–8, Fri 12–9, Sat 10–9, Sun 12–6 **Closed** Most public holidays, 25 Dec **Cards** Amex, Delta, Diners, MasterCard, Visa **Discount** 5% on 1 case **Delivery** Free within Central London (min. order £60); nationwide service available, phone for details of charges **Glass hire** Not available **Tastings and talks** Available, phone for details **£5**

Eamonn Smith isn't one to pull his punches. He proudly tells us that Moreno has 'The greatest selection of Fine & Rare Spanish wine in the world.' And when you see that the range includes nineteenth-century white Rioja, 1921 Vega Sicilia Unico, 1966 Torres Gran Coronas Reserva and a 1939

Pedro Ximénez, it's hard to argue with him. The range of old Riojas is especially impressive, and for those with significant birthdays or anniversaries in 2002, there are currently wines from 1952, 1942 and 1932 lurking in the cellars of the Maida Vale shop. Yet even without such mature delights, the Moreno selection is first class. The company is one of the major UK importers of Spanish wines, and chances are that you've already sampled some of the wines either at other merchants or in restaurants. There are wines specifically blended for the UK market, such as the Poema range and the astonishing La Pamelita sparkling red, made by the Scottish winemaker Pamela Geddes. The list features good-value reds from regions such as Toro and Navarra, and equally well-priced whites from Rueda and Alella. And then there are top-notch wines from Ribera del Duero, Priorato and Rioja, of course, but also from other DOs (Denominación de Origen) such as Tarragona (Castell de Falset), Costers del Segre (Castell del Remei) and Jumilla (Olivares Dulce). Non-Hispanophiles, despair not: you will find wines from other countries, although you might think about shopping elsewhere. But if Spain's your thing, then Moreno could very well satisfy your every need.

Look out for

- 'The greatest selection of Fine & Rare Spanish wine in the world'
- Vila Velha de Vilariça from the Portuguese bit of the Douro
- South American wines from Viña Casablanca, Navarro Correas and Toscanini.

Morris & Verdin

Unit 2, Bankside Industrial Estate,
Summer Street, London SE1 9JZ

Tel 020-7921 5300
Fax 020-7921 5333
Email sales@m-v.co.uk
Web site www.morris-verdin.co.uk

Open Mon–Fri 8–6 **Closed** Sat, Sun, public holidays **Cards** None accepted
Discount 10% on 1 unmixed case **Delivery** Free within Central London (min. 1 case); nationwide service available (min. 1 case), charge £10 + VAT, free for 4+ cases **Glass hire** Not available **Tastings and talks** Not available

---

'We have a few wines which are not expensive; we have a few decent wines which fit a price point. But if there is an overall philosophy of the company, it is to find producers whose wines we think are so damn good that we don't want to let any other importer get hold of them.' Jasper Morris has been peddling his floppy ginger-haired enthusiasm for more than 20 years now, and shows no signs of slowing down. His original plan was to concentrate on France, and French wines still take up the lion's share of the list. Burgundy has always been a speciality, and the array of growers includes many of the region's top names. Nor is the rest of the country ignored – with the selections from the Rhône and the Loire of particular note. Over the years, however, Jasper's plan has expanded to take in wines from other countries, in both the Old and New Worlds. Special mention should be made of his Californian selection, which is one of the best you'll find. Rumour has it that, in the near future, there will also be an influx of new talent from Italy and Australia. But whatever crops up on the next M&V list, or in the offers that appear throughout the year, you have Jasper's assurance that it will be 'damn good'.

Look out for
- Burgundies from Bachelet, Rion, Lafon and Fichet
- Loire range including Taille aux Loups, J-M Roger and Branchereau
- Rhône reds from Fauterie, Barrot and Chaume-Arnaud
- Rieslings from Germany, Alsace and Austria
- USA stars Ridge, Ramey, Au Bon Climat and Andrew Will
- Isabel, Gunn and Clos de Ste Anne from New Zealand.

Morrison Supermarkets

Wakefield 41 Industrial Estate, Wakefield,	*Tel* (01924) 870000
West Yorkshire WF2 0XF	*Fax* (01924) 875250
(110–120 branches nationwide)	*Web site* www.morereasons.co.uk

Open Mon–Fri 8–8, Sat 8–7, Sun 10–4, public holidays 9–5 (times vary between stores) **Closed** 25 & 26 Dec, 1 Jan, Easter Sun **Cards** Amex, Delta, Diners, MasterCard, Switch, Visa **Discount** Not available **Delivery** Not available **Glass hire** Free with order **Tastings and talks** In-store tastings by arrangement

'I'm thinking of not stocking £3 claret in the future with our name on, 'cos frankly, it's c**p.' Morrisons may have a reputation for being cheap and cheerful, but wine trading manager Stuart Purdie still doesn't like cutting too many corners where quality is concerned. This mainly northern chain has become the UK's sixth largest supermarket (and the fastest growing) by going out of its way to make shopping an easy and enjoyable experience – and this approach extends to the wine department. The wines on special offer receive top billing, and at Morrisons, the offers really are special. You'll usually find at least one red and one white at £1.99, as well as several other deals such as 'VAT-free prices'. As for the quality of the wines, we can't say that they're better or worse than at other supermarkets. With the accent very firmly on value-for-money, there are few £10+ bottles to provide window-dressing, and wines that rise above the £5 barrier are the exception rather than the rule. So if you're after something esoteric, head elsewhere, but if you're looking for simple everyday wines at great prices, then there's every reason to shop at Morrisons.

Look out for
- Jindalee, Yellow Tail and Rosemount from Australia
- Red and white Graves from Château St-Galier
- Well-priced Nathanson Creek California wines
- Spanish range including the delicious Vega del Rio Rioja
- Better-than-usual selection of Romanian wines
- 'Special' special offers.

James Nicholson Wine Merchant

27A Killyleagh Street, Crossgar, *Tel* 028-4483 0091
Co. Down, Northern Ireland BT30 9DQ *Fax* 028-4483 0028
 Email info@jnwine.com
 Web site www.jnwine.com

Open Mon–Sat 10–7 **Closed** Sun, 25 & 26 Dec, 1 Jan, Easter Mon **Cards** Amex,
MasterCard, Switch, Visa; personal and business accounts, James Nicholson Club Card
Discount Available, phone for details **Delivery** Free throughout Ireland (min. 1 case);
UK mainland, charge £6.95 per case **Glass hire** Free **Tastings and talks** Wide range
of tastings and talks, dinners with guest speakers **(£5)**

'This is my twenty-fourth year buying and selling wine. A life that revolves
around horse-racing (unsuccessfully), skiing (slowly), golfing (badly) and
wine buying (well, I hope!),' says James Nicholson. We think he buys wine
well – so well that we'd recommend mainland Britons to get on to this
mailing list too: James might cater for all of Ireland, but he still caters for we
outsiders as well.

The smart new wine list is a handy pocket-sized affair that's convenient
(and entertaining enough) for perusal while bored in a queue somewhere.
For starters, the Bordeaux selection includes all the top names (Talbot,
Lynch-Bages, Le Pin) and older vintages go back to 1982 Haut-Brion. This
kind of detail continues throughout the range, with a healthy smattering of
famous names and rare allocations from some of the best estates in the
world. France, Germany, Australia and California feature particularly
strongly, we feel. We shouldn't fail to mention value-for-money here either.
Every country selection starts at around the £5- or £6-a-bottle mark, and
James ensures there's always plenty under a tenner.

What really marks out this company is its high-energy approach to
communication. As James points out: 'In 1999/2000 we conducted no less
than 104 tastings and talks, six dinners with major winemakers Randall
Grahm, Frederic Jaboulet, Michel Dupont Fahn, André Ostertag, etc. We
have newsletters every six weeks and we also send out monthly email
updates with the latest news for those who want to receive it.' The
newsletters would give this country's glossy magazines a run for their
money and include all the background producer details and tasting notes
we could wish for on their chosen topic – plus there are usually some good
discounts to be had. It all makes compelling, and tempting reading, and
there's no way we'd miss a masterclass with Burgundy's Nicolas Potel if we
lived on Hibernian shores.

To celebrate 25 years of business, James Nicholson's Wine Week in April
2002 promises to be an exemplary affair, with tastings and dinners being
held at both branches, in Belfast and Dublin. A series of three-day
masterclasses sounds enticing too. We wish the team every success in this
event and for the next 25!

Look out for
- Top-quality New World Pinots: Mount Difficulty and Mount Edward
  from Central Otago, New Zealand, and Tom Rochioli from California's
  Russian River
- Fabulous Domaine Ostertag Heissenberg Riesling from Alsace

- *En primeur* Bordeaux from the 2000 vintage, personally selected by James Nicholson
- Quinta de la Rosa and Quinta do Crasto rich, ripe reds, from Portugal's Douro Valley
- Terrific California selection: Bonny Doon, Saintsbury and Ridge
- Delicious white Rhône Condrieu from Domaine André Perret, plus Côte-Rôtie and Hermitage from Jaboulet and Rostaing
- Upper-echelon burgundies from Vincent Girardin, Domaine Mugneret and Nicolas Potel.

Nickolls & Perks

37 High Street, Stourbridge,
Worcestershire DY8 1TA

Tel (01384) 394518
Fax (01384) 440786
Email sales@nickollsandperks.co.uk
Web site www.nickollsandperks.co.uk

Open Mon–Fri 9–6.30, Sat 9–6, Sun 10–2 **Closed** 25 & 26 Dec, 1 Jan, Easter Mon
Cards Amex, Delta, MasterCard, Switch, Visa; personal and business accounts
Discount 10% on 1 case of £60+ **Delivery** Free within 10-mile radius; nationwide
service available, charge £6 + VAT, free for 3+ cases **Glass hire** 20p per glass (min. 24
glasses) **Tastings and talks** Range available, phone for details **£5**

This list just oozes quality. Nickolls & Perks has one of the finest cellars of burgundy, Bordeaux and port back-vintages in the country and even offers storage facilities for customers who want to buy these treasures and keep them in perfect condition. Under their shop ('Ye Olde Corner Shoppe' – Dutch-gabled, bay-fronted, wonderful timbered buildings in central Stourbridge) are vaults dating back to the fifteenth century. Built on sandstone, these are ideal for storing and maturing wine. But, worry not. You can buy by the bottle too, and take your purchase straight home.

The emphasis at N&P is decidedly on fine, rare and traditional fare, but buyer William Gardener is also spreading the range out beyond Bordeaux and burgundy classics. It's obvious he's found his level, though, and is going to stick with it; whether from Argentina, Australia or Italy, there is nothing sub-standard here at all – which means fewer growers but of such quality as Dominus (California), Sassicaia (Italy) or Thelema (South Africa).

All this finery is complemented by a very active web site, on which all stock is upgraded daily – antique wine glassware will also soon be available via the site. Sales can be tailored to individual cellar plans and investment management. Plus there are *en primeur* offers and a major bin-end event every February. Newsletters every quarter complete the package. What more could any wine-loving West Midlander want?

Look out for
- Top wines (Château de Beaucastel and Chapoutier) from the Rhône, plus Châteauneuf-du-Pape vintages going back to 1959
- Fine Bordeaux from the illustrious 1961, 1982 and 1990 vintages
- Vintage port dating back to 1896 'Rare Lodge' tawny
- Sensational burgundy growers: Marquis d'Angerville, Jean Jacques Confuron and Jacques Gagnard-Delagrange

- Delicious Riesling from Germany (Schloss Vollrads, Deinhard) and Alsace (Trimbach, Hugel)
- Penfolds Bin 707, Wynns John Riddoch and De Bortoli Cabernets from Australia.

Nicolas UK

Head office
Unit 1, Gateway Industrial Estate, Hythe Road, London NW10 6RJ (25 branches in and around London)

Tel 020-8964 5469
Fax 020-8962 9829
Email dhanns@nicolas-wines.com
Web site www.nicolas-wines.com

Open Mon–Sun 10–10 **Closed** 25 Dec, 1 Jan **Cards** Amex, Delta, Diners, MasterCard, Switch, Visa; personal and business accounts **Discount** Available, phone for details **Delivery** Free delivery within Central London (min. order £50); nationwide service available, phone for details of charges **Glass hire** Free with order (min. 1 case) **Tastings and talks** Weekly in-store tastings; private tastings available

We like this shop for the cheerful staff: all French and all immensely knowledgeable about their wines – and who still always greet you with a 'bonjour' rather than a 'good morning'. Nicolas offers a refreshingly different style from the rest of the rather samey merchants on our high streets, which has to be a good thing. Added to which the wines are primarily French.

Not that there's anything wrong with a French theme – why would there be? – but with around 350 branches in France, plus others in Belgium, Poland, Germany and over 20 here in the UK, we think the buyers are spreading their wares too thin in trying to equip every shop with the same range. There'd be more individuality and more choice in the wines if smaller batches could be stocked and sold, even if that meant you couldn't find the same bottle in every store, or every time you visited. We think batches of wines from small growers would complete (and complement) the 'air of difference' these shops have.

Bordeaux is still the strongest section at Nicolas. We approve of the Rhône growers offered and the sparkling too – at the time of writing, a bottle of fizz can cost as little as £6.50 (Blanquette de Limoux) or as much as £50.99 (a Taittinger magnum). And, despite the attractive, self-professedly 'ever so funky' Petites Récoltes *vin de pays* range (each only £3.99 a bottle!), we still think it would be better to promote individual new estate names behind the wines rather than Nicolas' own. And what about putting more emphasis on those new exciting areas down in Mediterranean France and forgetting the (unnecessary) whisky selection? All in all we wish this selection was more exciting than it is.

Look out for

- Regular special offers – particularly on the champagne range
- Cheerful, reliable Beaujolais wines (not the Nouveau!)
- Less-often seen Savoie, Arbois, Bandol and Cahors
- Good *cru bourgeois* wines from Bordeaux.

Noble Rot Wine Warehouses

18 Market Street, Bromsgrove,
Worcestershire B61 8DA

Tel (01527) 575606
Fax (01527) 833133
Email info@nrwinewarehouse.co.uk
Web site www.nrwinewarehouse.co.uk

Open Mon–Fri 10–7, Sat 9.30–6.30, Sun 10–4 (Dec only) **Closed** Sun (exc. Dec), public holidays **Cards** Delta, MasterCard, Switch, Visa; business accounts **Discount** Available, phone for details **Delivery** Free within 10-mile radius (min. 1 case); nationwide service available, phone for details of charges **Glass hire** Free with order **Tastings and talks** Range of events including tutored and in-store tastings, winemaker dinners £5

'We make it easy for you' – just one of the mottos of this enthusiastic Midlands company, where good wines at sensible prices go hand in hand with a strong desire to please. Julie Wyres' business began in 1990, and we've been impressed with the way it has developed over the last decade. Much of her success can be traced to her never losing sight of her target audience, namely those who are looking for something beyond what supermarkets can offer. It's no surprise, then, that most of the bottles are well under the £10 mark, nor to hear that Australian wines now make up a third of the sales. Julie describes her selection as 'broad but sensible'; you'll find most wine countries represented, but may want to look elsewhere for more extensive selections of fine and rare wines, despite the occasional appearance of the likes of Vega Sicilia, classed-growth claret and Penfolds Grange. But for 95 per cent of your drinking requirements, Noble Rot can help, and can usually beat most other establishments on price, even before the regular special offers. If we have any criticism, it is that Julie sticks somewhat too closely to the ranges of certain wholesalers. A little more shopping around would, for us, pay dividends. But overall, we like Noble Rot, and would recommend Midlanders to take advantage of the many in-store tasting opportunities, as well as the annual tasting each November, which features around 100 wines.

Look out for

- Starvedog Lane, Charles Melton, Logan and many other Australian producers
- Spanish wines from Torres, Campo Viejo and Coto de Imaz
- Tuscan reds from La Parrina, Le Pupille and Capezzana
- Clos Malverne, Leef op Hoop and L'Avenir from South Africa
- South American selection, including Valle de Vistalba, Finca El Retiro and Las Casas del Toqui
- Niepoort ports and Lustau sherries.

The Nobody Inn

Doddiscombsleigh, nr Exeter, Devon EX6 7PS

Tel (01647) 252394
Fax (01647) 252978
Email inn.nobody@virgin.net

Open Mon–Sat 11–3, 6–11; Sun, public holidays 12–3, 7–10.30 **Closed** 25 & 26 Dec
Cards Amex, Delta, MasterCard, Switch, Visa; personal and business accounts
Discount 5% on 1 case **Delivery** Free within 25-mile radius (min. 1 case); nationwide
service available, charge £8 for 1 case, £2 extra per case for 2–5 cases, free for 5+ cases
Glass hire Free **Tastings and talks** Regular tutored tastings **£5**

Such was the allure of the Nobody Inn that former editor of the *Guide*, Susy
Atkins, has now taken up residence nearby, the better to take advantage of
the many wines that Nick Borst-Smith and his team have managed to pack
into the ancient Inn. Ask politely and Nick will tell you the rather convoluted
legend of how this excellent pub/restaurant/B&B acquired its name. Ask
again and he'll give you a copy of the smart new wine list, complete with
cover picture of the pub, circa 1910. This hefty document now functions as
the list for both the restaurant and the wine merchant business, so the listings
come with two different prices, depending on whether you want to drink a
wine *in situ* – and we can recommend the food – or take it away with you.

If you find the idea of an 80-page wine list rather daunting, try the more
user-friendly selection at the front of the list. However, we'd encourage you to
take the plunge into the pages that follow, since this is where the real
treasures lie. No one region outshines any other, since Nick has a passion for
any wine, as long as it's good. There are serious Old World wines, there are
serious New World wines. Looking through the range, you used to be able to
see where Nick's heart had overruled his head, and left him with stocks of
older wines that he was still trying to shift several years later. However, many
of these seem to have disappeared in recent years, although there are still
plenty of mature bottles to be had at very reasonable prices, especially if sweet
Loire whites are your thing. We'd recommend a trip to Doddiscombsleigh to
eat in the restaurant there. In the two hours or so it takes to finish your meal
(don't miss the cheeses), you could have read almost half the wine list.

Look out for

- Veenwouden, Boekenhoutskloof and Thelema from South Africa
- Classy Australian fare from Mountadam, Henschke and Penley Estate
- Super California reds from Calera, Jade Mountain and Dalla Valle
- Extensive selection of sweet Loire whites
- Colome, Weinert and Catena from Argentina
- A range of malt whiskies just as good as the wines.

Specialist and Regional Award Winners are listed on pages 12–15

Oddbins

Head office
31–33 Weir Road, Wimbledon, London SW19 8UG   *Tel* 020-8944 4400
(240 branches, in UK, Calais and Dublin)   *Fax* 020-8944 4411
Email customer.services@oddbinsmail.com
Web site www.oddbins.com

Open Varies between stores, phone for details **Closed** 25 Dec, 1 Jan **Cards** Amex,
Delta, MasterCard, Switch, Visa; personal and business accounts **Discount** Available,
phone for details **Delivery** Free within 10-mile radius (min. order £50); nationwide
service available, phone for details of charges **Glass hire** Free with order, refundable
deposit required **Tastings and talks** Regular in-store tastings; 2 wine fairs per year

We love Oddbins. From the colourful price lists and bohemian shops to the
dynamic get-you-anything, tell-you-everything web site, the formula still
works. Slick it might be, but it's not pushy; and that toned-down dress code
and hippyish, dusty floorboard atmosphere when you walk into a shop is as
chill-out-and-browse as ever. Wacky promotional leaflets ('Las Americas,
starring Charlie Chardonnay, Miguel Merlot and Teena Torrontés, at an
Oddbins near you') just add to the fun.

We're waiting eagerly to see the full results of the new venture between
Oddbins and Sainsbury's – Taste for Wine (q.v.) – launched in February
2001. As Oddbins has remained unchallenged for years as the UK's best
wine chain, it's probably about time something happened to bridge the gap
between this merchant and the rest. The aim of Taste for Wine is to pool the
knowledge of these two empires to create an outlet geared to the
adventurous wine buyer in need of some guidance … so watch this space.

What else has happened over the last year? Well, Argentina is generally
more available … Oddbins has expanded their range. There's been more
interest in Greece … Oddbins was there first of course. Bordeaux's shaping
up its act … Oddbins has the best of the new generic brands already and
some pretty delicious top châteaux too. We would be worried that they
haven't got in on the hip, biodynamic trend in Burgundy, but the wines
from those moon-governed vines are so expensive that Oddbins are
probably just saying 'be kind to your vines, but – please, be kind to your
public too!' Trailblazing, as we've always said, is second nature to this
company.

People want wines from one-off small parcels and special bin ends, and
that's what still gets delivered, despite the 240 UK stores from Inverness to
Truro, plus two more in Calais and Dublin. Not every store has everything
in it, but they all have access: so if you ask for it, you'll get it. The Oddbins
van will get to you within four working days (perhaps six if it's struggling
up to the Highlands or Islands). That means more obscure wines, such as
the Gaia Estate Aghiorghitiko from Greece, South African Vergelegen
Reserve Chardonnay from 1998, or Fabre Montmayou's delicious 1996
Argentinian Malbec, are available to you whether you're on Hoy or in
Hammersmith.

We're still extremely impressed by the range Oddbins has on offer, and
by the prices, the presentation and personalities behind the wine – from the
shop floor to that exuding from the bottles. It's the latter that's so critical,

and Oddbins always seem to capture it. In their own words: 'Will Barossa Shiraz be the most highly prized red wine in the world? Will Margaret River Chardonnay oust Le Montrachet from its pedestal? Who knows? Who cares? So long as growers keep producing wines with the same integrity and go-for-it attitude the future is safe.' There are good parallels to be drawn with merchants.

Look out for

- Regular weekly 'bottles open' for shoppers to taste
- Two Oddbins wine fairs a year: London and Edinburgh
- Fabulous array of South African wines: new-generation Chenin Blanc to oddities Fairview Zinfandel and Carignan
- Australian Riesling at affordable prices: d'Arenberg, Knappstein, Wirra Wirra and Annie's Lane
- Delicious Spanish whites from Rioja, Rías Baixas and Somontano
- Upmarket Spätlese and Auslese German wines – pushing the revival forward
- Châteaux Cantemerle, Léoville-Barton, Phélan-Ségur, d'Armailhac – top-rank Bordeaux
- 'Immensely lovable Alsace': Riesling, Pinot Gris, Gewurztraminer …
- A world of fabulous fizz, from Pol Roger and Perrier-Jouët to Prosecco di Valdobiadene and Angas Brut.

Partridges

Partridges of Sloane Street
132–134 Sloane Street, London SW1X 9AT

Tel 020-7730 0651
Fax 020-7730 7104

Partridges of Kensington
17–23 Gloucester Road, London SW7 4PL

Tel 020-7581 0535
Fax 020-7581 3449
Email partridges@partridges.co.uk
Web site www.partridges.co.uk

Open Daily 8am–10pm **Closed** 25 & 26 Dec **Cards** Amex, Delta, MasterCard, Switch, Visa; personal and business accounts **Discount** 10% on 1 case **Delivery** Free within Central London; nationwide service available, charge £15 **Glass hire** Free **Tastings and talks** Regular in-store tastings, outside tastings by arrangement; regular masterclasses

'We are very traditional,' says François Ginther, ex-French hotelier and now wine buyer for the two Partridges shops. Many people first sample the company's wines in one of their legendary hampers, which range from well under £100 to the decadent Royale at a cool £1,000. However, the range deserves attention on its own merits. Tradition dictates that the selection of claret, burgundy and champagne be extensive, but François has also assembled an equally impressive choice from Australia, Italy and Spain, as well as good-quality selections from most other countries. Some wines err on the side of caution – we'd like to see a few more names added to the burgundy section for example – but elsewhere, such as in the Italian wines and Riojas, there is a pleasing mix of ancient and modern. Prices are on the high side, but we suspect this isn't of major concern to most customers. And when the service is so polite and efficient, we're not going to complain either.

Look out for

- Besserat de Bellefon, Gallimard, Gimonnet and most of the top champagne houses
- Burgundies from Louis Latour, Faiveley and Champy
- Mittnacht, Trimbach and Schlumberger in Alsace
- Sileni, Kim Crawford and Cloudy Bay from New Zealand
- Western Australian wines – Moss Wood, Alkoomi and Plantagenet
- Riojas from Muga, Murrieta, Ijalba and Albina.

Thos Peatling Fine Wines

Head office

Westgate House, Bury St Edmunds, Suffolk IP33 1QS   *Tel* (01284) 755948
Fax (01284) 714483

37–39 Little London, Long Sutton,   *Tel* (01406) 363233
Lincolnshire PE12 9LE   *Fax* (01406) 365654

Open Mon–Fri 9–6, Sat 9–5, Sun (Dec only)   **Closed** Sun, public holidays   **Cards** Amex, Delta, MasterCard, Switch, Visa; personal and business accounts   **Discount** Available, phone for details   **Delivery** Local service within 30-mile radius (min. order £50), charge varies with distance; nationwide service available, charge £7.99 per case   **Glass hire** Free with order   **Tastings and talks** Regular tastings and talks, phone for details

Our hearts skipped a beat when Thos Peatling Fine Wines sent us their stock list dated 3rd April 1901 this spring – now that would have been something! In fact, what we have is the 2001 selection, and as this includes the likes of 1893 Château d'Yquem and 1902 Lafite, we're hardly in a position to be disappointed.

Peatlings have always had a fine stock of claret, port and burgundy, and a reputation to match. But since early 2000, when director Nicholas Corke (what better name?) led the management buy-out, taking Peatlings out of the Greene King fold and re-establishing it as an independent business for the first time since 1930, the range has become better and broader. We observed last year that work needed doing to breathe life back into the list after some tough times, and we're glad to report that this work is well under way. No longer is there an over-reliance on familiar brands and popular *négociants*. Burgundy (the biggest *négociant* trap) now lists the likes of Chandon de Briailles, Bonneau du Martray, Leflaive and Jean Marc Pillot. The range from Italy is varied and broad, and among a wide selection from Australia, at a variety of different price points, the likes of Petaluma, Tyrells and Vasse Felix all make a showing. There's perhaps a bigger reliance on old malt whisky, spirits and cognac than we'd like to see – but this is a wine guide, so we would say that wouldn't we? Perhaps more emphasis could be placed on the Americas instead, or Spain? And we'd like to see more description and detail in the wine list too. But there's no doubt that since last year, good progress has been made towards catching up with the high standards of fellow East Anglian merchants, Adnams, Noel Young and Lay & Wheeler. Staff brimming with enthusiasm for the wines they sell does more than a little to help things along their way.

Look out for
- Wonderful 1982, 1990 and 1995 Bordeaux
- Superb range of vintage and non-vintage champagne, plus other top-quality sparklers
- Lively varietals from Mediterranean and south-western France
- 'Less usual' wines from Lebanon, Romania and Switzerland
- Brunellos, Barolos and Barbarescos aplenty from Italy
- Delicious white burgundies, from top-rank Chablis and Corton to everyday Mâcon-Villages.

Peter Graham Wines

41–43 Elm Hill, Norwich NR3 1HG

Tel (01603) 625657
Fax (01603) 666079
Email louisa@petergrahamwines.com
Web site www.petergrahamwines.com

Open Mon–Sat 9.30–5.30 (wholesale 8–5.30)   **Closed** Sun (exc. Dec), public holidays
Cards Delta, MasterCard, Switch, Visa; personal and business accounts
Discount Available, phone for details   **Delivery** Free nationwide (min. 1 mixed case)
Glass hire Free   **Tastings and talks** Weekly tastings or wine dinners around Norfolk and Suffolk **(£)**

(Peter) Graham Donaldson aimed to publish his 2001 list in February, told us tentatively that it might appear in May and finally sent us a copy hot off the press in July. He did, however, have an excuse – or rather several excuses. He had been visiting suppliers both at home and abroad, as well as finding a new computer system and a bigger warehouse to cope with a business that expanded by more than 50 per cent in 2000 and shows no signs of slowing in growth. Graham puts the success down to personal service and an intimate knowledge of the wines. If you visit the Norwich shop, you'll find either him or his fellow buyer and director Louisa Turner behind the counter.

The quality of the wines could explain the popularity. It's not that you'll find wines here that are unavailable elsewhere, just that Graham and Louisa have put together a remarkably dud-free selection based on quality rather than reputation. We'd point you first of all to an impressive array of burgundies (Beaujolais included), but really you could dip your toe into any section and not be disappointed with what you found. There are several rather pricy wines, notably from Burgundy, the Rhône and Ribera del Duero, but there are also plenty of what Graham calls 'kitchen supper' wines; ones that have plenty to say but won't break the bank. No doubt by the time this appears there will be even more wines in the half-timbered Norwich shop. For those in the vicinity, a visit is recommended.

Look out for
- Emerging South African stars Whalehaven, Boekenhoutskloof and Mont Rochelle

- Mount Horrocks, Simon Gilbert and Vasse Felix from Australia
- Fine Burgundy from Billaud-Simon, Bertrand Ambroise and Boyer-Martenot
- Vajra, Allegrini and Le Pupille from Italy
- Good-value clarets from Patache d'Aux, Vieux Château Gaubert and Le Crock
- Alsace whites from Bott-Geyl and Burn.

Philglas & Swiggot

21 Northcote Road, Battersea,
London SW11 1NG

Tel 020-7924 4494
Fax 020-7642 1308
Email karen@philglasandswiggot.co.uk

Open Mon–Sat 11–7.30, Sun 12–5 **Closed** Public holidays **Cards** Amex, Delta, Diners, MasterCard, Switch, Visa; business accounts **Discount** 5% on 1 mixed case **Delivery** Free within 2-mile radius (min. 1 case); nationwide service available (min. 1 case), charged at cost **Glass hire** Free with order **Tastings and talks** Regular in-store tastings, outside tastings by arrangement **(£5)**

From the heart of Battersea's 'Nappy Valley', comes an extraordinary one-couple fight against Chardonnisation. Queenslander Karen Rogers and husband Mike very definitely dare to be different. They founded Philglas & Swiggot ten years ago, initially to specialise in Australian wines, but now they have a more general (and expanding) mission to 'seek out the most innovative and exciting wines from anywhere, and grab them on sight!' And so they do, gathering in at least 120 new wines each year, focusing on quality, value-for-money, style integrity and consistency.

That the guys at P&S have noticed an increasing tendency among customers to buy those much-maligned, vinous pariahs – Riesling, dessert wines and even sherry – is all credit to their ability to seek out good wine and to encourage people to understand it. As Karen says: 'We try to be welcoming and non-elitist, and help in any way that persuades customers to try something new.' The list reflects their success. It isn't the usual meander through the French classics (though they're all there) but a rip-roaring, open-top, wind-in-your hair ride around Australia (the biggest range of Margaret River wines in the UK, more than ten Rieslings, delicious food-matching Semillons, top Cabernet blends); Italian Super-Tuscans, Chiantis and Brunellos; the winding lanes of Burgundy for reliable, small-producer treasures; the mountain-fresh Grüner-Veltliners of Austria, etc. All of which you can feel free to discuss any time you want to pop into the shop. You might also like to try any of the bottles that might be open, or to join the P&S customer club, which offers a 12-bottle mixed case with tasting notes (bimonthly, monthly or quarterly) at a range of prices, and (we like this last touch), with an optional extra bottle for cellaring each time. Choices are reliable and thoughtful, and will inevitably include some of the rarer wines Karen and Mike have sought out.

'No … we don't have time to write a newsletter', says Karen, but the energy that goes into the physical presence of the wines more than makes up for this, and the frequently updated, chatty and informative list is available by email on request. A £12.55 average spend per bottle might not be so cheap, but as we've said before, there's no dead wood here. Everything listed is genuinely good!

Look out for

- Rare dessert wines from Italy, Austria and Australia (fabulous Rutherglen Muscats)
- Southern Italian reds from Sicily and Sardinia
- Recommendations under £6.99: cheerful, cheaper options from around the world
- A choice of 'non-blockbusting' California reds – Shafer, Stags' Leap, Saintsbury
- Carefully chosen Australian Chardonnays (the way they should be done, without blandness or big oak)
- More Australian fare – Mount Langi Ghiran, d'Arenberg's Dead Arm and Armagh Shiraz.

Christopher Piper Wines

1 Silver Street, Ottery St Mary, Devon EX11 1DB   *Tel* (01404) 814139
Fax (01404) 812100
Email sales@christopherpiperwines.co.uk

Open Mon–Fri 8.30–1, 2–6; Sat 9–1, 2.30–4.30   **Closed** Sun, public holidays   **Cards** Delta, MasterCard, Switch, Visa; personal and business accounts   **Discount** 5% on 1–2 cases, 7.5% on 3+ cases   **Delivery** Free within 25-mile radius (min. 1 case); nationwide service available, charged at cost   **Glass hire** Free   **Tastings and talks** Tutored tastings available **£5**

Founding fathers Chris Piper (large, jolly Beaujolais maker) and John Earle (thinner but just as passionate) continue to run this fine merchant following the same principles they had when they established the company back in 1979. This means that nothing gets on to the list by reputation alone, wines that speak of their terroir are favoured over ones that don't, and standards of service are paramount. As Chris says, 'CPW is NOT just Chris Piper, but a team of extraordinarily dedicated "winos" who realise the importance of service, individuality and a sense of humour.' All three qualities bubble to the surface in the monthly *Noble Rot* newsletters, which carry details of the many tastings, dinners and weekends held throughout the year, plus information about new arrivals and *en primeur* offers.

Regular visitors to Ottery St Mary will have noticed that the shop has recently expanded to double its former size. New manager Fred Ferguson has, according to Chris, '… set this side of the business alight'. Full marks to Fred, but also full marks to the four-strong buying team for giving him such a fine set of wines to work with. Chris and Co. wouldn't deny that France is their first love, so you'll find extensive selections from most regions, particularly Burgundy, where a love of Beaujolais is very evident – Mr P does, after all, make the wines at Château des Tours in Brouilly. There are also healthy ranges from Germany, Italy and Spain. In the New World, all countries are well served, with the Australian selection being the most extensive. Also extensive, and growing, is the number of 'eco-friendly' (although not necessarily certified organic) wines, denoted in the list by a smiley face. It's not a perfect range –

we'd like to see some wines from emerging regions such as Priorato in Spain or New Zealand's Central Otago, for example. But any wine drinker is guaranteed to find dozens of fine and interesting bottles here to slake his or her thirst, plus of course a friendly welcome from those 'dedicated winos'.

Look out for

- Fine selection of Burgundy, including Chavy, Lescure and Pinson
- Calera, Cuvaison and Ridge from California
- Some of South Africa's classiest from Paul Cluver, Glen Carlou and Jordan
- German Rieslings from Loosen, S A Prüm and Heyl zu Herrnsheim
- Puiatti, Ceretto and Candido from Italy
- Australian range featuring Brown Brothers, Pendarves, Simon Hackett and many others.

Terry Platt Wine Merchants

Council Street West, Llandudno, Conwy LL30 1ED *Tel* (01492) 874099
Fax (01492) 874788
Email plattwines@clara.co.uk
Web site www.terryplattwines.co.uk

Open Mon–Fri 8.30–5.30 **Closed** Sat, Sun, public holidays **Cards** Amex, Delta, MasterCard, Switch, Visa; personal and business accounts **Discount** Available, phone for details **Delivery** Free within 50-mile radius (min. 1 case); nationwide service available (min. 1 case), charged at cost for 1–4 cases, free for 5+ cases **Glass hire** Free with order **Tastings and talks** Available by arrangement **£5**

Jeremy Platt seems to have surprised even himself in publishing his Spring 2001 price list earlier than ever before, and he also seems to have been spending considerable time adding new wines to his range. He tells us that 'customers are still buying the "good-value wines", i.e. New World in the £4–£7 bracket', so the list kicks off with Australia and doesn't get on to Europe until it's been through the Americas, South Africa and New Zealand. We'd head for the California selection first – a rare thing to say about a UK merchant. Meanwhile, in Europe, it's the Spanish and French wines that draw our attention, with the Burgundy and Loire lists being the most enterprising. A little more life in the Italian and German sections would be welcome – if value-for-money is the thing, how about some wines from southern Italy? But we suspect that, in the near future, Jeremy will find time to plug the diminishing number of gaps in the range. Keep up with new arrivals via the newsletters, issued 'when we have something interesting to say!', or the recently launched and still slightly wobbly web site.

Look out for

- Burgundies from Lignier, Louis Latour and Pascal Bouchard
- Water Wheel, Wakefield and Brown Brothers from Australia
- Spanish reds from Ladubon, Lagunilla and Ochoa
- Villaudière, Jolivet and Roches Neuves in the Loire
- from California, Sonoma County's Mill Creek, Rodney Strong and St Francis
- Montes, Casa Lapostolle and Caliterra from Chile.

Playford Ros

Middle Park House, Sowerby, Thirsk,
North Yorkshire YO7 3AH

Tel (01845) 526777
Fax (01845) 526888
Email sales@playfordros.com
Web site www.playfordros.com

Open Mon–Fri 7.30–6, public holidays 9–4 **Closed** Sat, Sun, 25 & 26 Dec, 1 Jan
Cards MasterCard, Switch, Visa; personal and business accounts **Discount** Available,
phone for details **Delivery** Free within 75-mile radius; nationwide service available,
charges per case: £10 for 1, £6.50 for 2, £5.50 for 3, £4 for 4; free for 5+ cases
Glass hire Free within local delivery area **Tastings and talks** Regular tastings, phone
for details **(£5)**

Space is running out on the back of the Playford Ros catalogue to list
all the producers around the world for which the company is an agent or
distributor. While much of the business is selling to local hotels and
restaurants, nearly a third of all sales are now to those members of the
general public willing to buy a minimum of a dozen bottles. Looking
through the range, the only problem would seem to be confining your
choice to just 12 bottles – you may want to head for the half-bottle selection,
which means you can have 24 different wines. Not long ago, the focus was
more towards wines from classic European regions, but with increased
customer demand for New World wines, the range has evolved into a very
good all-rounder. While devotees of Australia, Bordeaux and Burgundy
have most reason to be pleased with the brisk selection on offer, there are
good-quality wines from most wine regions. Some companies may list more
wines, but it's difficult to discern holes in the Playford Ros range. If you can
'cover' Italy satisfactorily in 20 wines, why stock more?

Look out for
- Burgundy from Dampt, Olivier Leflaive and Christian Clerget
- Alsace whites from Trimbach, Krick and Rolly Gassman
- Amezola de la Mora, Breton and Chivite from Spain
- Classy New Zealand reds from Stonyridge, Esk Valley and Cloudy Bay
- Montes, Los Vascos and Infinitus from South America
- Australian producers such as Redbank, Oakridge and Grant Burge.

Le Pont de la Tour

Butlers Wharf Buildings, 36D Shad Thames,
London SE1 2YE

Tel 020-7403 2403
Fax 020-7403 0267
Email patriceg@conran-restaurants.co.uk
Web site www.lepontdelatour.co.uk

Open Mon–Sat 12–8.30, Sun, public holidays 12–6 **Closed** 25 Dec, 1 Jan **Cards**
Amex, Delta, Diners, MasterCard, Switch, Visa; business accounts **Discount** 7.5% on
1 case, 10% on large orders **Delivery** Local service within Greater London (min. 1 case
or £250), charge £10, free for 2+ cases; nationwide service available, charged at cost
Glass hire Available **Tastings and talks** Regular tastings, phone for details

A glance at the wine list still involves a sharp intake of breath, but content
yourself with knowing that in the restaurant upstairs, prices are even

steeper – though dining at Le Pont de la Tour, overlooking the Thames, is still the best way to experience these wines. Being part of Terence Conran's restaurant empire, precious allocations of the great Pauillac châteaux, Echézeaux, La Tâche and Richebourg burgundy should really come as no surprise.

The list is particularly strong – no, superb – on the French classics, but, food-matching being of utmost importance here, there are also good selections of whites from Austria and Germany, plus a handy range of Italian 'B's (Barolo, Barbera and Barbaresco) too. Head out to the New World for plenty more burly options – fine reds from Australia and California's Napa Valley – plus carefully chosen wines such as South Africa's Thelema estate Cabernet from Stellenbosch, Stagnari Tannat from Uruguay and Finca El Retiro Tempranillo from Argentina. These last, and other quirkier choices, not only dare to be different but also present less of a strain on the wallet. There's no getting away from it, however: fine wines are definitely the theme here.

Wine buyer Patrice Guillon cultivates an impressive team of knowledgeable staff, who are regularly seen on the London tasting circuit, and know all about the wines they're selling – lucky them! They host informal tastings of their wares every weekend and more formal affairs each month. Plus, keenness to communicate should reach its apotheosis in the new web site. Le Pont de la Tour is one of those merchants to commit to memory. When you have a lottery win and want to get hold of the best, the best will be here.

Look out for

- Five vintages of Cheval Blanc going back to 1962
- Delicious Raveneau Chablis and Bonneau du Martray Corton-Charlemagne
- 'Modern style' classics such as Guigal's Côte-Rôtie from the Rhône and Château Petit-Village Pomerol
- Top Australian Shiraz: Penfold's Grange, Henschke Hill of Grace and Jim Barry's Armagh
- Fascinating oddities such as English Chapel Down Bacchus, Swiss Petite Arvine and sweet Alsace Pinot Gris from Hugel
- Minervois, Madiran and Pays d'Oc Marsanne – good-value, interesting 'foodie' wines from southern France.

We love to hear your views on wine merchants. You can email your comments to us at: whichwineguide@which.net

---

Portland Wine Company

Head office

16 North Parade, Sale, Manchester M33 3JS

Tel 0161-962 8752
Fax 0161-905 1291

152A Ashley Road, Hale, Altrincham,
Cheshire WA15 9SA

Tel 0161-928 0357

82 Chester Road, Macclesfield,
Cheshire SK11 8DL

Tel (01625) 616147
Email portwineco@aol.com
Web site www.portlandwine.co.uk

Open Mon–Sat 10–10, Sun 12–9.30 **Closed** 25 & 26 Dec, 1 Jan **Cards** Amex,
MasterCard, Switch, Visa; personal and business accounts **Discount** 5% on 6 bottles,
10% on 1 case (not online orders) **Delivery** Free within 20/30-mile radius; nationwide
service available, charge £10 + VAT **Glass hire** Free with order **Tastings and talks**
Tutored and large tastings, phone for details **£5**

Wish you lived in Manchester? You would if you saw this astutely chosen
list. There can be few, if any, other merchants who so effectively run the
gamut from affordable to top-class wines in just about every category you
could dream of. Try Italian wines from sub-£5 Chianti to Aldo Conterno's
illustrious Bussia Soprana Barolo, or Spanish reds from a friendly £3.99 to
classy Vega Sicilia at (a bargain) £92.50 a bottle. Or burgundy from Latour's
straight Bourgogne to the elite Mommesin Clos du Tart.

It's obvious that the Portland Wine Company has the measure of its
customers' requirements, at whatever level, and Geoff Dickinson and his
friendly team ensure that communication goes both ways, with a regular
newsletter listing special offers and small bins – such as oddments of
burgundy so tiny that they'll never make it to the main list. Fortunately
for those of us elsewhere in the UK, PWC has an efficient web site and is
prepared to deliver around the country, so we can get in on this smart act.

'We are independent in every way and the world is our oyster. We are
also fortunate enough to visit many of the wineries to gain first-hand
experience,' says manager Judith Gilder. It's unsurprising she was
persuaded away from the teaching profession with this lot to tempt her; and
the experience she mentions shines through. She's also a good person to
have behind the helpful courses and frequent tastings on offer, and, as she
says, PWC's list is a perfect basis for customers to trade up, look around and
branch out in their wine choices. Ten out of ten!

Look out for
- Superb range of Chilean wines: Casa Lapostolle Clos Apalta, Montes
  Alpha Cabernet, Seña and many more
- Range of good-value regional French wines from the 'little guys'
- Château de Tracy and Pascal Jolivet's classy Sauvignons from the
  Upper Loire
- Bordeaux: stunning older vintages from the marvellous Château Figeac,
  Léoville-Las-Cases, Tour de By, among others
- A comprehensive selection of half bottles
- Wine lists printed on request.

R S Wines

Avonleigh, Parklands Road, Bower Ashton, Bristol BS3 2JW

Tel 0117-963 1780
Fax 0117-953 3797
Email rswines@talk21.com

Open Mon–Fri 9–7 **Closed** Sat, Sun, public holidays **Cards** None accepted; personal and business accounts **Discount** Negotiable **Delivery** Free within 50-mile radius (min. 1 case); nationwide service available (min. 3 cases), charge £4 per case **Glass hire** Free with order **Tastings and talks** Available, phone for details

Raj Soni's list represents, in his words, 'a personal journey in winedom'. For a trip that started with a £360 bank loan in 1985, that's quite some escapade. Sixteen years later, Raj has a list of wines to his name that would be the envy of many longer-established merchants. Smart burgundies such as Bonneau du Martray Corton-Charlemagne sit alongside cleverly chosen, up-and-coming châteaux names such as Rausan-Ségla, Phélan-Ségur and Kirwan. Such top Italian wines as Allegrini's Amarone della Valpolicella line up next to Selvapiana Chianti Ruffina. But the real advantage of this list is that there's plenty at the 'next level'. Raj is a good taster and buyer, with enough foresight to know just which names are the soon-to-be stars, and by buying these in, he offers good value for money.

Give Raj a call and he'll talk you through his selection. Though most of his business is wholesale, he's happy to sell wine by the case too, and happy to send out a list. You might not recognise all of the labels but we'd like to bet you soon will. The list is all in block capitals and we found reading it made our head spin, but these are head-spinning wines anyway.

Look out for
- Specially selected organic wines
- Bonny Doon, Ridge and Frog's Leap reds – top wines from California
- For something different, Mexican Petite Sirah from L A Cetto
- Exciting range of pre- and post-prandials: sherry, port, calvados, cognac
- Henschke Semillon, Charles Melton Shiraz and Yarra Yering Cabernet from Australia
- Bordeaux châteaux: reliable choices going back to 1985.

Arthur Rackham

Head office
The Church, 172 London Road, Guildford, Surrey GU1 1YR
(4 branches in Surrey; 3 shops, 1 wholesale)

Tel (01483) 458700
Fax (01483) 454677
Email jamesrackham@supanet.com

Open Mon–Sat 10–9, Sun, public holidays 11–7 **Closed** 25 & 26 Dec, Good Fri, Easter Sun & Mon **Cards** Amex, Delta, Diners, MasterCard, Switch, Visa; personal and business accounts **Discount** 10% on 1 case **Delivery** Available, phone for details of charges **Glass hire** Free with order **Tastings and talks** Local tastings available by arrangement

'We are fine wine merchants in the truest sense,' confess the team at Arthur Rackham. This is no empty claim: fine wines are aplenty here, ranging from the top-notch burgundies to a great selection from Alsace, a cluster of top-class Loire wines and a batch of superb German Rieslings. Bordeaux reach second growth rather than first, but the affordability element is strong and there are some very decent older vintages (1989 and 1990) too.

We particularly like the champagne selection, with everything from well-priced Jules Ferraud Brut at £14.50 a bottle to Krug 1989 and Louis Roederer Cristal 1994 at £99. There are in fact 66 sparkling wines to choose from here, including magnums of Lindauer Brut and the superb Pipers Brook Pirie from Tasmania. (Fizz for the cash-strapped comes in at a commendable £5.49 for a bottle of Australia's Great Western Brut – not bad!)

The Rackham's list has a good global span, and, for a chain of merchants, we think the scope and interestingness of the range is excellent. It is heartening to see attention reach out to the less-usual wine areas of the world – the wines of Luxembourg, Uruguay, Lebanon, Washington and Oregon. 'It is our mission to continually ferret out new treasures for our customers,' says Oliver Simpson: long may this attention to detail and impeccable, unhurried selection continue.

Look out for

- Cabernet, Merlot and Carmenère: juicy, fruity, Chilean varietal wines at easily accessible prices
- Superb range of Australian reds, including Capel Vale Kinnaird Shiraz, Penfold's Grange and Penfolds Bin 707 Cabernet Sauvignon
- Top South African growers represented: Hamilton-Russell, Thelema, Meerlust and Linton Park
- Excellent red burgundies from Drouhin, Faiveley, Jadot and Champy
- Port to lay down from the 1980s and 1990s – including Warres (by magnum), Niepoort and Fonseca tawnies, Dows, Grahams and Quinta de Vesuvio 1997
- Chewy, ripe California Zinfandels from Grgich Hills, Cline, St Francis and Lolonis.

Raeburn Fine Wines

Head office
21–23 Comely Bank Road, Edinburgh EH4 1DS

Tel 0131-343 1159
Fax 0131-332 5166

Cellars
The Vaults, 4 Giles Street, Leith,
Edinburgh EH6 6DJ

Tel 0131-554 2652
Email raeburn@netcomuk.co.uk
Web site www.raeburnfinewines.com

Open (Shop) Mon–Sat 9.30–6, Sun 12.30–5, public holidays 10.30–4 (Cellars open for tastings only)   **Closed** 25 & 26 Dec, 1 & 2 Jan   **Cards** Amex, Delta, MasterCard, Switch, Visa; personal and business accounts   **Discount** 2.5% on 1 mixed case, 5% on 1 unmixed case   **Delivery** Free within 10-mile radius (min. 1 case); nationwide service available, charged at cost   **Glass hire** Free with order   **Tastings and talks** Available, phone for details   **£5**

Inspired by a recent trip Down Under, Zubair Mohamed tells us that he has plans to expand his already respectable Australia and New Zealand ranges in the near future. Whether the new arrivals will appear on the annual list, however, is a different matter. Zubair did send us a copy of the Summer 2000 list, but the document only serves as a snapshot of his range at that particular time. Regular customers know that they need either to be on the mailing list, check the web site or, better still, make frequent visits to the shop to keep up with the many comings and goings in Comely Bank Road.

Zubair doesn't try to be comprehensive in his selection; instead, he focuses on high-class, small, usually family-run domaines throughout the world. Some regions, such as Burgundy, the Rhône, southern France and Italy, have many representatives. In others, such as Alsace and California, just one or two domaines contribute to the range. But quality throughout is impeccable. And while there are a number of wines which fall into the luxury bracket, plenty also come in at well under a tenner, especially from Portugal, southern France and Italy. At all quality levels, prices compare very favourably with those at other merchants. And if you fancy a change from this excellent range of wines, why not try the sherries and whiskies under Zubair's The Bottlers label?

Look out for
- Vast range of high-class burgundy
- Fine Rhône wines from Allemand, Barge, Florentin and Beaucastel
- New Zealand stars Dry River, Neudorf and Felton Road
- Classy German Riesling from Mönchhof, Selbach-Oster and Maximin Grünhaus
- Pfaffl, F X Pichler and Bründlmayer from Austria
- Entertaining selection of Portuguese reds.

Reid Wines

The Mill, Marsh Lane, Hallatrow,   *Tel* (01761) 452645
Bristol BS39 6EB   *Fax* (01761) 453642

Open Mon–Fri 9–5.30, Sat (by appointment only) **Closed** Sun, 24 Dec–2 Jan
Cards MasterCard, Visa **Discount** Not available **Delivery** Nationwide service available, charges per case: £6.50 for 1, £4 for 2, £3 for 3, £2 for 4, free for 5+ cases
Glass hire Not available **Tastings and talks** Talks by arrangement, phone for details

Pick up a copy of Reid's list and you'll be impressed – by the wonderful, old fine wine vintages: the ancient madeiras dating back to 1836, the 1890s clarets; and by the frank honesty – and dry humour – of the notes that describe them. For 1963 Château d'Yquem, read 'Should never have seen the light of day – a disgrace'; for 1956 Château Latour, 'From the period when Latour made good wine in "off vintages"'. The buying team don't just source and sell these wines, they know a good deal about them – and make strong recommendations about those that should be left to mature ('… keep off those 1988, 1989 and 1990 Sauternes … you know it makes sense'). With wines such as Leflaive's Puligny-Montrachet, Chapoutier's La Mordorée Côte-Rôtie and Château Pichon-Lalande available from recent vintages, we know it makes sense too.

France heads the country range here, followed by the Italian group (the Super-Tuscan selection shows the more modern side to Reid, as do the Apulia, Sardinia and Sicilian choices from the trendy south, and the wonderful

Montevertine Pergole Torte). Australia and California feature strongly with a plethora of expensive names, with wines listed by variety. The selections of port, sherry and Hungarian Tokaji are nothing if not spectacular.

And prices? Well, some of these are high, but given the quality and age of what's on offer, we'd expect that. But they accurately reflect Reid's estimations of the wines, for example: 'The Belle Epoque bottle should make a nice lamp when you've drunk it – 1975s are still good!' – your lamp and its Perrier-Jouët contents will cost you £350, but it is a jeroboam. 'Good kit this Bolly': the 1973 Bollinger will set you back £475 a magnum – fair enough. But the 'almost certainly dreadful' Château Lestage Listrac from 1936 will set you back a mere (mere?) £55; and the 'nasty looking 1920 white Bordeaux' is just £14.50 a bottle.

Look out for

- Excellent 1995 red burgundies to be laid down and aged
- Great-value 1990s Alsace from top-class producers Trimbach and Hugel
- Fabulous array of Australian greats: Penfold's Grange, St Hallett Old Block, Henschke Hill of Grace and Veritas Heysen
- *Cru classé* clarets to lay down and some recent vintage, lesser châteaux ready to drink
- Magnificent Barolo selection from Angelo Gaja and Aldo Conterno
- Ridge, Pahlmeyer, Arrowood and Dominus rare wines from California.

La Réserve

Head office
7 Grant Road, Battersea, London SW11 2NU

Tel 020-7978 5601
Fax 020-7978 4934

Knightsbridge
56 Walton Street, London SW3 1RB

Tel 020-7589 2020
Fax 020-7581 0250

Hampstead
29 Heath Street, London NW3 6TR

Tel 020-7435 6845
Fax 020-7431 9301

Marble Arch
47 Kendal Street, London W2 2BU

Tel 020-7402 6920
Fax 020-7402 5066

Fulham
203 Munster Road, London SW6 6BX

Tel 020-7381 6930
Fax 020-7385 5513
Email realwine@la-reserve.co.uk
Web site www.la-reserve.co.uk

Open Mon–Fri (Head office) 8.30–6.30 (Knightsbridge) 9.30–9.00 (Hampstead) 10–8 (Marble Arch) 10–8 (Fulham) 12–9.30; Sat, Sun varies between stores **Closed** Sun (some stores) **Cards** Amex, Delta, MasterCard, Switch, Visa; personal and business accounts **Discount** 5% on 1 case, negotiable on larger orders **Delivery** Nationwide service available, charge £7.50 per case, free for orders over £200 **Glass hire** Free with order **Tastings and talks** Tastings, wine courses and dinners, phone for details **£5**

'Not just another wine list. Not just another wine merchant.' The slogan at the top of this London company's literature speaks of confidence, and La

Réserve has this in spades. It also has a range of wines which merits that confidence. Mark Reynier and Simon Coughlin set up their business as recently as 1988, but this feels like a merchant of much longer standing. The selection of burgundies is a match for any in the UK, and plenty of venerable old bottles of claret and port adorn the shelves. In addition, there are excellent selections from most of the New World countries – only Germany and South Africa seem to lack less than comprehensive coverage. Another feature of the range is that La Réserve seems to get allocations of a large number of rare, 'sexy' wines, whether they be from Italy (such as Conterno Barolo), Spain (Abadia Retuerta), or the USA (Andrew Will). While many of these wines fall very firmly into the luxury bracket, there are plenty at more affordable levels, with the southern French section deserving particular mention.

Mention should also be made of the entertaining programme of tastings, ranging from 'How to Taste' introductions to head-to-head blind tastings of first growth clarets or *grand cru* burgundies. One of the best meal deals in London can be found in The Cellar at the Knightsbridge store. £10 buys you a buffet of Maître Philippe Olivier's cheeses plus pâtés, terrines, salads and fruit, and you can drink any wine in store at the on-the-shelf price. There, as in all of the stores (and there may be two more by the end of 2001), you'll find staff whom Simon describes as '… enthusiastic, well-trained professionals who can sell – there's no point in having the knowledge without the ability to sell.' This doesn't mean that devious tactics are used to persuade gullible punters to part with their precious cash; just that all efforts are taken to marry the right bottles with the right customers. Go on – let the folk at La Réserve twist your arm a little. You won't regret it.

Look out for

- Burgundies from more than 60 top growers
- Southern French wines from Domaine St Andrieu, Mas Brunet and Domaine La Colombette
- Top Spanish reds from Roda, Abadia Retuerta and Cims de Porrera
- Isole e Olena, Vietti and Coppo from Italy
- Rare West Coast reds from Andrew Will, Whitehall Lane and Talley
- New Zealand Pinot from Felton Road, Gibbston Valley and Kumeu River.

Howard Ripley

25 Dingwall Road, London SW18 3AZ

Tel 020-8877 3065
Fax 020-8877 0029
Email info@howardripley.com
Web site www.howardripley.com

Open Daily all hours **Cards** None accepted; personal and business accounts **Discount** Not available **Delivery** Nationwide service available (min. 1 case), charge £9.50, free for orders over £200 **Glass hire** Not available **Tastings and talks** Tastings and regular winemaker dinners; also by arrangement

Howard Ripley now has a new string to his bow. No longer is this merchant one of the finest places in the UK to buy burgundy – but he has now, since the arrival of Sebastian Thomas (ex-Laytons), branched out into German wines. In both areas the spotlight is on top growers, making everything from simple village wines and QbAs up to *grands crus* and *Trockenbeerenauslese*. This gives those of us with a little less disposable income the chance to sample wines from estates such as Maximin Grünhaus or Guy Amiot, and still have change from a tenner. However, good as the German range is, the burgundies are still the main event. The range is astonishing, and even though most wines come in at well over £10, the prices are not outrageous for the quality of the wines, even after you've added the VAT (please can it be included in your list next time round, Howard?). If you find the selection too large to contemplate, Howard and Sebastian have extensive knowledge of both the producers and the wines, and will happily talk you through the range. There are also tastings of the latest vintage each year (Burgundy in January, Germany in May) plus dinners involving visiting winemakers. Your wallet may regret making an acquaintance with the company, but your palate won't.

Look out for
- One of the finest burgundy selections you'll find
- German Riesling from Müller-Catoir, Egon Müller, J J Prüm and several other top estates.

Roberson

348 Kensington High Street, London W14 8NS

Tel 020-7371 2121
Fax 020-7371 4010
Email wines@roberson.co.uk
Web site www.roberson.co.uk

Open Mon–Sat 10–8 **Closed** Sun, public holidays **Cards** Amex, Delta, Diners, MasterCard, Switch, Visa; personal and business accounts **Discount** 10% on 1 mixed case, 5% on 1 unmixed case **Delivery** Free within Central London for 1+ cases or orders of £50+; nationwide service available (min. 1 case), charged at cost **Glass hire** Free with order **Tastings and talks** Available, phone for details

'We have an enormous range of wines from all over the world by the bottle. We stock rare French wines such as the classics from Bordeaux and Burgundy, and oddities such as Opitz's sweet dessert wines. We have exclusivity on wines from Chile, all good value. We have 1900 Lafite-Rothschild and 1900 Château d'Yquem,' says private sales manager J J Dearden. So that's all eventualities covered then – if you happen to be a wealthy film star living locally.

As befits its smart location, Roberson's begins its list with an incredible 115 different champagnes, culminating in a special edition jeroboam of Dom Pérignon at £1,950. Turn the page and there are a mere 20 that sparkle from the rest of the world. That just about sums this company up. It's the real thing, or not at all. There's no mediocrity here.

It all makes very seductive reading. And browsing the Gaudíesque shop shelves is made every bit as pleasant by their content – not to mention the modern but serious, otherworldly look and feel of the place. Imagine filling your shopping basket with a bottle of 1962 Latour here, 1945 Clos du Tart there, adding in a 1994 Conterno Barolo for fun. Well you could do all that and more besides at Roberson and, we suspect, nobody would bat an eye. There's not all that much that comes in under £10 and we find the average customer spend of £7.50 bottle a little hard to believe. We recommend shopping at (or ordering from) Roberson if you're a serious consumer of claret, champagne, burgundy or Italian wine – in fact if you're a serious consumer of wine at all. But bargain hunters should beware.

Look out for

- 1996 Red burgundy – a whole host of village, *premier* and *grand cru* wines from this sensational vintage
- Vintage port dating from 1995
- Thelema, Neil Ellis and Hamilton Russell South African estates
- Australia: the occasional Grange and Henschke Hill of Grace available to those with the cash
- From Spain: Rioja back to 1970 and Vega Sicilia back to 1981
- Top Hermitage and Côte-Rôtie from Guigal, Graillot and Gentaz-Dervieux
- White burgundy vintages back to 1961 Corton
- Bordeaux châteaux in vast quantities.

Safeway Stores

Head office

Safeway House, 6 Millington Road, Hayes,   *Tel* 020-8970 3821
Middlesex UB3 4AY   *Fax* 020-8970 3605
(480 outlets nationwide)   *Web site*s www.safeway.co.uk (main site)
  www.safewaywinesdirect.co.uk (wine site)

Open Mon–Sat 8–10, Sun 10–4 (times vary between stores) **Closed** public holidays (varies between stores), 25 Dec **Cards** Amex, MasterCard, Switch, Visa; personal and business accounts **Discount** 5% on 1 case of 6 **Delivery** Nationwide service available, via web site (min. 1 case of 6), charge £4.99 **Glass hire** Available, deposit of 10p per glass required **Tastings and talks** Available, phone local store for details

Safeway, as ever, is offering a feast for the supermarket wine buyer – at any level. Bottles might start at a barely believable £1.45 (you guessed it, German Niersteiner) but there's also a fair crop around the manageable £3 and £4 level (South Africa, Spain and Portugal do particularly well here), and a good selection of comforting £5-ish wines (which is where the impressive North and South American, and Australian wines kick in). Take the South Africa section as a good example of what's on offer. The May/June 2001 list has over 60 wines beginning with a £1.79 Chenin Blanc, and building up to top growers such as Fairview and Neil Ellis. Impressive.

Safeways are as strong as ever on Hungarian and Bulgarian wines, and while we think they could do better on Greece and Austria (are all these wines really too expensive?), there are some fascinating oddities from obscurer regions such as the Ukraine, Georgia and Montenegro. Oddities continue with a good range of Kosher and low-alcohol brands, and also some horrors – the unfortunately obligatory sweet British wine, Lambrusco, 3-litre boxes of Liebfraumilch.

As well as the bargain territory, there's also scope for Safeway customers to trade up and splash out. The buying team have been working hard on increasing their premium brand range (Domaine Jean Pillot's Chassagne-Montrachet and Rossignol-Trapet Gevrey-Chambertin from Burgundy look good to us!) and even have a fine wine range up and running in some of their outlets. The 'commitment to developing a range with a real difference and distinction' is bearing good fruit.

Safeway are also particularly strong on Bordeaux. Buyer Neil Sommerfelt (who has recently departed for Jeroboams) fully admits that this is tricky territory for the supermarket shopper, given the dreadful inconsistency recently of this illustrious region. But, as he says: 'Good £3–£4 value can be found and ring-fenced if time and effort are spent sourcing direct, and at £4–£6, better value and a sense of individuality and place really start to show.' Sommerfelt is taking his time with his choices and urges claret lovers to try out the Sovex, Calvet, Ginestet and Dourthe brands which are beginning to get their acts together, plus châteaux du Tasta, Tour du Mont, La Rose Brisson and d'Agassac. 'Well selected *petits châteaux* can offer good value and character!' he says. We'd say it's worth taking his advice.

Look out for

- A fair smattering of clearly labelled organic wines – from France especially
- Excellent £1 (and more) savings on gems such as Rosemount Shiraz and Peter Lehmann Semillon from Australia
- Australian Riesling, Verdelho, and blends of Mataro and Petite Verdot – more than just the mainstream grape varieties!
- Champagne, from J Bourgeois Père et Fils bargains to Bollinger Special Cuvée, plus other sparklers from around the world
- Good-value, warming French country wines
- From Italy, cool, crisp northern whites (Pinot Grigio, Orvieto) to sumptuous southern reds (Serina Primitivo, Sangiovese di Puglia), all at under £5 a bottle.

Sainsbury's

Head office
Stamford House, Stamford Street, London SE1 9LL   *Tel* 020-7695 6000
(435 stores throughout UK and Northern Ireland)   *Fax* 020-7695 7610
Web site www.sainsburys.co.uk

Open Mon–Fri 8am–10pm, Sat 8–8, Sun 11–5, public holidays 10–6 (times vary between stores) **Closed** 25 Dec **Cards** Amex, Delta, Diners, MasterCard, Switch, Visa **Discount** 5% on 6 bottles **Delivery** Not available **Glass hire** Free in selected stores **Tastings and talks** Tastings available, talks by arrangement, phone local store for details

'I cannot honestly recall a more exciting time in the industry.' Sainsbury's Director of Wines Allan Cheesman has never been short of words on matters vinous, but his sentiments from Spring 2001 are echoed in the current range from his company. Maybe Sainsbury's is not taking quite as many risks as it did at some points in the 1980s, but it does seem to be more adventurous now than for several years. This may be explained by the presence of two experienced and wine-mad Masters of Wine, Justin Howard-Sneyd and Laura Jewell, in the six-strong team of buyers. However, much of the credit must also go to Cheesman, who is almost as passionate about wine as he is about the Sainsbury's wine department.

As ever, you'll have to head for the largest branches to see the full extent of the buyers' efforts, and it's here that you'll find the much more expensive wines such as classed-growth clarets and limited-release Australian reds. But a competent range, plus a few stars, is available in most branches. We'd point you first of all towards the wines from Chile and South Africa, the pick of a generally reasonable New World selection. The disappointment is the rather tired Australian range, which is dominated by big names such as Penfolds, Rosemount and Hardy's.

In Europe, the Italian and Spanish wines include much of note, ranging from the juicy young reds of southern Italy to the soft oaky wines of Valdepeñas and Rioja. Some estate-bottled Rieslings are beginning to reappear among the new-wave German wines too, but it's France that offers the best choice. The clarets have been solid for many years, and there are some attractive Rhône reds, such as Frélin's Crozes Hermitage (one of a number of organic lines) and the Grande Bellane Valréas. The southern France range had tended to concentrate on varietal *vins de pays*, but more interesting AC wines are beginning to appear and, if you're near one of the top stores, you may even find an £11.99 Picpoul de Pinet and an £18.99 St-Chinian. Perhaps the most remarkable Sainsbury's wines we've tasted in recent months have been the own-label Cabernet and Syrah from Morocco, both bargains at £3.99.

So a good year for Sainsbury's, and we hope to see more zest appearing in the selection in the coming months. Keep a look out for the regular promotions that bring keen prices down to cut-throat levels. The larger stores often discount their fine wines to clear the shelves, and there are some incredible bargains to be had – we heard of 1996 Château Cantemerle being reduced from £27.99 to an astonishing £9.99 a bottle!

Look out for

- Vergelegen, Spice Route and Bellingham from South Africa
- Cono Sur, La Palmeria and Valdivieso from Chile
- Ochoa, La Rioja Alta and Albali from Spain
- Italian reds from A Mano, Cecchi and Castello di San Polo in Rosso
- Growing number of high-class wines from southern France
- Châteaux La Vieille Cure, Ségonzac and Coufran from Bordeaux, plus a delicious Clairet from Château Tassin.

Sandiway Wine Company

see deFINE Food & Wine Ltd

Specialist and Regional Award Winners are listed on pages 12–15

Seckford Wines

Dock Lane, Melton, Suffolk IP12 1PE

Tel (01394) 446622
Fax (01394) 446633
Email marcus@seckfordwines.co.uk
Web site www.seckfordwines.co.uk

Open Mon–Fri 9–6 **Closed** Sat, Sun, public holidays **Cards** Delta, MasterCard, Switch, Visa; personal and business accounts **Discount** Not available **Delivery** Free within 20-mile radius (min. 1 case); nationwide service available (min. 1 case), charge £11.75 per order **Glass hire** Not available **Tastings and talks** Available on request, phone for details

Yet another top-notch East Anglian wine merchant. More wholesale business is carried out than retail, but if you're willing to put together a mixed case from what Seckford has to offer (as we would be!), then you'll not be short of upper-echelon choices. The Bordeaux selection, for a start, is immensely good quality and offers something for everybody up to an *impériale* of Pétrus 1982 at £12,500. Added to which, as the buyer Marcus Titley tells us: 'Last year we sold an Yquem collection for £250,000! Every vintage produced from 1854 to 1995.' So that's the league we're in here.

We do stress, though, that the members of this team also know how to lay their hands on more-affordable fine wine, and an enticing range is available from which to take our pick. As well as left- and right-bank treasures, there are some superb red burgundies – the 1999 *en primeur* offer makes very tempting reading. We're slightly disappointed by the dearth of 1996 white burgundy, where such top wines would seem to be the speciality, but as it's such an extremely good vintage, we suspect Seckford's discerning customers (wine trade among them) have snapped it all up. To cheer us, we're pleased to see South Africa and Australia still making a good showing. Five vintages of Penfold's Grange always bode well from Down Under, and in South Africa, Paarl's Backsberg estate has equally impressive offerings from the Shiraz grape. Seckford tell us that they're particularly proud of their Rhône and Italian lines of late, and we can see why, with the likes of Allegrini, Antinori, Aldo Conterno and Ornellaia on offer.

Look out for

- Sauzet, Roumier, Leflaive, Jadot and Colin-Deleger top allocations from Burgundy
- First-class new wave claret: La Mondotte, Le Pin, Lynch-Bages, Gruaud-Larose and Vieux Château Certan
- Chave and Chapoutier, two of the Rhône Valley's finest growers
- Succinct but sensational selection from top Alsace grower Zind-Humbrecht
- Boutique-scale, quality Australian wines from Hollick, Yering Station and Coriole
- Plenty of 'birthday' wines – mature vintages right back to the 1950s and 1960s.

Selfridges

400 Oxford Street, London W1A 1AB	*Tel* 020-7318 3730
	Fax 020-7491 1880
1 The Dome, Trafford Centre, Manchester M17 8DA	*Tel* 0161-629 1220
	Web site www.selfridges.co.uk

Open Mon–Wed 10–7, Thur–Fri 10–8, Sat 9.30–7, Sun 12–6 **Closed** 25 Dec, Easter Sun **Cards** Amex, Delta, Diners, MasterCard, Switch, Visa; Selfridges Card **Discount** 8.5% on 1 case (further discounts for Selfridges Card holders) **Delivery** Nationwide service available, charge £5 within M25, £10 outside **Glass hire** Free with order **Tastings and talks** Weekly tastings, wine club, phone for details **£5**

Buyer Andrew Willy is proud of his list for its 'breadth and depth of range – from *vin de pays* to Pétrus' and of his staff for their skilful wine choosing and food-matching advice, pointing out they have a big food hall next door. He really does have a truly spectacular selection of wines. Starting off with one of the biggest ranges of champagne and sparkling wines we've seen (everything from halves of Krug, to a 20-bottle Nebuchadnezzar of Veuve-Clicquot), moving on to a fine wine list, with precious allocations of Bordeaux (Le Pin, 1982 Lafite, 1990 Pétrus), Domaine de la Romanée-Conti burgundy, Ridge and Opus One from California, and Grange from Australia – the illustrious names are all here. On the main list, there are wines you simply don't see anywhere else, and not all of them are at stratospheric prices – there's even a fair selection at less than a fiver. (Though we're certainly not suggesting this is a cheap place to buy wine.)

Last year we extolled the virtues of the Italian selection and this year our feelings haven't changed; but we'd like to add our praise for the very good ranges from South Africa and Australia. The latter selection is sensibly divided into regions, so that customers can get a feeling for what each of the different states has to offer. We'd like to see more in the way of South Australian Riesling, but other than this, Andrew Willy has carefully selected beyond the boring Cabernet/Chardonnay spectrum. There's also a plentiful selection from France, apart from the top-niche names mentioned above.

This is still one of the most comprehensive wine lists we know of, and we still rate it very highly indeed. There remain, however, a few or so grey areas that don't quite live up to the breadth of everything else: Argentina, Oregon and Greece. No doubt Selfridges are working on these.

There is to be a new Selfridges wine department opening in autumn 2002 in Manchester City centre, since branch two, down the road at the Trafford Centre, has fared so well. Two in Manchester? We don't doubt the rest of the country will start clamouring for this sort of wine quality soon too.

Look out for

- A worthy selection of organic choices including Mas de Daumas Gassac and Clare Valley wines from Australia
- Precious California reds: Shafer, Dominus, Ridge and Stags Leap
- Glittering Chilean stars: Almaviva, Seña, Casa Lapostolle and Don Maximiano
- Fabulous selection of top burgundy growers: Ramonet, Girardin, Leflaive, Sauzet and more

- Fine Alsace Rieslings, Pinots and Gewurztraminers from top growers
- Affordable Bordeaux by the bottle from trustworthy châteaux, plus the likes of top-class Pauillacs and Pomerols for finer/celebratory dining
- Hedonistic global range of sweet wines by the half bottle, not least Château d'Yquem at £140
- In-store informal tastings every week.

Edward Sheldon

New Street, Shipston on Stour,
Warwickshire CV36 4EN

Tel (01608) 661409
Fax (01608) 663166
Email finewine@edward-sheldon.co.uk
Web site www.touchoxford.com

Open Mon–Fri 9–7, Sat 9–5 **Closed** Sun, public holidays **Cards** Delta, MasterCard, Switch, Visa; personal and business accounts **Discount** Available, phone for details **Delivery** Free within 10-mile radius (min. 1 case); nationwide service available (min. 1 case), charge £6 per case **Glass hire** Free with order (min. 1 case) **Tastings and talks** Regular tastings and dinners, talks available by arrangement, phone for details

It's a case of swings and roundabouts at this Midlands merchant, according to co-buyer and shop manager Phil James. Wholesale trade is down but there has been more interest in the retail side of the business. The latter increase isn't just because Phil and his staff carry all shop case sales to customers' cars. No, the service may be very good, but it's the range of wines that attracts our attention, and this has been steadily improving for a number of years. It's not without its flaws – the Italian and Californian ranges would certainly benefit from a new broom. However, the selection from most other countries is generally good, and in some regions very good. Highlights are the Australian wines, which seem to have been chosen for subtlety rather than power, a Burgundy range where the accent is increasingly on high-class growers rather than *négociants*, and a selection of clarets that is impressive even without the annual *en primeur* offer. The wine dinners, advertised in the bimonthly newsletter *The Corker*, remain among the best value around. The most expensive in 2001 included a vertical tasting of Châteaux d'Angludet and Palmer plus the meal for an extremely reasonable £35.

Look out for
- Loire wines from Roches Neuves, de Tracy and Guy Saget
- Extensive selection of claret from most 1990s vintages
- Burgundies from Girardin, Parent and Louis Latour
- Bernard Chave, de Nalys and Courbis in the Rhône
- Western Australian wines from Howard Park, Devil's Lair and Cape Mentelle
- New Zealand range including Te Mata, Wither Hills and Montana.

Somerfield

Head office
Somerfield House, Whitchurch Lane,
Bristol BS14 0TJ
(600 branches nationwide)

Tel 0117-935 9359
Fax 0117-978 0629
Web site www.somerfield.co.uk

Open Mon–Fri 8–8, Sat 8.30–6.30, Sun, public holidays 10–4 (times vary between stores)
Closed 25 Dec, Easter Sun **Cards** Amex, Diners, MasterCard, Switch, Visa **Discount**
5% on 6 bottles **Delivery** Available within 5-mile radius, charge £3, free for orders of
£25+ **Glass hire** Not available **Tastings and talks** Monthly tastings in some stores **£5**

Angela Mount runs a slick programme of wine buying, as well she needs to
with 1,400 stores to supply. (That's 600 Somerfields nationwide and 800
Kwiksave shops, which have a more limited range.) 'We focus strongly on
the under-£5 sector, since this still accounts for the largest proportion of
wine sales, and pride ourselves on the quality of our wines at the lower-
priced end of the market. We focus on top quality at each price point and on
great offers to encourage customer trial,' she says.

Although we still don't know how Somerfield survives, the 'offers' being
as spectacularly cheap as they are, we are delighted to see Angela Mount's
list going from strength to strength. Down-to-earth, straightforward
enticement obviously works. And why wouldn't it, with delicious (and
unusual) Uruguayan Tannat/Cabernet Franc listed at £4.99, Argentinian
Syrah and Tempranillo at £3.99? Go for a Somerfield blend (Angela flies out
and supervises a lot of these herself; they're not bad either), and prices are
even cheaper. Somerfield Bulgarian Cabernet is £2.99, as is the Somerfield
Australian Dry White. Somerfield Prince William Champagne starts at £11.99
for the Blanc de Noir, which we think is pretty impressive too – or you can
go 90 per cent cheaper and pick up a sparkling Moscato fizz for an
incredible £1.99.

Key areas are listed as South Africa, South America, Italy and France, but
we think the Australian selection is very strong too, packed with steady,
reliable brands and delicious grape flavours. We hope Angela's next step is
to trade up, so we can enjoy some of the different regional flavours
emerging from this country, even if that inevitably involves less-inviting
prices. From France, though, all the regions are represented. Overall, then,
although we'd like to see more scope to splash out and understand the
classics, we think Somerfield is covering its pitch admirably well and
providing an invaluable service.

Look out for

- Primitivo reds from Italy's hot (and trendy) southern vineyards
- Argentina: try out red grapes with a difference (Cabernet, Malbec, Sangiovese and Shiraz)
- Romanian Pinot Noir and Hungarian Bull's Blood
- Spice Route South African Shiraz and Pinotage
- Lots of Languedoc reds and whites from France (including Somerfield's own blends)
- Cono Sur Pinot Noir from Chile.

Sommelier Wine Company

23 St George's Esplanade, St Peter Port,
Guernsey GY1 2BG

Tel (01481) 721677
Fax (01481) 716818

Open Mon–Thur 10–5.30, Fri 10–6, Sat 9.30–5.30 **Closed** Sun, public holidays **Cards**
Delta, MasterCard, Switch, Visa; personal and business accounts **Discount** 5% on 1
case **Delivery** Free within Guernsey (min. 1 case) **Glass hire** Free **Tastings and
talks** Available, phone for details **£5**

The two Richards, Allisette and Mathews, who with help from Fred ('a
slightly daft Austrian') run Sommelier, could justifiably have ticked nearly
all of the boxes on our questionnaire to indicate which wine regions they
specialised in. Theirs is a range that with the exception of German wines
('nothing personal, nothing political – they just won't sell', according to
Richard M) has virtually everything a wine lover could want. 'We buy only
those wines we would be happy to drink at home,' says Richard A, and the
consequences are there for all to see in the ever-expanding list, now not far
short of 150 pages, and including 22 rosés – can any other merchant beat
that? Pinks apart, other obvious areas of passion are the Loire (serious
Muscadet included), Burgundy ('we have more than we have space'),
Australia, where the range includes several hard-to-find estates, South
Africa (ditto) and Italy.

The Italian selection, in which sub-£5 Chiantis happily rub shoulders
with Sassicaia and Conterno Barolo, demonstrates another Sommelier trait,
that of offering decent wines at all prices. And the prices are very attractive,
largely because there is no duty on wines in the Channel Islands. Indeed,
the only drawback for the Guernsey wine lover is that local laws forbid the
opening of bottles for in-store tastings. Never mind, there are plenty of
tutored tastings and dinners over the course of the year to keep customer
morale up. Overall then, a very impressive performance, and we only wish
that the Richards had a branch or two on the UK mainland.

Look out for
- Champagnes from Philipponnat, Gardet and Jacquesson
- Loire selection including Vacheron, Metaireau and Champalou
- Burgundy from Gouges, Amiot and Domaine de la Vougeraie
- Classy Italian whites from Feudi di San Gregorio, Specogna and La
  Monacesca
- Australian rarities such as Greenock Creek, Noon, Fox Creek and
  Giaconda
- Louisvale, Steenberg and Veenwouden from South Africa.

South African Wine Centre

see Swig

Frank Stainton Wines

3 Berry's Yard, Finkle Street,
Kendal, Cumbria LA9 4AB

Tel (01539) 731886
Fax (01539) 730396
Email admin@stainton-wines.co.uk

Open Mon–Fri 9–5.30, Sat 9–5 **Closed** Sun, public holidays **Cards** Delta,
MasterCard, Switch, Visa; personal and business accounts **Discount** 5% on 1 mixed
case **Delivery** Free within 50-mile radius (min. 1 case); nationwide service available
(min. 1 case), charge £10 per case **Glass hire** Not available **Tastings and talks**
Available, phone for details

'Been there, drunk that, want to go again,' as one of Frank Stainton's four
key members of staff says – which is hardly surprising when you see the
wines this company lists. These four have been going back again day after
day, for 82 years now (between them, that's the total service they've notched
up). There are more than a few hotels and restaurants in the surrounding
Lake District that could claim equal loyalty – they make up 90 per cent of
Stainton's business.

FSW's wines are resolutely good quality. As we've said before, there's no
compromise just for the sake of hitting a certain price point. With restaurant
mark-ups being what they are these days, this might give rise to the odd
gasp for breath over the dinner table (what's new there!), but if you buy
your wines straight from the merchant instead, you'll be in good hands.
After all, not every company on these pages can boast stocks of 1995 Cheval
Blanc, Nicolas Joly's Savennières from the Loire or, from Italy, Allegrini's
very fine Amarone della Valpolicella.

We've been critical in the past of too much reliance on one producer per
region, but that is far from the case today – with the forgivable exception,
still, of Hugel in Alsace. There are plenty of different growers to choose
from, and while Bordeaux, California, Australia and Italy are still the
strengths, there are also exceptionally good wines to be had from Germany,
the Rhône and South America. It rather looks as if Frank Stainton Wines are
getting better and better!

Look out for

- Bordeaux vintages from 1983 to the present day – magnums too
- Great Zinfandel selection from California: includes Ridge, Clos du Val
  and Van Asperen
- Finca El Retiro wines new from Mendoza, Argentina
- Champagne from good-value, non-vintage wines to Bollinger Grand
  Année, and more
- Top wines of the Loire Valley: Château de Nozet, Nicolas Joly and
  Fournier Père et Fils
- Fabulous Australian selection: Shaw & Smith, Mount Horrocks, Mount
  Langi Ghiran and more.

Stevens Garnier Wine Merchants

47 West Way, Botley, Oxford OX2 0JF   *Tel* (01865) 263303
Fax (01865) 791594
Email shop@stevensgarnier.co.uk
Web site www.stevensgarnier.co.uk

Open Mon–Wed 10–6, Thur–Fri 10–7, Sat 9.30–6 **Closed** Sun, public holidays **Cards**
Amex, Delta, MasterCard, Switch, Visa; personal and business accounts **Discount**
Available, phone for details **Delivery** Free within 70-mile radius (min. 1 case);
nationwide service available, charge £10 **Glass hire** Free with order **Tastings and
talks** Range of tastings and dinners, phone for details **£5**

Even if you don't frequent this Oxford merchant, chances are that you've
drunk at least something from the Stevens Garnier range. The company
imports wines from well-known producers such as La Chablisienne
(Chablis), Vacheron (Loire), Carmen (Chile) and Sogrape (Portugal), and
distributes them widely throughout the UK. Indeed, the retail side is only a
small sector of the business, but visitors to the Botley shop will find a
friendly welcome, and a range of wines which extends beyond the
wholesale list in most wine regions. The most inspiring selection is that from
the less-prestigious regions of France, where the whites are just as notable as
the reds. Wines such as Jurançon, Picpoul de Pinet and Roussette de Savoie
aren't the most common, but you'll find tasty examples of each here.

The selections from the Loire, Burgundy, Bordeaux and South America
are worth a look too; and, while the choices from other regions are less
extensive, the wines on offer are decent and sensibly priced.

Look out for
- Carillon, Chaley and Guy Prieur in Burgundy
- Loire whites from Vacheron, Delaunay and Brisebarre
- South American offerings: Weinert, Carmen and Viniterra
- Enterprising range from regional France
- The excellent Selaks whites from New Zealand
- Some of Canada's finest from Château des Charmes.

Stratford's Wine Shippers & Merchants

High Street, Cookham, Berkshire SL6 9SQ   *Tel* (01628) 810606
Fax (01628) 810605
Email sales@stratfordwine.co.uk
Web site www.stratfordwine.co.uk

Open Mon–Fri 9–6.30, Sat 10–7 **Closed** Sun, public holidays **Cards** Amex, Delta,
Diners, MasterCard, Switch, Visa; business accounts **Discount** Available, phone for
details **Delivery** Free nationwide service available (min. 1 case) **Glass hire** Free with
order **Tastings and talks** Available, phone for details **£5**

For a merchant billed as an Australian specialist, we think Stratford's do
surprisingly well from the rest of the world too. In fact, in the last year
they've opened up their portfolio to include wines from the Americas and
now have the makings of a range to parallel their Australian selection.
Smaller estates producing interesting wines – not the churn-it-out-and-glug-

401

it kind – are exactly what we want to see from both these areas, and exactly what Stratfords have on offer. A healthy smattering of California's Bonny Doon estate, Hess Collection and Qupé wines bear witness – although all are well over the £10 mark. It's early days for the South American range but Argentinian reds from Finca El Retiro show things are off to a good start.

We're also impressed with Stratfords' French selection, which is strong in both Bordeaux and Burgundy, with all the decent vintages going back to 1982 (stunning St-Julien claret, snap it up if your pocket's deep enough). All the right champagnes are there too. There's a respectable nod to Spain, Italy, Germany and New Zealand, each with quality in mind – but the real treasures are, as ever, from Australia.

Stratford's are sole agents for poised, cool-climate wines from Wakefield in the Clare Valley, Nepenthe in the Adelaide Hills. Viv Thompson's amazing array of varietal wines from Great Western in Victoria are all there. Hunter Valley Verdelho, Margaret River Cabernet from Howard Park – you name it, and there's a good grower here to show you how Australian wine should be made the hands-on way. We're particularly pleased to see the finishing touch: sticky *botrytis* Semillon and Rutherglen Muscats – sweet, delicious but relatively unloved, so buy them while you can. The Down Under selection is skilfully chosen and broad ranging, and we'd hate to see it suffer at the expense of global coverage. We don't like to be greedy, but suspect there are other smaller Australian estates that would sit well on this specialist list – and that if anyone can get them, Stratfords can.

Look out for
- Handy web site – for ordering and keeping track of new wines
- Charles Cimicky's bold Barossa Valley reds for warming, winter drinking
- Maxwell's McLaren Vale varietal range, showing how good small-scale winemaking can be
- Carefully chosen, everyday Bordeaux from reliable châteaux – Tour de By, Pâtache d'Aux, Fourcas Dupré
- Perrin, Chapoutier and Beaucastel, plus Condrieu from the Rhône
- Delicious ports and sparkling wines to choose from.

Sunday Times Wine Club

see Laithwaites

Swig

5 & 6 Roxby Place, London SW6 1RU

Tel 020-7903 8311
Fax 020-7903 8313
Email imbibe@swig.co.uk
Web site www.swig.co.uk

Open Mon–Fri 8.30–6.30 **Closed** Sat, Sun, public holidays **Delivery** Free within M25 (min. order £60); nationwide service available, charge £10 for 1 case, £3 per extra case **Tastings and talks** Available, phone for details **£5**

The Swig shop in Haverstock Hill was one of London's sparkiest places to buy wines, and had a growing band of loyal customers. So why, early in 2001, did owner Robin Davis decide to sell the shop to Lea & Sandeman?

Simple. The laid-back Robin wanted a life in which he didn't have to be in a store from early in the morning till late each evening, and so decided to become a mail-order only merchant. With him in Swig's new incarnation is former shop manager Damon Quinlan, and the pair have spent the summer months of 2001 building up their new range of wines. At present, the focus is on three regions. Those who used to shop at the old Swig won't be surprised to see Robin specialising in wines from the Rhône and Italy, and doing so with some aplomb. The third area is South Africa. Robin has taken over the business of the former South African Wine Centre, which used to have the finest assortment of Cape wines in the UK. The summer 2001 Swig list featured 20 different producers – not as many as were at the SAWC in its prime, but still considerably more than most other merchants. We'll be keeping an eye on the newsletters and the web site to monitor Swig's progress. We've already seen Robin dabbling with some Alsace wines, and wouldn't be surprised to see further additions to an already tidy little selection in the future.

Look out for
- Rhône wines from Perret, St-Cosme and Janasse
- Italian estates such as Brancaia, La Spinetta and Planeta
- Rust-en-Vrede, Springfield, Boschendal and many other South African producers.

T & W Wines

51 King Street, Thetford, Norfolk IP24 2AU *Tel* (01842) 765646
Fax (01842) 766407
Email contact@tw-wines.com
Web site www.tw-wines.com

Open Mon–Fri 9.30–5.30, Sat 9.30–1 **Closed** Sun, public holidays **Cards** Amex, MasterCard, Visa; personal and business accounts **Discount** Not available **Delivery** Free within 15-mile radius (min. 1 case); nationwide service available, charge £10.95 for 1–4 cases, free for 5+ cases (surcharge for Highlands) **Glass hire** Free with order **Tastings and talks** Available, phone for details **(£5)**

We love this chunky list – for chunky it still is, and, we suspect, better organised than it has been in the past. Instead of odd pages of Chilean or South African wines punctuating the many devoted to France, there are suitably placed 'A Taste Of …' offers. An excellent idea, and a superb way of getting to know a region. 'A Taste of Red Burgundy', for example, offers a £99 case with four styles of Beaujolais (three bottles each); or £319 for a case of Volnay – three vintages each from four different growers; or £301 for a case of Côte de Nuits (three bottles of Gevrey-Chambertin, three of Chambolle-Musigny and more). Others to choose from include 'A Taste of the Loire', 'A Taste of Bordeaux' and 'A Taste of Biodynamics' – and small essays about favourite producers and the latest wine theories provide a good background to exactly what you're getting.

Trevor Hughes is not only an enthusiastic communicator (as an ex-restaurateur, this must be part of his skill set), he's totally dedicated to sourcing the very finest bottles he can find for this staggeringly large range of wines – and very successful at it too. This is a very personal selection and sticks resolutely to its strengths: Trevor is a Burgundy, not a Bordeaux man, he has his own vineyard in Meursault, so perhaps there's no surprise in this bias. Though there's a nod to New Zealand, California and Australia, the really exciting choices are from the place Hughes knows best, France. There's no compromise either when it comes to the provenance of older bottles, of which there are many.

One gripe, however: we wish these list prices would include VAT. Quality being as good as it is at T & W, some of the wines are expensive: adding on VAT at the till will more than likely double the shock to the poor buyer. In all other respects, though, we feel Trevor Hughes is fairly kind to the wine lover (nice wines, huge selection). If a hefty thud on the doormat heralds the arrival of this list in the post, we advise you to find a comfy chair as soon as possible – long and leisurely perusal is essential.

Look out for

- Fabulous Clos St-Hune Riesling back to 1981 – plus other treasures from Alsace
- Magnums and jeroboams of burgundy, from Grands Echézeaux to Clos de Vougeot, Volnay and Pommard
- White burgundy vintages from today back to 1966
- Huet, Dagueneau and Château de Fesles from the Loire
- Delicious Austrian wines from premier estate Willi Opitz
- Burgundy's top reds from the Domaine de la Romanée-Conti
- Fine German wine from the Mosel, up to *Beerenauslesen* and Eiswein level.

Tanners Wines

Head office

26 Wyle Cop, Shrewsbury,	*Tel* (01743) 234500
Shropshire SY1 1XD	*Fax* (01743) 234501
4 St Peter's Square, Hereford HR1 2PG	*Tel* (01432) 272044
	Fax (01432) 263316
36 High Street, Bridgnorth, Shropshire WV16 4DB	*Tel* (01746) 763148
	Fax (01746) 763148
Severn Farm Enterprise Park, Welshpool,	*Tel* (01938) 552542
Powys SY21 7DF	*Fax* (01938) 556565

Email sales@tanners-wines.co.uk
Web site www.tanners-wines.co.uk

Open Mon–Sat 9–5.30 (times may vary between branches), Sun (Dec only) **Closed** Sun (exc. Dec), public holidays **Cards** Amex, Delta, MasterCard, Switch, Visa; personal and business accounts **Discount** 5% on 1 case if collected **Delivery** Free within 60-mile radius (min. 1 case); nationwide service available, charge £5.95, free for orders of £80+ **Glass hire** Free, charge for washing if necessary **Tastings and talks** Range of tastings available, phone for details

---

Resisting the temptation to absorb ourselves in the 'Rarities, Classics and Odds and Ends' list (Bordeaux favourites going back to the 1970s, Spanish Vega Sicilia in magnum, top Burgundy domaines Potel, Roumier, Faiveley and Rousseau), we started this review with a glimpse at the smaller wine regions of the world to see whether Tanners was still taking them as seriously as it always has. It is. This is where you can reliably come to seek out the likes of delicious Nemea red from Greece, La Cetto Mexican wines, sweet Alsace Gewurztraminer, precious Albariño from the Spanish Rías Baixas. Plus, new and underrated vineyards are targeted with a will to seek out as much bargain territory as possible.

It's also good to see that Tanners' old-fashioned classics and good old-fashioned service are still very much to the fore. Inviting *en primeur* offers still regularly arrive through our letter-box. 'We ensure that you pay approximately 10 per cent below the price of the wine when it finally reaches our shelves,' says managing director James Tanner, a promise that makes buying wine lying abroad very appealing.

The folk at Tanners are never happy with their list, however, and are always looking to improve it, which means they always move with the times, as the strengthening selection of 'bio conscious' wines proves. Marked with a small butterfly are products made either organically, biodynamically or from vineyards with these processes at heart but 'tempered by pragmatism'. It's pleasing but not surprising to see top practitioners such as Domaine Leflaive and Chandon de Brialles from Burgundy, and Château de Beaucastel and Chapoutier from the Rhône, heading up the selection. 'We don't cut corners on the range: we buy wines that are unconfected and have genuine fruit and interest. And we prefer wines from single domaines where we can be sure of provenance,' says James. No bulk-buying or bland stuff here then – nor any cheating on the bio front.

Tanners has recently created a 12,000-square-foot fully air-conditioned warehouse to hold its stocks; the company publishes seven newsletters a year; sends out biannual lists annotated with producer profiles and up-to-date regional details (wines are divided into regional sections, so you know where you're buying from) – and is working on a new web site. It also holds six major tastings annually, plus other bespoke events. As an all-round wine merchant it can't be faulted and we still think it is one of the best in the country.

Look out for

- Detailed burgundy listings with when-to-drink advice
- Saintsbury, Pepperwood Grove and Cuvaison Pinot Noir from California
- Top Australian whites Petaluma Chardonnay, Shaw & Smith Sauvignon and Mitchell Riesling
- Delicious white Bordeaux, plus reds from the affordable (Lilian-Ladouys) to the illustrious (Margaux and Latour)
- Super-Tuscan Ornellaia, Sandrone Barolos and Isole e Olena from Italy
- Sumptuous, sweet Hungarian Tokajis from the Royal Tokay Wine Company
- Full, unabashed, unadulterated glorious Mosel Rieslings from perennially unfashionable Germany.

Tesco Stores

Head office
Tesco House, PO Box 18, Delamare Road,   *Tel* (01992) 632222
Cheshunt, Hertfordshire EN8 9SL

Customer service line   *Tel* (0800) 505555
(655 branches nationwide)   *Email* customer.service@tesco.co.uk
                                                              Web site www.tesco.com

Open Mon–Sat 8–6/10, Sun, public holidays 10–4 (times vary between stores – many
open 24 hours) **Closed** 25 & 26 Dec, 1 Jan, Easter Sun **Cards** Amex, Delta, Diners,
MasterCard, Switch, Visa **Discount** 5% on 6+ bottles **Delivery** Available within 20-
minute journey time of local store, charge £5 **Glass hire** Available, phone for details
Tastings and talks In-store tastings; other events through wine adviser service (25
stores), phone for details

We umm'ed and ahh'ed our way through the Spring 2001 tasting laid on by
Britain's most successful grocer. There was nothing wrong with the wines
on offer, classy or otherwise, nor with those we'd never tasted before. But …
there was little that had us jumping up and down, keen to rush back to the
computer to bash out words of praise about Tesco.

Success has its price. The sheer scale of the company means that it must
pursue wineries that are capable of supplying wine in quantity. Certain
countries, particularly those from the New World, are geared up for Tesco-
sized operations, and can back up the large volumes with money for the
promotions that every supermarket seems to need these days. However,
finding a winery elsewhere capable of providing thousands of cases of
consistent, reasonable-quality wine that can sell at £4.99 and then be
discounted to £3.99 for two months of the year is far more of a challenge.
We struggle to get excited about most of Tesco's southern French range in
particular.

Of course Tesco isn't alone in having difficulty finding European
suppliers capable of delivering quantity and quality. It is, though, still alone
in having one of its buyers, Master of Wine Phil Reedman, stationed in
Adelaide, from where he is able to sniff out deals earlier than his UK-based
rivals, and the ranges from both Australia and New Zealand (also Phil's
remit) are the ones we'd point you to first, followed by the bottles from
Chile and South Africa, and the pricier wines from Italy and Bordeaux. If the
array of Australian wines in particular is too large to contemplate – in the
top stores it's over 100 wines – then try the wines sporting the *Finest** neck
collars. The idea behind *Finest** is to designate those own-label wines that
the company thinks are the, er, finest, and that customers can buy with
confidence. The Australian range merits the adjective; but wines in other
areas – parts of France (again) and Germany in particular – do not.

One of the best times of the year to buy wine at Tesco is in the annual
wine festival each April, when smaller parcels of more interesting wines hit
the shelves. You'll also find a wider range of serious clarets and burgundies
appearing in some stores, but once again, it's Phil's Australian selection that
we've enjoyed most out of past wine festival purchases and which holds the
most appeal for customers. A final word to Ritchie Blackmore fans. If you're
looking for something to drink while head-banging to *Smoke on the Water*,

Tesco now offers an Argentinian wine called Deep Purple Shiraz. Just be careful you don't let your hair dangle in your glass though.

Look out for

- Australian range including Chapel Hill, Provenance and Tim Adams
- New Zealand wines from Jackson Estate, Montana and Millton
- Errázuriz, Cono Sur and MontGras from Chile
- Clarets from Lilian Ladouys, Maucaillou and Haut-Chaigneau in the top stores
- Chianti from Badia a Coltibuono and Selvapiana
- Fairview, Kanonkop and Thandi from South Africa.

Thresher Wine Shops

Head office

First Quench, Enjoyment Hall, Bessemer Road,   *Tel* (01707) 387200
Welwyn Garden City, Hertfordshire AL7 1BL   *Fax* (01707) 387416
(2,400 retail outlets nationwide)   *Web site* www.bottomsup.co.uk

Open Mon–Fri, Sun, public holidays 10–10, Sat 10am–10.30pm **Closed** 25 Dec **Cards** Amex, Delta, MasterCard, Switch, Visa; personal and business accounts **Discount** Available, phone for details **Delivery** Free within 10-mile radius (min. 1 case); nationwide service available, phone for details of charges **Glass hire** £5 per case deposit **Tastings and talks** Available locally on request; in-store tastings at weekends in Bottoms Up and Wine Rack **(£5)**

Last year we felt the dust had still not settled on the Thresher–Victoria Wine merger, and we were right. The last 12 months have seen even further rationalisation and change, with 3,000 outlets trimmed to 2,400 and, as of October 2000, new ownership by Nomura International. The First Quench group now comprises **Thresher**, where you can pick up your everyday bottles; The almost identical **Victoria Wine** (so similar that it is scheduled to disappear soon); **Wine Rack** for a more expensive range; and **Bottoms Up**, the same again, but with better-looking stores.

We think the range of wines chosen looks very healthy, considering these upheavals. While the 'R' word – rationalisation – might seem a harbinger of generic Chardonnay and dodgy red blends, we're pleased to see that many interesting wines are still on offer. Sub-£10 Bordeaux has a strong presence, with plenty of the reliable names to choose from. We still like the champagne range – although we can't see as many older vintages listed as we used to – and we're still impressed by the Australian, New Zealand, Chilean, South African and Argentinian selections, although in the first of these there's a noticeable dependence on the Southcorp stable. There are pockets of real inspiration, such as affordable burgundies from La Chablisienne and Louis Jadot, an educational range of New World sparkling and top-notch Chilean wines from Errázuriz, Cono Sur and Casa Lapostolle. Pricing is extremely reasonable and the accessibility of these wines is further enhanced by a twice-yearly, colourful, well-set-out wine list, easy on the eye and a pleasure to browse. Communications guru at Thresher, Jonathan Butt, tells us that customers are wanting 'more red and more Australian'. This could be why the focus is strong in both these areas and still weak on

407

Germany and California. Maybe now all that buy-out buzz has subsided, however, the sourcing team will look to enliven things even further. Perhaps too they'll rely less on the dependable big growers and more on the characterful, smaller ones. We'll be watching.

Look out for

- Reliable Australian wines from Rosemount, Penfolds and Wynns
- Rounded ripe Beaujolais – the real stuff, from the top villages; Duboeuf's are excellent
- Champagne favourites: Taittinger, Veuve Clicquot, Perrier-Jouët and Mumm
- Superb New Zealand Chardonnays from Te Mava, Church Road and Villa Maria
- New classics from Argentina: try wines from the Bonarda, Malbec and Torrontés grapes
- Bulgaria, Hungary and Romania: fruity varietal wines at low, low prices.

Turville Valley Wines

The Firs, Potter Row, Great Missenden,   *Tel* (01494) 868818
Buckinghamshire HP16 9LT   *Fax* (01494) 868832
                              Email chris@turville-valley-wines.com
                              Web site www.turville-valley-wines.com

Open Mon–Fri 9–5.30 **Closed** Sat, Sun, public holidays **Cards** None accepted
Discount Not available **Delivery** Nationwide service available (min. order £300),
charged at cost **Glass hire** Not available **Tastings and talks** Not available

Turville's aim is to dare to be different; to offer wines that are hard to find elsewhere – so if you ever find yourself in Great Missenden on a weekday, with a hankering for a bottle of Domaine de la Romanée-Conti, you'll be in luck. This is, undoubtedly, a classic selection of wines. Fine Bordeaux, madeiras and ports from past vintages, Sauternes back to 1967 and the most fabulous range from Burgundy's Romanée-Conti; plus Super-Tuscans, top Alsace and Penfold's Grange going back to 1979. We think you will find these wines elsewhere (Farr Vintners, q.v., for example), but few other merchants offer such an elite selection with such personal service.

Turville have recently seen a swing in customer preference towards burgundy, California and top Australian wines. Looking at the prices, we're sure this swing won't have been caused by increased affordability. All we can say is, costs here are commensurate with quality, and however it is that Michael Rafferty manages to get hold of these precious allocations of 'the greats', we're well impressed.

Look out for

- Opus One vintages back to 1981, plus 'impossible to find' Harlan Estate, Screaming Eagle and Dominus, all from California
- Top port houses, Taylor, Fonseca, Warre and Dow, from fine old vintages dating back to 1945
- Bordeaux from Mouton-Rothschild to Troplong-Mondot … big names and big vintages

- Guigal, Château de Beaucastel, Chave and Chapoutier from the Rhône
- Odds and ends by the bottle, including Errázuriz Syrah from Chile, South African Pinot Gris from Fairview and Sicilian Merlot from Planeta – showing a shrewd eye for anything 'interesting'
- Vega Sicilia vintages from Spain.

Uncorked

Exchange Arcade, Broadgate, London EC2 3WA

Tel 020-7638 5998
Fax 020-7638 6028
Email drink@uncorked.co.uk
Web site www.uncorked.co.uk

Open Mon–Fri 10–6.30 **Closed** Sat, Sun, public holidays **Cards** Amex, Delta, Diners, MasterCard, Switch, Visa; personal and business accounts **Discount** Available, phone for details **Delivery** Free within EC2; nationwide service available, charge £8.50 + VAT, free for orders of £150 **Glass hire** Free with order **Tastings and talks** Regular and tailored tastings **£5**

At some merchants, you feel that time has stood still. Not at Uncorked. As manager/buyer Jim Griffen says, 'Month to month, the emphasis changes completely. This never allows anyone – including staff – to become bored.' Whatever is this month's 'thing' at this central London shop, we can assure you that the quality will be of the highest order, since this is one of those rare merchants that pursues excellence regardless of region. You might find an opening offer of the latest vintages from the Rhône or Burgundy, the latest arrivals from in-demand producers from Australia or Italy, or maybe a parcel of mature Bordeaux that Jim has managed to pick up. He reckons he lists more than 350 *new* wines each year – some companies' entire range isn't so large. One thing that does remain constant is the enthusiasm for wine shown by the staff. Jim tells us that many customers come especially for the advice given; a wise move, since not everything on offer is a household name. Even so, he admits that the quality of the wines 'makes the rest easy'. You don't have to be a Londoner to take advantage of this exceptional range. Every couple of months there are lively newsletters (a recent one featured 'great wines, nerdishly sensible prices') to keep customers in touch with new arrivals and forthcoming tastings. With free delivery for orders over £150, what are you waiting for?

Look out for
- Benfield & Delamere, Isabel and Neudorf from New Zealand
- Exhaustive selection of fine burgundies
- Rhône reds from Gerin, Beaurenard and Brusset
- Top Piedmont estates such as Bruno Rocca, Paolo Scavino and Domenico Clerico
- Rare California offerings such as Behrens & Hitchcock, Brewer-Clifton and Neyers
- Lubiana, Fox Creek and Metier from Australia.

Unwins

Head office

Birchwood House, Victoria Road, Dartford,   *Tel* (01322) 272711
Kent DA1 5AJ   *Fax* (01322) 294469
(451 branches throughout southern England)   *Email* info@unwins.co.uk
                                                                                      Web site www.unwins.co.uk

Open Mon–Sat 10–10, Sun, public holidays 11–10 (varies between stores) **Closed** 25 Dec
Cards Amex, Delta, Diners, MasterCard, Switch, Visa; personal and business accounts
Discount 10% on 1 mixed case, 5% on 6 mixed bottles **Delivery** Free within 10-mile
radius of local store **Glass hire** Free with order **Tastings and talks** Available, phone
for details

In the wake of the 2000 takeover of Fullers, we were rather bullish about
Unwins, feeling that the traditionally rather stolid range had benefited
enormously from the addition of some ex-Fullers' wines. Then we attended a
press tasting in October 2000 which did the company no favours whatsoever.
There were very few wines which weren't readily available elsewhere and a
handful which really shouldn't have been available anywhere at all… Cut to
Spring 2001, when 41 new Italian wines suddenly appear, with precious few
duds among them. Will the real Unwins please stand up?

Examine the new Italian range more closely and you begin to get a
clearer picture of the company. The wines may be good, but they are for the
most part 'safe', so you won't find funky Friuli whites or new-wave
Piedmont reds. The buyers visited Italy 'several' times in putting the range
together, but really there's very little here that couldn't have been assembled
with a handful of UK phone numbers.

The safeness continues throughout most of the range, especially now
that some of the more interesting wines which were around after the merger
have disappeared from the shelves. For example, BRL Hardy, Southcorp
and Beringer Blass provide the bulk of the Australian wines, while Gallo,
Fetzer, Wente, Blossom Hill and Mondavi between them supply virtually
everything from California.

Sparks of originality can be found, such as the trio of reds from Pic St-
Loup, and the selections from the Loire and South Africa. And Bordeaux
fans will find a large selection of claret, with several classed-growth wines
available by the bottle at very attractive prices. A look at the rather
pedestrian burgundies brings you back down to earth, however. Buying
claret is easy – all you need is a shopping list of châteaux. Buying burgundy
is more of a challenge, and it's one that the Unwins' buyers have still not
addressed with gusto.

Servicing 451 shops (with some of the friendliest staff on the high street)
constricts the choice of wines available, and we also appreciate that this
family-owned chain sets great store by its long-term relationships with
suppliers. However, this isn't the most inspiring wine range around, and
we'd like to see the Unwins buying team exercising its considerable buying
muscle far more widely.

Look out for

- Keen prices on classy claret
- Spice Route, Beyerskloof and Clos Malverne from South Africa

- Vacheron, Pinard and des Forges in the Loire
- Italian range featuring Feudi di San Gregorio, Villa Cafaggio and Planeta
- Kiwi whites from de Redcliffe, Kumeu River and Sacred Hill
- Argentinian reds from Norton, Catena and Lurton.

Valvona & Crolla Ltd

Regional Award Winner – Scotland

19 Elm Row, Edinburgh EH7 4AA

Tel 0131-556 6066
Fax 0131-556 1668
Email sales@valvonacrolla.co.uk
Web site www.valvonacrolla.com

Open Mon–Wed, Sat 8–6, Thur, Fri 8–7.30 **Closed** Sun, 25 & 26 Dec, 1 & 2 Jan **Cards** Amex, Delta, MasterCard, Switch, Visa **Discount** 7.5% on 1–3 cases, 10% on 3+ cases **Delivery** Free within Edinburgh City (min. order £30); nationwide service available, charged at cost **Glass hire** Free with order **Tastings and talks** Available, phone for details

Anyone judging the wine range from this Edinburgh institution on the second half of its list alone would think that this was a good (but not great) place to buy decent bottles from around the world. Enthusiasts of wines from New Zealand, Australia and California should be especially happy, as should those with a penchant for Château d'Yquem – there are eight vintages on offer. The range of malt whiskies, running into hundreds, is impressive too. However, the main event here – as it has been since Benedetto Valvona set up shop in Edinburgh in the 1860s – is all matters Italian. In 1934, the business moved to its current premises, and Benedetto's son went into partnership with Alfonso Crolla, grandfather of current managing director, Philip Contini. Philip's *modus operandi* is 'work long hours and make customers happy', and the many awards that Valvona & Crolla wins for both food and wine show that his efforts are amply rewarded. Where wine is concerned, if it's good and Italian, you'll probably find it here, maybe hidden among the 17 Brunellos, 40 Chiantis and 51 Barolos. There is everything from a simple, juicy Veneto Merlot at £4.99 to double magnums of 1982 Gaja Barbaresco at £1,999. If you ever get bored with the wine – and you won't – there is the astonishing deli. And if while you shop you hear the strains of Neapolitan songs hanging in the air, it's probably Philip stretching his vocal chords. His face is never short of a smile, but if you buy a copy of his debut CD *Santa Lucia Luntana*, it will break into a broad grin.

Look out for

- The best selection of Italian wine in the UK
- Ridge, St Francis & Bonny Doon from California
- New Zealand wines from Mount Riley, Fromm and Kim Crawford.

Specialist and Regional Award Winners are listed on pages 12–15.

Helen Verdcourt Wines

Spring Cottage, Kimbers Lane, Maidenhead,   *Tel* (01628) 625577
Berkshire SL6 2QP

Open Daily all hours, phone first to check   **Cards** None accepted; personal and
business accounts   **Discount** Available, phone for details   **Delivery** Free within
Buckinghamshire & Berkshire; nationwide service available (min. 1 case), charged at cost
Glass hire Free   **Tastings and talks** Monthly tastings and talks for 3 wine clubs **£5**

If you are thinking of setting up in the wine business, draw inspiration from
Helen Verdcourt. She's been running her own wine business single-handed
since she acquired her WSET Diploma in 1978, and has assembled a range
which puts many larger companies to shame. She stocked burgundies from
Vincent Girardin long before he attained his current fame, and has been a
fan of Rhône wines since well before their current popularity. The choices
from Italy, Spain, Chile and Australia are also particularly noteworthy, but
wherever you look on the neat little list, you will find high-quality,
interesting wines from all the major wine-producing regions. Most fall in the
£5 to £15 range, but there are occasional forays into more expensive territory
for the likes of Ridge Montebello, the Super-Tuscan Camartina and Rostaing
Côte-Rôtie. Look on the back cover of the list and you'll see the three venues
where Helen gives her monthly tastings, as well as details of the tours she
occasionally runs to wine regions. Truly a small but perfectly formed
merchant.

Look out for
- Châteauneuf from Janasse, Pégaü and Les Cailloux
- Pervini, Paternoster and Librandi from southern Italy
- Spanish reds from Muga, Abadia Retuerta and Mauro
- Extensive selection of good-value Chilean wines
- Classy South African fare courtesy of Jordan, Clos Malverne and
  Simonsig
- Fine Australian offerings from Evans & Tate, Rockford and Bremerton.

Victoria Wine

see Thresher

La Vigneronne

Regional Award Winner – London

105 Old Brompton Road, London SW7 3LE	*Tel* 020-7589 6113
	Fax 020-7581 2983
	Email lavig@aol.com
	Web site www.lavigneronne.co.uk

Open Mon–Fri 10–8, Sat 10–6 **Closed** Sun, public holidays **Cards** Amex, Delta, Diners, MasterCard, Switch, Visa; personal and business accounts **Discount** Available, phone for details **Delivery** Free within 1-mile radius; nationwide service available, charge £10 per order, free for orders of £250+ **Glass hire** Not available **Tastings and talks** Twice-weekly and in-store tastings **(£5)**

A merchant run by adventurers, for adventurers. If you think you just about understand Bordeaux; you're baffled by, but have a general comprehension, of Burgundy; but you just can't get a grip on the many and varied wines coming out of southern France, then La Vigneronne is the place to come. Mike and Liz Berry have been sourcing interesting wine for their cheery 'local shop' on the Old Brompton Road for over 20 years now. They're well and truly *au fait* with the region (so much so that they now live there) and their list reflects their passion, knowledge and enthusiasm for all things Mediterranean. Cahors, Cevennes, Costières de Nîmes, Coteaux l'Ardèche, Lubéron, Jura, Madiran, Marmandais and Roussillon… they're all there. And soon, we suspect, to be joined by Liz and Mike's own wine.

Delving into the South is thoroughly to be recommended, but as Michael Warlow, running the shop in London, points out: 'Our customers are becoming increasingly adventurous, so we need to complement our strong speciality areas with fine wines from the rest of the world.' To this end, you can also pick up Grosset, Greenock Creek and De Bortoli wines from Australia; Arrowood, Shafer, Mondavi and Ridge from the States; plus top-notch Rhône, burgundy and champagne these days too. And that's just for starters.

At La Vigneronne they like to keep things many and varied – bringing in small batches of wine as and when they can get them; so you have to be on your toes to get hold of what you want. As well as the twice-weekly customer tastings, there are plenty of bottles open in the shop to sample and help your choice, but we advise you to buy then and there rather than relying on the twice-yearly lists. Wait for these and you'd be too late. Regular (three- to four-weekly) newsletters also help, and are more likely to deliver available goods! We have in front of us La Vigneronne's Fine and Rare list for March 2001, leading with Alsace Rieslings going back to 1982; we also have their 1999 Rhône offer and a list of April and May tastings, starting with a blind session of Pinot Noirs and a vertical selection of Savennières from Nicolas Joly going back to 1983. Thing don't get less mainstream and less commercial than this, so it's worth the attention. Intrepid wine travellers welcome!

Look out for

- Classic Mourvèdres from Bandol producers La Bégude, Tempier, Tardieu-Laurent and Lafron-Veyrolles
- Palette Blanc, Rosé and Rouge from fairy-tale Château Simone

- Mas de Daumas Gassac from the early days (1980) up until *en primeur* today
- Strange, old Spanish fortified wines (Solera Priorata from 1865), plus old ports and madeiras aplenty
- Claret and burgundy from top châteaux, domaines and vintages
- One of the country's best and most comprehensive selections of delicious Alsace wines.

Villeneuve Wines

1 Venlaw Court, Peebles EH45 8AE

Tel (01721) 722500
Fax (01721) 729922

82 High Street, Haddington EH41 3ET

Tel (01620) 822224
Fax (01620) 822279

49A Broughton Street, Edinburgh EH1 3RJ

Tel 0131-558 8441
Fax 0131-558 8442

Email wines@villeneuvewines.com
Web site www.villeneuvewines.com

Open (Peebles) Mon–Sat 9–8, Sun 12.30–5.30 (Haddington) Mon–Thur 10–7, Fri 10–8, Sat 9–8 (Edinburgh) Mon–Thur 10–10, Fri & Sat 9–10, Sun 1–8 **Closed** Sun (Haddington); 25 & 26 Dec, 1 & 2 Jan **Cards** MasterCard, Switch, Visa; personal and business accounts **Discount** 5% on 1 mixed case **Delivery** Free within 20-mile radius (min. 1 case); nationwide service available, charge £6, free for orders of £100+ **Glass hire** Free **Tastings and talks** Available on request **£5**

While many merchants are reporting a swing back towards European wines, the founder, director and buyer of Villeneuve, Kenneth Vannan tells us that his customers continue to clamour for New World wines. 'Central Otago Pinot Noir and Chardonnays from Napa and Carneros are being seen as better value than burgundy, whilst Chilean and South African wines are replacing Bordeaux.' This may be so, but we find it hard to fault his European range. From France, there's no shortage of claret, some decent growers tucked in among the burgundies, and some lovely Rhône reds. There are also good selections from Spain and Portugal, and few can better his range of Italian wines. However, Ken's prowess at wheedling out new and interesting wines really only comes to the fore once you hit the New World section. The Australian and South African bottles are a healthy mix of the familiar and the less familiar, while the New Zealand selection sees a welcome representation from the up-and-coming Central Otago region. Arguably the best selection is that from California, where Ken has cherry-picked from the ranges of several UK wholesalers (notably the Wine Treasury, q.v.), and then added in several of his own discoveries. We'll be watching out for further new arrivals from other countries in the coming months. In the meantime, we recommend a trip to one of the three shops. And while you're there, ask why the company logo is a rather disturbing-looking rooster.

Look out for

- Italian wines from Vajra, Fontodi, Planeta and Jermann
- California wines from MacRostie, Wild Hog, Truchard and Pecota

- Familiar Australian offerings, plus the less-famous Prince Albert, Stringy Brae and Parker Estate
- Central Otago wineries Felton Road, Mount Difficulty and Mount Edward
- Southern French wines from Trévallon, Puech-Haut and Clos Guirouilh
- Lebanese wines from Musar, Ksara and Kefraya.

Vin du Van Wine Merchants

Colthups, The Street, Appledore, Kent TN26 2BX

Tel (01233) 758727
Fax (01233) 758389

Open Mon–Fri 9–5 **Closed** Sat, Sun, public holidays **Cards** Delta, MasterCard, Switch, Visa **Discount** Not available **Delivery** Free within 10-mile radius (min. 1 case); nationwide service available (min. 1 case), charge £5.95 per order **Glass hire** Free **Tastings and talks** Not available

It is ten years now since ex-art director Ian Brown established Vin du Van and began selling 'unusual, rare, odd, quirky, esoteric and sometimes weird wines from all over Australia'. His latest list shows that it is very much business as usual, which means that you'll find the most extensive range of Down Under wines we know of, all described in a manner that has to be seen to be believed. For example, 1998 Chatsfield Mount Barker Shiraz – 'It was with a cautious nostril that we drifted in the direction of the "Up Up and Away" cesspool tanker. The doner kebab flagging us down belonged to our old chum Iggy Pilchard, frontperson with The Fish, and the driving force behind those loon-panted icons of progressive rock, the Jolly Jam Tarts …' Half a page later, those looking for actual information on said wine will be none the wiser, although they will probably have smiles on their faces. If the day-glo purple prose isn't to everyone's liking, the selection of wine will be. Anyone bored with the same old Australian names appearing on shelves up and down the UK should pore through Ian's range. Yes, the well-known producers are all here (although you won't find many of their cheaper offerings). But they are joined by much less widely seen wines from the likes of Bass Phillip, Nicholson River, Apsley Gorge, Mount Mary, The McAlister and Yeringberg. Add in a smattering of New Zealand reds and whites, and you have a superb selection which will rekindle the passions of anyone with Antipodean ennui. In Ian's own inimitable words, 'Break out the first aid kit Doris.'

Look out for

- The finest selection of Australian wines in the UK.

For an explanation of the symbols used at the top of some of the merchant entries, see page 303.

Vinceremos Wines & Spirits

19 New Street, Leeds LS18 4BH

Tel 0113-205 4545
Fax 0113-205 4546
Email info@vinceremos.co.uk
Web site www.vinceremos.co.uk

Open Mon–Fri 9–5.30, Sat (Dec only)   **Closed** Sat (exc. Dec), Sun, public holidays **Cards** Amex, Delta, MasterCard, Switch, Visa; business accounts   **Discount** 5% on 5–9 cases, 10% on 10+ cases   **Delivery** Nationwide service available (min. 1 mixed case), charge £5.95 per order, free for 5+ cases   **Glass hire** Free with order   **Tastings and talks** Available, phone for details **£5**

'I've always said that, whether or not it remains newsworthy, sustainable agriculture (and of course viticulture) is here to stay. It simply has to be,' says Jem Gardener, which is why Vinceremos was developed to promote and sell wines made with all possible kindness to the environment. (Not that vines as a monoculture are damaging in themselves – they've been grown on the banks of the Mosel in Germany for over 2,000 years to delicious effect; but the amount of pesticide, herbicide and artificial fertiliser over recent years has weakened many vineyards, and many wines.) Everything on the Vinceremos list is either officially organic, biodynamic, or made with holistic vineyard management in mind.

If all this sounds a bit wacky to you, think again. We strongly suspect there's a link between organic practices and brighter, fresher, cleaner grape flavours, and Jem's list gives us no reason to doubt our theory. A range of delicious Alsace, Australian and New Zealand wines bears positive witness. The Loire Valley, the Rhône and France's Mediterranean south are also strengths. For doubters or the faint-hearted, quotes and commendations from major press columnists are listed next to each wine. And if these aren't objective enough, then the increasing number of growers who are putting their chemistry sets away ought to be evidence enough.

Jem mentions that it's hard to get hold of organic and biodynamic wines these days, such is the demand. But this is not why he doesn't list wines of the most famous biodynamic proponents – Leflaive, Domaine Leroy and Dominique Lafon – it's because he simply can't sell burgundy. And Vinceremos wines stick resolutely around the £5 mark, because that's where customers like them.

Vinceremos also indicates whether or not a wine is suitable for consumption by vegetarians and vegans. Most of them are, but for those worried about the use of isinglass, gelatine or egg white for clarification, growers who don't use these are highlighted. Sulphur is near-essential in winemaking, and a natural part of wine, but growers who strive to use as little as possible are also noted.

Vinceremos is also proud supplier of wine to a new organically based restaurant in Leeds, The Mill Race, and to 'Org' – a new juice-bar and deli. It also supplies organic olive oil, juices and cordials, gin, rum, grappa and vodka. For those who are interested, Vinceremos started up in 1985 selling Russian vodkas from a bedroom; the name coming from the Spanish *venceremos* – we shall overcome.

Look out for

- Delicious Millton Vineyard varietals (for example, Riesling, Chardonnay, Chenin) and Richmond Plains Pinot from New Zealand
- Top Vouvray Le Haut Lieu Sec from Loire grower Gaston Huet
- Much-lauded Côtes du Rhône reds from Cave la Vigneronne Villedieu, Jacques Frélin and Domaine de la Grande Bellane
- Organic champagne from José Ardinat
- Superb range of organic Italian wine – Chianti, Barolo, Soave and Bardolino
- Penfolds organic wines from Australia
- Cider, port and English country wine (the likes of blackcurrant, elderflower, elderberry): all organic.

El Vino

Head office

Vintage House, 1–2 Hare Place, Fleet Street, London EC4Y 1BJ	*Tel* 020-7353 5384 *Fax* 020-7936 2367
Alban Gate, 125 London Wall, London EC2Y 5AP	*Tel* 020-7600 6377 *Fax* 020-7600 7147
6 Martin Lane, Cannon Street, London EC4R 0DP	*Tel* 020-7626 6876 *Fax* 020-7621 0361
30 New Bridge Street, London EC4V 6BJ	*Tel* 020-7236 4534 *Fax* 020-7489 0041 *Web site* www.elvino.co.uk

Open Mon–Fri 8.30am–10pm **Closed** Sat, Sun, public holidays **Cards** Amex, MasterCard, Visa **Discount** Not available **Delivery** Nationwide service available, charge £8.90 for up to 1 case, £9.90 for 1–2 cases, free for 2+ cases; £3 within EC1–EC4 and WC2 (1–2 cases) **Glass hire** Not available **Tastings and talks** Available, phone for details

By the time you read this, El Vino will have just about completed its hundred-and-twenty-second year of trading. This is the oldest wine merchant in the City of London, set up in 1879 by Alfred Bower, and still run by the same, founding family – now the Mitchells. The greatest thing about El Vino is its four Tasting Houses – all in the City, and all with a Dickensian air, they each capture the essence of London past. The newest 'El Vino' bar is in Alban Gate, the oldest, 'The Old Wine Shades' in Martin Lane, even pre-dates the 1666 Great Fire and frequently hosted Dickens himself – as well as smugglers surfacing from its tunnel to the river. And this (though exciting enough) is about as exciting as it gets. We're not going to be churlish about the claret selection – as befits a classic old merchant, it's very respectable, with one or two interesting older vintages too. And we're also not going to moan about the own-label wines: much as we'd like to know more about the growers, we know that what's in the glass is invariably of very good quality. But we think El Vino should really try and keep up with modern times. Of the 170 wines listed, only two come from California, and three from South Africa. Australia fares a little better, but on the whole, there's more emphasis on traditional port, sherry, German hock and moselle, and, of course, madeira. The special offers on the twice-yearly chatty newsletter are a little more adventurous, but we'd like to see more!

Look out for

- El Vino Tasting Houses – to sample wine and to dine
- Well-priced, village-quality Beaujolais
- Delicious choices from Burgundy – not least Clos de Tart from Mommessin
- Bordeaux: top châteaux listings including Latour, Lynch-Bages and Pichon-Lalande
- 1970 and 1977 port.

Vino Vino

Freepost SEA5662, New Malden, Surrey KT3 3BR   *Tel* (07703) 436949
Fax 020-8942 4003
Email vinovino@appleonline.net

Open Mon–Sun 8–8 **Cards** Delta, MasterCard, Switch, Visa **Discount** Not available
Delivery Free nationwide (min. 1 case) **Glass hire** Not available **Tastings and talks**
Not available **£5**

Derek Dornan has a fine history in wine indeed. He started vinous life working at Oddbins, progressed to The Winery (q.v.) and three years ago set up his own specialist mail-order business focusing on Italian wine. And what wines! His selection is as stunning as it is comprehensive and luxurious. And all from one country – well, two: there's now a new list from Spain as well.

Vino Vino has taken off on the basis that Italy is 'a great wine-producing country, producing every wine style imaginable, yet poorly represented in the UK'. Derek's right, too. This, now, is one of the only places from which you can gain a thorough A-to-Z understanding of Italian in no time – as long as you are prepared to spend over £5 a bottle. We wouldn't say the wines are overly expensive, but these are all quality examples, representing the best of what Italy can do. Our list falls open at pages 30 to 33: Banfi, Ruffino and Frescobaldi; need we say more? In terms of Italy, poor representation is now a thing of the past.

And if you won't find better Italian wines anywhere, you'll also do worse than go to Vino Vino to get a grip on Spain. This list was born in early 2001 and, at the time of writing, charts around 100 wines. It'll grow 'as soon as more wines of character and quality are found'. What there is follows the principles of the Italian selection: good-quality producers and a range of wine styles (and prices) from each. This way you're given the chance to explore the full scope of the regions and the growers – whom you really can get to know, as no detail, whether tasting note, older vintage or property profile, is spared. Stick at Italy and Spain for now, Derek – we'd hate to see this sort of attention to detail diluted!

Look out for

- Barolo from Voerzio, Vietti, Pio Cesare and more
- Special allocations of superb 1997 Chiantis
- Forgotten whites from the Marches, the Islands and the South of Italy: Greco di Tufo, Verdicchio and Vermentino di Gallura
- Don't ignore them! Classic sweet wines Marsala, Passito di Pantelleria, and more
- Ribera del Duero Spanish reds from Protos and Pesquera
- Top Rioja *bodegas*, Muga, Bilbainas, Ondarre and others.

Vintage Roots

Farley Farms, Reading Road,
Arborfield, Berkshire RG2 9HT

Tel 0118-976 1999
Fax 0118-976 1998
Email info@vintageroots.co.uk

Open Mon–Fri 8.30–5.30, Sat (Dec only) **Closed** Sat (exc. Dec), Sun, public holidays
Cards Delta, MasterCard, Switch, Visa; personal and business accounts **Discount** 5% on
5+ cases **Delivery** Free within 30-mile radius (min. 6 btls); nationwide service available
(min. 6 btls), charge £4.95 for 1 case, £5.95 for 2–5 cases, free for 6+ cases **Glass hire** £1
deposit per glass **Tastings and talks** Available on request, phone for details **£5**

'We offer the largest range of organic and biodynamic wines available in the
UK,' says Neil Palmer. When he and his chums founded Vintage Roots back
in 1986, all they possessed was an Enterprise Allowance grant and a desire to
promote matters organic. At the time, not much was known about the
organic movement, and it was a struggle to find decent wines. Today,
however, organic wine producers are springing up all over the world, and
the Vintage Roots' list gets bigger each time we take a look at it. Every wine,
including those in the expanding own-label range, comes from producers
who are certified as organic or biodynamic (and if you don't know the
difference between the two categories, take a look at the informative list,
where you'll also discover what constitutes vegan or vegetarian wines). The
spectrum of wines on offer may not be as large as at a conventional
merchant, but you'd have to be extremely picky to notice any gaps. And if
you should tire of the wines, head for the organic beers, among which is
Cannabia, the original hemp beer – Home Office approved, of course.

Look out for
- Fizz from Fleury, Achard Vincent and Albet y Noya
- Spanish wines from Ijalba, Mas Igneus and Viña Urubi
- Clarets from Falfas, Haut-Nouchet and La Grave
- An Australian organic selection from Glenara, Penfolds, Botobolar and
  Thistle Hill
- Chile's first organic red from Agricola Miraflores
- Italian reds from Viberti, Buondonno and Ottomarzo.

Waitrose

Head office
Southern Industrial Area, Bracknell,   *Tel* (01344) 424680
Berkshire RG12 8YA   *Fax* (01344) 825211

Waitrose Wine Direct   *Tel* (0800) 188881
Freepost SW1647, Bracknell RG12 8HX   *Fax* (0800) 188888
(136 branches nationwide)   *Email* customer_service@waitrose.co.uk
      Web site www.waitrose.com

Open Mon–Sat 8.30/9–7/8/9, Sun 10/11–4/5 (times vary between stores) **Closed** 25 Dec,
1 Jan **Cards** Amex, Delta, MasterCard, Switch, Visa; personal and business accounts
Discount 5% on 6+ mixed bottles **Delivery** Nationwide service available (Waitrose
Direct), charge £4.95, free for orders of £75+ **Glass hire** Free, charge for breakages
Tastings and talks Available, phone for details **(£5)**

The range on offer at Waitrose is not quite what you'd expect from a
supermarket list really: this is top merchant stuff and more besides, with a
buying team led by four MWs. Even from the bargain-basement areas –
(often boring) Eastern Europe and the Mediterranean – the wines, though
few in number, are interesting, nice and cheap, and carefully chosen as
being something different. Reliable Domaine Boyar Merlot and Cabernet
blends from Bulgaria, for example, come in at £2.99 and £3.49 respectively.
Linden Tree Merlot from Macedonia is also £3.49 and is a good illustration of
buyers' confidence to branch out into the less-usual winemaking areas of the
world. Reach for the low price, but still pause and think, 'Carnelian/Merlot
from California, well that sounds curious', or visit the sparkling
wine section, where you can pick up a bottle of Paul Trudel Brut from France for
£3.99 and, from the same outlet, a case of 1989 Krug champagne for £1,020.

Big-name wines aren't just the usual offerings either. Penfold Grange
and Roxburgh Chardonnay are here, but so too are the likes of Amarone
della Valpolicella from Zenato, Italy and *grand cru* Clos de la Roche
burgundy from Armand Rousseau, with top wines listed from every
country. As with any good merchant there are *en primeur* offers – the
delicious 1999 red burgundies are new out as we write. How many
supermarkets could say the same?

In short, Waitrose is still the most exciting supermarket for wine in the
UK, and still surpasses many more specialist outlets for the breadth,
imagination and adventurousness of its selection. Even the low-alcohol
wines manage to look interesting (well, some of them), and half bottles and
bag-in-box choices take no quality short-cuts. Better, and trendier, the
organic range has expanded yet again. There were nine in 2000, 21 in 2001
and now we can report 27 fully organic wines on the Waitrose shelves.
California features strongly here, as does France; you can even pick up an
organic champagne.

No less attention to detail is spent on the excellent mail-order service.
This is the way to pick up a tasty sub-£40 mixed case, '12 for the price of 11',
full of fresh, characterful New World flavours, or go for a case of
Chardonnays or Summer Reds. So, no excuses that your nearest Waitrose is
miles away, just phone Waitrose Wine Direct and have your wines delivered
straight to your door.

Look out for

- The web site – another way to put in a quick, easy order
- Australia: try out Jindalee Shiraz from Victoria for a bargain bottle, or the Eileen Hardy classy version from McLaren-Padthaway
- Tasty top-end German choices: Wehlener Sonnenuhr from J J Prüm and Dr Loosen
- Pommard, Volnay, Clos de Tart and Corton-Charlemagne – there's no stinting on burgundy
- Bordeaux: great names from lesser years, Cheval Blanc and Haut Brion are perennially exceptional, even in 1997
- Fairview Viognier, Hamilton Russell Pinot Noir and Spice Route Merlot: the best on offer from South Africa
- Tignanello from Antinori: sophistication peaks with a Super-Tuscan!

Weavers of Nottingham

1 Castle Gate, Nottingham NG1 7AQ

Tel 0115-958 0922
Fax 0115-950 8076
Email weavers@weaverswines.com
Web site www.weaverswines.com

Open Mon–Sat 9–5.45 **Closed** Sun, public holidays **Cards** Amex, Delta, Diners, MasterCard, Switch, Visa; personal and business accounts **Discount** 5% on 5 cases, 10% on 10 cases **Delivery** Free nationwide (min. 6 bottles); charge for 1–6 btls £3.94 within 50-mile radius, otherwise at cost **Glass hire** 20p per dozen if delivered **Tastings and talks** Available, phone for details **£5**

Very much a family wine company this. Fourth-generation mum and dad, Di and Alan Trease, are directors, daughter Mary is in charge of sales, and son Philip is the marketing (and the web site) man. And very cheery it is too. From the lively brochure, full of snapshots and producer profiles, to the regular tastings at their elegant Georgian town house down the road, and the special list of reliable 'everyday drinking' bottles around £5, it's all ultra-accessible and friendly. Only thing is, we're still not that excited about the wines. Safe, and lacklustre, are words we've used in the past, and we're not so sure, this year, whether we can do any better. All the sensible names and *négociants* are there, and just about all the wine world's covered (albeit in some brevity), but the only real attention to detail seems to come in the whisky section. For what it's worth, though, Weavers has one of the best selection of Lebanese wines we've seen, and it also has an imaginative range of 'tasting packs' – boxes of 12 comprising everything from 'Mid-week drinking wines', to 'Around the world with a glass of red' and 'Classic Claret'. We really wish they'd put some of that abundant family energy into some more-enthusiastic wine buying!

Look out for

- A wide range of fruit spirits, liqueurs, flavoured vodkas and alcoholic cordials
- Whiskey and whisky, and an impressive range of single malts, plus ten individual cask bottlings
- Rhône Valley classics from Guigal, Vidal Fleury and Château la Nerthe

- Top Alsace wines from the Trimbach estate
- Champagne and sparkling wines from around the world, including sparkling red burgundy.

Whitebridge Wines

Unit 21, Whitebridge Estate, Stone, Staffordshire ST15 8LQ

Tel (01785) 817229
Fax (01785) 811181
Email sales@whitebridgewines.co.uk
Web site www.whitebridgewines.co.uk

Open Mon–Fri 9–5.30, Sat 9–1 **Closed** Sun, public holidays **Cards** Delta, MasterCard, Switch, Visa; personal and business accounts **Discount** Not available **Delivery** Free within 15-mile radius (min. 1 case); nationwide service available (min. 1 case), charge £5.99 + VAT per case (surcharge for Highlands & Islands) **Glass hire** Free **Tastings and talks** Regular tastings, phone for details **£5**

Francis Peel swears that it's not just the name that has prompted him to become agent for Western Australian producer Peel Estate. He also tells us that after 18 years in business, Whitebridge Wines is 'simply the best in the Midlands'. While we know of a number of other merchants in the area who might dispute this, the range certainly contains much of note. No one region could be called a speciality, but there are wines from most of the major regions and countries, plus a few from more unusual places, such as Bolivia, Mexico and Uruguay. We'd point you first of all to the selections from New Zealand and Australia, and then towards the wines from Italy, Burgundy, Champagne, Spain and Portugal. With the exception of a rather lacklustre range from Germany, the choices from elsewhere are mostly good, and the staff ('all wonderful') will happily guide you through anything that is less than familiar.

Look out for
- Champagne from Gosset, Devaux and Joseph Perrier
- Catamayor, La Concepción and Viña Casablanca from South America
- Burgundies from Billaud-Simon, Michel Bouzereau and Jacques Cacheux
- Pago de Carraovejas, Navajas and Castel del Remei in Spain
- Australian reds from Simon Hackett, Grant Burge and Peel Estate
- New Zealand reds from Te Motu, Ata Rangi and Rippon.

Wimbledon Wine Cellar

1 Gladstone Road, Wimbledon, London SW19 1QU *Tel* 020-8540 9979
Fax 020-8540 9399

84 Chiswick High Road, London W4 1SY *Tel* 020-8994 7989
Email enquiries@wimbledonwinecellar.com
Web site www.wimbledonwinecellar.com

Open Mon–Sat 10–9 **Closed** Sun, public holidays **Cards** Amex, Delta, MasterCard,
Switch, Visa; personal and business accounts **Discount** 10% on 1 mixed case **Delivery**
Free within Central, South & West London (min. order £100); nationwide service
available (min. order £100), charge £16.50 **Glass hire** 20p refundable deposit per glass
Tastings and talks In-store tastings, group tastings and talks; phone for details

Since taking over the old Chiswick Cellars shop in 2000, Andrew Pavli now
has two shops in London crammed to the gills with fine wine. If you're
interested in seeing what's on offer, don't look at the web site – in July 2001
it still showed the Spring 1998 releases from Ridge, and Andrew tells us that
it brings in very little business. And don't ring up for a list. 'We don't
produce one,' says Andrew. 'However, we keep records of all our good
clients, and we phone them regularly.' Personal service is very important for
this team, and their efforts seen to be amply rewarded. The average bottle
spend here is considerably higher than that at several better-known
merchants.

So what will you find? Australia, California, Alsace, Bordeaux, Burgundy,
the Rhône, Italy and Spain are listed as areas of speciality, and with around
2,000 wines available, this isn't an exaggeration. Since the range changes
almost daily, in the absence of a list it's difficult to give details of specific
wines – but Wimbledon Wine Cellar is often the only stockist in the UK for
some bottles, especially for those from Italy.

If Italy is your thing, then watch out in the future for details of a possible
new venture in Tuscany. Andrew has plans to buy some properties there
and use them both as holiday homes and as bases for wine trips. It's another
enterprising venture from an enterprising merchant, which deserves to be
much better known.

Look out for

- Fine Piedmont reds from Fontanafredda, E Pira and Voerzio
- Large range of clarets dating back to the 1960s
- Burgundies from Jadot, Louis Latour and many other producers
- Loire whites from Dézat, de Ladoucette and Cailbourdin
- Ridge, Qupé and Hitching Post from California
- Australian wines from Henschke, Cape Mentelle and Shaw & Smith.

For an explanation of the symbols used at the top of some of the
merchant entries, see page 303

Wine Cellar

Head office

Parisa Group, PO Box 476, Loushers Lane, *Tel* (01925) 454545
Warrington, Cheshire WA4 6RQ *Fax* (01925) 454546
(480 branches nationwide) *Email* david.vaughan@parisa.com
Web site www.winecellar.co.uk

Open Mon–Fri 10–10 (times may vary between stores) **Closed** Sat, Sun, public
holidays **Cards** MasterCard, Switch, Visa; business accounts **Discount** 10% on 1 case
Delivery Free within 10-mile radius; nationwide service available, charge £4.99 for up
to 1 case, free for 1+ cases **Glass hire** Free **Tastings and talks** Regular tastings,
phone for details

The 65 Wine Cellar shops form a small part of the Parisa Group. Other parts
of the company you may come across are **Booze Buster** (basic local off-
licences); **Parisa Café Bars**, of which there are now 16, serving decent food
along with 250 wines from the Wine Cellar range with a very low mark-up;
and, if you're in Manchester, **PerSia**, which puts the Café Bar concept into a
'Persian bazaar' setting. Why Persia? Simply because that's where Parisa's
chief executive and guiding light Nader Haghighi hails from.

While there's little of the Persian in the typical Wine Cellar branch, there
is a competent if rarely thrilling selection of wines. Other companies of
comparable size have several buyers, but for a number of years, the lion's
share of the buying duties at Wine Cellar has fallen to David Vaughan.
Having so much on his plate gives him less time to source hoards of
interesting wines, but we are also aware that the typical Wine Cellar still
doesn't attract quite the number of ABC1 customers that Haghighi had in
mind when he launched the first Wine Cellar stores in 1994. We gather that
many of the more interesting wines, which were bought in the early stages,
could still be found some years later gathering dust on shelves either in the
shops or in the warehouse.

The upshot is that well-known names dominate the range. Quality-wise,
there's nothing wrong with the wines, but this isn't the exciting place to buy
wine that we thought it may turn into when the stores first appeared. If
you're looking for a little more originality, it *can* be found. We'd point you
towards the reds from southern France, some of the mid-priced clarets and
some of the less-familiar Australian reds. We'd also recommend you keep an
eye on the special offers – the '20 per cent off any three bottles' campaign in
Spring 2001 was a very good deal.

Look out for

- Southern French reds from Coste Blanque, Temple and Villemajou
- Norton, MontGras and Villard from South America
- South African offerings – Clos Malverne, Jordan and Graham Beck
- Chalet, Jadot and Vallet Frères burgundies
- Viñas del Vero, Bagordi and Ochoa from Spain
- Australian range including Capel Vale, Cleveland and Grant Burge.

Wine Rack

see Thresher

Wine Raks (Scotland)

21 Springfield Road, Aberdeen AB15 7RJ

Tel (01224) 311460
Fax (01224) 312186
Email enq@wineraks.co.uk
Web site www.wineraks.co.uk

Open Mon–Sat 10–8, Sun (Dec. only), public holidays 12–6 **Closed** Sun (exc. Dec)
Cards Delta, MasterCard, Switch, Visa; business accounts **Discount** Available, phone
for details **Delivery** Nationwide service available, charge £2.50–£5 within 25-mile
radius, otherwise at cost (£8.80+) **Glass hire** Free with order **Tastings and talks** 2
major tastings per year, private tastings at cost

Ex-engineer Tariq Mahmood has always promoted his range with
enthusiasm, but over the last few years we've seen a marked improvement
in his choice of wines. Maybe the upturn can be traced back to the arrival of
ex-Adnams man Mike Corser in 1997; maybe not. Whatever the reason,
Wine Raks is now a very good place for Aberdonians (and those further
afield) to buy wine. The finest selection is that from Australia, where the 30-
odd producers include several less-familiar but nevertheless classy estates.
The New Zealand, South American and South African arrays include more
quality producers. In Europe, lovers of Italian, Spanish and German wines
will also find much to please them, while claret fans won't be disappointed
with the choice from vintages of the 1990s (and if the regular range doesn't
extend as far as you'd like, ask for the Fine and Rare Wines supplement).
You'll find decent wines elsewhere in the French list, but not at present to
the same depth – although we wouldn't be surprised if that hasn't changed
next time we take a look at Wine Raks. If developments continue at the
current rate, Tariq and Mike could soon be in the running for the Scottish
Merchant of the Year Award.

Look out for
- Loire wines from Gitton, Pellé and Chéreau Carré
- Good stocks of clarets from recent vintages
- Italian wines from Trappolini, Burlotto and Valchiaro
- Heymann-Lowenstein, Paul Anheuser and Schloss Johanissberger from
  Germany
- Boschendal, Steenberg and Clos Malverne from South America
- Lesser-known Australian estates such as Prentice, Milbrovale and
  Kangaroo Island.

The Wine Society

Gunnels Wood Road, Stevenage,
Hertfordshire SG1 2BG
(1 outlet in Hesdin, France)

Tel (01438) 740222
Fax (01438) 761167
Email memberservices@thewinesociety.com
Web site www.thewinesociety.com

Open Mon–Fri 8.30–9, Sat 9–2 **Closed** Sun, public holidays **Cards** Delta,
MasterCard, Switch, Visa **Discount** £1 on orders of 5+ cases **Delivery** Nationwide
service available, charge £4, free for 1+ cases or orders of £75+ **Glass hire** Free
Tastings and talks Over 70 tastings per year nationwide and in northern France

For the scale of this operation (well over 80,000 satisfied customers at the last count), we think this is a class act. Despite its necessary solidity, the Wine Society's widely sourced list still manages the odd foray into adventurousness. Take the Australia section for starters. As well as cheerful favourites, such as Penfolds Rawson's Retreat at pocket-friendly prices, mouthwatering Grosset Polish Hill Riesling and Piccadilly Chardonnay show up too. d'Arenberg's Ironstone Pressing (£17.50 a bottle) sits side-by-side with Wattles Grenache-Shiraz (£5.75) in the reds. From California, there's the same crop of chewy, chunky everyday wines, peppered with the likes of Ridge Lytton Springs Zinfandel, and top-quality Sanford and Saintsbury Pinot Noir. And so it goes on. The balance between workadays and classics is just right. Of course, as befits a merchant in its 128th year, there's plenty to be pleased about in the Bordeaux (traditional) section too. We do wish there was more burgundy; but then, maybe buyer Sebastian Payne MW is a claret man?

Maybe it's also a question of being able to supply those 80,000 … did we say customers? We meant shareholders/members. The Wine Society is in fact a very large co-operative, and if you want to buy its wine, you have to join. For a fee of £40, you become a member for life. This might seem a lot of money if all you wanted was to pick up a £4.50 bottle of Stormy Cape Chenin, but, again, if it works for those 80,000, it can't be that bad a deal. Bear in mind the advantages: access to some top-class wines including blue-chip classics that you can have stored in the Society's Members' Reserve cellar; regular tastings; mixed-case offerings (18 different selections to choose from, including one of half bottles); and a second showroom in France from which purchases can be made at French VAT and duty rates, with significant savings. All this for just a one-off payment you'll have forgotten about by Christmas – or, perhaps, be given as a Christmas present?

We like the appearance of the list better this year – the colour has improved greatly! And one other comment we feel we must add is that it's a relief to see a page devoted to rosé wine. Although they're not at all fashionable, we love them for drinking on a summer's day. In fact, we wish we had a glass to hand right now…

Look out for
- Bordeaux: châteaux Figeac, Gruaud-Larose, Pichons Baron and Lalande; vintage choices including 1982
- Bordeaux second labels: Réserve de la Comtesse, Ségla, Les Pagodes de Cos, for earlier drinking and less of a dent in your pocket

- Enticing French country wines; oddities such as Arbois Pinot Noir from the Jura
- Mouthwatering Italian choices: Selvapiana Chianti, Salice Salentino from Apulia, and many more
- A wide range of well-priced Chilean and Argentinian wines
- Daring to be different: English wines and a full range of delicious, top-class fino, amontillado and oloroso sherry.

The Wine Treasury

69–71 Bondway, London SW8 1SQ

Tel 020-7793 9999
Fax 020-7793 8080
Email jdoidge@winetreasury.com
Web site www.winetreasury.com

Open Mon–Fri 9.30–6.30 **Closed** Sat, Sun, public holidays **Cards** MasterCard, Visa; business accounts **Discount** Available, phone for details **Delivery** Nationwide service available (min. 1 case), charge £6, free for 2+ cases (England and Wales); for Scotland, phone for quote **Glass hire** Not available **Tastings and talks** Available on request, phone for details

We've noticed a general trimming of the range at The Wine Treasury in recent years. The Austrian whites have disappeared, as have the wines from Utah(!), and there are no longer quite as many burgundies as was once the case. However, we haven't noticed any reduction in quality, which remains resolutely high. The number one passion here is California, and the 23 wineries represented are among the finest in the state. You'll also find some excellent small Australian estates, some of the smartest names in Italy, and tidy offerings from all the major regions in France – so despite the more compact range, you won't have any problem assembling a mixed case. The Wine Treasury has never been known for its cheap prices – this is, after all, the company that offered 2000 Léoville-Barton *en primeur* at £95 per bottle – but you can reduce the pain to your wallet by joining the Syndicate. £60 a year may sound like a lot of money to join a customer club, but since it entitles you to discounts of around 25 per cent, and other special offers, it could be worth your while.

Look out for
- Rare California wines such as Blockheadia Ringnosii, Bacio Divino and Luna
- Penley, Paradise Enough and Stoney from Australia
- Burgundies from Chevillon, Drouin and Etienne Boileau
- Rhône range featuring excellent Côtes du Rhône (red and white) from Rocher
- Piedmont stars La Spinetta, Voerzio and Sandrone
- Superb Loire Chenin Blanc from Patrick Baudouin.

We love to hear your views on wine merchants. You can email your comments to us at: whichwineguide@which.net

The Winery

4 Clifton Road, Maida Vale, London W9 1SS

Tel 020-7286 6475
Fax 020-7286 2733
dmotion@globalnet.co.uk

Open Mon–Sat 11–9.30, Sun, public holidays 12–8 **Closed** 25 & 26 Dec, 1 Jan
Cards Delta, MasterCard, Switch, Visa; personal and business accounts **Discount** 5%
on 1 case **Delivery** Free within 2-mile radius (min. 1 case); nationwide service
available, charge £8.50 per case for 1–2 cases, free for 3+ cases **Glass hire** Free with
order **Tastings and talks** Weekly in-store tastings, wine course, phone for details **£5**

David Motion is more likely to be found dabbling among his Dolcettos than
at his music stand these days. Though he still keeps up lyrical appearances
working as a composer, his heart is more and more to be found in France or
Italy, or California – sourcing the next new addition to this expansive wine
list. Perhaps you'd expect it from a musician, but the end result is one of the
most imaginative ranges in this *Guide*.

As we've said before, David is only truly happy when he finds something
different and exclusive, so while quite a few of the upmarket Bordeaux,
Burgundy and Italian names are there, the most exciting choices are from
the names you might not have heard of before. Barolos come from Veglio,
Grimaldi and Alessandria, for example; St-Emilion Bordeaux from châteaux
Prieuré-Lescours, Bonnin and du Rivallon. Selection gets even braver from
Burgundy (where we're always told to watch our grower to get good
quality) with Chambolle and Vougeot from the much-criticised Sirugue
estate, now turning a new leaf; plus smaller growers such as Philippe
Jambon and Domaine Servin. Far from making us nervous, we're full of
admiration for this adventurousness, and are excited about the new wines to
be tried out.

What makes us even more confident about the risks taken at The Winery
is the ultra-talented staff David has on hand. Olivier Varichon is a qualified
winemaker, Vincent Barat is a skilled sommelier and Brice Mancelet has a
wealth of wine retail experience. In addition, top sommelier Catherine
Nicolas has been brought in to run regular wine courses at the shop. The
skills of this team not only afford invaluable advice to customers (not least in
food matching), but are also pooled to assist in the buying effort.

Since purchasing the shop in 1996, things have gone (and are going) from
strength to strength. More tastings (they're free on Saturdays), wine courses
and more wines are all on the cards, but space is needed to expand. David
tells us that two new properties he's had his eye on have fallen through
before completion. We hope it's third-time lucky for you David; but in the
meantime, we're happy to pick up our vinous prescriptions from the old
chemist's shop.

Look out for:

- Robert Sinskey's delicious, elegant wines from California, especially The
  Adventures of Commander Zinskey (the Zinfandel)
- Small-family Alsace wines from Mittnacht-Klack
- Stunning array of burgundies from the affordable to the illustrious, with
  plenty of fabulous 1996s among them

- Rare wines from top of Italy to the toe
- Unusual Rhône wines, from Condrieu to Cairanne, with classy Côte-Rôties among them
- Carefully selected range of right-bank Bordeaux from the impressive 1998 vintage.

Wines of Interest

46 Burlington Road, Ipswich, Suffolk IP1 2HS

Tel (01473) 215752
Fax (01473) 406622
Email woi@fsbdial.co.uk
Web site www.winesofinterest.co.uk

Open Mon–Fri 9–6, Sat 9–1 **Closed** Sun, public holidays **Cards** Delta, MasterCard, Switch, Visa; personal and business accounts **Discount** Available, phone for details **Delivery** Free within Suffolk, Norfolk, north Essex and Central London (min. 1 case); nationwide service available (min. 1 case), charged at cost **Glass hire** Free with order **Tastings and talks** Available, phone for details **£5**

'At Wines of Interest, we fly a flag for wines which impress with finesse rather than firepower.' Hear, Hear – we're in full agreement with the two Jonathans, Hare and Williamson, who took over WoI in June 2000. They've retained several of the principles of their predecessor Tim Voelcker, such as concentrating on quality, not being wooed by fancy names (no *grande marque* champagne, for example) and keeping the majority of wines well under the £10 mark. However, they've also found time to introduce new items, such as a selection of Austrian whites from Tscheppe. The range isn't huge, and there are some countries, such as Italy and Argentina, that get a slightly raw deal. Overall, however, we have few complaints.

Prior to taking over the business, Jonathan W had worked here for 14 years, and we're pleased to see that he's continued with the Sampling Club. Members pay £1.35 a month, and have the opportunity to buy a sample bottle of the red and white wines of the month for half price. Subsequent orders of the same wine can be bought that month at the 'sealed case' rate, usually five per cent off the normal price. The only thing we can't understand about this deservedly popular idea is why other merchants haven't followed suit.

Look out for
- Burgundies from Roux and Fourrier
- Albert Belle and Domaine de la Mordorée in the Rhône
- Mas Montel, Guillaume and Château de Peyrade from southern France
- Fine German wines from Leitz, Diel and Wolf
- Australian range featuring Grant Burge, Hollick and Mitchelton
- South African wines from Delheim, Wildekrans and Jordan.

For an explanation of the symbols used at the top of some of the merchant entries, see page 303

The Wright Wine Company

The Old Smithy, Raikes Road, Skipton,
North Yorkshire BD23 1NP

Tel (01756) 700886
Fax (01756) 798580
Email bob@wineandwhisky.co.uk
Web site www.wineandwhisky.co.uk

Open Mon–Sat 9–6, Sun (Dec only), public holidays 10–4 **Closed** Sun (exc. Dec)
Cards Delta, MasterCard, Switch, Visa; personal and business accounts **Discount** 5%
on 1 mixed case **Delivery** Free within 35-mile radius; nationwide service available
(min. 1 case), charged at cost **Glass hire** Free with order **Tastings and talks** Not
available **(£5)**

'Foot and mouth will cause the first downturn in sales in our 19 years of
trading,' said Bob Wright, early on in 2001. But that would be the only cause,
for the wines Bob supplies are, as ever, first rate.

This is still an encyclopaedic selection (though only the wine names are
printed, with nothing about them, so perhaps 'encyclopaedic' is not the
right word!). Australian reds extend from precious Penfolds Grange (not
badly priced, at only just over the £100 a bottle mark!) to Capel Vale West
Australian Merlot; South African whites include Jordan, Uitkyk and
Meerlust estate wines, plus many, many more. Burgundy also runs the
gamut, spanning a wide price range from £6 to £72 a bottle. The Alsace,
Champagne and Loire selections are pretty clever too – though we'd like to
see a few more stellar names among the clarets. The very useful list of over
150 half bottles is impressive. Overall, New World and Old are covered with
equal enthusiasm – and, in terms of old, we're particularly impressed to see
madeiras dating back to 1842. We wouldn't mind living in Skipton, with this
kind of choice on our doorsteps, but fortunately the Wright Wine Company
has a good delivery service. (There's also a web site, but buying on this is
only encouraged if you're thinking of whisky.)

Look out for

- Top burgundies from Mongeard-Mugneret, Faiveley, Latour and
  Bonneau du Martray
- Greece, Hungary, Uruguay, Argentina and the Lebanon all represented
- Cloudy Bay, Jackson Estate plus Hunter's wines from New Zealand
- Fabulous dessert wines: Coteaux du Layon, Tokaji Aszú (6 puttonyos),
  Heggies Eden Valley *botrytis* Riesling, and more
- Vintage port from the 1970s, 1980s and 1990s
- Liqueurs from Aalborg Akvavit to Wisniowka Cherry Cordial, plus spirits
  and whiskies galore.

Wrightson & Co Wine Merchants

Manfield Grange, Manfield, nr Darlington,	*Tel* (01325) 374134
North Yorkshire DL2 2RE	*Fax* (01325) 374135

Email ed.wrightson.wines@onyxnet.co.uk
Web site www.thatwineclub.co.uk

Open Mon–Fri 9–5.30 **Closed** Sat, Sun, public holidays **Cards** MasterCard, Switch, Visa; personal and business accounts **Discount** 5% on accounts settled within 7 days **Delivery** Free within 40-mile radius (min. 2 cases); nationwide service available, charge £7.50 for 1 case, £10 for 2 cases, free for 3+ cases **Glass hire** Free with order **Tastings and talks** Tastings available, phone for details

Simon Wrightson is proud to offer a very personal service of 'good, yet inexpensive wines'. Yet this is a wine lovers' list. Everyday bottles – under £5 a bottle, under £6 a bottle and under £10 a bottle – kick things off with some well-chosen but fun offerings such as Mad Fish Shiraz and Guigal's simple Côtes du Rhône, cheerful Beaujolais and South African boutique wines such as Hunting Family Slaley Shiraz. Then follows the backbone of classics: Bordeaux and red and white burgundy are covered in as fine detail as possible, with careful tasting notes and helpful when-to-drink symbols – the range includes such stars as Châteaux Léoville-Barton, Belair (St-Emilion), Cos d'Estournel and Clos de l'Oratoire. There's also a good smattering from the Bordeaux Côtes – good-value wines at less than half the price of the aforementioned! Beginning with Olivier Leflaive's wines does the burgundy section no harm, and we'd reiterate what we said last year that, overall, this selection is the 'paragon of good taste'. Simon also dips into Chile, Argentina, Australia and California but without quite the same passion as for South Africa – from which he selects some real bargains and, we suspect, future shining stars. This well-thought-out range is supplemented by three newsletters a year, three tastings and a tempting January bin-end sale. Simon is even considerate enough to plan out your Christmas present list for you, with a range of seasonal Orkney smoked salmon packs, a damson gin gift pack, and small (and large) pre-selected wine cases. We'll be leaving the Wrightson list fully visible when relatives visit this autumn…

Look out for

- Delicious, well-priced Sauternes wines
- 1980s red Bordeaux – some treasures from 1982, 1988 and 1989
- Bargain burgundies from the Mâconnais: Rully, Givry and Montagny, plus more illustrious bottlings from further north, starting with Corton
- Serious Napa Valley red from Dominus (price on application!)
- Fantastic Barbadillo sherries from Sanlúcar
- Ten Christmases' worth of presents – decanters, corkscrews, whiskies, armagnacs, glasses and fruit liqueurs.

Specialist and Regional Award Winners are listed on pages 12–15.

Peter Wylie Fine Wines

Plymtree Manor, Plymtree, Cullompton,	*Tel* (01884) 277555
Devon EX15 2LE	*Fax* (01884) 277557

Email peter@wylie-fine-wines.demon.co.uk
Web site www.wyliefinewines.co.uk

Open Mon–Fri 9–6 **Closed** Sat, Sun, public holidays **Cards** None accepted
Discount Available, phone for details **Delivery** Nationwide service available, charge
£20 for 1 case or for up to 3 cases in London; larger orders charged at cost **Glass hire**
Not available **Tastings and talks** Not available

Know anyone born in 1909? If so, we can think of a superb birthday present for them – a half bottle of Mouton Rothschild or a full one of Latour from their birth year. Come to think of it, you could toast the memory of someone born in 1811, if you logged on to Peter Wylie's web site. The only trouble is you'd be around £15,000 poorer for it – this wine is an Yquem, of course; few others but Sauternes survive this long.

This really is a stunning set of wines. Peter Wylie has been 40 years in the business, and in that time he's probably developed one of the most fascinating speciality ranges in the country. Needless to say, old vintages being the theme, attention is mostly fixed on Bordeaux; with burgundy, port and madeira putting in distinguished appearances. Impressive old Swiss, German and American wines, plus elderly Cloudy Bays from New Zealand, also crop up.

We suspect Peter doesn't get to taste his wares nearly as often as he'd like (they exist in such small quantities), but his imagination is surely fed, day to day, as much as ours as we write this review. What was going on in the cellar-master's mind as he bottled his 1914 Château Pontet Canet? Was 1966 as good a year in Burgundy for Monsieur Grivelet as it was for British football? Were Croft's port *bodegas* reachable by anything other than donkey in 1912, or Barbeito's madeira cellars by anything other than sailing ship in 1834? It will cost you to feed your day-dreams any further, but most of these wines come in at under £500 a bottle (thank goodness), and there's a pretty interesting range under £50 too. Modern vintages are all here as well. The more recent you go, the more likely you are to get your choice in double magnum, jeroboam or *impériale* – there's a fabulous array of these big bottles on hand. Peter presents his list with all the appropriate detail: neck measures and label condition for the old bottles, Parker points for the 1982 clarets (the vintage that made the name of this world-feared critic). And, if you contact Peter by email, he'll advise you how, when and with what to drink them.

Look out for

- 1926 Pavillon Blanc de Château Margaux (which will make you look at your two-year-old Sauvignon Blanc in a new light)
- Over 60 wines from the mammoth 1961 vintage
- Double magnums of Lafite-Rothschild and Latour from the 1970s
- Rare Bordeaux from the war-time vintages: 1914, 1916, 1918, 1940, 1943, 1944 and 1945
- Stunning selection of Sauternes, from 1811 to the present day
- 1990 burgundies from top domaines Leflaive, Laguiche, Latour and Drouhin.

Yapp Brothers

The Old Brewery, Mere, Wiltshire BA12 6DY

Tel (01747) 860423
Fax (01747) 860929
Email sales@yapp.co.uk
Web site www.yapp.co.uk

Open Mon–Sat 9–5 **Closed** Sun, public holidays **Cards** Delta, MasterCard, Switch, Visa; personal and business accounts **Discount** Available on 6+ cases, also £3 per case if collected **Delivery** Nationwide service available (min. 1 case), charge £3 for 1 case, free for 2+ cases **Glass hire** Free **Tastings and talks** Tastings available, phone for details

Have there been any significant changes to your business in the last year?, we asked in our questionnaire. 'No,' came the answer from Mere. This isn't strictly true, as we spotted a Chablis in a recent offer – a rare excursion into Burgundy for this Rhône and Loire specialist. But otherwise, the pace of change *chez* Yapp is as slow as the wines are good. Robin Yapp did his research many years ago, and assembled an impressive band of growers in his two favoured regions, since when there has been little need to add to the range. Not that new domaines don't appear. The southern French selection in particular seems to expand each time we look at the list. However, here as in other areas, the additions tend to be from small, quality-minded, family-run domaines that make wines for drinking rather than tasting. 'Our own evaluation … is whether or not we can happily consume the contents of a bottle (or two) in one session.' If you visit Mere only once a year, make it in early March. Not only will you be able to pick up a copy of the new list, but you'll also be able to taste your way through several attractively priced bin-ends from the previous edition of the list.

Look out for
- Monthly tutored tastings at The Old Brewery
- Rhône stars Vernay, Jasmin, Chave and Clape
- Lecointre, Druet, Filliatreau and Vatan from the Loire
- Roussillon reds from Ferrer-Ribière and Canteranne
- Superb Australian Shiraz from Jasper Hill
- The best of Provence from Château Simone, Bunan and Trévallon.

Noel Young Wines

Regional Award Winner – East of England

56 High Street, Trumpington, Cambridge CB2 2LS

Tel (01223) 844744
Fax (01223) 844736
Email admin@nywines.co.uk
Web site www.nywines.co.uk

Open Mon–Thur 10–8, Fri & Sat 10–9, Sun 12–2 **Closed** Public holidays **Cards** Amex, Delta, MasterCard, Switch, Visa; business accounts **Discount** Available, phone for details **Delivery** Free within 25-mile radius (min. 1 case); nationwide service available, charge £7 for 1 case, £4 per extra case, negotiable for larger orders **Glass hire** Free with order, phone for details **Tastings and talks** Tutored tastings; talks by arrangement, phone for details **£5**

Here is a man who loves his Syrah. You'll find it everywhere on this list … Ever tried 'S' Syrah from Graf Hardegg in Austria? Or Dominio de Valdepusa Syrah from Marqués de Griñon in Spain? See what we mean? Of course, the Syrah thing really gets going in France (and California, and New Zealand, and Italy), and as Shiraz in Australia. It's the latter that has the most impressive selection of all, and this even includes Magpie Estate Shiraz, blended by Noel himself at his joint venture project in the Barossa Valley. Flying from Trumpington to Tanunda, Australia, might seem crazy, but he could do far worse than team up with the inimitable Rolf Binder of Veritas to make wine, and the distance travelled is a measure of his passion.

'No snobbery. Excellent advice. Always looking for good new taste sensations,' is Noel Young's summary of his business. And we'd agree that new sensations abound. Tabs are kept on everything on offer from Australia, with quality offerings such as Garry Crittenden's unusual Arneis, Cullen's perfect interpretation of Chardonnay. California choices are also strong, as are those from France and Italy. From the rest of the world, Noel's abundant energy goes into sourcing quality offerings from as many different growers and unusual locations as possible.

Such is the constant turnover and frequency of new wines at Noel Young Wines, we find the best approach is to keep the fine wine list to hand and regularly read the bimonthly newsletters. You'll find treasures such as Bonny Doon ancient-vine Carignan from California, which need to be snapped up as soon as spotted. We also like the mixed-case offers at around £50. For this small sum you can try a tasting case of New Zealand Sauvignon from different estates, a South African red selection from various grapes, or a total mixture 'for entertaining'.

This merchant is as vinously switched-on as ever: visiting the shop, or attending one of the regular tastings, will prove it.

Look out for

- Stocks of mature Bordeaux, Burgundy and vintage port from the Douro Valley
- Stellar newcomer from Tasmania, Stefano Lubiana (makes great, sparkling, non-vintage *brut*)

- Chunky Australian Shiraz and strapping Cabernets too
- Carefully chosen South African list, including Thelema and new estate Veenwouden
- Delicious white Rhône wines: Condrieu, Hermitage and white Châteauneuf-du-Pape
- Small but perfectly formed Austrian selection focusing on the impeccable wines of Alois Kracher.

ALSO RECOMMENDED

The merchants in this section are establishments that come with our recommendation, but which we felt merited briefer profiles. We would be delighted to receive feedback on merchants in this section, and indeed on any merchants we have omitted altogether that you feel should be in the Guide. You can email us your comments to whichwineguide@which.net

A & A Wines

Mansfield Park, Guildford Road
Tel (01483) 274666
Cranleigh, Surrey GU6 8PT
Fax (01483) 268460
Email aawines@aol.com
Web site
www.spanishwinesonline.co.uk

Smatterings from France and South America apart, the two Andrews (Bickerton and Connor) concentrate on their first love, which is wines from Spain. Andrew B reckons he has 'the best range of Spanish wines in the UK at all price levels.' Those looking for Rioja will find a solid set of wines dating back to 1970 Viña Tondonia Gran Reserva from López de Heredia, one of eleven bodegas from the region represented on the list. Most other regions get a look in too. Highlights include the Yllera wines from Castilla-León, Cavas from Marques de Monistrol and a set of Hidalgo sherries. **£5**

For an explanation of the symbols used at the top of some of the merchant entries, see page 303.

A & B Vintners Ltd

Little Tawsden, Spout Lane,
Brenchley,
Kent TN12 7AS
Tel (01892) 724977
Fax (01892) 722673
Email info@abvintners.co.uk
Web site www.abvintners.co.uk

In a world where even the simplest corner-shop off-licence now stocks wines from a dozen different countries, A & B stands as a model of focused excellence. John Arnold and Ken Brook set up their business in August 1998 and have continued to specialise in wines from Burgundy, the Rhône and the Languedoc-Roussillon. Indeed, apart from Riedel glasses, no other items appear on their annual list. While the list includes several great wines, and shows the high calibre of the producers John & Ken deal with, it doesn't show A & B at its best. Many wines are available in such small quantities that they are only featured in the separate offers published throughout the year (and at very attractive prices too). For fans of wines from these three fascinating regions, this is one mailing list you should definitely be on. **£5**

Ambleside Wine Store

see Windermere Wine Stores

Amey's Wines

83 Melford Road, Sudbury,
Suffolk CO10 1JT
Tel (01787) 377144

A draft copy of Peter Amey's
Summer 2001 list had us reaching
for our magnifying glass, so small
was the print. However, our squints
were halted by the pleasing
selection of 'personally chosen
wines which are selected for quality,
individuality and value, and can be
sold with confidence.' The list nods
its head to most parts of the wine
world, and especially vigorously
where Australia, Italy, southern
France and South Africa are
concerned. Even where the range
from a particular region isn't
especially large, the calibre of the
producers is usually high – witness
the Californian reds from Fife and
Franus, and Alsace whites from Sorg
and Mittnacht.

Amps Fine Wines

6 Market Place, Oundle,
Peterborough PE8 4BQ
Tel (01832) 273502
Fax (01832) 273611
Email info@ampsfinewines.co.uk
Web site www.ampsfinewines.co.uk

Sports-mad Philip Amps stocks a
good solid selection of wines in his
Oundle shop. From the Old World,
you'll find familiar names such as
Guigal, Torres, Laroche, Trimbach
and Dr Loosen, plus an expanding
Italian range and a small but
interesting set of Portuguese reds.
From the New World, South Africa
is the current area of passion, the
result of a recent trip to the Cape,
and Whalehaven, Verdun and
Boschendal are just three of the
producers highlighted. Other
countries feature more well-known
faces – Penfolds, Babich and
Caliterra to name but three – and
while we can see where Philip
sources most of his range, we're not
going to complain about the
standard of the wines. **£5**

The Antique Wine Company of Great Britain

see The Cellar D'Or

Arkell's Vintners

Kingsdown Brewery, Stratton St
Margaret, Swindon SN2 6RU
Tel (01793) 823026
Fax (01793) 828864
Email vintners@arkells.com
Web site www.arkells.com

The wine selection from this
Swindon brewer may not be the
most enterprising around, but it
runs to several hundred labels, and
should fulfil most of the needs of all
but the choosiest customers. From
classic regions, there's no shortage
of vintage port, claret from the mid-
1990s vintages, nor burgundies from
Louis Latour and Jaffelin. Elsewhere
the list is dotted with good-quality
producers such as Dopff Au Moulin,
Pellé (Menetou Salon), Chapoutier,
Ochoa, Jackson Estate, Grant Burge
and Mondavi. While we understand
that wine will always be a sideline
for a brewer, someone here clearly
has an eye (and a palate) for a good
wine. It wouldn't take an awful lot
more effort for Arkell's to become a
decent merchant in its own right.

Arriba Kettle & Co

Buckle Street, Honeybourne,
nr Evesham, Worcestershire
WR11 5QB
Tel (01386) 833024
Fax (01386) 833541
Email arribakettle@talk21.com

Ex-architect Barry Kettle apologised
for the absence of wines from
Menetou Salon and Sancerre in his
2000/1 list , but '… the quality of the
1999 vintage is very modest and the
prices are up and I see no merit in
expecting customers – who rely on
our integrity – to buy an inferior
vintage at a higher price than they
paid for the previous good one.' In
its place, he offers Sauvignon from
Neil Ellis, who joins Simonsig, de
Wetshof and Kanonkop in a tidy
little South African range. Other
highlights of Barry's list are sherries
from Barbadillo, burgundies from
Mouton and Lumpp, Loire wines
from Domaines de la Chanteleuserie
and Brisebarre, and champagnes
from the houses of Blin and Pierre
Paillard.

Benson Fine Wines

96 Ramsden Road, London SW12 8QZ
Tel 020-8673 4439
Fax 020-8675 5543
Email bensonwines@
  connectingbusiness.com
Web site www.bensonfinewines.co.uk

The trio of 1990s' Australian reds
seems curiously out of place in the
middle of Clare Benson's list. We
think of this as a treasure trove for
fine wine oddments from classic
regions, especially Bordeaux and
Burgundy. Given the age of the
wines on offer, prices are very fair,
even after VAT has been added.
With wines available in such small
quantities – two bottles of this, four

of that – it's best to ring Clare to find
out what's in stock. And while you're
on the phone, ask for details of the
tastings and dinners organised by
the associated Wine & Dine Society,
as they are very good value.

Booths of Stockport

62 Heaton Moor Road, Heaton
Moor, Stockport SK4 4NZ
Tel 0161-432 3309
Fax 0161-432 3309
Email johnbooth@lineone.net

Booths continues to offer an eclectic
choice – reaching beyond the
narrow range of Sauvignon Blanc
and Chardonnay, Cabernet
Sauvignon and Merlot, because: 'If
restaurants worked on this basis we
would only have steak, lamb,
chicken and salmon. There would
be no duck, guinea fowl or 20-odd
fish from trout to turbot, and this
we consider to be disastrous.'

Buyer/manager John Booth is
undeterred by his location in the
midst of supermarkets in Stockport.
His mission to rediscover Pinot Gris,
Chenin, Riesling and 'trendier'
varieties such as Albariño and
Marsanne has seen some success
over the last year. Plus, his growing
conviction that New World wines
are becoming too expensive has
generated an increasing demand for
the value-for-money wines of
Argentina. Iberia and south-western
France feature as strongly as ever,
and, despite his reservations, so do
Australia and New Zealand. What
this small-scale merchant lacks in
breadth, it makes up for in
infectious enthusiasm – and we
recommend that, where possible,
customers bypass those
supermarkets altogether – because
Booths also doubles up as a
delicatessen.

Bordeaux Index

6th Floor, 159–173 St Johns Street,
London, EC1V 4QJ
Tel 020-7253 2110
Fax 020-7490 1955
Email sales@bordeauxindex.com
Web site www.bordeauxindex.com

Yes, Dylan Paris and his chums ('a
right clever bunch, and very good-
looking to boot') have plenty of
claret on their books, and offer it at
very competitive prices. But Mr P is
slightly irked that people are
ignoring his exciting range of
burgundies, which features rising
stars such as Denis Mortet, Nicolas
Potel and Vincent Dancer. He can
also offer some top-notch Piedmont
reds (Scavino, Sandrone, Ceretto),
equally fine Rhône wines (Rayas,
Chave, Chapoutier) and in-demand
wines from other parts of the world.
The minimum purchase of £500 will
deter many, but if you have money
to splash out on fine wine, Bordeaux
Index is certainly worth a call.

The Bottleneck

7 & 9 Charlotte Street, Broadstairs,
Kent CT10 1LR
Tel (01843) 861095
Fax (01843) 861095
Email info@thebottleneck.co.uk
Web site www.thebottleneck.co.uk

'I apologize for the tear-stained
cases, but some of the wines are
being sold at less than cost.' Chris &
Lin Beckett approach the wine
business with a good sense of
humour, but it doesn't stop them
putting together a range of wines
that is for the most part serious.
Australia is their speciality, and
you'll find wines from Evans & Tate,
St Hallett, Chapel Hill and many
more on the shelves. The New
Zealand range, featuring Jackson
Estate, Grove Mill and Babich, also
deserves a mention. Other
highlights of a good rather than
great range are the Languedoc
wines of Puech-Haut, the Simonsig
South Africans, Nyetimber's
excellent sparklers and possibly 'the
first wine on sale from Uruguay in
Thanet'.   **£5**

Budgens

Stonefield Way, Ruislip,
Middlesex HA4 0JR
Tel 020-8422 9511
Fax 020-8864 2800
Web site www.budgens.co.uk

(180 branches throughout south-east
England)

Since she moved to Budgens
towards the end of 1999, one of the
major tasks undertaken by Christine
Sandys has been to reduce the wine
range from around 500 wines to less
than 300. 'In supermarket terms, our
stores are relatively small,' says
Christine, ex-wine buyer for Co-
operative Retail Services (CRS), 'so it
is difficult to be "out of the
ordinary". Considering our space
restrictions, I think we provide a
carefully chosen, well-priced range.'
For novelty, go elsewhere, as the
selection tends to favour well-
known names, such as Rosemount,
Montana, Gallo, James Herrick and
Mouton Cadet. But for low prices –
sub-£5 is the rule rather than the
exception here – plus the occasional
excursion into finer territory, such
as Caronne Ste Gemme at £11.99,
then the Budgens range deserves a
look.

Burgundy Shuttle

168 Ifield Road, London SW10 9AF
Tel 020-7341 4053
Fax 020-7244 0618
Email
  peter@burgundyshuttle.ltd.uk
Web site www.burgundyshuttle.co.uk

It's not quite all Burgundy in Peter Godden's corner of south-west London. His list includes some fine Loire whites, including Crochet for Sauvignon and de Fesles for Chenin; some sensibly priced Bordeaux reds; and smatterings from other parts of France. But Burgundy is the main event, and we counted not far short of sixty growers from the region on his March 2001 list. Some of them are well-known – Henri Clerc, Vincent, Drouhin-Laroze, for example – while others have yet to make a name for themselves. If you need to be guided through the range, Peter will be happy to assemble a mixed dozen for you, and there are also large tastings twice a year.　**£5**

Cape Province Wines

77 Laleham Road, Staines,
Middlesex TW18 2EA
Tel (01784) 451860
Fax (01784) 469267
Email capewines@msn.com
Web site www.capewinestores.co.uk

Peter Loose reckons he has the best selection of South African wine in the UK. Certainly his range of 130 wines, including estates such as Meerlust, Plaisir de Merle, Simonsig and Klein Constantia, is one of the largest you'll find. It also deserves commendation for, by and large, avoiding the rather basic wines at the cheaper end of the price scale. However, we'd like to see Mr Loose expanding his horizons to take in the emerging stars of the Cape. Where, for example, are producers such as Spice Route, Veenwouden, Warwick and Steenberg? Maybe they'll appear on the next list, maybe not.　**£5**

Les Caves de Pyrene

Pew Corner, Old Portsmouth Road, Artington, Guildford, Surrey GU3 1LP
Tel (01483) 538820
Fax (01483) 455068
Email
  enquiries@lescavesdepyrene.com
Web site www.lescavesdepyrene.com

'We are selling something that we love, not a product – genuine enthusiasm helps!' says Douglas Wregg in answer to our questionnaire. To this end, Les Caves prides itself on one of the best selections of regional French wines in the country. It's good to see the wines of Faugères, Pic St-Loup and Irouléguy taking centre stage at the front of the list, rather than the usual Bordeaux clarets! And we can't think of anywhere else where the *petits châteaux* wines of Lussac-St-Emilion, Blaye and Castillon would take precedence over the *crus classés* either. Les Caves' refreshingly different take on wine has now extended to the rest of Europe and the New World too, with Spain, Italy, Australia and Uruguay largely represented with the same off-beat choices, wry-humoured tasting notes and reasonable prices. Visit the web site for the monthly newsletter and you'll see what we mean.　**£5**

Ceci Paolo

The New Cook's Emporium,
21 High Street, Ledbury,
Herefordshire HR8 1DS
Tel (01531) 632976
Fax (01531) 631011
Email
  patriciaharrison@compuserve.com
Web site www.cecipaolo.com

Not many merchants in this *Guide*
have both a wine list and a list of
oils and vinegars. But then Patricia
Harrison's business fully merits the
word 'emporium' – if you're a
foodie, this is a great place to shop.
As for the wines – occasional
sightings of Australian bottles have
been reported, but the list is
exclusively Italian, with the entire
range coming from Liberty Wines
(q.v.). With producers such as
Pieropoan, Vajra and Fontodi, we
can't fault the quality, but we'd
encourage Patricia to cast her
buying net to a wider range of
suppliers. Keep an eye out for the
lively programme of food and wine
tastings.   **£5**

The Cellar D'Or   ♛

37 St Giles Street, Norwich NR2 1JN
Tel (01603) 626246
Fax (01603) 626256
Email
  wine@cellardor.co.uk (Cellar D'Or)
  vintages@antiquewine.org
  (Antique Wine Company)
*Web site*s www.cellardor.co.uk
  (Cellar D'Or)www.antique-wine.net
  (Antique Wine Company)

A newcomer to the *Guide* which, if
the list is anything to go by, we'll be
saying a lot more about in the
future. The French range includes
serious Rhône reds (Jasmin, Pégaü),
equally fine Burgundies (Leflaive,
Arnoux) and healthy selections from

other regions; and the Italians and
Spaniards, though less numerous,
maintain the quality. In the New
World, the highlight is the
Australian selection, which features
wines from some less widely seen
producers such as Prentice and
Torbreck. The choices from
Argentina and the USA could be a
little more vibrant, but overall the
range is a good one. And for anyone
looking for something to celebrate a
particular anniversary or birthday,
the associated Antique Wine
Company of Great Britain can
provide bottles of wine (or spirits)
from virtually every vintage in the
twentieth century.

Chandos Deli

6 Princess Victoria Street, Clifton,
Bristol BS8 4BP
Tel 0117-974 3275
Fax 0117-973 1020

121 Whiteladies Road, Bristol BS8 2PL

97 Henleaze Road, Henleaze, Bristol
BS9 4JP
Email info@chandosdeli.com
Web site www.chandosdeli.com

The folk at Chandos are on a
mission, they are determined to
disprove that Italian offerings are the
'ugly ducklings' of the wine world.
Well, we never thought they were
ugly, but should any Bristol residents
be so opined, we suggest that a trip
to any of the three shops (soon to be
four) will change their minds. This is
a succinct little list, but it includes the
likes of Jermann, Pieropan and
Cornell northern whites, and the
ever-captivating Allegrini Amarones
(not to mention their Recioto della
Valpolicella too). There's a real
treasure trove from Tuscany,
including sweet *vin santo* and the
marvellous Isole e Olena Chianti
Classico, plus a good long look at the

fashionable South and Islands too. With these as ammunition (not to mention the forays into France and Australia) the doubters should soon be convinced. **£5**

Châteaux Wines

Head office
Paddock House, Upper Tockington Road, Tockington, Bristol BS32 4LQ
Tel (01454) 613959
Fax (01454) 613959

Châteaux Wines Warehousing & Distribution
c/o Octavian, Eastlays Warehouse, Gastard, Nr Corsham, Wiltshire SN13 9PP
Email cheryl.miller@bris.ac.uk
Web site www.chateauxwines.co.uk

Take out the Laurent Perrier and Château Musar, and there are fewer than 40 wines on the Miller family's list. Highlights of this compact range are the Château Roi de Fombrauge in St Emilion, the Simmonet-Febvre Chablis, André Pelletier's Juliénas and Le Vieux Micocoulier from Tricastin. Yes, apart from Musar and a couple of Chilean wines from Viña Alamosa, everything here is French. Londoners who would like to sample the wines have an opportunity at the annual tasting each November. **£5**

Brian Coad Fine Wines

Grape Expectations, Stray Park, off Park Street, Ivybridge, Devon PL21 9DW
Tel (01752) 896545
Fax (01752) 691160
Email
  briancoadfinewines@lineone.net

Brian Coad confesses that he's 'very much a Francophile', which goes a long way towards explaining his

healthy selections from Burgundy, the Loire, the Rhône and Bordeaux. He gives no explanations, however, for his smaller but still commendable ranges from other parts other Europe, where the Pecorari wines from Friuli and the Esporño range from Portugal deserve a mention. And Brian doesn't let his predilections stop him putting together a decent set of New World wines, with the choices from Australia (including Elderton and Brookland Valley) and New Zealand (Alana, Te Mata) standing out in particular. So while your mixed case may include several French wines, there's plenty from other countries to fill any remaining gaps. **£5**

Cochonnet Wines

Trengilly Wartha Inn, Constantine, Falmouth, Cornwall TR11 5RP
Tel (01326) 341013
Fax (01326) 340332
Email trengilly@compuserve.com
Web site www.wineincornwall.co.uk

'We do not need to sell dull wines to cover our overheads,' says buyer and partner Nigel Logan. Cochonnet is part of the Trengilly Wartha Inn set-up, so no doubt this can be done in other ways. The selection here is certainly eclectic rather than dull. How good it is to see Collioure and Cahors, Bandol and Bourgueil from France, rather than the usual array of boring old *vin de pays* blended red! The Bordeaux châteaux dare to be different too, with some good *cru bourgeois* estates on offer. France is a major strength, but there are equally adventurous Spanish wines, and an impressive range from Austria put together for ABC (Anything But Chardonnay) followers. The choice of New World estates is more mainstream but nonetheless top quality, and every bit as enticing.

Cockburn & Campbell Ltd

see Young's Wine Direct

Colombier Vins Fins

Colombier House, Cadley Hill
Industrial Estate, Ryder Close,
Swadlincote, Derbyshire DE11 9EU
Tel (01283) 552552
Fax (01283) 550675
Email
  enquiries@colombiervinsfins.co.uk
Web site www.colombiervinsfins.co.uk

The philosophy of this rather quirky
Derbyshire company is to bypass
well-known brands and concentrate
on '... the best individual wineries in
the world, "not the most well
known, but known by the best".'
Despite a few familiar faces such as
Guigal and Brown Brothers, and a
host of well-known clarets, most of
what is on offer tends to be exclusive
to the company, not least the range
from managing director Jehu Attias's
own domaine near Chagny in
Burgundy, and the wines from
Colombier's own Beaune-based
négociant business. Because of this,
we confess that we're not familiar
with everything in the range, but
we've generally been impressed with
those we have tasted, particularly
from Burgundy, Bordeaux and Italy.

Constantine Stores

30 Fore Street, Constantine,
Falmouth, Cornwall TR11 5AB
Tel (01326) 340226
Fax (01326) 340182
Email sales@drinkfinder.co.uk
Web site www.drinkfinder.co.uk

Falmouth is almost as far from
Scotland as you can go in the UK,
but that hasn't stopped Andrew
Rowe assembling a formidable
range of malt whiskies. The wine
selection put together by this
'young, dynamic wine lover' (his
words, not ours) is also extensive.
Much of the range is given over to
well-known names such as Louis
Latour, Oxford Landing and
Caliterra, but Andrew also finds
space for a few more esoteric
offerings such as Domaine de Nalys
Châteauneuf and a collection of
high-class Portuguese reds. Since
the launch of the web site paper lists
are a thing of the past, so to keep up
with the range, either go on-line or
drop into the store. **(£5)**

Rodney Densem Wines

Shop
4 Pillory Street, Nantwich,
Cheshire CW5 5BD
Tel (01270) 626999
Fax (01270) 626999

Wholesale & Admin
Regent House, Lancaster Fields,
Crewe Gates Farm Estate,
Crewe, Cheshire CW1 6FF
Email sales@onestopwine.com
Web site www.onestopwine.com

While the bulk of Rodney Densem's
business is wholesale, several
thousand cases of wines are sold
each year at the smart Nantwich
shop. The selection errs throughout
on the side of caution, and familiar
names such as Torres, Louis Latour,
Brown Brothers, Warre's and
Duboeuf are very much the order of
the day. The choices from Argentina
and South Africa are a little more
adventurous, but overall we'd like
to see a touch more verve in the
range. Still, the firm puts great
emphasis on customer service, and
the friendly, helpful staff should be
able to find something to suit the
palates of most customers. **(£5)**

Drinks Etc

36 High Street, Boroughbridge,
North Yorks YO5 9AW
Tel (01423) 323337
Fax (01423) 323353
Email andy@drinks-etc.co.uk
www.drinks-etc.co.uk

New shop, new web site, new entry
in the *Guide*. Under the energetic
guidance of Andrew Saxon, Drinks
Etc is taking Boroughbridge by
storm with its very wide range of
wine – some of very high quality
indeed. We'd happily come here to
pick up our favourite Australian
bottles (Mount Horrocks, Langi
Ghiran, Shaw & Smith, d'Arenberg);
we like the Italian wines (Orvieto to
Super-Tuscan choices here); and
we're intrigued by the other 'drinks
etc' that are on offer … whisky,
cider, beer, spirits, vermouth, rum,
gin, cognac – you name it. Andrew
puts out a bimonthly newsletter to
keep customers abreast of what he's
up to, and we feel sure that his hard
work and fabulous array of carefully
chosen wines will meet with
enthusiastic return visits very soon,
if they haven't already.   **£5**

Eckington Wines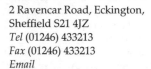

2 Ravencar Road, Eckington,
Sheffield S21 4JZ
Tel (01246) 433213
Fax (01246) 433213
Email
  qandrewloughran@supanet.com

How better to buy your wine than
from a self-professed 'old duffer
who enjoys selling what he drinks'
(or … drinking what he should be
selling)'? That's the kind of personal
recommendation we like to see.
Andrew Loughran chooses well, and
we're as impressed as ever with the
fabulous range of Australian estates

he gets his hands on – 16 vintages of
Grange, Penfold's Magill, St Hallett
Old Block, Rockford Basket Press,
Shiraz classics aplenty! There aren't
many merchants who can claim
seven vintages of Le Pin and 11 of
Italy's Sassicaia either. Judging by
these, and other top-rank wines,
Eckington customers obviously have
considerable spending power; but
there's a fair selection on offer too
for those still cutting their vinous
teeth and not out to spend too much
on a caseful. Tastings are held on the
first Tuesday of each month, and the
biannual Eckington newsletter gives
helpful recommendations, tips and
background details – another nice
personal touch.   **£5**

Edencroft Fine Wines

Hospital Street, Nantwich, Cheshire
CW5 5RJ
Tel (01270) 629975
Fax (01270) 625302
Email sales@edencroft.co.uk
Web site www.edencroft.co.uk

It's meat that first greets you when
you enter Mark Brookshaw's shop.
Turn left, however, and you'll see a
room crammed with wine. Pretty
good wine it is too. The Australian
wines are probably the most
numerous, and you'll find some
older vintages of Eileen Hardy
Shiraz on offer amid more recent
offerings; but there are also strong
showings from other parts of the
world. We'd point you first of all
towards the Californians (Crichton
Hall, Ridge), Rhône reds
(Colombier, de Vallouit) and
Italians (La Spinetta, Fonterutoli,
Planeta) – but really there are no
duds on Mark's shelves. And if
you need something to eat with
your purchases, there's all that fine
food just on the other side of the
store.   **£5**

English Wine Centre

Alfriston Roundabout, East Sussex
BN26 5QS
Tel (01323) 870164
Fax (01323) 870005
Email bottles@englishwine.co.uk
Web site www.englishwine.co.uk

The name says it all. If you're
looking for the largest selection of
our home-produced wines,
Christopher Ann has them here in
his 'lovely old buildings in beautiful
grounds in the Sussex countryside'.
Nearly 20 wineries are represented,
and while our favourites of these
are Breaky Bottom, Chapel Down,
Hidden Spring and Valley
Vineyards, plus of course the
sparkling-only Nyetimber and
Ridgeview, we'd encourage you to
try anything from the range. And
don't be shy of the red wines either
– they're improving with each
vintage, and Christopher tells us
that interest in them is growing.
While England may be the main
event, you'll now find a couple of
dozen wines from other countries.
Good as these are, we'd still urge
you to be patriotic and drink for
England. **£5**

Evington's Wine Merchants

120 Evington Road, Leicester
LE2 1HH
Tel 0116-254 2702
Fax 0116-254 2702
Email evingtonwine@fsbdial.co.uk
Web site www.evingtons-wines.com

After more than 40 years in the
trade, Simon March is still fighting
to convince his customers that it's
worth spending that little bit extra.
And, backed up by a decent set of
wines – the strongest we can ever
remember from this Leicester
company – he reckons he's getting
there. While his selection isn't large
(only Rioja and Portuguese reds
could be called real specialities),
both New and Old Worlds are
accorded a fair degree of attention.
Throughout the range, you'll find
gems such as Loire wines from
Baumard, New Zealand reds from
Crab Farm and some fine Austrian
whites from Freie Weingärtner
Wachau. Some prices err on the
high side, but overall, this is a very
good place to buy wine. **£5**

Ferrers le Mesurier and Son

Turnsloe, North Street, Titchmarsh,
Kettering, Northamptonshire
NN14 3DH
Tel (01832) 732660
Fax (01832) 732660

The Dower House, Parish Road,
Stratton Strawless, Norfolk
NR10 5LP
Tel (01603) 279975
Email blaiselm@aol.com

This is a highly personal selection:
small, but refusing to pander to
'tedious New World varietals' and
overpriced Bordeaux. As far as
Ferrers is concerned, too many
people are 'downtrading'; he's sad
about it, but refuses to let it deter
him from presenting the wines he
admires – from France. The Loire,
Burgundy, Beaujolais and the
Rhône are the regions to watch
here, with some carefully chosen,
admirable growers, as burgundy
from Anne Gros and Crozes-
Hermitage from Alain Graillot bear
witness. Very little hits the list at
over £10 a bottle, and there's a
southern French group at under £5.
After 26 years in the trade, Ferrers
knows a good wine when he sees it.

Irma Fingal-Rock

64 Monnow Street, Monmouth
NP25 3EN
Tel (01600) 712372
Fax (01600) 712372
Email irmafingalrock@msn.com
Web site www.pinotnoir.co.uk

Irma Fingal-Rock provides the intriguing name, but it's her husband Tom Innes whose effusive personality pervades at this South Wales establishment. We're every bit as entertained by the detailed accounts of his buying trips as his customers obviously are, and to sample the resulting burgundies, we'd go back again and again too. Ex-barrister Tom has collected over 90 burgundies – red, white and Chablis – and more than a few wines from the Rhône, Bordeaux and other French regions. The list is broad and the prices low; and we're impressed by the number of less-usual grower names Tom has managed to wheedle out of the French woodwork. There's also a great selection from outside France: Henschke, Tyrrells and Rolf Binder from Australia are never a bad sign, and the same goes for Gaja and Biondi-Santi from Italy. There are only three wines from South Africa, but Hartenberg and Rust-en-Vrede show similar discernment. We're glad to see IFR supporting the local wine and cider makers (Offa's Vineyard and Monnow Valley for the former) and our only quibble is we'd like to see more scope to splash out and trade up – but that may seem churlish in the light of such enthusiasm. We also applaud the talent of their 12-year-old daughter, as illustrated by her designs for the price list covers.

Le Fleming Wines

19 Spenser Road, Harpenden,
Hertfordshire AL5 5NW
Tel (01582) 760125
Fax (01582) 760125
Email
  cherry@lefleming.swinternet.co.uk

We especially like Le Fleming's New World collection. Cherry Jenkins has done herself proud. The full spectrum of Australian regions are on show, with growers such as Cullen from Western Australia; Henschke, Rockford and Yalumba from the Barossa Valley; Mount Horrocks from Clare; Best's from Victoria … Price-wise, we'd go so far as to say this is one of the best and broadest Australian selections in the country. Cherry also comes up trumps with her South African choices, and Ridge, Saintsbury and Frog's Leap from California too. As she says, 'I know 90 per cent of all the producers personally, so am able to offer in-house knowledge to my wine imbibers,' – to add to the depth already offered here. As for the French classics, choices are barely any less in calibre and are at the same time resolutely affordable. All credit to the enthusiasm of this one-woman merchant, who is 'open all hours via the answer-phone'. She's a braver person than we are.

For the Love of Wine

Flint Cottage, High Rougham, Bury St Edmunds, Suffolk IP30 9LN
Tel (01359) 270377
Fax (01359) 271483
Email
  for.the.love.of.wine@dial.pipex.com
Web site
  www.for-the-love-of-wine.co.uk

The Steel family's love of wine currently only extends to two countries. Italy was the first love, and the company has some excellent growers on its books. Among our favourites are Casa Emma and La Campana in Tuscany, and Abbona and Volpi in Piedmont, but we've not been disappointed with anything we've tried from the range. In addition, the Steels have also been flirting recently with Switzerland, and now represent six producers there. The highlight of what could be the largest range of Swiss wines in the country are the Pinot Noir and Petite Arvine from René Favre, so why not add some of these to your mixed case?　**£5**

Forth Wines

Crawford Place, Milnathort, Kinross
KY13 9XF
Tel (01577) 866001
Fax (01577) 866020
Email enquiries@forthwines.com

Important wholesaler and mail-order operator recently purchased by Matthew Clark plc. It's business as usual, however, and Forth don't intend to let the personal service they've always offered slip. Arabella Woodrow (a doctor and MW to boot!) heads up the team, so we're not surprised that the wines are impressive. And we're particularly pleased to see a company's imagination stretch as far as Idaho, Austria and fascinating Alsace red. Some of the grower names err towards the 'boring' – there's lots of Latour burgundy here – but for every 'less exciting' wine there's a fascinating older vintage from Bordeaux or Portugal to redress the balance. There's also – for the bulk or by-the-glass drinkers out there – a large selection of bag-in-box wines.

John Frazier

Head office
Stirling Road, Cranmore Industrial Estate, Shirley, Solihull,
West Midlands B90 4NE
Tel 0121-704 3415
Fax 0121-711 2710

New Inn Stores, Stratford Road, Wooten Wawen, Solihull,
West Midlands B95 6AS
Tel (01564) 794151

2 Old Warwick Road, Lapworth, Solihull B94 6LU
Tel (01564) 784695

Main Street, Tiddington, nr Stratford-upon-Avon CV37 7AN
Tel (01789) 262398
Email sales@fraziers.co.uk
Web site www.fraziers.co.uk

The results of a tuck-and-trim quality drive two years ago, in which the company dropped a couple of its branches, appear to be very good indeed. Fraziers are as much the all-rounders as ever, and their prices are every bit as competitive, but we think they've gone the extra mile on their upper-echelon wines. Five vintages of Penfolds Grange, a selection of Allegrini's Italian bottles, and some of the grandest names from Bordeaux all bear witness. It's great to be able to get hold of these treasures, and good to have the advice on hand to guide your choice. John Frazier still maintains that he's a New World specialist and we wouldn't deny that he is – particularly in light of his broad Australian selection – but we wouldn't want anyone to get the idea that this Midlands chain offered anything less than a world-ful.　**£5**

Friarwood

26 New Kings Road, London
SW6 4ST
Tel 020-7736 2628
Fax 020-7731 0411
Email sales@friarwood.com
Web site www.friarwood.com

Friarwood's forte has traditionally
been the ability to offer older
vintages from well-known
properties in Bordeaux and
Burgundy. This continues to be true,
and the Burgundy section now
includes a slightly larger selection of
producers than was once the case,
but wine buyer Edward Bowen tells
us that this Fulham company is now
extending its selection from Spain,
Italy and the New World. While we
like the Californian range (Ridge,
Qupé, Bonny Doon) and the South
African wines from Count Agusta
and Meerlust, it would still be those
classics that had us coming back
here. Those and the caviar, cigars
and Roxton's Original Sloe Gin.

Garrards Wine & Spirit
Merchants

49 Main Street, Cockermouth,
Cumbria CA13 9JS
Tel (01900) 823592
Fax (01900) 823592
Email chris@garrards-wine.co.uk
Web site www.garrards-wine.co.uk

Christopher Garrard has few hard
and fast rules at his Cumbrian
establishment. 'If we can assist in
getting that "special bottle" etc, we
will!' We'd say he already has a few
special bottles on his list, and
recommend that locals (and
holidaymakers) peruse these shelves
regularly for the cut-price offers that
crop up from time to time. It's not
all wine here either. There's a rather
splendid selection of whiskies, beers

and lagers at the back of the list too
– not least among them, Black
Sheep and Riggwelter from over the
border in North Yorkshire. We
applaud Garrards' diversity and aim
to please at all levels, with a range
that comprises good-quality, well-
priced offerings from across the
globe – Alsace to Australia,
Bordeaux and beyond.

Goedhuis & Co Ltd

6 Rudolf Place, Miles Street,
London SW8 1RP
Tel 020-7793 7900
Fax 020-7793 7170
Email enquiries@goedhuis.com
Web site www.goedhuis.com

The effusive Tom Stopford-Sackville
reckons his customers are suffering
New World fatigue. Not that the
New World has ever been a major
feature on the Goedhuis list
(although we wouldn't find the
Nepenthe Australians, Bernardus
Californians and Casa Lapostolle
Chileans too tiring). This is a place
where France receives top billing,
and the offerings from Burgundy
and Bordeaux are top class, with the
expanding Rhône selection not far
behind. In all three regions, you'll
have to get in early when the
opening offers are released to secure
the top wines, but the 'residue' is
still worth a close look. There's also
plenty for Italian fans to get their
teeth into, such as Sandrone's
Barolo and the Chianti Classico
from Monte Bernardi. Look out too
for the bin-end sale each March –
serious savings on serious wines.

The Good Wine Shop

391 St Margaret's Road, Isleworth,
Middlesex TW7 7BZ
Tel 020-8892 7756
Fax 020-8892 2260

203 Waldegrave Road, Teddington,
Middlesex TW11 8LX
Tel 020-8977 2161
Email daniel@gws2.demon.co.uk.

Make that the Good Wine *Shops*.
This is a new venture run by Daniel
Thorold, ex-manager of the El Vino
wine bar in Fleet Street, and Paul
Thomas, formerly of Cockburns of
Leith. The Isleworth shop opened
early in 2000; the Teddington outlet
was established the following
November. The focus is on value-
for-money with a slightly quirky
edge, so you'll find a good selection
of southern French reds, sensibly
priced burgundies, and some less
familiar wines from South Africa.
And if the wines don't catch your
eye, you can always go for the many
beers, Breton ciders and specialist
foods, including 'the outstanding
Benenden sauce', a sweet garlic
salad dressing.

Gordon & MacPhail

58–60 South Street, Elgin, Moray
IV30 1JY
Tel (01343) 545110
Fax (01343) 540155
Email
  info@gordonandmacphail.com
Web site
  www.gordonandmacphail.com

We get the impression that whisky
still comes first here (Gordon &
Macphail have been suppliers of
such for over 100 years) but wine is
a closer second than ever. There are
certainly vinous choices from
everywhere, but we're still

disappointed to see single (large)
producers dominating the ranges
from some of the regions. There's
more to South Africa than the KWV,
for example (however much they've
improved), and there's certainly
more to California than Kendall-
Jackson. However, we're pleased to
see less-usual areas such as Mexico,
Uruguay and Canada represented,
and admire what the buyers (David
and Ian Urquhart) have managed to
wheedle out of Bordeaux and
Australia. Port, madeira, champagne
and sparkling wine all get fairly
good exposure too, so you're
certainly not limited to whisky for
pre- and post-prandial delectation.

Grapeland

27 Parkfield, Chorleywood,
Hertfordshire WD3 5AZ
Tel (01923) 284436
Fax (01923) 286346
Email info@grapeland.uk.com
Web site www.grapeland.uk.com

Graham Cork (good name that) is
still in his first year of business, but
already has an impressive list to
offer. We particularly like the wines
he's chosen from Australia and
South Africa – Simonsig's range
from the latter is one of the best
from that country. Once similarly
fleshed out, we don't doubt the
Californian and South American
selections will be equally pithy.
Starting life with a good range of
classics has also been important to
Graham, as is obvious from the
quite upper-crust choices from
Burgundy and Bordeaux. We like
the way it all kicks off with
'Grapeland's Special Selection
Claret' at £4.99, too, though such
keenly priced wines are rare on this
list. 'Service, service, service', is
Graham's motto. The company
already has a web site, newsletters

are on the way, and tastings, glass hire and free local delivery all complete the picture. And Graham is happy to offer advice in the event of any dilemmas while deciding on a mixed case. **(£5)**

Peter Green

37A/B Warrender Park Road, Edinburgh EH9 1HJ
Tel 0131-229 5925
Fax 0131-229 5925

Michael Romer is responsible for buying the wines at this fine Scottish establishment, with some top-notch Alsace wines and affordable Bordeaux and burgundies making a fine start to the list. Indeed, affordability seems to be the watchword across the range, and we appreciate the way this doesn't preclude the likes of Allegrini, Masi and Rizzardi when it comes to Italy – all stunning estates, making stunning wines. Michael shows no fear of trying out something new, and the result includes some fascinating choices from Somontano, Priorat and trendy new regions of Spain, plus a healthy smattering of less-mainstream Australian estates (and thank heaven for them!). Michael's eye for a trend also encompasses a couple of Uruguayan Tannats – excellent for accompanying the fieriest of barbecue fare. We do find the California selection a little more pedestrian, but this can be forgiven in view of the unusual Greek, Israeli and Canadian wines available, and for the impeccable (and brave) range of delicate Mosel wines and top sherries. **(£5)**

Hall Batson & Co

28 Whiffler Road, Norwich NR3 2AZ
Tel (01603) 415115
Fax (01603) 484096
Email info@hallbatson.co.uk
Web site www.hallbatson.co.uk

Hall Batson continues to progress with its appealing mix of known and unknown wines from around the world, and it doesn't seem far from taking up a place among the other top-notch East Anglian wine merchants. The classics are all here, in good quantity, and there's added breadth given by offerings from Spain (stretching to trendy Galicia in the north-west), Portugal, an excellent selection from South Africa, and careful choices from California and Australia. Added assets are the detailed tasting notes, and the overall affordability this wine merchant offers, making it a great alternative to regular high-street shops – particularly given the option of delivery service. Gourmet dinners, grower visits and regular in-house tastings all add to the high standard of service.

Roger Harris Wines

Loke Farm, Weston Longville, Norfolk NR9 5LG
Tel (01603) 880171
Fax (01603) 880291
Email sales@rogerharriswines.co.uk
Web site www.beaujolaisonline.co.uk

Roger Harris' first shipment of Beaujolais was a barrel of Fleurie that he had ordered to be sent to him in Nairobi. By the time it arrived, it was oxidised beyond recognition, so he christened it 'fire water' and drank every drop anyway. Whatever it tasted like it must have been a seductive brew, as

Roger has been importing Beaujolais (from his Norfolk red-brick farmhouse) for 26 years now. Thankfully the wines are all delicious these days, with nothing more fiery than a fine de Bourgogne among them.

We love this list. Not all that many merchants take the trouble to focus in so closely on one region, and anyone browsing through this selection will quickly realise that Roger is passionate about these wines. We can think of no better place to gain a full understanding of Beaujolais – serious Gamay, that is, not the third-Thursday-of-November Nouveau mouthwash. But back to that wine list: the ten *crus* or village wines are all there, with a number of good growers from each; plus Beaujolais Blanc (from Chardonnay), Beaujolais rosé (we like the sound of that for summer/picnic drinking) and a selection of wines from the Mâconnais (again, excellent, but not as trend-bucking as the Beaujolais choices). Our message hasn't changed. We heartily recommend purchasing a mixed case from this wholesale outlet and delving in as deep as Roger has. Most of the wines come in at under £100 a case, so this is bargain territory too. **£5**

Richard Harvey Wines

Bucknowle House, Wareham, Dorset BH20 5PQ
Tel (01929) 481437
Fax (01929) 481275
Email harvey@lds.co.uk

As befits a Master of Wine and consultant to Bonhams and Brooks auctioneers, Richard Harvey's Bordeaux selection is excellent. It's competitively priced enough to see the wine trade returning time after

time, so we suggest private buyers do too. There's ample choice from every important vintage since 1961, with all the top names making a showing. Monthly claret offers cover both classed growth and good *crus bourgeois* châteaux, and there is an annual *en primeur* release, for which Richard uses his buying skills to select characterful options from the smaller estates. So successful has Bordeaux been at Richard Harvey Wines that a similar focus on Burgundy, the Rhône and Italy is promised soon. For those looking to mix and match in their (minimum) single case purchases, there's a handy choice of quality bottles from beyond the Gironde. Not many, but of enough character for us to hope that expansion plans come to fruition soon. **£5**

Haslemere Cellar

16 West Street, Haslemere, Surrey GU27 2AB
Tel (01428) 645081
Fax (01428) 645108
Email hcellar@haslemere.com

A small but impeccably formed little list, focusing on France and good prices, and running the gamut from the everyday to every dinner party. Richard Royds is a busy man – he travels as often as he can in order to choose these wines – but we hear good things have been going on. August 2001 saw Haslemere Cellar moving to new premises and joining forces with the local cheese specialists, Cheesebox. The produce of this union is already obvious in the mouth-watering 'Haslemere Hampers' mail-order sideline. We wouldn't mind a hamperful of what this outlet has to offer, and would happily make a start on the delicious German wines before tucking into the clarets (1961 Pichon Baron among them, if you please) and cheddar. **(£5)**

Heyman, Barwell Jones Ltd

24 Fore Street, Ipswich, Suffolk
IP4 1JU
Tel (01473) 232322
Fax (01473) 212237
Email sales@heyman.co.uk

This smart wholesale operation is another of those distinguished East Anglian acts. Their wealth of experience is reflected in the good old brewing names, such as Cobbold and Beamish, which crop up in the list of directors. Among the very reasonably priced wines are some top-notch ones too: Château Bellegrave, Pomerol; Langoa-Barton St-Julien from Bordeaux; plus some very fine burgundies and one or two smart Australian choices. We like the fact that there's something from everywhere here, and that your mixed case really could range from Alsace Gewurztraminer to Zinfandel. We don't know some of the growers listed and can't vouch for their reliability, but we feel sure that with an experienced buyer such as Annette Duce at the helm (she's ex-Fortnum & Mason), they'll be nothing less than very sound.

Hicks & Don

4 Old Station Yard, Edington, Westbury, Wiltshire BA13 4NT
Tel (01380) 831234
Fax (01380) 831010
Email mailbox@hicksanddon.co.uk
Web site www.hicksanddon.co.uk

'This selection has been made by three Masters of Wine, Ronnie Hicks, Robin Don and Anthony Barne, together with Richard Simpson who manages the business. In it you will not see wines that Robert Parker finds "profound", but affordable wines that we think you will enjoy drinking ...' There's no doubt about it, this list gets off to a good start on that basis. Wines are set out by style in sensible categories such as 'Rhône and Shiraz' and 'White Burgundy and other Chardonnays'. If you order a mixed case, you can enjoy choosing them as much as drinking them, as the range is broad, intelligent, and occasionally unusual. Look out for the regular bin-end offers too – therein lie gems and bargains. **(£5)**

High Breck Vintners

11 Nelson Road, London N8 9RX
Tel 020-8340 1848
Fax 020-8340 5162
Email hbv@richanl.freeserve.co.uk
Web site www.hbvwines.com

Andrew and Linda Richardson took over the running of High Breck in 1999, and have been slowly expanding what was already an admirable range from smaller French producers. Highlights include Bauget-Jouette in Champagne, Gitton in Sancerre, Tijou in Anjou and Wiederhirn in Alsace, and there's always a good selection of clarets available. The choice from other countries is much more limited, but you'll still find good-quality wines from Grant Burge in Australia, Barbadillo and Valdespino in Jerez, and Antinori in Italy. While there's only one list produced each year, the chatty newsletters keep customers up to date with new arrivals and special offers. Look out for the bin-end sales, which bring already attractive prices down to even more friendly levels.

George Hill Ltd of Loughborough

59 Wards End, Loughborough,
Leicestershire LE11 3HB
Tel (01509) 212717
Fax (01509) 236963
Email info@georgehill.co.uk
Web site www.georgehill.co.uk

Customer service is obviously
important at this Leicestershire
merchant. 'You get a better class of
insult at George Hill,' says Andrew
Hill, grandson of the company's
founder and now managing director
and wine buyer. His array of wines
is a solid one in which he aims to list
'… nothing that is boring and
overpriced'. We'd like to see a little
more life in the selections from up-
and-coming places such as southern
France and Portugal, but we've no
problems with the ranges from
South Africa (Jordan, Louisvale,
Glen Carlou) and Spain (Rioja from
Urbina and others, plus fine sherries
too). The Australians and Italians
are also worth a look. **£5**

Hopton Wines

Hopton Court, Cleobury Mortimer,
Kidderminster, Worcestershire
DY14 0EF
Tel (01299) 270734
Fax (01299) 271132
Email hoptoncourt@hotmail.com
Web site www.hoptoncourt.co.uk

Christopher Woodward laments
that many locals prefer to go to
France to do their wine shopping
rather than visit him in Cleobury
Mortimer. Those who do make it to
his shop will find a solid range
featuring producers such as
Niepoort, Backsberg, Château de
Tracy and Hunters. If anything
could be called Hopton's speciality
it would be Bordeaux – try the

sensibly priced wines from châteaux
such as Cap de Haut, l'Hurbe and
Prieuré Lescours. And do find time
for the excellent value champagnes
from the houses of Marguet-
Bonnerave and Launois.

Ian G Howe

35 Appletongate, Newark,
Nottinghamshire NG24 1JR
Tel (01636) 704366
Fax (01636) 610502
Email
  howe@chablis-burgundy.co.uk
Web site
  www.chablis-burgundy.co.uk

Ian and Sylvia Howe do sell a little
champagne and a selection of
Crème de Fruits, but their passion is
very much the wines of Chablis. The
Howes' list runs to about 16
different producers, all of them high
class, with famous names such as
Dauvissat and Raveneau rubbing
shoulders with up-and-coming
domaines such as Boudin and
Tribut. There are also other wines of
the district, including the excellent
Sauvignon de St-Bris from Goisot.
For the last few years, Ian has been
expanding his range of Côte de
Beaune burgundies, so you'll now
find reds from Sérafin and Tardy,
and whites from Pillot and Bzikot.
But good as these are, we'd still
steer you towards the Chablis first.

Inspired Wines

West End, High Street, Cleobury
Mortimer, Shropshire DY14 8DR
Tel (01299) 270064
Fax (01299) 270064
Email info@inspired-wines.co.uk
Web site www.inspired-wines.co.uk

Inspiration and momentum are
gathering at this small merchant.
Tim Cowin and his wife Sue have

453

now moved their business into a wine warehouse (from a small shop), they have launched a new quarterly newsletter (and very cheerful/informative it is too) and took on their first part-time member of staff in January 2001. The Cowins still maintain they're having trouble shifting French wine – although their selection is good, the Shropshire locals would rather choose from elsewhere. However, these customers shouldn't have a problem finding something 'inspired' from other parts of the world – with the likes of Allegrini and Masi making a showing from Italy, Pipers Brook from Australia and Bonny Doon from the States. We're also pleased to see top English sparkling wine, Nyetimber, listed. Anybody in the dark about some of the more 'adventurous' names on this list will have their questions quickly answered, either at one of the regular tastings or by opening a bottle in the shop. **£5**

Irvine Robertson Wines

10 & 11 North Leith Sands, Edinburgh EH6 4ER
Tel 0131-553 3521
Fax 0131-553 5465
Email irviner@nildram.co.uk
Web site www.irwines.co.uk

General manager Graeme White describes himself as 'Scottish, independent and proud of it!'. He can also be proud of his range of wines. New World wines are gaining in popularity, and Graeme offers particularly good selections from South Africa (Märeson, Rocheburg), Australia (Water Wheel, Evans & Tate) and the USA (Stag's Leap Wine Cellars, St Francis). However, he doesn't neglect the classic regions of Europe. You'll find Muga Riojas,

Rhône reds from Guigal and a selection of burgundies which majors on *négociants*, but also growers such as Michel Bouzereau and Chavy. And for those who prefer something fortified, there's port from Churchill, madeira from Henriques & Henriques and Hidalgo sherries. **£5**

Michael Jobling Wines

Baltic Chambers, 3–7 Broad Chare, Newcastle upon Tyne NE1 3DQ
Tel 0191-261 5298
Fax 0191-261 4543
Email
  mjw@michaeljoblingwines.co.uk
Web site
  www.michaeljoblingwines.co.uk

Michael Jobling might have terrible handwriting (we could barely read his reply to our questionnaire this year!) but through his selection of wines, the message is clear: quality counts. This list might not be lengthy, but it is good. As we've mentioned before, buying by the case is not a problem when there is such a stunning range of growers to choose from. Right from the best champagnes (Krug, Bollinger), through Hugel and Trimbach from Alsace, Jaboulet-Aîné from the Rhône, Stag's Leap and Saintsbury from California, we're impressed by the calibre of what's on offer. It's a selection made all the more useful by the sub-£4 'easy-drinkers' at the start of the list and the range of half bottles at the back. As Michael says: 'Wine is to be enjoyed without being pompous about it.' From his list, there's every opportunity for enjoyment. **£5**

Richard Kihl

Slaughden House, 142–144 High
Street, Aldeburgh, Suffolk IP15 5AQ
Tel (01728) 454455
Fax (01728) 454433
Email sales@richardkihl.ltd.uk
Web site www.richardkihl.ltd.uk

This superb array of Bordeaux (just
about every vintage covered from
1865 to the present day) is available
from 'Richard Kihl' if you're buying
by mail order, or Slaughden Wines
if you live locally to the shop. And
we wish we lived locally: Richard
Kihl moved his premises from
London to Aldeburgh on the Suffolk
coast six years ago – very nice too!
This has made little difference to the
quality of service: customers are still
supplied from the London
warehouse, enthusiastic staff are still
on hand to offer in-depth broking
and purchasing advice, and regular
tastings and newsletters still crop up
from time to time. As well as the
best names from Bordeaux, top
burgundy is on offer, plus
champagne, the odd Super-Tuscan
and plenty of old-vintage port and
madeira. Prices for this classy lot are,
well, extremely classy! £5

Luvians Bottle Shop

93 Bonnygate, Cupar, Fife KY15 4LG
Tel (01334) 654820
Fax (01334) 654820

66 Market Street, St. Andrews, Fife
KY16 9NT
Tel (01334) 477752
Fax (01334) 477128
Email luvians@freeuk.com

In truth it's the vast range of
whiskies that is the most impressive
feature of the Luvians' list; however,
there's plenty for those who prefer
grape to grain. The selections from
Bordeaux, Burgundy, Italy and
Australia are vast, and the quality
on offer is pretty high. Other
regions and countries may offer
slightly shorter (but by no means
small) ranges, but again we can't
faulty producers such as Allende in
Rioja, Ostertag in Alsace and Neil
Ellis in South Africa. A Luvians
speciality seems to be ready-made
vertical tastings – seven vintages of
Cos d'Estournel; nine of Opus One.
Don't miss out on the fortified
wines either – some lovely Lustau
sherries plus ports back to Taylor
1924. £5

F & E May

Viaduct House, 16 Warner Street,
London EC1R 5HA
Tel 020-7843 1600
Fax 020-7843 1601
Email sales@fandemay.com
Web site www.fandemay.com

It's a toss-up whether Bordeaux or
Germany is the main event at this
London company. From the latter,
you'll find good selections from
producers such as von Buhl,
Maximin Grünhaus and St
Urbanshof. From the former, there
are good stocks of well-known
châteaux covering several vintages.
However, you'll also find some fine
wines from Spain, such as
Manzaneque and David Moreno
Peña, plus the excellent Don Zoilo
sherries. Other countries and
regions get a look-in, and we
recommend the Rhône reds of
Revol and Bastide, the Alsace whites
of Klipfel and the higher-priced
wines from the Mondavi range. £5

For an explanation of the
symbols used at the top of
some of the merchant entries,
see page 303

Mayfair Cellars

Miniver House, 19–20 Garlick Hill,
London EC4V 2AL
Tel 020-7329 8899
Fax 020-7329 8880
Email sales@mayfaircellars.co.uk

July 2000 saw the champagne house Jacquesson take the controlling stake in Mayfair Cellars, since which time one or two changes have been made. What was a classy operation before has, we suspect, got a little classier. It's too early to tell for sure, of course, but the new range of Austrian wines from the Freie Weingärtner in the Wachau, and the Bordeaux châteaux additions to the list all seem to bode well. Mayfair's goals haven't altered all that much. It still offers brokering services, and the aim is still to specialise in boutique producers who don't sell to high-street chains. There are still four to five tastings a year and client lunches. And Mayfair still has a busy branch in Hong Kong. But we suspect the takeover has afforded some more intrepid buying forays into the New World for a start. It's good to see Jacquesson giving the nod to Clover Hill Tasmanian sparkling, and it's equally encouraging to see the likes of Leeuwin and De Bortoli making an appearance from Australia. Mayfair continues to focus on the classics first and foremost – the burgundies are expensive but Bordeaux and Rhône choices offer less wallet-strain. And from Italy the range is broader than ever – now including Tenuta di Riseccoli olive oil.   **£5**

Mayor Sworder

7 Aberdeen Road, Croydon, Surrey
CR0 1EQ
Tel 020-8686 1155
Fax 020-8686 2017
Email sales@mayorsworder.co.uk
Web site www.mayorsworder.co.uk

The very smart and handy-sized list – full of useful details, helpful tasting notes and clever illustrations – makes for good first impressions of this Surrey-based merchant. This is well substantiated by the wines on offer, especially those from France. Martin Everett, Master of Wine, chooses well here, with an enticing range of Rhônes, top Bordeaux châteaux (watch out for the well-priced *en primeur* offers) and burgundy from basic Bourgogne Aligoté to Bâtard-Montrachet. Good, mainstream names come from the rest of the world too – with the occasional top-notch properties such as South Africa's Kanonkop. As the list now begins with French country, Australian and other New World wines, we're tempted to think Martin's trying to shed the France-first image and go more global … good for him!

Mills Whitcombe

The Sett, Lower Maescoed,
Herefordshire HR2 0HS
Tel (01873) 860222
Fax (01873) 860444
Email floyd@millswhitcombe.co.uk

A newcomer to the last edition of the *Guide*, Mills Whitcombe has just completed (as we write) its first year of business. In this time it's managed to pull together a tidy selection including the illustrious likes of Josmeyer from Alsace, Finca El Retiro from Argentina and Dirk

Niepoort's quality ports. That it's struck gold quite so soon is hardly surprising given the pedigree of the start-up team: Becky Whitcombe, Floyd Mills and Judy Kendrick are all experienced wine-traders. They've even managed to entice winemakers such as Trevor Mast (Mount Langi Ghiran) and Charlie Melton from Australia up to Hereford to speak at Mills Whitcombe tastings. Not bad for starters! That they know what they're looking for is obvious from the calibre (and price) of the wines listed. This, regular newsletters, and lively, friendly and enthusiastic service, all bodes well for a cracking future. **(£5)**

Milton Sandford Wines

The Old Chalk Mine, Warren Row Road, Knowl Hill, Berkshire RG10 8QS
Tel (01628) 829449
Fax (01628) 829424
Email
    sales@milton-sandford.demon.co.uk

A mail-order merchant with a difference. Not only does Milton Sandford operate from an old chalk mine, but it offers one of the best selections of its kind in the UK. When we asked Richard Sandford to list the wines he was most proud of, and he came back with 'Grosset wines, including Polish Hill and Watervale Rieslings, Pierro West Australian Chardonnay, Bott Geyl from Alsace and Stags Leap from California', we knew that the MSW quality pitch was as strong as ever. Australia still tops the bill, but France, especially Champagne, come up trumps too. There's a short but classy selection of Bordeaux (including châteaux Beychevelle and Malescasse) and a snappy range

of Rhône reds. We're pleased to see some lesser-known wine names and smaller producers here, and feel confident that even if you haven't heard of the grower, the wine will be well worth drinking.

The Moffat Wine Shop

8 Well Street, Moffat, Dumfriesshire DG10 9DP
Tel (01683) 220554
Email moffwine@aol.com
Web site www.moffattown.com/
    moffat/traders/mwines

Moffat wines are sensibly chosen, keenly priced; and an ever-increasing proportion of them come from the New World. The Australia section is where wine buyer A K McIlwrick really gets going (and it's growing and growing) but we're also impressed with the range of offerings from New Zealand and Chile. Moffat doesn't dwell too long on France, but the Spanish selection has the greatest number of new additions this year – Tempranillos from Navarra and Toro look tasty – and there's been a further foray into Hungary (Castle Island Furmint and Hárslevelü are both worth a try). The recently launched wine tastings/suppers now run on two consecutive nights – such is their popularity – and, as ever, the whisky list goes from strength to strength. We particularly like the new regional colour-coding of the malts to highlight their source. **(£5)**

We love to hear your views on wine merchants. You can email your comments to us at: whichwineguide@which.net

New Zealand Wines Direct

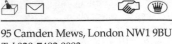

95 Camden Mews, London NW1 9BU
Tel 020-7482 0093
Fax 020-7267 8400
Email
  margaret.harvey@btinternet.com
Web site www.fwnz.co.uk

Much of the credit for the popularity of New Zealand wines today must go to Margaret Harvey, MW (Master of Wine) and MNZM (Member of the New Zealand Order of Merit). She began importing wines from her home country into the UK in 1985, developing what was a hobby into a fully fledged business. Over the years she has been responsible for introducing several top producers to the UK, and continues to do so – a newcomer this year is the excellent Pegasus Bay from Canterbury. Such is the demand for wines from some of her growers – Stonyridge, Rippon, Ata Rangi and Te Motu in particular – that her stocks rapidly run out. However, she'll be happy to suggest alternatives, and we're sure you'll be satisfied with her choices.

Pallant Wines Ltd

17 High Street, Arundel,
West Sussex BN18 9AD
Tel (01903) 882288
Fax (01903) 882801
Email contact@pallantwines.co.uk

'Personality!' That's the key to Pallant wines, according to managing director and wine buyer Marian Huntingdon. Her establishment is both a wine shop and a high-class deli, so you need go no further to find everything for a good meal. The range runs to around 400 different wines, but since turnover is brisk, you'll have to pay a visit to the shop for a browse. We'd head first for the Hamilton Russells from South Africa, the New Zealand Pinot Noirs, the champagnes from Delbeck, Jacquesson and Billecart-Salmon, and an alternative fizz from nearby Nyetimber.

Palmers Wine Store

The Old Brewery, Bridport, Dorset
DT6 4JA
Tel (01308) 422396
Fax (01308) 421149
Email enquiries@palmerbrewery.com
Web site www.palmerbrewery.com

While beer is the main event at the Old Brewery in Bridport, Cleeves Palmer has assembled a decent array of wines for the company established by his great-grandfather in the nineteenth century. Well-known names such as Penfolds, Concha y Toro, Drouhin and Campo Viejo abound, but the inclusion of offerings from the likes of Verget, Clos Malverne and Selvapiana spice up the stock. The selections from Australia, Chile and South Africa are the largest, but you could dive into the range at any point and come up with a good (if not necessarily great) bottle of wine.

Thomas Panton

The Wine Warehouse, Hampton Street, Tetbury, Gloucestershire
GL8 8JN
Tel (01666) 503088
Fax (01666) 503113
Email
  panton@winewhse.force9.co.uk
Web site www.wineimporter.co.uk

'Our main interest is in French wines because we believe that they are more subtle in flavour and being from small growers have much more to say for themselves,' explains Tom Panton. To that end, this neat little list has an adept range of Bordeaux, burgundy and Beaujolais (some top growers among them; Michel Rolland and Château Léoville-Barton to name but two), and sound choices from the Rhône, Loire and Provence. It also dips into some fascinating smaller areas such as Savoie, and has a fine selection of Alsace wines from Domaine Albert Mann. Although the rest of the coverage doesn't delve as deep, Tom chooses well-made wines (often discovered while visiting the regions himself), and if the £10-a-bottle threshold is broken there's normally a good (quality) reason for it. Tom's team pride themselves on being youngish and on the ball (there's a very new web site now up and running), and on being small-scale enough to offer good personal service.

Parfrements

68 Cecily Road, Cheylesmore, Coventry CV3 5LA
Tel (02476) 503646
Fax (02476) 506406
Email gerald@parfrements.co.uk
Web site
  www.parfrements.co.uk/parfrements

Gerald Gregory is self-confessedly 'tall, dark and handsome, interested in metaphysics, philosophy and wine appreciation', and also very proud of his merchant's business. 'We don't sell run-of-the-mill plonk here!' He's also a passionate communicator. Parfrements issues four wine lists a year, gives free advice as and when it's called for, has a monthly bulletin page on its web site, and offers regular tastings to customers – plus, Gerald heads up his brochure with a useful

glossary of 'terminology explained'. This isn't the lengthiest list of wines we've seen but it's one of the quirkiest. It starts at A (for Absinthe, believe it or not!) and works around the world alphabetically, without pandering to the me-firstness of Bordeaux and Burgundy. Special attention is paid to Italy and Portugal, and we rate the California choices highly too.   **(£5)**

Peckham & Rye

Head Office
18 Bogmoor Place, Glasgow G51 4TQ
Tel 0141-445 4555
Fax 0141-445 5511
Email sbatpeck@aol.com
Web site www.peckhams.co.uk

(9 stores located in Glasgow and Edinburgh)

The Peckhams empire now runs to ten stores in Scotland, and we'd be happy to live near any one of them. The range is packed with plenty of good-quality, familiar names such as Hugel, Faiveley, Marqués de Murrieta, Pipers Brook and Brown Brothers. However, the company does not bypass more rarefied wines, so you'll find more esoteric gems – such as burgundies from Latour-Giraud, Hewitson's solid Barossa reds and the Mission Hill wines from Canada – on the shelves. There's something here for everyone, and quality is generally high. Indeed, our only regret is that there aren't some stores south of the border. And if you don't find the wines a moving experience, Peckhams is the only merchant we know selling 'Bowel Essence' (£3.99 for 30ml).

Penistone Court Wine Cellars

The Railway Station, Penistone,
Sheffield, South Yorkshire S36 6HP
Tel (01226) 766037
Fax (01226) 767310
Email pcwc@dircon.co.uk
Web site www.cellars-direct.com

For all its humble beginnings this is
now a nicely balanced list, bringing in
everything from £3.45-a-bottle
cheerful Spanish numbers to £125
Château Cheval Blanc (well, at least
you know you can get it!). In terms of
satisfying customers who want mid-
to high-price big names, we think
Chris Ward is doing increasingly
well, but we hand out due credit for
the (more interesting) bargain areas
too. Alsace, for example: £5 and £6
wines are hard to come by from this
region but Chris has managed to find
them. Italy is as impressive as ever, as
is the sizeable collection of wines
from the USA. In Australia, Chile and
Argentina, Chris tends to rely on just
a handful of producers but
nonetheless still shows a good eye for
departing from the norm.   **£5**

C A Rookes Wine Merchants

7 Western Road Industrial Estate,
Stratford-upon-Avon CV37 0AH
Tel (01789) 297777
Fax (01789) 297752
Email bottle@carookes.co.uk
Web site www.carookes.co.uk

John Freeland likes wines that 'have
been made with the hands and the
heart, and not designed in a
laboratory and made in a factory'.
We couldn't agree more. He also
prefers to sell them to people he
likes, so if you're a fan of French
wine it'll be worth getting on the
right side of him. Muscadet features
largely here, and if you're not
convinced about this wine, turn up

at one of the regular Saturday
tastings to find out more. Otherwise,
there's Bordeaux aplenty to delve
into (including good-priced
châteaux second labels), a wide
range of burgundy, and tasters from
the rest of the world. France is the
speciality, but if you want to try
Uruguayan Tannat (for example), it's
there on the list.

Sapsford Wines

33 Musley Lane, Ware,
Hertfordshire, SG12 7EW
Tel (01920) 421492
Fax (01920) 467040
Email sapsfordwines@aol.com

The Sapsford team (Mary and Barry)
want their wines to be 'agricultural,
not industrial' products, and their
quest for the right ones is clearly
nothing if not a consuming passion.
We like the prices and we like the
wholesome smattering of growers
we haven't heard of before. That the
Sapsfords began as Loire specialists
is still evident, as these wines
dominate the front of the list, but
they've branched out too. Popular
demand from customers has seen
the addition of Corbières to their
forays, as well as the rest of France,
and the new Italian and Portuguese
selections show an equally good eye
for a bargain. Talks, tastings and
advice are always available.   **£5**

Savage Selection

The Ox House, Market Place,
Northleach, Cheltenham,
Gloucestershire GL54 3EG
Tel (01451) 860896
Fax (01451) 860996
Email info@savageselection.co.uk
Web site www.savageselection.co.uk

'Great wine is not about cosmetics, it
is about originality,' says Mark
Savage, and his range is about as

original as they come. There are no concessions to fashion here, just a collection of wines that he has ferreted out in his four decades in the trade. France is clearly his happiest hunting ground, and he has especially close relationships with certain producers, such as Thévenet in Burgundy, Tempier in Bandol and François Mitjavile in Bordeaux. However, he also finds time to source excellent wines from other parts of Europe (the Italian choices are especially impressive) and various parts of the New World, including Idaho. Even if some of his wines are less than mainstream, we've never been disappointed with anything we've tried. So if you want 'real wine rather than processed grape juice', just put yourselves in the hands of a Savage. **£5**

Scatchard

Head Office
Kings Dock Street, Wapping,
Liverpool L1 8JS
Tel 0151-709 7073
Fax 0151-709 1500

36 Exchange Street East, Liverpool
L2 3PS
Tel 0151-236 2955
Fax 0151-236 6838

11 Albert Road, Hoylake, Wirral
CH47 2AB
Tel/Fax 0151-632 0507
Email info@scatchard.com

Well known as Spanish specialists, Scatchard are now making inroads into Italy too, and we're far from disappointed by the rest of this global selection. What Spain and Italy have in quantity, the Alsace, California and New Zealand choices add to in quality. For example, there's no white Rías Baixas from Spain, more's the pity, but we think the Cloudy Bay and Isabel estate

Chardonnays from New Zealand make up for this loss. Business errs slightly more on the wholesale than the retail side – the aim being to supply restaurant-friendly options to local eateries – but by-the-bottle customers are treated to regular Friday tastings, and their pursuit of the sub-£2 bargain, if not indulged, is striven for as far as possible. Scatchard have three outlets now, all with the same broad and interesting range. **£5**

Ashley Scott

PO Box 28, The Highway,
Hawarden, Flintshire CH5 3RY
Tel (01244) 520655
Fax (01244) 520655

A succinct but highly respectable list from this Flintshire duo (Jean and Michael Scott) is impressive firstly for its stylish presentation – a handy size and a smart red and gold cover. Appearances aside, delve in and you'll find something from almost everywhere. Treasures such as Alsace's Willm estate sit alongside Hazendal from South Africa and Corbans from New Zealand. If there's anything left unexplained by the detailed notes, the Scotts are more than happy to advise. Pricing is exceptionally fair (even the Bordeaux rarely top £10 a bottle) and while you don't get the big labels here, Ashley Scott's two lists a year show a great deal of attention to detail, which is what you would expect after 38 years in the business.

For an explanation of the symbols used at the top of some of the merchant entries, see page 303.

Sebastopol Wines

Sebastopol Barn, London Road,
Blewbury, Oxfordshire OX11 9HB
Tel (01235) 850471
Fax (01235) 850776
Email sebastopol wines@aol.com

Merchant-in-a-barn it may be, but
Sebastopol's list is strictly upper crust,
and upper crust only. Generous
reserves from the likes of châteaux
Angélus, Valandraud and Margaux in
Bordeaux all point the way. The
burgundy selection is pitched at the
same level, as are those from the
Rhône and Australia, and
champagnes are no less illustrious
than Krug, Salon and Dom Pérignon.
There must be some very deep
pockets around Blewbury in
Oxfordshire, or how else would
Barbara and Caroline Affleck be able
to maintain such an impressively
classy selection? We'd say we were
being generous to put the average
bottle-spend here at £20 – it's
probably more like £30. And while the
cheapest bottle, a manzanilla sherry,
comes in at £6.09, it just so happens to
be Barbadillo, which, quality-wise,
once again is as good as it gets.

Slaughden Wines

see Richard Kihl

Spar UK

Head office
Hygeia Building, 66–68 College
Road, Harrow, Middlesex HA1 1BE
Tel 020-8426 3700
Fax 020-8426 3701/2
Web site www.spar.co.uk
(2,650 branches nationwide)

Cheap and cheerful and open till
late (24 hours a day in some cases) –
but, as we said last year, Spar is not
our first choice of outlet for wine

shopping. There's plenty of big-
brand reliability here, but very little
excitement, and 'anything but
Chardonnay' customers will be out
of luck. Rosemount, Hardy's and
Gallo feature all through the list,
and are supported by a gluggable
stash of own-brand, £3-ish wines.

Springfield Wines

Springfield Mill, Norman Road,
Denby Dale, Huddersfield HD8 8TH
Tel (01484) 864929
Fax (01484) 864929

Springfield is run by an enthusiastic
husband-and-wife team, Richard
and Lesley Brook (with occasional
help from their daughters), who
offer, throughout, a very personal
touch. Their carefully handwritten
list adds to the homespun charm of
it all – as does the fact that the
business is based in a converted
textile mill. (An unintentional pun!)
France features most strongly here –
a real passion for the place is
reflected in unusual and fascinating
offerings from the Jura and oddities
such as sparkling Alsace. What's
nicest about this list is its resolute
attempt at being global but
attainable, with all the wines, bar
the burgundies on the first page,
sticking steadfastly (or as nearly as
possible) to the £5 and £10 mark.

John Stephenson & Sons
(Nelson)

254 Manchester Road, Nelson,
Lancashire BB9 7DE
Tel (01282) 698827
Fax (01282) 601161
Email wbannp@aol.com

A succinct but insightful list
featuring everything from top claret
and burgundy from older vintages
to Israeli Merlot and Argentinian

Torrontés. We like the fact that, despite the range of familiar names here (Hardy's and Brown Brothers from Australia, Sutter Home and Woodbridge from the States), John Stephenson also dares to be different – and occasionally this means it stumbles, at fortuitous prices, on real quality. Walter Schug's Carneros Pinot Noir, for example, is a treasure at £14.30. The aim, overall, is to be keenly priced, but we're not overly impressed by the selection of cheap but bland German and Italian wines: sometimes we think it's possible to stoop too low. We like the rationale though. **£5**

Taste For Wine

Customer Call Centre
Tel (0800) 917 4092
Fax (0800) 917 4095
Web site www.tasteforwine.co.uk

Ex-*Guide* editor Claire Gordon-Brown was lured away from us early in 2001 to head up the buying team for this joint venture between Sainsbury's and Oddbins. The aim is to have about 1,000 wines available through conventional mail order or via the Internet. At present, the range runs to around 500 wines, which unsurprisingly includes many of those available on the shelves of the two parent companies. The venture concentrates on the £5-to-£10 bracket, rather than the cheaper end of the market. The largest selection is from Australia, but most countries receive decent coverage. If you shop regularly at Sainsbury's and Oddbins, you probably don't need Taste for Wine. However, the instigators feel they have identified a need for a 'reliable middle-market direct wine company' and are seeking to exploit that. Expect some

very attractive mixed-case offers in the coming months, or simply pick a dozen wines from the list and then add in a thirteenth bottle – for free.

Trout Wines

The Trout, Nether Wallop, Stockbridge, Hampshire SO20 8EW
Tel (01264) 781472
Fax (01264) 781472
Email
anthonywhitaker@waitrose.com

'Our service is a very personal one and all our wines are chosen by us because we like them and not because they fit in price-wise,' says Anthony Whitaker, hand on heart; and while he's not going to win any prizes for quantity, we would happily dip into this selection for its sheer quality or just to try out something new. We detect, from some of his unusual but flavourful choices, that Anthony has a very good palate, and are particularly impressed by the New World wines on offer. This is a wine merchant for 'Hampshire-ites': it's one to pop into – not only for its charming situation in a large thatched cottage, but because there's invariably a bottle of something tasty open to guide your choice. Watch out for the regular bin-end offers. **£5**

Vine Trail

266 Hotwell Road, Hotwells, Bristol BS8 4NG
Tel 0117-921 1770
Fax 0117-921 1772
Email enquiries@vinetrail.co.uk
Web site www.vinetrail.co.uk

France is still the order of the day at Vine Trail – a surprise when you know that Nick Brookes graduated in Spanish and Italian! – and his passion for French wines is obvious in the thorough detail set out in his list. If variety is a measure of quality, then the unusual regions (such as Savoie, Jurançon, Madiran, Gaillac and Quincy) featured in this range make it top-notch. We find we recognise only a few of the growers selected, but a glimpse at the array of first-class restaurants Vine Trail supplies with its wines (The Fat Duck in Bray, Ransome's Dock in Battersea, Bibendum in Fulham, to name but three) seems to indicate the choice is good, just not well known! **£5**

Vintage Cellars

33 Churton Street, Pimlico, London SW1V 2LT
Tel 020-7630 6254
Fax 020-7233 7536
Email shop@winecellarsales.co.uk
Web site www.vintagecellars.co.uk

No significant changes at Heiko Vermeulen's Pimlico establishment, which means that this is still the place to come for Brocard Chablis and other burgundies from Gérard Chavy and Coste Caumartin, plus a wide range of clarets (four vintages of Mouton for the well-heeled; Lamothe-Cissac for mere mortals). Other European highlights include Austrian wines from Freie Weingärtner Wachau and Lang, and Barolo from Borgogno, most venerable of an interesting set of Italian wines. If you're after New World wines, look out for the Trinity Hill and Forefathers from New Zealand, or head for the selection from America's Pacific North west and try the Washington Cabernets and Semillons from L'Ecole No. 41, and the Oregon Pinot and Gewurztraminer from Amity Vineyards. **£5**

Waterloo Wine Company

Shop
61 Lant Street, London SE1 1QN
Tel 020-7403 7967
Fax 020-7357 6976

Office and warehouse
6 Vine Yard, London SE1 1QL
Tel 020-7403 7967
Fax 020-7357 6976
Email sales@waterloowine.co.uk
Web site www.waterloowine.co.uk

With the gentrification of SE1, that area south of the Thames, Paul Tutton of Waterloo Wine Company has an increasing number of local residents on his doorstep. Those who manage to locate the Lant Street shop will find a small but attractive selection of wines, which chooses to focus on specific regions rather than offer blanket cover of the world. Paul is proudest (and justifiably so) of the range from Waipara West in New Zealand, which is owned and run by him, his sister and their respective partners. Other highlights include Domaine de la Tour Boisée in Minervois, Hewitson in the Barossa Valley, Piedmont wines from Punset and Settimo, Le Brun de Neuville champagne, burgundies from Perrot-Minot and Roger Belland, and an extensive selection from the Loire Valley.

Waters of Coventry

Collins Road, Heathcote, Warwick CV34 6TF
Tel (01926) 888889
Fax (01926) 887416
Email info@waters-wine-merchants.co.uk
Web site www.waters-wine-merchants.co.uk

Two-hundredth birthday greetings go to this company, founded by David Shakespeare Waters in June

1802. If we were to pick wines from the range for the celebrations, we'd bypass the rather basic Italian and German offerings, pause slightly longer among the Spanish bottles, including Hidalgo sherries, but settle with the selections from France. Here, highlights include a number of vintages from Du Tertre in Margaux, burgundies from Germain, Harmand-Geoffroy and Dampt, Rhône wines from Ogier, Bernard Chave and Cuilleron, and the sumptuous Coteaux du Layon from Domaine des Sablonnettes. A few New World wines could get a look in, maybe the Chilean Viña La Rosa, the Whitehaven Sauvignon Blanc from Marlborough, and the appetising reds from Water Wheel in Central Victoria. And when it's time for the toasts, we'd fill our glasses with the toothsome champagne from Bonnaire.   **(£5)**

Wessex Wines

88 St Michael's Estate, Bridport, Dorset DT6 3RR
Tel (01308) 427177
Fax (01308) 424383
Email wessexwines@btinternet.com

Individuality and value for money are the watchwords at Wessex, and we're certainly impressed by the strong selection from France. The list kicks off with some enticing-sounding *vins de pays* – Fox Wood Bruno's Block Chardonnay, Wild Trout Vin de Pays d'Oc – and then gets into some seriously off-beat choices from Bordeaux, Alsace, the Loire, Côtes du Rhône, and more. Experimentation isn't quite so liberal from the rest of the world but there's the same eye to cost, and sightings over £10 a bottle are rare indeed. It wouldn't be difficult to fill a case with this imaginative range to choose from.   **(£5)**

Whitesides of Clitheroe

Shawbridge Street, Clitheroe, Lancashire BB7 1NA
Tel (01200) 422281
Fax (01200) 427129

Pithy and succinct we said, when we reviewed this merchant in the 2000 edition of the Guide, and our feelings haven't changed. We like the fact that the list starts with around 20 wines under £5 – snappy, crisp varietals, everything from South African Pinotage to Portugal's Fernão Pires – and we're impressed with the cheerful New World selection thereafter. Whitesides tend to stock a whole range from one producer rather than running the gamut and introducing a few more names, but there's no less variety in doing this. French, Spanish and Italian classics get less of a showing, but there are appealing choices nonetheless. We reckon filling a case would be an easy and pleasurable task here.

Windermere Wine Stores

Windermere Wine Store
11 Crescent Road, Windermere, Cumbria LA23 1EA
Tel (01539) 446891
Fax (01539) 488001

Ambleside Wine Store
Compston Road, Ambleside, Cumbria LA22 9DJ
Tel (01539) 434558
Email sales@windermere-
  wine.co.uk
Web site
  www.windermere-wine.co.uk

You can find the odd bottle of £100+ Mouton Rothschild lurking on the shelves at this Lake District merchant, but mostly the focus is on well-known names at under £10 a bottle. While a selection featuring the likes of Louis Latour, Sutter Home, KWV and Rosemount is hardly ground-breaking, there are a few more interesting wines – such as Pascal Jolivet in the Loire, West Brook in New Zealand and Lorentz in Alsace. There's also plenty of whisky, as anyone checking out the *www.themaltroom.co.uk* web site will testify.

The Wine and Beer Company

1 Armoury Way, Wandsworth, London SW18 1TH
Tel 020-8875 9393
Fax 020-8875 1925
Email info@wine-beer.co.uk
Web site www.wine-beer.co.uk
(Branches in Calais, Cherbourg, Le Havre)

'One of London's biggest selections of exciting wines from around the world. All at fantastic prices,' proclaims the latest wine list. And that's exactly our summary too. What's really enticing for us is the 20 per cent discount on six bottles or more – for example, Château Talbot 1995 reduced from £35.99 to £28.79 a bottle, or the likes of Taittinger *brut* non-vintage champagne reduced from £24.99 to £19.99. Buyer Simon Delannoy has put together a particularly impressive range from France, but Chile, Argentina and Australia feature quite strongly too, although the selections are based on the usual big-name estates. If you can't find something on the list, a continual selection of bin-ends might fill the gap. This is an excellent stop for the party planner (glasses on hire, ice supplies; as well – of course – as canned and premium bottled beer!), but the prices are certainly enough to make any purchaser's mouth water.

The Wine Shop

7 Sinclair Street, Thurso, Caithness KW14 7AJ
Tel (01847) 895657

And The Whisky Shop and The Beer Shop – Martine Hughes has good selections of all three beverages. Where wine is concerned, she's especially proud of her selection of Muscats, and offers everything from dry to syrupy sweet from France, Spain, Australia and California. Elsewhere, her range isn't the largest around, and is hardly ground-breaking. However, we're not going to say anything against a collection based on good, reliable producers such as Dr Loosen, Trimbach, Jackson Estate, Cape Mentelle, Concha y Toro, Torres and Tedeschi. Look out in the near future for a new web site, *www.thursowineshop.co.uk*, plus a newsletter to keep customers up to date with new arrivals – and the monthly food and wine tastings at the nearby North Highland College.

£5

Wines of Westhorpe

Marchington, Staffordshire ST14 8NX
Tel (01283) 820285
Fax (01283) 820631
Email wines@westhorpe.co.uk
Web site www.westhorpe.co.uk

We were confused. Was that a hefty £18.60 a bottle for Oriachovitza Bulgarian Cabernet Sauvignon? No indeed: it's £18.60 a case. You don't believe it? Well, neither did we at first, but take our word for it, there's plenty more where that came from. Alan Ponting chooses to specialise in Eastern European wines, and by doing so can keep his prices right down. Wines of Westhorpe is one of the country's best stockists of Hungarian wine (Alan rates this country higher than France), with top-quality offerings from winemaker Tibor Gál and some sumptuous bottles of Tokaji. Bulgaria also features strongly, and there are some impressive cheapies from Chile, South Africa and South Australia too.

Winos Wine Shop

63 George Street, Oldham, Lancashire OL1 1LX
Tel 0161-652 9396
Fax 0161-652 9396

'We're constantly surprised by what we have,' confesses Mark Acton, one of a number of people who help 'iconoclastic winemonger' Phil Garrett at this bustling Oldham shop. Mark and Phil probably couldn't say how many different wines they have in stock – we reckon the range may run into four figures. Those who enjoy expensive wines from classic regions will find them somewhere on the groaning shelves, but Phil's real pleasure is in selling 'decent good-value wines to real Oldhamers'. The ranges from Chile, Australia, southern France, Italy (whites are currently popular) and Spain are arguably the best, but chances are that you'll find a good example of whatever you fancy. Look out for the lively tastings ('no spitting out') and dinners, often in conjunction with the award-winning White Hart restaurant.

We love to hear your views on wine merchants. You can email your comments to us at: whichwineguide@which.net

Woffenden Wines

103 Chapeltown Road, Bromley Cross, Bolton, Lancashire BL7 9LZ
Tel (01204) 308081
Fax (01204) 308081
Email norman@woffendenwines. fsnet.co.uk
Web site www.capewines-bolton.co.uk

Dr Norman Woffenden, an ex-ICI man, is keen on everything South African and has been trading in that country's wines since Nelson Mandela was released from prison. This isn't a long list, but it's justifiably growing in esteem as people become more inquisitive about this highly individual wine-producing country. We're pleased to see the likes of Thelema Cabernet Sauvignon, Kanonkop Pinotage and Fairview Malbec flying the flag for the reds, and highly recommend trying out Neil Ellis's Sauvignon Blanc and the De Wetshof Chardonnay. We still think you'll get a better bottle here than you will at many a supermarket, where choice centres around the larger estates. Locals should keep an eye out for one of Norman's tasting events. **(£5)**

Young's Wine Direct

20–30 Buckhold Road
London SW18 4AP
Tel 020-8875 7008
Fax 020-8875 7009
Email wine_direct@youngs.co.uk
Web site
  www.youngswinedirect.co.uk

Given the quality of the beers, we'd fully understand if Young's eschewed the grape and stuck to the grain in any of the 200 Young's pubs dotted around south-east England. However, if you do fancy a glass of wine, the selection of 15 to

20 wines served by the glass puts most brewers to shame and deserves applause. A further 180 wines are also available via Young's Wine Direct. Stars of the range are the Provence reds, a set of burgundies from good growers at attractive prices, the Chiantis from Nittardi, Domaine Cauhapé Jurançon, Loire whites from Bourgeois and Vacheron, and a pair of fine *vins de pays* under the Le Sanglier label. If you pick the wines up from your nearest Young's pub, you don't have to pay for delivery either.

ONLINE-ONLY

ChâteauOnline

29 Rue Ganneron, 75018 Paris
Tel (0800) 169 2736
Fax +33 (0) 155303063
Email customer.service@
  chateauonline.com
Web site www.chateauonline.co.uk

Château Online may be a French company, but we're pleased to say that the *.co.uk* version of the web site is written in English English (as opposed to translated French). Heading up the site is Jean-Michel Deluc, ex of the Paris Ritz, and one of a team of (mostly French) sommeliers around Europe responsible for choosing the wines. Not surprisingly, the French range is the best on offer, even without *en primeur* campaigns, but other countries get more than just a look in, and the general standard of the wines is good. The site isn't quite as efficient as it could be – on our last visit, there were only three wines listed on the '5 Best-Selling Reds' page, for example. However, it is certainly worth a browse, and the delivery charge of £5.99 regardless of the size of your order is very reasonable.

ItsWine.com

11 Upper Wingbury Courtyard,
Wingrave, Aylesbury
Buckinghamshire HP22 4LW
Tel (01296) 682600
Fax (01296) 682500
Email sales@itswine.com
Web site www.itswine.com

Speedy, succinct and successful, this web site takes a cheery approach and aims for affordability and accessibility. We like the case offers for as little as £49.99, and also the rapidity with which the search engine tackles its requests. We were a little distressed when our search for top-end whites came up with Penfolds Grange mistakenly under the Australian Riesling section (at £109.99 a bottle, though we were glad to see the wine was listed), but the rest of our searches went swimmingly: the top-end whites include burgundies from Latour and de Ladoucette's Pouilly-Fumé. Master of Wine Jonathan Pedley checks through everything in this range as an extra guarantee of quality, and we know how exacting he is. For those wanting wine news, gossip and helpful hints, Julie Arkell is the in-house wine writer – she also has a regular recommendation slot, in which she picks out less well-known, good-quality options; always well priced of course. It's worth logging on to the site for the sheer affordability of everything – and it's worth joining the wine club for the tempting discounts!

madaboutwine.com

Regal House, 70 London Road, Twickenham, London TW1 3QS
Email
  contactus@madaboutwine.com
Web site www.madaboutwine.com

'If you're mad about wine, we're crazy about you,' is the opening gambit, which goes some way to capturing the friendly feel of this web site, and its breadth of service. Pre-selected mixed cases are the favourite customer purchase here, and we're not surprised – the staff at madaboutwine are skilled and choose them wisely. As we write, for example, there are a couple of great 13-bottle promotion cases: one of New World reds and another that's a 'European Showcase' – each comes with a free bottle of champagne, and the latter case is just £79.95. While this is very much the place to surf for a bargain, you can also 'ask the expert' your vinous queries, browse through the monthly newsletter and find out the most favourable food and wine matches. Plus this year there's a new dimension to the site, with the introduction of the Virtual Cellar: you tour it by mouse and click on a bottle of whatever you fancy. Clever stuff! And, as with all the very best wine merchants, there's also a fine wine broking service. 'We list over 5,000 wines from the finest and rarest in the world, through to high-street brands,' says director John-Paul Cockain. He isn't wrong, there's a wealth on offer here. The

future looks well assured, too, as the team is now branching out into direct mail-order sales.

Virgin Wines Online

48 Leicester Square, London WC2H 7LT
Tel (0845) 603 6363
Fax 020-7484 4444
Email help@virginwines.com
Web site www.virginwines.com

'We launched in June 2000 and are now the leading Internet wine retailer in the UK,' says marketing director Chris Mitchell; and with 17,500 wines on offer, and with the list updated daily, we say that's pretty impressive. As you'd expect from the Virgin empire, the motto 'no waffle, no jargon, just plain English' is taken … well, we were going to say seriously, but everything about this site is light-hearted, non-intimidating and fun. Via the Wine Wizard search facility, wine recommendations are tailored to customers' own taste preferences ('if you like this, then you'll love these…' is the approach). We've tasted some of Virgin's wines recently and the choice is getting better and better. There's now a new range made especially for this site, and there's a quality selection from South African 'empowerment projects'. The new online magazine is as bright, breezy and brash as the rest of the site – from celebrity interviews on wine to hangover cures to, yes, an educational 'the language of wine' – we love it. More depth? A 'fine wine' search and an 'advanced' search are at your disposal too. Plus, in terms of advanced service, how many merchants offer to deliver between 7pm and 10pm, if that's most convenient for you? Not many. And we like the 'if we recommend and you don't like, you don't pay' attitude too.

Part V

Find out more about wine

FIND OUT MORE ABOUT WINE

There are more opportunities than ever to learn about wine, as its popularity grows and it becomes increasingly accessible. A great deal of wine-related material is to be found on the Internet (see 'Web sites' on page 482). Wine societies operate all over the UK, offering tutored tastings, seminars, dinners and other events. Tours to vineyards and wine regions enable you to indulge in local cuisine and extend your knowledge in the company of like-minded people; some travel companies deal exclusively in wine-related tours and holidays. Wine courses are available for both absolute novices and knowledgeable enthusiasts, and may include general wine appreciation and tasting technique, an introduction to winemaking and vine-growing, or examinations leading to a certificate. Many merchants also run mail-order 'wine clubs'.

WINE SOCIETIES

Association de la Jurade de St-Emilion (Grande Bretagne) *Peter Shamash, 7 Tower Court, Overstone Park, Northants NN6 0AS Tel: (01604) 642379* A regular series of gastronomic dinners, lunches, tastings and visits to St-Emilion, intended to increase knowledge and appreciation of that region and its wines.

Central London Wine Society *Paul Mapplebeck, 65 Grange Gardens, Pinner HA5 5QD Tel: 020–8866 9314* Meetings on every second and fourth Wednesday evening at the Civil Service Club, Great Scotland Yard, Whitehall, London. Beginners are welcome. There is no membership charge; payment is made for each tasting attended. All members are invited to comment on product quality.

Harrogate Medical Wine Society *Dr Bernard Dias, 86 Station Parade, Harrogate HG1 1HH Tel: (01423) 503129 Fax: (01423) 884426* Although originally open solely to members of the medical and related professions, membership is now extended to wine enthusiasts outside that sphere. Tastings are held at least once a month. The Society arranges wine tours and the Harrogate Consumer Wine Festival. Membership is £10 a year, with a charge for each tasting.

The International Wine & Food Society *Philip Clark, 9 Fitzmaurice Place, Berkeley Square, London W1J 5JD Tel: 020–7495 4191 Fax: 020–7495 4172 Email: sec@iwfs.com Web site: www.iwfs.com* Founded in 1933; membership terms on application; special rates for members under 35. 20 UK branches, from 140 branches in 30 countries worldwide, organise tastings, dinners and vineyard visits. Regular newsletters, gastronomic monographs and an annual *Vintage Guide* to wine buying are free to members; other benefits include discounts at hotels, restaurants and gastronomic events.

The Lincoln Wine Society *Norman Tate, 8 Green Lane, North Hykeham, Lincoln LN6 8NL Tel: (01522) 680388* Meetings held once a month; activities include guest experts and wine merchants, fine wine and food evenings, trips to merchants and wine areas and a grand annual function. Annual membership £7 (£12 joint). (See also The Lincoln Wine Course, in *Courses*, below.)

Morley College Wine Club *Vivienne Franks, 18 Hazel Gardens, Edgware, Middlesex HA8 8PB Tel/fax: 020–8958 3319 Email: Morleywineclub@aol.com* Regular meetings held in South London from September to June. People who enjoy wine and want to learn more about it are welcome.

Northern Wine Appreciation Group *DM Hunter, 21 Dartmouth Avenue, Almondbury, Huddersfield HD5 8UR Tel: (01484) 531228* Meetings weekly from September to June. Graded tutored tastings and special events are held for new members. Activities include group dinners and visits to merchants for tastings.

Rochester Wine Society *John Lamb, 1 Boundary Road, Chatham ME4 6TS Tel: (01634) 308488* The Society meets on the second Monday of the month; phone John Lamb for details. Payment is made for each tasting attended, and members are encouraged to comment on product quality. Beginners welcome.

Tanglewood Wine Society *John Trigwell, Tanglewood House, Mayfield Avenue, New Haw, Addlestone KT15 3AG Tel: (01932) 348720 Fax: (01932) 350861 Email: john@tanglewoodwine.co.uk Web site: www.tanglewoodwine.co.uk* The Society has branches in Cobham and Reigate, and holds regular monthly tastings and social events. Annual membership £7.50 (£12 joint at the same address). A charge is made at each tasting: average £12 per person. (See also Tanglewood Wine Tours, in *Travel and tours*, below.)

Lilyane Weston *'Owlet', Templepan Lane, Chandlers Cross, Rickmansworth WD3 4NH Tel/Fax: (01923) 264718 Email: lilyaneweston@skynow.net* A selection of courses and fine wine tastings (£20 per session); also Gourmet Evenings and training for restaurant staff. Available to lecture to business and social clubs, consumer groups, colleges and universities and wine trade events throughout the UK. Personally guided tours to vineyards worldwide – recent visits to Argentina, Australia, Austria, Brazil, Bulgaria, California, Chile, Corsica, the Czech Republic, France, Germany, Italy, Madeira, New Zealand, Portugal, Sicily, Slovenia, Spain, South Africa, Turkey and Uruguay.

The Wine Club *3 Oak Street, Heeley, Sheffield S8 9UB Tel: 0114–255 3301/6611 Fax: 0114–255 1010* A wide range of tutored tastings, hosted by guest speakers; cheese and wine tastings and dinners are also organised. Fully hosted vineyard visits to Champagne, Burgundy and Bordeaux, and a weekend away, are arranged every year. Themed dinners are held at the Manor House Hotel and Restaurant, Dronfield, and an annual week-long gastronomic 'Scottish House Party' at Glen House, Peeblesshire. All events are paid for individually and are open to all on a first-come-first-served basis.

The Wine & Dine Society *Clare Benson, 96 Ramsden Road, London SW12 8QZ Tel: 020–8673 4439* Weekly tastings with guest speakers and theme dinners are held at various locations in London. Tasting/educational workshops are also held regularly. Tasting evenings start at £15 per person.

The Winetasters *Mrs I Prideaux (Secretary), Denver, 8 Bulstrode Way, Gerrards Cross SL9 7QU Tel: (01753) 889702* Non-profit-making club offering tastings, seminars, dinners and tours. Meetings are held in London. Annual membership £12 (£5 if you live more than 50 miles from London).

TRAVEL AND TOURS

ACT (A la Carte Tours & Accompanied Cape Tours) *Virginia Carlton, Hill House, Much Marcle, Ledbury HR8 2NX Tel: (01531) 660210 Fax: (01531) 660494 Email: vcarlton@actours.fsnet.co.uk* ACT arranges wine tours to the Western Cape for parties of four or more; Independent holidays to the Cape Winelands start at £1,200 a person. Combine wine tasting in the Cape with a visit to a private game reserve in the Eastern Transvaal.

Arblaster & Clarke *Wine Tours Ltd, Clarke House, Farnham Road, West Liss GU33 6JQ Tel: (01730) 893344 Fax: (01730) 892888 Email: sales@winetours.co.uk Web site: www.arblasterandclarke.com* A wide selection of wine tours worldwide, including Argentina, Australia,

California, Chile, France, Hungary, Italy, New Zealand, Oregon, Portugal, South Africa and Spain, is available throughout the year. Parties are escorted by knowledgeable wine guides – usually Masters of Wine – and a bilingual tour manager. All trips include visits, tastings and meals at wineries. Trips range from a weekend in Champagne to two weeks in Chile and Argentina. A full range of walking trips throughout France is available, as are gourmet holidays. Private tours can be arranged for companies, individuals and wine societies.

DER Travel Service Ltd *18 Conduit Street, London W1R 9TD Tel: 020–7290 1111 Fax: 020–7629 7442 Email: sales@dertravel.co.uk Web site: www.dertravel.co.uk* DER offers air, rail and motoring holidays to Germany's and Austria's wine-growing regions as well as Rhine and Danube cruises. Local wine festivals are held in the Rhine and Moselle region in September and October. Seven-night holidays in the Moselle region start from £329 per person including bed and breakfast, ten nights using your own car on the Romantic and Castle Road from £479 per person, and the Rhineland Explorer tour by rail from £459 per person. All prices are based on two people sharing.

Eurocamp Travel Ltd *Hartford Manor, Greenbank Lane, Northwich CW8 1HW Tel: (01606) 787878* Eurocamp arranges self-drive camping and mobile home holidays at 186 sites in Europe, many of which are 'among the grapes'. These include Bergerac, Cahors, Bordeaux and the Rhineland.

Friendship Wine Tours *Bullimores House, Church Lane, Cranleigh GU6 8AR Tel: (01483) 273355 Fax: (01483) 268621* Specialists in 'tailor-made' escorted tours to the 'Fine Wine' regions of Europe and beyond. Relaxed and informative visits provide an insight into wine-production in Alsace, Bordeaux, Burgundy, Champagne, Languedoc, the Loire and the Rhône in France; Piedmont and Tuscany in Italy; Galicia, Navarra and Rioja in Spain; Costa Verde and Douro in Northern Portugal; and Baden, the Mosel and the Rhine in Germany.

Great Escapes *27–29 West Street, Storrington RH20 4DZ Tel: (0800) 7312921(reservations) (01903) 748140 (brochures)* Great Escapes offers holidays based in hotels chosen for their setting, cuisine, character and comfort, including a 'unique' selection of hotels with their own vineyards. Regions include Alsace, Burgundy, Champagne and the Loire Valley.

Jon Hurley's Wineweekends.com *Jon and Heather Hurley, Upper Orchard, Hoarwithy HR2 6QR Tel: (01432) 840649* Stay at various country houses in the Wye Valley in Herefordshire. Inclusive prices range from £175 to £300 per person. Each location includes a walk, led by Heather Hurley, with a pub halfway and lots of wine tasting.

Wink Lorch *5 Drovers Way, Seer Green, Beaconsfield HP9 2XF Tel: (01494) 677728 Fax: (01494) 677729 Email: winklorch@hotmail.com* Regular holidays in the French Alps, which include visits to Savoie and Swiss vineyards, local Savoie meals, mountain walks and tastings of wines from other regions. Ski and Wine trips are held in the winter season. (See also *Courses*, below.)

Moswin Tours *Moswin House, 21 Church Street, Oadby LE2 5DB Tel: 0116–271 4982 Fax: 0116–271 6016 Email: germany@moswin.com Web site: www.moswin.com* Tailor-made wine tours for groups to Germany by air or coach. Some are arranged around special events such as the Bernkastel Wine Festival or the Mosel Harvest. Tastings and lectures included. The Mosel Harvest tour is available for individual travellers, and offers the chance to get involved in vineyard work. Other areas covered for groups include the Rhine and Ahr Valley, Franconia, Baden, Elbe Wineland and Saale-Unstrut Wineland.

Ski Gourmet *Greenways, Vann Lake, Ockley, Dorking RH5 5NT Tel: (01306) 712111 Fax: (01306) 713504 Email: sales@winetrails.co.uk Web site: www.winetrails.co.uk* Ski Gourmet offers a selection of (mostly guided) ski holidays in France and Austria, with other areas under consideration. Accommodation is in private chalets and small hotels, with fine food and wine from each area, including informal chats and tastings from local wine growers and their wines, and occasional guest chefs for cookery class weeks.

Sunday Times Wine Club Tours *Clarke House, Farnham Road, West Liss GU33 6JQ Tel: (01730) 895353 Fax: (01730) 892888 Email: clubtours@winetours.co.uk* Sunday Times Wine Club Tours offers a series of tours each year ranging from Australia to Italy, Spain and France (Bordeaux, Burgundy, Champagne).

Tanglewood Wine Tours *Tanglewood House, Mayfield Avenue, New Haw, Addlestone KT15 3AG Tel: (01932) 348720 Fax: (01932) 350861 Email: jean@tanglewoodwine.co.uk Web site: www.tanglewoodwine.co.uk* This family business specialises in coach tours to the vineyards of all the major wine regions of France, as well as the Piedmont area of northern Italy and Ribera del Duero in Spain. Tours are available to California. (See also Tanglewood Wine Society, in *Wine societies*, above.)

UK Vineyards Association *Ian Berwick, Church Road, Bruisyard, Saxmundham IP17 2EF Tel: (01728) 638080 Fax: (0870) 136 3708* Many English and Welsh vineyards are open to the public and offer guided tours, tastings and sales. Free details are available from the above address (please send an s.a.e.).

Wessex Continental Travel *1 King Edward Road, Saltash PL12 4EQ Tel/Fax: (01752) 846880 Web site: www.wessexcontinental.co.uk* Described as 'holidays with wine', a range of 7- and 8-day coach tours are offered around France. Prices are from £575, with a maximum of 36 people per tour. For private/corporate groups, independent arrangements can be made to other wine regions of the world. Also wine cruises to Rioja in Spain: seven days from £515.

WineShare *Glebelands, Vincent Lane, Dorking RH4 3YZ Tel: (01306) 742164 Fax: (01306) 743936 Email: enquiries@wineshare.co.uk Web site: www.wineshare.co.uk* For a yearly payment of £65, guaranteed not to increase for 10 years from date of subscription, WineShare offer rental of 50 vines in one of three vineyards producing either a Rhône-, Bordeaux- or Beaujolais-style wine. Wine produced can be delivered in the UK or collected in France. Gift subscriptions, including the WineShare video and two personalised bottles of red and white wine from the relevant vineyard, are £95. Vintage weekends for picking are held in September; tastings in April and October, a day trip to Calais, and dinners in both France and England are held throughout the year.

Winetrails *Greenways, Vann Lake, Ockley, Dorking RH5 5NT Tel: (01306) 712111 Fax: (01306) 713504 Email: sales@winetrails.co.uk Web site: www.winetrails.co.uk* Winetrails offers a variety of wine tours and gentle walking and cycling holidays in grape-growing territory around the world. The emphasis is on good food, wine, nature and local culture. Destinations include Alsace, Andalucia, Australia, Auvergne, Bordeaux, Bulgaria, Burgundy, Champagne, Chile, Cilento, Cyprus, Hungary, Jerez, Languedoc, the Loire Valley, Madeira, Navarra, New Zealand, Piedmont, Portugal, Provence, the Rhône Valley, Rioja, Roussillon, Savoie, Switzerland, South Africa's Cape, Tuscany, Umbria and the UK. Private tailor-made trips worldwide are available on request.

WINE COURSES

Association of Wine Educators *18 Hazel Gardens, Edgware, Middlesex HA8 8PB Tel: 020–8931 1128 Fax: 020–8958 3319 Email: admin@wineeducators.com Web site: www.wineeducators.com* An independent professional group of specialist wine presenters who offer courses, workshops, tutored tastings, tailor-made special events and wine holidays. The Association has over 50 members located throughout the UK.

Christie's Wine Course *Victoria von Struensee, 5 King Street, St James's, London SW1V 6QS Tel: 020–7747 6800 Fax: 020–7747 6801* An Introduction to Wine Tasting course is offered over five consecutive Monday or Tuesday evenings, and comprises comparative tastings of French wines with reference to the New World. Seven courses are held throughout the year, and the cost is £200. Master Classes, concentrating on fine and rare wines, are also available at a cost of £65 to £80. Tailor-made wine tastings for groups are offered, as well as wine seminars abroad.

Connoisseur *23A West End Lane, London NW6 4NU Tel: 020–7328 2448 Fax: 020–7681 9905 Email: tastings@connoisseur.org Web site: www.connoisseur.org* The introductory course, offered over five sessions, focuses on the major grape varieties and the differences between New World wines and their Old World counterparts. The intermediate course of six sessions looks at the regional styles of the major wine-producing countries. The cost of the courses (£155 for the introductory and £185 for the intermediate) includes eight wines per session as well as tasting glasses and course notes. Tailor-made wine courses and tastings are also on offer.

German Wine Academy *Sabine Stock, Deutsches Weininstitut, Postfach 1660, 55006 Mainz, Germany Tel: 0049 6131 2829 42 Fax: 0049 6131 2829 50* A twelfth-century German monastery, Kloster Eberbach, is the setting for courses (delivered in English), which include lectures by wine experts, vineyard visits and tastings. The seven-day course is run in September and October.

Grape to Glass Workshops *Philip MacGregor, 31 Southview Avenue, London NW10 1RE Tel/Fax: 020–8450 5388* Practically-oriented tutored tastings (with little theory but much tasting), and Food and Wine seminars. Dinners and corporate entertainment on a wine theme also organised.

Heart of England School of Wine *18 Gilbert Scott Court, Towcester NN12 6DX Tel: (01327) 350711 Fax: (01327) 353637 Email: hoesow@aol.com* Providing consumer wine courses and tutored tastings, the qualified team of tutors will host everything from a themed tasting or dinner to a wine weekend or ten-week appreciation course. Courses can be informal, or structured to include Wine and Spirit Education Trust (WSET) qualifications. The aim of the School is wine education in an informal and entertaining way. Vineyard visits are also arranged, for example a seven-day break in Bordeaux or Austria.

Leith's School of Food and Wine *21 St Alban's Grove, London W8 5BP Tel: 020–7229 0177* Evening courses, priced £252, leading to the award of Leith's Certificate in Wine (roughly analogous to the WSET's Certificate, without the sessions on licensing and labelling laws), and the Leith's Intermediate Certificate in Wine, priced £265. Other courses are occasionally available, for example Matching Food with Wine, and cost £45.

The Lincoln Wine Course *Norman Tate, 8 Green Lane, North Hykeham, Lincoln LN6 8NL Tel: (01522) 680388* Wine appreciation course at North Hykeham Evening Institute, starting in September each year. This is a two-term course (two hours a week), with the emphasis on tasting and gaining a good general knowledge of wine. Participants can take the Wine and Spirit Education Trust's Certificate and Higher Certificate examinations. The cost is divided between the course fee and a weekly supplement to cover the cost of the tastings. (See also The Lincoln Wine Society, in *Wine societies*, above.)

Wink Lorch *5 Drovers Way, Seer Green, Beaconsfield HP9 2XF Tel: (01494) 677728 Fax: (01494) 677729 Email: winklorch@hotmail.com* Wine educator and writer, Wink Lorch is a regular speaker for wine and social clubs, offering tutored tastings on all wine subjects. Her specialities include the Loire Valley, South Africa, Chile, Argentina and California. Tailor-made wine events, courses and holidays are provided for a wide range of individual and corporate customers. Member of the Association of Wine Educators. (See also *Travel and tours*, above.)

Northern Ireland Wine and Spirit Institute *Martin Sayliss, 10 Glenshane Park, Newtownabbey, Co. Antrim BT37 0QN Tel: 028–9086 2483 Email: mh.sayliss@ulst.ac.uk* The Institute offers a programme of talks, tastings and wine-related activities to members, from January to June and from September to December. Occasional study tours to wine-producing areas have also been arranged, including Catalonia and, most recently, Languedoc-Roussillon. The cost of membership is currently £50, and is open to all those who demonstrate an enthusiasm for and interest in wine; guests are welcome to attend individual meetings, for which there is a small charge.

Plumpton College *Chris Foss, Ditchling Road, Plumpton, nr Lewes BN7 3AE Tel: (01273) 890454 Fax: (01273) 890071 Email: staff@plumpton.ac.uk Web site: www.plumpton.ac.uk* Plumpton College offers courses in Wine Studies, wine production and the wine trade for both amateurs and professionals. These include an HND in Wine Studies, the Vinegrower's Course, the Winemaker's Course, Introduction to Vine Growing, Sensory Evaluation of Wine, Introduction to Winemaking and occasional seminars on particular aspects of wine. Plumpton College is an approved training centre for the Wine & Spirit Education Trust and offers the Advanced Certificate and the Diploma in Wines and Spirits. The college has a commercial vineyard and a dedicated Wine Studies centre with a commercial winery.

The School of Hospitality, Leisure and Tourism *Huddersfield Technical College, New North Road, Huddersfield HD1 5NN Tel: (01484) 536521 Fax: (01484) 511885* Evening courses in wine appreciation are held from September to June. The WSET Intermediate Certificate and Advanced Certificate courses are also available. Short courses and tastings can be arranged to suit requests. Gourmet evenings and tastings are also held every six months.

Sotheby's Wine Department *34–35 New Bond Street, London W1A 2AA Tel: 020–7293 5727 Fax: 020–7293 5961* Varietal and Regional Wine Courses alternate and run throughout the year (except during the summer holiday period) on consecutive Monday evenings. The cost is £200 per course of six sessions. Wine Seminars and Tutored Tastings with top wine producers are also held. Sales of Fine and Rare Wines take place monthly in London, six times a year with Aulden Cellars in New York, and five times a year in Chicago.

The Wine & Spirit Education Trust *Five Kings House, 1 Queen Street Place, London EC4R 1QS Tel: 020–7236 3551 Fax: 020–7329 8712 Email: wset@wset.co.uk Web site: www.wset.co.uk* The aim of the Trust is to promote education and training among those working in the drinks and allied industries. Courses are also open to the general public. Trade courses are offered at three levels: Intermediate Certificate, Advanced Certificate and Diploma. Seminars are also offered, as well as summer appreciation schools, evening wine courses, food and wine matching workshops and tutored tastings, which all cater for interested consumers. In addition, the Trust approves external examination centres and tutors to conduct WSET examinations and courses.

Wine Education Service *Sandy Leckie, 9 Bermuda House, Mount Park Road, Harrow HA1 3XH Tel: 020–8423 6338 Email: info@wine-education-service.co.uk Web site: www.wine-education-service.co.uk* Offers introductory, intermediate and advanced wine courses for the consumer in London, Manchester, Edinburgh and a number of other UK locations. Courses combine tasting with both structured tuition and informal discussion. The introductory course is made up of 10 two-hour sessions, features 60 wines and costs £175.

Winewise *Michael Schuster, 107 Culford Road, London N1 4HL Tel: 020–7254 9734 Fax: 020–7249 3663* Winewise runs two regular tasting courses and a programme of individual tastings (details are mailed three times a year). The Beginners' Course costs £165 for six evenings, once a week. Forty wines are tasted from around the world, priced from £3 to £20; slides are used to illustrate regional vineyards, viticulture and winemaking practices. The Fine Wine Course costs £250 for six evenings, and is devoted to the classic wines of France. Both courses emphasise tasting technique.

WEB SITES

compiled by Tom Cannavan

This is without a doubt a golden age for the wine-lover with a thirst for information. A combination of twenty-first-century attitudes and twenty-first-century technology means that not only do the world's wine makers, writers and enthusiasts want to share information freely, but the Internet has given them the means to do so. A great Bordeaux château is just as likely to have a web site as its New World counterpart, and a plethora of professional sites joins the legions of knowledgeable *amateurs du vin* in using the power of the Internet to present a wealth of browsing possibilities.

No other food or beverage subject has so much cyberspace devoted to it. There are literally thousands of web sites out there catering for every wine whim, from general wine information resources, to sites that celebrate the most specialised and obscure of vinous subjects. And best of all, almost everything is offered free.

There are caveats of course: the web is a self-publishing medium, and for every high-quality and fascinating site, there's another that barely merits a few minutes of precious surfing time. Some sites are slick on design, but shallow on content, others carry outdated or unreliable information, and yet others are published by those who hide a vested interest behind a veneer of impartiality.

The following sites are listed in no particular order. We hope that this sample will encourage you to explore further. Happy browsing.

General information/online magazines

www.decanter.com

Online version of the UK's most influential print journal on wine, with news and features including wine tasting, serving and cellaring advice. Some areas, such as 'My Cellar' where you can record your own wines, require you to hand over name and email address. Premium content, such as the Fine Wine Price Tracker, requires a paid subscription (from £160 per annum).

www.winespectator.com

It's love it or hate time for this sprawling online edition of the top US wine magazine, but there's a wealth of information here on wine and 'gracious living'. Extended features, such as accessing all 87,000 wine reviews instead of a small sample, requires a paid subscription ($39.95 per annum).

www.bath.ac.uk/~su3ws/wine-faq/

Typing the address is a bit of a trial, but this simple, text-based resource of Frequently Asked Questions and answers is one of the oldest and most thorough wine resources on the Web.

www.wineanorak.com

British-based e-zine with lots of editorial on wine-related subjects. There are wine tips and quality content pertinent to the UK consumer, though some of the content lives up to the 'anorak' billing. Includes a useful guide to UK wine shops.

www.jancisrobinson.com

The doyenne of British wine writing takes her recently launched site seriously, and though content is still a little thin, it is independent, regularly updated and is much more than a promotional puff.

www.winepros.co.uk

UK-branded branch of an Australian site. Good articles, but some of the most interesting features of this commercial site – including an online edition of *The Oxford Companion to Wine* – require a paid subscription (AU$66.00 per annum).

www.thewinedoctor.com

Wine-loving UK medic's site includes wine tips, educational material and restaurant reviews. The most original feature is a year-long saga to explore the wines of Alsace and Germany.

www.wineontheweb.co.uk
The main thing going for this rather patchy site is a series of 'Radio Postcard' audio reports on wine-related topics; ideal for visually impaired surfers.

www.wineoftheweek.com
Slightly odd name for a New Zealand site with lots more to it than just a wine of the week. Presentation is a little amateurish, but it is clear and contains very good Antipodean news, reviews and features.

www.wrathofgrapes.com
The site of a bunch of Dublin-based enthusiasts, with lots of tasting notes but also good information on wine tastings, feature articles and a huge collection of humorous and thought-provoking wine quotations.

Tasting notes/wine recommendations

www.finewinediary.com
Every web site has tasting notes from budding Robert Parkers, but here two Edinburgh- and Oxford-based wine-loving brothers have amassed a formidable collection, almost exclusively on fine wines. Scores are awarded for current drinking quality and development potential in the huge, searchable archive.

www.superplonk.com
Notes garnered from Malcolm Gluck's *Guardian* column on low- and medium-priced wines. Possibly the largest collection of 'everyday' wine reviews on the Web. The database-driven site offers some neat ways to search and browse the collection.

www.andys-scribblings.co.uk
Weekly email newsletter featuring a wide selection of tasting notes and recommendations on wines, beers and other drinks.

Learning and enjoying

www.wset.co.uk
The Wine & Spirit Education Trust (WSET) runs both vocational and leisure courses in wine, up to Diploma level. Courses and tutored tastings are held in central London and various regional centres. Self-teach versions of their courses can be ordered online from this functional web site.

www.winetours.co.uk
What nicer way to learn about wine than to visit the wine regions in expert company? Arblaster & Clarke (see entry in 'Travel and tours') are past-masters at such organised tours, led by well-known figures from wine writing and the wine trade. Tours span the globe, from weekends in Champagne to exploring South America. The simple but attractive web site has good information, but no online booking as yet.

www.localwineevents.co.uk
Of course the best way to learn about wine is by tasting. Many web sites carry information about organised tastings, but try here for events in your area. The site lists only those events that are submitted by their organisers, so coverage is a bit patchy.

Wine talk

www.ukwineforum.com
Many forums on the Web are severely under-used, but the friendly, civilised and lively group that constitutes the UK Wine Forum makes it the number-one spot for online discussion of wine from a distinctly British angle. There is also a community tasting notes archive.

www.wldg.com
Huge US-centred discussion group with international participation, but some may find it too biased towards a North American viewpoint.

Wineries

www.haut-brion.com
Almost every wine producer has a web site, but some try harder than others. This venerable estate does more than it needs to, and does it well with videos, web-cams, a discussion forum and a wonderful pictorial almanac of a year in the vineyard.

www.thevintageportsite.com
The Symington family (Dow's, Graham's, Warre's) offers excellent information on the history of port, styles, storage and serving, as well as vintages back to 1900.

www.moet.com
If you have a fast Internet connection this ultra-stylish, high-tech site presents a gorgeous multimedia introduction to how Champagne is made.

Links

www.vine2wine.com
A huge resource with hundreds of reviews for wine-related sites. Sites are categorised and rated from one to three stars, and the directory is kept bang up to date.

More than the hard sell

Many e-commerce wine sites have spent considerable time and money developing editorial content with regional guides, wine courses, quizzes and more. Amongst those with most worthwhile content are:

www.virginwines.com – 'Wine Zone' magazine section
www.everywine.co.uk – articles from well-known journalists
www.chateauonline.co.uk – 'My Wine World'
www.bbr.co.uk – Quizzes and wine FAQ
www.bringmywine.com – 'All About Wine'.

And finally ...
www.wine-pages.com
My own site. One of the biggest and most popular wine e-zines in the world, it is updated daily and includes a six-part wine appreciation course, tricky quizzes to test your knowledge, guides to the world's wine regions, several thousand tasting notes, wine recommendations, essays, free competitions and more.

(Tom Cannavan is the publisher of wine-pages.com and author of *The Good Web Guide to Wine*.)

GLOSSARY

almacenista (Spain) a small-scale sherry stockholder

amarone (Italy) dry PASSITO wine from Valpolicella

amontillado (Spain) an aged FINO sherry on which yeast FLOR has ceased to grow but which is matured further without *flor* to develop delicate, nutty flavours; commercial 'medium amontillados' are not made in this way, but are blended, sweetened sherries

appellation contrôlée (**AC**) (France) the best-quality category of French wine, with regulations defining the precise vineyard area according to soil, grape varieties, yields, alcohol level, and maybe vineyard and cellar practices

Ausbruch (Austria) dessert wine, between *Beerenauslese* and *Trockenbeerenauslese,* from nobly rotten grapes

Auslese (Germany/Austria) usually sweet wine from selected ripe grapes, possibly with noble rot (*see* BOTRYTIS CINEREA)

barrique 225-litre barrel, usually of French oak, in which both red and white wines are matured and white wines sometimes fermented. Normally replaced every 2–3 years, as new *barriques* have more effect on taste

bâtonnage (France) the operation of stirring the LEES

Beerenauslese (BA) (Germany/Austria) wine from specially selected ripe berries, probably with noble rot

biodynamics (Burgundy, and elsewhere) an extreme form of organic viticulture, based on the teachings of Rudolf Steiner, which takes into account the influence of the cosmos on a vine

blanc de blancs white wine or champagne made from white grapes only

blanc de noirs white wine or champagne made from red grapes vinified without skin contact (the juice of most red grapes is colourless; all the colouring matter is found in the skins)

bodega (Spain) cellar, winery

botrytis cinerea a form of rot that shrivels grapes and concentrates their sugars ('noble rot')

brut (Champagne) dry or dryish (up to 15g sugar/litre)

Bual (Madeira) sweetest style of madeira after Malmsey; must now legally be made from 85% Bual/Boal grapes

canopy management training and pruning a vine in such a way as to optimise the exposure of the grapes to the sun and air

carbonic maceration fermentation of whole bunches of grapes in a vat filled with carbon dioxide to give fruity wines with low tannin

Cava (Spain) champagne-method sparkling wines; now a DO in its own right

chaptalisation the addition of sugar to the must to increase the final alcohol content of the wine

classico (Italy) heartland of a DOC zone, producing its best wines, e.g. Soave

clos (France) vineyard site that was walled in the past, and may still be walled

colheita (Portugal) vintage (table wine); single-vintage tawny (port)

cream (Spain) sweet sherry

crianza (Spain) basic wood-aged wine, with a minimum of six months' oak-cask ageing and one year's bottle- or tank-ageing; can only be released after two full calendar years

cru (France) literally 'growth', meaning either a distinguished single property (as in Bordeaux) or a distinguished vineyard area (as in Beaujolais or Burgundy) *cru bourgeois* (Bordeaux) 'bourgeois growth', indicating a wine from the bottom tier of the Médoc region's secondary classification system

cru classé (Bordeaux) sometimes *grand cru classé*, 'classified growth', indicating a wine from the Médoc's primary classification system, divided into five strata (*premiers*, *deuxièmes*, *troisièmes*, *quatrièmes* and *cinquièmes crus classés*); or from the classification systems of the Graves, Sauternes or St-Emilion

crusted/crusting (Portugal) a blend of port of different years for short-term cellaring; needs decanting

cuve (France) vat or tank

cuve close a method of making sparkling wines by carrying out the second fermentation inside a sealed tank rather than in bottle. Also known as the 'tank method' and 'Charmat method'

cuvée (France) term applied to a batch of wine, usually of superior quality but with no precise legal definition

demi-sec (Champagne, Loire) sweet (up to 50g sugar/litre)

denominação de origem controlada (**DOC**) (Portugal) the Portuguesec equivalent to France's AC category

denominación de origen (**DO**) (Spain) wines of controlled origin, grape varieties and style

denominación de origen calificada (**DOCa**) (Spain) as DO, but entails stricter controls including bottling at source; so far, only Rioja has been given a DOCa status

denominazione di origine controllata (**DOC**) (Italy) wine of controlled origin, grape varieties and style

denominazione di origine controllata e garantita (**DOCG**) (Italy) wine from an area with stricter controls than DOC

domaine (Burgundy) estate, meaning the totality of vineyard holdings belonging to a grower or *négociant*

doux (Champagne, Loire) sweet to very sweet (over 50g sugar/litre)

Eiswein (Germany) wine made from frozen grapes

en primeur (Bordeaux) agreeing to buy in advance of a wine's being released for sale

Erstes Gewächs (Germany) 'first growths', regions' own system of classification of vineyards

extra-brut (Champagne) absolutely dry (no added sugar)

extra-dry (Champagne) off-dry (12–20g sugar/litre)

fino (Spain) light, dry sherry matured under FLOR

flor (Jura, Spain) the layer of yeast growing on wine or sherry in a part-empty butt

frizzante (Italy) lightly sparkling

garrafeira (Portugal) better-than-average table wine given longer-than-average ageing; a producer's selection of his best wine; a colheita port given bottle as well as cask age

grand cru (Alsace) classified vineyard site

grand cru (Burgundy) finest category of named vineyard site

grand cru classé (Bordeaux) 'fine classed growth'; in St-Emilion indicates wine from the second level of the classification system

grand vin (Bordeaux) 'fine wine': the top wine of a Bordeaux château, blended from selected *cuvées* only, as opposed to the 'second wine', which is blended from less successful *cuvées* and perhaps the wine of younger vines, and which is generally sold at a lower price; in other regions the term is used more loosely

gran reserva (Spain) wine aged for a minimum of two years in oak cask and two years in bottle; can only be released after five full calendar years

Halbtrocken (Germany) semi-dry

indicação de proveniência regulamentada (**IPR**) (Portugal) similar to France's VDQS status

indicazione geografica tipica (**IGT**) (Italy) wine of controlled origin, grape varieties and production methods, with less stringent regulations than DOC. Now covers many SUPER-TUSCANS

Kabinett (Germany/Austria) first category of PRÄDIKAT wine, light and delicate in style

late-bottled vintage (LBV) (Portugal) a medium-quality red port of a single year

late harvest sweet wine made from grapes picked in an over-mature or maybe *botrytised* condition

lees dregs or sediment that settles at the bottom of a container

lutte raisonée (France) a balanced approach to vine growing which respects the environment. A long way along the road to being organic viticulture

maceration process of leaving grapes to 'stew' on their skins before, during and after fermentation

Malmsey (Madeira) the most sweet and raisiny of madeiras; now must legally be made from 85% Malvasia grapes

malolactic fermentation a secondary, non-alcoholic 'fermentation' that converts malic acid into lactic acid. The process is accomplished by bacteria rather than yeast

manzanilla (Spain) salty fino from Sanlúcar de Barrameda

manzanilla pasada (Spain) aged MANZANILLA

méthode cap classique (**MCC**) (South Africa) champagne-method sparkling wines

méthode traditionnelle (France) the Champagne method of producing sparkling wines

mis en bouteille par (France) bottled by

moelleux (France) medium-sweet to sweet

mousse (France) term used to describe the effervescence in sparkling wine

mousseux (France) sparkling

must a mixture of grape juice, stem fragments, grape skins, seeds and pulp prior to fermentation

négociant (France) wholesale merchant and wine trader

noble rot *see* BOTRYTIS CINEREA

non vintage (nv) a wine or champagne made from a blend of wines of different years

nouveau (France) new wine which in Beaujolais is sold from the third Thursday in November after the harvest. Other areas may be earlier

oloroso (Spain) sherry aged oxidatively rather than under FLOR

organic wine wine produced according to eco-friendly principles in both the vineyard and the winery, and which has received accreditation from one of a number of official bodies

palo cortado (Spain) light and delicate style of OLOROSO

passerillage (France) the process of leaving grapes to dry and dehydrate on the vine with the eventual aim of producing a dessert wine from them

passito (Italy) dried or semi-dried grapes or wine made from them

petits châteaux (Bordeaux) properties modest in reputation and price, but which can provide some of the best wine value in the region

phylloxera aphid which kills vines by attacking their roots. Phylloxera devastated Europe's vineyards in the second half of the nineteenth century, since when vines have had to be grafted on to disease-resistant rootstock

pipe (Portugal) a port cask containing between 534 litres (shipping pipe) and 630 litres (lodge pipe)

Prädikat (Germany, Austria) a category of wine with a 'special attribute' based on natural sugar levels in must, such as *Kabinett, Spätlese, Auslese, Beerenauslese, Trockenbeerenauslese* or *Eiswein*

premier cru (Burgundy) second highest category of named vineyard site. If no vineyard name is specified, wine made from a number of different *premier cru* sites

premier grand cru classé (Bordeaux) 'first fine classed growth', indicating a wine from the top level of the St-Emilion classification system

Qualitätswein bestimmter Anbaugebiete (**QbA**) (Germany) quality wine from a specific region

Qualitätswein mit Prädikat (**QmP**) (Germany) quality wine with a 'special attribute' (*see* PRÄDIKAT)

quinta (Portugal) farm, estate. In the port context, any style may be branded with a *quinta* name, but *single quinta* port generally refers to a single-farm port from a lesser year

recioto (Italy) sweet PASSITO wine from the Veneto

récolte (France) harvest

reserva (Portugal) better-than-average wine; slightly higher (0.5%) in alcohol than legal minimum; at least one year old

reserva (Spain) wine aged for a minimum of one year in oak cask and one year in bottle; can only be released after three full calendar years

riserva (Italy) wines aged for longer than normal. If DOC wines are riserva, then a minimum (but variable) ageing period is laid down. Usually the best wines are held back for *riserva*

Schilfwein (Austria) sweet wine made from grapes dried on racks of lakeside reeds which become shrivelled and concentrated before being crushed, the equivalent of France's VIN DE PAILLE

sec (Champagne, Loire) medium-dry (17–35g of sugar per litre of wine); (other wines) dry

secco (Italy) dry

seco (Portugal, Spain) dry

second wine (Bordeaux) *see* GRAND VIN

Sekt (Germany, Austria) sparkling wine

sélection de grains nobles (Alsace) wine made from *botrytis*-affected grapes (*see* BOTRYTIS CINEREA)

semi-seco (Spain) medium dry

Sercial (Madeira) the driest madeira, though cheap examples are rarely fully dry; must now legally be made from 85% Sercial grapes

sin crianza (Spain) without wood-ageing

solera (Portugal, Spain) sherry ageing system which, by fractional blending, produces a consistent and uniform end product

sous-marque (France) a wine sold or labelled under a secondary, possibly fictional, name

Spätlese (Germany/Austria) wine from late-picked grapes, possibly with noble rot

special reserve (Madeira) madeira with a minimum age of ten years

spumante (Italy) sparkling

sulfites (US) sulphur dioxide, present in all wines (including organic wines), used as a preservative and disinfectant

supérieur (France) higher alcohol content than usual

superiore (Italy) wine with higher alcohol than usual, and sometimes more age

Super-Tuscan (Italy) usually non-DOC wine of high quality from Tuscany. Most now fall under IGT category

sur lie (Loire) this should refer to a wine (generally Muscadet) bottled directly from its lees, without having been racked or filtered. It may contain some CO_2

Süssreserve (Germany) unfermented grape juice

Tafelwein (Germany) table wine

tank method *see* CUVE CLOSE

tawny port (Portugal) basic light port. True wood-aged tawny ports are either marketed as COLHEITAS or as Ports with an Indication of Age

terroir (France) term encompasses a number of factors, including the soil, climate aspect, altitude and gradient, all of which can affect the way a vine grows and therefore the taste of the ultimate wine

Trocken (Germany) dry

Trockenbeerenauslese (**TBA**) (Germany/Austria) very sweet wine from grapes affected by noble rot

varietal a wine based on a single grape variety

vecchio (Italy) old

velho (Portugal) old

vendange tardive (Alsace) 'late harvest', meaning wine made from especially ripe grapes

Verband Deutscher Prädikatsweingüter e.V. (VDP) (Germany) group of estates whose members have agreed to a set of regulations

verde (Portugal) 'green', meaning young

Verdelho (Madeira) medium-dry madeira; must now be made from 85% Verdelho grapes

viejo (*muy*) (Spain) old (very)

vigneron (France) wine grower

viña (Spain) vineyard

vin de paille (France) sweet wine made from grapes which have been allowed to dry out, traditionally on straw (*paille*)

vin de pays (France) literally translates as country wine, and describes wine that is better than basic *vin de table*, with some regional characteristics. Usually *vins de pays* are determined by administrative geography, with more flexible regulations than for APPELLATION CONTRÔLÉE

vin de table (France) the most basic category of French wine, with no provenance other than country of origin given on the label

vin doux naturel (France) sweet wine made by adding spirit partway through the fermentation process before all the grape sugar has been converted to alcohol

vinho de mesa (Portugal) table wine

vinho regional (**VR**) (Portugal) equivalent to VIN DE PAYS

vinho verde (Portugal) literally, green wine (after the greenness of youth); can be white or red

vino da tavola (**VdT**) (Italy) table wine: wine that is neither DOCG, DOC nor fortified nor sparkling nor low in alcohol. Many SUPER-TUSCANS used to come under this category

vino de la tierra (Spain) country wine

vino de mesa (Spain) table wine

vin santo (Italy) type of PASSITO wine from Trentino, Tuscany and Umbria

vintage champagne champagne made from a blend of a single year, sold after at least three years' ageing

vintage character (Portugal) medium- to premium-quality ruby port

vintage madeira (Madeira) the finest madeira from one specific year

vintage port (Portugal) very fine port, bottled young and requiring long cellaring (8 to 40 years); needs decanting

Vitis vinifera the species of the *Vitis* genus in which virtually all of the major wine grape varieties are found

VDQS (France) (*Vin Délimité de Qualité Supérieure*) covers the very much smaller category, below APPELLATION CONTRÔLÉE, with very similar regulations

VQPRD (Italy) 'quality wine produced in a specified region'; EU term indicating AC, DOC, DOCG, DO, DOCa and other similarly controlled quality categories

WSET (Wine and Spirit Education Trust) (UK) training courses, resulting in wine qualifications. (For details, see *Find out more about wine*.)

INDEX

ROLL OF HONOUR

PAST EDITORS OF
THE *WHICH? WINE GUIDE*

1981 Which? Wine Guide	Jancis Robinson
1982 Which? Wine Guide	Jancis Robinson
1983 Which? Wine Guide	Jane MacQuitty
1984 Which? Wine Guide	Jane MacQuitty
1985 Which? Wine Guide	Kathryn McWhirter
1986 Which? Wine Guide	Kathryn McWhirter
1987 Which? Wine Guide	Roger Voss
1988 Which? Wine Guide	Roger Voss
1989 Which? Wine Guide	Roger Voss
1990 Which? Wine Guide	Roger Voss
1991 Which? Wine Guide	Andrew Jefford
The Which? Wine Guide (published 1992)	Rosemary George MW and Christine Austin
The Which? Wine Guide (revised 1993)	Rosemary George MW and Christine Austin

There was no *1994 Which? Wine Guide*

The Which? Wine Guide 1995	Harry Eyres, contributing editor Simon Woods
The Which? Wine Guide 1996	Harry Eyres, contributing editor Simon Woods
The Which? Wine Guide 1997	Susy Atkins and Simon Woods
The Which? Wine Guide 1998	Susy Atkins and Simon Woods

There was no *Which? Wine Guide 1999*

The Which? Wine Guide 2000	Susy Atkins and Simon Woods
The Which? Wine Guide 2001	Simon Woods and Claire Gordon-Brown MW